American Vital Records
from The Gentleman's Magazine

1731 – 1868

$\mathcal{A}$MERICAN
VITAL RECORDS
FROM THE
GENTLEMAN'S MAGAZINE

1731 – 1868

Compiled by David Dobson

CLEARFIELD

Reprinted for
Clearfield Company by
Genealogical Publishing Co.
Baltimore, Maryland
2007

ISBN-13: 978-0-8063-1177-7
ISBN-10: 0-8063-1177-0

Made in the United States of America

THE
Gentleman's Magazine:
OR,
Monthly Intelligencer.

VOLUME I.

For the YEAR M.DCC.XXXI.

CONTAINING,

I. ESSAYS *Controversial*, *Humorous*, and *Satirical*; *Religious*, *Moral*, and *Political*: Collected chiefly from the *Publick Papers*.

II. Select Pieces of POETRY.

III. A succinct Account of the most *remarkable Transactions* and *Events*, Foreign and Domestick.

IV. *Births*, *Marriages*, *Deaths*, *Promotions*, and *Bankrupts*.

V. The Prices of *Goods* and *Stocks*, and Bill of *Mortality*.

VI. A Register of Books.

VII. Observations in *Gardening*.

With proper INDEXES.

By SYLVANUS URBAN, Gent.

PRODESSE & DELECTARE.   E PLURIBUS UNUM.

LONDON:
Printed by EDW. CAVE, jun. at St JOHN's GATE.

Title page of volume for 1731.

THE

Gentleman's Magazine

AND

HISTORICAL REVIEW.

Aliusque et idem.—*Hor.*

ST. JOHN'S GATE, CLERKENWELL.
The Residence of Cave, Founder of the Gentleman's Magazine, 1731.

By SYLVANUS URBAN, Gent.

NEW SERIES.

VOL. V., JAN.—MAY, 1868.

(BEING THE TWO-HUNDRED-AND-TWENTY-FOURTH SINCE THE COMMENCEMENT.)

London:

BRADBURY, EVANS, & CO., 11, BOUVERIE STREET.
1868.

Title page of volume for 1868.

Note

he *Gentleman's Magazine* was founded in London in 1731. The first publication of its type, it featured a broad mix of news, essays, poetry, parliamentary debates, book reviews, and antiquarian notes.

For the genealogist it is an absolute treasure-house of useful data. From the day of its inception until 1868 it published columns listing births, marriages, and deaths, enabling people throughout the English-speaking world to keep abreast of friends and relatives at home and abroad. These columns contain thousands of entries relating to North America which have now been extracted to form a unique source of genealogical reference material for the period from 1731 to 1868.

The *Magazine* was issued in a number of series, which is reflected in the system of referencing used in this book. Entries extracted from the original series bear references which comprise, first, the volume number, then the page number, while in subsequent series the volume number is prefixed *NS*, meaning *New Series*, or *NS2*, meaning *Second New Series*, etc.

Abbreviations

NORTH AMERICA

Ala	Alabama
BC	British Columbia
BNA	British North America
Cal	California
Conn	Connecticut
Del	Delaware
Fla	Florida
Ga	Georgia
Mass	Massachusetts
Md	Maryland
Miss	Mississippi
NA	North America
NB	New Brunswick
NC	North Carolina
NE	New England
NFD	Newfoundland
NH	New Hampshire
NJ	New Jersey
NS	Nova Scotia
NY	New York
Pa	Pennsylvania
PEI	Prince Edward Island
RI	Rhode Island
SC	South Carolina
Tenn	Tennessee
Va	Virginia
Vt	Vermont
WI	West Indies
Wisc	Wisconsin

GREAT BRITAIN

Abdns	Aberdeenshire
Beds	Bedfordshire
Bucks	Buckinghamshire
Glocs	Gloucestershire
Hants	Hampshire
Hunts	Huntingdonshire
Lancs	Lancashire
Leics	Leicestershire
Lincs	Lincolnshire
Northants	Northamptonshire
Perths	Perthshire
Staffs	Staffordshire
Wilts	Wiltshire
Worcs	Worcestershire
Yorks	Yorkshire

Adm	Admiral
b	born
Brig	Brigadier
bro	brother
Cap	Captain
ch	child/children
C in C	Commander in Chief
CO	Commanding Officer
Col	Colonel
Comm	Commissary/ Commander
d	died
dau	daughter
Dep	Deputy
est	estate
ex	from
fa	father
gdau	granddaughter

Gen	General	PMG	Postmaster General
gfa	grandfather	Prof	Professor
gmo	grandmother	QC	Queen's Counsel
Gov	Governor	QM	Quarter Master
gs	grandson	RA	Royal Artillery
HEICS	Honourable East India Company Service	RE	Royal Engineers
		Reg	Regiment
HM	His/Her Majesty	RHA	Royal Horse Artillery
inf	infant	RM	Royal Marines
jr	junior	RN	Royal Navy
Lt	Lieutenant	s	son
m	married	Sec	Secretary
Maj	Major	sis	sister
MD	Doctor of Medicine	Univ	University
mo	mother	wid	widow
MP	Member of Parliament	WS	Writer to the Signet
PC	Privy Council	yngr	younger
plant	plantation	yngs	youngest

VITAL RECORDS FROM THE GENTLEMAN'S MAGAZINE

ABINGER Lord William Frederick m. Helen, 2nd dau. Captain
Magruder, Montreal, 23 Dec.1863.   (NS2/10:245)

ABBOTT ..., s. Charles T Abbott, surgeon, 39th Reg.,
b. St George, Bermuda, 11 March 1861.   (NS2/10:566)

ABBOTT Jeannie, b.1840, w. C T Abbott, surgeon, 39th Reg.,
d. St George, Bermuda, 15 May 1861.   (NS2/11:94)

ABBOT Millicent Cariton, only ch. Samuel Abbot, m. Edmund
Jermyn, Ipswich, Charleston, SC, 24 May 1818.   (88:464)

ABBOTT Susan Mary, dau. late John Abbott, solicitor, London,
m. William M Neill, merchant, NY, London, 22 Nov.1858.
                                                    (NS2/6:89)

ABBOTT William, b. Bath, 1788, comedian, d. Baltimore,
7 June 1843.   (NS20:324)

ABERNETHIE Margaret, dau. late Dr Abernethie, Banff, m.
Colquhoun Grant, Jamaica, 28 Jan.1798.   (68:168)

ABERNETHY Patrick, d. Jamaica, 1791.   (61:186)

ABICHAM John Anthony, Jamaica, d. Uxbridge, 1790.   (60:478)

ACLAND Arthur, b. 1808, judge, Huron Co., Ct., d. Chatham,
Upper Canada, 21 April 1854.   (NS42:90)

ADAIR John George, Bellegrove, Queen's Co., m. Cornelia, wid.
Col. Ritchie, USA, dau. Gen. Wadsworth, Geneseo, USA, Paris,
30 May 1867.   (NS3/4:102)

ADAMS Mrs Abigail, b. 1740, dau. Rev. W Smith, Weymouth,
Dorset, w. John Adams, late US President, d. Quincy,
Boston, 1818.   (88:638)

ADAMS Benjamin Clairmonte, b. 1835, 6th s. John C Adams,
Bedford, d. Barbados, 12 Sep.1852.   (NS38:655)

ADAMS C B, Prof., Amherst, Mass., d. St Thomas, WI,
19 Jan.1853.   (NS39:448)

ADAMS John, b. Boston, 1736, ex US President, d. 4 July 1826.
                                                      (96:271)

ADAMS John Quincy, US Ambassador, Berlin, s. John Adams, US
President, m. Louisa, 2nd dau. Joshua Johnson, Great Tower
Hill, 26 July 1797.   (67:709)

ADAMS John Quincy, b. 1766, s. John Adams, ex US President,
d. Washington, 23 Feb.1848.   (NS29:658)

ADAMS Mrs, wid. John Quincy Adams, ex US President,
d. Washington, 14 May 1852.   (NS38:321)

ADAMS Peter, Barbados, d. 24 May 1772.   (42:247)

ADAMS Mr, Newington, Surrey, m. Miss Ross, London, dau.
late Peter Ross, Dominica, 18 July 1799.   (69:1189)

ADAMSON Mary, dau. late Constantine Adamson, merchant, NY,
ex Gateshead, Co. Durham, d. Fordham, NY, 15 Aug.1865.
                                                         (NS2/19:527)

ADAMSON Sophia, dau. Rev. Dr Adamson, Christ Church Cath., m.
Rev. David Lindsay, s. late James Lindsay, London, Montreal,
30 April 1851.   (NS36:79)

ADCOCK George Henry, b. 1803, d. St Kitts, 13 Nov.1850.
                                                         (NS35:222)

ADCOCK ..., s. Cap. Adcock, 16th Reg., b. Toronto, 6 Nov.1864.
                                                         (NS2/18:93)

ADDIS Charles jr., barrister, late Lincoln's Inn, d.
St Vincent, 2 Dec.1845.   (NS25:222)

ADDISON Alexander, counsellor, Western Bar, d. Pittsburgh,
1808.   (78:371)

ADDISON Rev. George Augustus, Manchester, m. Anna, 2nd dau.
late Charles Farquharson, Clarendon, Jamaica, 4 Feb.1851.
                                                         (NS35:545)

ADYE Dr, St Kitts, d. Exeter, 2 April 1804.   (74:388)

ADYE Abraham Charles, Attorney General, d. Grenada,
4 May 1815.   (85:646)

AERY Dr Thomas, d. Jamaica, 1790.   (60:1214)

AFFLECK Miss, dau. late Dr Affleck, sis. J Affleck, barrister,
Spanish Town, Jamaica, d. Spanish Town, 8 Nov.1802.   (73:83)

AGAR W Talbot, only s. late W Agar, QC, m. Leonora Matilda,
only dau. late W Reed, St Vincent, Lymingston, 29 July 1843.
                                                         (NS20:428)

AGG William, Maj., 51st Light Inf., only s. W J Agg, Hewlett,
Glocs., m. Beatrix Shedden, yngst. dau. John Barr, Bermuda,
Cheltenham, 7 Nov.1861.   (NS2/11:678)

AGNEW William James, s. Dr Agnew, Bristol, d. Dominica,
23 Oct.1848.   (NS31:222)

AIKIN Roger, d. Jamaica, 1790.   (60:1053)

AIKMAN Alexander, jr., HM Printer, Jamaica, m. Charlotte, 2nd
dau. Robert Cory, attorney, late Mayor of Great Yarmouth,
Mount Hybla, Jamaica, 7 April 1805.   (75:582)

AIKMAN Alexander, b. Bo'ness, 23 June 1755, 2nd s. Andrew
Aikman and Ann Hunter, emigrated to SC 1771, Loyalist,
settled Jamaica 1778, printer & publisher, d. Prospect Pen,
St Andrews, Jamaica, 6 July 1838.   (NS10:556)

AIKMAN Louisa Susanna, b. Charleston, SC, 1755, 2nd dau.
Alexander Aikman, late printer, Jamaica, d. West Cowes,
29 Nov.1831.   (101:571)

AINSLIE John, m. Lady Mary, dau. Earl of Cromarty, wid.
Thomas Drayton, Charleston, SC, 17 June 1762.   (32:390)

AINSLIE Mary Arthur, b. 1816, 2nd dau. late R A Worsop,
Howdenhall, Yorks., w. George Hewitt Ainslie, d. Hamilton,
Upper Canada, 4 Nov.1837.   (NS9:334)

AINSLIE Thomas m. Miss Martin, Boston, 1772.   (42:495)

AINSLIE ..., dau. Thomas Ainslie, Collector of Quebec,
b. 30 May 1773.   (42:412)

AINSLIE ..., dau. Thomas Ainslie, b. Quebec, Feb.1776.
                                                       (46:385)

AINSLIE ..., s. Thomas Ainslie, Collector of Quebec,
b. Boston, 30 June 1774.   (44:446)

AINSLIE ..., s. & dau. Thomas Ainslie, Collector of Quebec,
b. 22 March 1782.   (53:92)

AINSLIE Mrs, w. Thomas Ainslie, Collector of Quebec,
d. 24 Dec.1787.   (58:366)

AIR Charles James, Member of House of Representatives,
d. Charleston, SC, 6 March 1803.   (73:478)

AIREY Louisa Anne, eldest dau. Lt. Col. Airey, 34th Reg.,
d. Port Talbot, Canada West, 1 Jan.1849.   (NS31:446)

AITKIN Jane, dau. late Charles Aitkin, St Croix, m. James
Mudie, London, North Tarry, Angus, 11 Dec.1798.   (68:1082)

AITKEN John, d. Havanna, 11 March 1856.   (NS45:545)

AITKIN Robert m. Ann Emily, eldest dau. late R Dasent,
Attorney General, St Vincent, 13 Oct.1847.   (NS29:80)

AKENSYDE Mr, 'the oldest packhorse trader in Georgia',
d. 1767.   (37:478)

AKERS George Alexander, 3rd s. late Aretas Akers, St Kitts,
d. Kentish Town, 9 Jan. 1799.   (69:83)

AKERS J Ramsay, s. J R Akers, Tunbridge Wells, d. Lake
Ontario, 9 April 1864.   (NS2/16:805)

AKERS Miss, dau. late Aretas Akers, St Kitts, m. William J.
Morton, Marylebone, 23 Jan. 1799.   (69.78)

AKERS ..., dau. Cap. Akers, RE, b. Lewis, Quebec,
15 Dec. 1865.   (NS3/1:264)

ALBONY Augusta Sophia, wid. James Hill Albony, London, m.
Thomas Norton, ex Chief Justice, Newfoundland, Paris,
18 Oct. 1852.   (NS39:86)

ALBAUGH Zachariah, b. Md. 1748, d. Licking Co., Ohio,
8 Nov. 1857.   (NS2/4:112)

ALCOCK Henry, b. 1762, s. Henry Alcock, Birmingham, Chief
Justice, Lower Canada, d. Quebec, 8 Feb. 1808.   (78:557)

ALDEBORT John, b. Poland 1687, d. Mass. May 1792.   (62:673)

ALDERSON Thomas, Hertford, Jamaica, m. Miss Boulby, dau.
late Henry Boulby, Newcastle, Denham, Norfolk, 12 May 1789.
                                                      (59:467)

ALDRICH Charlotte, w. Rev. Pelham Stanhope Aldrich, dau.
late Benjamin Bridges, Hollisley, Suffolk, d. Bahamas,
17 March 1844.   (NS22:110)

ALEXANDER Evan, late NC Congressman, d. Oct. 1809. (79:1236)

ALEXANDER Mary, w. J J Alexander, St Lucia, wid. Robert
Cullen, Lord of Session & Justiciary in Scotland, d. St Lucia,
10 Feb. 1818.   (88:569)

ALEXANDER Mary Bell, yst. dau. late R Alexander, Kentucky,
sis. S C A Alexander, Airdrie, m. Henry C Deedes, Marylebone,
20 July 1859.   (NS2/9:186)

ALEXANDER Robert, bro. Sir William Alexander, Airdrie, d.
Frankfort, Kentucky, 1 Feb. 1841.   (NS15:670)

ALEXANDER Robert S C A, b. 1819, son of late Robert
Alexander, Kentucky, neph. late Sir William Alexander, Airdrie,
d. Woodford, Kentucky, 1 Dec. 1867.   (NS3/5:254)

ALEXANDER Mrs, mo. Earl of Stirling, d. NY, 18 April 1760.
                                                      (30:297)

ALEXANDER William, b. 1726, Earl of Stirling, Viscount of
Canada, US Maj. Gen., d. Albany, NY, 12 Jan. 1783. (53:541)

ALEXANDER William, late St Vincent, d. London,
18 Jan. 1814.   (84:299)

ALEXANDER ..., dau. Maj. B J Alexander, Rifle Brigade,
b. Quebec, 8 Dec. 1866.   (NS3/3:235)

ALISON Margaret, dau. late Rev. Archibald Alison, m. William
Burge, HM Counsel, Jamaica, Edinburgh, 11 Aug. 1841.(NS16:424)

ALKIN Daniel, b. 1728, d. Wexford, Canada West, 1848.
                                                   (NS30:335)

ALLAN Alexander, d. Jamaica, 1790.   (60:1148)

ALLAN Bessie Rea, daughter Andrew Allan, Montreal, m.
William Henry Benyon, 23rd Royal Welsh Fusiliers, Montreal,
21 Nov. 1867.   (NS3/5:103)

ALLAN Louisa Maude, b. 1826, dau. Chief Justice Robinson,
w. George W Allan, Toronto, d. Rome, 13 May 1852. (NS38:107)

ALLAN G., Colonial Bank, Kingston, Jamaica, m. Charlotte,
dau. late Rev. W F Ireland, Cardiff, 15 Nov. 1836. (NS7:92)

ALLAN Robert, b. Kilbarchan, 1786, poet, to America April
1841, d. NY, 1842.   (NS18:331)

ALLANSON James, St Kitts, ex Liverpool, drowned on passage
from St Eustatia to Boston, 1818.   (88:90)

ALLCOCK Mrs, w. Henry Allcock, judge, d. Yorktown, Upper
Canada, 1803.   (73:87)

ALLEN Benjamin, d. Jamaica, 1791.   (61:971)

ALLEN Charles, late Bristol, d. Dominica, 1795.   (65:794)

ALLEN Ethan, Brig. Gen. Militia, d. Vermont, 13 Feb. 1789.
                                                   (59:466)

ALLEN Frances, 3rd dau. Lt. Col. Thomas H Ball, 81st Reg.,
w. Harry George Acklom Allen, London, Canada, d. London,
Canada, 28 June 1863.   (NS2/15:247)

ALLEN J A, Colonial Treasurer, m. Sarah, yst. dau. late Hugh
Leach, Bristol, Port of Spain, Trinidad, 15 June 1843.
                                                   (NS20:312)

ALLEN Col. John, Backhall, Barbados, d. London, 29 Oct. 1737.
                                                   (7:701)

ALLEN John, late Kingston, Jamaica, d. Newingston, Surrey,
6 Oct. 1816.   (86:467)

ALLEN J, s. Rev. T Allen, Stradbroke, Suffolk, m. Catherine
Maria, dau. late Rev. E Barlee, Warlingworth, Suffolk, North
Douro, Canada West, 11 April 1861.   (NS2/10:694)

ALLEN Margaret, dau. John Foster Allen, m. David Hall,
Barbados, 21 May 1811.   (81:187)

ALLEN Mary Ann, b. 1835, 2nd dau. late George Paine, Kent,
w. W D Allen, d. Goderich, Canada West, 18 Dec. 1861.
                                                 (NS2/12:238)

ALLEN Peggy, Philadelphia, m. George Hammond, Plenipotentiary
to USA, Philadelphia, 1793.   (63:669)

ALLEN Samuel, pilot, d. Port Royal, Jamaica, 1793. (63:1152)

ALLEN Miss, est. dau. William Allen, m. John Penn, Lt. Gov.
of Penn., 31 May 1766.   (36:342)

ALLEN Cap., USS Argus, d. Mill Prison, Plymouth, 18 Aug. 1813.
                                                    (83:401)

ALLENSON Elizabeth, b. 1783, w. Samuel Allenson, late London,
d. Philadelphia, 5 Dec. 1857.   (NS2/4:225)

ALLEY W H , late Cap. 4th Reg., special justice, d. Jamaica,
24 Aug. 1837.   (NS9:222)

ALLEYNE Annie, 2nd dau. Sir Reynold Alleyne, Alleynedale
Hall, Barbados, m. W Fitzherbert, est. s. Sir H Fitzherbert,
Barbados, 20 Feb. 1836.   (NS5:544)

ALLEYNE Christian Dottin, 4th dau. late John Gay Alleyne,
Barbados, m. Rev. H Withy, Cheltenham, 26 April 1829.(99:366)

ALLEYNE Douglas, Cap. 37th Reg., eldest son Henry Alleyne,
Barbados, m. Ada Graves, only ch. Charles Twisleton Graves,
ex Cap., Royal Irish Fusiliers, ggdau. 10th Lord Saye & Sele,
Kensington, 11 Jan. 1865.   (NS2/18:237)

ALLEYNE Elizabeth Gibbons, w. John Foster Alleyne, President
Council of Barbados, d. Clifton, Glocs., 12 Feb. 1820.(90:282)

ALLEYNE Fitzherbert, 2nd s. Sir Reynolds A Alleyne, m. Anna
Maria Best, 2nd dau. Sir R Bowcher Clarke, Chief Justice of
Barbados & St Lucia, Barbados, 23 March 1854.   (NS42:70)

ALLEYNE Maria Louise, yst. dau. late H G Alleyne, Barbados,
m. John Fordyce, Bengal Artillery, Paris, 16 Feb. 1842.
                                                   (NS17:541)

ALLEYNE Mary Spire, eldest dau.   Sir John Gay Alleyne,
Barbados, d. Weston-super-Mare, 10 Jan. 1862. (NS2/12:242)

ALLEYNE Phillippa, daughter Sir R A Alleyne, m. Hampden
Clement, Barbados, July 1831.   (101:268)

ALLEYNE Thomas, d. Barbados, 13 May 1775.   (45:255)

ALLEYNE ..., s. J G Newton Alleyne, b. Turner's Hall,
Barbados, 16 May 1852.   (NS38:193)

ALLEYNE ..., s. Bouverie Alleyne, Colonial Secretary,
b. St Vincent, 14 Jan. 1861.   (NS2/10:453)

ALLHUSEN B E , 15th Reg., 2nd s. Christian Allhusen,
Newcastle-on-Tyne, m. Isabelle, only dau. William Wright,
Advocate Gen., NB, Fredericton, NB, 18 Oct. 1864.(NS2/17:780)

ALLHUSEN ..., dau. Cap. Allhusen, 15th Reg., b. Fredericton,
NB, 30 July 1865.   (NS2/19:501)

ALLIN Miss, dau. Jacob Allin, Jamaica, m. Samuel Whitcomb,
Lillington, Dorset, 27 May 1749.   (19:236)

ALLISON Anne, yr. dau. Thomas Pope, London, w. Forbes F
Allison, Detroit, d. 28 Aug. 1859.   (NS2/7:431)

ALLPORT Richard, merchant, Bristol, d. Trinidad, 26 July 1829.
                                                    (99:286)

ALPRESS Samuel, HM Council Jamaica, d. Jamaica, 1784.(53:797)

ALPRESS Mrs, wid. Samuel Alpress, Jamaica, d. Bath, 18 March
1797.   (67:354)

ALPRESS Mrs m. Dr Cholmondley Dering, SC, 1766.   (36:550)

ALSTON Harold, b. 1846, yst. s. late Cap. H F Alston, 79th
Reg., late 4th Va. Cav., CSA, d. Richmond, Va., 22 April 1865.
                                                    (NS2/19:118)

ALLSTON Washington, b. England, 1789, artist, d. Cambridge,
America, 1843.   (NS20:324)

ALVES Alexander, 2nd s. Dr John Alves, Inverness, d. Jamaica,
1797.   (67:171)

ALVES William Gemmill, St Vincent, late Cap. 29th Reg., d.
Brighton, 22 April 1860.   (NS2/8:641)

AMBLER John, Representative, James Town, Barbados, d.1766.
                                                    (36:405)

AMBROSE Sophia, 2nd dau. late Mr Stoneham, Chelmsford, wid.
C Ambrose, d. Hamilton, Canada West, 24 May 1856.(NS2/1:255)

AMBURG Van, lion-tamer, d. Philadelphia, 29 Nov. 1865.
                                                    (NS3/1:151)

AMES Charles, b.1778, yst. s. late Mr Ames, Colchester, Essex,
d. Bridgetown, Barbados, 1 July 1806.   (76:874)

AMHERST William, Col. 32nd Reg., Gov. St John, NFD, bro. Lord
Amherst, d. 13 May 1781.   (51:243)

AMHERST William Pitt, 2nd Lord Amherst, d. Montreal,
28 March 1804.   (74:387)

AMPHLETT William, Lt., RN, b. 1819, yst. s. Rev. William
Amphlett, Wychbold, Worcs., 'died by the explosion of the
steam packet Glencoe at St Louisville, Mississippi'
3 April 1852.   (NS38:106)

AMWYL Lt. Col., 4th Reg., m. Senhouse, dau. J Barrow,
Barbados, 22 Oct. 1822.   (92:560)

ANDERSON Dr Alexander, Botanical Garden Superintendent,
d. St Vincent, 7 Sep. 1811.   (81:657)

ANDERSON Alexander, b. 1805, 2nd s. Alexander Anderson,
Belize, Honduras, d. Plumland, Cumberland, 17 Sep. 1829.
                                                      (99:380)

ANDERSON Andrew, Tortula, m. H Hetherington, dau.R Hetherington,
Tortula, Durham, 25 April 1799.   (69:525)

ANDERSON Hannah, w. Andrew Anderson, d. Tortula, 7 Aug. 1813.
                                                      (83:621)

ANDERSON J, late Tobago, d. Aberdeen, 13 Dec. 1817. (87:631)

ANDERSON James, b.1791, Port-au-Prince, d.Bermuda, 25 June
1820.   (90:187)

ANDERSON James, FRSE, Edinburgh, m. Ann, yst. dau. Robert
Watt, Jamaica, Stratford Bow, 30 Dec. 1840.   (NS15:199)

ANDERSON Mary Anne, only ch. James Anderson, Piccadilly, m.
William Skiddy, NY, Isleworth, Middlesex, 26 Nov. 1841.
                                                      (NS17.205)

ANDERSON Richard Oswald, Woodford, Georgetown, SC, d. Bath,
11 Oct. 1852.   (NS38:656)

ANDERSON Mrs Susannah, w. Thomas Anderson, d. Vere, Jamaica,
Nov. 1801.   (72:181)

ANDERSON Thomas, MD, b.1793, d. Trinidad, 1868. (NS3/5:408)

ANDREWS J D, Port Antonio, m. Eliza Panton, Manchineal,
Jamaica, 1800.   (70:1283)

ANDREWS William, b.1793, late Jamaica, d. Kensington,
27 Nov. 1854.   (NS43:109)

ANGE Francis, b. Stratford-on-Avon, 1633, d. Md., 1767.
                                                      (37:478)

ANGELO Michael, War Office, m. Ann Bell, 4th dau. late
William Grant, barrister, Barbados, Paddington, 24 April 1802.
                                                      (NS2/12:775)

ANNESLEY William Grove, Cap. 6th Reg., 4th s. late Gen.
A G Annesley, Co. Cork, m. Eliza, 2nd dau. John Taylor,
Good Hope Estate, Jamaica, St Michael's, Port Royal
Mountains, Jamaica, 8 March 1866.   (NS3/1:737)

ANSTEY Sophia Caroline, 3rd dau. William Jekyll Anstey, late
Postmaster General, Jamaica, m. William Castle Smith, MD,
Bideford, London, 19 Nov. 1846.   (NS27:195)

ANSTRUTHER Miss, late WI, d. Cheshunt, 1 July 1787. (57:641)

ANTHONY George, nephew Lt. Gen. Sir John Wilson, d. Jamaica,
15 Nov. 1844.   (NS23:222)

ANTOMARCHI Dr, ex physician to Napoleon, d. St Jago de Cuba,
3 April 1838.   (NS10:342)

ANTROBUS Cap., late Bristol, d. Kingston, Jamaica, 10 Feb.
1811.   (81:492)

APEY John, Judge Advocate & Principal Secretary to Gen.
Amherst, NY, d. 15 Oct. 1761.   (21:603)

APTHORP Rev. East, s. Boston, NE, merchant, m.(1) Elizabeth,
dau. Eliakim Hutchinson, Mass. judge (2) Anne, dau. John
Crich, Suffolk, d. Cambridge, 16 April 1816.   (86:468)

APTHORP Charles, Boston, d.1758.   (28:611)

APTHORP Charles Ward, ex NY Council, d. Bloomingdale, NY,
1797.   (67:619)

ARABIN Frederick, Cap. RA, s. H Arabin, Maglare, Co. Meath,
m. Eliza Mountain, d. Bishop of Quebec, Quebec, 31 May 1823.
                                                 (93:367)

ARAGO Gen., d. Mexico, 1836.   (NS6:669)

ARBUTHNOTT James, d. NY, 8 July 1732.   (2:877)

ARCEDECKNE Andrew, Jamaica, d. 1 Oct. 1763.   (33:518)

ARCHER Edward, b. 1798, s. late W Archer, d. Jamaica,
18 June 1818.   (88:373)

ARCHER F G, m. Eliza Anne Isabel, dau. John Brixtowe, Belize,
British Honduras, 5 Sep. 1867.   (NS3/2:670)

ARCHER John Vassell, only s. John Giddies Archer, Barbados,
d. Clifton, 26 Oct. 1806.   (76:1169)

ARCHER Mrs, b. 1777, dau. late John Vassall, Bath, w. John
Gittons Archer, Barbados, d. Clifton, 27 Dec. 1806.(76:1254)

ARCHIBALD S G W, b.1779, Master of the Rolls, Admiralty
Judge, d. Halifax, NS, 28 Jan. 1846.   (NS25:559)

ARDAGH Rev. S B, Rector of Barrie, m. Helena, 4th dau.
W Durie, Inspector of Hospitals, Toronto, 6 Dec. 1859.
                                               (NS2/8:178)

ARMOUR John, est. s. John Armour, merchant, Edinburgh,
d. Heywood Hall, St Mary's, Jamaica, 16 March 1805. (75:677)

ARMOUR Robert jr., b.1807, Advocate, Lower Canada,
d. Montreal, 4 Oct. 1845.   (NS24:666)

ARMSTRONG Eliza, b.1798, daughter. Edmund Armstrong, St Croix,
d. St Croix, 30 Oct. 1818.   (88:87)

ARMSTRONG Mary Redfern, daughter Rev. Dr Bunting, London,
w. H Armstrong, d. Antigua, 21 Oct. 1835.   (NS5:335)

ARMSTRONG Nenon, ex army paymaster, s. Gen. Armstrong, Bath,
d. NJ, 9 July 1851.   (NS36:329)

ARMSTRONG T G, b.1810, 3rd s. J Armstrong, Bath, ex Cap. 66th
Reg., Militia Maj., d. Woodstock, Upper Canada, 31 March 1838.
                                               (NS9:670)

ARMSTRONG William, s. late W Armstrong, merchant, Glasgow,
d. St Vincent, 22 Sep. 1800.   (70:1214)

ARNETT S, b.1754, s. A S Arnett, silkmercer, Cornhill,
d. Nassau, New Providence, 1813.   (83:595)

ARNOLD Fanny Carolina, 3rd dau. John Arnold, Toronto, m.
Richard Edmonds, s. late Rev. Edmonds, Woodleigh, Devon,
21 Sep. 1853.   (NS41:76)

ARNOLD Mrs Margaret, wid. Brig. Gen. Arnold, dau. Edward
Shippen, Chief Justice, Penn., London, 24 Aug. 1804.(74:885)

ARNOLD William, late Grenada, d. London, 8 April 1807(77:489)

ARNOLD William, MD, b.1791, d. Kingston, Jamaica, 20 June 1848.
                                               (NS30:446)

ARNOLD William Fitch, m. Elizabeth Cecilia, only dau. late
Alexander Ruddach, Tobago, 19 May 1819.   (88:480)

ARNOTT Archibald J, Royal Canadian Rifles, s. George Arnott,
MD, Cheltenham, m. Caroline Martha, yst. dau. Rev. Jones,
St Johns, Canada East, 19 Nov. 1863.   (NS2/16:244)

ARNOTT Mrs Mary, b.1757, d. Brooklyn, 27 Sep. 1867(NS3/2:685)

ASHE Edward, Lt., RN, m. Marcella, daughter Rev. Gilbert
Percy, St Peter'S,Quebec, Quebec, 28 May 1851.   (NS36:188)

ASHE Mary Gertrude, dau. A Ashe, Bath, m. Edward Arnold
Cumberbatch, Barbados, 6 Aug. 1822.   (92:178)

ASHER Allan, b.1809, New Orleans, d. Camden Town, 6 July 1856.
                                                   (NS2/1:261)

ASHBRIDGE George, Representative, Philadelphia, d.1773.
                                                    (43:254)

ASHLEY Joseph Biscoe, b.1814, s. John Ashley, Ashley Hall,
Jamaica, d. Gloucester, 15 May 1837.   (NS8:100)

ASHTON John, Grange, Cheshire, m. Mary, dau. John Jarrett,
Jamaica, Liverpool, 1790.   (60:474)

ASHTON William, late merchant, St Croix, d. Islington, 1814.
                                                    (84:300)

ASHWELL Charles, Grenada, m. Fanny, yst. dau. Edward
Whitehouse, Surrey, 18 Aug. 1792.   (62:766)

ASPEN Mathias, late merchant, Philadelphia, d. Holborn,
9 Aug. 1824.   (94:189)

ASPINWALL Eliza King, dau. Col. Aspinwall, ex US Consul Gen.,
London, m. William Henry Domville, Lincoln's Inn, yr. s.
Sir William Domville, Wandsworth, 14 Dec. 1853.   (NS41:309)

ASPINWALL Frances Allan, b. 1822, dau. Col. Aspinwall, US
Consul, London, d. Wandsworth, 1 April 1848.   (NS29:564)

ASPINWALL Louisa Elizabeth, daughter Col. Aspinwall, US
Consul, London, b. 1816, d. 7 April 1842.   (NS17:563)

ATCHERLEY Francis Topping, Maj. 30th Reg., m. Emma Arabella,
2nd dau. Francis H Heward, Toronto, 4 June 1863. (NS2/15:99)

ATCHERLEY ..., s. Lt. Col. F T Atcherley, 30th Reg., b.
Toronto, 8 Jan. 1865.   (NS2/18:362)

ATCHERLEY ..., s. Col. Francis Atcherley, b. Prescott,
Canada, 15 Oct. 1866.   (NS3/2:819)

ATCHERLEY ..., s. Lt. Col. F T Atcherley, b. Brockville,
Canada West, 2 Jan. 1868.   (NS3/5:382)

ATHERTON N, solicitor, London, m. Sabina, dau. late David
Bernard, Jamaica, 20 April 1824.   (94:368)

ATHILL E, yst. dau. late James Athill, Antigua, m. John
Vassall, 13 May 1799.   (69:526)

ATHILL James, Lt., RN, m. Ellen, dau. late George Redhead,
ex Cap. 3rd Foot Guards, Antigua, London, 13 March 1850.
                                                   (NS33:657)

ATHILL Joseph Lyons, Assemblyman & judge, Antigua,
d. 18 Sep. 1790.   (60:1052)

ATHILL Samuel, b. 1786, est. s. Samuel Athill, Antigua,
barrister, d. Antigua, 21 Oct. 1811.   (81:657)

ATHILL Miss, dau. late Dr Athill, m. Cap. Bickerton,
HMS Sybil, Antigua, 1788.   (58:1181)

ATHILL Miss, dau. Samuel Athill, Antigua, m. Charles Turner,
London, 13 Jan. 1804.   (74:86)

ATKINS Edmund,Superintendent, Indian Affairs, d. 8 Oct. 1761.
                                                    (21:603)

ATKINSON Augustus Williams Henry, Lt., 99th Reg., m.
Pauline Rivers, est. dau. William C Hunter, NY, Hong Kong,
1 March 1864.   (NS2/17:106)

ATKINSON Fanny, Lancaster, m. Mr Willock, merchant, Antigua,
16 March 1777.   (47:147)

ATKINSON George, Secretary of Jamaica, m. Susannah Mackenzie
Dunkley, Clarendon, Jamaica, 1794.   (64:956)

ATKINSON Thomas jr., Glasgow, author, d. on passage to
Barbados, 10 Oct. 1833.   (104:670)

ATWOOD Francis William, son of Rev. T G P Atwood, Froxfield,
Wilts., d. San Francisco, 22 June 1867.   (NS3/2:539)

ATTWOOD Thomas, ex Chief Judge, Dominica & Bahamas, d. King's
Bench Prison, 27 June 1793.   (63:676)

AUCHENLECK Mrs Elizabeth, wid. Samuel Auchenleck, late
Customs Collector, Antigua, d. Antigua, 31 Aug. 1819.(89:284)

AUCHMUTY Nicholas, bro. Maj. Gen. Sir Samuel Auchmuty,
d. RI, Jan. 1813.   (83:660)

AUDAIN ..., s. John Audain, Richmond Hill, St Vincent,
b. Notting Hill, 13 Dec. 1860.   (NS2/10:94)

AUDOBON John James, b. New Orleans, 1774, naturalist,
d. NY, 27 Jan. 1851.   (NS35:440)

AUGIER Mrs, b.1777, dau. Dr Lyon, Liverpool, St Lucia, d. on
passage to Liverpool, 1803.   (73:1254)

AUSTIN Charlotte Teresa, only dau. Thomas Austin, m.J J Bury
Lt., RE, bro. Earl of Charleville, Chambly, Canada, 24 June
1852.   (NS38:302)

AUSTIN Eliza Howard, d. Bridgetown, Barbados, 16 Nov. 1848.
                                                    (NS31:222)

AUSTIN Emmeline, dau. late W Austin, Boston, Mass., m.
H S Le Strange, Norfolk, Boston, 26 Dec. 1866.   (NS3/3:239)

AUSTEN Rev. H Morland, Crayford, Kent, m. Mary, yst. dau.
William Parke, The Thickets, Jamaica, Sturminster, Dorset,
15 Sep. 1853.   (NS40:628)

AUSTIN John, Barbados, m. Letitia Cartwright, Notting Hill,
17 April 1801.   (71:371)

AUSTIN Rev. Preston Bruce, St George's, Demerara, s. Rev.
W S Austin, Gt. Bentley, Essex, m. Anna Eliza, only ch. late
R S Griffith, Barbados, 9 Dec. 1854.   (NS43:301)

AUSTIN Miss, dau. late Rev. Hugh William Austin, Barbados,
m. Cap. Goldfinch, Oxford Militia, Bath, 17 Jan. 1807.(77:88)

AUTON Lt. Col., b.1779, d. Bell Vue, Barbados, 9 Sep. 1856.
                                                 (NS2/1:657)

AXTELL William, b. Jamaica, 1720, NY Loyalist, d. Chertsea,
Sussex, 2 Sep. 1795.   (65:794)

AYLMER Henrietta, b.1819, w. George Edward Aylmer, Cap. 93rd
Highlanders, d. Toronto, 3 March 1844.   (NS21:670)

AYNSLEY William, Chief Justice, NJ, d.1758.   (28:452)

AYRE Christopher, Marshal of Vice Admiralty Court,NFD, m.
Eliza, est. dau. Nicolas Mitchell, Plymouth, 13 Oct. 1847.
                                                 (NS29:80)

AYTON A, b.1772, late Lynn, d. St Vincent, 2 July 1801.
                                                 (71:859)

BABINGTON Lucas, Newry, bro.-in-law R Lawrenson, Mt. Drummond,
s.-in-law late Charles Pasley, Dublin, d. St Louis, Mo., 1851.
                                                 (NS36:216)

BACHE Alexander Dallas, b. Philadelphia, July 1806,
scientist, d. Newport, RI, 17 Feb. 1867.   (NS3/3:541)

BACKHOUSE George Canning, b.1818, s. John Backhouse, Under-
Secretary of State, judge, d. Havanna, 30 Aug. 1855.
                                                 (NS54:553)

BACKHOUSE William, only s. William Backhouse, Sedburgh, Yorks.
d. Trinidad, 24 May 1800.   (70:901)

BACON Frances Hall, 2nd dau. Maj. Bacon, Seafield, m. Rev.
Henry MacDougall, Nassau, Bahamas, Isle of Man, 26 Aug. 1851.
                                                 (NS36:647)

BADHAM Arthur B, ex Trinity College, Dublin, d. on passage to
WI, 4 Feb. 1836.   (NS5:567)

BADNEDGE Edward, Judge Advocate, d. St Elizabeth, Jamaica, 1794.
                                                 (64:768)

BAGOT Sir Charles, b. 23 Sep. 1781, 2nd s. Lord Bagot, late
Gov. Gen. B.N.A., d. Kingston, Canada, 18 May 1843.(NS20:201)

BAGOT Georgina, yst. dau. late Sir Charles Bagot, Gov. Gen.
Canada, m. Lt. Col. Fraser, N.A.Staff, London, 21 Sep. 1843.
(NS20:539)

BAIJER Mrs, wid. John Otto Baijer, Antigua, d. Exeter,
April 1796.   (66.444)

BAILEY Joseph Gatcomb, Dyersville, USA, m. Frances Sophia,
yst. dau. late W H Collings, Paddington, 16 March 1858.
(NS2/4:544)

BAILEY William, b.1787, late Jamaica & Horton Lodge, Bucks.,
d. 16 Sep. 1819.   (89:379)

BAILLIE Annette, only dau. late Evan Baillie, barrister, m.
John Cameron, Tempe Estate, Grenada, 19 Jan. 1852.(NS37:509)

BAILLIE G, ex merchant, St Vincent, d. Brighton, 28 July 1809.
(79:785)

BAILLIE James, surveyor, d. Clarendon, Jamaica, 12 Oct. 1789.
(60:179)

BAILLIE James, ex merchant, Eustatia, d. Ealing, 7 Sep. 1793.
(63:869)

BAILLIE John, Sherwood Park, m. Anne, yst. dau. late
R Wilson, St Kitts, Southampton, 16 July 1806.   (76:774)

BAILLIE John, late Torquay, d. on passage from Falmouth to
Jamaica, 1832.   (102:94)

BAILLIE Samuel Crookshanks, d. Jamaica, 1790.   (60:476)

BAILLIE Thomas, b.1797, ex Surveyor Gen., NB, d. Boulogne-
sur-Mer, France, 3 June 1863.   (NS2/15:112)

BAILLIE William Douglas Hall, 24th Reg., est. s. Thomas
Baillie, Surveyor Gen., NB, m. Hannah Maria Anne, est. dau.
John Greensill, HM Ordnance storekeeper, Purfleet, Thurrock,
Essex, 11 July 1854.   (NS42:386)

BAILEY Mr, d. Jamaica on passage to Jamaica, 10 May 1798.
(68:903)

BAIN Alexander, d. WI, 1798.   (68:909)

BAIN Alexander, b.1767, ex Bahamas, late London, d. Wiesbaden,
Germany, 1846.   (NS25:111)

BAIN Donald, b. Thurso, Caithness, 1774, surgeon, d. St Jago,
Savanna, Clarendon, Jamaica, June 1801.   (72:83)

BAINBRIDGE Miss, dau. late Thomas Bainbridge, Jamaica, m.
George Wyatt, Hatton Garden, 25 July 1796.   (66:614)

BAIRD Adam, d. Jamaica, 1790.   (60:1214)

BAIRD Michael, d. York, Penn., 1816.   (86:629)

BAKER Charles Osborne, Cap., RMLI, m. Georgina Ann, only dau.
late John C Isaacs, Colonial Secretary, Tortula, Cornwall,
12 Oct. 1858.   (NS2/5:629)

BAKER Hugh Cossart m. Emma, daughter Henry Wyatt, ex Long
Ditton, Surrey, Canada, 15 Nov. 1845.   (NS25:199)

BAKER Hugh Cossett, Hamilton, Canada West, d. 2 March 1859.
          (NS2/6:546)

BAKER Mrs, late Boston, Mass., d. 27 Sep. 1786.   (56:908)

BAKER Mrs, wid. John Proculus Baker, Jamaica, d. Exeter,
3 March 1800.   (70:389)

BAKER Mrs, daughter late John Hammond Cole, Norwich, w.
George W Baker, ex Cap., RA, d. Bytown, Ottawa River,
Canada West, 24 Oct. 1851.   (NS37:106)

BAKER ..., s. Cap. R B Baker, 39th Reg., b. St George,
Bermuda, 7 March 1862.   (NS2/12:770)

BALDERSON Joseph, Virginian planter, d. 27 Sep. 1780.(50:447)

BALDING Joseph, b. 1741, d. Zanesville, Ohio, 1862.
          (NS2/13:791)

BALDWYN Edmond, NY, m. Sophia Griswold, 5th dau. late James
Nainby Hallett, NY, 18 Sep. 1843.   (NS20:539)

BALDWIN Eliza, b.1831, w. W W Baldwin, gdau. James MacQueen,
Kensington, d. Larchmore, Upper Canada, 27 Sep. 1855.
          (NS24:666)

BALDWIN John, Nassau Assemblyman, d. Nassau, Bahamas,
7 Jan. 1788.   (58:366)

BALDWIN Robert, statesman, d. Toronto, 9 Dec. 1858.(NS2/6:216)

BALDWIN William Warren, d. Toronto, 1844.   (NS21:671)

BALDWIN William Willcocks, son of Robert Baldwin, Canada, m.
Eliza, est. dau. late Alexander McDougall, Weston Hall,
Grenada, gdau. James MacQueen, Kensington, 29 Aug. 1854.
          (NS42:617)

BALDWIN Cap., 4th Reg., m. Miss Prescot, dau. Gov. in Chief,
BNA, Quebec Chateau, Aug. 1797.   (67:979)

BALDWIN Mrs, w. Cap. Baldwin, dau. Gov. Prescott, d.
Quebec, 1798.   (68:814)

BALFOUR Henry Lowther, Cap., RA, m. Blanche Anne, yst. dau.
Frederick Widder, Canadian Land Co., Toronto, 12 May 1863.
                                               (NS2/15:97)

BALFOUR Mrs, w. Lt. Col. William Balfour, 57th Reg., d.
Trinidad, 6 July 1802.   (72:878)

BALFOUR ..., s. Cap. Balfour, RA, b. Montreal, 21 Jan. 1866.
                                               (NS3/1:576)

BALFOUR ..., s. Cap. Balfour, RA, b. Toronto, 1 Jan. 1868.
                                               (NS3/5:382)

BALLENDEN Lord m. Sarah Cumming, wid., Montego Bay, Jamaica,
Leith, 26 June 1787.   (57:638)

BALME Mary Ann, daughter Paul Balme, London, m. Alfred Lowe,
US Consul, Civita Vecchia, Roman States, Ramsgate, 22 Aug.
1851.   (NS36:647)

BALTIMORE ..., dau. Lord Baltimore, b. Annapolis, Md.,
7 May 1733.   (3:325)

BANCKER Chr., NY, d. 13 April 1763.   (33:314)

BANKES Sutton, b.1749, yst. s. Robert Bankes, Sleaford, Lincs.
d. Lynwood Plant., Miss., 30 July 1803.   (73.1803)

BANKS Charles, b. Cadboll, Ross, merchant, Charleston, SC,
d. Philadelphia, 23 May 1813.   (83:592)

BANKS Mrs, w. Charles Banks, d. Charleston, SC, 14 May 1813.
                                               (83:592)

BANNATYNE Archibald m. Leonora, est. dau. S B Windsor,
Solicitor Gen., St Vincent, 1814.   (84:674)

BANNISTER Marianne, dau. John Bannister, Congressman, niece
Theodore Bane, Va. Congressman, m. Dr George Wilson,
Stotenleigh, late Edinburgh, 19 March 1789.   (59:761)

BARCLAY Alexander, b. Knockleith, Auchterless, s. Charles
Barclay, Receiver Gen., Jamaica, d. Kingston, Jamaica,
30 Oct. 1864.   (NS2/18:114)

BARCLAY Bathia, 2nd dau. Charles Barclay, Inchbroom, Moray,
m. Thomas McNeel, Custos, Westmoreland, Jamaica, 25 Jan. 1842.
                                               (NS17:429)

BARCLAY John Smith, b.1822, Cap., 39th Madras Native Infantry,
s. Alexander Barclay, Receiver Gen., Jamaica, Pegu, 31 Jan.
1859.   (NS2/6:653)

BARCLAY Margaret, 2nd dau. late George Barclay, Barbados, m.
Charles Taddy, 2nd s. Rev. John Taddy, Beds., 8 May 1843.
                                               (NS20:87)

BARCLAY Dr, Trinity Church, NY, d.20 Aug. 1764.   (34:498)

BARING Charles, b.1773, late Courtlands, Devon, d. Flat Rock,
NC, 7 Dec. 1865.   (NS3/1:438)

BARING Henry, 3rd s. Sir Francis Baring, m. Miss Bingham,
dau. Mr Bingham, US Senator, Philadelphia, 1802.   (72:684)

BARING Thomas Charles, son of Bishop Of Gloucester & Bristol,
m. Susan Carter, est. dau. Robert Bowne Minturn, NY,
15 Nov. 1859.   (NS2/8:176)

BARKER Isabella, 3rd dau. late George Barker, Leamington
Priory, Warwicks., m. James Lamond Smith, Glen Millan,
Abdns., Guelph, 22 Oct. 1844.   (NS23:196)

BARKER Rev. J C, St George, chaplain to Bishop of Barbados,
d. Tortula, 1842.   (NS18:101)

BARKER Cap., RA, ADC Gov., m. Mary Anne, est. dau. Walter
George Stewart, Island Secretary, Spanish Town, Jamaica,
16 March 1852.   (NS37:612)

BARLEE Catherine Maria, dau. late Rev. E Barlee, Worling-
worth, Suffolk, m. J Allen, s. Rev. T Allen, Stradbroke,
Suffolk, North Douro, Canada West, 11 April 1861.(NS2/10:694)

BARNABY Sir William, Cap., RN, m. Mrs Wood, wid. J Wood,
Bermuda, 2 May 1816.   (86:632)

BARNARD William Henry, son of late William Barnard,
Norwich, d. Autlan, Mexico, 2 June 1849.   (NS32:446)

BARNES Hannah, b.1766, wid. Joseph Barnes, Judge Supreme
Court Jamaica, ex Mayor, Kingston, Jamaica, d. Bristol,
13 Jan. 1841.   (NS15:331)

BARNES John Barker, d. St Croix, 12 Jan. 1807.   (77:376)

BARNETT Charles, yst. s. late H Barnett, Cobrey, Herefords.,
d. Jamaica, 17 Sep. 1853.   (NS40:649)

BARNETT Edward, late London, d. NA, 1813.   (83:505)

BARNETT Frances, Jamaica, m. Edward Woolery, Isleworth,
18 Sep. 1760.   (30:490)

BARNETT Harry Frederick, b.1815, surgeon, yst. s. late Dr
Barnett, Worcester, d. Trinidad, 30 Dec. 1853.   (NS41:439)

BARNETT Mary Ann, wid. Hugh Barnett, Sportsmanhall Estate,
Jamaica, d. Barnstaple, Devon, 26 Oct. 1846.   (NS26:665)

BARNETT Morris, comedian, d. Montreal, 18 March 1856.
                                                    (NS45:541)

BARNET Samuel, d. Jamaica, 1800.   (70:905)

BARNET William, Jamaica, m. Miss Wooling, Jamaica,
11 Sep. 1764.   (34:497)

BARNETT ..., daughter W Barnett, Jamaica, m. Rev. J Smith,
Chaplain to House of Commons, 9 Aug. 1803.   (73:788)

BARNETT Mr, Chief Justice, d. St Anne's, Jamaica, 1781.(51:394)

BARNETT Hugh, ex Jamaica, d. Kingsdown, 6 May 1823. (93:477)

BARNSDALE Bennall, b.1803, printer & publisher, 'The Baptist
Herald & Friend of Africa', d. Falmouth, Jamaica, 13 Sep.1841
                                                        (NS17:118)

BARR Beatrix Shedden, daughter late John Barr, Bermuda, m.
Maj. William Agg, 51st Light Inf., only s. W J Agg,
Hewletts, Glocs., Cheltenham, 7 Nov. 1861.   (NS2/11:678)

BARR Louisa Caroline, 5th dau. late John Barr, Bermuda, m.
William Clegg, Lt., 11th Reg., Brighton, 6 Feb. 1861.
                                                      (NS2/10:331)

BARR William Shedden m. Charlotte Eleanor Burnaby, dau. Rev.
John Lough, St George, Bermuda, 1 Jan. 1861.   (NS2/10:454)

BARRETT George Goodin, judge, politician & militia officer,
d. Cambridge Pen, St Thomas East, Jamaica, Oct. 1795.
                                                       (65:1112)

BARRETT George H, b.1794, tragedian, d. NY, 5 Sep. 1860.
                                                      (NS2/9:560)

BARRETT S, Jamaica, m. Margaret Gillies, dau. Robert Storey,
Arcot, Northumberland, 7 March 1812.   (82:288)

BARRETT Mrs Starr, b. Spain, 1699, d. Charleston, America,
9 Jan. 1820.   (90:377)

BARRETT S M, ex Carlton Hall, Yorks., d. Cinnamon Hill,
Jamaica, 23 Dec. 1837.   (NS9:334)

BARRETT W, staff-surgeon, m. Mary Anne, 2nd dau. Thomas Molson
Montreal, 3 June 1858.   (NS2/5:185)

BARRETT Miss, only dau. late Wisdom Barrett, Jamaica, m.
James Trant, Montserrat, Chelsea, 1798.   (68:1147)

BARRON Comm., USS Chesapeake, d. Norfolk, Va., 1810.(80:589)

BARRON Eustace, b.1791, d. Mexico City, 11 April 1859.
                                                      (NS2/9:89)

BARROW Eliza, dau. late J H Barrow, m. William Grassett,
Barbados, 26 March 1818.   (88:368)

BARROW Francis, b.1824, 10th s. John Barrow, Wedmore,
Somerset, d. Jamaica, 1842.   (NS18:335)

BARROW Senhouse, dau. J Barrow, Barbados, m. Lt. Col.Amwyl,
4th Reg., Barbados, 22 Oct. 1822.   (92:560)

BARRYMORE William, pantomime author, d. Boston, USA,
16 Feb. 1845.   (NS23:678)

BARTHROP William, est. s. late William Warner Barthrop,
Parham Hall, Suffolk, d. St Catherine, Upper Canada, Nov. 1850.
                                                  (NS36:216)

BARTLETT Clara Helena, only dau. J Bartlett, Belleville, m.
Frederick Charles Emberson, headmaster, Ontario College,
Picton, Belleville, Canada West, 8 July 1867.   (NS3/2:383)

BARTLETT Rev. Thomas Marsh, MA, chaplain to the forces at
Kingston, m. Sarah Baillie, est. dau. late Lt. Col. Duncan
Cameron, York Mills, Canada, 26 Sep. 1843.   (NS20:646)

BARTLETT Mrs, b.1817, w. Rev. T H M Bartlett, York Mills, d.
Toronto, 1842.   (NS19:110)

BARTON Henry Charles Benyon, only s. late Cap. Robert Cutts
Barton, RN, Burrough, Devon, m. Mary Ann, 2nd dau. late
Thomas Whitfoot O'Neal, Barbados, Cheltenham, 1 July 1845.
                                                  (NS24:415)

BARTON Jeremiah, politician & militia officer, d. Old Harbor,
Jamaica, 4 Nov. 1792.   (62:1220)

BARTRUM Rev. Joseph Plura, b.1781, ex St Kitts, d. London,
19 Sep. 1860.   (NS2/9:559)

BARWICK Andrew Hay, b.1834, 4th s. late Maj. James Barwick,
79th Reg., d. Mountblairy, Upper Canada, 9 Dec. 1851.
                                                  (NS37:312)

BASDEN Robert Home, b.1799, d. Dominica, 21 Nov. 1852.
                                                  (NS39:216)

BATEMAN Thomas George, b.1828, 4th s. Lt. Col. Bateman, d.
Kingston, Jamaica, 1 Dec. 1842.   (NS19:556)

BATEMAN Miss, actress, m. Mr Crow, surgeon, London, NY,
31 Oct. 1866.   (NS3/2:826)

BATES Joshua, b. Weymouth, Mass., 1788, merchant, d. 24 Sep.
1864.   (NS2/18:251)

BATSON Stanlake, Winfield, Berks., m. Miss Ricketts, only
dau. late Gov. Ricketts of Barbados, 14 Sep. 1818. (88:274)

BATSON William Nicholas, b.1819, New Orleans, d. London,
27 Aug. 1859.   (NS2/7:431)

BATTEN Rev. Charles Hamilton, b.1826, yngs. s. late Rev.
Joseph Hallet Batten, Principal, Haileybury College, d.
Kingston, Jamaica, 14 Nov. 1852.   (NS39:215)

BATY James, ex London, d. NY, March 1807.   (77:383)

BAXTER Margaret Maria, dau. late George Thomas Baxter, step-
dau. James Anderson, London, m. James Thompson, Halifax, NS,
Chapel of Royal Hospital, Bridewell, 14 May 1850. (NS34:200)

BAYER John Otto, b.1741, ex 82nd Reg., councillor, Antigua,
d. 10 May 1817.   (87:569)

BAYLEY Charles Thomson, s. late Rev. Henry Bayley, Tansor,
Northants., d. Peterborough, Canada West, 2 Nov. 1853.
                                                    (NS41:217)

BAYLEY Charlotte Augusta, dau. late Alexander Bayley, Wood
Hall, Jamaica, m. Charles Lyall, Barbados, yngs. s. John
Lyall, Brighton, Stapleton, Glocs., 21 Aug. 1845. (NS24:521)

BAYLEY Robert Souper, d. Spanish Town, Jamaica, 1800.(70:905)

BAYLISS Sarah Elizabeth, Spitalfield, m. Charles Stayner,
Gov., Churchill Factory, Hudson Bay, 5 Jan. 1798.   (68:83)

BAYLY Diana Sarah, dau. late Nathaniel Bayly, Jamaica, m.
Rev. Samuel Holworthy, MA, Croxall, Derbys., Cheshunt,
6 April 1811.   (81:392)

BAYLY Nathaniel, Bath, m. Melusina Warburton, dau. late
Arthur Freeman, Antigua, 24 Aug. 1795.   (65:703)

BAYLY Sophia Maria, dau. late N Bayly, Bayly's Vale, Jamaica,
m. Thomas Raikes jr., London, 24 May 1802.   (72:469)

BAYLY Miss, dau. late Nathaniel Bayly, Jamaica, d. Bath,
29 April 1857.   (2/2:740)

BAYNE Alexander, b.1830, only s. late Alexander Bayne, Board
of Ordnance, d. NY, 14 Aug. 1857.   (2/5:536)

BAYNES Edward Dacres, ex President of Montserrat, eldest s.
late Thomas Baynes, Com., RN, bro. Vice Adm. Sir R L Baynes,
d. Antigua, 5 Nov. 1864.   (NS2/16:129)

BAYNES Sarah Ann, w. Edwin Baynes, d. Grenada, 4 Sep. 1866.
                                                  (NS3/2:695)

BAYNTUN Charles, b.1814, eldest s. Edward Bayntun, Bromham,
Wilts., d. Jamaica, 16 Jan. 1833.   (103:479)

BAYNTUN Thomas, Jamaica, m. Miss Porter, Cheshunt, 4 Nov. 1758.
                                                    (28:556)

BAYS Peter Payne, b. Cambridge, 1784, shipmaster & author, d.
NY, 7 Feb. 1864.   (NS2/16:535)

BAZALGETTE Catherine Louise, 3rd dau. Col. Bazalgette, late
Dep. QM Gen., NS, m. Cap. Arthur Gove, 71st Highland Light
Inf., eldest s. Lt. Gen. Charles Gove, C.in C., NS,
Halifax, NS, 19 July 1854.   (NS42:499)

BAZALGETTE Herbert Sawyer, eldest s. Col. Bazalgette, C.O.
HM Forces, NS, d. Halifax, NS, 2 Sep. 1852.   (NS38:546)

BEACH Thomas, Attorney Gen. Jamaica, d.1774.   (46:446)

BEACHCROFT Robert Zoffannie, London, m. Emma, dau. E W Payne,
late NY, Merewith, Kent, 30 Nov. 1842.   (NS19:197)

BEALE Othniel, d. Charleston, America, 1773.   (43:303)

BEALL John Yates, Cap. CSN, d. NY, 24 Feb. 1865. (NS2/18:661)

BEALL Miss, Lewisham, dau. Edward Beall, late master shipwright, Jamaica, m. Martin Morryson, Greenwich Hospital,
Lewisham, Kent, 16 Feb. 1788.   (58:178)

BEARE James, ex Topsham, Devon, d. Grenada, 4 Jan. 1842.
                                                    (NS18:223)

BEARE Thomas, b.1823, eldest s. Samuel Shalders Beare,
Norwich, d. Bermuda, 26 Oct. 1843.   (NS21:334)

BEARE Thomas John, b.1819, eldest s. Samuel S Beare,
Norwich, d. St Domingo, 20 Oct. 1843.   (NS21:110)

BEAUCHAMP William, d. Philadelphia, 1798.   (68:1086)

BECHER Frances Anna Maria, eldest dau. Henry C R Becher, QC,
London, Canada, m. Cap. Stewart Hervey Bruce, 91st Reg.,
London, Canada, 19 Jan. 1864.   (NS2/16:378)

BECKELS Henry, Barbados, m. Miss Maxwell, 28 Sep. 1762.
                                                     (32:503)
BECKFORD Ballard, Jamaica, d. 23 May 1760.   (30:394)

BECKFORD Juliers, eldest s. Mr Beckford, estate owner,
Jamaica, m. Miss Ashey, dau. Solomon Ashey, MP, Bridport,
17 Jan. 1739.   (9:46)

BECKFORD Thomas, Jamaica, m. Mrs Burrel, Asted, Surrey,
11 Feb. 1745.   (15:108)

BECKLES H., s. President of Barbados, m. Susannah Beckles, dau.
late William Henry, Barbados, Marylebone, 17 July 1838.
                                                    (NS10:439)
BECKLES John Alleyne, ex President of Barbados, d. 14 July
1840.   (NS14:446)

BECKLES R., 3rd WI Reg., only s. Robert Beckles, Barbados,
gs. late John Alleyne Beckles, President of Barbados, m.
Helen, yngt. dau. late John Rogers, Westbury-on-Tyne,
20 Jan. 1852.   (NS37:401)

BECKWITH Clementina, w. Maj. Gen. Sir Sidney Beckwith, QM
Gen., NA, d. Canada, 19 March 1815.   (85:471)

BECKWITH John, b.1826, 2nd s. late Rev. H A Beckwith,
Collingham, d. Astoria, Oregon, 24 Dec. 1850.   (NS35:574)

BECKWITH Susan, 2nd dau. J Beckwith, The Bower, Halifax, m.
Cap. G Evatt, 55th Reg., NB, 31 May 1812.   (82:186)

BECKWITH Tarply, only s. Sir Marmaduke Beckwith, Va.,
d. 27 Dec. 1748.   (18:572)

BEDDOME Josephus, Hamilton, Upper Canada, b.1808, s.
Josephus Beddome, Manchester, gs. Com. Gen. Martin Petrie,
d. London, Canada West, 8 Nov. 1854.   (NS43:105)

BEDFORD Gunning, Gov., Del., d. America, 1797.   (67:1072)

BEDFORD James, Laugharne, South Wales, s. Col. Bedford,
Bengal Army, m. Sarah Elizabeth, eldest dau. Thomas Perch,
Barbados, Bath, 3 Feb. 1864.   (NS2/16:380)

BEDFORD John, b.1779, Vice Adm. Judge, d. Barbados,
30 Sep. 1807.   (77:1172)

BEDFORD Mrs, wid. John Bedford, late Vice Adm. Judge,
Barbados, d. on passage from Barbados, 23 March 1808.(78:459)

BEDINGFIELD Philip, RA, m. Arabella Gertrude, 2nd dau. Lt.
Col. Payne, Fredericton, NB, 28 Oct. 1851.   (NS37:181)

BEDWARD George jr., Spring Garden Est., Westmoreland, Jamaica,
d. on passage from Jamaica on Elizabeth, 1787.   (57:837)

BEECH Thomas, surgeon, ex Bracknell, Berks., d. Dominica,
Oct. 1812.   (83:284)

BEED Esther, w. William G Beed, dau. Rev. John Bishop,
Sussex, d. Hampton, Iowa, 21 March 1864.   (NS2/16:805)

BEEVER Rev. F J Holt, b.1830, d. banks of Missouri River,
29 July 1863.   (NS2/15:660)

BEGBIE Alexander, b.1757, Comm. Gen. Bahamas, d. Nassau, New
Providence, 22 April 1814.   (84:189)

BEGBIE Hariot, wid. Alexander Begbie, Comm. Gen. Bahamas,
d. London, 21 May 1842.   (NS18:106)

BEGBIE Hariot, dau. late Alexander Begbie, Comm. Gen.
Bahamas, d. Bayswater, 10 Feb. 1852.   (NS37:318)

BEGG William, b. Scotland, 1796, schoolmaster, Goderich,
d. Clinton, Canada, 1864.   (NS2/17:256)

BELCHER John, Gov., NJ, d. 31 Aug. 1757.   (27:531)

BELCHER Mary Anne, b.1796, eldest dau. Andrew Belcher, late
Halifax, NS, d. Westminster, 5 Feb. 1812.   (82:195)

BELFOUR Rev. Hugo John, b.1802, Jamaica, neph. late Okey
Belfour, St John's Wood, d. Jamaica, Sep. 1827.   (97:570)

BELISARIO A M, m. Esther, dau. Alexander Lindo, Kingston,
Jamaica, 1791.   (61:774)

BELL Aline, yngs. dau. Thomas Bell, ex Stockton-on-Tees,
President of Dominica, m. John Richard Walcot, Black Bay Est.
Grenada, 15 Dec. 1859.   (NS2/8:289)

BELL Miss Elizabeth, ex Glasgow, m. John Campbell, Lanethall,
Jamaica, 1790.   (60:1213)

BELL Rev. Frederick, Clifton, yngs. s. late Thomas Bell, MD,
Dublin, m. Mary Pennington, yngs. dau. late Edward Bullock,
Jamaica, Clifton, 16 March 1843.   (NS19:528)

BELL James, MD, ex Kelso, d. Bluecastle, Westmoreland,
Jamaica, 15 Jan. 1801.   (71:372)

BELL James Alexander, b.1801, Bermuda, d. Liverpool,
23 Sep. 1838.   (NS10:564)

BELL John, Chief Justice, Portland, Jamaica, d. Kingston,
Jamaica, 10 July 1774.   (44:446)

BELL John Frederick, 47th Reg., s. Frederick Brown Bell,
Norfolk, m. Maria Aletta, dau. Maj. Gen. George Napier,
Toronto, 16 Oct. 1862.   (NS2/13:770)

BELL Richard, d. Boston, Mass., 18 Oct. 1757.   (27:577)

BELL Russell, 8th s. late Thomas Bell, Hackney, of Hermann &
Co., d. Norfolk, Va., 15 Sep. 1845.   (NS24:666)

BELL Thomas, Comm. Dept., s. late T Bell, London, d. Trinidad
6 May 1817.   (87:638)

BELL Thomas, b.1800, President of Dominica, d. Dominica,
14 Oct. 1861.   (NS2/11:692)

BELL Gen., b.1749, Trelawney, Jamaica, d. London,30 Oct. 1816
                                                   (86.471)

BELLAIRS William, Maj., 49th Reg., m. Emily Craven, eldest
dau. William Barton Gibbons, Barbados, 16 Sep. 1857.
                                                   (NS2/3:673)

BENGER Elliot, Dep. PMG America, d. Va., 1751.   (21:427)

BENISON Georgina, dau. Maj. Benison, 39th Reg., m. Cap.
Allan Elliot Lockhart, RE, St George, Bermuda, 4 June 1864.
(NS2/17:234)

BENJAMIN Caroline, yngs. dau. Robert W Benjamin, m. Thomas
Holmes, Customs Collector, Grenada, Demerara, 19 Nov. 1841.
(NS17:321)

BENJAMIN Henry, b.1806, Quebec, d. Finsbury, 5 April 1857.
(NS2/2:629)

BENNET Beverley, b.1779, d.Tinderhook, America, 1804. (74:87)

BENNETT Emma, eldest dau. Robert Ward, Brighton, w. Charles
Bennett, magistrate, d. St Lucia, 19 Oct. 1839.   (NS13:333)

BENNETT Henry Edward, s. Rev. H Bennett, Sparkford, Somerset,
m. Louisa Birchall, yngs. dau. Chief Justice MacAulay,
Toronto, 26 Nov. 1857.   (NS2/4:207)

BENNET James, Barbados, d. Thame, 6 Feb. 1758.   (28:94)

BENNETT Marshall, Appleby House, Isle of Wight, d. Honduras,
3 Oct. 1839.   (NS13:110)

BENNETT Mary Sophia, w. D Bennett, 2nd dau. late Gen. Legge,
Chaxhill, Glocs., d. NB, Nov. 1841.   (NS17:230)

BENNET Richard, d. Wye River, America, 1749.   (20:43)

BENNET Samuel, Jamaica, d. 22 Jan. 1755.   (25:43)

BENNETT Thomas, eldest s. Alderman Bennett, Shaftesbury, m.
Hannah Hutchings, niece Col. Williams & Maj. Skinner, RA,
St Johns, NFD, 5 Jan. 1828.   (98:175)

BENNET William, late Kingsdownparade, Bristol, d. on passage
to America, 1 March 1807.   (77:485)

BENNET William, yngs. s. Philip Bennet, Rougham, Norfolk,
d. Weston, Canada, 25 July 1849.   (NS32:447)

BENNY James, Demerara, d. Barbados, 15 Dec. 1820.   (91:186)

BENSON W J C, Quebec, b.1816, d. Whitehall, Lake Champlain,
2 Dec. 1850.   (NS35:334)

BENT Cap., 5th Reg., m. Elizabeth Paul, dau. Gov. St Vincent,
1822.   (93:79)

BENTALL Mrs Henry, b.1775, d.Bridgetown, Barbados, at her
son Alexander Stewart's residence, 25 June 1845.   (NS24:326)

BENYON Thomas, Thorp Arch, Yorks., m. Julia, 2nd dau. late
John Waterhouse, Kingston, Jamaica, Brenchley, Kent,
9 July 1862.   (NS2/13:225)

BENYON William Henry, 23rd Royal Welsh Fusiliers, m. Bessie
Rea, eldest dau. Andrew Allan, Montreal, 21 Nov. 1867.
(NS3/5:103)

BERESFORD Elizabeth Keturah, b.1785, wid. James Beresford,
Royal York Rangers, 1st WI Reg., 2nd dau. late Barwick Bruce,
MD, Barbados, d. at home of s. Barwick Beresford, MD,
3 March 1852.   (NS37:530)

BERESFORD Lady, w. Sir John Beresford, Com. HMS Poitiers,
d. Bermuda, 1 July 1813.   (83:195)

BERKELEY Alexander Henry Hastings, b.1824, 2nd s. Gen. Sir
George Berkeley, British Attache, d. Mexico, 8 July 1854.
(NS42:206)

BERKELEY Anne, eldest dau. Lt. Gen. S H Berkeley, C.O., WI,
ggdau. Dr Alexander Bruce, Barbados, m. Cap. A Carden, 60th
Rifles, Barbados, 4 Aug. 1847.   (NS28:533)

BERKELEY Frederick George, Cap., 47th Reg., 2nd s. Charles
Berkeley, London, m. Mary Louisa, 2nd dau. William Dickson,
Niagara, Canada, Guelph, 28 Sep. 1865.   (NS2/19:640)

BERKELEY Mary, wid. Thomas Berkeley, Grenada, m. Maj. W H
Hartman, 9th Reg., London, 12 July 1842.   (NS18:312)

BERKLEY S H, Lt. Col., 16th Reg., Dep. Adjutant, Windward &
Leeward Islands, m. Elizabeth, 2nd dau. William Murray,
Barbados, 24 Feb. 1818.   (88:464)

BERKELEY Mrs, b.1792, wid. John Berkeley, Grenada, d. Datehill
Antigua, the residence of her s. Rev. A Berkeley, St George,
26 Feb. 1856.   (NS45:545)

BERNAL Mrs, wid. J I Bernal, Jamaica, d. London, 7 Jan. 1832.
(102:92)

BERNARD Charles, d. Jamaica, 1790.   (60:1148)

BERNARD Charles Edward, MD, b. Jamaica, d. Bristol, 18 Nov.
1842.   (NS19:93)

BERNARD David, planter, Barbados, d.1773.   (43:581)

BERNARD Daniel P., ex Jamaica, d.24 Dec. 1816.   (87:374)

BERNARD Francis, Boston, NE, d.1770.   (40:591)

BERNARD Sir Francis, Nettleham, Lincs., ex Gov. Mass.,
d. 16 June 1779.   (49:327)

BERNARD Sir John, b.1745, 2nd s. late Sir Francis Bernard,
Gov. NJ & Mass., d. WI, 1810.   (80:92)

BERNARD Rachel, yngs. dau. late D Bernard, Jamaica,
d. Cheltenham, 2 March 1832.   (102:284)

BERNARD Sabina, dau. late David Bernard, Jamaica, m.
N Atherton, solicitor, London, 20 April 1824.   (94:368)

BERNARD Thomas James, judge, St Anne's, Jamaica, d. Jamaica,
3 March 1850.   (NS33:558)

BERRY Dorothy, w. Curtis Philip Berry, d. Jamaica, 5 June
1835.   (NS4:335)

BERRY John, NY, m. Miss Smear, eldest dau. Rev. Christopher
Smear, Frostenden, Suffolk, 24 Oct. 1795.   (65:878)

BERTIE Brownlow Charles, b.1820, yngs. s. Earl of Abingdon,
ex 9th Lancers & 2nd Life Guards, d. on passage from
Panama to San Francisco, 30 Dec. 1852.   (NS39:448)

BERTHON Miss, London, m. George Hammond, ex Jamaica,
6 Aug. 1793.   (63:859)

BERTHONNEAU John, d. Jamaica, 1791.   (61:186)

BERTRAND E R, Tabery, Dominica, m. Frances Elizabeth, dau.
R Newton, Coldrey, Hants, Froyle, Hants., 1 Feb. 1823.(93:272)

BERTRAND Frances Elizabeth, eldest dau. late Robert Newton,
Coldry, Hants., d. Tabery, Dominica, 7 Dec. 1842. (NS19:556)

BEST Arthur, b.1800, Hertford, d. Anotta Bay, Jamaica, 1821.
                                                     (91:648)

BEST Frances Maria, 2nd dau. John Rycroft Best, Barbados, m.
S R Wybault, Charlton Kings, 2 June 1846.   - (NS26:197)

BEST Rev. George, ex Westminster, m. Elizabeth, dau. Bishop
NS, Halifax, NA, 21 Aug. 1820.   (90:464)

BEST George Granville, HMS Imaum, b.1826, 2nd s. late Archdeacon Best, Fredericton, NB, d. Jamaica, 17 Feb. 1849.
                                                    (NS31:558)

BEST H Compton, Lt., RN, 2nd s. George Best, Surrey, m.
Henrietta Jane, 2nd dau. Lt. Gen. St John A Clarke, Dublin,
Halifax, NS, 25 July 1865.   (NS2/19:373)

BEST Rev. Robert Stanser, b.1823, eldest s. late Archdeacon
Best, Fredericton, NB, gs. late Rev. Robert Stanser, Bishop,
NS, d. Malta, 1848.   (NS29:446)

BETHUNE Angus, merchant, ex Charleston, SC, m. Miss Horton,
dau. John Horton, merchant, London, 14 March 1792. (62:278)

BETHUNE Rev. Charles J S, s. Archdeacon, Toronto, m. Harriet
Alice Mary, dau. late Lt. Col. Forlong, Gore Vale, Toronto,
21 April 1863.   (NS2/15:96)

BETHUNE Rev., b. Scotland, missionary, d. Jamaica, 1800.
                                                     (70:905)

BETHUNE Rev. J, b. Scotland, 1750, ex chaplain 84th(Royal
Highland Emigrants)Reg., d. Williamstown, Upper Canada,
23 Sep. 1815.   (85:635)

BEVAN Sophia, 5th dau. late Robert Bevan, m. Jacob George
Mountain, Principal, St Johns College, NFD., Rougham,
5 Sep. 1854.   (NS42:617)

BEWES ..., 3rd s. Thomas Bewes, MP, Plymouth, d. Jamaica,
30 June 1835.   (NS4:446)

BEWLEY Mrs Mary Anne, wid. T H Bewley, d. Stewart's Town,
Jamaica, 9 Sep. 1838.   (NS10:671)

BEWLEY Rev. T H, Gen. Supt. Weslayan Mission Schools, Jamaica
d. Stewart's Town, Jamaica, 14 July 1838.   (NS10:671)

BICKERTON Cap., HMS Sybil, s. Sir Richard Bickerton, m. Miss
Athill, dau. late Dr Athill, Antigua, 1788.   (58:1181)

BICKERTON Lady Hussey, b.1769, dau. James Athill, Antigua,
wid. Adm. Sir Richard Hussey Bickerton, d. Bath, 2 March 1850.
                                                    (NS33:453)

BIDDLE Nicholas, ex President US Bank, d. Philadelphia, 1844.
                                                    (NS21:657)

BIDEWELL Rev. E T, Orcheston St Mary, Wilts., m. Frederica
Emma Laura Spencer, 2nd dau. late Rev. F H Carrington,
St Johns, NFD, Shoreditch, 26 Oct. 1843.   (NS20:648)

BIDWELL Charles Toll m. Amelia, yngs. dau. late Manuel Jose
Hurtado, Columbia, Panama, 12 Jan. 1861.   (NS2/10:330)

BIGNALL Mrs, theater owner in Charleston, Norfolk & Richmond,
m. James West, ex Theater Royal, Bath, Norfolk, SC, 22 May
1795.   (65:701)

BILENFANTE Deborah m. Simon Meffiat, Barbados, 1768. (38:198)

BILLINGHURST Joseph, Yapton, Sussex, m. Margaret Elizabeth,
eldest dau. Dr Alexander Melville, MD, St Vincent, 28 March
1827.   (96:557)

BINGHAM Maria Matilda, dau. William Bingham, USA, m.
Le Marquis du Blaisel, Chamberlain to the Emperor of Austria,
17 April 1826.   (96:461)

BINGHAM William, b.1752, Philadelphia, US Senator, d. Bath,
6 Feb. 1804.   (74:188)

BINGHAM Miss, dau. Senator Bingham, Philadelphia, m. Henry,
3rd s. Sir Francis Baring, 1802.   (72:684)

BINGLEY Peregrine Taylor, 2nd s. late T B Bingley, Bengal Horse Artillery, m. Caroline Haughton Clarke, dau. late John H James, Jamaica, wid. Lt. Col. Clarke, Grenadier Guards, Bayswater, 20 Oct. 1852.   (NS39:86)

BINHAM H, s. Dr Binham, Hanover, d. Iron Shore Wharf, Jamaica, 22 June 1798.   (68:811)

BINNEY Charles, RE, m. Emma Louisa, dau. J T Walford, ex 64th Reg., Halifax, NS, 27 Nov. 1845.   (NS25:199)

BINNEY Rev. Hibbert, Bishop, NS, m. Mary, dau. William Blower Bliss, Supreme Court judge, Halifax, NS, 4 Jan. 1855.
                                                     (43:302)

BINNEY J, Lt., RN, s. H N Binney, NS, m. Anna, dau. late Rev. Edward Marshall, Jamaica, Putney, 1822.   (92:640)

BINNS Edward, MD, d. Jamaica, 10 Feb. 1851.   (NS35:574)

BIRCH Margaret Fanny, w. William John Birch, Oxfordshire, d. Philadelphia, 11 Jan. 1857.   (NS2/2:369)

BIRCH Richard, late Kingston, d. Falmouth, Jamaica, Nov. 1801.
                                                     (72:181)

BIRCH R J Wryley, Cap., 30th Reg., 2nd s. G W Birch, Wretham, Norfolk, m. Catherine Leonora Margaret, 2nd dau. late Alex. Vass, Montreal, 31 Oct. 1867.   (NS3/5:102)

BIRD James, b.1775, Chief Factor, Hudson Bay Co., Red River Settlement, d. 18 Oct. 1856.   (NS2/2:248)

BIRRELL George, ex Attorney Gen. St Lucia & Bahamas, d. Nassau, New Providence, 9 March 1837.   (NS7:670)

BIRT Jabez Sheen, b.1790, Tewkesbury, surgeon to Emperor Christophe, d. Haiti, 1825.   (95:647)

BISCOE Caroline Octavia, yngs. dau. late Joseph Seymour Biscoe, Pendhill, Surrey, m. Justice Stevenson, Supreme Court Jamaica, Barnwood, 9 June 1852.   (NS38:195)

BISCOE Catherine Mary, eldest dau. late Maj. V Biscoe, RE, Kent, m. Cap. Edward Osborne Hewett, RE, Toronto, 4 Feb. 1864
                                                     (NS2/16:520)

BISHOP Anne, wid. Sir H R Bishop, m. M Schultz, NY, London, 20 Dec. 1859.   (NS2/6:91)

BISHOP Mrs, dau. Charles Craven, ex Gov. SC, d. Fairford, Glocs., 1816.   (86:473)

BLACK George, Cap., Royal Canadian Rifles, m. Louisa Philips, 3rd dau. Cap. Sir John Marshall, Gillingham, Kent, 5 Oct. 1841.
                                                     (NS16:648)

BLACKALL Mrs, w. Lt. Gov. Blackall, d.Dominica, 2 May 1853.
                                                     (NS40:98)

BLACKBURN Col. Thomas, d. Rippon Lodge, Va., 17 July 1807.
(77.889)

BLACKHOOF, b.1717, Shawnee Chief, d. Wapaghkonnett, 1 Nov.
1831.   (101:478)

BLACKMAN John Lucie, Barbados, d. Leeward Islands, 1780.
(50:445)

BLACKWELL Fanny Merriman, eldest dau. Thomas E Blackwell,
Clifton, England, & Montreal, m. Gilbert Prout Girdwood,
surgeon, Grenadier Guards, Montreal, 9 April 1862.(NS2/12:773)

BLACKWELL Cap., eldest s. Maj. Gen. Blackwell, m. Elizabeth,
only dau. late Francis Johnston, London, Tobago, 26 April
1832.   (102:172)

BLACKWOOD John, late Quebec, d. Bath, 25 June 1819.   (89:89)

BLACKWOOD John, b.1762, late Canada, d. London, 29 March
1835.   (105:555)

BLACKWOOD Percy, Col. Sec. Tobago, b.1840, yngs. s. Sir
Henry M Blackwood, d. Southsea, Hants., 1 June 1866.
(Ns3/2:119)

BLAGROVE Ann, b.1753, wid. John Blagrove, late Jamaica, d.
London, 16 Jan. 1834.   (104:228)

BLAGROVE Charles Campbell, 2nd s. J Blagrove, Cardiffhall,
Jamaica, d. Rotterdam, 26 Oct. 1815.   (82:671)

BLAGROVE Henry John, s. late F R Coore, London, m. Eliza,
eldest dau. Utten J Todd, The Ridge, Jamaica, 25 July 1850.
(NS34:540)

BLAGROVE Peter, 3rd s. John Blagrove, Jamaica, d. Orange
Valley Est., St Anne's, Jamaica, 1812.   (82:192)

BLAIR Adam Johnston Ferguson, Canada, 2nd s. Adam Ferguson
Blair, Balthayock, Perths., d. Ottowa, 29 Dec. 1867.
(NS3/5:259)

BLAIR Rev. James, Commissary Bishop London, President William
& Mary College, Va., d.1743.   (13:443)

BLAIR James, bro. late Dr Blair, late partner Blair Napier
& Co, Charleston, SC, d. Brighton, 1815.   (85:91)

BLAIR James Bannatyne, Lt., 6th Reg., m. Helen Josephine, dau.
late George Geddes, Halfway-tree Church, Jamaica, 5 Oct.1865.
(NS3/1:117)

BLAIR John, late Worthy Park, Jamaica, d. London, 15 Dec.
1846.   (NS27:213)

BLAKE Daniel, s. William Blake, London, m. Miss Middleton,
dau. late Arthur Middleton, Congressman, SC, 1800.   (70:484)

BLAKE Edward, barrister, Toronto, eldest s. Chancellor of
Upper Canada, m. Margaret, 2nd dau. Bishop of Huron,
London, 6 Jan. 1857.   (NS2/4:326)

BLAKE N, b.1712, Wrentham, Mass., d. Keene, USA, 4 Aug. 1811.
                                                        (81:390)

BLAKE P., Sevenoaks, Kent, m. John Sober, Barbados,
6 Nov. 1760.   (NS18:102)

BLAKE Rev. Robert, b.1771, ex Yorks. & Lancs., settled
Piermont, NH, 1819, d. Woodburn, Macoupin Co., Ill.,
21 March 1842.   (NS18.102)

BLAKE Lt. Col., 20th Light Dragoons, m. Miss Hanson, dau.
late John Hanson, Jamaica, Hampton, 1814.   (84:392)

BLAND John B. m. Mary Maud, 2nd dau. Rev. Dr Porter, Exeter,
ex President, King's College, NS, Halifax, NS, 30 May 1848.
                                                        (NS30:198)

BLAND Mr, hus. Mrs Bland, Theatre Royal, Drury Lane, bro. Mrs
Jordan, d. Boston, USA, 1807.   (77.1075)

BLANSHARD Jane, yngs. dau. late John Blanshard, HEICS, m.
Thomas Pemberton, St Kitts, Broadstairs, 12 Aug. 1846.
                                                        (NS26:420)

BLAQUIERE Louise Emily, dau. B P Blaquiere, m. Arthur A
Farmer, Huntingford, Canada West, 2nd s. late W M Farmer,
Nonsuch Park, Surrey, Kingston, Canada West, 3 Feb. 1846.
                                                        (NS25:534)

BLATCH Emily, b.1804, eldest dau. late George Roberts,
Warminster, w. George Blatch, d. St Johns, NFD, 27 July 1844.
                                                        (NS22:446)

BLAYDES Hugh Marvel, eldest s. late Hugh Blaydes, Banby Hall,
Notts., d. Halifax, NS, 1835.   (NS5:446)

BLEAKLEY Mary Ann, b.1818, dau. late Stephen Yarwood, RN,
w. John Bleakley, d. Montreal, 8 Nov. 1850.   (NS35:223)

BLENKARNE Amelia Louisa, yngr. dau. Cap. Blenkarne, Ordnance
Dept., ex 14th Reg., m. Douglas, 23rd Fusiliers, eldest s.
Stephen Grantham, Ryders Wells, Sussex, Montreal, 10 Nov.1848.
                                                        (NS31:80)

BLENMAN Jonathan, Solicitor Gen., Barbados, d.13 Feb. 1807.
                                                        (77.484)

BLENMAN Jonathan, b.1785, s. John Blenman, Solicitor Gen.,
Barbados, barrister, d. Penzance, 22 July 1843.   (NS20:329)

BLENMAN Mrs, wid. Rev. Timothy Blenman, late Barbados, d.
Clifton, Bristol, 27 Nov. 1820.   (90:571)

BLICHENDON Arthur, planter, Jamaica, d.1780.   (50:155)

BLINDSHALL Henry Booth, Jamaica, d. London, 1794.   (64:865)

BLINSHALL Mrs, wid. Thomas Blinshall, Clarendon, Jamaica,
d. Hastings, 11 Jan. 1802.   (72:93)

BLISS Mary, dau. William Blowers Bliss, Supreme Court judge,
m. Rev. Hibbert Binney, Bishop of NS, Halifax, NS, 4 Jan.1855.
                                                    (NS43:302)
BLISS Samuel, b.1647, Springfield, NE, d.27 July 1749.(19:429)

BLIZARD Stephen, b.1702, Speaker, Antiguan Assembly, Militia
Col., Chief Justice, d.24 Nov. 1777.   (47:556)

BLOMFIELD Francis, b.1827, 3rd s. C J Blomfield, Bishop of
London, d. wreck of Northerner, Cape Menocino, Cal.,
5 Jan. 1860.   (NS28:415)

BLOUNT George, Henley-on-Thames, m. Esther Thibou, Antigua,
2 Jan. 1753.   (23:51)

BLUCKE R., 4th s. late Rev. Robert Blucke, Edlesborough,
Bucks., d. Tobago, 11 Nov. 1833.   (104:343)

BLYTH Miss, niece J Betts, m. Chevalier D'Estimauville,
Canada, Boston, Lincs., 3 June 1796.   (66:523)

BOAK William, merchant, Hart & Boak, NY, d. London, 1 Aug.1838.
                                                    (NS10:338)
BOCHER Alexander, Lt., HMS Prosperine, m. Frances, dau. late
Rev. Scott, Port Royal, Jamaica, 1793.   (63:860)

BODDEN William, b.1722, Chief Magistrate, Grand Cayman Island,
d.23 April 1789.   (59:670)

BODDINGTON Mr, ex Portsmouth, gun-carriage foreman, d.
Washington, USA, Oct. 1810.   (80:283)

BOERUM Simon, Delegate to Continental Congress, d.11 July 1775
                                                       (45:407)
BOGARD Abraham, b. Del., 1715, d. Maury Co., Tenn., 14 June
1833.   (103:286)

BOGLE Allan James, Bogle & Co., Jamaica, drowned, 1814(84:508)

BOLAND Mr, d. St George's Bay, NFD, March 1856.   (NS2/1:775)

BOLDERO Eutychia Ann, b.1759, dau. Rev. Thomas Harmer,
Wattisfield, Suffolk, wid. Edmund Boldero, Bury St Edmonds,
d. Berlin, USA, at house of Rev. C A Goodrich, 27 March 1842.
                                                    (NS17:678)

BOLDERSON Joseph, planter, Va., d.27 Sep. 1780.   (50:447)

BOLTON Robert jr., gs. Rev. William Jay, Bath, m. Elizabeth R
Brenton, niece Adm. Brenton, late Newport, RI, Eastchester,
NY, 8 Jan. 1838.   (NS9:424)

BOLTON Sophia, 2nd dau. Henry Bolton, Chief Justice, NFD.,
m. James, Lt. Col., 43rd Light Inf., 2nd s. late W Furlong,
Wellshot House, Lanarks., Toronto, 15 June 1842.   (NS18:199)

BOLTON William Jay, Caius College, Cambridge, 2nd s. Rev.
R Bolton, NY, m. Susanna, 2nd dau. late William Welch,
Stoke Newington, Lynn, 26 Sep. 1849.   (NS32:639)

BOND P., b.1748, ex HM Consul, Mid & South USA, d. London,
29 Dec. 1815.   (85:643)

BOND Rebecca, b.1758, late USA, d. Brighton, 16 July 1843.
                                                 (NS20:332)

BOND Williamina, b.1728, mo. Phineas Bond, HM Consul Gen.,
d. Philadelphia, 30 Jan. 1809.   (79:278)

BONHAM Lt. Col., 69th Reg., m. Agnes Skeete, niece William
Bishop, Gov. Barbados, Bridgetown, Barbados, 26 Feb. 1800.
                                                  (70:588)

BONNELL William Franklin, Digby, NS, m. Anna, dau. H Collins,
London, 10 Dec. 1808.   (78:1126)

BONNYCASTLE Charles, b.1797, Prof., Univ. Charlottesville,
Va., d. Charlottesville, 31 Oct. 1840.   (NS15:110)

BONTEIN Mrs, w. Thomas Bontein, Jamaica, d. 10 June 1806.
                                                  (76:678)

BOONE Phoebe, b. SC, w. W J Boone, Bishop Shanghai, d. Suez,
20 Jan. 1864.   (NS2/16:401)

BOON Col., d. Missouri, July 1818.   (88:469)

BOOTH James, b.1807, Boston, USA, d. London, 14 April 1850.
                                                 (NS33:680)

BOOTH Robert, Asst. Comm. Gen., s. late Rev. R Booth, Rodmill,
Sussex, d. Jamaica, 1 Nov. 1867.   (NS3/5:112)

BOOTH Cap., Gov. Montserrat, d. Montserrat, 30 Aug. 1853.
                                                 (NS41:438)

BORDEN Abraham, Gen. Treasurer RI, d. 30 Dec. 1732. (3:102)

BORLEBROG Anne, actress, d. Charleston, NA, 1827.   (97:94)

BORROWES Erasmus, 97th Reg., eldest s. Rev. E Borrowes, m.
Frederica Esten, eldest dau. Lt. Col. Hutchison, 97th Reg.,
Bellevue, Halifax, NS, 14 Aug. 1851.   (NS36:533)

BOSWELL David, d. Montego Bay, Jamaica, 18 Jan. 1790.(60:372)

BOTECOURT Lord, Gov. Gen. Va.; d. 1770.   (40:591)

BOUCHER Richard, b.1754, d. Jamaica, 12 Dec. 1832. (103:190)

BOUCHETTE Joseph, b.1774, Surveyor Gen. Quebec, Militia Col,
d. Montreal, 8 April 1841.   (NS15:671)

BOUGHEY George Fenton Fletcher, Cap., 59th Reg., 3rd s.late
Sir J F Boughey, m. Matilda Elwin, 4th dau. George
Weatherill Ottley, Parry's, Antigua, 16 Dec. 1842. (NS19:311)

BOUGHTON Jane Anne, eldest dau. Thomas Boughton, Peckham,
Surrey, m. Rev. J C Harvey, St Johns, NFD., 4 Aug. 1842.
                                                  (NS18:420)

BOULBY Miss, dau. late Henry Boulby, Newcastle, m. Thomas
Alderson, Hertford, Jamaica, Denham, Norfolk, 12 May 1789.
                                                  (59:467)

BOULDIN Judge, successor to late John Randolph of Roanoke,
d. House Reps., NY, 1834.   (104:454)

BOULTON Henry John, s. H J Boulton, Toronto, late Chief
Justice, NFD, m. Charlotte, dau. Henry Rudverd, Colne House,
Iver, Bucks., 23 Sep. 1852.   (NS38:631)

BOULTON Jane, 2nd dau. Col. James Graham, gdau. Gen. Samuel
Graham, Stirling Castle, w. Forster Boulton, d. Port Hope,
Canada West, 16 Dec. 1863.   (NS2/16:263)

BOULTON Rev. William, b.1807, yngs. s. D'Arcy Boulton,
barrister, d. Toronto, 31 May 1834.   (104:441)

BOULTON William Somerville, b.1831, eldest s. late Rev.
William Boulton, Upper Canada College, Toronto, gs. late
Cap. Henry Carew, RN, Devon, d. wreck Hungarian, Sable Island
NS, 20 Feb. 1860.   (NS2/8:524)

BOULTON ..., s. Chief Judge Boulton, b. St Johns, NFD.,
4 May 1834.   (104:101)

BOURKE John, b.1776, late Kingston, Jamaica, d. Knightsbridge
20 Oct. 1814.   (84:503)

BOURKE Maria m. James B Thomason, s. Thomas Thomason, Tortula
St Croix, 15 Oct. 1791.   (61:1157)

BOURKE Nicholas, Jamaica, d.1772.   (42:151)

BOURNE Emily, b.1832, dau. late J G H Bourne, Chief Justice,
NFD., d. London, 24 Oct. 1846.   (NS26:663)

BOURNE Rev. Samuel Whitbread m. Mary Caroline, eldest dau.
late Henry R Cassin, MD, Nevis, Islington, 24 March 1852.
                                                  (NS37:512)
BOURNE Sylvanus, NE, d.18 Sep. 1763.   (33:565)

BOVELL Mary, only dau. late J Bovell, MD, Barbados, m. Rev.
H Payne Hope, Christon, Somerset, 16 July 1834.   (104:312)

BOWDEN Rev. Edward, b.1796, s. J S Bowden, Hull, d. St George
Bermuda, 14 Aug. 1817.   (87:561)

BOWDINE William, d. Boston, Mass., 4 Sep. 1747.   (17:544)

BOWDITCH Nathaniel, President American Academy Arts Science,
d. Boston, America, 1838.   (NS10:446)

BOWDOIN James, ex Gov. NE, d. Boston, NE, 6 Nov. 1790.
                                                    (60:1147)

BOWDOIN James Temple, b.1776, 2nd s. late Sir John Temple,
gs. Gov. Bowdoin, Mass., d. Twi:kenham, 31 Oct. 1842.
                                                    (NS18:674)

BOWEN Dr Francis, s. Edward Bowen, Chief Justice Quebec, m.
Constantia Caroline, 2nd dau. late Robert Shore Milnes
Sewell, Quebec, gdau. Jonathan Sewell, ex Chief Justice
Quebec, Chilver's Cotton Vicarage, 8 Jan. 1861. (NS2/10:201)

BOWEN Rev. John,St Vincent, only s. Rear Adm. J Bowen,
Ilfracombe, Devon, m. Dorothy, only dau. late E Bullock,
Jamaica, St George's, Bloomsbury, 27 April 1830.   (100:460)

BOWEN J Townsend, Trinidad, m. Jessie, yngs. dau. T Courthope
London, Camberwell, 14 June 1838.   (NS10:207)

BOWEN Joseph, eldest s. Joseph Bowen, d. Jamaica, 4 Sep. 1833
                                                    (104:118)

BOWEN Richard Lawrence, d. Montego Bay, Jamaica, 23 May 1829.
                                                    (99:94)

BOWEN Sarah Fenwick, only ch. W S Bowen, Naseby Woolley,
Northants., gdau. late Thomas Fenwick, Barrow, Lancs., m.
Edward Mathew Reid, 2nd s. late E J Reid, Jamaica, Naseby,
6 Oct. 1841.   (NS16:648)

BOWERBANK Edward, b.1790, ex Lothbury, d. NY, 30 March 1842.
                                                    (NS17:678)

BOWES Col., Yorks., 6th Reg., m. Miss Johnson, 2nd dau. Sir
John Johnson, Montreal, 13 April 1805.   (75:676)

BOWLES Maj., Cherokee chief, bro. Carrington Bowles, print-
seller, St Paul's Churchyard, d. Havanna Prison, 25 Dec.1805.
                                                    (76:281)

BOWMAN Elizabeth, dau. John Grove, Ashgrove, m. John Weir,
HM Comm. Gen., Dominica, 1776.   (46:578)

BOWRING Charles, d. Norfolk, Va., 21 June 1823.   (93:478)

BOWRING Grace W, b.1825, dau. late William Bowring, Paradise
Est., Nevis, gdau. Rear Adm. Gourlay, RN, d. St Kitts,
1 Jan. 1854.   (NS41:329)

BOWRING John Christian, Guadaloupe-y-Calvo, Mexico, m.
Jeanna Hay, eldest da. Adolphus Hay, Antwerp, 11 Nov.1843.
                                                    (NS23:91)

BOWTEIN Thomas, Jamaica, m. Miss Cudden, dau. Thomas Cudden,
Master Chancery, 12 Sep. 1777.   (47:459)

BOXILL William, MD, b.1777, late Barbados, d. London,
16 Oct. 1846.   (NS26:663)

BOYD Dr George Frederick, surgeon, late 84th Reg., d.
Halifax, NS, 2 March 1789.   (59:373)

BOYD James, 4th s. late Dr William Boyd, Martinhall,
Galloway, merchant, London, d. Guadaloupe, 14 Sep.1794.
                                                   (64:1150)

BOYD John, Councillor, Bahamas, d. Nassau, New Providence,
13 Sep. 1792.   (62:1152)

BOYD Mary, Jamaica, m. Robert Kalley, merchant, Glasgow,
3 Aug. 1795.   (65:702)

BOYER Gen., ex President Haiti, d. Paris, 9 July 1850.
                                                   (NS34:231)

BOYLE ..., s. Cap. Cavendish Boyle, b. Barbados, 11 Aug.1847.
                                                   (NS28:422)

BOYLE ..., s. Cap. Cavendish Bcyle, b. Barbados, 29 May 1849.
                                                   (NS32:197)

BOYFIELD Anna Maria, Lee, Kent, m. Thomas Peters Fearon,
Jamaica, 2 March 1782.   (52:149)

BOYFIELD Miss m. Thomas Woodyer, St Kitts, 1785.   (55:1005)

BRACE James, planter, d. Clarendon, Jamaica, 2 June 1795.
                                                   (65:791)

BRACEBRIDGE Miss, Weddington, m. George Hemming, Jamaica,
19 Sep. 1769.   (39:462)

BRADBURY Catherine Emma, 3rd dau. William Bradbury, Montreal,
m. Robert Faed Kirkpatrick, 2nd s. William Kirkpatrick,
Brighton, Montreal, 21 May 1852.   (NS38:89)

BRADFORD Thomas, b.1743, 'the oldest printer in America',
successor to Benjamin Franklin, d. Philadelphia, 7 May 1838.
                                                   (NS10:230)

BRADFORD William, author, printer & soldier, d. Philadelphia,
1792.   (62:88)

BRADFORD William, Attorney Gen. USA, d. Philadelphia,
23 Aug. 1795.   (65:879)

BRADLEY Rev. William Gardner, St Mary Cayon, St Kitts,
eldest s. Rev. W Bradley, Nether Whitacre, Warwicks.,d.1851.
                                                   (NS37:105)

BRADLEY William Henry, Bombay medical staff, m. Eleanor
Lawrence Simpson, eldest dau. John Simpson, Tilston,
Jamaica, Bycullah, 16 Nov. 1840.   (NS15:311)

BRADSHAW Richard, ex Moss-side, Manchester, d. La Chute,
Canada East, 29 Oct. 1861.   (NS2/12:236)

BRADY John, b.1792, s. Cap. Cornelius Brady, Hull, drowned
on passage from Savanna to NY, 14 April 1824.   (94:574)

BRAINE Daniel H, Cap. Frances of NY, d.16 July 1807. (77.782)

BRAITHWAITE Elizabeth Jane, eldest dau. Miles Braithwaite,
Barbados, m. Ledeatt Redwood, eldest s. George Washington
Redwood, Antigua, Islington, 13 Jan. 1846.   (NS25:308)

BRAITHWAITE Rev. Francis Gretton C., s. Rev. Francis Robert
Braithwaite, ex Archdeacon St Kitts, m. Frances, 4th dau.
late Thomas Brown, Barbados, London, 14 Aug. 1861.(NS2/11:320)

BRAITHWAITE Mary Blanche, yngr. dau. Rev. F R Braithwaite,
Basseterre, Archdeacon St Kitts, m. George Pilgrim Toppin,
London, 23 July 1863.   (NS2/15:369)

BRAITHWAITE Miles, 3rd s. late M Braithwaite, Barbados, d.
Fort Twiss, Hythe, Kent, 26 March 1837.   (NS2/2:627)

BRAMFIELD Andrew, b.1741, ex Lt. Col. Militia, Jamaica, bro.
Stephen Bramfield, Hassington Mains, Berwicks., d. Hoxton,
11 March 1807.   (77.383)

BRAMLEY Joseph, Stamford Hill, m. Mrs E Kellerman, wid.
J Kellerman, Jamaica, Hackney, 2 May 1801.   (71:479)

BRANDER Mr, Grenada, killed in a duel, St George, Grenada,
16 April 1799.   (69:621)

BRANDER John, Grenada, d. Tortula, 18 May 1806.   (76:776)

BRANT Mrs Catherine, b.1760, wid. Joseph Brant, Chief Six
Nations, d. Mohawk Village, Upper Canada, 1838.   (NS10:664)

BRASIER Lucy, yngs. dau. Kilner Brasier, Saffronhill, Co. Cork
m. Bertie Entwistle Jarvis, Councillor, Antigua, Watergrass
Hill, 23 Nov. 1843.   (NS21:88)

BRAUGH C, b.1772, merchant, ex Barbados, d. Bristol,
9 Feb. 1812.   (82:391)

BRAY George Frederick Campbell, Cap., 96th Reg., 2nd s. Col.
Bray, 39th Reg., m. Charlotte Frances, dau. late Edward Pope,
Archdeacon Jamaica, Guildford, 27 April 1859.   (NS2/6:638)

BRAY John, b.1782, emigrated England to USA 1805, comedian,
Boston, d. Leeds, 19 June 1822.   (92:647)

BRECKEN John, late PEI, d. Hull, 6 March 1827.   (96:285)

BREDIN ..., dau. Maj. Edgar Grantham Bredin, RA, b. Gunhill,
Barbados, 8 Sep. 1865.   (NS3/1:220)

BREMRIDGE Richard, b.1826, yngr. s. late R Bremridge, London,
d. NY, 30 June 1849.   (NS32:335)

BRENAN Thomas, Barbados, d. Westerham, Kent, 17 Feb. 1814.
(84:410)

BRENTON Elizabeth R, niece Adm. Brenton, ex Newport, RI, m.
Robert Bolton jr., gs. Rev. William Jay, Bath, Eastchester,
NY, 8 Jan. 1838.   (NS9:424)

BRERETON Robert, d. Jamaica, 1790.   (60:1214)

BRETT Miss E, d. America, 1804.   (74:1174)

BRETTINGHAM Lt. R W m. Harriot Frances Josephine, yngs. dau.
late William Sheppard, Clifton, BristoL, St Johns, NFD.,
22 June 1846.   (NS26:314)

BRIDEKIRK John, ex naval architect, New Providence, Bahamas,
d. North Shields, 1816.   (86:570)

BRIDGE Mary, b.1716, d. Jamaica, 26 May 1827.   (97:477)

BRIDGE Thomas Finch Hobday, b.1807, Archdeacon, NFD & Labrador
d. St Johns, NFD, 29 Feb. 1856.   (NS45:543)

BRIDGEWATER E, ex physician, St Kitts, d. London, 5 Sep.1811.
(81:293)

BRIDGHAM Miss, b.1771, American loyalist, m. Sir John Hatton,
Long Stanton, Cambridges., St Giles, 17 Jan. 1788.   (58:81)

BRIDGMAN Sophia Catherine, w. John Bridgman, Customs
Collector, St Lucia, d. St Lucia, 20 Dec. 1812.   (83:181)

BRIGGS Robert, b.1784, settled Antigua 1802, fa. Mrs Neville,
Bristol, d. Green Castle, Antigua, 3 May 1841.   (NS16:334)

BRINDLEY Mrs Mary, wid. George Brindley, Comm. Gen. BA,
'descendent of ancient family of Wentworth in Yorks.' d.
Halifax, NS, 6 Jan. 1819.   (88:279)

BRINLEY Mrs Elizabeth, wid. Thomas Brinley, late Boston, NE,
d.1793.   (63:283)

BRINLEY Mary Hadley m. Thomas D'Avenant Cotton, Royal
Fusiliers, Halifax, NS, 25 June 1810.   (80:485)

BRINLAY William Birch, b.1771, d. Halifax, NS, 11 June 1812.
(82:90)

BRISBANE Thomas Stewart James, 3rd s. Sir C Brisbane, Gov.
St Vincent, d.1812.   (82:493)

BRISSET Miss, dau. J Brisset, Jamaica, d. London,
25 Dec. 1789.   (59:1214)

BRIXTOWE Eliza Anne Isabel, dau. John Brixtowe, m. F G Archer,
Belize, British Honduras, 5 Sep. 1867.   (NS3/2:670)

BROAD Charles, ex machinery superintendant, Drury Lane
Theater, d. St Vincent, 15 Oct. 1837.   (NS7:447)

BROADBETT Miss, Jamaica, m. Cap. Raymond, 21st Light Dragoons
Chudleigh, Devon, 25 April 1798.   (68:441)

BROCK Charles, yngs. s. W W Brock, MD, late Jamaica,
d. Liverpool, 13 June 1836.   (NS6:108)

BROCK George William John, b.1814, late Toronto, d. Colchester
31 Jan. 1854.   (NS41:334)

BROCK Susan Margaret, 2nd dau. late W W Brock, MD, Jamaica,
m. James Burnett, late HM Consul in Brazil, Torquay,
9 Aug. 1860.   (NS2/9:318)

BROCK T R, b.1811, eldest s. W W Brock, MD, Clifton,
d. Guelph, Canada, 3 Oct. 1850.   (NS34:679)

BROCK W W, b.1780, late Jamaica, d. Clifton, Glocs.,
10 Nov. 1851.   (NS37:106)

BROCKLESBY Charles M, s. late Cap. Brocklesby, Quebec, m.
Caroline, 2nd dau. John Cooke, Guildford, 10 Feb. 1846.
                                                         (NS25:422)

BRODBELT Francis Rigby m. Miss Milward, dau. John Gardner
Milward, Spanish Town, Jamaica, 25 July 1803.   (74:277)

BRODIE Alexander Oswald, b.1788, merchant, NY, d. Edinburgh,
9 Sep. 1856.   (NS2/1:526)

BRODIE Charlotte B, late preceptress, Raleigh Academy, m.
Maj. Smith, Prince Edward Co., Va., Williamsburg, Granville
Co., America, 1812.   (81:188)

BRODIE Oswald, Flamstead Est., d. St Anne's, Jamaica,
9 Aug. 1818.   (88:469)

BROOKE Celeste Althea Armantine, b.1834, w. Robert Lawrence
Brooke, USA, d. London, 22 May 1856.   (NS2/1:124)

BROOKE Frances, yngs. dau. late Rev. William Brooke, Kirby,
Bedon & Swainsthorpe, m. Rev. J Mountain, eldest s. Bishop
Quebec, Beaconsthorpe, 12 Oct. 1812.   (82:390)

BROOKES Thomas, b.1767, s. John Brookes, Calsthorpe, Lincs.,
d. Fort Johnson, Cape Fear R., NC, 16 Sep. 1802.   (73:691)

BROOKING Frances, 2nd dau. A H Brooking, Customs Collector, m.
Cap. Francis Maude, RN, yngs. bro. Vicount Hawarden,
St Johns, NFD., 4 Sep. 1827.   (97:364)

BROOKS Caroline Broughton, dau. Dr Burt, Harwich, w. Rev.
George B Brooks, Blenheim, Jamaica, d. 14 Dec. 1857.
                                                         (NS2/4:337)

BROOKS Charles, Representative Jamaican Assembly, d.1777.
(47:295)

BROOKS George, MD, b.1810, d. Spanish Town, Jamaica,
28 May 1854.   (NS42:201)

BROOKS H, trader, St Albans, 'shot while smuggling goods
from Canada to Vermont', 3 Nov 1811.   (82:89)

BROOKS Peniston, logwood-cutter, d. Honduras, 1767. (37:563)

BROOKS Preston R, d. Washington, DC, 27 Jan. 1857.(NS2/2:497)

BROOM Rev. Frederick, missionary, m. Catherine Elizabeth,
eldest dau. Lt. Col. Napier, Indian Affairs Secy.,
Montreal, 18 Jan. 1842.   (NS17:429)

BROWN Maj. Alexander, Gov. Tobago, d. 1766.   (36:405)

BROWNE Anne, b.1775, only dau. John White, Jamaica, w. Lt.
Col. John Browne, d. Bath, 23 April 1851.   (NS35:685)

BROWN Arthur Fountain, b.1846, 4th s. Rev. James L Brown,
Holbeck, Leeds, d. Hamilton, Canada West, 24 April 1867.
(NS3/4:114)

BROWN Claude Scott, b.1795, Asst. Comm. Gen., d. Kingston,
Upper Canada, 7 July 1821.   (91:283)

BROWN Edward, s. John Brown, merchant, Glasgow, d. Grenada,
18 July 1796.   (66:880)

BROWNE Elizabeth, b.1785, 2nd dau. John Browne, Grenada,
d. Reigate, 23 March 1858.   (NS2/4:566)

BROWN Frances, 4th dau. late Thomas Brown, Barbados, m.
Rev. Francis Gretton C Braithwaite, s. Rev. Francis Robert
Braithwaite, late Archdeacon St Kitts, London, 14 Aug. 1861.
(NS2/11:320)

BROWN George Lomax, s. late J R Brown, Camberwell, d. Chicago
1854.   (NS42:413)

BROWN George Wright, s. Mr Brown, Five Bells, Pinchbeck,
Lincoln, d. America, 8 Feb. 1804.   (74:596)

BROWN Henry, barrister, d. Jamaica, 1790.   (60:476)

BROWN Henry sr., d. Jamaica, 1790.   (60:766)

BROWN H, d. on passage from Grenada to England, 25 July 1803.
(73:987)

BROWN Mrs Hawkins, b.1753, w. Isaac H Brown, MP, dau. late
Edward Hay, Gov. Barbados, d.11 April 1802.   (72:473)

BROWN James sr., ex merchant, St Augusta, Ga., d.Paisley,1810
(80:590)

BROWN James William, b.1792, ex St Vincent, d. London,
2 Feb. 1847.   (NS27:328)

BROWN Jean, dau. late Campbell Brown, Antigua, m. Lt. W
Hamersley, 3rd Garrison Bat., 20 Sep. 1817.   (87:362)

BROWN Jeannie, dau. late William Brown, glover, m. John Smith
ex Hanover, Jamaica, Glasgow, 1792.   (62:181)

BROWN John, b.1784, s. James Brown, tanner, Stamford, Lincs.,
d. St Domingo, 30 Nov. 1807.   (78:170)

BROWN John, b. Belfast, ex Dublin merchant, captured by the
French on passage from Antigua, d. Marigalante Island, WI,
Sep. 1808.   (78:1126)

BROWN John, Halifax, NS, drowned Halifax, 15 July 1813.(83.40)

BROWN John Robert, Jamaica, m. Elizabeth, eldest dau. John
Holder, Cubberly House, Hereford, Bath, 19 Dec. 1848.
                                                        (NS31:310)

BROWN Letitia, b.1769, w. John Brown, Sportsmanhall,
Trelawney, Jamaica, d. Bristol, 30 May 1817.   (87:571)

BROWN Louise, dau. late C Brown, St Johns, m. Matthew
Beachcroft Harrison, 62nd Reg., only s. Rev. M Harrison,
Basingstoke, Hants., St Johns, NB, 7 April 1859. (NS2/6:637)

BROWN Margaret McHaffie, b.1786, wid. Jonathan Brown,
Jamaica, d. Portobello, Edinburgh, 17 Aug. 1852.   (NS38:434)

BROWN Mary Anne Fuller, dau. late John Fuller Brown, Mulberry
Gardens, Spanish Town, Jamaica, m. Joseph Johnstone, Bengal,
1797.   (67:710)

BROWN Mary, yngs. dau. late William Brown, Gov. Bermuda, m.
John Harvey, eldest s. James Tucker, Bermuda, 1 Aug. 1803.
                                                        (73:788)

BROWNE Mary Isabella, wid. James Browne, Customs Controller,
Savanna-la-Mar, Jamaica, m. Lt. Frederick Jelly, RN,
Hatfield Pen, Savanna-la-Mar, Jamaica, 11 Oct. 1820. (91:83)

BROWN Mather, b. America, artist, d. London, 1 June 1831.
                                                        (101:182)

BROWNE Otway Cuffe, 3rd s. Dean of Fenns, d. Jamaica, 1836.
                                                        (NS6:446)

BROWN Patrick, b.1769, d. Nassau, New Providence, Bahamas,
15 June 1845.   (NS24:326)

BROWNE Salwey, ex Cap., 68th Light Inf., s. late William Browne
Herts., m. Elizabeth, eldest dau. William Stevenson, Quebec,
11 May 1848.   (NS30:314)

BROWN Samuel, b.1715, d. Norwich, Conn., 1805.   (75:877)

BROWN Susan, d. Cobourg, Canada West, 23 Nov. 1852.(NS39:216)

BROWNE Susan Harriet, only dau. Col. Thomas Bruce, m. Allan
MacDowell, MD, St Vincent, 4 July 1818.   (88:273)

BROWN Thomas, b.1760, d. St George, Grenada, 30 Sep. 1846.
                                                        (NS27:110)

BROWN T James, b.1792, Assemblyman, Jamaica, d. on passage to
England, 20 April 1823.   (93:478)

BROWN William, Lochwinnoch, Renfrews., d. Antigua, Oct. 1835.
                                                         (NS5:678)

BROWNE William Patrick, PC, Chief Magistrate, Maj. Gen.
Militia, Col. St Catherine Reg., d. Browne's Hall, Jamaica,
1789.   (59:372)

BROWNELL Thomas Church, b. Bristol, Mass., 19 Oct. 1779,
eldest s. Sylvester Brownell, Westport, Mass., Bishop Conn.,
d. Hartford, 13 Jan. 1865.   (NS2/18:371)

BROWNRIGG ..., s. Cap. Brownrigg, Military Sec. Gov. Gen.,
b. Montreal, 5 July 1845.   (NS24:299)

BRUCE Archibald, MD, b.1778, Prof. Minerology, NY Medical
Inst., d. NY, Feb. 1818.   (88:569)

BRUCE Barwick, MD, s. Joseph Osborne Barwick, judge, Barbados,
and his wife Jane, d. Hartford, Conn., 31 May 1841.(NS18:331)

BRUCE Sir F W N, b.1814, d. NY, 19 Sep. 1867.   (NS3/2:549)

BRUCE James, Barbados, d.19 Sep. 1749.   (19:429)

BRUCE James, Lt. Gov. Jamaica, m. Margaret, dau. John
Thompson, Spring Garden, Edinburgh, 1798.   (68:1147)

BRUCE James, Lt. Gov. Dominica, d. London, 22 April 1808.
                                                          (78:464)

BRUCE James, late St Vincent, d. Bath, 14 April 1815.(85:473)

BRUCE J S, customs officer, b.1805, s.S B Bruce, surgeon,
Ripon, d. Grenada, 12 Dec. 1833.   (104:454)

BRUCE Stewart, 32 years resident, d. Kingston, Jamaica,
26 Jan. 1807.   (77:376)`

BRUCE Stewart Hervey, Cap. 91st Reg., m. Frances Anna Maria,
eldest dau. Henry Becher, QC, London, Canada West, 19 Jan.1864.
                                                      (NS2/16:378)

BRUCE Thomas, b.1812, yngr. s. late George Bruce, Chelsea,
d. Philadelphia, 27 Oct. 1853.   (NS40:653)

BRUCE ..., s. Countess of Elgin, b. Spencer Wood, Upper
Canada, 26 April 1853.   (NS40:84)

BRUCE-GARDYNE Thomas M, Middleton, Angus, late Lt., 40th Reg.
m. Annie, yngs. dau. late Charles Willard, Kingston, Canada
West, 6 April 1858.   (NS2/4:664)

BRUEKNALL William, late Jamaica, d.22 Sep. 1746.   (16:558)

BRUERE Elizabeth, wid. George James Bruere, Gov. Bermuda,
d. London, 8 Aug. 1788.   (58:757)

BRUERE Mary, eldest dau. J Bruere, London, m. Richard
Alexander Tucker, BA, Dep. Paymaster Gen., NS, 10 March 1808.
                                                       (78:270)

BRULEY James, d. Tortula, 1 June 1792.   (62:673)

BRULEY James, b.1777, d. Tortula, 2 Jan. 1805.   (75:282)

BRULEY Joseph, d. St Croix, 15 May 1818.   (88:373)

BRUNE John Ernest, Los Hermanos, Madruga, Cuba, yngs. s.
Frederick William Brune, Blankenburg, Brunswick, d. Hermita,
Cuba, 9 Oct. 1819.   (90:281)

BRYAN Rev., Manchioneal, d. Jamaica, 1790.   (60:1214)

BRYNE Andrew, d. Jamaica, 1791.   (61:971)

BUCHAN Alexander, merchant, Glasgow, d. Grenada, 3 July 1795.
                                                       (65:968)

BUCHANAN Archibald Shannan, Drumhead, Dunbarton, d. Antigua,
18 Sep. 1791.   (61:1062)

BUCHANAN Rev. Arthur John Pilgrim, Carriacou, s. late Cap. Co
Colin Buchanan, 62nd Reg., m. Margaret Ann, dau. Francis
Jemmitt, Richmond Est., Grenada, 4 Feb. 1847.   (NS27:542)

BUCHANAN George, late Jamaica, d. Glasgow, 14 Jan.1801.
                                                       (71:185)

BUCHANAN Georgina Bruce, only dau. late Cap. Colin Buchanan,
62nd Reg., ggdau. James Bruce, Chief Judge, Barbados, m.
William Downes Jewill, Barbados, 26 Nov. 1844.   (NS23:420)

BUCHANAN James, Glasgow, m. Mary Anne, eldest dau. late
William Finlayson, St Elizabeth, Jamaica, 7 Aug.1819.(89:178)

BUCHANAN John, d. Jamaica, 1790.   (60:476)

BUCHANAN John, s. late John Cross Buchanan, Auchintoshan,
Dunbarton, m. Rosa Henrietta, 2nd dau. late Thomas Jenken, MD
Zacatecas, Mexico, British Consulate, 4 March 1865.(NS2/18:778)

BUCHANAN Sophia Louisa, eldest dau. A C Buchanan, m. George
Tudor Pemberton, 2nd s. George Pemberton, Quebec, 25 Sep.1867
                                                       (NS3/2:671)

BUCHANAN W, d. St Anne's, Jamaica, 1810.   (80:498)

BUCHANAN Mrs, wid. John Buchanan, late Md., merchant, London,
d. Bromley, Kent, 1784.   (54:73)

BUCKE Clarissa, b.1797, dau. late Joseph Andrews,
Mildenhall, w. Rev. H W Bucke, d. London, Upper Canada,
25 Jan. 1845.   (NS23:677)

BUCKE Helen Augusta, dau. Rev. Horatio Walpole Bucke, d.
Moore, Lambton, Canada, 24 Feb. 1856.   (NS45:659)

BUCKE Rev. Horatio Walpole, b.1802, d. at residence s. George
Walpole Bucke, Moore, Lambton, Canada, 31 March 1856.(NS45:659)

BUCKE Walter Lewis, b. Bungay, 1780, settled Nevis 1802,
d. Nevis, 23 Feb. 1857.   (NS2/2:624)

BUCKLEY Augusta m. John Prettejohn, Barbados, 23 Nov.1801.
                                                        (71:1209)

BUDD Septimus, b.1820, 7th s. late Samuel Budd, N.Tawton,
Devon, bro. Dr William Budd, Bristol, d. Toronto, 3 April 1847.
                                                        (NS27:679)

BULFINCH Dr, physician, NE, d.1758.   (28:46)

BULL Cap. John, 'last survivor of those who made the
expedition into the Cherokee country in 1715', d. SC, 1767.
                                                        (37:524)

BULL John, d. Montego Bay, Jamaica, 31 Oct.1801.   (72:181)

BULL William, b.1683, Lt. Gov. NC, d. March 1755.   (25:236)

BULL W, b. SC, 1709, ex Lt. Gov. SC, settled GB 1782,
d. London, 4 July 1791.   (61:684)

BULLER Edward, Cap., RN, m. Gertrude Van Cortland, Halifax,
NS, 15 March 1789.   (59:371)

BULLER William, Customs Collector, d. Trinidad, 10 June 1802.
                                                        (72:781)

BULLOCK Edmund, Jamaica, m. Dorothy, dau. late Thomas
Harrison, Attorney Gen. Jamaica, Bath, 1796.   (66:789)

BULLOCK Dorothy, elder dau. late E Bullock, Jamaica, m. Rev.
John St Vincent Bowen, only s. late Rear Adm. J Bowen,
Ilfracombe, Devon, London, 27 April 1830.   (100:460)

BULLOCK Eliza, w. Joseph Bullock, Comm. Gen. WI,
d. Martinique, 12 June 1809.   (79:679)

BULLOCK Mary Pennington, yngs. dau. late Edward Bullock,
Jamaica, m. Rev. Frederick Bell, Clifton, yngs. s. late
Thomas Bell, MD, Dublin, Clifton, 16 March 1843.   (NS19:528)

BULLOCK Richard, b.1809, 2nd s. late Edward Bullock, London,
late Jamaica, d. Windsor, 3 April 1847.   (96:474)

BULLOCK St George, b.1813, 2nd s. late Rev. John Bullock,
Radwinter, d. Otterville, Canada, 31 May 1853.   (NS40:209)

BULLOCK Mrs, w. Joseph Bullock, Comm. Gen., d. Martinique,
1810.   (80:283)

BUNCH Robert, HM Consul Carolinas, eldest s. Robert H Bunch, Newprovidence, m. Charlotte Amelia, dau. late Samuel Craig, NY, 18 Oct. 1853.   (NS41:78)

BUNNETT Edward Charles, b.1819, yngs. s. Henry James Bunnett, MD, d. Spanish Town, Jamaica, 10 May 1854.   (NS42:201)

BUNTER Louisa, yngs. dau. late Cap. R B Young, RN, Exeter, w. William Bunter, Bristol, d. Cleveland, E. Tenn., 28 Oct. 1854.   (NS45:96)

BUNTING Rev. George Anthony, b.1839, s. late Rev. Anthony Bunting, Port Antonio, Jamaica, d. Leicester, 31 May 1855.
                                                       (NS44:104)

BUNTING Jane Elizabeth, b.1795, wid. Rev. Anthony Bunting, Port Antonio, Jamaica, d. Newport Pagnall, 9 Jan. 1857.
                                                     (NS2/2:254)

BUONAPARTE Jerome Napoleon m. Susan Mary, dau. late Benjamin Williams, Baltimore, 2 Nov.1829.   (99.558)

BURCH Miss, dau. late Mr Burch, Bermuda, m. Cap. Weston, RN, Bermuda, 4 Oct.1794.   (64:1148)

BURGE B Milnard, barrister, d. Spanish Town, Jamaica, 26 June 1819.   (89:185)

BURGE William, HM Counsel, Jamaica, m. Margaret, dau. late Rev. Archibald Alison, Edinburgh, 11 Aug.1841.   (NS16:424)

BURGESS Henry Gilbert, Ordnance Dept., b.1824, eldest s. late H W Burgess, London, d. St Kitts, 21 April 1848.   (NS30:110)

BURKE Charlotte, eldest dau. Francis Burke, d. Woodlands, Montrino, WI, 24 July 1849.   (NS32:446)

BURKE Denis, MD, b. Ireland, 1752, late assistant surgeon, West Point, d. Washington, 29 June 1852.   (NS38:433)

BURKE Edmund Plunkett, b.1805, late Inner Temple, London, Caius College, Cambridge, Judge, St Lucia, d. Dominica, 1835.
                                                        (105:222)

BURKE Francis m. Rosina, 4th dau. late Dr West, Antigua, Montserrat, 22 Oct.1844.   (NS23:196)

BURKE John, late Kingston, Jamaica, d. Brighton, 13 Dec.1824.
                                                         (95:190)

BURN John, Charleston, m. Mrs Burn, wid. Rev. Burn, 1768.
                                                          (38:93)

BURN John, Councillor, SC, d. Edinburgh, 28 Dec.1774. (45:46)

BURN Mrs, wid. Rev. Burn, m. John Burn, Charleston, 1768.
                                                          (38:93)

BURNETT Edward Sydney, Cap., RA, m. Marion Grasett, yngs. dau. Thomas D Harris, Toronto, 17 Oct.1865.   (NS2/19:776)

BURNETT ..., s. Cap. E S Burnett, RA, b. Montreal, 13 Sep.1867
                                                     (NS3/2:667)

BURNETT James, ex HM Consul, Brazil, m. Susan Margaret, 2nd
dau. late W W Brock, MD, Jamaica, Torquay, 9 Aug.1860.
(NS2/9:318)

BURNLEY William Hardin, b.1780, d.29 Dec.1850, Port of Spain,
Trinidad.   (NS35:334)

BURNLEY ..., dau. Joseph Hume Burnley, 1st Sec. British
Legation, b. Washington, 5 Nov.1865.   (NS3/1:112)

BURR Rev. Aaron, President NJ College, d.24 Sep.1757.(27:531)

BURR Col. Aaron, b.6 Feb.1756, d. Staten Island, NY, 1836.
(NS6:655)

BURR Miss, dau. late candidate US Presidency, d.America,1801.
(71:675)

BURREL Miss, Asted, Surrey, m. Thomas Beckford, Jamaica,
11 Feb. 1745.   (15:108)

BURRELL Peter, ex Antigua, d. London, 4 June 1766.   (36:294)

BURRIDGE William, b.1783, ex banker, Portsmouth, d. Troy, NY,
9 Oct. 1825.   (95:478)

BURROWS Charles, Jamaica, d.1767.   (37:524)

BURROWES Arnold Robinson, Benarth, N Wales, late Cap. Cold-
stream Guards, d. Strathmore, Canada West, 28 Aug.1851.
(NS36:553)

BURROW Miss, only dau. late James Burrow, Councillor, NS, m.
Lt. Smith, 57th Reg., Halifax, NS, 27 Oct.1791.   (61:1157)

BURT ..., dau. Archdeacon P Burt, b. St Kitts, 9 Sep.1865.
(NS2/19:635)

BURT ..., s. A P Burt, QC, b. St Kitts, 18 March 1867.
(NS3/3:804)

BURTENSHAW Mr, eldest s. late Henry Burtenshaw, Lewes,
d. Jamaica, 4 Sep.1794.   (64:1150)

BURTON Harriet Emma, 4th dau. late Rev. William Burton,
Trelawney, Jamaica, m. Charles A Cunningham, MD, London,
Upton, Bucks., 15 Sep.1852.   (NS38:630)

BURTON Launcelot, 2nd s. T Burton, Bracondale, d. WI, 1801.
(71:1212)

BURTON Robert, ex London, d. Richmond, Va., 12 Feb.1806.
(76:283)

BURTON Rev. William, ex Horsfield, Norfolk, d. Montego Bay,
Jamaica, 12 Dec.1808.   (79:278)

BURTON Rev. W G P, 2nd s. Rev. W Burton, St Thomas in Vale,
Jamaica, d. Spanish Town, Jamaica, 29 July 1847. (NS28:549)

BURWELL Carter, Va., d.24 Sep.1775.   (45:503)

BURY Alfred, 69th Reg., 3rd s. Earl of Charleville, m. Emily
Frances, 3rd dau. Lt. Gen. Wood, CO Windward & Leeward
Islands, Barbados, 20 June 1854.   (NS42:384)

BURY J J, Lt., RE, bro. Earl of Charleville, m. Charlotte
Teresa, only dau. Thomas Austin, Chambly, Canada, 24 June
1852.   (NS38:302)

BUSHE Robert, b.1790, Trinidad, d. London, 20 Oct.1844.
                                                   (NS22:664)

BUSHBY Arthur T, Registrar Ge. BC, yngs. s. J Bushby, London,
m. Agnes, 3rd dau. James Douglas, Gov. BC, Victoria,
Vancouver Island, 8 May 1862.   (NS2/13:222)

BUSHBY Joseph, Dep. Comm. Gen. St Domingo, d. Kingston,
Jamaica, April 1799.   (69:716)

BUSHE John Scott, eldest s. late Robert Bushe, Dublin, m.
Martha MacNamara, eldest dau. Archdeacon Cummings, gniece late
Adm. MacNamara, Port of Spain, Trinidad, 6 June 1848.
                                                   (NS30:199)

BUSHE Rev. Thomas Francis, Russah, 4th s. late Robert Bushe,
Trinidad, d. Folkestone, 19 May 1858.   (NS2/4:681)

BUSHNELL William Avery, Conn., m. Catherine Hayes, vocalist,
London, 8 Oct.1857.   (NS2/3:557)

BUSNEY Frederick, ex merchant, Philadelphia, d. London,
15 Oct.1786.   (56:911)

BUSSELL Anne, w. W I Bussell, d. Jamaica, 8 Nov.1852.
                                                   (NS39:216)

BUTLER Catherine Morden, 2nd dau. Col. Edward K S Butler,
Hants., m. James Urquhart, 17th Reg., 3rd s. late Thomas Moss,
Knockfinne, Queen's Co., ex Cap., Royal Scots, gs. late Lt.
Gen. B Forbes Gordon, Balbithan, Abdns., Windsor, NS,
26 Oct. 1865.   (NS2/19:777)

BUTLER Elizabeth, w. Col. Edward K S Butler, yngs. dau. late
Col. Baget, Nurney, Kildare, d. NS, 4 Nov.1846.   (NS27:111)

BUTLER Eliza Mary, eldest dau. Col. Butler, Hants., NS, m.
Francis Ironside Rawlins, 15th Reg., Windsor, NS, 16 Nov.1865.
                                                   (NS3/1:117)

BUTLER James, b.1738, American loyalist, late Ga., d.4 May 1817
                                                    (87:477)

BUTLER John Button, Comm. Gen., d. Halifax, NS, 2 JUly 1834.
                                                   (104:447)

BUTLER Robert m. Mary, yngs. dau. late Anthony Stokes, late
Chief Justice Ga., 13 Oct.1800.   (70:1003)

BUTLER Pierce, b. Philadelphia, 1807, lawyer, d. Ga.,15 Aug.
1867.   (NS3/2:539)

BUTLER Col., Martock, m. Elizabeth, yngs. dau. late
Benjamin Cobb, New Romney, Aylesford, NS, 17 Sep.1850.
(NS34:651)

BUTTER John, b.1806, ex Bristol, late surgeon, Trinidad, d.
NY, 19 June 1848.   (NS30:447)

BUTTERFIELD Rosalie, only dau. Nathaniel Butterfield,
Bermuda, m. Charles William Gray, Tonbridge Wells, 7 Sep.
1843.   (NS20:538)

BUTTERFIELD Thomas, President Bermuda, d. Hamilton, Bermuda,
23 Jan.1861.   (NS2/10:469)

BYAM Sir Ashton, Attorney Gen. Jamaica, d.25 Dec.1790.(61:184)

BYAM Edward, b.1766, Cedarhill, Antigua, Assemblyman,
d. Antigua, 1795.   (65:794)

BYAM Edward, b.1740, Judge Court Vice Admiralty, d. Antigua,
8 Feb.1817.   (87:374)

BYAM M, ex Antigua, d. Kew, 22 April 1836.   (NS5:676)

BYAM Mrs, b.1750, wid. William Byam, Cedarhill, Antigua, d.
London, 28 Jan.1794.   (64:183)

BYAM William, barrister, b.1828, 2nd s. William Byam,
d. Antigua, 30 June 1853.   (NS40:537)

BYAM Rev. Dr, Antigua, d. at sea 1757.   (27:435)

BYNG Robert, Gov. Barbados, d. 6 Oct.1740.   (11.50)

BYRNE Ellen, eldest dau. F H Byrne, PEI, m. W Edward Jones,
barrister, Lincoln's Inn, only s. William Jones, Springhill,
Staffs., London, 7 Sep.1853.   (NS40:627)

BYRNE Maria, only dau. N Byrne, London, m. C Thomson,
Attorney Gen. St Kitts, London, 10 Jan.1832.   (102:78)

BYRNE Mary, b.1786, dau. P Byrne, bookseller, d. Philadelphia
24 July 1804.   (74:88)

BYRNE William, bookseller, s. Patrick Byrne, bookseller,
ex Dublin, d. Philadelphia, 21 Dec.1805.   (76:182)

BYRNE Cap. m. ... Thady, sis. Col. Thady, NY, 1763. (32:313)

CABB Richard, editor & proprietor 'St Kitts Advertiser',
d. St Kitts, Feb.1830.   (100:382)

CABOT Harriett Charlotte Sarabella, eldest dau. James Cabot,
Mexico City, m. James Graham, merchant, British Legation,
Mexico, 24 Sep.1846.   (NS27:78)

CADE Joseph, b.1801, ex British Consul Panama, d. Tonbridge
Wells, 24 Aug.1860.   (NS2/9:441)

CADWALADER Williamina, b.1754, wid. Gen John Cadwalader, mo.
Gen. Thomas Cadwalader, Philadelphia, & Fanny, w. Lord Erskin
d. Holmbush, Sussex, 9 Sep.1838.   (NS9:220)

CAHUSAC Rev. Thomas Barry m. Mary Pattison, 3rd dau. Dr Rob,
Water Valley, Jamaica, 1 May 1845.   (NS24:189)

CAHUSAC William, b.1786, d. Montreal, 10 March 1840.(NS13:669)

CALCRAFT Cap. Granby Hales, yngr. s. John Calcraft, d. NY,
16 Jan.1855.   (NS43:438)

CALDER Rev. L m. Maria, eldest dau. John Sharpe, late
Attorney Ge. Grenada, Tempsford, Beds., 1812.   (82:288)

CALDER Mary, wid. Dr Calder, La Chine, 2nd dau. late Joseph
Plimsoll, Plymouth, d. Montreal, 29 June 1852.   (NS38:322)

CALDWELL Hugh, ex British Army doctor, d. NY, 6 Sep.1853.
                                                      (NS40:537)

CALDWELL Gen. John, Lt. Gov. Kentucky, d. Frankfort,
Kentucky, 9 Nov.1804.   (74:1244)

CALDWELL William, Assemblyman St Dorothy, Alderman Kingston,
d. Kingston, Jamaica, 29 Jan.1819.   (88:376)

CALHOUN John Caldwell, b. Abbeville, SC, 18 March 1782, ex
US Vice President, d. Washington, 31 March 1850.   (NS33:665)

CALLAGHAN Catherine, only ch. H Callaghan, Pusey Hall, Vere,
Jamaica, m. Reginald Henry Elliot, 3rd s. James Elliot,
Dymchurch, Kent, Vere, 16 Sep.1863.   (NS2/15:635)

CALLENDER James, b. Scotland, editor 'The Recorder', drowned
James River, Va., 7 June 1803.   (73:882)

CALLOW Mrs, w. Lt. Col. Callow, Lt. Gov. Quebec, d. Sep.1804.
                                                        (74:979)

CALVERT Benedict Leonard, bro. Lord Baltimore, proprietor Md.
ex Gov. Md., d. on passage to England, 1 June 1732.   (2:826)

CALVERT Cornelius, b. Norfolk, Va., 1785, d. Dolphin Tavern,
Falmouth, 27 Jan. 1804.   (74:185)

CALVERT Edward, headmaster, Trinidad, m. Emily Wisset, wid.
A Middleton, marine surveyor, London, 17 Feb.1859.(NS2/6:317)

CALVERT Emily Wisset, w. Edward Calvert, Queens School,
d. Port of Spain, Trinidad, 4 Sep.1859.   (NS2/7:54)

CAMAC William, b.1804, Greenmount, Co.Down, d. Philadelphia,
7 March 1842.   (NS17:678)

CAMBRIDGE Mary, wid. John Cambridge, d. PEI, 6 Dec.1832.
(103:190)

CAMERON Alexander, Cap., 6th WI Reg., d. Dominica,
28 Jan. 1813.   (83:660)

CAMERON Allan, d. Kingston, Jamaica, 27 May 1796.   (66:615)

CAMERON Catherine, wid. Lt. Col. D Cameron, d. Toronto,
24 Aug.1865.   (NS2/19:654)

CAMERON CHristian, only dau. Kenneth Cameron, Asst. Comm. Gen
m. Norris Godhard, Inspector Gen. Dept., Toronto, 3 June 1858
(NS2/5:304)

CAMERON Mrs, b.1738, wid. Donald Cameron of Lochiel, d. New
Providence, 4 April 1806.   (76:583)

CAMERON John, Tempe Est., Grenada, m. Annette, only dau. late
Evan Baillie, barrister, Grenada, 19 Jan.1852.   (NS37:509)

CAMERON J, b. Paisley, 1763, planter Antigua 1782-1812, d.
Whitehaven, 25 Aug.1812.   (82:298)

CAMERON Mackay Hugh Baillie, 2nd s. late Lt. Col. D Cameron,
79th Highlanders, d. Lyndally, Toronto, 10 Nov.1847.(NS29:110)

CAMERON Sarah Baillie, eldest dau. late Lt. Col. Duncan
Cameron, m. Rev. Thomas Marsh Bartlett, MA, military chaplain
Kingston, York Mills, Canada, 26 Sep.1843.   (NS20:646)

CAMERON Dr, d. Kingston, Jamaica, 23 Aug.1800.   (70:1214)

CAMERON ..., s. Lt. Eugene Hay Cameron, RA, b. Barbados,
23 May 1863.   (NS2/15:94)

CAMPBELL Archibald, Knockbuy, d. Minard, Jamaica, 8 July 1798
(68:811)

CAMPBELL Archibald David, d. Staten Island, NY, 29 Jan.1857.
(NS2/2:497)

CAMPBELL Archibald Hamilton, banker, Montreal, s. late John
Campbell, Carbrook, Stirlings., m. Louisa, yngs. dau. Henry
Fisher, MD, Hillhead, Dunkeld, Perths., Hillingdon,
Uxbridge, 3 April 1856.   (NS45:629)

CAMPBELL Colin, of Campbell & O'Hara, d. Tandragee Castle,
Kingston, Jamaica, Sep.1808.   (78:952)

CAMPBELL Colin, MD, d. Kingston, Jamaica, 1825.   (94:574)

CAMPBELL Colin, late High Sheriff, Charlotte Co., NB, d.
St Andrews, NB, 30 Aug.1843.   (NS20:670)

CAMPBELL Cap. Dougal, d. Jamaica, 1791.   (61:187)

CAMPBELL Dugald, Saltspring, d. on passage from Jamaica,
19 June 1817.   (87:87)

CAMPBELL Duncan, St Anne's, Jamaica, d.1791.   (61:1065)

CAMPBELL Duncan, Knapdale, Jamaica, d. Aux Cayes, Domingo,
1795.   (65:1057)

CAMPBELL Duncan, St Vincent, d. Clifton, 15 Sep.1797.(67:895)

CAMPBELL Elizabeth, dau. Alexander Campbell, Jamaica, wid.
D Davies, London, m. Rev. H W Marychurch, London, 5 Sep.1849.
                                                       (NS32:529)

CAMPBELL Elizabeth, b.1766, dau. Angus Campbell, Jamaica, d.
Bristol, 18 Sep.1850.   (NS34:560)

CAMPBELL Emily Georgina, b.1825, eldest dau. late John
Chilton, w. John Montgomery Campbell, d. Grafton, Canada
West, 15 Aug.1852.   (NS38:655)

CAMPBELL Frances Elizabeth, dau. Maj. J Campbell, 60th Rifles
m. James Crofton Uniacke, yngs. s. Andrew Mitchell Uniacke,
Halifax, NS, Kensington, 16 Nov.1865.   (NS3/1:117)

CAMPBELL G Montgomery m. Sophia Storie, dau. John Simcoe
Saunders, Fredericton, NB, 9 June 1858.   (NS2/5:185)

CAMPBELL Grace, 4th dau. late Angus Campbell, Maryhill,
Tobago, gdau. late Elphinstone Piggott, Chief Justice Tobago,
m. Rev. Henry Martyn Capel, school-inspector, Ryde, Isle of
Wight, 23 Aug.1867.   (NS2/17:512)

CAMPBELL Helen, 2nd dau. Maj. Gen. Sir Archibald Campbell, Lt
Gov. NB, m. Augustus Almeric Spencer, Cap., 43rd Reg., 3rd s.
Lord Churchill, Fredericton, NB, 6 Feb.1836.   (NS5:544)

CAMPBELL Dr James, b. Lincs., 1777, doctor Hedon, Yorks., 1798
settled Montreal 1824, Kingston 1836, d. 25 Jan.1842.(NS18:332)

CAMPBELL James, Jamaica, d. Rotherhithe, 7 Feb.1766. (36:103)

CAMPBELL John, Jamaica, m. Miss Storer, dau. Thomas Storer,
London, 10 March 1774.   (44:141)

CAMPBELL John, Lancithall, m. Elizabeth Bell, ex Glasgow,
Jamaica, 1790.   (60:1213)

CAMPBELL John, b.1731, Glendaruel, Argyll, Supt. Indian Affairs
Lower Canada, d. 23 June 1795.   (65:703)

CAMPBELL John, Indian Agent Upper Miss., killed in a duel by
R Crawford, British agent in Miss., 13 Aug.1808.   (78:1126)

CAMPBELL Rev. John, b.1749, St Andrews, Jamaica, d. London,
13 Oct. 1813.   (83:406)

CAMPBELL John, Auchenwillie, Argyll, d. Besancon, Three Rivers
Upper Canada, 11 Oct.1819.   (89:568)

CAMPBELL John, Colesbay, Cape of Good Hope, m. Sarah, only
dau. late William Henry West, Jamaica, London, 1 Nov.1842.
                                                       (NS19:86)

CAMPBELL Sir John, b.27 Nov.1807, s. Sir John Campbell, Lt.
Gov. St Vincent, d. Kingston, St Vincent, 18 Jan.1853.
(NS39:542)

CAMPBELL Robert, b. Edinburgh, bookseller & stationer,
Philadelphia, d. Frankford, 14 Aug.1800.   (70:1107)

CAMPBELL Gen. Robert Blair, ex US Consul London, d. Ealing,
13 July 1862.   (NS2/13:237)

CAMPBELL Lord William m. Miss Izard, Charleston, SC, 1763.
(32:313)

CAMPBELL Lord William, Gov. SC, d.1773.   (43:416)

CAMPBELL Mrs, b.1713, wid. George Campbell, Orange Grove,
Jamaica, d. Enfield, 28 Dec.1801.   (71:1217)

CAMPBELL ..., Gov. Bermuda, d.22 Nov.1796.   (67:252)

CAMPBELL Lady, wid. Sir William Campbell, Chief Justice,
Upper Canada, d. Toronto, 15 Feb.1843.   (NS19:558)

CAMPBELL ..., s. Lt. Col. Sir John Campbell, b. Jamaica,
19 June 1846.   (NS26:313)

CAMPE Rev. Charles, Port of Spain, Trinidad, only s. late
Charles Campe, Essex, m. Rebecca, dau. Richard Sharp, Maidstone, Kent, Trinidad, 15 April 1847.   (NS28:198)

CAMSON John, b.1704, d. Patrick Co., Va., 1824.   (95:94)

CANNING Elizabeth, transported to NE Aug.1754, d. Weathersfield
Conn., 22 July 1773.   (43:413)

CANON Richard, Annapolis, Md., d. 17 Nov.1768.   (38:543)

CAPEL Arthur Douglas, Lennoxville, 4th s. Rev. T R Capel,
Wareham, Dorset, m. Rebekah, 3rd dau. Rev. John Mais, Tintern
Parva, Monmouth, Lennoxville, Canada, 26 Dec.1861.(NS2/12:220)

CAPEL Rev. Henry Martyn, schools inspector, m. Grace, 4th dau.
late Angus Campbell, Maryhill, Tobago, gdau. Elphinstone
Piggott, Chief Justice Tobago, Ryde, Isle of Wight,
23 Aug.1867.   (NS2/17:512)

CAPEL ..., s. A D Capel, Bishop's College, b. Lennoxville,
Canada, 1 Nov.1862.   (NS2/13:768)

CAPPELL Mrs, wid. William Cappell, Jamaica, d. Yarmouth, Isle
of Wight, 1814.   (84:99)

CARDEN Cap. A, 60th Rifles, m. Anne, eldest dau. Lt. Gen.
S H Berleley, C.O. WI, ggdau. Dr Alexander Bruce, Barbados,
4 Aug.1847.   (NS28:533)

CARDINALL Hannah, b.1821, sis. Mr J Cardinall, Halstead, d.
Inagna, Bahamas, 24 Nov.1855.   (NS45:433)

CARDOZU Abraham Rodriques, b.1703, d. Jamaica, 1791. (61:682)

CAREW Margaret Bishop, dau. late Rev. W Carew, Grenada, d.
Bath, 28 May 1833.   (103:573)

CAREY William, b.1780, Water Wheel, Westmoreland, Jamaica,
d. Winchester, 24 Nov.1842.   (NS19:106)

CARLISLE Mrs, Woodford Bridge & Antigua, m. John Gray,
London & Jamaica, July 1752.   (22:336)

CARLOW James Townsend, eldest s. late James Carlow, Sitting-
bourne, d. Canada, 16 Aug.1842.   (NS19:110)

CARLTON Gen., Gov. Quebec, m. Maria Howard, sis. Earl of
Effingham, 21 May 1772.   (42:246)

CARLETON Dudley, b.1789, Chateau St Louis, Canada, s. late
Lord Dorchester, d. Newbury, Berks., 1820.   (90:378)

CARMICHAEL James Charles Edward, only s. late John Edward
Carmichael, gs. Charles Douglas Smith, late Lt. Gov. PEI,
m. Eliza Jane, eldest dau. John Williston, Miramachi, NB,
19 May 1853.   (NS40:304)

CARMICHAEL John, Lt., 53rd Reg., m. Margaret Anne, dau. late
Dr Falside, St Vincent, 1797.   (67:1127)

CARMICHAEL Mrs, w. J Wilson Carmichael, St Vincent, d. London
3 Aug.1814.   (84:198)

CARNE Susan, dau. late John Carne, Falmouth, m. Rev. Edward
Montague Hamilton, 2nd s. late Cheney Hamilton, Receiver Gen.
Jamaica, Stoke Damerel, 17 April 1844.   (NS21:645)

CARPENTER Philip, merchant, Jamaica, d.1769.   (39:270)

CARPENTER R W m. Susan, dau. late Benjamin Waterhouse,
Kingston, Jamaica, Bath, 3 April 1846.   (NS25:639)

CARR Roseanna, yngs. dau. late J T Carr, Newcastle-on-Tyne,
d. Port of Spain, Trinidad, 13 April 1859.   (NS2/9:89)

CARR Thomas, merchant, s. John Carr, watch-manufacturer,
Coventry, d. Jamaica, 12 June 1807.   (77:780)

CARR William Hay, bro. Earl of Errol, m. Miss Elliot, 3rd dau.
Samuel Elliot, Antigua, 27 July 1796.   (66:701)

CARRE Henry, eldest s. Rev. Carre, Raphoe, m. Louisa
de Quincy, 3rd dau. Rev. F J Lundy, Grimsby, Upper Canada,
gdau. Jonathan Sewell, Chief Justice Lower Canada, Stirling,
Upper Canada, 9 Aug.1866.   (NS3/2:539)

CARRINGTON Frederica Emma Laura Spencer, 2nd dau. late Rev.
F H Carrington, St Johns, NFD, m. Rev. E T Bidewell,
Orcheston St Mary's, Wilts., Shoreditch, 26 Oct.1843.(NS20:648)

CARRINGTON Julia Eliza, 3rd dau. late Rev. F H Carrington, m. Charles Crowdy, surgeon, NFD., 23 Sep.1850.   (NS34:652)

CARRINGTON Paul, Barbados, d. London, 13 May 1812.   (82:597)

CARRINGTON Robert Charles, The Admiralty, Whitehall, m. Sarah Jane, 2nd dau. Ebenezer B Pewtress, Buffalo, NY, Hammersmith, 15 June 1861.   (NS2/11:82)

CARRINGTON Rosamond, dau. Rev. Hamilton Carrington, m. Cap. H C Marriott, St Johns, NFD., 18 April 1849.   (NS32:84)

CARROLL Charles, b.1736, 'last survivor of the signees of the Declaration of Independence', Carrollton, USA, d. Nov.1832.
                                                   (102:658)

CARROLL Louisa, 2nd dau. Col. Charles Carroll, Md., gggdau. Charles Carroll, Carrollton, m. George Cavendish Taylor, late 95th Reg., Baltimore, 28 Dec.1858.   (NS2/6:313)

CARRUTHERS George, eldest s. late James Carruthers, Dunwoodie Green, d. Dundee Est., Trelawney, Jamaica, 15 July 1796.   (66:880)

CARSON Jacobina, dau. late John Carson, MD, Philadelphia, m. Robert Forsyth, advocate, Edinburgh, 12 July 1803.(73:690)

CARTER Amelia, wid. Dr Carter, (nephew Sir Isaac Brock), dau. late John Coward, Ordnance storekeeper, Canada, m. John Edward Johnstone, MD, Montreal, 28 Jan.1851.   (NS35:545)

CARTER Anne, Crutched Friars, m. Richard Coleston, America, 6 July 1745.   (15:444)

CARTER Ellen, yngs. dau. William Carter, Troy, Jamaica, m. Lt. Col. G W Green, 2nd East Bengal Fusiliers, 3rd s. Rev. G W Green, Carmarthens., London, 16 June 1859.   (NS2/9:82)

CARTER Emma, w. James Carter, judge, NB, yngs. dau. Rev. Charles Wellbeloved, York, d. Fredericton, NB, 29 July 1842.
                                                   (NS19:110)

CARTER Jane Caroline, 3rd dau. Robert Carter, RN, Assemblyman m. Peter German Tessier, St Johns, NFD., 4 Feb.1849.(NS31:534)

CARTER Julia Mary, 2nd dau. Robert Carter, RN, Colonial Treasurer, m. Charles Durnford, s. Rev. Robert Newman, Coryton, Devon, St Johns, NFD., 31 Dec.1850.   (NS35:421)

CARTER Robert, President Council, d. Va., 4 Aug.1732.(2:1082)

CARTER Mrs, wid. Lt. Col. Carter, d. St Johns, Antigua, 24 June 1807.   (77:888)

CARTER William, b.1752, Vice Admiralty judge NFD., d. NFD., 18 March 1840.   (NS13:669)

CARTERET Henrietta, Gloucester, m. Thomas Priestley, Jamaica, 18 Oct.1767.   (37:523)

CARTWRIGHT Letitia, London, m. John Austin, Barbados,
17 April 1801.   (71:371)

CARTWRIGHT Letitia, b.1826, only dau. late Daniel Boscombe,
Bermuda, w. Henry Cartwright, HM Commr. Massarurbe, d.
Grand Cay, Bahamas, 1854.   (NS43:327)

CARY Lucius, Jamaica, d. Clifton, 26 Aug.1826.   (96:284)

CARY Rev. Samuel, b.1785, colleague Rev. Dr Freeman, King's
Chapel, Boston, NE, d. Royston, 22 Oct.1815.   (85:636)

CASSIN Henry R, MD, m. Mrs Catherine Watts, wid. late Thomas
Watts, HEICS, Antigua, 30 May 1819.   (89:271)

CASSIN Mary Caroline, eldest dau. late Henry R Cassin, MD,
Nevis, m. Rev. Samuel Whitbread Bowne, London, 24 March 1852.
                                                     (NS37:512)

CASTLE Tudor, Stapleton Grove, Glocs., m. Anne, 3rd dau. late
George Cunningham, Trelawney, Jamaica, London, 14 Oct.1845.
                                                     (NS24:650)

CASTLES John, d. on passage from Grenada, 1791.   (61:778)

CASWELL Albert, Trowbridge, Wilts., m. Mary Elizabeth, 2nd
dau. David Paine, Ingersoll, Canada West, Woodstock, Canada
West, 7 Oct.1851.   (NS37:83)

CASWELL Richard, Speaker Senate, d. Fayetteville, NC, 1790.
                                                      (60:373)

CASWELL Thomas, b.1817, 4th s. late Rev. R C Caswell, West
Lavington, Wilts., d.NY, 5 March 1862.   (NS2/13:112)

CATHCART Miss, dau. Lady Georgina Cathcart, b. Chambly,
Lower Canada, 1840.   (NS15:89)

CATON Mrs, mo. Duchess of Leeds, Marchioness Wellesley, Lady
Stafford, d. John McIntosh, her son-in-law, Md., 15 Nov.1846.
                                                     (NS27:222)

CATOR Albemarle Bertie, b.1831, s. late Adm. Bertie Cator,
d. Victoria, Vancouver Island, 17 Oct.1864.   (NS2/18:114)

CATTON Charles, b. GB, 1754, Royal Academician, settled NY
1801, d. New Paltz, Ulster Co., NY, 1819.   (88:655)

CATON Louisa Catherine, 3rd dau. R Caton, Md., m. Col.
Felton Bathurst Hervey, 24 April 1817.   (87:466)

CATON Thomas Moore, d. on passage to America, 1802. (72:785)

CATTLEY Henry Beaumont, Doctors Commons, m. Caroline, 2nd dau.
William Swabey, PEI, ex RHA, London, 12 June 1854. (NS42:294)

CAULFIELD Rev. Charles, Bishop of Nassau, d. Nassau, New
Providence, Bahamas, 4 Sep.1862.   (NS2/13:647)

CAULFIELD Gov., NY, d. 14 Aug.1767.   (37:430)

CAVAN Michael, b.1780, merchant, d. Barbados, 6 June 1832.
                                                       (102:94)

CAVE John, b.1790, 2nd s. Stephen Cave, Clevehill, Bristol,
d. Barbados, 18 Jan.1808.   (78:364)

CAW James jr., St Thomas, m. Frances, yngs. dau. late
William Ruan, MD, St Croix, 14 Sep.1859.   (NS2/7:529)

CAYMER John, d. NY, 1798.   (68:1086)

CEAN James, Assemblyman, d. Kingston, Jamaica, 1781. (51:489)

CERF Amelia, dau. Henry Cerf, Worton Hall, ex Jamaica, m.
M Deby, barrister, Brussels, Bath, 9 Feb.1825.   (95:177)

CERF Henry, b.1757, late Isleworth & Jamaica, d. Brussels,
18 Nov.1840.   (NS15:110)

CHABOT James, b.1778, ex Malta, d. Mexico, 20 June 1850.
                                                     (NS34:455)

CHABOT Mary Ann Julia, yngr. dau. late James Chabot, Mexico,
m. Alexander F Low, Tizapan, Mexico, British Residence Mexico
24 July 1852.   (NS38:519)

CHADBAND J, ADC Gov., d. Tobago, 1831.   (101:652)

CHADS Augusta Cornell, 4th dau. Lt. Col. Chads, Virgin Islands
m. James Watson, s. late James Dunlop, Glasgow, Tortula,
13 March 1854.   (NS41:636)

CHADS Eliza West, yngs. dau. Lt. Col. Chads, Virgin Islands,
m. Charles Girdlestone, s. Rev. H Girdlestone, Landford,
Tortula, 13 March 1854.   (NS41:636)

CHADS Lt. Col. John Cornell, b.1794, President British
Virgin Islands, d. Tortula, 28 Feb.1854.   (NS41:444)

CHADWICK Louisa, b.1808, 5th dau. Jonathan Bell, Kensington,
w. John Craven Chadwick, d. Ancaster, Canada West, 24 March
1845.   (NS23:678)

CHAIRES Russell, w. Joseph Chaires, Tallahassee, dau. James
Ormond, Leith, d. Florida, 29 Aug.1841.   (NS17:118)

CHALLET Samuel, Customs Collector, d. Trinidad, 13 May 1814.
                                                       (84:189)

CHALMERS George Canning, b.1829, only s. George Chalmers,
Trafalger, d. Waterdown, Canada West, 24 June 1864.(NS2/19:795)

CHALMERS John, Antigua, d.1757.   (27:189)

CHALMERS Thomas, Customs Collector, d. Tobago, 5 Oct.1801.
                                                      (71:1211)

CHALMERS Miss, American descendant Dr Chalmers, SC physician,
d. on road to Paris, 1783.   (54:721)

CHAMBERLAIN Robert, b.1802, eldest s. Robert Chamberlain,
Millet Est., Jamaica, d. London, 28 Oct.1821.   (91:477)

CHAMBERLAIN Samuel, b.1714, ex St Anne's, Jamaica, d. London,
27 Feb.1794.   (64:281)

CHAMBERS John, bro. Edward Chambers, Devon, d. Jamaica, 1770.
                                                     (40:344)

CHAMBERS Samuel, Cap., RN, m. Susan Matilda, eldest dau.
William Wylly, Attorney Gen Bahamas, Nassau, New Providence,
10 March 1807.   (77.585)

CHAMBERS Hugh Best, Cap., Royal Newfoundland Co., 4th s. late
David Chambers, London, d. NFD., 23 Jan.1851.   (NS35:575)

CHAMBERS Miss, eldest dau. late Edward Chambers, Bachelorshall, Jamaica, m. James Weeks jr.·, Bristol, 4 July 1792.
                                                     (62:672)

CHAMPION Richard, ex Paymaster Gen. & china-manufacturer in
Bristol, d. Camden, SC, 7 Oct.1791.   (61:1158)

CHAMPION Richard Lloyd, 2nd s. late R Champion, ex Bristol,
d. Rocky Branch, Camden, SC, Nov.1813.   (84:298)

CHANDLER George Lee, Cap., RA, m. Alice Maria Elizabeth, only
dau. Rev. William Mayhew, St Andrews, Jamaica, Halfwaytree
Church, Jamaica, 4 Dec.1862.   (NS2/14:369)

CHANDLER Isaac B, medical student, Charleston, SC, d.
Edinburgh, 1801.   (71:576)

CHANDLER William Botsford, barrister, eldest s. E B Chandler,
Dorchester, NB, d. 11 June 1847.   (NS28:105)

CHANDLER ..., dau. Maj. Chandler, RA, b. Jamaica, 21 Sep.1863.
                                                    (NS2/15:769)

CHANDLER ..., dau. Lt. Col. Chandler, RA, b. Quebec,
10 Sep.1867.   (NS3/2:667)

CHAPMAN Sir R, Gov. Bermuda, m. Caroline, dau. late Rev.
G Pyke, Essex, Boyton, Wilts., 9 Nov.1835.   (NS4:646)

CHAPMAN William Bloom, b.1776, eldest s. Deputy Chapman,
London, d. Jamaica, 1794.   (64:1155)

CHARLTON Charles Henry, yngs. s. late Cap. John Charlton, RA,
d. Jamaica, 12 Nov.1841.   (NS17:231)

CHARLTON Cornelius, b.1824, ex Strood, Kent, printer Paris
Star, d. Paris, Canada West, 1 June 1855.   (NS44:110)

CHARNLEY William, s. Mr Charnley, Blackburn, Coroner Lancs.,
d. Jam., 1795.   (65:880)

CHARNOCK John, b.1722, ex Barbados, d. Bath, 16 July 1809.
                                                     (79:686)

CHASE Judge, d. Md., 1811.   (81:292)

CHASE Rev. Philander, b. NH, 1775, Bishop Ill., d.20 Oct.1852
                                                   (NS38:641)

CHATTERTON Henry, b.1821, s. Edward Chatterton, Rye, Sussex,
d. Cleveland, America, 1854.   (NS43:218)

CHAUNCEY Isaac, Com. USN, d. Washington, 1840.   (NS13:670)

CHERBORNE Cap., merchant, New Providence, d. Dec.1753.(23:591)

CHERRIMAN John Bradford, Prof. Nat. Phil., Toronto, m. Julia
yngs. dau. E Malone, Plymouth, London, 12 June 1858.(NS2/5:84)

CHETWYND Walter, MP & Gov. Barbados, d. 4 Feb.1732.   (2:630)

CHEW Sophia, dau. Judge Benjamin Chew, m. Henry Philips,
Manchester, Philadelphia, 18 Oct.1796.   (66:1054)

CHEYNE George, b.1788, Cap., RN, d. Fredericton, NB,
11 Aug.1866.   (NS3/2:551)

CHILDERS Leonard, 4th s. Mrs Childers, Henley, d.Panama,
15 July 1826.   (96:381)

CHISHOLM Daniel, d. Jamaica, 1791.   (61:682)

CHISHOLM George, b.1743, settled Canada 1769, d. East Flam-
borough, Canada, 1843.   (NS19:558)

CHOATE Rufus, Mass., ex US Attorney Gen., d. Halifax, NS, en
route for England, 14 July 1859.   (NS2/7:314)

CHOLMLEY Mrs, wid. Robert Cholmley, Barbados, m. Thomas
Workman, Barbados, 1757.   (27:530)

CHOPPIN Caroline, eldest dau. James Choppin, St Vincent, m.
James Protheroe, Bristol, Bath, 27 Aug.1806.   (76:873)

CHOVET Abraham, MD, b.1704, settled Jamaica, moved Philadelphia
1770, d. Philadelphia, 24 March 1790.   (61:279)

CHRISTIAN F H, b. Yverdun, Berne, Switzerland, Westminster,
d. Mexico, 13 Oct.1818.   (88:638)

CHRISTIE Fairlie, Assemblyman, d. Fairfield House, Jamaica,
Dec.1806.   (77:376)

CHRISTIE Francis C, d. Belize, Honduras, 10 Aug.1854.
                                                   (NS42:528)

CHRISTIE Miss, niece Fairlie Christie, m. Michael Parys,
Kingston, Jamaica, July 1800.   (70:1001)

CHRISTOPHE, King of Haiti, b.1767, d. Sans Souci, Haiti,
8 Oct.1820.   (90:565)

CHURCH Sarah, wid. Benjamin Church, physician, Boston,
America, d. 8 Aug.1788.   (58:757)

CLACKTON Joseph, Jamaica, d. 9 Sep.1763.   (33:565)

CLAPHAM Rev. John Henry, Port of Spain, d. Trinidad,
3 Jan.1835.   (105:441)

CLARE Michael Benignus, MD, Physician Gen.Jamaica, m.
Margaret, eldest dau. Col. C D Graham, Lt. Gov. St Mawe's,
Twickenham Park, Jamaica, 18 March 1817.   (87:465)

CLARE Sarah, b.1812, dau. late Sir Michael B Clare, Jamaica,
d. the Deanery, Wolverhampton, 1838.   (NS9:669)

CLARKE A, b.1763, ex Trinidad, d. Belmont, Co. Donegal,
16 April 1836.   (NS6:110)

CLARKE Alexander Ross, Lt., RE, m. Frances Maria, yngs. dau.
Col. Matthew C Dixon, RE, Canada, Montreal, 1 Nov.1853.
                                              (NS41:184)

CLARKE Alice A, eldest dau. late Thomas Clarke, Norfolk, Va.,
m. Joseph Valentine, s. late Thomas J Smedley, gs. late
Valentine Smedley, Hawesville, Kentucky, 8 June 1854.(NS42:294)

CLARKE Anna Maria Best, 2nd dau. Sir R Bowcher Clarke, Chief
Justice Barbados & St Lucia, m. Fitzherbert, 2nd s. Sir
Reynold A Alleyne, Barbados, 23 March 1854.   (NS42:70)

CLARK Ann Eliza, eldest dau. James Clerk, MD, Dominica, m.
John Sim, MD, London, 9 Oct.1817.   (87:466)

CLARKE Caroline Haughton, dau. late John H James, Jamaica,
wid. Lt. Col. Clarke, Grenadier Guards, m. Peregrine Taylor,
2nd s. late T B Bungay, Bengal Horse Artillery, London,
20 Oct.1852.   (NS39:86)

CLARKE David, of Rouse & Clarke, merchant, d. Jamaica,
3 June 1818.   (88:373)

CLARKE E Lee, dau. late G I Clarke, Hydehall, m. I Hodgson,
only s. A Hodgson, Jamaica, Stockport, 9 Aug.1831. (101:171)

CLARKE Rev. Edward William, Great Yeldham, Essex, eldest s.
late Dr Edward Daniel Clarke, d. Belize, Honduras, 1843.
                                              (NS20:326)

CLARK Elizabeth, 3rd dau. Sir Bowcher Clark, Chief Justice
Barbados, m. Cap. Dugald Stewart Miller, 67th Reg., QM Gen.,
eldest s. Dr Miller, Exeter, Barbados, 20 May 1858.(NS2/5:185)

CLARKE Elizabeth Anne, b.1804, only dau. late Josias Clarke,
Jamaica, d. Hotwells, 16 July 1825.   (95:189)

CLARKE Elizabeth Grasett, 2nd dau. Foster Clarke, Barbados, m.
Thomas Louis, 2nd s. late Adm. Sir Thomas Louis, Barbados,
2 Oct. 1828.   (98:558)

CLARKE Elizabeth Staples, eldest dau. William Clarke, NY, m.
Col. T H Packenham, 30th Reg., NY, 25 Feb.1862. (NS2/12:497)

CLARKE Emily Mary, 2nd dau. William Clarke, MD, Tweedside,
Barbados, m. Cap. Peter Edward Hill, RA, Barbados, 26 Oct.1864.
(NS2/16:108)

CLARKE Emily Spooner, eldest dau. Sir R B Clarke, Chief
Justice Barbados, m. Charles Edward Michel, Maj., 66th Reg.,
Barbados, 19 Nov.1850. (NS35:196)

CLARKE Godney jr., Barbados, m. Miss Lascelles, neice Adm.
Holbourne, 15 Oct.1762. (32:503)

CLARKE Gedney, Customs Collector, Barbados, d. 27 Aug.1764.
(34:498)

CLARKE George m. Susan, 2nd dau. Charles Kelsal, Jamaica,
Westham, Essex, 12 Feb.1776. (46:142)

CLARK Hannah, b.1737, wid. Maj. Gen. Elijah Clark, d. Wilkes
Co., USA, 1827. (97:574)

CLARKE Henrietta Jane, 2nd dau. Lt. Gen. St John A Clarke,
Dublin, m. Lt. H Compton Best, RN, Halifax, NS, 25 July 1865.
(NS2/19:373)

CLARKE Henry, b.1803, Hackney, d. on passage from NY,
24 Feb.1840. (NS13:669)

CLARK Joseph, b.1781, late Wetherby, Yorks., d. Cincinatti,
USA, 1 July 1858. (NS2/5:313)

CLARKE Rev. J, St Catherine, Upper Canada, d. 1840.(NS14:550)

CLARK James, MD, FRS, ex Councillor Dominica, d. London,
21 Jan.1819. (88:184)

CLARKE John, b.1739, Tobago, d. Berwick-on-Tweed,
24 Jan.1807. (77:185)

CLARKE John, ex Jamaica, d. 16 Feb.1814. (84:410)

CLARKE Joseph Charles, Jamaica, d. Brighton, 12 Nov.1828.
(98:476)

CLARK Josiah, b.1699, d. Northampton, Mass., May 1789.(61:279)

CLARK Josiah, b. 1697, Northampton, d. Philadelphia, 1789.
(59:955)

CLARKE Martha, dau. Thomas Clarke, Antigua, m. Cap. Robilliard
RN, 12 July 1820. (90:84)

CLARKE Mary Ogle, b. 1845, yngs. dau. Sir R Bowcher Clarke,
Chief Justice Barbados & Windwards, d. Haynes Hill,
Barbados, 17 March 1861. (NS2/10:585)

CLARKE Rev. Richard, b. 1719, St Philips, Charleston, SC,
late Hartley, Kent, d. 31 June 1802.   (72:785)

CLARKE Samuel T, Spencer's Plant., d. Barbados, 3 Sep.1837.
                                                       (NS9:222)

CLARKE Mr, Scotland, catechist, d. Jamaica, 1800.   (70:905)

CLAUDET Francis George, yngs. s. A Claudet, London, m. Fanny,
eldest dau. Charles Fleury, Weymouth, Dorset, Victoria,
Vancouver Island, 22 Sep.1864.   (NS2/16:107)

CLAXTON Robert, barrister, m. Frances Young, eldest dau.
William Stephen, St Kitts, 26 Oct.1816.   (86:622)

CLAXTON Robert, b.1792, late Customs Collector, Antigua, d.
Bristol, 1841.   (NS16:664)

CLAXTON Robert, b. 1796, Chief Justice St Kitts, d. London,
18 March 1849.   (NS31:551)

CLAY Henry, b. 12 April 1777, Hanover Co., Va., late US Secy.
State, d. Washington, 29 June 1852.   (NS38:197)

CLAYTON Septimus, editor 'American Daily Advertiser', d. Md.,
1798.   (68:1086)

CLAYTON Thomas, Potterhill, Paisley, d. Poplar Grove,
Wilmington, SC, 1 Oct.1793.   (63:1214)

CLEGG William, Lt., 11th Reg., m. Louisa Caroline, 5th dau.
late John Barr, Bermuda, Brighton, 6 Feb.1861.   (NS2/10:331)

CLELAND Alexander B, MD, Royal Canadian Rifles, m. Fanny
Kemp, yngs. dau. J Roberts, customs surveyor, Bristol, NY,
3 June 1845.   (NS24:190)

CLEMENT Hampden m. Philippa, eldest dau. Sir R A Alleyne,
Barbados, July 1831.   (101:268)

CLEMENT Henry, 3rd s. Thomas Clement, solicitor, Alton,
Customs Collector Tortula, d. Tortula, 21 Aug.1821. (91:475)

CLEMENTSON Samuel, b. 1733, late merchant, Boston, Mass.,
d. Windsor, 7 April 1782.   (52:206)

CLIEFE William, b.1813, Customs Collector, Morant, Jamaica,
s. Thomas Cliefe, nephew J Cliefe, Yorkhill Castle, Herefords.
d. Morant, 1841.   (NS15:670)

CLIFTON Rev. George Hill, Ripple, Worcs., m. Helen Frances,
only ch. late W Burt Wright, Jamaica, London, 16 Aug.1842.
                                                     (NS18:421)

CLINCKETT Rev. G M, Claremont, yngs. s. Abel Clinkett,
Barbados, m. Jane, yngs. dau. late Rev. William Henry,
Tooting, Surry, Jamaica, 10 Jan.1851.   (NS35:545)

CLINTON Gen. J, b. 1737, d. Orange Co., America, Feb.1813.
(83:387)

CLINTON George de Witt, b. NY, 1740, Gov. NY, d. NY, Feb.1828.
(98:465)

CLOETE Sir Abraham Josias, CO Windwards & Demerara, m. Anne
Woollcombe, eldest dau. Thomas Louis, Culloden, Barbados,
gdau. Rear Adm. Sir Thomas Bent, Cadwell, Barbados,
8 July 1857.   (NS2/3:328)

CLOGSTOUN Anthony, Marshal Trinidad, m. Georgina, dau.
Ashton Warner, late Chief Justice Trinidad, Trinidad, 1840.
(NS14:650)

CLOGSTOUN Letitia, wid. Robert Clogstoun, ex Antigua, d.
London, 11 April 1810.   (80:494)

CLOSE Eliza Crespigny, b.1831, only dau. Octavius Williams,
Truro, w. Cap. Close, RA, d. Montreal, 12 May 1860.(NS2/9:100)

CLOUSTOUN Anne Rose, 2nd dau. Edward Cloustoun, Stromness,
Orkney, m. Edward Reilly, Hudson Bay Co. Service, York
Factory, Hudson Bay, 28 Aug.1849.   (NS32:638)

CLUTSAM George, b.1793, eldest s. Cap. G Clutsam, drowned
Jamaica, 14 June 1813.   (83:194)

CLUTTERBUCK Charles, b.1815, yngs. s. Charles Caspar Clutterbuck, North Cadbury, Somerset, d. Jamaica, Feb.1832.(102:575)

COATES Alexander, d. Antigua, 12 Nov.1807.   (78:1188)

COATES Rev. Henry, b.1831, ex Worcester College, Oxford, d.
Spanish Town, Jamaica, 28 July 1853.   (NS41:214)

COATES R, s. Alexander Coates, Antigua, d. Towcaster, 1810.
(80:676)

COBB Elizabeth, yngs. dau. late Benjamin Cobb, New Romney, m.
Col. Butler, Martock, Aylesford, NS, 17 Sep.1850. (NS34:651)

COBB James, s. late J Cobb, Kettering, d. WI, 1813. (83:183)

COBHAM Francis, MD, b.1798, d. Barbados, 29 May 1831.(101:94)

COBHAM Richard, Judge Vice Adm. Court, m. Katherine Anne
Hinds, dau. Richard Skinner, Barbados, 30 March 1819.(88:480)

COCHRAN Alexander, bro. Earl of Dundonald, m. Lady Wheate,
wid. Sir Jacob Wheate, NY, April 1788.   (58:561)

COCHRAN Isabella, wid. Rupert John Cochran, late NY, d.
Edinburgh, 5 Sep.1851.   (NS36:446)

COCHRAN Maria, yngs. dau. Archdeacon Cochran, m. Rev. Charles
Hillyer, Church Missionary Society, Red River, 13 Dec.1854.
(NS43:408)

COCHRAN Justice, b. Halifax, NS, 1777, eldest s. Thomas
Cochran, Councillor, NS, asst. judge, Upper Canada, d.
Oct.1804.   (75:875)

COCHRAN William, s. Cap. Cochran, Greenock, d. Quebec, 1803.
                                                    (73:1254)

COCK Elizabeth Stewart, eldest dau. Lt. R Cock, RN, Seymour
East, Canada West, m. Herbert Henry Matkarsie, RN, 7 April
1852.   (NS38:87)

COCKAYNE Octavius, b.1826, 8th s. Rev. John Cockayne, Bath,
d. Montreal, 15 Sep.1861.   (NS2/11:572)

COCKBURN Alexander, b.1740, d. Grenada, 1816.   (86:638)

COCKBURN Miss, eldest dau. Dr Alexander Cockburn, Grenada, m.
William Baillie Rose, Edinburgh, 23 April 1798.   (68:441)

COCHRANE Thomas, b.1795, printer & bookseller, NY, bro. John
Cochrane, bookseller, Melksham, d. NY, 1832.   (103:94)

CODD John Morse, 3rd s. Cap. Codd, War Office, d. Barbados,
1 Oct.1809.   (79:1174)

CODMAN Stephen, b. Norwich, 1796, cathedral organist, d.
Quebec, 6 Oct.1852.   (NS38:656)

CODRINGTON Anne, only dau. John Codrington, Manchioneal, m.
James Tyrrell, Portland, Jamaica, 23 June 1792.   (62:1151)

COE B D, b.1790, Buffalo, NY, d. London, 26 Nov.1852.
                                                    (NS39:107)

COFFIN John, b.1751, 3rd s. Nathaniel Coffin, customs cashier,
Boston, NE, American loyalist, British Army Gen., d. NB,
12 June 1838.   (NS10:321)

COFFIN Mary Aston, yngs. dau. Gen. Coffin, Walmer, Kent, m.
Charles Richard Ogden, Solicitor Gen. Canada, 29 July 1824.
                                                    (94:176)

COFFIN Cap. Zacheus, Nantucket, captured on passage from
Dunkirk to Philadelphia 1785, prisoner in Algiers, d.Nov.1787.
                                                    (57:1127)

COGSWELL Rev. William, b.1810, d. Halifax, NS, 5 June 1847.
                                                    (NS28:328)

COHEN Andrew, d. Jamaica, 1790.   (60:1214)

COLBURN Susannah, w. James S Colburn, merchant, Boston, USA,
dau. Mr Lorimer, London, d. on passage to Boston, 19 Oct.1802.
                                                    (72:1161)

COLDEN Mrs, w. Cadwallader Colden, Gov.NY, d.17 Jan.1762.
                                                    (32:145)

COLDEN Cadwallader D, b.1769, gs. Cadwallader Colden, Gov. NY
& historian, d.7 March 1834.   (104:567)

COLE Laura, yngs. dau. Charles Cole, Paston Hall, m. John
Prettejohn, Barbados & Harehatch, Berks., Paston, Northants.,
8 April 1840.   (NS13:536)

COLE Thomas, landscape-painter, d. Catskill, NY, 1848.
                                                       (NS30:214)

COLE ..., dau. Lt. Col. A Lowry Cole, 17th Reg., b. Quebec,
6 Aug.1857.   (NS2/3:454)

COLEBROOKE Emma Sophia, w. Col. Sir William Colebrooke, RA,
Gov. Windward Islands, d. Barbados, 19 April 1851. (NS36:99)

COLEBROOKE Frances Elizabeth, eldest dau. Sir William
MacBean George Colebrooke, m. Alfred, 3rd s. late Frederick
Reade, London, NB, 8 Oct.1844.   (NS23:311)

COLEBROOKE Lady Mary, b.1730, dau. Patrick Gaynor, Antigua,
m. Sir George Colebrook, d. Hampstead, 13 Aug.1818. (88:282)

COLEMAN Harriett, b.1802, dau. Cap. George Dawson, wid. James
Coleman, Elizabeth, Lancaster Co., Penn., d. Philadelphia,
19 Jan.1865.   (NS2/18:392)

COLEMAN J G, Dep. Naval Officer Barbados, d. on passage from
Trinidad to St Kitts, 24 Jan.1810.   (80:491)

COLEMAN Mr, inventor 'Aeolian attachment', d. America on
return from England, 1845.   (NS24:103)

COLERIDGE Georgina Blackstone, inf. dau. Rev. W H Coleridge,
Bishop Barbados, d. Devon, 29 Sep.1835.   (NS4:556)

COLES Jeremiah, b. England, bosun Oliver Elsworth, drowned
NY, 28 July 1805.   (75:881)

COLES R C, Royal Reg., yngs. s. Rev. J Coles, Silchester,
Hants., m. Fanny, only dau. J Morris, Halifax, NS,
22 July 1852.   (NS38:305)

COLES William, b.1771, d. on passage from WI, 16 Feb.1835.
                                                       (105:446)

COLESTON Richard, America, m. Anne Carter, Crutched Friars,
6 July 1745.   (15:444)

COLLICK Henry, yngs. s. William Collick, Shripney, Sussex, m.
Elizabeth Croasdaile, eldest dau. David Mignot, MD, Kingston,
Jamaica, Chelsea, 13 Oct.1846.   (NS27:79)

COLLIER Catherine Gregorie, b.1794, wid. James Morris Collier,
Tobago, London, 6 Oct.1853.   (NS40:650)

COLLIER William, Barbados, m. Miss Warren, Wotton, Berks.,
18 Sep.1760.   (30:490)

COLLINGS Frances Mary Sophia, yngs. dau. late W H Collings, m.
Joseph Gatcomb Bailey, Dyersville, USA, London, 16 March 1858.
                                                       (NS2/4:544)

COLLINS Anna, dau. H Collins, Marylebone, m. William
Franklin Bonnell, Digby, NS, 10 Dec.1808.   (78:1126)

COLLINS John, 2nd s. W Collins, MP, Warwick, Comm. Service, d.
London, Upper Canada, 17 Dec.1840.   (NS15:670)

COLLYER Charlotte Ann, 3rd dau. Rev. J B Collyer, m. Rev.
J H Harris, Principal York College, Upper Canada, Hackford,
Norfolk, 25 Aug.1829.   (99:270)

COLQUHOUN Walter m. Miss McAlister, Logon, Dominica, 1776.
          (46:435)

COLQUHOUN Walter, Camstraden, d. Antigua, 12 Feb.1802.(72:374)

COLT Col. Samuel, b. Hartford, Conn., 19 July 1814, inventor,
d. Hartford, Conn., 9 Jan.1862.   (NS2/12:380)

COLTMAN John, b.1780, 3rd s. late John Coltman, Beverley, d.
Portneuf, Lower Canada, 12 Aug.1812.   (82:670)

COLTMAN William Bachelor, late Chairman, Quebec Audit Board,
Councillor Lower Canada, d. 2 Jan.1826.   (96:92)

COLVILLE Eden m. Ann, 3rd dau. Col. Maxwell, Montreal,
4 Dec.1845.   (NS25:199)

COMBE Charles, yngs. s. Dr Combe, London, d. Tortula,
29 Sep.1808.   (78:1039)

CONCANEN Matthew, late Attorney Gen. Jamaica, d. 22 Jan.1749.
          (19:44)

CONNELL Rev. Thomas Griffith, Barbados, m. Maria Jane, wid.
John P Poyer, Barbados, Windsor, 1 Sep.1853.   (NS40:626)

COOKE Caroline, 2nd dau. John Cooke, m. Charles M Brocklesby,
s. late Cap. Brocklesby, Quebec, Guildford, 10 Feb.1846.
          (NS25:422)

COOKE George Frederick, b.1755, Berwick-on-Tweed, tragedian,
d. NY, 26 Sep.1812.   (82:494)

COOK J Early, Nunnery, Cheshunt, m. Sarah, dau. Isaac Munt,
Jamaica, 5 Feb.1820.   (90:272)

COOKE Martha, wid. William Cooke, Burgh House, Lincoln, m.
Rev. Sir George W Crawford, Barbados, 3 May 1849.   (NS32:84)

COOK Mary, w. Asst. Comm. Gen. Cook, d. Barbados, 27 Oct.1811.
          (82:488)

COOKE Richard, Farmhill, m. Miss Kellerman, dau. Jacob
Kellerman, planter, Jamaica, Stroud, Glocs., 19 June 1793.
          (63:575)

COOKE William Percy, b.1809, eldest s. late Maj. William Percy
Cooke, 6th Native Inf., Advocate Gen. Bengal, d. Belize,
Honduras, 3 Aug.1842.   (NS19:110)

COOKMAN George, b.1774, ex Mayor Hull, fa. late Rev. George
Cookman, chaplain US Senate, d. Stepney Lodge, 17 April 1856.
(NS45:662)

COOKSON Mary, w. Rev. James Cookson, d. Greenwich, King's Co.,
NA, 7 Jan.1848.   (NS29:566)

COOPER Bernard John, Com., RN, m. Bessie, wid. W B Perine,
Baltimore, dau. late Z Collins Lee, Baltimore, 15 Aug.1867.
(NS3/2:527)

COOPER Caroline Maria, w. Rev. Charles Alfred Cooper, 2nd
dau. Rev. John Cherton, Worcs., d. Jamaica, 9 July 1843.
(NS20:446)

COOPER Rev. George Frederick, ex Liverpool, d. San Francisco,
Cal., 25 Dec.1857.   (NS2/4:564)

COOPER James Fenimore, b.15 Sep.1789, Burlington, NJ,
novelist, d. Cooperstown, NY, 14 Sep.1851.   (NS36:546)

COOPER Samuel, b.1788, 4th s. late Robert Cooper, Woodbridge,
Suffolk, d. Kingston, Jamaica, 15 June 1814.   (84:292)

COORE Mrs Isabella, b.1786, 3rd dau. John Blagrove, Jamaica,
d. London, 1831.   (101:187)

COOSENS Miss, Lambeth, m. Alexander Hutton, Jamaica, 22 Aug.
1775.   (45:406)

COPE John, b.1725, Supreme Court judge, d. Westmoreland,
Jamaica, 1 March 1792.   (62:479)

COPE John, attorney & clerk of peace, Westmoreland, d.
Kingston, Jamaica, 1793.   (63:1152)

COPE Col., Gov. Placentia, d. Jamaica, 1742.   (13:51)

COPELAND Mary Harris, eldest dau. late Joseph Leacock,
Barbados, w. George Ford Copeland, d. Cheltenham, Glocs.,
14 Feb.1842.   (NS17:450)

COPELAND Peter, Nevis, d.4 Aug.1767.   (37:430)

COPEMAN Louisa Mary, dau. late Edward Robert Copeman, New
Buckenham, Norfolk, m. Cap. Frederick Hutton, Bermuda,
28 Jan.1858.   (NS2/4:437)

CORBETT Lt., ex 4th Veteran Bat., Town Maj. Kingston, d.
Kingston, Upper Canada, 24 Jan.1832.   (102:649)

CORLET James, Assembly Speaker, Dominica, Lt. Col. St George
Militia Reg., d. 1840.   (NS14:676)

CORMACK John Rose, MD, Edinburgh, m. Eliza Anne, 2nd dau.
late William Hine, Jamaica, London, 4 Nov.1841.   (NS17:92)

CORRINGTON Cobourg, customs officer, St Johns, yngs. s. Cap.
William Henry Corrington, ex barrack-master, Weymouth, m.
Catherine, dau. late James Reed, Partridge Island, St Johns,
NFD, 23 Dec.1843.   (NS21:309)

CORY Charlotte, 2nd dau. Robert Cory, attorney & ex mayor,
Great Yarmouth, m. Alexander Aikman, printer to Jamaican
Assembly, Mount Hybla, Jamaica, 7 April 1805.   (75:582)

COSBY J P, Cap., 14th Reg., m. Annie Houldworth, eldest dau.
Rev. Charles Fyfe, Port Royal, Jamaica, 26 Nov.1862.
                                                  (NS2/14:230)

COSENS Grace, wid. G H Cosens, Jamaica, d. Exeter, Dec.1821.
                                                     (91:647)

COSNAN Maj., town-maj. Quebec, m. Mrs Palmer, wid. Herbert
Palmer, 1762.   (32:93)

COSTER Anna, dau. late George Coster, Archdeacon NB, m.
Henry Filkes Hooper, 76th Reg., yngs. s. late Rev. John
Hooper, Albury, Surrey, Christchurch, Fredericton, NB,
3 Oct.1860.   (NS2/9:547)

COSTIN Barry Alexander Boyd, b.1831, ex Bagshot, Surrey,
drowned in wreck Hungarian, Sable Island, NS, 19 Feb.1860.
                                                   (NS2/8:524)

COTTER George Sackville, b.1838, eldest s. Lt. Col. Cotter,
Madras Artillery, b. Kingston, Canada West, 9 Jan.1859.
                                                   (NS2/6:328)

COTTER James, d. on passage to Martinique, 1798.   (68:539)

COTTER Peter, b.1815, d. Belle Plane, St Lucia, 2 Dec.1842.
                                                   (NS19:556)

COTTERELL Mr, d. St Kitts, Jan.1768.   (36:103)

COTTINGHAM Nockalls Johnson, s. late Lewis Nockalls Cottingham, architect, drowned in wreck Arctic on passage to NY,
27 Sep.1854.   (NS42:639)

COTTLE Grace Camilla, dau. late Thomas Cottle, Nevis, m.
James Selfe, Trewbridge, Wilts., Camberwell, 14 Nov.1797.
                                                    (67:1126)

COTTLE Thomas John, b.1761, Councillor Nevis, d. Round Hill,
Nevis, 1 Feb.1828.   (98:382)

COTTLE William, ex tailor & habit-maker, Bath, d. on Orange
on passage to NY, Oct.1793.   (63:1149)

COTTON Selina Harriet, b.1800, w. Maj. Francis Ringler Thomson
RE, d. Sorel, Canada West, 18 June 1843.   (NS20:334)

COTTON Thomas D'Avenant, Royal Fusiliers, s. late Dean of
Chester, m. Mary Hadley Brinley, Halifax, NS, 25 June 1810.
                                                     (80:485)

COULL William, ex St Vincent, d. Cullen, Banffs.,30 Sep.1815.
                                                     (85:635)

COULTHURST Elizabeth, w. Matthew Coulthurst, Barbados,
d. 12 Oct.1820.   (90:473)

COURTHOPE Jessie, yngs. dau. T Courthope, London, m.
J Townshend Bowen, Trinidad, Camberwell, 14 June 1838.
                                                      (NS10:207)

COVENHOGEN Nicholas, judge, King's Co., Long Island, d.
New Utrecht, 6 March 1793.   (63:479)

COWANS Mrs, b.1704, d. Schenectady, America, Sep.1807.
                                                      (77:1173)

COWAN Samuel, Kingston, Upper Canada, m. Katherine Annabell,
2nd dau. Hugh Alexander Emerson, late Solicitor Gen. NFD.,
London, 4 Sep.1858.   (NS2/5:414)

COWARD John, late Ordnance storekeeper, Isle Aux Noirs,
Canada, d. Tiverton, 3 Oct.1831.   (101:379)

COWDRY William, eldest s. Thomas Cowdry, surgeon, Torrington,
d. Coburg, Canada West, 1856.   (NS45:101)

COWELL Editha, dau. David Espenett, Tenterden, w. George
Cowell, d. Cleveland, Ohio, 15 April 1854.   (NS41:666)

COWIE R, ex Hudson Bay Co., d. Montrose, 6 June 1859.
                                                      (NS2/9:92)

COWIE ..., dau. David Cowie, b. St Vincent, 30 April 1867.
                                                      (NS3/4:98)

COX George Herbert, 53rd Reg., m. Jane, 2nd dau. late
Thomas Melville, St Vincent, Twickenham, 17 May 1848.(NS30:88)

COX Harriet, 2nd dau. Lt. Col. William Cox, RA, d. Kingsey,
Canada, 11 March 1854.   (NS41:554)

COX Henry, b.1776, Assemblyman St Mary's, Custos Rotulorum
St Anne's, Jamaica, d. Devonport, 20 Dec.1844.   (NS23:215)

COX Mrs Letitia, b.1678, d. Bybrook, Jamaica, 26 June 1838.
                                                      (NS10:454)

COXE Sarah, b.1752, wid. Daniel Coxe, ex NJ, d. Brighton,
31 July 1843.   (NS20:332)

COX Susan Elizabeth, b.1786, yngs. dau. late I L Cox,
Barbados, d. Clifton, Glocs., 21 Nov.1847.   (NS29:107)

COX ..., s. Maj. Cox, RE, b. St John, NB, 15 Aug.1866.
                                                      (NS3/2:682)

COXWORTHY Victoria Williams, dau. E T Coxworthy, Dep. Comm.
Gen., m. Cap. Alexander Dirom, RE, Halifax, NS, 19 Aug.1862.
                                                      (NS2/13:485)

CRADDOCK Miss, Bridgenorth, m. Henry Talbot, Barbados,
3 Dec.1758.   (28:611)

CRAIG Charlotte Amelia, dau. late Samuel Craig, NY, m.
Robert Bunch, HM Consul Carolinas, eldest s. Robert H Bunch,
New Providence, NY, 18 Oct.1853.   (NS41:78)

CRAIG Sir James Henry, late Gov. BNA, Gov. Blackness Castle,
Col., 78th Reg., d. London, 12 Jan.1812.   (82:92)

CRAIG Mr, planter, Tobago, d. London, Nov.1794.   (64:1060)

CRAMOND James, d. NY, 28 Sep.1799.   (69:993)

CRAMP Anne, dau. late William Burls, Lower Edmonton, w. Rev.
Dr Cramp, President Acadia College, d. Wolfeville, NS,
26 July 1862.   (NS2/13:505)

CRANE John Stafford Chilton, s. Rev. P Crane, Essex, d.
Havanna, 28 June 1854.   (NS42:314)

CRANSTOUN Lord James, Gov. Grenada, d. Fareham, 22 Aug.1796.
                                                    (66:798)

CRANSTOUN Lord m. Miss Macnamara, eldest dau. John Macnamara,
St Kitts, 25 Aug.1807.   (77:886)

CRANSTOUN ..., dau. Lord Cranstoun, b. St Kitts, 15 Aug.1808.
                                                   (78:1125)

CRANSTOUN ..., s. Lord Cranstoun, b. Cranstoun House, St Kitts,
12 Aug.1809.   (79:789)

CRANSTOUN Lord James Edmond, d. St Kitts, 5 Sep.1818.(88:470)

CRASKELL Robert, d. Jamaica, 1790.   (60:1053)

CRAVEN Charles, uncle Lord Craven, Gov. SC under Queen Anne,
d. 27 Dec.1754.   (24:579)

CRAUFORD Rev. Sir George W m. Martha, wid. William Cooke,
Burgh House, Lincoln, Barbados, 3 May 1849.   (NS32:84)

CRAWFORD Henry James, yngs. s. David Crawford of Cartonbank,
d. Jamaica, June 1803.   (73:882)

CRAWFORD Col. James, late Gov. Bermuda, d. NY, 22 March 1811.
                                                    (81:596)

CRAWFORD Joseph Tucker, HM Consul Gen. Cuba, m. Joanna
Frederica, dau. late Mr Jacobson, advocate, Altona, step-
dau. C D Tolme, Havanna, Havanna, 28 May 1845.   (NS24:189)

CRAWFORD John, d. Kingston, Jamaica, 1797.   (67:804)

CRAWFORD John Frame, b.1750, Antigua, d. Kilburn Wells,
10 April 1800.   (70:397)

CRAWFORD Mrs Judith, b.1679, d. Spanish Town, Jamaica,
21 Nov.1830.   (100:381)

CRAWFORD Lawrence, Jamaica, m. Patty Redman, London, May 1750.
(20:284)

CRAWFORD Ninian, d. Jamaica, 1790.   (60:1214)

CRAWFORD Thomas, b. NY, 1814, sculptor, d. London, 8 Oct.1857.
(NS2/3:564)

CRAWSHAY Isabel, 2nd dau. William Crawshay, Cyfartha Castle,
m. Gerard Ralston, Philadelphia, Pendeylan, Glamorgan,
18 Sep. 1838.   (NS10:656)

CRAY Harrison, b.1711, ex treasurer & receiver NA, d. London,
1794.   (64:1156)

CREASE Mary Maberly, eldest dau. Cap. Crease, RN, gdau.
Edward Smith, Ince Castle, Cornwall, d. Matanzas, Cuba,
Aug.1853.   (NS40:649)

CRELE Joseph, b. Detroit, 1725, d. Caledonia, Wisc., 27 Jan.
1866.   (NS3/1:596)

CREMORNE Philadelphia Hannah, b. Philadelphia, 1740, gdau.
William Penn, wid. Viscount Thomas Cremorne, Baron Dartrey,
Ireland, d. London, 14 April 1826.   (96:380)

CRICHLOW Hannah, b.1770, wid. Charles Crichlow, Barbados,
d. Exeter, 10 April 1856.   (NS45:661)

CRICHTON Elizabeth Dundas, dau. Patrick Crichton, Jamaica,
m. William Lambie, Jamaica, Edinburgh, 1820.   (90:563)

CRIDLAND Frederick J, HM Consul Alabama & Florida, m. Harriet
Aurelia, dau. Marion Cutler, Avon, NY, Mobile, Alabama,
29 Oct.1866.   (NS3/3:104)

CROCKER ..., s. Surgeon Maj. Alfred Crocker, b. Barbados,
5 Aug.1864.   (NS2/17:510)

CROFT Grace, only ch. Sir Thomas Elmsley Croft, gniece Lord
Denman, m. Edward, 2nd s. Henry Murray, London, gs. late
Henry Murray, Trinidad, London, 5 March 1846.   (NS25:535)

CROFT Miss, eldest dau. Sir Arthur Croft, Barbados, m. James
Woodcock, Jamaica, 1777.   (48:237)

CROMARTIE Constance Edwards, 2nd dau. F M Cromartie, Dep.
Spt. Military Stores, m. Richard William Charles Winsloe,
Cap., 21st Royal North British Fusiliers, Barbados, 12 Sep.
1861.   (NS2/11:557)

CROOK Edward, b. Wilts., settled SC 1781, planter, d. Santee
River, SC, 15 April 1796.   (66:614)

CROOKE Samuel, Councillor, St Kitts, d. 17 March 1772.(42:151)

CROSBY Rev. S Oliver, St Philips, Barbados, m. Catherine, 3rd
dau. Rev. John Warneford,Caldicott Hill,Herts., Barbados,
30 May 1848.   (NS30:314)

CROSBY William, d. NY, 1780.   (50:494)

CROSKEY Joseph Rodney, US Vice Consul, Cowes, m. Sarah, yngs.
dau. T Roper, West Cowes, Northwood, 25 Sep.1843.   (NS20:539)

CROSSE John MacArtney, b.1825, eldest s. late J G Crosse, MD,
Norwich, d. Galt, Canada West, 19 Aug.1856.   (NS2/1:522)

CROSSMAN James, d. Jamaica, 1791.   (61:186)

CROUCHER Samuel, NY, d.3 July 1757.   (27:338)

CROW Mr, surgeon, London, m. Miss Bateman, actress, NY,
31 Oct.1866.   (NS3/2:826)

CROWDY Charles, surgeon, 3rd s. James Crowdy, Colonial Sec.,
m. Julia Eliza, 3rd dau. late Rev. F H Carrington, NFD,
23 Sep.1850.   (NS34:652)

CROWE ..., s. Cap. T C Crowe, RA, b. Montreal, 7 Nov.1867.
                                                      (NS3/5:99)

CROWTHER Rev. G D, d. Jamaica, 12 Sep.1848.   (NS30:663)

CRUCHLEY William, London, m. Mrs Schaw, wid. Charles Schaw,
Schawfield, Jamaica, 19 Oct.1795.   (65:878)

CRUDEN John, merchant, America, Comm. Sequestrated Est. SC,
d. on passage from Turk's Island to Nassau, 1787.   (57:1193)

CRUGER Bertram Peter, b.1774, NY, d. Brompton, 3 Sep.1854.
                                                      (NS42:529)

CRUGER Henry, b.1739, ex Bristol MP, settled USA 1789, d. NY,
24 April 1827.   (97:94)

CRUGER John, b.1770, Assembly Speaker, Mayor NY, d.20 Dec.1791.
                                                      (62:182)

CRUIKSHANK George, Jamaica, d. London, 22 May 1818. (88:640)

CRUIKSHANK James, MD, b.1762, d. London, 25 Nov.1831.(101:569)

CRUIKSHANK John, Ballard's Valley, Jamaica, d. London,
2 Nov.1787.   (57:1127)

CRUIKSHANK J, Ballard's Valley, d. Berry Hill, St Mary's,
Jamaica, 31 March 1812.   (82:594)

CRUIKSHANK William, late Jamaica, d. Arbroath, 15 Sep.1817.
                                                      (87:472)

CUBBISON Charles, b. Ayr, d. on passage from Jamaica,
2 Aug.1810.   (80:288)

CUDDEN Miss, dau. Thomas Cudden, Master Chancery, m. Thomas
Bowtein, Jamaica, 12 Sep.1777.   (47:459)

CULLOW Thomas, merchant, ex Tobago, d. Havre de Grace,
28 May 1803.
                                                      (73:601)

CULLEN Rachel, elder dau. R D Cullen, Philadelphia, m.
George Nicholson Saunders, Bengal Army, s. Robert John
Saunders, Eltham, Brighton, 7 Aug.1862.   (NS2/13:358)

CUMBERBATCH Edward Arnold, Barbados, m. Mary Gertrude, dau.
A Ashe, Belvidere, Bath, 6 Aug.1822.   (92:178)

CUMBERLAND Louisa, 3rd dau. late Adm. Cumberland, gdau. late
Richard Cumberland, m. Edward, s. late James Potter Lockhart,
ex President Dominica, Dominica, 18 May 1843.   (NS20:427)

CUMINE Rev. Alexander, St Catherine's, d. Spanish Town,
Jamaica, 18 July 1791.   (61:969)

CUMMING Alexander, b.1772, Rabaco Est., St Vincent, d.
St Vincent, 27 Sep.1853.   (NS40:650)

CUMMING Emily, dau. A Cumming, m. J M Grant, Lt., RE, yngs. s.
Col. Grant, RA, St Vincent, 19 April 1849.   (NS32:83)

CUMMING John William, American seaman, d. Guy's Hospital,
London, March 1809.   (79:384)

CUMMING Margaret, 3rd dau. Alexander Cumming, St Vincent, m.
Cap. Caledon Richard Egerton, 89th Reg., s. late Rev. Sir
Philip Grey Egerton, Georgetown, St Vincent, 30 May 1843.
          (NS20:199)

CUMMINGS Martha Macnamara, eldest dau. Archdeacon Cummings,
gniece late Adm. Macnamara, m. John Scott, eldest s. late
Robert Bushe, Dublin, Port of Spain, Trinidad, 6 June 1848.
          (NS30:199)

CUMMINGS Patrick, d. St Johns, Antigua, June 1795.   (65:703)

CUMING Ralph, MD, surgeon, HM Naval Hospital, English Harbour,
Antigua, ex Romsey, Hants., & s. Ralph, d. Antigua,
24 June 1808.   (78:851)

CUMMING Sarah, wid., Montego Bay, Jamaica, m. Lord Ballenden,
Leith, 26 June 1787.   (57:638)

CUMMING Lt. m. Baroness Judith, eldest dau. Baron Frederick
de Bretton, St Croix, Guadaloupe, 1811.   (81:188)

CUMMING Mrs, wid. Asst. QM Gen. Barbados, dau. late Baron de
Bretton, St Croix, d. St Anne's, Barbados, 12 July 1821.
          (91:283)

CUMMINS John Ashley, b.1819, Dep. Asst. Comm. Gen., d.
Barbados, 1 Jan.1853.   (NS39:448)

CUMMINS Sarah, 2nd dau. George Cummins, Archdeacon Trinidad,
m. Lord George Francis Harris, Gov. Trinidad, Trinidad,
16 April 1850.   (NS34:200)

CUMMINS William Alves Travers m. Susan Elizabeth, 2nd dau.
late Joseph Cunard, NB, niece late Sir Samuel Cunard, Southport, Lancs., 10 Oct.1866.   (NS3/2:689)

CUMMINS Miss, dau. Judge Cummins, American authoress, d.
Canada, 1867.   (NS3/3:266)

CUNARD Margaret Ann, 2nd dau. Samuel Cunard, Halifax, m.
William Leigh Mellish, Cap., Rifle Brigade, eldest s. late
Rev. Edward Mellish, Dean of Hereford, Halifax, NS,
19 Oct.1843.   (NS20:648)

CUNARD Lady Mary, dau. Bache McEvers, NY, w. Sir Edward
Cunard, d. NY, 26 May 1866.   (NS3/2:116)

CUNARD Susan Elizabeth, 2nd dau. late Joseph Cunard, NB,
niece late Sir Samuel Cunard, m. William Alves Travers Cumins,
Southport, Lancs., 10 Oct.1866.   (NS3/2:689)

CUNNINGHAM Alexander Fairlie, 2nd s. Sir William Cunningham
of Robertland, d. Tobago, 30 June 1795.   (65:791)

CUNNINGHAM Anne, 3rd dau. late George Cunningham, Trelawney,
Jamaica, m. Tudor Castle, Stapleton Grove, Glocs., London,
14 Oct.1845.   (NS24:650)

CUNNINGHAM Archibald, d. NY, 13 Sep.1799.   (69:993)

CUNNINGHAM Charles A, MD, London, m. Harriet Emma, 4th dau.
late Rev. William Burton, Trelawney, Jamaica, Upton, Bucks.,
15 Sep.1852.   (NS38:630)

CUNNINGHAM Charlotte Elizabeth, eldest dau. Col. Cunningham,
Scots Brigade, m. Frances Carteret Scott, Customs Collector,
Montego Bay, Jamaica, 1801.   (71:1051)

CUNNINGHAM George, b.1789, Maxfield & Greenside Est., d.
Jamaica, 9 Oct.1843.   (NS21:110)

CUNNINGHAM G, b.1767, ex newspaper proprietor, Cheltenham,
d. Brooklyn, NY, 1854.   (NS41:335)

CUNNINGHAM James, American loyalist, pilot to Lord Howe's
fleet, d. 2 Oct.1783.   (53:895)

CUNNINGHAM James, Jamaica, m. Mrs Smart, wid. R Smart,
Jamaica, eldest dau. John Willis, London, 17 Nov.1818.(89:80)

CUNNINGHAM John, b.1738, settled Jamaica pre 1762, Col.
St James Reg. Militia, d. Montego Bay, Jamaica, 27 Sep.1812.
                                                          (82:670)

CUNNINGHAM John, b.1818, eldest s. George Cunningham, Greenside & Maxfield Est., Trelawney, Jamaica, late Bath, d.
Falmouth, Jamaica, 3 June 1843.   (NS20:334)

CUNNINGHAM Rebecca Anne, w. C T Cunningham, Colonial Sec., d.
Barbados, 2 Aug.1837.   (NS8:551)

CUNNINGHAM Robert, St Kitts, d. 1762.   (32:45)

CUNNINGHAM Samuel, b.1780, d. Roslin Castle, Trelawney,
Jamaica, 26 Dec.1844.   (NS23:334)

CUNNINGHAM William, Jamaica, d. 30 June 1761.   (21:334)

CUNNINGHAM William, eldest s. George Cunningham, Inspector Gen.
Customs Scotland, d. Nassau, New Providence, 9 Aug.1799.
                                                        (69:900)

CUNNINGHAM William, merchant, ex Kingston, Jamaica, d. Somers-
town, 28 Aug.1805.   (75:884)

CUNSTANCE Mrs Elizabeth, b.1797, dau. J White, Paulsgrove,
Hants., d. Spanish Town, Jamaica, 28 May 1822.   (92:382)

CUPPAGE Cap. Adam, b.1794, Justice Barbados, d. Barbados,
14 Feb.1859.   (NS2/6:546)

CUPPAGE Margaret Hughes, only dau. Adam Cuppage, judge, m.
John Hampden King, barrister & Assemblyman, Barbados,
30 Oct.1850.   (NS35:195)

CURLL Henry, Dep. Asst. Comm. Gen., Barbados, m. Marianne
Ellen, 2nd dau. John Edward Tillett, ex Liverpool, London,
23 Dec.1848.   (NS31:311)

CURREY John, Barbados, d. London, 19 Dec.1770.   (40:591)

CURRIE Andrew, s. late George Currie, Customs Controller of
Newcastle, d. Jamaica, 1 June 1822.   (92:382)

CURRIE Dr James, Richmond, m. Mrs Ingles, Princess Anne Co.,
Norfolk, Va., 12 Nov.1789.   (60:178)

CURRIE Margaret Ann, 2nd dau. Henry M MacLean, Tortula, wid.
Alexander Currie, m. Henry James Mills, Port of Spain,
Trinidad, 1 Jan.1863.   (NS2/14:369)

CURRIE Thomas, Lowlands, Tobago, d.1801.   (71:576)

CURTIS Daniel Sargent, Boston, USA, m. Ariana Randolph, yngs.
dau. late Rear Adm. R R Wormely, RN, Newport, RI, 3 Nov.1853.
                                                        (NS41:185)

CURTIS Roger William, 3rd s. Adm. Sir Lucius Curtis, East
Cosham, Hants., d. Trinidad, 23 Sep.1859.   (NS2/7:654)

CURTIS Dr Thomas, b.1788, Limestone Springs, SC, editor, d.
North Carolina, Chesapeake Bay, 29 Jan.1859.   (NS2/6:438)

CURWEN Henry Fraser, eldest s. Edward Stanley Curwen,
Workington Hall, Cumberland, m. Susie, yngs. dau. late Col.
Charles C Johnson, Argenteuil, Canada East, London, 30 April
1863.   (NS2/14:784)

CUTHBERT Ann, wid. George Cuthbert, Jamaica, d. London,
30 Dec.1814.   (84:679)

CUTHBERT George, President Council Jamaica, d. Jamaica,
25 May 1835.   (NS4:222)

CUTHBERT James, b.1769, d. Manor House, Berthier, Montreal,
5 March 1849.   (NS32:334)

CUTHBERT Jane, wid. Lewis Cuthbert, Castlehill, Inverness, &
Jamaica, d. Clifton, Glocs., 28 Sep.1830.   (100:380)

CUTHBERT Lewis, Castlehill, Inverness, Provost Marshal Jamaica,
d. Clifton Est., Jamaica, 28 Oct.1802.   (72:1162)

CUTLER Harriet Aurelia, dau. Francis Marion Cutler, Avon, NY,
m. Frederick J Cridland, HM Consul Alabama & Florida, Mobile,
29 Oct.1866.   (NS3/3:104)

CUYLER H, d. Green Bush, Albany, NY, 5 Feb.1803.   (73:382)

DA COSTA Moses Mendes, b.1780, d. Barbados, 8 Nov.1845.
                                                    (NS24:665)

DACRES R J, Cap., RA, s. late Vice Adm. Sir R Dacres, m.
Frances Brooking, only dau. Henry P Thomas, merchant,
St Johns, NFD., 3 Nov.1840.   (NS15:90)

DADE Rev. C, MA, Fellow Caius College, Cambridge, m. Helen,
2nd dau. Rev. Thomas Philips, late Vice Principal Upper
Canada College, Winston, Upper Canada, 14 March 1840.(NS13:645)

DADLEY James, b.1808, Bath, d. Barking Lodge, Jamaica, 1839.
                                                    (NS13:110)

DAKINS Lydia, wid. Thomas Dakins, Trinidad, d. Pembury, Kent,
6 Dec.1843.   (NS21:107)

DALBY John, Derby, m. Miss Livius, Richmond, Surrey, dau.
late Chief Justice Quebec, 5 Dec.1800.   (70:1288)

DALLAS Charles Robert King, Jamaica, late 32nd Reg., m. Julia
Maria, dau. Robert Charles Dallas, St Adriesse, Normandy, &
Jamaica, Paris, 3 July 1821.   (91:85)

DALLAS Dr Colin, late St Vincent, d. 26 Jan.1810.   (80:91)

DALLAS George Mifflen, b. Philadelphia, 10 July 1792, ex US
Minister in London, d. Philadelphia, 31 Dec.1864.(NS2/18:373)

DALLAS Julia Maria, dau. Robert Charles Dallas, St Adriesse,
Normandy, & Jamaica, m. Charles Robert King Dallas, Jamaica,
ex 32nd Reg., Paris, 3 July 1821.   (91:85)

DALLAS Robert m. Mrs John Hewitt, wid., Jamaica, 20 April 1769.
                                                    (39:215)

DALLAS Susan Seil, b.1770, wid. Charles Stuart Dallas, Belle
Cou, Jamaica, d.Stratton, Cornwall, 20 Aug.1843.   (NS20:554)

DALLAS ..., s. A G Dallas, Gov. Rupert's Land, b. Fort Garry,
Red River, 23 Feb.1863.   (NS2/14:650)

DALRYMPLE-CRAWFORD ..., s. Mrs Dalrymple-Crawford, b.Erie
Mount, Upper Canada, 20 March 1843.   (NS20:86)

DALRYMPLE Hugh, Attorney Gen. Grenada, d. 9 March 1774.
                                                   (44:239)

DALRYMPLE John Hamilton, Customs Collector Jamaica, s. late
Hugh Dalrymple of Nunraw, d. Montego Bay, Jamaica, 7 Aug.1804.
                                                   (74:978)

DALRYMPLE Robert, Customs officer, d. Barbados, 26 May 1808.
                                                   (78:749)

DALY M Bowes, s. Sir Dominick Daly, m. Joanna, dau. Edward
Kenny, President Council NS, Halifax, NS, 4 July 1859.
                                                   (NS2/7:302)

DALY Richard, b.1798, bro. Col. Daly, 4th Light Dragoons, 12
years a Jamaican magistrate, d. Demerara, 30 Nov.1846.
                                                   (NS27:222)

DALYELL John Thomas, Maj., 21st Royal North British Fusiliers,
s. Lt. Col. Thomas Dalyell, 42nd Native Infantry, m.
Constance Louisa, 5th dau. Thomas Parry, Bishop Barbados,
Barbados, 7 Feb.1861.   (NS2/10:567)

DALZELL Mary Elizabeth, dau. late Allan Dalzell, Barbados, m.
Maj. W T Savary, Bengal Service, Leckhampton, Glocs.,
4 April 1850.   (NS33:658)

DAMPIER Mary Bowyer, b.1795, w. Cap. William Dampier, late
Brunton, Somerset, d. Toronto, 14 July 1840.   (NS14:446)

DANA Francis, Chief Justice Mass., d. Boston, 1811. (81:657)

DANCER Thomas, MD, physician & botanist, d. Kingston, Jamaica,
1 Aug.1811.   (81:390)

DANDRIDGE Bartholomew, US Consul Southern St Domingo, d.
Aux Caves, 17 July 1802.   (72:974)

DANIELL Thomas, Attorney Gen. Dominica, d. Lynn, Norfolk,
17 March 1806.   (76:293)

DANIELL Miss, only dau. Thomas Daniell, Attorney Gen.
Dominica, m. John Holmes jr., Belfast, Snesham, Norfolk,
1 April 1802.   (72:373)

DANNY William, b.1798, only s. late Dr William Danny, d.
St Kitts, 10 Sep.1818.   (88:270)

DANVERS James, ex London, d. Port au Prince, St Domingo,
18 June 1821.   (91:283)

DARBY John Lewis, b.1792, ex Consul Gen. for Monte Video NY,
d. Slaugham, Sussex, 28 June 1857.   (NS2/3:229)

DARDEN M, d. Henderson Co., Tenn., 1857.   (NS2/3:349)

DARE Louisa Caroline, b.1763, dau. William Julius, Mansion Est., St Kitts, wid. Pholion Dare, Long Ashton, d. London, 22 Sep.1845.   (NS24:544)

DARKEN Edward John, MD, eldest s. John Darken, Holt, d. NY, 30 Jan.1853.   (NS39:448)

DARLING Ann Wilhelmina, b.1813, eldest dau. late Allen Dalzell, w. Lt. C H Darling, 57th Reg., d. Govt. House, Tobago, 16 Oct.1837.   (NS9:222)

DARLING Henry Charles, Maj. Gen., Lt. Gov. Tobago, d. Tobago, 7 Sep.1835.   (NS5:317)

DARLINGTON Samuel, ex Tobago, d. Cornhill, 18 Nov.1777. (48:551)

DARLOT Henry, Foreign Post Office, m. Miss Troup, Jamaica, 6 March 1800.   (70:282)

DARRACOTT Dora, b.1811, w. Thomas Bligh Darracott, Trinidad, ex Kingsbridge, Devon, d. Bermuda, 5 Nov.1834.   (NS5:335)

DARRELL Henry, merchant, New Providence, d. Dec.1753.(23:591)

DARRELL Susan Matilda, 2nd dau. Thomas Darrell, Barbados, m. John McArthur, Bristol, Clifton, 8 Sep.1842.   (NS18:651)

DARROCH ..., s. Maj. Gen. Darroch, b. Halifax, NS, 1814.
                                                      (84:673)

DARUSMONT Fanny Wright, b. 1795, Dundee, political agitator, w. M Darusmont, d. Cincinnatti, 13 Jan.1853.   (NS39:551)

DASENT Rev. Alexander, 4th s. late J R Dasent, Attorney Gen. St Vincent, m. Caroline Mayer, 2nd dau. George Colquhoun Grant, St Vincent, 13 Oct.1847.   (NS29:80)

DASENT Ann Emily, eldest dau. late J R Dasent, Attorney Gen. St Vincent, m. Robert Aitken, St Vincent, 13 Oct.1847.
                                                      (NS29:80)

DASENT George Webbe, 3rd s. late John Roche Dasent, Attorney Gen. St Vincent, m. Frances Louisa Delane, 3rd dau. W F A Delane, London, 4 April 1846.   (NS25:639)

DASHWOOD Mr, Postmaster, d. Jamaica, 1793.   (63:866)

DAUNCEY Rev. Francis, St James, Jamaica, d. Montego Bay, 28 April 1795.   (65:614)

DAVENEY Eliza, eldest dau. C B Daveney, Norwich, m. R B Ficklin, Royal Canadian Rifles, 3 May 1849.   (NS32:84)

DAVENPORT Joseph, ex Va., d.27 March 1783.   (53:452)

DAVENPORT Mr, theater lessee, fa. Miss Davenport, actress, d. Cincinnatti, America, 16 July 1851.   (NS36:331)

DAVIDSON Dr Charles, s. late John Davidson of Tillyhetly,
d. St George, Grenada, 2 Oct.1804.   (74:1242)

DAVIDSON Diana, 2nd dau. Dr Davidson, Leeds, m. Hector
Mackenzie, NY, s. late Kenneth Mackenzie of Redcastle, Edinburgh, 29 March 1800.   (70:588)

DAVIDSON Elizabeth Isabella, only dau. John Davidson, Dumfries,
m. Rev. Philip Wood Loosemore, Prince William, Dumfries, NB,
30 Nov.1858.   (NS2/6:197)

DAVIES Decima Isabella Catherine, only dau. late Thomas
Davies, MD, Newbattle, Jamaica, m. Charles Inman, 3rd s.
Charles Inman, Liverpool, East Barnet, 15 Sep.1853.(NS40:628)

DAVIES Edward Whitacre, Lt., Royal Canadian Rifles, only s.
Rev. E Acton Davies, Malvern Link, m. Kate Rebecca, 4th dau.
C S Peirce, St Johns, Canada East, 22 Aug.1866.   (NS3/2:541)

DAVIES Harriet, dau. late Rev. John Davies, Pedworth, Berks.,
m. Charles Richard Orgill, Portland, Jamaica, Salisbury, 1800.
                                                  (70:1284)

DAVIS Rev. Dr Daniel Gateward, b. St Kitts, 1788, s. Rev. W
David, Bishop Antigua, d. London, 25 Oct.1857.   (NS2/3:675)

DAVIS Frances Jane, dau. B Brown Davis, St Kitts, m.
C Hamilton Mills, eldest s. G Galway Mills, St Kitts, 21 July
1820.   (90:272)

DAVIS Gateward Coleridge, barrister, eldest s. late Daniel G
David, Bishop Antigua, m. Elizabeth Gordon, 4th dau. William
Walrond Jackson, Bishop Antigua, St Johns, Antigua, 21 Jan.
1864.   (NS2/16:520)

DAVIS John Gwynne, b. Llanvirnach, Pembroke, d. Va., 5 Feb.
1841.   (NS15:670)

DAVIS Maria, wid. Henry Davis, Customs Collector, d. Jamaica,
Aug. 1845.   (NS24:665)

DAVISON Dr J, surgeon, d. Montreal, 1813.   (83:505)

DAVY William, US Consul, Hull, d. Leeds, 11 Sep.1827.(97:285)

DAWES William, Tuftonhall, Grenada, Lt., RN, d. St George,
Grenada, 14 April 1819.   (88:585)

DAWES Rev. William, b.1809, St Johns, Montreal, d. 5 Sep.1847.
                                                  (NS28:661)

DAWES ..., b.1792, s. Judge Dawes, drowned Boston,USA, July
1815.   (85:278)

DAWS Dr, b. Huntingdon, 1778, surgeon, Wisbech, Cambridge, to
USA 1819, d. Washington, 10 March 1852.   (NS37:629)

DAWSON Eleanor, wid. William Dawson, ex Consul Md., dau.
Richard Lee, President of last British Council Md., d.
Brighton, 29 Dec.1833.   (104:669)

DAWSON Eliza, dau. James Dawson, London, m. Henry R Morgan,
ex Jamaica, 10 Dec.1821.   (91:641)

DAWSON Rev. James, St John's, Jamaica, d. Kingston, Jamaica,
30 June 1851.   (NS36:327)

DAWSON James Hewitt Massy, Ireland, m. Miss Dennis, eldest
dau. late Francis Dawson, Jamaica, 11 March 1800.   (70:282)

DAWSON Philip Thomas, b.1805, 5th s. late W Dawson, Wakefield,
Yorks., d. Baltimore, USA, 17 March 1843.   (NS20:110)

DAWSON Samuel, b.1788, s. late Elliot Dawson, Hinckley, Leics.,
d. St Bartholemew, WI, 23 Oct.1809.   (80:87)

DAY Thomas, b.1815, merchant, ex Liverpool, d. NY, 7 May 1851.
                                                        (NS36:100)

DAY Miss, dau. late John Day, Antigua, m. Thomas Loddington,
22 Sep.1791.   (61:873)

DAYRELL Paul, s. late Rev. Dr Dayrell, Lillington-Dayrell,
Bucks., d. NA, 23 April 1803.   (73:987)

DAYTON William, b. NJ, 1807, US Minister to France, d. Paris,
1 Dec.1864.   (NS2/18:122)

DEACON George, b.1825, eldest s. late Edward E Deacon,
barrister, Inner Temple, d. Porto Rico, 24 July 1850.(NS34:565)

DEAN James, ex Bolton-le-Moors, Lancs., d. NY, 30 April 1843.
                                                         (NS20:222)

DEAN John, b.1828, only s. Rev. Edmond N Dean, Gloucester, d.
Hamilton, Canada, 8 Feb.1855.   (NS43:442)

DEANE Catherine, w. Thomas Deane, merchant, Kingston,
Jamaica, dau. late Dr Walker, Physician Gen. Jamaica, d.
St Johns, Jamaica, 1826.   (96:191)

DEANE Silas, b.1736, Groton, Conn., US Ambassador France, d.
on board the Boston Packet, the Downs, 23 Sep.1789. (59.866)

DEANS R, s. Adm. Deans, m. Rachel, dau. Samuel Jackson,
Catherine Hall, Jamaica, Spanish Town, Jamaica, 10 April 1820.
                                                         (90:562)

DEANS Rachel Susanna, wid. Alexander Deans, Master Chancery,
Jamaica, m. A Peyton Phelps, London, 12 May 1835.   (NS4:88)

DEARE George, b.1820, Cap., Royal Canadian Rifles, d.Niagara,
Canada West, 8 Dec.1851.   (NS37:209)

DEAS John, Grand Master Mason SC, d.1790.   (60:1149)

DE BALINHARD ..., dau. W C De Balinhard, 47th Reg., b.
Montreal, 11 May 1862.   (NS2/13:92)

DE BEGNIS Guisseppe, b. Lugo, Italy, 1795, d. NY, Aug.1849.
                                                     (NS33:446)
DE BERDT Dennis, NY Agent, d. 18 April 1770.   (47:190)

DE BLAQUIERE Henry, s. Peter Boyle De Blaquiere, m. Margaret
Lucretia, 4th dau. Col. Light, ex 25th Reg., Lytis, Carey,
Woodstock, Upper Canada, Woodstock, 11 Oct.1848. (NS31:198)

DE BLOIS Lewis, late merchant, Boston, NE, d. Holburn,
9 Feb.1799.   (69:173)

DE BORJA Migoni Francisco, Mexican Consul Gen. England, d.
7 Dec.1831.   (101:570)

DE BRETTON Baroness Judith, eldest dau. Baron Frederick de
Bretton, St Croix, m. Lt. Cumming, Guadaloupe, 1812. (81:188)

DEBY M, barrister, Brussels, m. Amelia Cerf, dau. Henry Cerf,
Warton Hall, late Jamaica, Bath, 9 Feb.1825.   (95:177)

DE CHAIR Dudley Raikes, yngr. s. late Rev. Frederick De Chair,
East Langdon, Kent, m. Frances Emily, eldest dau. Christopher
Rawson, Helmwood, Lennoxville, Canada East, Lennoxville
10 Dec.1863.   (NS2/16:244)

DE CLUGNY Amelia Constance Gertrude Etiennette, only ch. late
Baron De Clugny, Gov. Guadaloupe, wid. M Raymond Godet, m.
Andrew Cochrane Johnson, s. late Earl of Dundonald, s.in-law
Earl of Hopetoun, Martinique, 21 March 1803.   (73:689)

DE COLLEVILLE Chevalier le Sieur, s. Marchioness De Colleville,
Normandy, French infantry officer, m. Miss McIntosh, yngs. dau.
William McIntosh, Grenada, Ostend, 1791.   (61:1061)

DEEDES Edmund, yngs. s. late William Deedes, Sandby Park, Kent,
m. Annie Bruce, yngs. dau. late Robert Kelly, gdau. late Sir
A MacDowall, Toronto, 20 Oct.1846.   (NS27:193)

DEEDES Henry C m. Mary Bell, yngs. dau. late R Alexander,
Kentucky, sis. S C A Alexander, Airdrie, London, 20 July 1859.
                                                    (NS2/9:186)
DEFFALINES, Emperor of Haiti, King of St Domingo, d.1805.
                                                     (75:1074)

DE GAESBEKE Baron, Bruges, m. Ellen Claiborne, eldest dau.
Thomas Higham, Charleston, SC, Margate, 23 May 1844.(NS22:86)

DE HACKENBERG Baron Frederick, b.1720, Hessian Maj. Gen.,
d. NY, 29 Aug.1783.   (53:893)

DEHANY Mary Fravell, 2nd dau. late George Dehany, Jamaica, m.
G H C Scott, London, 27 Nov.1833.   (104:102)

DE KETELHODT Baron, Custos, St Thomas-in-the-East, Jamaica,
d. Jamaica, 11 Oct.1865.   (NS3/1:142)

DE LA BASECQUE Count m. Mrs Scott, wid. Michael Scott,
Grenada, Artois, France, Nov.1792.   (84:697)

DE LA CADENA Mariano Velasquez, b.1778, Prof. Spanish Lit.,
Columbia College, d. NY, 25 Feb.1860.   (NS2/8:525)

DELAGAL Elizabeth, b.1748, wid. Henry Sacheverell Delagal,
Barbados, d. London, 4 Jan.1811.   (81:88)

DELAMERE Julia Mary, only dau. Cap. P Herbert Delamere, 3rd
WI Reg., m. Lt. Walter Roberts, 3rd WI Reg., Kingston,
Jamaica, 6 July 1867.   (NS3/2:383)

DE LA MORE Louisa Maria, wid. Cornelius Hendrickson Kortright,
St Croix & Porto Rico, mo. late Count Arthur de la More, d.
18 Jan.1867.   (NS3/3:394)

DELANCEY James, Lt. Gov. NY, d. 31 July 1760.   (30:443)

DELANCEY Brig. Gen. Oliver, late NY, d. Beverley, 27 Aug.1785.
                                                     (55:919)

DELANCEY Gen. Oliver, b. America, loyalist, Col. 17th Dragoons
d. Sep.1822.   (92:372)

DELANCEY Peter, Westchester, America, d.1770.   (40:590)

DELANCEY Philia, b.1722, wid. late Brig. Gen. Oliver Delancey
NY, d. London, 8 March 1811.   (81:397)

DELANCEY Stephen, late Chief Justice Bahamas, Gov. Tobago,
d. Dec.1798.   (69:165)

DELANCEY William Heathcote, b. Westchester Co., NY, 8 Oct.
1797, Bishop Western NY, d. Geneva, NY, 6 April 1865.
                                                 (NS2/18:789)

DELANCEY Miss, NY, m. Sir William Draper, 1770.   (40:590)

DELANE Frances Louisa, 3rd dau. W F A Delane, m. George Webbe
3rd s. late John Roche Dasent, Attorney Gen. St Vincent,
London, 4 April 1816.   (NS25:639)

DELANEY Daniel, b.1730, d. St Kitts, 1803.   (73:1254)

DELAP Robert, Chief Justice Jamaica, d. 20 April 1767.(37:279)

DELAP Robert, Assemblyman, Jamaica, d.29 Jan.1768.   (38:47)

DE LA PAGERIE Madame, mo. Madame Buonaparte, d. Martinique,
1 July 1807, buried Les Trois Islets.   (77:888)

DELAPOER-BERESFORD Henry Clement, 69th Reg., yngs. s. late
John Delapoer-Beresford, Col. Sec. St Vincent, m. Matilda,
yngs. dau. Francis Hincks, Gov. Windwards, Barbados,
23 July 1857.   (NS2/3:456)

DELAROCHE Mary Ann, dau. late John Delaroche, Carisbrook
Castle, Jamaica, wid. Henry Coote, m. Richard Ferris,
Bristol, Cheltenham, 29 April 1852.   (NS38:87)

DE LA SOMET John, b.1636, d. Va., 1766.   (36:599)

DELESSER Aaron, Grandmaster York Masons Jamaica, d. Kingston,
Jamaica, 1813.   (83:595)

DEL CASTILLO Juan, b. Jaca, Aragon, Spain, 1744, Principal
Apothecary Royal Hospital, Porto Rico, Mexico, & botanist,
d, Porto Rico, 26 July 1793.   (66:880)

DE LISLE Mary Jane, 2nd dau. Frederick De Lisle, London, m.
Thomas Ritchie Grassie, Halifax, NS, London, 17 March 1842.
                                                       (NS17:541)

DELPRATT Agnes, b.1774, wid. Samuel Delpratt, Jamaica, d.
Old Charlton, 8 Sep.1850.   (NS34:452)

DE MARGUERITE Julia, dau. Dr A B Granville, London, w.
Baron De Marguerite, d. Philadelphia, 1866.   (NS3/2:282)

DE MELFORT Count Edward, Paris, m. Mary Sabina, dau. late
Thomas Nasmyth, Jamaica, London, 11 Jan.1826.   (96:80)

DEMETRES John, b.1698, d. Montego Bay, Jamaica, Nov.1801.
                                                       (72:181)

DE MONTENACH Mary Ann Jessy, 3rd dau. late M. De Montenach,
Fribourg, Switzerland, & Mary Elizabeth, gdau. late
Baroness de Longeuil, m. Lt. Col. Whyte, 7th Hussars,
Montreal, 9 Sep.1842.   (NS18:651)

DE MONTMORENCY Raymond Harvey, Cap., 32nd Light Infantry, m.
Rachel Mary Lumley Godolphin, eldest dau. Lt. Gen. Sir John
Michel, Montreal, 25 April 1866.   (NS3/1:901)

DE MONTMORENCY ..., s. Cap. R H De Montmorency, 32nd Light
Infantry, b. Montreal, 5 Feb.1867.   (NS3/3:522)

DENNE Thomas m. Mary Anne, dau. late John Laidlaw, Dominica,
Downe, Kent, 19 Oct.1852.   (NS39:86)

DENNIS Mary, b.1750, wid. Francis Dennis, Jamaica, d.London,
2 Jan.1832.   (102:92)

DENNIS Miss, eldest dau. late Francis Dennis, Jamaica, m.
James Hewitt Massy Dawson, Ireland, 11 March 1800.   (70:282)

DENNISTON John, merchant & Assemblyman, Nassau, d. Long
Island, America, 15 Aug.1794.   (64:1150)

DENNY Col. William, 71st Reg., Highland Light Infantry, grand
nephew late Sir Barry Denny, m. Euretta, dau. late James
Richardson, Belle Rive, Montreal, 15 Dec.1846.   (NS27:418)

DENYSE Mr, b. New Utrecht, 18 Oct.1760, d. Flatbush, Indiana,
20 July 1856.   (NS2/1:391)

DEOLPH Maj. Ezra, b.1710, late Toland, Conn., d. Hopkinton,
NH, 16 Aug.1811.   (81:657)

DE PASS Abraham Daniel, 4th s. Daniel De Pass, London, m.
Judith, eldest dau. Abraham Lazarus, Kingston, Jamaica,
8 July 1846.   (NS26:418)

DE QUADE John Henry Baron, b. Albany, NA, 1694, settled
London 1788, d. 1791.   (61:383)

DERING Annie Louisa, b.1845, dau. Cap. Cholmeley Dering, ex
85th King's Light Infantry, d. Halifax, NS, 22 March 1850.
                                                      (NS34:110)

DERING Dr Cholmondley, SC, m. Mrs Alpress, 1766.   (36:550)

DERING Edward Cholmeley, b.1849, s. Cap. C. Dering, ex 85th
King's Light Infantry, d. Halifax, NS, 26 March 1850.
                                                      (NS34:110)

DERING Jane Barrington, b.1843, dau. Cap. C Dering, ex 85th
King's Light Infantry, d. Halifax, NS, 20 March 1850.(NS34:11)

DESAGULIERS Gabriel, Barbados, d.1768.   (38:198)

DESBOROUGH Grace Alice, inf. dau. Col. Desborough, RA, d.
Gordon Town, Jamaica, 24 Sep.1867.   (NS3/5:112)

DES BRISAY Rev. Theophilius, clergyman, d. PEI, 14 March 1823.
                                                        (93:653)

DE SINIER Marie Victoria Harline, only dau. Olivier Perrault
De Sinier, Montreal, m. Cap. E St George Smyth, 30th Reg.,
Montreal, 9 July 1867.   (NS3/2:383)

DESPARRE Madame, St Domingo, d. London, 15 Nov.1798. (68:992)

D'ESTIMAUVILLE Chevalier, Canada, m. Miss Blyth, niece
J Betts, Boston, Lincs., 3 June 1796.   (66:523)

DEVILER Mrs Grace, b.1711, d. Jamaica, 1791.   (61:1065)

DEWAR Edward, Clapham, Surrey, d. St Thomas, WI, 16 June 1800.
                                                        (70:694)

DE WINTON Cap., RA, m. Evelyn, 2nd dau. Christopher Rawson,
Lennoxville, Canada East, 9 June 1864.   (NS2/17:234)

DE WINTON ..., s. Cap. F De Winton, RA, b. Lennoxville, Canada
East, 10 Feb.1865.   (NS2/18:497)

DE WINTON ..., dau. F De Winton, b. Halifax, NS, 19 July 1867.
                                                     (NS3/2:524)

DICK William, Jamaica, m. Eliza, yngs. dau. Thomas Lane,
London, 5 Sep.1811.   (81:284)

DICKINSON Edward, b.1795, Whitely Melksham, d. on passage
from Jamaica, 4 July 1849.   (NS32:446)

DICKENSON Gabriel, planter, Jamaica, d. 21 Oct.1779. (49:520)

DICKENSON Henry King, St Johns, NFD, m. Mary, dau. Cap.
Tolloh, RN, Waterford, 16 July 1851.   (NS36:316)

DICKENSON Maria, wid. Cap. Dickenson, 86th Reg., dau. late
John Gray, Treasurer Honduras, m. John Hodge, Great St Helens,
St Pancras, 1 July 1846.   (NS26:314)

DICKINSON Rev. R S Stores, ex Philadelphia, d. Edinburgh,
28 Aug.1856.   (NS2/1:519)

DICKSON Dr D J H, physician, Leeward Islands, m. Miss Tracy,
1812.   (82:188)

DICKSON Horatio Nelson, Halifax, NS, m. Emma Jane, yngs. dau.
Lt. John Wise, RN, Chatham, 8 Feb.1853.   (NS39:427)

DICKSON Horatio N, b.1819, West Brompton, d. Halifax, NS,
14 Oct.1858.   (NS2/5:647)

DICKSON Mary Louisa, 2nd dau. William Dickson, Niagara, m.
Cap. Frederick George Berkeley, 47th Reg., 2nd s. Charles
Berkeley, London, Guelph, Canada, 28 Sep.1865.   (NS2/19:640)

DIGGLE Frederick W, b.1816, yngr. s. Col. Diggle, late Cap.
82nd Reg., d. Gratton, Canada West, 31 Dec.1851.   (NS37:312)

DIGGS Cole, Councillor, Va., d. 1745.   (15:220)

DIGNUM Caroline Redwar, wid. Andrew Graham, dau. late Rev.
Lewis Bowerbank, d. Spanish Town, Jamaica, 29 March 1867.
                                                     (NS3/3:819)

DIGNUM ..., s. Andrew Graham Dignum, Spanish Town, Jamaica,
b. Cirencester, 22 Oct.1845.   (NS24:634)

DILL Mrs Anne, wid. Dr Dill, York Co., NY, m. Rev. Dr Witherspoon, President NJ College, Philadelphia, 1791.   (61:774)

DILLON ..., dau. Maj. R Dillon, 30th Reg., b. Montreal,
5 May 1864.   (NS2/17:104)

DINWIDDIE Robert, Gov. Va., d. 28 July 1770.   (40:393)

DIROM Cap. Alexander, RE, m. Victoria Williams, dau. E T Coxworthy, Dep. Comm. Gen., Halifax, NS, 19 Aug.1862.(NS2/13:485)

DISMORE Jane, b.1727, wid. Edward Dismore, ex PMG Jamaica,
d. Kingston, Jamaica, 28 Aug.1818.   (88:379)

DISTIN Henry, b.1783, ex Jamaica, d. Elgin, 7 Dec.1851.
                                                     (NS37:209)

DISTIN Mary Catherine, only dau. Henry Distin, Jamaica, m.
Francis Hamilton, Kensworth, Herts., London, 17 March 1840.
                                                     (NS13:535)

DIXON Charles Cranstoun, b.1786, late Lt. Col., 90th Reg.,
d. Kingston, Canada, 19 June 1866.   (NS3/2:397)

DIXON Frances Maria, yngs. dau. Col. Matthew Dixon, RE,
Canada, m. Lt. Alexander Ross Clarke, RE, Montreal,
1 Nov.1853.   (NS41:184)

DIXON Henry, Glasgow, d. Cave Valley, Hanover, Jamaica,
5 Jan.1801.   (71:371)

DIXON Thomas, bro. Rev. William Dixon, Tong, d. New Orleans,
2 March 1854.   (NS41:554)

DIXON Mrs, b.1780, w. John Dixon, Mount Pleasant, d. Barbados,
27 May 1805.   (75:774)

DOANE Dr A S, Health Officer NY, d.27 Jan.1852.   (NS37:316)

DOANE Eliza, b.1789, wid. Bishop Doane, NJ, d. Florence,
10 Nov.1859.   (NS2/8:190)

DOANE Rev. George Washington, b. Trenton, NJ, 27 May 1799,
Bishop NJ, d. Burlington, NJ, 27 April 1859.   (NS2/6:647)

DOBBYN Anne, b.1800, w. William Augustus Dobbyn, late Bath &
Dragoon Guards, d. Philadelphia, 21 April 1844.   (NS21:671)

DOBIE Richard, b. Libberton, Edinburgh, 1730, merchant,
Montreal, d. Montreal, 23 March 1805.   (75:773)

DOBIE William D, d. Falmouth, Jamaica, 8 Dec.1819.   (90:186)

DOCKER Robert Noble, b.1810, eldest s. Thomas Docker, Dover,
d. Toronto, 12 Dec.1848.   (NS29:455)

DOCKER William, MD, s. George Docker, Birmingham, d. Commerce,
Scott Co., Missouri, Sep.1856.   (NS2/2:117)

DODD Archibald, Chief Judge Cape Breton, bro. late Mr Dodd,
surgeon, Bath, d.1831.   (101:477)

DODD Mrs Elizabeth, b.1738, settled NY & Florida, loyalist,
settled NB 1784, d. St Stephen, NB, 21 July 1849. (NS32:446)

DODS Joseph, Stanford, m. Caroline, only dau. late E James
Reid, Saltpond, Spanish Town, Jamaica, Hornsy, 31 May 1860.
                                              (NS2/9:86)

DODSON Georgina, dau. late George Dodson, Lichfield, Staffs.,
m. Rev. Henry Patton, Cornwall, Canada West, Prescott,
Canada West, 2 Dec.1846.   (NS27:303)

DODSON Miles, s. Cap. Thomas Dodson, b.1779, d. Charleston,
America, 1801.   (71:770)

DOHERTY Col. Sir Richard m. Rachel Sophia, wid. Gilbert
Munro, St Vincent, London, 8 July 1845.   (NS24:416)

DOMAN Nicholas, Greenvale Pen, Jamaica, d. Trelawney,
Jamaica, 13 April 1829.   (99:94)

DOMAN Webb, merchant, d. Falmouth, Jamaica, 1812.   (82:193)

DOMVILE Cap. J Russell, Customs Collector Trinidad, s. Rev.
H B Domvile, Pencombe, Herefords., d. Trinidad, 1 May 1853.
                                                        (NS40:98)

DOMVILLE William Henry, Lincoln's Inn, yngr. s. Sir W
Domville, m. Eliza King, dau. Col. Aspinwall, ex US Consul
Gen. London, Wandsworth, 14 Dec.1853.   (NS41:309)

DONALD David, b.1739, ex planter, Hanover, Jamaica, d.
London, 30 July 1807.   (77:985)

DONALDSON Alexander, Jamaica, d. on passage to Jamaica,
24 March 1807.   (77:487)

DONALDSON William, merchant, d. Kingston, Jamaica, 5 Dec.1789.
                                                         (60:179)

DONEY George, b. Virginia, d. Cashiobury, Sep.1809.   (79:892)

DONNE Elizabeth, wid. Rev. Theophilius Donne, Clarendon,
Jamaica, d. Bromley, Kent, 17 Feb.1859.   (NS2/6:438)

DONNE Rev. Theophilius, d. Clarendon, Jamaica, 18 Jan.1823.
                                                         (93:379)

DONOVAN Francis, Tibberton, Glocs., d. on passage to WI,1811.
                                                         (81:599)

DONOVAN Richard, b.1767, Tibberton Court, Glocs., barrister,
d. Antigua, 1816.   (86:571)

DOUGLAS Agnes, 3rd dau. James Douglas, Gov. BC, m. Arthur T
Bushby, Registrar Gen. BC, yngs. s. J Bushby, London,
Victoria, Vancouver Island, 8 May 1862.   (NS2/13:222)

DOUGLAS Alice, 4th dau. James Douglas, Gov. BC, m. Charles, 2nd
s. Rev. Henry Good, Wimbourne, Dorset, Victoria, Vancouver
Island, 31 Aug.1861.   (NS2/11:675)

DOUGLAS Campbell, Jamaica, m. Agnes, dau. Robert Marshall,
merchant, Glasgow, Hamilton, 1 July 1793.   (63:670)

DOUGLAS Charles Irvine, yngs. s. late Lord William Douglas, m.
Margaret Elizabeth, dau. Arthur Holmestead, Toronto, 4 March
1862.   (NS2/12:640)

DOUGLAS David, Assembly Printer, Master in Chancery, Judge,
d. Spanish Town, Jamaica, 8 August 1789.   (59:955)

DOUGLAS Cap. Dunbar, s. Earl of Selkirk, d. St Kitts, Nov.
1796.   (67:80)

DOUGLAS James, Jamaica, d. on Hope of Bristol on passage for
Jamaica, 19 July 1791.   (61:873)

DOUGLAS James, only s. James Douglas, MD, Quebec, m. Naomi, 3rd dau. late Walter Douglas, Glasgow, Frankfort-on-Main, 15 Nov.1860.   (NS2/9:664)

DOUGLAS John, Provost Marshal Grenada, d. Grenada, 31 July 1838.   (NS10:566)

DOUGLAS J, Provost Marshal Grenada, m. Ellen Hardey, Brixton Hill, Brixton, 2 Jan.1837.   (NS7:201)

DOUGLAS Naomi, 3rd dau. late Walter Douglas, Glasgow, m. James Douglas, only s. James Douglas, MD, Quebec, Frankfort-on-Main, 15 Nov.1860.   (NS2/9:664)

DOUGLAS Robert, Gov. St Kitts, d.24 Oct.1780.   (50:50)

DOUGLAS Susan, 2nd dau. late George Cleghorn, Weens, Roxburgh, w. G M Douglas, d. Quebec, 21 Nov.1860.   (NS2/10:112)

DOUGLAS Miss, dau. Col. Douglas of Greencroft, m. Col. Maxwell, Gov. St Kitts & Virgin Islands, Lockerbie House, Dumfries, 5 April 1821.   (91:372)

DOW William. s. Rev. Dow, Blairgowrie, d. Antigua, 7 July 1803.   (73:882)

DOWDNEY Rev. John, NY, d. Fortrose, Ross-shire, 14 Jan.1867.   (NS3/3:264)

DOWLING Rev. T E, Douglas, NB, 2nd s. late Rev. J G Dowling, Gloucester, m. Caroline Jane, only dau. late Benjamin Wolhampton, Sheriff of York, Fredericton, NB, 4 April 1864.   (NS2/16:792)

DOWNER Mrs, w. Col. Downer, Portland, Jamaica, d. London, 27 Sep.1800.   (70:1110)

DOWNES Miss, London, m. William Franklin, Gov. NJ, 5 Sep.1762.   (32:448)

DOWNIE J, Clarendon, Jamaica, d.14 Dec.1812.   (83:386)

DOWNIE M, Demerara, d. Barbados, 17 May 1818.   (88:87)

DOWNING A J, NY, writer, d. River Hudson, 1852.   (NS38:437)

DOWNMAN Maria, only dau. late John Richards, Boston, USA, gdau. late John Richards, Hambledon, Hants., d. Horndean, 2 Nov.1858.   (NS2/5:652)

DOYLE Mary, w. Lt. Gen. Doyle, dau. late William Smith, Chief Justice Canada, d.26 Aug.1819.   (89:283)

DRAKE Montague William, 2nd s. late Rev. George Tyrwhitt Drake, Malpas, Cheshire, m. Joanna, 2nd dau. late James Tolmie Campbelltown, Argyll, Victoria, Vancouver Island, 12 March 1862.   (NS2/13:222)

DRAPER Sir William m. Miss De Lancey, NY, 1770.   (50:590)

DRAYTON Thomas, nephew late Lord MacLeod, d. America,
May 1801.   (71:672)

DRAYTON William, ex Chief Justice East Florida, District
Judge SC, d. Charlestown, 18 May 1790.   (60:669)

DRAYTON William, late Barbados, d. London, 26 Dec.1846.
                                                   (NS27:214)
DREW James, d. Tobago, 2 June 1798.   (68:811)

DREW Stephen Tregea, 3rd s. late Stephen Drew, barrister,
Jamaica, d. Saltash, Cornwall, 19 Dec.1834.   (105:218)

DRIVER William, Shrewsbury, missionary, d. St Eustatia, 1813.
                                                   (83:505)
DRUMMOND Charles Spencer, eldest s. late Rev. Arthur
Drummond, Charlton, Kent, m. Mary, eldest dau. late John S
Innes, Grafton, Canada West, Grafton, 28 Oct.1862.(NS2/13:771)

DRUMMOND James, botanist, Glasgow, d. Cuba, 1835. (NS4:667)

DRUMMOND Dr John, d. Westmoreland, Jamaica, 14 Aug.1804.
                                                   (74:690)
DRUMMOND Robert, ex Maj., 2nd Bat., NJ Volunteers, d. London,
31 Jan.1789.   (59:182)

DRURY Charles, b.1800, only s. Adm. Drury, gs. Rev. George
Drury, Claydon, Suffolk, d. Jamaica, 1822.   (92:574)

DRURY Kingsmill Henry, b.1825, s. late Cap. C J Cheshyre
Drury, 32nd Reg., d. Adairville, Kentucky, 11 Nov.1853.
                                                   (NS41:217)
DRURY Mrs, b.1760, wid. Adm. Thomas Drury, aunt late Cap.
Augustus Vere Drury, RN, d. Kingston, Jamaica, 20 Dec.1845.
                                                   (NS25:558)
DUANY Edmund, planter, Jamaica, d.24 Nov.1776.   (46:579)

DUBART Peter, "the greatest Protestant French merchant in
Canada", d.1767.   (37:524)

DUBELLAMY Mr (alias Evans), singer, d. NY, Aug.1793.(63:1149)

DUBERRY Thomas, Montserrat, d.1764.   (34:46)

DU BLAISEL Le Marquis, Chamberlain to Emperor of Austria, m.
Maria Matilda, dau. William Bingham, USA, 17 April 1826.
                                                   (96:461)
DUCHE Jacob, b.1708, ex Philadelphia, fa. Rev. Duche, chaplain,
d.28 Sep.1788.   (58:936)

DUCHE Mrs, w. Rev. Jacob Duche, ex chaplain St George's fields
Asylum, d. Philadelphia, 1797.   (97:531)

DUCKETT Rev. William, St Agnes, Nassau, m. Charlotte, wid.
D White, Madras Civil Service, eldest dau. S Nicholls,
Tiverton, Forest of Dean, 8 Jan.1855.   (NS43:302)

DUFF William, London, m. Catherine McGiffog, Jamaica, 1793.
(63:956)

DUFFUS Mary Ann, dau. John Duffus, Halifax, m. Cap. Alex.
Dingwall Thomson, 16th Reg., s. Lt. Col. Thomson, 16th Reg.,
Halifax, NS, 17 Aug.1864.   (NS2/17:512)

DULANY Walter, Comm. Gen. & Councillor, Annapolis, Md.,
d.1773.   (44:46)

DUMMER Jeremy, author & late agent for Mass., bro. Gov. Mass.,
d.19 May 1739.   (9:273)

DUNBAR Alexander, ex merchant, Nairn, d. Kingston, Jamaica,
1794.   (64:768)

DUNBAR Asa, lawyer, d. NH, 1787.   (58:366)

DUNBAR Charles, merchant, d. Curacao, 1813.   (83:670)

DUNBAR Robert, b.1785, eldest s. late William Dunbar, London,
d. Dominica, 7 Sept.1804.   (74:1168)

DUNCAN Charles, Westerfield Co., Va., d. London, 29 Jan.1808.
(78:175)

DUNCAN James, merchant, d. NY, 16 Nov.1799.   (70:283)

DUNCAN Mrs, wid. John Duncan, Jamaica, m. E Tovey, Somerset,
4 Jan.1817.   (87:32)

DUNCAN Mrs, w. Thomas Duncan, Councillor, d. Grenada,
25 June 1818.   (88:373)

DUNCANSON James, only s. Walter Duncanson, town-clerk,
Dunbarton, d. Jamaica, 5 April 1797.   (67:528)

DUNKERLEY Mrs, b.1772, w. James Dunkerley, Kingston, Jamaica,
d. Surrey, 1 Nov.1801.   (71:1061)

DUNKLEY Susannah Mackenzie, Clarendon, Jamaica, m. George
Atkinson, Sec. Jamaica, Clarendon, 1794.   (64:956)

DUNLOP James Watson, s. late James Dunlop, Glasgow, m.
Augusta Cornell, 4th dau. Lt. Col. Chairs, President Virgin
Islands, Tortula, 13 March 1854.   (NS41:636)

DUNLOP John, merchant, d. St Croix, 25 July 1805. (75:881)

DUNLOP Susan Elizabeth, eldest dau. James Dunlop, m. Rev.
Andrew F Freeman, s. Bishop of Arkansas, Petersburg, Va.,
8 July 1858.   (NS2/5:304)

DUNLOP ..., s. Lt. Col. Dunlop, 2nd WI Reg., b. St James,
Trinidad, 15 Nov.1865.   (NS3/1:113)

DUNN Charlotte, w. John Henry Dunn, Receiver Gen. Upper
Canada, d. Toronto, 9 Dec.1835.   (NS5:445)

DUNN F W, s. J Dunn, London, d. Havanna, 3 May 1819. (88:586)

DUNN Sarah, b.1772, wid. Thomas Dunn, Jamaica, d. Crediton,
Devon, 15 Feb.1849.   (NS31:329)

DUNN Thomas, 2nd s. late William Dunn, baker, Dublin, d.
St Croix, 1798.   (68:724)

DUNN ..., s. Cap. Dunn, Royal Canadian Rifles, b. Kingston,
Upper Canada, 29 Nov.1865.   (NS3/1:114)

DUNSCOMB J M, s. J Dunscomb, NFD, m. Caroline B, yngs. dau.
Maj. Gen. Durnsford, RE, London, 26 April 1840.   (NS13:646)

DUNSFORD Rev. James Hartley, ex Fretherne, Glocs., Peterborough
Canada, d.25 July 1852.   (NS38:320)

DUNSFORD Mr, s. Mr Dunsford, cutler, Exeter, d. on passage to
WI, 1800.   (70:1008)

DUNSTONE James, Assemblyman & Custos, Trelawney, Jamaica, d.
Trelawney, 12 April 1853.   (NS40:97)

DUPONT DE NEMOURS M., d. Elantekenan, Wilmington, USA,
10 Aug.1817.   (87:376)

DUPORT Gideon, merchant, Charlestown, d.1785.   (55:489)

DUPORTAIL Louis Joseph Le Becque, b. France, Maj. Gen. in
American Revolution, d. on passage from NY to Havre de Grace
on Sophia of NY, 11 August 1801.   (71:960)

DURAY James, Cap. Provincial Army under General Braddock,
d. 4 Dec.1777.   (48:45)

DURHAM Frances Eliza, only dau. late William Hall Durham,
barrister, St Vincent, m. W Tawzia, yngs. s. Col. W J T Savary
London, 1828.   (98:267)

DURHAM Jessie Isabella, 4th dau. late Edward Durham, Cape of
Good Hope, m. William C Stephens, Sec. Great Western Railway
Canada, 2nd s. late Cap. Edward L Stephens, RN, Hamilton,
Canada West, 15 June 1858.   (NS2/5:304)

DURHAM William Hall, barrister, St Vincent, d. Kingston,
St Vincent, 3 Nov.1807.   (78:86)

DURIE Helena, 4th dau. W Durie, Inspector Hospitals, m. Rev.
S B Ardagh, Barrie, Toronto, 6 Dec.1859.   (NS2/8:178)

DURIE Helena, b.1783, w. William Durie, ex RA, d. Toronto,
29 Aug.1862.   (NS2/13:507)

DURNFORD Caroline B, yngs. dau. Maj. Gen. Durnsford, RE, m.
J M Dunscomb, s. J Dunscomb, St Johns, NFD, London, 26 April
1840.   (NS13:646)

DURNFORD Elizabeth, 3rd dau. Maj. Gen. Durnford, RE, m.
Rev. Willoughby, 2nd s. late Chief Justice Sewell, Montreal,
Canada, 24 July 1843.   (NS19:85)

DURNING John, planter, d. Dromilly Est., Jamaica, 14 Sep.1794.
                                                        (64:1150)

DURRANT Sir Thomas, Scottow, Norfolk, m. Miss Steenbergen,
late St Kitts, 5 Oct.1799.   (69:900)

D'WARRIS Fortunatus, MD, Custos, St George, d. Jamaica, 1790.
                                                        (60:476)

D'WARRIS William, b.1752, Golden Grove, St George, Jamaica,
d. Stanmore, 4 Oct.1813.   (83:505)

DWYER Francis, merchant, Jamaica, bro. James Dwyer, Bristol,
d. Martha Brae, Jamaica, 2 Dec.1806.   (77:179)

DYDE Robert, late London, d. Montreal, Canada, 1819. (88:655)

DYER Hugh McNeill, Lt., RN, s. Cap. Dyer, RN, m. Marianne
Elizabeth, dau. late William Cole Loggin, Woolfodesworthy,
Bermuda, 15 May 1858.   (NS2/5:185)

DYER M, b.1749, ex Tortula, d. Alphington, Devon, 15 Oct.
1832.   (102:483)

DYER William, ex editor 'Jamaica Courier', s. late Robert
Dyer, merchant, Bristol, d. Falmouth, Jamaica, 26 Nov.1843.
                                                       (NS21:223)

DYKE Rev. Henry Grey, b.1799, eldest s. Rev. Jerome Dyke,
Burback, Leics., to NY July 1833, d. Quebec, 26 Aug.1834.
                                                       (104:552)

DYMOCKE Rev. James, ex St David's, Jamaica, d. Edinburgh,
31 Jan.1815.   (85:278)

DYNELEY Mary Frederica, b.1794, dau. Edward, Lord Ellen-
borough, w. Col. Dyneley, RA, d. Bytown, Canada East,
16 Sep.1851.   (NS36:554)

DYSON Rev. Henry Jeremiah, Barking, Essex, d. St Kitts,
27 March 1854.   (NS41:663)

DYSON Matilda, w. Rev. H J Dyson, d. St Kitts, 26 March 1854.
                                                       (NS41:663)

EARDLEY-WILMOT ..., dau. Col. F Earldley-Wilmot, b. Montreal,
3 April 1861.   (NS2/10:692)

EARDLEY-WILMOT ..., dau. Col. Eardley-Wilmot, b. Montreal,
18 March 1862.   (NS2/12:637)

EARLE Rev. Alfred, only s. late W Earle, Tunbridge Wells, m.
Alice Margaret, 3rd dau. G C Harvey, Bermuda, Halifax, NS,
5 Dec.1867.   (NS3/5:104)

EARLE ..., dau. Lt. Col. William Earle, Grenadier Guards, b.
Montreal, 30 Aug.1865.   (NS2/19:502)

EAST Edward Hinton, Lt., RA, m. Charlotte Mary Elizabeth
Brace, only dau. Rev. William Strachan, Christ Church,
Nassau, New Providence, 5 Nov.1850.   (NS35:195)

EAST Hinton, Receiver Gen., Public Treasurer, Judge Advocate
Gen. Militia, d. Liguanea, Jamaica, Jan.1792.   (62:279)

EAST Hinton, s. Edward East, b. Jamaica, 1784, d. St Andrews,
Jamaica, 14 Jan.1866.   (NS3/1:595)

EAST Isabella Anne, 2nd dau. Hinton East, Councillor, Jamaica,
niece Sir Edward Hyde East, m. Oscar Marescaux, Colonial Bank,
eldest s. Adolphe Marescaux, St Omer, France, Woodford,
Jamaica, 15 March 1864.   (NS2/16:650)

EASTERBY Dr John, d. Jamaica, 1790.   (60:1214)

EASTON Abel, yngs. s. George Easton, Strathfieldsaye, Hants.,
m. Louisa, dau. late William Thorn, Turnham Green, Middlesex,
Broadway, NY, 5 July 1860.   (NS2/9:314)

ECCLES Anna, eldest dau. Cap. Eccles, Dublin & Bath, m. John
Bower Lewis, Niagara, 17 Oct.1840.   (NS15:90)

ECCLES W, d. Port of Spain, Trinidad, 20 Aug.1859.(NS2/7:430)

EDE Job, Southampton, d. Nevis, 1 July 1844.   (NS22:334)

EDEN Anna, w. Lt. Col. John Eden, d. Montreal, 16 Nov.1841.
                                                   (NS17:230)

EDEN Fanny Louisa, eldest dau. Col. W H Eden, Gov. Bermuda, m.
Cap. Edward F Hare, 56th Reg., s. Maj. W H Hare, Plymouth,
Bermuda, 28 Oct.1852.   (NS39:194)

EDEN Sir Robert, ex Gov. Md., bro. Sir John Eden, & of w.
Archbishop Canterbury, d. Annapolis, Md., 2 Sep.1784.(55:876)

EDGAR Mrs, wid. Dr Handasyde Edgar, late Jamaica, d. London,
13 July 1819.   (89:93)

EDMONDS Rev. Charles Cresford, Glamorgan, m. Emma, yngs. dau.
late Jacob Aemilius Irving of Bonshaw, Newmarket, Upper
Canada, 14 July 1866.   (NS3/2:398)

EDMONDS Frederic, MD, Guanaxuato, Mexico, m. Elizabeth Mary,
3rd dau. Rev. John Curnow Millett, Penpoll, Phillack,
Cornwall, 21 Oct.1846.   (NS27:80)

EDMONDS Richard, s. late Rev. R Edmonds, Woodleigh, Devon, m.
Fanny Caroline Arnold, 3rd dau. John Arnold, Toronto, 21 Sep.
1853.   (NS41:76)

EDSON Calvin, d. Randolph, NY, 1833.   (103:191)

EDWARDS Brian, b.1807, magistrate, Westmoreland, Jamaica, d.
Jamaica, 13 Nov.1835.   (NS5:335)

EDWARD Hugh, Antigua, d. London, 31 May 1856.   (NS2/1:125)

EDWARDS J K, editor 'Montreal Transcript', m. Jane Somers,
eldest dau. late Colin Galbraith, writer, Edinburgh, on the
John Bell, Montreal, 3 Aug.1859.   (NS2/7:414)

EDWARDS William, merchant, Bristol, d. St Vincent, Jan.1810.
                                                  (80:384)

EDWARDS Zachary Hume, only s. late Bryan Edwards, d. on the
Montague on passage from WI, 29 August 1812.   (82:400)

EDWARDS ..., b.1776, eldest s. Bryan Edwards, Jamaica, d.
Winchester College, 9 March 1794.   (64:284)

EDWARDES John Pusey, Pusey Hall, Jamaica, d. London, 30 May
1822.   (92:572)

EFFINGHAM Countess Catherine, w. Earl of Effingham, Gov.
Jamaica, d. on passage from Jamaica to NY, 14 Oct.1791,
buried Spanish Town, Jamaica.   (61:1234)

EGAN Francis, ex Jamaica, d. London, 30 July 1849. (NS32:327)

EGAN Hanby m. E Forster, dau. Maj. Forster, RA, NS, Halifax,
NS, 15 Oct.1820.   (90:562)

EGEDE Paul, b.1708, s. Hans Egede, Denmark, settled Greenland
1720, Bishop of Greenland, d. 3 June 1789.   (59:1209)

EGERTON Caledon Richard, Cap., 89th Reg., s. late Rev. Sir
Philip Grey Egerton, m. Margaret, 3rd dau. Alexander Cumming,
St Vincent, Georgetown, St Vincent, 30 May 1843. (NS20:199)

ELAM Joseph, ex merchant, Leeds, d. Philadelphia, 24 Oct.1793.
                                                  (63:1149)

ELCOCK Margaret, wid. Edward Elcock, Barbados, d. Bath,
19 Dec.1831.   (101:651)

ELDRIDGE Richard Burroughes, b. Great Yarmouth, Assemblyman,
d. St Johns, Antigua, 18 Sep.1852.   (NS38:655)

ELGIN Countess, dau. Maj. Cumming Bruce, MP, d. Jamaica,
7 June 1843.   (NS20:334)

ELLEGOOD Rev. J, St Ann's, Montreal, 3rd s. late Jacob
Ellegood, Dumfries, m. Harriett Elizabeth, eldest dau. late
George Taylor, London, Fredericton, NB, 10 Sep.1849.(NS32:638)

ELLERY C, ex planter, Nevis, wine-merchant, London, d.
19 Aug.1811.   (81:286)

ELLETSON Goodin, ex Jamaica, d. NC, 10 Nov.1789.   (60:179)

ELLETSON Roger Hope, Lt. Gov. Jamaica, m. Miss Gamon, London,
17 April 1770.   (47:190)

ELLETSON Roger Hope, Lt. Gov. Jamaica, d.29 Nov.1775.(45:607)

ELLETSON Roger Hope, b.1679, Merryman's Hill, St Andrews,
Jamaica, d. Hope Est., Jamaica, 31 May 1819.   (89:185)

ELLETSON Mrs, b.1739, w. Roger Hope Elletson, Lt. Gov.
Jamaica, d.1767.   (37:279)

ELLIOT Reginald Henry, 3rd s. James Elliot, Dymchurch, Kent,
m. Catherine, only ch. H Callaghan, Pusey Hall, Vere,
Jamaica, 16 Sep.1863.   (NS2/15:635)

ELLIOTT James, Dep. Inspector Gen. Army Hospitals,d.Montreal,
4 Oct.1843.   (NS20:670)

ELLIOT James Sutton, b.1806, late Principal Military Storekeeper, d. NY, 23 Aug.1860.   (NS2/9:441)

ELLIOT Miss, niece Sir Gilbert Elliot, Navy Treasurer, m.
James Jauncey, s. James Jauncey, Assemblyman, NY, 1773.
                                                      (44:45)

ELLIOT Miss, 3rd dau. Samuel Elliot, Antigua, m. William Hay
Carr, bro. Earl of Errol, 27 July 1796.   (66:701)

ELLIS Caroline Charlotte, eldest dau. Cap. F W Ellis, RN, m.
Robert Alexander Strickland, Douro, Canada West, eldest s.
Maj. Strickland, Southwold, Suffolk, 25 March 1856.(NS45:514)

ELLIS Charlotte Mary Jane, 2nd dau. late Cap. F W Ellis, RN,
Southwold, m. Charles E, 5th s. T A Stewart, Douro, Canada
West, Southwold, Suffolk, 9 Aug.1860.   (NS2/9:318)

ELLIS Emma Louisa, b.1842, w. Francis Ellis, Queen's Advocate
for Turks & Caicos Islands, d. Turks Island, 15 Dec.1867.
                                                    (NS3/5:255)

ELLIS John, Fellow Royal Society, Carolina naturalist, West
Florida agent, d.5 Oct.1776.   (56:483)

ELLIS J, merchant, d. NY, 1811.   (81:285)

ELLIS William B, attorney, Portland Assemblyman, d. Spanish
Town, Jamaica, June 1795.   (65:791)

ELLISON Robert, Customs Collector, NY, d.16 July 1732.(2:877)

ELLISON Robert, eldest s. Henry Ellison, Egremont, Cumberland,
d. Norfolk, Va., 1787.   (57:1024)

ELMES H L, b.1815, only s. James Elmes, Port of London
surveyor, architect, London, d. Jamaica, 26 Nov.1847.(NS29:21)

ELMSLIE Hannah, Philadelphia, m. Charles Godfried Paleske,
Prussian Consul Gen. US, Philadelphia, 1792.   (62:574)

ELMSLY John, b.1762, Chief Justice Lower Canada, d. Montreal,
29 April 1805.   (75:677)

ELMSLIE John, ex Jamaica, d. Windsor, 23 July 1829. (99:188)

ELRINGTON ..., dau. Col. Elrington, Rifle Brigade, b.
Montreal, 26 Nov.1865.   (NS3/1:114)

ELTON C B, s. late Rev. J Elton, Dublin, d. Philadelphia, 1802.
                                                   (72:785)

ELWES Henry jr., ex NA, nephew Sir William Elwes, d. 15 Dec.
1773.   (43:622)

ELWIN H S, b.1820, eldest s. Rev. T H Elwin, East Barnet,
Herts., d. Boteau, Dominica, 1 June 1838.   (NS10:342)

ELWYN Thomas Langdon, b. Canterbury, 1774, educated Trinity
College, Oxford, son-in-law John Langdon, Gov.NH, d. Portsmouth, NE, 22 March 1816.   (86:474)

EMBERSON Frederick Charles, headmaster, Ontario College,
Picton, m. Clara Helena, only dau. J Bartlett, Belleville,
Canada West, 8 July 1867.   (NS3/2:383)

EMERSON Katherine Annabell, 2nd dau. Hugh Alexander Emerson,
late Solicitor Gen. NFD., m. Samuel Cowan, Kingston, Upper
Canada, London, 4 Sep.1858.   (NS2/5:414)

EMERSON Ruth, b.1769, wid. Rev. W Emerson, Boston, mo. Ralph
Waldo Emerson, d. Concord, Mass., 16 Nov.1853.   (NS41:106)

EMMETT Mr, counsellor, projector Irish Rebellion 1791, d.
NY, 1827.   (97:647)

EMRANSON Sylvester, WI, m. Alice Exton, Ireland, 13 Sep.1747.
                                                   (17:447)

ENDERBY Miss, London, m. Nathaniel Wheatly, Boston, NE,
10 Nov.1773.   (53:581)

ENGLAND Mary Catherine, yngs. dau. late Maj. England, 75th
Reg., niece Gen. Sir Richard England, m. Com. George A W
Welch, RN, eldest s. George Asser White Welch, Cheltenham,
Montreal, 1 June 1864.   (NS2/17:108)

ENTWISTLE Ernie, b.1733, d. Antigua, April 1803.   (73:691)

ERGAS Ralph, d. Kingston, Jamaica, 20 March 1782. (52:206)

ERSKINE John, late merchant, Greenock, d. Kingston, Jamaica,
17 Sep.1795.   (65:969)

ERSKINE ..., eldest s. Thomas Erskine, m. niece late George
Washington, America, 1800.   (70:484)

ESDAILE Archibald, President St Kitts, Master in Chancery,
Admiralty Judge, d. St Kitts, 25 Oct.1796.   (67:164)

ESPINASSE Reuben, 2nd s. Maj. Espinasse, Dundrum, Co. Dublin,
m. Madeline Josephine Ellen, only dau. late J T Gillmer,
Philadelphia, Gravesend, 11 Feb.1868.   (NS3/5:387)

ESTEN Charles Phillips, b.1840, 2nd s. Vice Chancellor Esten,
Toronto, d. Maplewood, Newmarket, Canada West, 29 July 1857.
(NS2/3:467)

ESTEN Esther Strangeways, wid. J C Esten, Chief Justice
Bermuda, d. Toronto, 9 Sep.1849.   (NS32:559)

ESTEN James Christie Palmer, b. St George, Bermuda, 1808,
Vive Chancellor, d. Toronto, 24 Oct.1864.   (NS2/17:803)

ESTEN J P, barrister, eldest s. J C Esten, Chief Justice
Bermuda, m. Ann F, dau. J Hutchison, late Bermuda, 11 Jan.
1832.   (102:78)

ESTON James Christie Palmer, b.1772, late Chief Justice
Bermuda, ex Exeter, d. Toronto, 9 Aug.1838.   (NS10:566)

ESTRIDGE John, Councillor St Kitts, d. Weymouth, 3 Oct.1773.
(48:495)

ETHERIDGE James, b.1814, s. late Thomas Etheridge, Sibtonhall,
Suffolk, d. Jamaica, 14 Dec.1853.   (NS41:439)

ETHERIDGE Thomas, b.1772, s. Rev. Robert Etheridge, Starston,
Norfolk, d. Port Royal, Jamaica, 23 March 1797.   (67:528)

ETTLES John, merchant, late Havanna, d. London, Nov.1846.
(NS27:102)

EUSTIS George, b. Boston, Mass., 20 Oct.1796, s. Jacob &
Elizabeth Eustis, Chief Justice Louisiana, d. New Orleans,
22 Dec.1858.   (NS2/9:188)

EVANS Charles, b.1825, eldest s. Charles Evans, d. Belize,
Honduras, 2 Nov.1845.   (NS25:222)

EVANS Dawson R, Cap., 6th Royal Reg., m. Sara, 2nd dau. George
McGrath, Charlemont, Jamaica, St Thomas-in-the-Vale, Jamaica,
4 May 1865.   (NS2/19:106)

EVANS Cap. Henry m. Mrs Leith, wid. Cap. Leith, 69th Reg.,
only dau. late Gov. Seton, St Vincent, 6 Oct.1807.   (77:976)

EVANS Mrs Mary Martin, ex Kingston, Jamaica, d. Bucks.,
12 Dec.1812.   (82:672)

EVANS W J, MD, m. Marianne, 2nd dau. late A T Perkins,
London, Barbados, 1 Feb.1838.   (NS9:539)

EVATT G, Cap., 55th Reg., m. Susan, 2nd dau. J Beckwith, the
Bower, Halifax, NB, 31 May 1812.   (82:186)

EVELYN Lyndon Howard, Customs Collector, Savannah-la-Mar, m.
Alice, dau. Benjamin Samuda, ex Jamaica, Lund, Westmoreland,
Jamaica, 3 March 1821.   (91:467)

EVERARD Lt, RN, magistrate, Jamaica, d.20 Aug.1834. (105:222)

EVERETT Edward, b. Dorchester, Mass., 11 April 1794, s.
Rev. Oliver Everett, scholar & statesman, d. Boston, USA,
15 Jan.1865.   (NS2/18:515)

EVERSHED Frances, 4th dau. late Thomas Evershed, Pallingham,
Sussex, m. Alexander Geddes, Annandale, Jamaica, London,
22 Dec.1852.   (NS39:305)

EWART James B, b.1801, d. Dundas, Canada West, 17 Dec.1853.
                                                 (NS41:219)

EWART John, Nevis, d. London, 1821.   (91:572)

EWING Robert, b.1785, only s. Walter Ewing jr., merchant,
Glasgow, d. Trinidad, 6 June 1802.   (72:781)

EWING Rev. Dr, d. Philadelphia, 1803.   (73:87)

EXTON Alice, Ireland, m. Sylvester Emranson, WI, 13 Sep.1747.
                                                  (17:447)

EYRE Col. Lyttleton, Va., d.1768.   (38:446)

EYRE ..., s. Lt. Gov. Eyre, b. Kingshouse, Spanish Town,
Jamaica, 5 Feb.1863.   (NS2/14:512)

EYRE ..., dau. Gov. Eyre, b. Flamstead, Jamaica, 22 Dec.1865.
                                                 (NS3/1:416)

EZARD Cap., master Valiant of Hull, d. PEI, 7 June 1818,
buried Charlottetown.   (88:373)

FAGAN Rev. Henry Stuart, headmaster, Burton-on-Trent Grammar
School, m. Emily, eldest dau. James Kinnear, MD, NY, London,
23 July 1851.   (NS36:423)

FAGAN John, d. NY, 1798.   (68:1086)

FAHIE Rear Adm. m. Mary Esther, dau. A W Harvey, Councillor,
Bermuda, July 1823.   (93:368)

FAHIE Sir W C, Vice Adm., b.1763, d. Bermuda, 11 Jan.1833.
                                                 (103:561)

FAHIE Matilda, dau. Rear Adm. Fahie, m. Cap. Hoare, sloop
Dotteral, Bermuda, 15 March 1823.   (93:562)

FAIRBAIRN Henry, MD, d. Antigua, 15 Nov.1795.   (65:166)

FAIRCHILD John, Chief Justice, St Michaels, Barbados, d.
12 Sep.1757.   (27:46)

FAIRFAX Lord Thomas, b.1693, Scottish Peer, d. Va., 1782,
bro. Robert Fairfax, Leeds Castle, Kent.   (52:149)

FAIRFAX Lord Thomas, b.1742, s. Rev. Bryan Fairfax, fa.
Charles Snowden Fairfax, Woodbourne, Md., d. Vaucluse,
Fairfax Co., Va., 21 April 1846.   (NS27:81)

FAIRFAX Col. William, President, Va., d.2 Sep.1757. (27:531)

FAIRLIE James, ex Kingston, Jamaica, d. Bellfield,
19 May 1819.   (88:586)

FALCONER James C E, master, Hamilton Academy, d. Bermuda,
14 Oct.1853.   (NS41:439)

FALKNER Elizabeth, w. William Falkner, d. Coburg, Upper
Canada, 13 Aug.1828.   (98:382)

FALKNER Cap., 29th Reg, Sec. NC, m. Miss Hudson, London,
April 1763.   (32:257)

FALL Richard m. Eliza, dau. late Andrew Whiteman, Grenada,
17 June 1820.   (90:636)

FALSIDE Margaret Anne, dau. late Dr Falside, St Vincent, m.
Lt. John Carmichael, 53rd Reg., St Vincent, 1797. (67:1127)

FANNIN James, ex Montego Bay, Jamaica, d. London, 12 June 1808.
                                                    (78:565)

FANSHAWE Charles Gascoyne, 3rd s. John G Fanshawe, Parloe,
Essex, d. Jamaica, 1801.   (71:187)

FARLEY (?) Mary Anne, gdau. late G Farley, Henwick, Worcs.,
m. Robert Joseph Kerr, Grand River, Upper Canada, 7 July
1822.   (92:88)

FARMER Arthur A, Huntingford, Canada West, 2nd s. late W M
Farmer, Nonsuch Park, Surrey, m. Louise Emily, dau. B P
Blaquiere, Kingston, Canada West, 3 Feb.1846.   (NS25:534)

FARMER Reginald Onslow, RA, yngs. s. late W M Farmer, Nonsuch
Park, Surrey, m. Geraldine, dau. Cap. J S Farrell, RA,
Bytown, Canada, 1 Oct.1851.   (NS37:181)

FARMER Robert, b.1798, s. Alexander Farmer, Helmington, Suffolk,
chief-mate, ship Friends, d. Salt River, Jamaica, 27 May 1821.
                                                    (91:187)

FARNHAM Ralph, b.1756, d. Acton, Maine, 26 Dec.1860.
                                                    (NS2/10:348)

FARQUHARSON Anna, 2nd dau. late Charles Farquharson, m. Rev.
George Augustus Addison, Manchester, Clarendon, Jamaica,
4 Feb.1851.   (NS35:545)

FARQUHARSON Elizabeth Frances, only dau. late Matthew
Farquharson, St Elizabeth, Jamaica, m. Robert Henry Robertson
2nd s. Duncan Robertson, St Elizabeth, London, 19 March 1864.
                                                    (NS2/16:521)

FARQUHARSON James Alexander, Maj. Gen., Gov. St Lucia, d.
St Lucia, 23 Jan.1834.   (104:317)

FARQUHARSON John, MD, ex Charleston, SC, d. Old Aberdeen,
18 Oct.1790.   (60:1053)

FARRELL Geraldine, dau. Cap. J S Farrell, RA, m. Reginald
Onslow Farmer, yngs. s. late W H Farmer, Nonsuch Park,
Surrey, Bytown, Canada, 1 Oct.1851.   (NS37:181)

FARR Mrs, b.1735, wid. John Farr, Gov. NS, d. Preston, 1814.
(84:100)

FARRELL John Richard, Barbados, d. Lamplighter Hall,
30 Dec.1824.   (95:189)

FARREN Henry, eldest s. William Farren, English comedian,
settled USA 1856, St Louis theater manager, d. 18 Jan.1860.
(NS2/8:307)

FARRINGTON Frances Sarah, yngs. dau. late James W Farrington,
Nassau, m. Ralph H Potts, Lt., 1st WI Reg., yngs. s. late
Radford Potts, Beverley, Yorks., Nassau, Bahamas, 20 Dec.
1864.   (NS2/18:364)

FAULKNER Thomas, Oxted, Surrey, NC Sec., d.21 April 1782.
(52:207)

FAUQUIER Francis, Lt. Gov. Va., d.1768.   (38:199)

FAVEY Lucy Jane, 3rd dau. late Charles Favey, merchant, m.
Francis Horatio, 4th s. Cap. Henry Pryce, RN, Antigua,
13 Jan.1848.   (NS29:421)

FAWCETT Rev. John, chaplain to Adm. Parker, Fellow Queens
College Oxford, Vicar Milford Hants., d. WI, 1795.   (65:794)

FEARON Elizabeth, b.1728, w. Benson Fearon, Pentonville, sis.
late John & Thomas Foxcroft, NY, joint postmaster gen. USA
with Dr Franklin, d.10 Nov.1801.   (71:1062)

FEARON Thomas Peters, Jamaica, m. Anna Maria Boyfield, Lee,
Kent, 2 March 1782.   (52:149)

FEILDEN ..., s. Maj. Feilden, 60th Rifles, b. Quebec,
13 March 1863.   (NS2/14:650)

FELLERSON Michael, b.1689, d. Mass., 1793.   (63:186)

FELLOWES Frances Georgina, w. William Henry Fellowes, d.
Canada West, 4 July 1855.   (NS54:330)

FENN Andrew, d. Jamaica, 1790.   (60:766)

FENN Margaret Anne, b.1837, w. Rev. Nathaniel V Fenn, d.
Woodstock, Canada West, 17 Sep.1867.   (NS3/2:683)

FENNER James, b.1770, ex Gov. RI, d. Providence, 11 April
1846.   (NS26:222)

FENWICK James, Customs Controller, St Vincent, d.1777.(48:391)

FERGERSON Faude, b.1706, d. Trinidad, 15 June 1836. (NS6:223)

FERGUS Lucy, b.1744, dau. Patrick Fergus, Montserrat, d. Bury,
24 March 1824.   (94:381)

FERGUSON Adam, ex Woodhill, Perth, advocate, d. Woodhill,
Canada East, 25 Sep.1862.   (NS2/13:788)

FERGUSON Mrs Frances, b. NA, 1730, emigrated Va. to GB, 1750, d. Hampton, Middlesex, 1810.   (80:192)

FERGUSON George, b.1814, eldest s. late George Ferguson, Houghton Hall, Cumberland, ex Cap., 23rd Reg., d. Montreal, 5 March 1847.   (NS27:679)

FERGUSON James, s. Sir James Ferguson, d. Tobago, 1777.(48:45)

FERGUSON John, MD, late Kingston, Jamaica, d. Clapham, 22 July 1856.   (NS2/1:391)

FERGUSON Dr Thomas, b.1706, d. Jamaica, 1791.   (61:1065)

FERGUSON-BLAIR A J, b.1815, s. late Adam Ferguson, Woodhill, Perths., statesman, d. Canada, 1 Jan.1868.   (NS3/5:542)

FERMOR Lady Juliana, yngs. dau. Earl of Pomfret, m. Thomas Penn, Prop. Pa., 22 Aug.1751.   (21:427)

FERNANDEZ David, ex Lambeth, d. St Thomas, 1810.   (80:281)

FERNS Jonathan Gore, ex Maj., 76th Reg., eldest s. late T Burgh Ferns, Co. Dublin, d. Halifax, NS, 26 May 1856.
                                                    (NS2/1:124)

FERRIS Richard, Bristol, m. Mary Ann, dau. late John Delaroche Carisbrook Castle, Jamaica, wid. Henry Coote, Cheltenham, 29 April 1852.   (NS38:87)

FICKLIN R B, Royal Canadian Rifles, m. Eliza, eldest dau. C B Daveney, Norwich, 3 May 1849.   (NS32:84)

FIDLER Rev. Daniel, Westmoreland, Jamaica, headmaster Manning Free School, d. The Castle, Savanna-la-Mar, 11 April 1863.
                                                    (NS2/14:80)

FIELD Henry, b.1809, late London, d. Berbice, 1850.(NS35:110)

FIELD ..., dau. Cap. Field, 6th Reg., b. Newcastel, Jamaica, 16 Oct.1865.   (NS3/1:112)

FIELD ..., s. Rev. Alfred Field, b. Belize, British Honduras, 30 Sep.1867.   (NS3/2:805)

FIELDEN Cap. Henry Wemyss, 2nd s. Sir William H Fielden, Feniscowles, Lancs., m. Julia, dau. late David McCord, Columbia, SC, Greenville, SC, 27 Oct.1864.   (NS2/18:234)

FINDLATER Alexander James, Jamaica, d. London, 8 Jan.1815.
                                                    (85:180)

FINDLATER Rev. John, ex St Vincent, d. London, 1809.(79:1238)

FINNIAN Robert, ex Jamaica, d. Clifton, 15 Sep.1800.(70:1107)

FISHER Louisa, yngs. dau. Henry Fisher, MD, Dunkeld, Perths., m. Archibald Hamilton Campbell, banker, Montreal, s. late John Campbell, Stirling, Uxbridge, 3 April 1856.   (NS45:639)

FISHER Mr, fa. Clara Fisher, d. NY, 1843.   (NS19:556)

FITZGERALD Charles Lionel John, Lt., 1st WI Reg., eldest s.
Lt. Col. Fitzgerald, late RA, m. Laura, yngs. dau. Henry
Sharpe, Chief Justice St Vincent, St George, St Vincent,
12 March 1863.   (NS2/14:781)

FITZPATRICK Mrs Elizabeth, b.Scotland, 1707, d.Brooklyn, NY,
1 April 1852.   (NS37:632)

FITZGERALD Fanny, yngs. dau. Thomas Fitzgerald, Greenbank,
Falmouth, m. Rev Edward Jordan, Nassau, New Providence,
3 Aug.1843.   (NS20:428)

FITZGERALD Pamela, wid. Lord Edward Fitzgerald, m. Mr Pitcairn
American Minister, Hamburg, 1800.   (70:1283)

FITZHERBERT Ellen Margaret, w. Cap. Fitzherbert, Rifle
Brigade, d. Halifax, NS, 21 May 1845.   (NS24:214)

FITZHERBERT W, eldest s. Sir H Fitzherbert, m. Annie, 2nd
dau. Sir Reynold Alleyne, Alleyne Dale Hall, Barbados,
20 Feb.1836.   (NS5:544)

FITZROY Mary Caroline,.only dau. Sir Charles Fitzroy, niece
Duke of Richmond, m. K Stewart, Com., HMS Ringdove, bro.
Earl of Galloway, PEI, 9 July 1841.   (NS16:422)

FLANAGAN Dr William, d.Kingston, Jamaica, 1793.   (63:1152)

FLEMING Sir Collingwood, Va., d.17 April 1764.   (34:250)

FLEMING Rev. J & w. Amelia, dau. Charles Talmadge, mercer,
Oxford, d. Belize, 13 Sep.1824.   (95:190)

FLEMING Laura Amanda, only dau. late J H Fleming, Anguilla, m.
Berkeley, eldest s. Adolphus Pugh Johnson, London, 17 June
1847.   (NS28:312)

FLEMING Dr, RC Bishop NFD., d. St Johns, NFD., 14 July 1850.
                                                   (NS34:455)

FLETCHER Alexander, ex Cap., 84th Reg., d. St John Island,
NA, Sep.1793.   (63:1149)

FLETCHER Arthur, s. Joseph Fletcher, Liverpool, agent Brown,
Danson & Co., London, d. Mill Creek, Cincinnati, USA,
17 Feb.1834.   (104:454)

FLETCHER Elizabeth, b. Jamaica, 1690, wid. Jacob Fletcher,
Whitehall Est., St Anne, Jamaica, d. Gay's Hill, Jamaica,
1 Feb.1810.   (80:384)

FLETCHER Mary Munnings, b.1822, eldest dau. John Campbell Lees
Chief Justice Bahamas, w. Rev.John Fletcher, King's College
School, Nassau, d. Nassau, New Providence, 13 July 1844.
                                                   (NS22:334)

FLETCHER Thomas Howard, 15th Reg., m. Helen, only dau. late
Charles Simonds, St Johns, NB, 27 April 1867.   (NS3/2:383)

FLEURY Fanny, eldest dau. Charles Fleury, Weymouth, Dorset,
m. Francis George, yngs. s. A CLaudet, London, Victoria,
Vancouver Island, 22 Sep.1864.   (NS2/16:107)

FLOUD Mary, sis. Thomas Floud, Mayor of Exeter, m. Samuel
Mitchell, Preseident, Grenada, 7 Sep.1802.   (72:877)

FLOWER Francis, b.1783, ex Hammersmith, d. St Croix, 26 June
1811.   (81:285)

FLUCKER Miss, dau. Thomas Flucker, Sec. Mass. Bay, m. James
Urquhart, Cap., 14th Reg., 1774.   (45:46)

FLUCKER Thomas, ex Sec. Mass. Bay, d.15 Feb.1783.   (53:182)

FLYNN Mrs Sarah, d. NY, 1798.   (68:1086)

FOHIS Utyenti, b.China, 1703, d.Canada, 1805.   (75:188)

FONTENELLE Miss (Mrs Wilkinson), actress, ex London, d.
Charleston, SC, 1800.   (70:905)

FOORD Edward, Councillor, d. Kingston, Jamaica, 1776.(47:295)

FOOT George Forrester, b.1799, d. Clarendon, Jamaica,
4 Dec.1820.   (91:475)

FOOT Richard, b.1780, surgeon, d. Jamaica, 1802.   (72:785)

FORBES Alexander, Jamaica, d. on passage to England, 1803.
                                                   (73:1254)

FORBES Alexander, ex Maj., 79th Highlanders, d. Kingston,
Canada West, 30 March 1851.   (NS36:216)

FORBES Alexander, b.1778, ex Tepic & San Blas, Mexico, d.
Basildon, 17 Dec.1862.   (NS2/14:134)

FORBES Duncan, d. Grenada, 10 Nov.1791.   (62:88)

FORBES Euphemia, eldest dau. late Patrick Forbes, Grenada, d.
Glasgow, 16 Feb.1806.   (76:284)

FORBES Francis, Barbuda, m. Miss Lindsay, 30 April 1764.
                                                    (34:250)

FORBES Francis, s. Sir C Forbes, d. San Francisco, 30 Dec.1849.
                                                   (NS33:559)

FORBES George, planter, d. Tobago, 30 Aug.1786.   (57:89)

FORBES George, b.1801, barrister, d. St Kitts, 3 Nov.1825.
                                                    (94:647)

FORBES Henry, d. Bermuda, 26 Oct.1757.   (27:482)

FORBES Henry, Barbados, d. Bristol, 24 Oct.1757.   (27:531)

FORBES Henry jr m. Mary Anne, yngs. dau. James Smith, gdau.
Alexander Aikman, Kingston, Jamaica, 2 Nov.1831.   (101:644)

FORBES John, Gov. Bahamas, barrister, ex Drogheda MP, d.
Nassau, New Providence, 13 June 1797.   (67:711)

FORBES Martha Frances, only dau. J A Forbes, Santa Clara, Cal.,
m. Alfred Boyce, s. T Tomkin, MD, Witham, Essex, Santa Clara,
24 Aug.1859.   (NS2/8:176)

FORBES Mary m. Lt. Thomas Winslow, 47th Reg., Bermuda,
6 Sep.1794.   (64:1052)

FORBES Mary Sophia, dau. late John Forbes, New Providence, m.
Thomas B Williams, Jamaica, 24 June 1820.   (90:636)

FORBES Mungo, ex Jamaica, d. Bristol, 6 April 1807. (77:489)

FORBES Thomas, d. Nassau, New Providence, 13 Feb.1808.(78:364)

FORBES Mrs, b.1763, d. Ashfield, Mass., 1866.   (NS3/1:930)

FORD Sir Francis, Ember, Surrey, d. Barbados, 7 June 1801.
                                                    (71:859)

FORD Gilbert, Attorney Gen. Jamaica, d.29 Jan.1768. (38:47)

FORD Rev. John, b.1786, ex St Nicholas, Gloucester, & Romsey,
Hants., d. NY, 17 Feb.1855.   (NS43:436)

FORDE P, b. France, d. Norfolk, America, 1816.   (86:629)

FORD William, ex Barbados, d. Liverpool, 21 June 1802.(72:783)

FORD Mr, d. Dumfries, Md., 1799.   (69:904)

FOORD Edward, Councillor, Kingston, Jamaica, d.1777. (57:295)

FORDYCE John, Bengal Artillery, m. Maria Louise, yngs. dau.
late H G Alleyne, Barbados, Paris, 16 Feb.1842.   (NS17:541)

FOREMAN John, b.1820, s. J Foreman, Belfast, merchant &
Assemblyman, d. Antigua, 14 June 1866.   (NS3/2:269)

FORLONG Harriet Alice Mary, dau. late Lt. Col. Forlong, Gore
Vale, Toronto, m. Rev. Charles J S Bethune, s. Archdeacon
Toronto, 21 April 1863.   (NS2/15:96)

FORREST Joanna, only ch. late Peter Forrest, London, m.
William W Irving, PEI, Halifax, NA, 17 Nov.1846.   (NS27:195)

FORSAN James, Leeward Islands, d.20 Oct.1758.   (28:556)

FORSTER Mr, attorney, Wallbrook, ex America, d. Sep.1783.
                                                    (53:805)

FORSTER E, dau. Maj. Forster, RA, NS, m. Hanby Egan, Halifax,
NS, 15 Oct.1820.   (90:562)

FORSTER John, b.1747, Jamaica, d. London, 25 Dec.1840.
                                                   (NS15:216)

FORSTER Matthew Frederick, Cap., 4th WI Reg., d. St George,
Grenada, 7 May 1796.   (66:701)

FORSTER William, b.1784, Quaker, Norwich, d. Knox Co., Tenn.,
27 Jan.1854.   (NS41:664)

FORSYTH John, b.1761, Councillor, Montreal, d. London,
27 Dec.1837.   (NS9:217)

FORSYTH John, b. Fredericksburg, Va., Oct.1781, late Sec.
State, USA, d. Washington, 21 Oct.1841.   (NS17:324)

FORSYTH Robert, advocate, m. Jacobina, dau. late John Carson,
MD, physician, Philadelphia, Edinburgh, 12 July 1803.(73:690)

FORT Mr, merchant, d. Pittsburgh, 1803.   (73:87)

FORTHTON James, b. Bordeaux, 1645, settled WI, 1694, m. in
St Kitts, Martinique 30 years, Grenada 40 years, d. Grenada,
1773.   (43:154)

FORTYE Jane Athol Gordon, wid. Maj. Thomas Fortye, 8th Reg.,
dau. late John Campbell, Argyll, d. Toronto, 22 March 1864.
                                                     (NS2/16:805)

FOSTER Alice Jane, b.1844, eldest dau. William Foster, d.
Mandeville, Jamaica, 29 Aug.1848.   (NS30:670)

FOSTER Archibald, d. Jamaica, 1791.   (61:186)

FOSTER John, 4th s. late Charles Foster, Lancaster, Jamaica,
& Montreuil-sur-Mer, d. Sacramento, Cal., 16 Oct.1849.
                                                       (NS33:342)

FOSTER Thomas, MP, Bossiney, Cornwall, m. Miss Haldane, dau.
John Haldane, St Kitts, 2 June 1741.   (11:331)

FOSTER William, d. Mandeville, Jamaica, 7 Sep.1848.(NS30:670)

FOSTER W, 2nd s. Rev. Foster, Ryall, Rutland, d. WI, 1796.
                                                        (66:882)

FOSTER Mrs, w. John Foster, merchant, dau. late Mr Gandy,
Kendal, Westmoreland, d. Richmond, Va., 21 Oct.1806. (77:89)

FOTHRINGHAM Alexander m. Judith, 2nd dau. late Dr Alexander
Garden, Charleston, SC, 24 Nov.1791.   (61:1061)

FOUDIRNIER Paul, merchant, St Kitts, d. 1 Aug.1770. (40:393)

FOULKS Arthur, Brockenhurst House, m. Mary, 2nd dau. G Mackenzie
Clarendon, Jamaica, Downton, Wilts., 20 Oct.1803.   (73:1252)

FOULKES Arthur, Jamaica, m. Louisa Locke, eldest dau. Archdeacon Glenie, London, 15 June 1841.   (NS16:201)

FOULKS Arthur, yngs. s. late Arthur Foulks, Bristol, d.
Spanish Town, Jamaica, 15 July 1842.   (NS19:110)

FOURDRINIER Henry John, Montreal, m. Mary, 2nd dau. George
Usborne, Portage-du-fort, Quebec, Portage-du-fort, 9 May
1860.   (NS2/9:84)

FOWLES Daniel, b.1717, publisher 'The NH Gazette', d. Portsmouth, NH, 8 June 1787.   (57:741)

FOX Henry Stephen, b.1791, only s. Gen. Henry Edward Fox,
British Envoy, d. Washington,Oct.1846.   (NS27:82)

FOXCRAFT Francis, NE, d.1768.   (38:302)

FOXCRAFT John, Dep. Post Master Gen., NA, m. Miss Osgood,
London, 2 Aug.1770.   (40:392)

FOXCROFT John, ex NY joint postmaster, agent for British
packets, d. NY, 5 May 1790.   (60:570)

FOXCROFT Thomas, ex Post Master Gen., Philadelphia, d.
29 April 1785.   (55:572)

FRANCIS Elizabeth, dau. late S Francis, Newington Est.,
Jamaica, m. Cap. T Scott, RM, London, 26 Oct.1837.   (NS8:648)

FRANCISCO Henry, b. England, 1686, settled America 1730,
d. Whitehall, NY, 25 Oct.1820.   (90:570)

FRANCK Richard, American planter, d.22 June 1775.   (45:304)

FRANCKEN Henry Andrew, assistant judge, Port Royal, Jamaica,
d. Kingston, Jamaica, May 1795.   (65:791)

FRANCKLIN James Boutineau, b.1764, d. Halifax, NS, 22 May 1841.
                                                         (NS16:446)

FRANCKLYN Peter, Customs Collector, Kingston, m. Mrs
Elizabeth Harding, Weston Favel Est., Trelawney, Jamaica,
Sep.1794.   (64:1052)

FRANKLIN Ellen, only dau. late William Franklin, ex Gov. NJ,
m. Capel Hanbury, Royal Scots Reg., 8 June 1818.   (88:562)

FRANKLIN Mary, w. William Franklin, ex Gov. NJ, s. Dr Franklin,
d. 3 Aug.1811.   (81:196)

FRANKLIN Peter, Dep. Post Master, Philadelphia, bro.
Benjamin Franklin, d. 15 Aug.1766.   (36:391)

FRANKLIN Thomas, ex Jamaica, d.26 July 1767.   (37:524)

FRANKLIN William, Gov. NJ, m. Miss Downes, London, 5 Sep.1762.
                                                          (32:448)

FRANKLIN William, b.1731, ex Gov.NJ, d. London, 16 Nov.1813.
                                                          (83:510)

FRANNIS Robert, d. Pa., 1791.   (61:1235)

FRANTHAM Mrs Betsey, b. Germany, 1680, settled NC, 1710,
d. Mauray Co., Tenn., 10 Jan.1834.   (104:222)

FRASER Charles Shuldham, b.1783, magistrate, St George,
Grenada, d. Grenada, 4 Oct.1850.   (NS34:678)

FRASER Duncan, Jamaica, m. Mrs Slater, Richmond, 1 Aug.1794.
                                                  (64:764)

FRASER Elizabeth, w. Benjamin Dewoff Fraser, MD, dau. R I
Coster, Witheridge, Devon, d. NS, 28 Jan.1842.   (NS18:332)

FRASER George, s. late George, Lord Saltoun, d. Nevis,
8 Jan.1799.   (69:254)

FRASER Dr John, eldest s. James Fraser, Glasgow, d. Kingston,
Jamaica, 1794.   (64:788)

FRASER John, d. Halifax, NS, 8 May 1795.   (65:614)

FRASER John James, b.1805, late singer, England, d. Philadelphia, 18 June 1863.   (NS2/15:246)

FRASER Lionel M, Lt., 41st Reg., m. Louise Amenaide, 2nd dau.
Jose Guiseppi, Consul to Venezuela, Port of Spain,
Trinidad, 21 Nov.1857.   (NS2/4:207)

FRASER Simon jr, only s. S Fraser, London, d. Dominica,
6 Aug.1793.   (63:958)

FRASER Simon, St Vincent, yngs. s. late William Fraser of
Culbuckie, d. Bermuda, 12 Oct.1798.   (69:252)

FRASER Simon, late Ordnance Dept., Bermuda, d. Edinburgh,
16 Feb.1819.   (88:279)

FRASER William, late Cap., Prince of Wales Fencibles, d.
Jamaica, June 1803.   (73:882)

FRASER Maj., ADC Lt Gen. Nugent, m. Miss Rowland, Jamaica,
Liverpool, 13 April 1807.   (77:375)

FRASER Lt Col., NA staff, m. Georgina, yngs. dau. late Sir
Charles Bagot, Gov. Gen. Canada, London, 21 Sep.1843.(NS20:539)

FREEBAIRN Thomas, d. Jamaica, 1790.   (60:1214)

FREEMAN Rev. Andrew F, s. Bishop of Arkansas, m. Susan
Elizabeth, eldest dau. James Dunlop, Petersburg, Va.,
8 July 1858.   (NS2/5:304)

FREEMAN Charles, b. USA, 1817, 'the American giant', d.
Winchester, 18 Oct.1845.   (NS24:649)

FREEMAN James, d. Jamaica, 1790.   (60:1053)

FREEMAN John, MD, b.1810, ex Framlington, d. Boston, Texas,
14 Jan.1857.   (NS2/2:624)

FREEMAN Joseph, late corn-factor, London, merchant,
Barbados, d. Barbados, April 1808.   (78:639)

FREEMAN Melusina Warburton, dau. late Arthur Freeman,
Antigua, m. Nathaniel Bayly, Bath, 24 Aug.1795.   (65:703)

FREEMAN Mr, WI, d. Bath, 15 Dec.1794.   (64:1158)

FREEMAN ..., s. W Peere Williams Freeman, b. Washington, USA,
18 May 1867.   (NS3/4:98)

FRENCH Edward A, b.1798, yngs. s. John Lynch French, St Kitts,
& Elizabeth, dau. Harry Darrell, Calehill, Kent, bro. Andrew
Lynch French, St Kitts, d. St Kitts, 9 Oct.1859. (NS2/7:654)

FRENCH John, Sec. Gov. Moore, NY, d.1768.   (38:494)

FRENCH Nathaniel Bogle jr, Dulwich, Surrey, m. Elizabeth.
only ch. late William Jackson, Chief Justice Jamaica,
5 Jan.1811.   (81:85)

FRENCH William, ex Jamaica, d. London, 14 Sep.1808. (78:861)

FRENCH Miss, dau. Nathaniel French, Antigua, m. Cap. Palmer,
Guards Reg., s. Sir Charles Palmer, 25 Oct.1752.   (22:478)

FRENCH Councillor, d. Kingston, Jamaica, 1758.   (29:45)

FRENCH Miss m. Cap. Stehelin, RA, Spanish Town, Jamaica,
Nov.1790.   (60:1213)

FRENCH Mrs, b.1740, dau. late Thomas Nicholas, Antigua,
ggdau. Sir Edward Nicholas, Sec. State Charles II, d.
Cavendish, Suffolk, 1815.   (85:378)

FRENCH Mrs, b.1746, wid. William French, Montserrat, d.
London, 1818.   (88:644)

FRERE John, Barbados, d.1759.   (29:497)

FRERE Miss, dau. John Frere, London, m. Sir John Ord, late
Gov. Jamaica, 3 Dec.1793.   (63:1148)

FRIERSON Philip, Entaw Springs, St Matthew's parish, Rep. in
House of Assembly, d.3 June 1788.   (58:752)

FRITH Lizzie, yngs. dau. late H Frith, Stonehaven, Bermuda,
m. Rev. C A Jenkins, Pembroke, Bermuda, 31 March 1864.
                                               (NS2/16:792)

FROST James, b.1775, late Norwich, engineer, d. Brooklyn,
USA, 31 July 1851.   (NS36:442)

FROST Rev. Thomas, b. Pulham, Norfolk, 1759, to America 1785,
Rector, St Philip's Church, d. Charleston, SC, 1805. (75:187)

FRYE Sarah, b.1775, dau. late John Ravel Frye, Montserrat,
d. London, 9 March 1844.   (NS21:440)

FRYE William, President, Montserrat, d.17 May 1736.   (6:423)

FRYER James Joseph, solicitor, eldest s. late James Robert
Fryer, York, killed by Indians, Humboldt, Cal., 30 Oct.1850.
                                                     (NS35:222)

FUGE John, b.1687, d. Savanna-la-Mar, Jamaica, 9 May 1827.
                                                     (97:285)

FULFORD Alice Mary, only dau. Bishop of Montreal, m. Henry
Martyn Lower, Archdeacon NFD, Hemmingford, Canada East,
12 Aug.1858.   (NS2/5:412)

FULFORD ..., s. Francis Drummond Fulford, b. the See-house,
Montreal, 6 Jan.1863.   (NS2/14:367)

FULFORD ..., dau. Francis Drummond Fulford, b. the See-house,
Montreal, 25 May 1865.   (NS2/19:104)

FULLER Charlotte Matilda, b.1799, wid. Lt. Col. Francis
Fuller, 59th Reg., d. Coburg, Canada West, 14 Jan.1855.
                                                     (NS43:438)

FULLER Frances Elizabeth, yngs. dau. late Lt. Col. F Fuller,
59th Reg., m. Charles, eldest s. Charles Gifford, Exmouth,
Coburg, Canada West, 12 Jan.1855.   (NS43:408)

FULLER Henry, b.1781, late Attorney Gen., d. the Rookery,
Maraval, Trinidad, 23 Sep.1854.   (NS42:638)

FULLER Margaret, dau. Timothy Fuller, lawyer, Boston, Mass.,
w. Marquis d'Ossoli, drowned wreck Elizabeth, NY, July 1850.
                                                     (NS34:446)

FULLERTON Mr, English comedian, d. Philadelphia, March 1802.
                                                     (72:469)

FULTON Robert, b.1769, steam-boat inventor, d. NY, 1815.
                                                     (85:92)

FURBUR Thomas, ex Stock Exchange, d. Honduras, 2 Oct.1824.
                                                     (95:190)

FURLONG James, Lt. Col., 43rd Light Infantry, 2nd s. late
W Furlong, Wellshot House, Lanarks., m. Sophia, 2nd dau.
Henry Bolton, Chief Justice NFD., Toronto, 15 June 1842.
                                                     (NS18:199)

FURLONGE William jr, Councillor, Montserrat, d. Montserrat,
7 April 1813.   (83:660)

FURY Rebecca, b.1687, d. Falmouth, Jamaica, 7 April 1827.
                                                     (97:94)

FUSSELL John C, Warminster, Wilts., m. Margaret, dau. late
J B Skeete, President, Barbados, Brighton, 15 Dec.1864.
                                                     (NS2/18:98)

FYFE Annie Houldsworth, eldest dau. Rev. Charles Fyfe, m.
Cap. J P Cosby, 14th Reg., Port Royal, Jamaica, 26 Nov.1862.
                                                     (NS2/14:230)

FYFE Mrs Catherine, wid. William Fyfe, Jamaica, d. London,
4 Oct.1818.   (88:473)

FYFFE Charles, yngs. s. David Fyffe, Drumgeith, d. Jamaica,
15 Oct.1804.   (74:86)

FYFE Robert, s. Barclay Fyfe, merchant, Leith, d. Kingston,
Jamaica, 1 Aug.1794.   (64:958)

FYFE William, d. Kingston, Jamaica, 6 Jan.1810.   (80:284)

FYNMORE Sarah Garway, yngs. dau. late Lt. William Fynmore,
m. Edward Way, Montreal, Southampton, 22 April 1851.(NS35:659)

GADSDEN Christopher Edward, Bishop of SC, d.1852. (NS38:321)

GAGE Mrs Margaret, b.1734, dau. Peter Kemple, President, NJ,
m. T Gage, CinC, HM Forces NA (d.2 April 1788), d. London,
9 Feb.1824.   (94:380)

GAGE Col., NA, m. Miss Kemble, Brunswick, 1759.   (29:93)

GAINS ..., dau. G E Gains, surgeon, 6th Royal Reg., b.
Newcastle, Jamaica, 31 May 1864.   (NS2/17:231)

GAIRDNER Alexander, judge, Councillor, d. Tobago, Dec.1848.
                                                          (NS31:446)

GALBRAITH Archibald, d. WI, 1798.   (68:909)

GALBRAITH Rev. Edward, Hanover, Jamaica, d. Lucca, Jamaica,
19 June 1859.   (NS2/9:196)

GALBRAITH Jane Somers, eldest dau. late Colin Galbraith,
writer, Edinburgh, m. J K EDwards, editor 'Montreal Transcript'
on board John Bell, Montreal, 3 Aug.1859.   (NS2/7:414)

GALBRAITH Dr, d. Kingston, Jamaica, 1793.   (63:1152)

GALE Flora, b.1672, d. Savanna-la-Mar, Jamaica, 7 Feb.1792.
                                                          (62:479)

GALE William, Jamaica, d. London, 4 Dec.1795.   (65:1057)

GALES Joseph, b. Sheffield, 1786, printer. d. Washington,
28 July 1860.   (NS2/9:326)

GALLAGHER Martin, printer & publisher 'Trinidad Gazette',
d. Trinidad, 21 Oct.1819.   (89:278)

GALLAN Gilbert, St Vincent, d. London, 26 Jan.1809. (79:187)

GALLAWAY Tobias Wall, planter, St Kitts, d.2 Dec.1767.(37:611)

GALLIMORE Julia, dau. late J Gallimore, m. Sir John Gordon of
Earlston, Water Valley, Jamaica, Dec.1811.   (81:585)

GALLIMORE Miss, dau. Jarvis Gallimore, Jamaica, m. James
Scarlet, 28 July 1791.   (61:774)

GALVEZ Count, Viceroy of Mexico, d. April 1787.   (57:548)

GAMBLE Mrs, w. John Gamble, Richmond, Va., d. on passage
to Madeira, 5 Sep.1809.   (79:893)

GAMBLER John, late Lt. Gov. Bahamas, d.7 April 1782. (52:206)

GAMON Miss, London, m. Roger Hope Elletson, Lt. Gov. Jamaica,
17 April 1770.   (47:190)

GARDEN Dr Alexander, ex Charleston, SC, d. London, 15 April
1791.   (61:389)

GARDEN Judith, 2nd dau. late Dr Alexander Garden, Charleston,
SC, m. Alexander Fothringham, 24 Nov.1791.   (61:1061)

GARDINER Elizabeth, dau. David Gardiner of Kirktonhill, m.
William Richardson, late St Vincent, Kirktonhill, 7 Oct.1789.
                                                     (59:954)

GARDINER Robert Barlow, b.1818, Chief Engineer Roads & Bridges
Jamaica, d. Spanish Town, Jamaica, 14 June 1859. (NS2/7:314)

GARDNER Archibald, d. NY, 1798.   (68:1086)

GARDNER Charlotte, wid. James Gardner, sis. Sir Thomas
Picton, d. NY, May 1853.   (NS40:209)

GARDNER Dr Sylvester, b.1704, late America, m. Catherine, b.
1756, dau. Thomas Goldthwait, late Penobscot, NE, Poole,
26 Oct.1784.   (55:875)

GARLAND John Slyfield m. Tryphena Glanville, yngs. dau.
Samuel Glanville, ex Jamaica, Ottley St Mary, 28 Oct.1851.
                                                    (NS37:84)

GARLAND Mrs, b.1683, mo. Charles Garland, Customs Collector,
NFD., d. Harbour Grace, NFD, 1801.   (71:675)

GARNETT Rev. James, BA, Trinity College, Cambridge, s. Rev.
W Garnett, Barbados, d. Scarborough, Tobago, 4 Jan.1842.
                                                    (NS17:557)

GARRAWAY Frederick Hervey, b.1791, late Dominica, d. London,
3 July 1856.   (NS2/1:260)

GARRETT Rev. T, Vere, m. Sarah, 4th dau. late Rev. S H Stewart,
Trelawney, Spanish Town, Jamaica, 8 July 1854.   (NS42:385)

GARRIDO Maria Trinidad, b.1754, d. Havanna, 1860. (NS2/9:327)

GARTH Miss, only dau. Arthur Garth, Jamaica, m. James
Jefferies, Staunton Dew, Somerset, London, 6 Sep.1796.(66:789)

GASKIN John S, Bushy Park, Barbados, m. Mary Matilda, 3rd dau.
Thomas S Protheroe, Clifton, Jersey, 4 June 1844. (NS23:311)

GASKIN Mary Elizabeth, w. John Sheape Gaskin, Councillor,
Barbados, d. London, 18 March 1840.   (NS13:442)

GASKIN Sarah Eliza, yngs. dau. late Thomas Gaskin, Barbados,
m. Edward Gunning, 24 Aug.1819.   (89:272)

GATES Horatio, b.1728, Lt. Gen. Revolutionary Army, d. NY,
10 April 1806.   (76:583)

GATES Maj. Gen. Horatio, wife & son, d. America, Sep.1782.
                                                         (52:550)

GAYNER John, b.1746, magistrate, settled Jamaica 1760, d.
Lulloden Est., St Anne's, Jamaica, 3 May 1823.   (93:478)

GEDDES Alexander, Annandale, Jamaica, m. Frances, 4th dau.
late Thomas Evershed, Pallingham, Sussex, London, 22 Dec.
1852.   (NS39:305)

GEDDES Eleanor, w. George Geddes, Woodford Bridge, d.
Jamaica, 12 July 1852.   (NS38:433)

GEDDES Helen Josephine, dau. late George Geddes, Councillor,
m. Lt. James Bannatyne Blair, 6th Royal Reg., Halfwaytree
Church, Jamaica, 5 Oct.1865.   (NS3/1:117)

GEGG Rev. Henry W, b.1813, ex Trelawney, d. Rookesby Park,
St Anne's, Jamaica, 11 Aug.1850.   (NS33:102)

GEGG Rev. John Henry, b.1785, ex Uphill, Somerset, d. Jamaica
11 May 1842.   (NS19:215)

GEGG Rev. Joseph m. Anna Maria Louisa Levison Doria, eldest
dau. late William Gordon, MD, Jamaica, 7 Jan.1847. (NS27:541)

GEORGE Augustus, yngs. s. Philip George, Bristol, d. St Johns
NB, 22 March 1828.   (98:574)

GEORGE Margaret, b.1762, dau. Thomas Cochran, Halifax, NS,
wid. Sir Rupart George, d. Cheltenham, 22 March 1835.(105:556)

GIBBES Samuel Osborne, yngs. s. Sir Philip Gibbes, HM Receiver,
Grenada, d. Grenada, Jan.1807.   (77:376)

GIBBONS Caroline, 2nd dau. late Edward Howard Gibbons,
Arundel, Sussex, m. Benjamin Walker, St Thomas, Canada West,
London, Canada West, 6 Nov.1858.   (NS2/6:88)

GIBBON Mrs E, b. Port Royal, 1690, d. Jamaica, 1790.(60:1148)

GIBBONS Emily Craven, eldest dau. William Barton Gibbons,
Barbados, m. William Bellairs, Maj., 49th Reg., Barbados,
16 Sep.1857.   (NS2/3:673)

GIBBON George, Glasgow, d. St Anne's Bay, Jamaica, Oct.1800.
                                                        (70:1214)

GIBBONS Mary Bishop, w. William B Gibbons, 3rd dau. late
President Skeete, d. Mangrove Plant., Barbados, 5 July 1843.
                                                      (NS20:334)

GIBBONS Thomas, Tobago, d.1773.   (43:154)

GIBBONS Sir William, Speaker, Barbados Assembly, Lt. Gen.,
d. April 1760.   (30:297)

GIBBONS W B m. Anne Maxwell Hinds, eldest dau. late John Abel
Jackson, niece Samuel Hinds, late Speaker, Barbados Assembly,
Barbados, 5 April 1845.   (NS23:645)

GIBBS Daniel, b.1781, settled Grenada pre 1797, Councillor,
d. Grenada, 29 Dec.1837.   (NS9:447)

GIBBS Edward, b.1791, ex Brixton, Surrey, d. Grenada, 31 Aug.
1855.   (NS54:553)

GIBBS Sarah, b.1796, w. E Gibbs, London & Grenada, d. London,
12 July 1831.   (101:91)

GIBBS Mrs, w. Samuel Osborn Gibbs, formerly Miss Bishop, Exeter
d. Grenada, 20 Aug.1804.   (74:1071)

GIBNEY William Augustus, b.1823, eldest s. Dr Gibney,
Cheltenham, d. Kingston, Jamaica, 1848.   (NS30:110)

GIBSON A P, late US Consul St Petersburg, d. London, 30 Nov.
1852.   (NS39:108)

GIBSON Edward Inman, s. Rev. J G Gibson, Holybourne, Hants.,
d. Antigua, 1828.   (98:286)

GIBSON Georgina Eliza, dau. W Clarke, MD, Tweedside, w. Cap.
Edgar Gibson, 3rd Buffs, d. Barbados, 20 Nov.1865.(NS3/1:147)

GIBSON James, merchant, d. Boston, NE, Aug.1754.   (24:435)

GIBSON Dr Robert, d. Belvidere, Hanover, Jamaica, 4 June 1797.
                                                   (67:800)

GIFFORD Charles, eldest s. C Gifford, Exmouth, m. Frances
Elizabeth, yngs. dau. late Lt. Col. F Fuller, 59th Reg.,
Coburg, Canada West, 12 Jan.1855.   (NS43:408)

GILBERT Mrs Eliza (alias Lola Montez), b. Ireland, 1819, d. NY,
17 Jan.1861.   (NS2/10:349)

GILBERT John, d. Philadelphia, 1798.   (68:1086)

GILBERT Mary, b.1811, yngs. dau. James Gilbert, Lydd, Kent,
sis. James Gilbert, book-seller, London, d. Philadelphia,
24 Jan.1853.   (NS39:332)

GILBOURNE Rev. James Luffingham, b.1823, military chaplain,
d. Barbados, 31 Aug.1862.   (NS2/13:647)

GILES Miss, London, m. Joseph King, St Kitts, Jan.1772.(42:46)

GILLARD Eliza, yngs. dau. late Malcolm McNeill, 17th Lancers,
w. Josias Gillard, d. Grafton, Haldimand, Canada, 25 May 1865.
                                                   (NS2/19:122)

GILLBANKS Joseph, Dep. Post Master Gen., d. Bridgetown,
Barbados, 24 June 1858.   (NS2/5:313)

GILLESPIE Thomas, merchant, d. Kingston, Jamaica,
29 April 1799.   (69:621)

GILLIATT Thomas, b. England, 1764, settled Richmond, Va., d.
NY, 3 July 1810.   (80:189)

GILLMER Madeline Josephine Ellen, only dau. late J T Gillmer,
MD, Philadelphia, m. Reuben, 2nd s. Maj. Espinasse, Dundrum,
Co. Dublin, Gravesend, 11 Feb.1868.   (NS3/5:387)

GILLON John, b. London, 1749, late Dominica, d. London,
14 Jan.1810.   (80:89)

GILPIN ..., s. J Gilpin, Philadelphia, b. Lancaster, 1801.
                                                         (71:478)

GILPIN R, b.1760, customs officer, Falmouth, Jamaica, &
St Lucia, d. Falmouth, Jamaica, 25 May 1819.   (89:88)

GILSMAN Miss, d. Tobago, 8 April 1811.   (81:88)

GIRARD Stephen, Philadelphia, d.1832.   (102:287)

GIRDLESTONE Charles, s. Rev. H Girdlestone, Landford, m.
Eliza West, yngs. dau. Lt. Col. Chads, President, Virgin
Islands, Tortula, 13 March 1854.   (NS41:636)

GIRDLESTONE George William, b.1809, eldest s. late Rev. W E
Girdlestone, Kelling & Salthouse, d. London, Canada West,
20 April 1858.   (NS44:105)

GIRDWOOD Gilbert Prout, surgeon, Grenadier Guards, m. Fanny
Merriman, eldest dau. Thomas E Blackwell, Clifton, England,
& Montreal, Montreal, 9 April 1862.   (NS2/12:773)

GIRDWOOD ..., s. G P Girdwood, surgeon, Grenadier Guards, b.
Montreal, 20 April 1864.   (NS2/16:789)

GITTENS Martha Elizabeth, b.1777, dau. late Benjamin Gittens,
Chief Judge Barbados, Bow, Middlesex, 5 Dec.1854.   (NS43:110)

GIUSEPPI Matthew, surgeon, London & Trinidad, d.13 Jan.1846.
                                                         (NS25:219)

GLADSTONE Alexander, b.1809, ex St Elizabeth, Jamaica, d.
Carlisle, 18 Aug.1856.   (NS2/1:521)

GLANVILLE Tryphena, yngs. dau. Samuel Glanville, ex Jamaica,
m. John Slyfield Garland, Ottley St Mary, 28 Oct.1851.
                                                         (NS37:84)

GLASGOW George Mark, ex Cap., RA, d. Kingston, Canada West,
26 Jan.1851.   (NS35:454)

GLASGOW Mrs, w. Col. Glasgow, RA, sis. Mrs T Esdaile, London,
d. Quebec, 1810.   (80:388)

GLASS James W, b.1784, HM Consul, d. Tampico, Mexico,
12 Nov.1848.   (NS31:223)

GLEN William Cunningham, barrister, m. Eliza, eldest dau.
John Nethersole, Jamaica, London, 15 Dec.1848.   (NS31:200)

GLEN Dr, bro. Gov. SC, m. wid. James Grame, late Chief
Justice SC, 1755.   (25:428)

GLENIE Louisa Locke, eldest dau. Archdeacon Glenie, m. Arthur
Foulkes, Jamaica, London, 15 June 1841.   (NS16:301)

GLOSTER Archibald, Attorney Gen. Trinidad, m. Miss Thompson,
Tooting, Surrey, 22 Oct.1806.   (76:978)

GLOSTER Russel, wid. Archibald Gloster, MD, Antigua, d.
London, 2 July 1808.   (78:661)

GLOSTER Sarah, b.1786, wid. Archibald Gloster, Chief Justice
Dominica, d. Nantes, 15 Dec.1855.   (NS43:327)

GLOSTER William Jarvis, s. Archibald Gloster, Attorney Gen.
Trinidad, d. London, 22 Sep.1806.   (76:984)

GLOVER William, b.1794, yngr. s. Rev. Richard Glover, Ilford,
Essex, d. WI, 1810.   (80:395)

GLYN ..., dau. Cap. J P Carr Glyn, Rifle Brigade, b. Quebec,
30 July 1867.   (NS3/4:381)

GODDARD James, Comm. Dept., d. Quebec, 11 Aug.1814. (84:400)

GODDEN Rev. Thomas, late Baptist missionary, Spanish Town,
Jamaica, d. Bristol, 30 Nov.1824.   (95:187)

GODFRY Arthur Henry, d. Canada West, 12 March 1857.(NS2/2:737)

GODFREY Robert William, d. Sherbrooke, Canada, 3 Aug.1851.
                                                (NS36:442)

GODHARD Norris, Inspector Gen. Dept., m. Christiana, only dau.
Kenneth Cameron, Asst. Comm. Gen., Toronto, 3 June 1858.
                                                (NS2/5:304)

GODWIN Joseph, Assemblyman, Bahamas, d.1772.   (42:151)

GOLDFINCH Cap., Oxford Milita, m. Miss Austin, dau. late Rev.
Hugh William Austin, Barbados, Bath, 17 Jan.1807.   (77:88)

GOLDTHWAIT Catherine, b.1756, dau. Thomas Goldthwait, late
Penobscot, NE, m. Dr Sylvester Gardner, b.1704, ex America,
Poole, 26 Oct.1784.   (55:875)

GOLDWYER George, yngs. s. late Henry Goldwyer, Bristol, d.
on passage from WI, 29 June 1826.   (96:190)

GOMEZ Antonio, ex Councillor, Trinidad, d. Philadelphia,
20 June 1843.   (NS20:334)

GOMEZ Philip, Registrar, Trinidad, eldest s. late Antonio
Gomez, judge, Trinidad, d. Port of Spain, 23 July 1866.
                                                (ns3/2:695)

GOOCH Henry, b.1817, 2nd s. Henry Gooch, Camberwell, d.
Jamaica, 21 May 1845.   (NS24:214)

GOOD Charles, 2nd s. Rev. Henry Good, Wimbourne, Dorset, m.
Alice, 4th dau. James Douglas, Gov. BC, Victoria, Vancouver
Island, 31 Aug.1861.   (NS2/11:675)

GOODHUE Maria Elizabeth, dau. E J Goodhue, London, Canada West,
m. Lt. Alexander Tovey, RE, s. Alexander Tovey, 24th Reg.,
London, Canada West, 14 April 1864.   (NS2/16:792)

GOODRICH Edward, Councillor, Bermuda, d. Bermuda, 1817.
                                                  (87:573)

GOODRICH Margaret, b.1730, wid. John Goodrich, Va., d.
Topsham, Devon, 1810.   (80:494)

GOODRICH Samuel Griswold (alias Peter Parley), b. Conn., 1793,
author, d. NY, 9 May 1860.   (NS2/9:100)

GOODSIR Joseph, customs officer, St Lucia, m. Louisa, dau.
P Berne, Castries, St Lucia, 24 Nov.1841.   (NS17:321)

GOODSIR Thomas, b.1827, s. Thomas Goodsir, customs officer,
Barbados, d. Greenwich, 9 May 1847.   (NS28:104)

GOODWIN Charles, yngs. s. late Samuel Goodwin, Spath,
Stafford, d. Antigua, 1810.   (80:500)

GOODWIN George, b.1671, d. Jamaica, April 1776.   (46:240)

GOODWIN Matthew, St Kitts, d. London, 1773.   (43:622)

GOODYEAR Charles, b.1801, inventor, d. NY, 1 July 1860
                                                  (NS2/9:323)

GORDON Alexander, Belmont, Tobago, yngr. bro. Baron Gordon,
the Exchequer, Scotland, d. Bath, 11 Jan.1801.   (71:92)

GORDON Catherine, 2nd dau. Alexander Gordon, Campbelltown, m.
Walter Irvine, Tobago, Deebank, 1797.   (67:798)

GORDON Charles, British Vice Consul, d. Port-au-Prince,
29 Aug.1826.   (96:477)

GORDON Mrs Frances, b.1753, mo. late William Whitehorne,
Laurence Park, Jamaica, d. Jamaica, 30 Oct.1837. (NS7:447)

GORDON Francis, Kenmore, Jamaica, only bro. Sir John Gordon of
Earlston, d. Spanish Town, Jamaica, 27 July 1823. (93:647)

GORDON George, President Berbice Court Justice, d. Berbice,
15 Nov.1820.   (91:185)

GORDON George W, Jamaica, m. Maria Jane, dau. late W T Shannon,
Co. Clare, London, 28 Oct.1846.   (NS27:193)

GORDON George, b.1789, s. late John Gordon, Bristol, d. Moor-
park, Jamaica, 23 May 1850.   (NS34:454)

GORDON James Alexander, d. Jamaica, 1757.   (27:338)

GORDON James, ex Tobago, d. London, 23 March 1806.   (76:385)

GORDON Jane Eliza, yngs. dau. late G G Gordon, Antigua, niece
late Sir W Ashton, m. Cap. Knox, 11 Dec.1817.   (87:628)

GORDON John, Assemblyman, St Anne, Jamaica, d.1774.   (44:494)

GORDON of EARLSTON Sir John, m. Julia, dau. late J Gallimore,
Water Valley, Jamaica, Dec.1811.   (81:585)

GORDON John Salmon, 96th Reg., m. Frances Charlotte, 3rd dau.
late Rev. John McIntyre, St James, Jamaica, Hackney, 22 Feb.
1849.   (NS31:535)

GORDON Mary, b.1764, wid. William Gordon, Banff & Dominica,
d. Eastry, Kent, 16 July 1854.   (NS42:314)

GORDON Peter, Grenada, 'killed by Mr Proudfoot in a duel',
1768.   (38:446)

GORDON Robert, Demerara, ex Gov. Berbice, d. Martinique,
10 Jan.1814.   (84:515)

GORDON Robert, ex Jamaica, d. Windsor, 12 Feb.1833. (103:187)

GORDON Robert, b.1740, President, St Vincent, d. St Vincent,
16 Sep.1830.   (100:381)

GORDON William, Montego Bay, Jamaica, d.1766.   (36:390)

GORDON Mrs, w. John Gordon, d. NY, 11 May 1798.   (68:903)

GORDON Mrs, w. Cap. Gordon, QM Trinidad, d. Trinidad, 13 Sep.
1817.   (87:561)

GORE Francis, b.1767, ex Gov. Bermuda & Upper Canada, d.
Brighton, 3 Nov.1852.   (NS38:661)

GORE James Arthur, Cap., 71st Highland Light Infantry,
eldest s. Lt. Gen. Charles Gore, CO NS, m. Catherine Louise,
3rd dau. Col Bazalgette, ex Dep. QM Gen. NS, Halifax, NS,
19 July 1854.   (NS42:499)

GOULD Arthur, Councillor, NS, Militia Col., d. Halifax, NS,
1792.   (62:576)

GOULD Maj. Samuel, b.1767, ex Senator, d. Branford, Conn.,
1848.   (NS30:671)

GOULD William, ex Glasgow, Lt., 5th WI Reg., d. Belize, Bay
of Honduras, 11 May 1801.   (72:181)

GOULDSBURY Valesius Skipton, MD, eldest s. Valesius Gouldsbury,
Longford, Ireland, gs. I A Gouldsbury, Auchnogare, m. Isabel
Charlotte, 3rd dau. late Edmund Thomas Perrott, Worcs., ggs.
Lord John St John, Barbados, 8 Sep.1867.   (NS2/17:647)

GOURLAY Dr William, physician, Madeira, m. Catherine, dau. Maj. Philip Van Costland, NY, Madeira, 25 April 1787.(57:637)

GOVETT Mrs, d. St Kitts, 23 Jan.1794.   (64:385)

GOWDIE Thomas Ovington, b.1817, s. David Gowdie, silk gauze manufacturer, Glasgow, d. Tobago, 28 Feb.1854.   (NS42:407)

GOWER S L, Little Hempston, Devon, m. Agnes Bonham, 3rd dau. late E Skeete, Barbados, Wells, 1 Sep.1840.   (NS14:424)

GRAEME Frances Sarah, eldest dau. Maj. Lawrence Graeme, Lt. Gov. Tobago, m. John Paul Thornton, Col. Sec., 3rd s. late Thomas Thornton, Constantinople, nephew Sir Edward Thornton, Tobago, 25 May 1846.   (NS26:196)

GRAME Mrs, wid. James Grame, ex Chief Justice SC, m. Dr Glen, bro. Gov. SC, 1755.   (25:428)

GRAHAM Brice, b.1783, ex merchant, Kingston, Jamaica, d. Latimer's Pen, Jamaica, 19 May 1849.   (NS32:334)

GRAHAM Edward, 2nd s. Sir Robert Graham, Esk, Cumberland, m. Adelaide Elizabeth, yngs. dau. late James Dillon Tully, MD, Inspector Gen. Hospitals Jamaica, London, 3 Aug.1844.
                                                   (NS22:422)

GRAHAM Sir Edward, b.1820, d. Montreal, 27 May 1864.
                                                 (NS2/17:122)

GRAHAM George, ex St Croix, d. Glasgow, 13 June 1798.(68:542)

GRAHAM James, ex 64th Reg., d. SC, 1803.   (73:87)

GRAHAM James F, Assemblyman, St Thomas-in-the-Vale, Jamaica, d. Villa Pen, Spanish Town, Jamaica, 1 Feb.1820.   (90:281)

GRAHAM James, merchant, m. Harriett Charlotte Sarabella, eldest dau. James Cabot, Mexico City, British Legation, Mexico, 24 Sep.1846.   (NS27:78)

GRAHAM Joanna, b.1702, d. Rio Bueno, Jamaica, 1827.   (97:94)

GRAHAM John, settled Jamaica 1749, d. Kingston, Jamaica, 15 March 1799.   (69:527)

GRAHAM Margaret, eldest dau. Col. C D Graham, Lt. Gov.St Mawe, m. Michael Beniques Clare, MD, Physician Gen. Jamaica, Twickenham Park, Jamaica, 18 March 1817.   (87:465)

GRAHAM Robert, Auckland, NZ, m. Sophia, dau. Edward Swann, surgeon, Weedon Military Prison, San Francisco, 13 June 1850.
                                                   (NS34:540)

GRAHAM William Martin, b.1827, eldest s. late Joseph Graham, Port of Spain, Trinidad, d. Stonehouse, Jan.1845. (NS23:216)

GRAHAM ..., s. G GRaham, 21st Fusiliers, b. Barbados, 11 May 1861.   (NS2/11:77)

GRAHAM Miss, only dau. late Charles Graham, Williamsfield, Jamaica, m. Maj. McDonald, London, 27 April 1805.   (75:485)

GRANGER William, d. Boston, NE, 7 July 1756.   (26:361)

GRANT Alexander, b.1734, d. Gross Point, Detroit, 1814.
                                                      (84:299)

GRANT Amelia, dau. Harry Grant, American Consul Northern
Scotland, d. Baltimore, 6 Oct.1803.   (73:993)

GRANT Andrew, d. Grenada, 1780.   (50:153)

GRANT Barbara Mary, yngs. dau. G Colquhoun Grant, Treasurer,
St Vincent, m. Cap. Dawson Stockley Warren, 14th Reg., Morne
Est., St Lucia, 24 Feb.1863.   (NS2/14:515)

GRANT Caroline Mayer, 2nd dau. George Colquhoun Grant, m.
Rev. Alexander, 4th s. late J R Dasent, Attorney Gen.
St Vincent, St Vincent, 13 Oct.1847.   (NS29:80)

GRANT Charlotte, b.1791, wid. Charles Grant, Trinidad &
Martinique, d. Dawlish, 27 Dec.1859.   (NS2/8:198)

GRANT Colquhoun, Jamaica, m. Margaret, dau. late Dr Abernethie,
physician, Banff, 28 Jan.1798.   (68:168)

GRANT David, Finsbury, d. Lucca, Jamaica, 13 May 1842.
                                                     (NS18:335)

GRANT Edward Butler Thomas, b.1752, ex merchant, Manchester,
d. Shrewsbury, NJ, 28 Nov.1825.   (96:95)

GRANT E C, Cap., 60th Rifles, m. Hester Maria, 2nd dau. late
A C Hamilton, St Catherine, Canada West, Hamilton, Canada
West, 2 June 1866.   (NS3/2:252)

GRANT Frederick, b.1779, ex Quebec, d. Mount Cyrus, Montrose,
Angus, 1 Nov.1842.   (NS19:109)

GRANT George Cole, surgeon, 7th s. Rev. Dr Grant, Dundee, d.
Jamaica, June 1801.   (71:960)

GRANT Gregory, Quebec, m. Miss Wood, London, 1777.   (48:606)

GRANT Harry, Charleston, SC, d. NY, 18 Dec.1814.   (85:373)

GRANT Henrietta, dau. late Andrew Grant, London & Grenada,
d. Clifton, Glocs., 30 Sep.1840.   (NS14:672)

GRANT Isabella Elizabeth, only dau. late A Grant of Tulloch-
griban, m. Maj. Gen. Sir Lewis Grant, Gov. Trinidad,
Trinidad, 31 July 1832.   (102:263)

GRANT James, s. Rev. Grant, Kilmanivaig, d. NY, 9 Sep.1799.
                                                      (69:993)

GRANT James, b.1773, St Vincent, d. London, 5 June 1837.
                                                      (NS8:99)

GRANT John, Kilgraston, ex Chief Justice Jamaica, d. Edinburgh
1793.   (63:377)

GRANT John, b.1778, Wallebow, St Vincent, d. London, 3 March
1820.   (90:284)

GRANT J M, Lt., RE, yngs. s. Col. Grant, RA, m. Emily, dau.
A Cumming, St Vincent, 19 April 1849.   (NS32:84)

GRANT Lachlan, d. Jamaica, 1791.   (61:1065)

GRANT Maj. Gen. Sir Lewis, Gov. Trinidad, m. Isabella
Elizabeth, only dau. late A Grant of Tullochgrigan,
Trinidad, 31 July 1832.   (102:263)

GRANT Peter, Sgt.-at-Arms, House of Assembly, s. Sir Ludovick
Grant of Dalvey, d. Salt Ponds, Jamaica, 25 Aug.1820.(90:473)

GRANT Virginia, w. James Meyer Grant, d. St Lucia, 12 Jan.1868.
                                               (NS3/5:396)

GRANT Mrs, w. Peter Grant, Jamaica, d. London, 9 May 1807.
                                               (77:493)

GRANT Cap., b.1814, ex Stourbridge, Worcs., d. Houston, Texas,
28 Dec.1852.   (NS39:656)

GRANT ..., dau. Cap. J M GRant, RE, b. New Westminster, BC,
2 Aug.1862.   (NS2/13:767)

GRANTHAM Douglas, 23rd Fusiliers, eldest s. Stephen Grantham,
Ryders Wells, Sussex, m. Amelia Louisa, yngr. dau. Cap.
Blenkarne, Ordnance Dept., ex 14th Reg., Montreal, 10 Nov.
1848.   (NS31:80)

GRANTHAM Rev. Thomas Aubrey, MA, 2nd s. late John Grantham,
Croydon, Surrey, missionary, Yarmouth, NS, 1816, d. Boston,
USA, 1841.   (NS16:214)

GRASSETT William, Councillor, Barbados, m. Eliza, dau. late
J H Barrow, 26 March 1818.   (88:368)

GRASSIE Thomas Ritchie, Halifax, NS, m. Mary Jane, 2nd dau.
Frederick de Lisle, London, 17 March 1842.   (NS17:541)

GRAVES Ada, only ch. Charles Twisleton Graves, ex Cap.,
Royal Irish Fusiliers, ggdau. 10th Lord Saye & Sele, m. Cap.
Douglas Alleyne, 37th Reg., eldest s. late Henry Alleyne,
Barbados, London, 11 Jan.1865.   (NS2/18:237)

GRAVES Nancy m. Cap. William Graves, Caswell Co, NC, 1820.
                                               (90:83)

GRAVES Cap. William m. Nancy Graves, Caswell Co, NC, 1820.
                                               (90:83)

GRAY Rev. Benjamin G, military chaplain, d. St John, NB, 1854.
                                               (NS41:552)

GRAY Charles William m. Rosalie, only dau. Nathaniel T Butterfield, Bermuda, Tonbridge Wells, 7 Sep.1843.   (NS20:538)

GRAY Elizabeth, dau. late Robert Gray, judge, PEI, m. Chief
Justice Jarvis, Charlottetown, PEI, 12 Dec.1843. (NS21:309)

GRAY Fanny, yngs. dau. Dr Gray, Bishop of Bristol, d.Barbados,
20 Feb.1827.   (96:478)

GRAY Henry August, b.1815, Public Treasurer, d. Belize,
Honduras, 14 Nov.1846.   (NS27:222)

GRAY John, London & Jamaica, m. Mrs Carlisle, Antigua, July
1752.   (22:336)

GRAY Rev. John William Dering, Trinity, St Johns, NB, d.
Halifax, NS, 1 Feb.1868.   (NS3/5:542)

GRAY John W, Port Maria, Jamaica, d.1854.   (NS43:218)

GRAY Joseph Bowers, b.1819, ex Chalmsford, Essex, Principal
Berwick College, d. South Berwick, Maine, 1 Dec.1856.
                                                  (NS2/2:116)

GRAY Martha Anne, wid. Rev. Archibald Gray, d. Halifax, NS,
3 June 1862.   (NS2/13:115)

GRAY Rebecca Harriott, w. Rev. John Gray, dau. late John
Fraser, Farraline, advocate, d. Kingston, Canada West,
10 Feb.1851.   (NS35:455)

GRAY T, St Kitts, eldest dau. Marquis of Tweedale, d.1757.
                                                    (27:338)

GRAY Cap. Walter, Com. American brigantine, d.21 July 1767.
                                                    (37:383)

GRAY William, ex Provost Marshal Jamaica, Port Royal Assemblyman, d. Jamaica, April 1788.   (58:658)

GRAYDON George, Col., RE, d. Montreal, 27 Jan.1852.(NS37:425)

GRAYFOOT Rachel Susan, only dau. late John Grayfoot, m.
Plunkett Standish Lyne Preston, merchant, Bridgetown,
Barbados, 3 Jan.1846.   (NS25:421)

GREATHEAD Richard & wife, St Kitts, d.23 Dec.1763. (33:619)

GREEN Annie Eliza, dau. late Henry Green, Titley, Herts., m.
William Stewart, PEI, Pavenham, 4 May 1844.   (NS21:646)

GREEN G W G, Lt. Col., 2nd East Bengal Fusiliers, 3rd s. Rev.
G W Green, Carmarthen, m. Ellen, yngs. dau. William Carter,
Troy, Jamaica, London, 16 June 1859.   (NS2/9:82)

GREENE Henry Charles, b.1821, 4th s. Benjamin Greene, Bury
St Edmund, d. St Kitts, 7 Aug.1840.   (NS14:446)

GREEN Joseph, ex Councillor, Boston, NE, d. London, 11 Dec.
1780.   (50:590)

GREEN J, ex Lt. Col., 26th Reg., d. Quebec, 1835. (105:558)

GREEN Nathaniel, Maj. Gen. US Army, d. Savanna, 19 June 1786.
                                                    (56:713)

GREEN William, Gov. RI, d.1758.   (28:244)

GREENE William. ex Sec. Grand Canal Co., Dublin, d.Baltimore,
1805.   (75:677)

GREEN W, d. Jamaica, 1812.   (82:603)

GREEN Maj. Gen., d. Shrewsbury, USA, 14 Sep.1811.   (81:657)

GREENSHIELDS Janet, 2nd dau. Thomas Greenshields, m. Andrew
Houston Young, Quebec, Kilmarnock, 12 Jan.1841.   (NS15:200)

GREENSILL Hannah Maria Anne, eldest dau. John Greensill, HM
Ordnance storekeeper, Purfleet, m. William Douglas Hall
Baillie, 24thReg., eldest s. Thomas Baillie, Surveyor Gen.,
NB, West Thurrock, Essex, 11 July 1854.   (NS42:386)

GREENWAY Dr Jchn, b.1759, settled Dominica 1788, d. Rosseau,
Dominica, 11 Dec.1828.   (99:190)

GREENWAY John, NY, late Monte Video & Rio de Janeiro, m.
Martha Elizabeth Anne, eldest dau. Lt. George Courtney
Greenway, RN, Clifton, 30 March 1853.   (NS39:647)

GREENWAY Martha Elizabeth Anne, eldest dau. Lt. George
Courtney Greenway, RN, m. John Greenway, NY, late Monte
Video & Rio de Janeiro, Clifton, 30 March 1853.   (NS39:647)

GREIG John, b. Scotland, 1781, settled NY, 1799, d. Canan-
daigua, NY, 1 April 1858.   (NS2/4:682)

GREIG Walter, ex Jamaica, d.17 Feb.1784.   (54:236)

GREIG Miss, dau. late W Greig, St Vincent, m. Lt. Col. White,
80th Reg., 1810.   (80:383)

GRENHOLME Laurence, 4th Bat., 60th Reg., m. Miss Wadman,
Bridgetown, WI, May 1790.   (60:667)

GRESHAM Caroline, 2nd dau. Robert Gresham, Beds., m. John
Alleyne Simmons, Vaucluse, Barbados, Crampton, Beds.,
8 Feb.1855.   (NS43:410)

GREY Alexander, Attorney Gen. Quebec, d. London, 7 Dec.1790.
                                                    (60:1215)

GREY Rev. William, chaplain Bishop NFD, m. Harriet, yngs. dau.
Rev. F H White, Abbot's Anne, Hants., 25 June 1849.(NS32:313)

GREY ..., s. F D Grey, Maj., 63rd Reg., b. Fredericton, NB,
1 Feb.1861.   (NS2/10:329)

GRIERSON James m. Mrs Isabel Parker, wid. late Henry Parker,
Jamaica, London, 1788.   (58:269)

GRIFFIN Richard Griffith, b.1827, 3rd s. late Cap. C W Griffin,
RN, Falmouth, d. Mexico, 3 Jan.1853.   (NS39:559)

GRIFFITH Ann Bell Grant, 4th dau. William Griffith, barrister,
Barbados, m. Michael Angelo, War Office, London, 24 April 1862.
                                                   (NS2/12:775)
GRIFFITH Anna Eliza, only ch. late R S Griffith, MD, m.
Rev. Preston Bruce Austin, Demerara, s. Rev. W S Austin, Essex,
Barbados, 9 Dec.1854.   (NS43:301)

GRIFFITHS Edward, Solicitor Gen. 'of the ceded islands',
d. Antigua, 24 Jan.1766.   (36:47)

GRIFFITH Rev. G, Trelawney, Jamaica, d.1846.   (NS25:327)

GRIFFITH Susan, dau. Rear Adm. Griffith, Newbrook House, Hants.,
m. Cap. Charles C Johnson, 85th Light Infantry, 3rd s. Sir
John Johnson, Montreal, 8 Jan.1818.   (88:81)

GRIFFITH Thomas Harrison d. Spanish Town, Jamaica, 28 June
1795.   (65:791)

GRIGGS John, b.1788, eldest s. James Griggs, Enfield, Middlesex, surgeon, d. Surinam, 25 Dec.1809.   (79:478)

GRISWOLD John, b.1784, merchant shipowner, d. Hyde Park, NY,
6 Aug.1856.   (NS2/1:520)

GRISWOLD R, Gov. Conn., d. Norwich, NA, 1812.   (83:183)

GROSETT Mary Henrietta, eldest dau. John Rock Grosett, ex
Lacock Abbey, Wilts., d. Petersfield, Jamaica, 31 Jan.1833.
                                                      (103:479)
GROSSETT Walter R, d. St George, Jamaica, 1824.   (94:382)

GROVES Thomas, s. John Groves, London, d. Grenada, 1796.
                                                       (66:969)
GROVES Webber, b.1695, d. NH, Jan.1793.   (63:281)

GRUBB Ann Elizabeth, 5th dau. late John Grubb, ex Horsenden
House, Bucks., late Charlottetown, m. Thomas Heath Haviland,
Charlottetown, PEI, 5 Jan.1847.   (NS27:541)

GRUMLY Mary Ann, eldest dau. late William Grumly, of David
Ross & Co., Tortula, Oystermouth, Glam., 16 Feb.1852.(NS37:426)

GRYMES Henry, Bath Co., Va., d.26 April 1804.   (74:784)

GUILD Dr George, Tobago, d. on passage to Baltimore,
30 Sep.1801.   (71:1211)

GUILDING Clarissa Elizabeth, 3rd dau. late Rev. Landsdown
Guilding, St Vincent, m. Denzil John Holt Ibbetson, 3rd s.
Denzil Ibbetson, Dep. Comm. Gen. Malta, Bromley, Kent,
28 May 1846.   (NS26:197)

GUISEPPI Louise Amenaiche, 2nd dau. Jose Guiseppi, Consul to
Venezuela, m. Lt. Lionel M Fraser, 41st Reg., Port of Spain,
Trinidad, 21 Nov.1857.   (NS2/4:207)

GULSTON Mrs, wid. Joseph Gulston, sis. Rev. Woodham,
St Catherine, Jamaica, d.20 Nov.1806.   (77:179)

GUNNING Edward m. Sarah Eliza, yngs. dau. late Thomas Gaskin,
Barbados, 24 Aug.1819.   (89:272)

GUNTER Henry, b.1814, ex Liverpool, d. San Francisco, 19 Oct.
1856.   (NS2/2:117)

GUNTHORPE Jeanetta Maria, 3rd dau. late Rev. William
Gunthorpe, Antigua, m. Frederick, 3rd s. late Ashton Warner,
Chief Justice Trinidad, London, 20 June 1843.   (NS20:200)

GUNTHORPE Mr, Antigua, d. on passage to England, 11 June 1766.
(36:342)

GURLEY Mrs, wid. Peter Gurley, St Vincent, dau. Sir William
Johnston of Custobers, Scotland, d. Needham Market, 23 March
1819.   (88:378)

GUTHRIE William, ex Jamaica, d. Edinburgh, 1814.   (84:195)

GWYER Matthew Wright, 3rd s. William O Gwyer, Bristol, d.
St Vincent, 26 March 1842.   (NS18:335)

GZOWSKI Helen, eldest dau. C S Gzowski, Toronto, m. Cap. E P
Bingham Turner, RA, yngs. s. late Lt. Gen. Turner, 19th Reg.,
Toronto, 20 Aug.1863.   (NS2/15:499)

HABERSHAM James, President, Georgia, d.1775.   (45:502)

HACKETT Ada Campbell, yngs. dau. James Hackett, Lennoxville,
m. John Adams, eldest s. late Jonathan W Walsh, Walsh Park,
Tipperary, Lennoxville, Canada East, 2 Sep.1861. (NS2/11:557)

HADDEN Ann, b.1785, w. David Hadden, d. NY, 3 Sep.1845.
(NS24:666)

HADDOW James, London, d. Grenada, 11 Sep.1802.   (72:116)

HAFFENDEN Mary Anderson, w. Thomas Haffenden jr, Hanwell, d.
Jamaica, 8 Nov.1847.   (NS29:334)

HAFFIE ..., d. Jamaica, 22 Jan.1753.   (23:51)

HAGART Charles jr., ex St Thomas, d. London, 12 Dec.1812.
(82:672)

HAGARTY James, b.1790, US Consul Liverpool, d. Lancaster,
24 Aug.1844.   (NS22:443)

HAGERMAN C A, judge, Canada, m. Caroline, 3rd dau. late
William George Daniel Tyssen, Foley House, Kent, London,
12 Aug.1846.   (NS26:420)

HAGERMAN Christopher Alexander, b.1792, judge, Upper Canada,
d. Toronto, 14 May 1847.   (NS28:223)

HAGERMAN Emily, dau. Justice Hagerman, d. Toronto, 1842.
(NS18:333)

HAGUE Rev. D G, Moravian missionary, d. Jamaica, 1825.(95:479)

HAGUE James, 2nd s. Barnard Hague, York, d. River Otanebee,
Upper Canada, 3 March 1843.   (NS20:222)

HAITI Prince John of, b.St Lucia, 1786, Grand Adm. Haiti, d.
Haiti, 1817, buried St Lucia.   (87:573)

HALDANE ..., dau. John Haldane, St Kitts, m. Thomas Foster,
MP Bossiney, Cornwall, 2 June 1741.   (11:331)

HALDANE Gov., Jamaica, d.26 July 1759.   (29:497)

HALE Edward, b.1789, yngs. s. Gen. John Hale, Yorks., d.
Quebec, 15 Oct.1862.   (NS2/13:789)

HALE Harriet, yngs. dau. John Hale, Receiver Gen. Lower
Canada, m. John Orlebar, RN, Quebec, 5 Feb.1838. (NS9:539)

HALE ..., s. John Hale, b. Quebec, 9 Jan.1800.   (70:384)

HALE William Amherst, ex Cap., 52nd Light Infantry, d. St Ann,
Canada, Sep.1844.   (NS22:670)

HALIBURTON Alexander Fowden m. Augusta Louisa Neville, dau.
Justice Haliburton, Windsor, NS, 27 June 1854.   (NS42:384)

HALIBURTON Elizabeth, yngs. dau. Sir Brenton Haliburton, late
Chief Justice, m. Richard M Poulden, ex Maj., RA, Halifax, NS,
5 June 1861.   (NS2/11:196)

HALIBURTON Louisa, w. Justice Haliburton, only dau. late Cap.
W L Neville, 19th Light Dragoons, d. Clifton, Windsor, NS,
27 Nov.1841.   (NS18:331)

HALL Ann, dau. late Thomas Dehany Hall, Kingston, Jamaica, d.
London, 17 Oct.1859.   (NS2/7:654)

HALL Charles, d. Pleasant Prospect, Liguena, Kingston, Jamaica,
25 Aug.1795.   (65:968)

HALL Rev. Clarence, St Dorothy's, Jamaica, eldest s. Cap.
Edward Hall, RN, d. Marlie, Jamaica, 23 Aug.1867. (NS3/2:682)

HALL Copley, d. Jamaica, 1790.   (60:476)

HALL David m. Margaret, dau. John Foster Allen, Barbados,
21 May 1814.   (81:187)

HALL Edward, Attorney Gen. Grenades, d. Antigua, 1766.(36:247)

HALL Emily, 3rd dau. late Samuel Hall, Seigneur of Chambly, m.
Thomas Richard Mills, ex Lt., 1st Dragoon Guards, eldest s.
William Mills, Saxhamhall, Suffolk, Chambly, 31 May 1843.
                                                  (NS20:199)

HALL Enoch, Newbiggin, Northumberland, Chancellor SC,
d. 18 Oct.1753.   (23:492)

HALL Frederick, Lt., RA, s. Lt. Col. Hall, RE, m. Amelia
Caroline, eldest dau. Lt. Col. Montgomery Williams, RE,
Bermuda, 15 Feb.1855.   (NS43:519)

HALL George Abbot, Customs Collector, d. Charleston, SC,
1 Aug.1791.   (61:969)

HALL James, Jamaica, m. Elizabeth, dau. Lord Lisle, Dawlish,
Devon, 1800.   (70:1284)

HALL Jasper, d. Jamaica, 24 Nov.1796.   (67:252)

HALL Margaret Salter, w. David Hall, London, dau. Forster
Alleyne, Barbados, d. 7 May 1823.   (93:572)

HALL Nathaniel, b. Bristol, 1747, Customs Collector New
Providence, d. Nassau, 8 July 1807.   (77:977)

HALL Susannah, dau. late William Hall, Kingston, Jamaica, m.
James Henry, St Anne's, Jamaica, Assemblyman, 1801. (71:763)

HALL William James, Councillor, d. Jamaica, 18 Dec.1827.
                                                         (98:286)

HALL Mr, ex singer Covent Garden, d. Morant Bay, Jamaica,
June 1817.   (87:184)

HALL Mrs, b.1751, wid. William Hall, Jamaica, d. Bury
St Edmonds, Suffolk, 30 Dec.1842.   (NS19:221)

HALLECK Fitz Greene, b.1790, poet, d. NY, 19 Nov.1867.
                                                       (NS3/5:113)

HALLETT Sophia Griswold, 5th dau. late James Nainby Hallett,
m. Edmond Baldwin, NY, 18 Sep.1843.   (NS20:539)

HALLEWELL Edmond G, Lt., 20th Reg., m. Sophia Lonsdale, 3rd
dau. Lt. Col. Reid, Gov. Bermuda, Bermuda, 11 May 1843.
                                                        (NS20:87)

HALLEY Thomas. b. Pontefract, Yorks., merchant, d. Petersburg,
Va., 13 July 1802.   (72:878)

HALLIBURTON Brenton, Chief Justice NS, d. Halifax, 16 July
1860.   (NS2/9:324)

HALLIDAY William, St Kitts, d.1759.   (29:497)

HALLIDAY Mrs, wid. William Halliday, St Kitts, d. London,
7 Oct. 1810.   (80:493)

HALLIS R, b.1787, ex Cap., 1st Dragoon Guards, later Royal
Canadian Rifles, d. Shambley, Canada, 7 March 1856.(NS45:660)

HALLOWELL Benjamin, b.1724, Commr. American Board Customs, fa.
Cap. Hallowell, HMS Swiftsure, d. York, Upper Canada,
28 March 1799.   (69:621)

HALTON Rev. John, St Peter's, Chester, m. Margaret, dau. late
N Taylor, Antigua, 1822.   (92:88)

HALY Edward B, b.1799, ex Barbados, late London, d. on passage
to WI on SS Solway, 7 April 1843.   (NS20:110)

HALY William W, s. late James Haly, Cork, d. Philadelphia,
26 Dec.1851.   (NS37:312)

HAMBLEDON Rev. John, Holloway, m. Sophia Anglin, dau. late
George Lawrence, St James, Jamaica, London, 9 Dec.1834.
                                                        (105:204)

HAMILTON Alexander, MD, d. Annapolis, Md., 1756.   (26:412)

HAMILTON Amey, Barbados, m. William Hemming, merchant,
Dublin, 1 May 1755.   (25:236)

HAMILTON Andrew, estate owner, Mass. Bay, d.1767.   (37:563)

HAMILTON Charles, ex Tobago, m. Miss Macdonnell, dau. late
Charles Macdonnell, Newhall, Co. Clare, 23 Oct.1799.(69:1192)

HAMILTON Charles, Leasowes, Shropshire, d. WI, 1817. (87:187)

HAMILTON Cheney, Receiver Gen. & Public Treasurer Jamaica, d.
Kingston, Jamaica, 17 Jan.1820.   (90:377)

HAMILTON Rev. Edward Montague, 2nd s. late Cheney Hamilton.
Jamaica, m. Susan, dau. late John Carne, Falmouth, Stoke-
Damerel, 17 April 1844.   (NS21:645)

HAMILTON Francis, Kensworth, Herts., m. Mary Catherine, only
dau. Henry Diston, Jamaica, London, 17 March 1840. (NS13:535)

HAMILTON Gavin Major, eldest s. William Hamilton, merchant,
London, d. Quebec, 6 May 1819.   (88:654)

HAMILTON Henry, Gov. Dominica, d. Antigua, 29 Aug.1796.
                                                        (67:164)

HAMILTON Hester Maria, 2nd dau. late A C Hamilton,
St Catherine, Canada West, m. Cap. E C Grant, 60th Rifles,
Hamilton, Canada West, 2 June 1866.   (NS3/2:252)

HAMILTON John, b.1780, eldest s. John Hamilton, Lord Provost,
Glasgow, d. Kingston, Jamaica, 4 Dec.1801.   (72:181)

HAMILTON Col. John, ex Consul in Va., d.12 Dec.1817. (87:472)

HAMILTON Mary Anne, dau. late Dr Robert Hamilton, Grenada, m.
Andrew Loughnan, London, 21 June 1798.   (68:535)

HAMILTON Mary Ann, wid., ex Edinburgh, m. Edward Marshall, alias
Peter Fisher, St John, NFD., 23 Feb.1815.   (85:   )

HAMILTON Mary Ann, only ch. late Andrew Hamilton, Woodlands,.
Philadelphia, m. Cap. S H Palairet, 29th Reg., Broad Mayne,
Dorset, 18 April 1843.   (NS19:643)

HAMILTON Mary, b.1742, wid. Robert Hamilton, MD, Grenada, d.
London, 29 Oct.1815.   (85:636)

HAMILTON Mary, b.1803, only dau. late Robert Hamilton,
Queenstown, Upper Canada, d. London, 5 Nov.1823.   (93:477)

HAMILTON Paul, b.1725, American loyalist, d. London,
11 Dec.1797.   (67:1076)

HAMILTON P, eldest s. Gen. Alexander Hamilton, d. NY,
24 Oct.1801.   (72:85)

HAMILTON Robert, Vineyard Pen, Jamaica, Col. Kingston
Militia, magistrate, St Andrew, Jamaica, d.1814.   (84:197)

HAMILTON William Leslie, Attorney Gen. Leeward Islands,
Councillor, St Kitts, d.9 Oct.1780.   (50:495)

HAMILTON Mrs, b.1748, w. Mr Hamilton, merchant, St Kitts,
dau. Benjamin Vaughan, prizebroker, d. Enfield, 14 March 1782.
(52:151)

HAMILTON Mr, d. Jamaica, Oct.1792.   (62:1220)

HAMILTON ..., dau. Gov. Hamilton, b. Dominica, 1797. (67:433)

HAMMELL William, d. Barbados, 12 Jan.1811.   (81:395)

HAMMERSLEY William, merchant, NY, d.1752.   (22:478)

HAMERSLEY W, Lt., 3rd Garrison Bat., m. Jean Brown, dau. late
Campbell Brown, Antigua, 20 Sep.1817.   (87:362)

HAMMERTON Col., Naval Officer, SC, d.14 Aug.1732.   (2:930)

HAMMET Frederick James Gordon, b.1805, 2nd Viscountess de
Rosmordue, nephew late Sir Ralph Woodford, ex Gov. Trinidad,
d. Trinidad, 11 Jan.1834.   (104:558)

HAMMOND George, HM Plenipotentiary to USA, m. Peggy Allen,
Philadelphia, 1793.   (63:669)

HAMMOND George, ex Jamaica, m. Miss Berthon, London, 6 Aug.
1793.   (63:859)

HAMMOND James, merchant, Kingston, Jamaica, d.25 Aug.1812.
(82:670)

HAMMOND Thomas J, b.1800, ex Eton, d. Panama, 9 Dec.1850.
(NS35:334)

HAMMOND William, s. William Hammond, solicitor, Ipswich, d.
at sea off Jamaica, 1820.   (90:188)

HAMMOND W J, b.1799, comedian, d. NY, 23 Aug.1848 (NS30:559)

HAMPDEN R Dickson, Councillor, Barbados, d. Barbados, 8 May
1852.   (NS38:317)

HAMPDEN Sarah, b.1772, wid. Jarrett Hampden, Barbados, uncle
Bishop of Hereford, d. Drumlanford House, Ayr, 5 Feb.1848.
(NS29:454)

HAMPSON Sir George Francis, Jamaica, d.24 Dec.1774. (45:46)

HAMPSON William, b.1784, eldest s. Edward Hampson, Baldock,
Herts., d. Barbados, June 1807.   (77:888)

HANBURY Capel, Royal Scots Reg., m. Ellen, only dau. late
William Franklin, ex Gov. NJ, 8 June 1818.   (88:562)

HANCE James, Jamaica, d. on board The John on passage to
Jamaica, 1812.   (82:193)

HANCOCK John, President Continental Congress, m. Miss
Quincy, Boston, 1775.   (45:502)

HANCOCK John, Gov. NE, d. Boston, 8 Oct.1793.   (63:1051)

HANCOCK Thomas, d. Boston, NE, 1 Sep.1764.   (34:498)

HANDFIELD George J, b.1824, 4th s. late Cap. Handfield, RN,
gs. Col. Charles Handfield, Comm. Gen. Ireland, ggs. Col.
John Handfield, Gov. Fort Pitt, Canada, 1761, Archdeacon,
d. Spanish Town, Jamaica, 3 Feb.1864.   (NS2/16:533)

HANNA Eleanor, b.1744, dau. Mr McEntee, Co. Monaghan, wid.
Thomas Hanna, settled US 1808, d. NY, 18 Dec.1856.(NS2/2:368)

HANNAFORD Eliza Gay, eldest dau. Stephen Hannaford, m. William
Tabois Smith, Jamaica, 7 April 1846.   (NS26:528)

HANSBROW Henry, d. Kingston, Jamaica, 1796.   (66:618)

HANSON Charles Simpson, Constantinople, m. Charlotte, dau.
Robert Smith, Speaker Assembly Tobago, Woodford, Essex,
Sep.1829.   (99:270)

HANSON Eliza, w. Mr Hanson, London, dau. John Pennock, Kingston, Jamaica, d.19 June 1820.   (90:638)

HANSON Mrs John T, b.1786, niece Oliver Goldsmith, d. West
Hoboken, NJ, 21 Sep.1866.   (NS3/2:698)

HANSON Olivia Augusta Gilbert, only dau. Jesse Jones, wid.
Cap. George Scott Hanson, 56th Reg., Somerset Isle, Bermuda.
m. Cap. Walter Fitzgerald Kerrich, 26th Cameronians, eldest
s. John Kerrich, Geideston Hall, Somerset, 2 July 1857.
                                                 (NS2/3:456)
HANSON Miss, dau. late John Hanson, Jamaica, m. Lt. Col.
Blake, 20th Light Dragoons, London, 1814.   (84:392)

HANWELL Cap., b.1748, Hudson Bay Co. Service, d.12 Nov.1826.
                                                   (96:478)

HARBOTTLE William, d. Jamaica, 1791.   (61:682)

HARDEN Thomas, b.1781, eldest s. George Harden, Talbot Inn,
Ripley, Surrey, d. WI, 8 Dec.1806.   (77:586)

HARDEY Ellen, Brixton Hill, m. J Douglas, Provost Marshal
Grenada, Brixton, 2 Jan.1837.   (NS7:201)

HARDIE Henry, d. Quebec, 23 Aug.1803.   (73:987)

HARDING Charles, portrait painter, d. Boston, USA, 1866.
                                                 (NS3/1:930)
HARDING Mrs Elizabeth, Weston Favel Est., Jamaica, m. Peter
Francklyn, Customs Collector, Kingston, Trelawney, Jamaica,
Sep.1794.   (64:1052)

HARDING Jessy, eldest dau. late Henry Harding, HM Customs,
Nevis, m. Rev. F L Lloyd, Aldworth, Berks., Tamworth,
10 Feb.1859.   (NS2/6:316)

HARDING Mrs Maria, d. Gloster, NJ, 1868.   (NS3/5:790)

HARDWICH Mary Augusta, Baldwin Co., Alabama, dau. late James
Hardwich, Bristol, niece William Lovell Hardwich, Camden
Town, m. John S McIntyre, Baldwin Co., Ala., Mobile, Ala.,
18 Aug.1858.   (NS2/5:628)

HARE Charles, b.1789, s. late Cap. Charles Hare, RN, Lt. RN,
d. St Johns, NB, 31 March 1859.   (NS2/6:653)

HARE Edward F, Cap., 56th Reg., s. Maj. W H Hare, Plymouth,
m. Fanny Louisa, eldest dau. Col. W H Eden, Acting Gov.
Bermuda, Bermuda, 28 Oct.1852.   (NS39:194)

HARE Fanny Louisa, b.1833, eldest dau. Col. W H Eden, 56th
Reg., wid. Cap. Edward F Hare, 56th Reg., d. St George,
Bermuda, 17 Sep.1853.   (NS40:649)

HARE Richard, 'an eminent brewer & justice for Middlesex. His
son has carried porter brewing to the highest perfection in
Philadelphia.', d.1 July 1776.   (46:335)

HARE N C, s. Lt. Col. Hare, 53rd Reg., b. London, Ontario,
22 Jan.1868.   (NS3/5:383)

HARFORD Samuel, b.1766, Quaker, Bristol, d. NY, 1 Aug.1838.
                                                  (NS10:566)

HARISOU Dorothy, dau. late Thomas Harisou, Attorney Gen.
Jamaica, m. Edmund Bullock, Jamaica, Bath, 1796. (66:789)

HARLOCK Joseph, WI, d. Sep.1763.   (33:565)

HARMAN Beversham, d. brigantine Wellington of Cork on return
from St Vincent, 29 Sep.1822.   (92:649)

HARMAN Pettus, eldest s. T R Harman, London, d. Washington,
USA, 22 Nov.1843.   (NS21:222)

HARMAN Mrs, wid. Samuel Harman, Antigua, d. Cheltenham,
3 March 1820.   (90:284)

HARPER Cornelia Elizabeth, b.1783, w. Thomas Harper, Sec.
St Kitts, d. St Kitts, 16 Feb.1819.   (88:485)

HARPER Gen. R G, b.1765, d. Baltimore, 1824.   (95:652)

HARRIES Rev. John, garrison chaplain 20 years, d. St John,
NFD., 22 Jan.1810.   (80:384)

HARRINGTON Caroline Barney, dau. George Harrington, US
minister Switzerland, m. Horace Rumbold, British Legation Sec.,
Berne, 15 July 1867.   (NS3/2:383)

HARRINGTON Sarah Jameson, London, m. William Joplin, Newcastle
-on-Tyne, Halifax, NS, 19 Aug.1820.   (90:562)

HARRIOTT John, 2nd s. William Harriott, Clifton, d. Spanish
Town, Jamaica, 30 July 1813.   (83:400)

HARRIS Charlotte Ann, w. Rev. Joseph H Harris, Principal,
Upper Canada College, d. York, Upper Canada, Feb.1834.
(104:670)

HARRIS Edward, hosier, Leicester, m. Miss Ustick, dau. Rev.
T Ustick, Philadelphia, 19 Dec.1796.   (67:251)

HARRIS Edward, b.1763, Judge Supreme Court NC, d. Lumberton,
NC, 1813.   (83:94)

HARRIS Lord George Fraser, Gov. Trinidad, m. Sarah, 2nd dau.
George Cummins, Archdeacon, Trinidad, 16 April 1850.(NS34:200)

HARRIS James, Stipendiary Magistrate St Kitts, m. Mary
Augusta, eldest dau. Nathaniel Hart, Col. Treasurer, Paris,
19 June 1851.   (NS36:315)

HARRIS Jane Caroline, dau. late George Gordon, Croughty,
Banff, w. John Wallace Harris, & their eldest ch. Charlotte &
Harry, d. Jamaica, Aug.1842.   (NS19:110)

HARRIS John F J, eldest s. John Harris, RN, m. Elizabeth,
yngs. dau. Lt. Col. Loring, Toronto, 9 Nov.1859. (NS2/8:176)

HARRIS Rev. J H, Principal York College, Upper Canada, m.
Charlotte Ann, 3rd dau. Rev. J B Collyer, Hackford, Norfolk,
25 Aug.1829.   (99:270)

HARRIS Marion Grasett, yngs. dau. Thomas D Harris, Toronto, m.
Cap. Edward Sydney Burnett, RA, Toronto, 17 Oct.1865.
(NS2/19:776)

HARRIS Philip, 2nd s. Francis Coleman Harris, m. Philipina
Van Koughnet, eldest dau. Col. Philip Van Koughnet,
Cornwall, Canada, 12 Oct.1845.   (NS24:650)

HARRIS Rev. Samuel, b.1767, 3rd s. Alderman Harris, Bristol,
ex Wigan, Lancs., d. Aurora, NA, 9 Oct.1832.   (102:652)

HARRIS Sarah, b.1831, yngs. dau. George Cummins, Archdeacon
Trinidad, d.Worthing, Barbados, 6 March 1853.   (NS39:560)

HARRIS William Fortescue, Maj. Port Royal Militia, d.Kingston,
Jamaica, July 1793.   (63:862)

HARRIS ..., s. Lady Harris, b. Trinidad, 1851.   (NS35:420)

HARRISON Christopher, s. late T Harrison, Attorney Gen.,
d. Jamaica, 11 Dec.1811.   (82:488)

HARRISON Edward, Councillor, d. Quebec, 1794.   (64:1205)

HARRISON Henry, b.1813, 2nd s. Rev. William Harrison,
Manchester, d. NY, 16 Dec.1853.   (NS42:89)

HARRISON John, London, d. Kingston, Jamaica, 1799. (69:624)

HARRISON Margaret A, dau. late Thomas Harrison, Attorney Gen.
Jamaica, m. Henry Veitch, Madeira, 1808.   (78:1187)

HARRISON Matthew Beachcroft, 62nd Reg., only s. Rev.
M Harrison, Basingstoke, Hants., m. Louise, dau. late
C Brown, St Johns, NB, 7 April 1859.   (NS2/6:637)

HARRISON Samuel, b.1786, Asst. Comm. Gen., d. Grenada,
8 Oct.1817.   (87:562)

HARRISON S B, b.1802, barrister, d. Toronto, 23 July 1867.
                                              (NS3/2:400)

HARRISON Thomas, HM Attorney Gen. Jamaica, yngr. s. late Sir
T Harrison, Chamberlain London, bro. Benjamin Harrison,
Christ's Hospital treasurer, d. Spanish Town, Jamaica,
12 Feb.1792.   (62:279)

HARRISON William Dyne, Stratford, s. Rev. W M Harrison,
Clayhanger, Devon, m. Lucy, 3rd dau. Daniel Tye, Wilmot,
Galt, Upper Canada, 10 May 1851.   (NS36:79)

HARRISON William Henry, b. Va., 9 Feb.1773, s. Benjamin
Harrison, US President, d. Boston, 4 April 1841.   (NS15:649)

HARROLD Fanny E, yngs. dau. late Alfred Harrold, Birmingham,
m. J Colvin Randall, Philadelphia, Edgbaston, 7 Nov.1860.
                                              (NS2/9:663)

HARRY Cap. John, master Wilson of Liverpool, d. Jamaica,
5 Oct.1794.   (64:1150)

HART Catherine, dau. late Rev. John Hart, Kirkenner, m.
William Pagan, Dominica, 23 June 1791.   (61:871)

HART Francis, Lambeth, surgeon, d. Martinique, 6 March 1798.
                                              (66:439)

HART Mary Augusta, eldest dau. Nathaniel Hart, Col. Treasurer,
m. James Harris, magistrate, St Kitts, Paris, 19 June 1851.
                                              (NS36:315)

HART Rebecca, dau. Lemon Hart, London, m. W J Levi, Barbados,
2 Feb.1820.   (90:272)

HART Dr, b.1753, ex physician St Kitts, d. Walcot, Somerset,
1813.   (83:668)

HARTLEY Mrs Catherine, w. Thomas Hartley, d. NY, 1798.(68:1086)

HARTLEY James, ex St Vincent, d. London, 24 Oct.1798.(68:995)

HARTLEY Mary Ann, w. Joseph Tucker Crawford, HM Consul Cuba,
d. Havanna, 16 Dec.1844.   (NS23:334)

HARTMAN W H, Maj., 9th Reg., m. Mrs Mary Berkeley, wid.
Thomas Berkeley, Grenada, London, 12 July 1842.   (NS18:312)

HARVEST Edward Douglas, 97th Reg., gs. Charles Douglas Smith,
Lt. Gov. PEI, m. Theresa Maria, dau. Cap. Ambrose Lane, PEI,
Charlottetown, PEI, 26 May 1853.   (NS40:304)

HARVEST Hector, Shepperton, m. Susanna Elizabeth, dau. Lt.
Gov. Smith, PEI, 18 Nov.1819.   (90:368)

HARVEY Alice Margaret, 3rd dau. G C Harvey, Bermuda, m.
Rev. Alfred Earle, only s. W Earle, Tunbridgewells, Halifax,
NS, 5 Dec.1867.   (NS3/5:104)

HARVEY Elizabeth, only dau. Sir Hohn Harvey, Lt. Gov. NB, &
niece Gen Lord Lake, m. Cap. Tryon, 43rd Light Infantry,
Northants, NB, 25 Nov.1837.   (NS9:205)

HARVEY Elizabeth, 3rd dau. Gerrard, Viscount Lake, w. Sir
John Harvey, Lt. Gen. NS, d. Halifax, NS, 10 April 1851.
                                                    (NS36:99)

HARVEY Harriett, 2nd dau. J A Harvey, Ordnance storekeeper,
m. Lt. F S Seale, RA, yngs. s. late Sir J H Seale, Kingston,
Canada, 24 April 1851.   (NS36:78)

HARVEY James J P, b.1816, bro. Thomas Harvey, solicitor, ex
Falmouth, d. Niagara, 9 Oct.1851.   (NS37:106)

HARVEY Jane, w. Rev. J C Harvey, dau. Thomas Boughton,
Nunhead, Surrey, d. NFD., 21 July 1843.   (NS20:447)

HARVEY John Noble m. M Tucker, eldest dau. J Tucker, Speaker
Bermuda Assembly, 1800.   (70:484)

HARVEY John, b.1753, ex President Grenada, d. Castle Semple
House, 23 Aug.1820.   (90:283)

HARVEY Lt. Gen. Sir John, b.1778, Col., 59th Reg., Lt. Gov.
NS, d. Halifax, NS, 22 March 1852.   (NS37:620)

HARVEY Rev. J C m. Jane Ann, eldest dau. Thomas Boughton,
Peckham, Surrey, St Johns, NFD, 4 Aug.1842.   (NS18:420)

HARVEY Louisa Archer, 2nd dau. G Cockburn Harvey, Halifax, m.
Com. William Jardine,RN, 2nd s. Sir William Jardine of Applegirth, Halifax, NS, 16 June 1864.   (NS2/17:234)

HARVEY Mary Esther, dau. A W Harvey, MD, Councillor, Bermuda,
m. Rear Adm. Fahie, Bermuda, July 1823.   (93:368)

HARVEY Robert, ex Grenada, d. Exeter, 29 July 1791. (61:777)

HARVEY Thomas, Comm. Dept., d. on passage from St John, NB,
on board the Isaac Todd, 11 Oct.1820.   (90:570)

HARVEY Mrs, w. Robert Harvey, Liverpool, dau. late Dr Andrew
Turnbull, MD, SC, d.2 April 1814.   (84:420)

HASERMANN Alexander, Solicitor Gen. Upper Canada, m.
Elizabeth Emily, dau. Walter Merry, Cheltenham, late Dep. Sec.
War, London, 15 April 1834.   (104:551)

HASLEWOOD George Henry, b.1802, Islington, d. WI, 31 Dec.1822.
                                                    (92:648)

HASTLER Edward, inf. s. Edward J Hastler, ex Liverpool, d.
San Francisco, Cal., 26 Nov.1850.   (NS35:334)

HASTLER Mary, b.1817, w. Edward J Hastler, ex Liverpool, d. San Francisco, Cal., 29 Nov.1850.   (NS35:334)

HASWELL Rev. William Jepson, b.1779, late Corpus Christi College, Oxford, chaplain HMS Pique, d St John's Rectory, Jamaica, 9 Aug.1817.   (87:561)

HATHAWAY Silas, b.1751, ex Jamaica, d. London, 9 Sep.1826.
                                                (96:284)

HATHWAY S, s. Late R Hathway, Hereford, d. Nevis, 1800.
                                                (70:1112)

HATTON Sir John, Long Stanton, Cambridge, m. Miss Bridgham, b.1771, American loyalist, London, 17 Jan.1788.   (58:81)

HAUGHTON Samuel Williams, Speaker Jamaica Assembly, d. Westmoreland, Jamaica, 12 Aug.1793.   (63:1051)

HAVELOCK Alice Margaret, b.1866, d. Tadousac, Quebec, 9 July 1867.   (NS3/2:399)

HAVELOCK ..., dau. Lady Alice Havelock, b. Montreal, 1 Nov. 1867.   (NS3/5:99)

HAVILAND John, b.15 Dec.1792, Gundenham, Somerset, architect & engineer, settled USA 1816, d. Philadelphia, 28 March 1852.
                                                (NS37:629)

HAVILAND Thomas Heath, Charlottetown, PEI, m. Ann Elizabeth, 5th dau. late John Grubb, formerly Hosenden, Bucks., late Charlottetown, Charlottetown, PEI, 5 Jan.1847.   (NS27:541)

HAVIN William Gordon, b.1800, eldest s. late Stephen Havin, Bahamas, d. London, 1 Nov.1809.   (79:1175)

HAWKES Edward, b.1806, ex Dudley, late surgeon, US consulate, Oahu, Sandwich Islands, d. Weston-super-Mare, 5 July 1852.
                                                (NS38:323)

HAWKINS George Charles, only s. late Thomas Vincent Hawkins, Chelsea, d. Tobago, 4 Dec.1850.   (NS35:222)

HAWLEY William Hanbury, Maj., 14th Reg., m. Eliza Jane, 2nd dau. late Henry Warner, barrister, Trinidad, Port-of-Spain, Trinidad, 10 March 1864.   (NS2/16:650)

HAWORTH John Smith, 3rd s. Joshua Haworth, Hull, d. Savanna-la-Mar, Jamaica, Jan.1802.   (72:374)

HAWTAYNE Catherine Elizabeth, b.1831, w. W H Hawtayne, 3rd WI Reg., d. Nassau, Bahamas, 9 Aug.1853.   (NS40:537)

HAWTAYNE W H W, Cap., 39th Reg., only s. late John Hawtayne, Archdeacon of Bombay, m. Julia, eldest dau. late Thomas Healey, 32nd Reg., Quebec, 22 July 1858.   (NS2/5:412)

HAWTAYNE ..., s. Cap. Hawtayne, b. St George, Bermuda, 3 Aug. 1860.   (NS2/9:423)

HAWTHORNE Nathaniel, b. Salem, Mass., 4 July 1804, novelist, d. Plymouth, NH, 19 May 1864.   (NS2/17:245)

HAY Charles, Clifton Pen, Jamaica, d. Aberdeen, 14 Aug.1805.
(75:882)

HAY Charles, Nevis, m. Georgina Augusta, yngs. dau. late Rev.
W Mair, London, 10 March 1847.   (NS27:648)

HAY Sir James, d. Kingston, Jamaica, Aug.1794.   (64:1054)

HAY Jeanna, eldest dau. Adolphus Hay, Antwerp, m. John
Christian Bowring, Guadaloupe-y-Calvo, Mexico, Antwerp,
11 Nov.1813.   (NS23:91)

HAY Cap. Lewis James, yngs. s. late Lewis Hay, Edinburgh,
Chief Magistrate, Port-of-Spain, d. Trinidad, 9 Sep.1834.
(105:222)

HAY Michael, Kingston, Jamaica, d.12 Dec.1762.   (32:241)

HAY Thomas, Sec. Jamaica, d.28 Jan.1769.   (39:110)

HAY Mr, Gov. Barbados, d.1780.   (50:50)

HAYE George, Barbados, d. Bath, 11 April 1759.   (29:242)

HAYES Anne, b.1763, eldest dau. Henry Whyte, Councillor, NY,
wid. Sir John Hayes, MD, military physician NA, Cheltenham,
18 Jan.1848.   (NS29:327)

HAYES Catherine, vocalist, m. William Avery Bushnell, Conn.,
London, 8 Oct.1857.   (NS2/3:557)

HAYNES Henry Higgenson, 2nd s. Robert Higgenson, Thimbleby
Lodge, Yorks., d. Barbados, 15 Jan.1853.   (NS39:330)

HAYNES John, Jamaica, d.1758.   (28:556)

HAYWOOD Elizabeth, b.1679, d. Spanish Town, Jamaica, 30 Oct.
1809.   (79:182)

HEAD Lady, w. Sir Edmond Head, Charleston, SC, d.12 June 1775.
(45:406)

HEAD .., dau. Sir Edmond Head, b. Govt. House, Fredericton,
NB, 6 Feb.1849.   (NS31:418)

HEALE Rev. W J m. Catherine, yngs. dau. late Col. Stephens,
St Lucia, Berrow, Worcs., 28 Nov.1837.   (NS9:88)

HEALEY Julia, eldest dau. late Thomas Healey, 32nd Reg., m.
Cap. W H W Hawtayne, 32nd Reg., only s. late John Hawtayne,
Archdeacon of Bombay, Quebec, 22 July 1858.   (NS2/5:412)

HEAPY John, ex London, d. Philadelphia, 1811.   (81:292)

HEATH Elizabeth Snow, 2nd dau. Thomas Snow, London, m. Rev.
John Scotland, 2nd s. John Scotland, Chief Judge Trinidad,
London, 10 Jan.1849.   (NS31:312)

HEATH Helen, b.1808, 2nd dau. late J Ritchie, w. W Heath,
Spring Mount Est., Jamaica, d. Jamaica, 29 Aug.1841.(NS16:668)

HEATHCOTE Edmond, Lt., HMS Eurydice, 3rd s. Rev. Samuel Heathcote, New Forest, Hants., m. Elizabeth Lucy, eldest dau. Lt. Col. Law, Royal Newfoundland Company, St Johns, NFD., 13 July 1844.   (NS22:421)

HEATHCOTE John, merchant, London, d. Baltimore, 6 April 1814.
                                                     (84:698)

HEATHCOTE Miss, eldest dau. Sir William Heathcote, m. Langford Lovell, Antigua, 28 April 1798.   (68:441)

HEAVEN James, b.1804, s. Thomas Heaven, WI, merchant, Bristol, d. on passage from Jamaica, June 1836.   (NS6:223)

HECTOR William, b.1788, surgeon, drowned off Iceland in wreck of Autumn of Dundee on passage from Quebec, 29 Oct.1818.
                                                     (88:568)

HEDDON James, late Venue Master Tobago, d.2 June 1817.(87:183)

HEMMING George, Jamaica, m. Miss Bracebridge, Weddington, 19 Sep.1769.   (39:462)

HEMMING William, merchant, Dublin, m. Amey Hamilton, Barbados, 1 May 1755.   (25:236)

HENCKELL John, Chief Justice Jamaica, d.4 Dec.1802. (72:272)

HENDERSON Charles A, HM Consul Panama, m. Helen Elizabeth, yngs. dau. Robert Power, Tasmania, Surbiton, 14 Nov.1860.
                                                     (NS2/9:664)

HENDERSON Elizabeth, wid. Benjamin Henderson, St Ann's, Jamaica, d. Bristol, 16 Aug.1851.   (NS36:443)

HENDERSON I, b.1710, d. Fishkill, America, 12 Dec.1812.
                                                     (82:488)

HENDERSON Jane, wid. Thomas Henderson, Dominica, d. Woolwich, 5 April 1822.   (92:380)

HENDERSON John, s. Sir Robert Henderson, m. Miss Robertson, dau. Gen. Robertson, Gov. NY, 1781.   (51:242)

HENDERSON John Charles, b.1826, 2nd s. John Robert Henderson, Walkern, Herts., d. Hamilton, Canada West, 12 March 1857.
                                                     (NS2/2:625)

HENDERSON Rev. Matthew, b. Kinross, minister, Charties & Buffalo, Pittsburgh, Penn., d. Oct.1795.   (65:1112)

HENNEN Lucy Cobham, w. Dr John Hennen, yngs. dau. late Thomas Howard Griffith, Barbados, d. London, 13 Sep.1845. (NS24:543)

HENRIQUES A Q, b.1775, ex Jamaica, d. Shirley, Hants., 30 May 1840.   (NS14:110)

HENRY Emma, eldest dau. Bernard Henry, Philadelphia, m. George eldest s. Lord Wood, Court of Session, Edinburgh, Philadelphia 17 April 1845.   (NS24:72)

HENRY James, Assemblyman, St Anne's, Jamaica, m. Susannah,
dau. late William Hall, Kingston, Jamaica, 1801.   (71:763)

HENRY Jane, yngs. dau. late Rev. William Henry, Tooting,
Surrey, m. Rev. G M Clinckett, St Matthew's, Claremont,
yngs. s. Abel Clinckett, Barbados, Jamaica, 10 Jan.1851.
                                                 (NS35:545)
HENRY J, ex Aberdeen, d. Halifax, NS, 1813.   (83:670)

HENRY P., Va., d.6 June 1799.   (69:717)

HENRY Philip, ex SC, d. London, 11 Aug.1797.   (67:717)

HENRY Robert, 5th s. late Joseph Henry, Dublin, m. Ann, 2nd
dau. late Nathaniel Thomas Ramsay, Barbados, London,
10 Nov.1853.   (NS41:185)

HENRY Susannah Beckles, dau. late William Henry, Barbados,
m. H Beckles, Barbados, London, 17 July 1838.   (NS10:439)

HENRY W, b.1806, yngs. s. Alexander Henry, Pentonville, d.
Jamaica, 17 July 1835.   (NS4:446)

HENSHAW J P K, b.1792, Bishop RI, d. Frederick, Md.,
20 July 1852.   (NS38:320)

HENSLEY Joseph, Attorney Gen., m. Frances Ann Dover, only dau.
Robert Hodgson, Chief Justice PEI, PEI, 8 Sep.1853.(NS40:628)

HENSLEY Louisa Margaretta, 2nd dau. Charles Hensley, PEI, m.
William Hamilton Hobkirk, Milton, 21 July 1848.   (NS30:421)

HENWOOD Samuel, b.1779, bro. James Henwood, Hull, late
Charleston, SC, York, d. London, 15 Oct.1844.   (NS22:664)

HEPBURN William, St Vincent, d. Clifton, 25 Jan.1846.
                                                 (NS25:332)
HERBERT Charles, b.1764, ex Grenada, d.25 Dec.1806. (76:1253)

HERBERT Henry William, b. London, 7 April 1807, eldest s. Rev.
William Herbert, author, d. Broadway, NY, 17 May 1858.
                                                 (NS2/5:200)

HERBERT Rev. John, s. Rev. David Herbert, Llansaintffread,
Cardigan, d. Kenyon College, Ohio, 1830.   (100:645)

HERBERT John Cottle, b.1801, 5th s. R M Herbert, Bristol, d.
Jamaica, 17 March 1830.   (100:651)

HERBERT John Richardson, President Nevis, d. Nevis, 18 Jan.
1793.   (63:373)

HERBERT Joseph, President Nevis, d.1768.   (38:47)

HERBERT Magnus Morton, Nevis, d. Brussels, 31 Oct.1834.
                                                 (105:446)
HERBERT Mrs, w. Joseph Herbert, Montserrat, d.3 Dec.1796.
                                                 (66:168)

HERCHMER Laurence William, eldest s. Rev. W Herchmer, m.
Mary Helen, 2nd dau. H Sherwood, Attorney Gen. Upper Canada,
Kingston, Canada, 8 Nov.1866.   (NS3/3:238)

HERDENBERG Rev. Jacob, President, Queen's College, NJ, d.
Brunswick, 1790.   (60:1214)

HERIOT ..., dau. J Heriot, Dep. Paymaster, Windward & Leeward
Islands, d. White Park, Barbados, Nov.1811.   (81:658)

HERON N, b. Wigtonshire, merchant, d. Petersburg, Va.,
16 Aug.1816.   (86:376)

HERVEY Col. Felton Bathurst m. Louisa Catherine, 3rd dau.
R Caton, Md., 24 April 1817.   (87:466)

HERVEY John, Grenada, d.6 Dec.1770.   (40:591)

HESELTINE John Woodhouse, b.1829, s. Charles Heseltine,
Customs Collector, Bermuda, Paymaster Fife Artillery, d.
Bermuda, 9 Oct.1858.   (NS2/5:647)

HESELTINE Samuel, Govt. Steam Inspector, eldest s. S R
Heseltine, London Stock Exchange, d. Victoria, Vancouver
Island, 5 Sep.1859.   (NS2/7:653)

HESLOP Alexander, only s. W Heslop, Jamaica, m. Emma, eldest
dau. Maj. Gen. Kemp. East Hottley, Sussex, London, 1842.
                                                 (NS18:313)

HESTER Mrs Agnes Helm, b. Nevis, 1726, d. Walworth, Surrey,
1806.   (76:90)

HETH Joice, b.1674, ex nurse George Washington, d. NY,
22 Feb.1836.   (NS5:446)

HETHERINGTON H, dau. R Hetherington, Tortula, m. Andrew
Anderson, Tortula, Durham, 25 April 1799.   (69:525)

HETHERINGTON Miss, Durham, dau. Richard Hetherington, Tortula,
m. Francis Johnson, Gray's Inn, 29 Dec.1801.   (71:1210)

HEVERIN George Francis, d. Kingston, Jamaica, 1793. (63:1152)

HEWARD Emma Arabella, 2nd dau. Francis H Heward, Toronto, m.
Maj. Francis Topping Atcherly, 30th Reg., Toronto, 4 June 1863.
                                                 (NS2/15:99)

HEWETT Edward Osborne, Cap., RE, 2nd s. Col. John Hewett,
Glamorgan, m. Catherine Mary, eldest dau. late Maj. V Biscoe,
RE, Kent, Toronto, 4 Feb.1864.   (NS2/16:520)

HEWETT Eliza, w. Rev. Edward Hewett, 2nd dau. late William
Stower, London, d. Jericho, St Thomas-in-the-Vale, Jamaica,
9 June 1846.   (NS26:334)

HEWITT John, Jamaica, d.20 April 1769.   (39:216)

HEWITT Mrs. John, wid., Jamaica, m. Robert Dallas, 20 April
1769.   (39:215)

HEWETT Thomas, ex St Kitts, d. London, 23 June 1766. (36:294)

HEWITT William, Comm. 'for the ceded islands', bro. Lord
Chancellor Ireland, d. Barbados, 1781.   (51:489)

HEWITT William Kellit, ex Jamaica, d. Exeter, 11 June 1812.
                                                    (82:605)

HEWETT ..., dau. Cap. Edward Osborne Hewett, RE, b. Halifax,
NS, 10 Feb.1865.   (NS2/18:497)

HEWETSON John, London, m. Adelaide Amelia Leslie, only dau.
late George Henry French, Richmond Hill, St Vincent,
Hampstead, 15 March 1859.   (NS2/6:424)

HEY William, Customs Commissioner, m. Miss Paplay, Jamaica,
5 April 1783.   (53:363)

HIATT John, b.1722, Chief Justice, St Ann's, Jamaica, d.
Mt. Plenty, Jamaica, 14 Sep.1820.   (90:570)

HIBBARD Ashley, ex Lt. Col., Canada Militia, Montreal, m.
Anne Sarah, 2nd dau. Rev. Ambrose Lane, Pendleton, 9 Feb.1864.
                                              (NS2/16:381)

HIBBERT Henry Roberts, yngs. s. George Hibberts, London, d.
Kingston, Jamaica, 14 July 1825.   (95:286)

HICHENS Mary, 2nd dau. William Hichens, m. John Hockin,
Dominica, 3rd s. Rev. William Hockin, Phillack, Cornwall,
London, 24 June 1847.   (NS28:312)

HICKES William John, b.1817, s. Lt. Col. Hickes, Bombay Army,
d. Hamilton, Canada West, 1 June 1856.   (NS2/1:125)

HICKS Julia Sarah, dau. Cap. A Bond, wid. Cap. G W S Hicks, m.
Herbert Taylor, s. Thomas Neville Usher, Consul Gen. Haiti,
Tunbridge Wells, 17 Oct.1854.   (NS43:76)

HICKS R L, Nevis, d. on passage from WI, 22 March 1785.
                                                    (56:440)

HIGGENSON John m. Helen, eldest dau. Alexander Thurburn, ex
Alexandria, Egypt, Duoro, Canada West, 5 Dec.1861.(NS2/12:220)

HIGGIN Isaac, Tooting, Surrey, d. Jamaica, 11 Feb.1832.
                                                   (102:383)

HIGGIN John, 2nd s. John Higgin, London, d. on passage to
Jamaica, 28 March 1824.   (94:647)

HIGGIN John, b.1815, eldest s. late Isaac Higgin, d.
Llandovery Est., Jamaica, 17 Aug.1853.   (NS40:537)

HIGGIN Thomas, b.1830, 4th s. late Isaac Higgin, London, d.
Jamaica, 9 Feb.1853.   (NS39:560)

HIGHAM Ellen Claiborne, eldest dau. Thomas Higham, Charleston,
m. Baron de Gaesbeke, Bruges, Margate, 23 May 1844. (NS22:86)

HIGHAM John, s. Thomas Higham, Charleston, SC, & Margate, Kent, m. Letitia, dau. Col. William Lyster, ex Greenford, Middlesex, Llanlligan, 24 Jan.1844.   (NS21:309)

HIGHATT Elizabeth, wid. Richard Highatt, Bristol, dau. late J John Stody, Jamaica, d.23 March 1812.   (82:395)

HIGHATT Henry, eldest s. late Richard Highatt, Bristol, d. Martha Brae, Jamaica, 23 Jan.1810.   (80:384)

HIGINBOTHAM Anne, eldest dau. Ralph Higinbotham, Baltimore, m. Granville Sharp Oldfield, merchant, ex England, Baltimore, 5 Aug.1819.   (89:562)

HILYARD William John, b.1818, eldest s. Rev. William Hilyard, Beverley, d. Hilo, Byron's Bay, Sandwich Islands, 1 Nov.1854.
                    (NS43:437)

HILL Annie, 2nd dau. Stephen J Hill, Gov. Leewards, m. Thomas Jarvis, Mt. Joshua, St Johns, Antigua, 15 Dec.1863.(NS2/16:244)

HILL Aramuta, 3rd dau. Cap. Hill, 69th Reg., m. Rev. Henry James Petry, Daviville cum Tingwick, Ottawa, 10 Jan.1867.
                    (NS3/3:377)

HILL Edward, ex Jamaica, d. bristol, 8 Feb.1815.   (85:278)

HILL Francis, b.1773, ex Broxbourne, Herts., d. Jamaica, 31 Jan.1850.   (NS33:558)

HILL James, merchant, d. Port Roseau, Dominica, 1803. (73:87)

HILL Jane, only ch. Robert A Hill, Hamilton, Canada West, m. Albert Arthur Erin, ex 13th Light Dragoons, 3rd s. Sir John Hesketh Lethbridge, Hamilton, 11 Oct.1862.   (NS2/13:770)

HILL Julia Caroline, 2nd dau. late Cap. Henry Hill, 57th Reg., m. Rev. John Leslie Mais, Spanish Town, Jamaica, St Andrews, Jamaica, 29 Jan.1856.   (NS45:512)

HILL Nicholas, d. Montserrat, 8 June 1813.   (83:194)

HILL Peter Edward, Cap., RA, m. Emily Mary, 2nd dau. William Clarke, MD, Tweedside, Barbados, 26 Oct.1864.   (NS2/16:108)

HILL Thomas, b.1779, Councillor, Montserrat, d. Montserrat, 26 Oct.1825.   (96:191)

HILL William, Customs Controller, d. Port Antonio, Jamaica, April 1793.   (63:671)

HILL Father, bro. Lord Hill, d. Cincinatti, 1830. (100:190)

HILLYER Rev. Charles, Church Missionary Society, m. Maria, yngs. dau. Archdeacon Cochran, St Andrews, Red River, 13 Dec.1854.   (NS43:408)

HILTON Miss m. Gov. Wentworth, NH, 15 March 1760.   (30:297)

HINCKLEY Mrs, w. D Hinckley, eldest dau. Joseph Outram, Alfreston, Derby, d. Boston, America, 5 Jan.1812.   (82:488)

HINCKS Matilda, yngs. dau. Francis Hincks, Gov. Windwards, m.
Henry Clement, 69th Reg., yngs. s. late John de la Poer-
Beresford, Col. Sec. St Vincent, Barbados, 23 July 1857.
(NS2/3:456)

HINCKSMAN Richard, ex Glasgow, merchant, d. Jamaica, June 1797.
(67:711)

HINDLE Thomas, b.1775, d. Trinidad, 27 June 1802.   (72:974)

HINE Eliza Anne, 2nd dau. late William Hine, Jamaica, m. John
Rose Cormack, MD, Edinburgh, London, 4 Nov.1841.   (NS17:92)

HINGSTON Selina Maria, b.1830, w. Cap. C H Hingston, 3rd WI
Reg., d. Jamaica, 11 April 1854.   (NS42:90)

HINKSON Rev. Samuel William, b.1816, ex Farthinghoe, Northants,
d. Colleton Est., Barbados, Sep.1842.   (NS19:102)

HIRE Isabella, 2nd dau. Lt. Henry Hire, RN, m. John Scott, 3rd
s. late Joseph Tucker, Naval Surveyor, Bermuda, 6 March 1845.
(NS23:538)

HISLOP Lawrence, ex Trelawney, Jamaica, d. Edinburgh,
4 Jan.1856.   (NS45:213)

HITCHINGS Edward, b.1814, barrister, Kingston, Canada,
drowned Lake Ontario, 1 Nov.1842.   (NS19:110)

HOARE Cap., sloop Dotteral, m. Matilda, dau. Rear Adm. Fahie,
Bermuda, 15 March 1823.   (93:562)

HOBART George, Magistrate St Andrews, Master in Chancery, d.
Jamaica, 19 Jan.1793.   (63:281)

HOBART John Sloss, judge NY, d. NY, 4 Feb.1805.   (75:283)

HOBART George Vere, Gov. Grenada, 2nd s. Earl of Buckingham,
d. Grenada, 5 Nov.1802.   (72:1225)

HOBBS Charles, ex Lambeth, d. WI, Feb.1815.   (85:373)

HOBKIRK William Hamilton, MD, m. Louisa Margaretta, 2nd dau.
Charles Hensley, PEI, Milton, 21 July 1848.   (NS30:421)

HOBBS ..., dau. Cap. J C Hobbs, 30th Reg., b. Toronto,
15 March 1863.   (NS2/14:650)

HOBBS ..., s. Col. T F Hobbs, 6th Royal Reg., b. Newcastle,
Jamaica, 18 Feb.1865.   (NS2/18:497)

HOBSON John, House of Representatives, NE, d.1770. (47:239)

HOCKIN John, Dominica, 3rd s. Rev. William Hockin, Phillack,
Cornwall, m. Mary, 2nd dau. William Hichens, Camberwell,
24 June 1847.   (NS28:312)

HODGE Dr Hugh, physician, Philadelphia, d.1798.   (68:909)

HODGE John, Great St Helens, m. Maria, wid. Cap. Dickenson,
86th Reg., dau. late John Gray, Treasurer Honduras, London,
1 July 1846.   (NS26:314)

HODGE Langford Lovell, Councillor, Antigua, d.1817.   (87:379)

HODGES Edward, Doctor of Music, ex Bristol, m. Sarah Anne,
dau. late William Moore, MD, niece Dr Moore, late Bishop of
NY, NY, 11 April 1844.   (NS21:644)

HODGES Miriam, b.1825, 2nd dau. Edward Hodges, Doctor of
Music, ex Bristol, d. NY, 29 Jan.1842.   (NS18:332)

HODGKINSON Mrs, ex Miss Brett, Bath Theatre, d. America, 1804.
                                                   (74:1174)

HODGSON Abraham, b.1765, Custos Rotulorum & Assemblyman,
St Mary, d. Jamaica, 11 April 1837.   (NS8:102)

HODGSON Frances Ann Dover, only dau. Robert Hodgson, Chief
Justice PEI, m. Joseph Hensley, Attorney Gen., PEI, 8 Sep.
1853.   (NS40:628)

HODGSON Frances Margaret, 2nd dau. John Hodgson, m. Cap.
George Oldmixon, RN, St Johns, NFD., 8 Oct.1854.   (NS43:76)

HODGSON I, only s. A Hodgson, Jamaica, m. E Lee Clarke, dau.
late G I Clarke, Hydehall, Stockport, 9 Aug.1831. (101:171)

HODGSON Joseph, b.1795, ex Falmouth, Jamaica, d. Barnes,
25 Sep.1843.   (NS20:557)

HODGSON Robert, ex Causewayfoot, Keswick, Cumberland,
Speaker PEI Assembly, d. PEI, 1811.   (81:680)

HOFFMAN Ogden, b.1794, s. Josiah O Hoffman, NY, Attorney Gen.
NY, d. NY, 1 May 1856.   (NS2/1:119)

HOFFNER Jacob, d. Philadelphia, 1798.   (68:1086)

HOGAN Maj., b. England, planter Cuba, settled Washington, d.
Philadelphia, 13 June 1810.   (80:189)

HOGG Robert, yngs. bro. Ettrick Shepherd, d. on passage to NA,
24 June 1833.   (103:286)

HOLBROOK G P, Surveyor Gen. NFD., m. Miss Prarl, 5th dau.
P Prarl, Hampton Court, Conn., St Johns, NFD., 4 June 1817.
                                                   (87:274)

HOLBROOK George Papps, Surveyor Gen. NFD., bro. Dr Holbrook,
Cheltenham, d.1832.   (102:649)

HOLDEN Charles, alias Charles E Somerville, b.1839, yngs. s.
late Henry George Holden, Public Record Office, London, 13th
NJ Volunteers, d. between Acquia Creek & Fairfax, Va.,
15 June 1863.   (NS2/15:245)

HOLDEN Robert, Little Eastcheap, eldest s. Robert Holden, ex
Jamaica, m. Anne, 3rd dau. Jacob Kellerman, ex Jamaica,
Worthing, Sussex, 17 Jan.1801.   (71:83)

HOLDER Elizabeth, eldest dau. John Holder, Hereford, m. John
Robert Brown, Jamaica, Bath, 19 Dec.1848.   (NS31:310)

HOLDER Elizabeth Murray, b.1766, wid. Rev. Henry Holder,
Barbados, d. Clifton, 3 April 1848.   (NS29:561)

HOLDER Mrs, wid. William Holder, sis. late Mrs Pring,
Crediton, d. Jamaica, 16 Jan.1832.   (102:383)

HOLDFORD Jane Maria, Greenwich, m. Josiah Stevens, WI,
13 March 1752.   (22:191)

HOLDRIGHT Mary Jane, dau. Edward Holdright, Monkstown, m.
Philip Francis Little, judge, NFD., Kingstown, Dublin,
4 May 1864.   (NS2/16:795)

HOLDSWORTH Frederick, b.1799, late Mexico City, d. Toronto,
17 Aug.1857.   (NS2/3:467)

HOLLAND Henry, b.1808, yngs. s. Rev. Richard Holland,
Spreyton, d. Occaguan, America, 25 Jan.1852.   (NS37:425)

HOLLIGAN James R, barrister, m. Mary, 3rd dau. George N
Taylor, Barbados, West Teignmouth, 3 Dec.1853.   (NS41:308)

HOLLINGSWORTH David, b.1766, settled Jamaica 1784, Assemblyman Manchester, Militia Col., d. Jamaica, 30 July 1840.
                                                   (NS14:676)

HOLLINGSWORTH Thomas, b.1774, d. Barbados, 8 March 1815.
                                                    (85:566)

HOLLIS Alicia, dau. late Cap. Hollis, King's Dragoon Guards,
m. George Rowley, 23rd Royal Welsh Fusiliers, Montreal,
27 Sep.1867.   (NS3/2:808)

HOLLOWAY C W Elphinstone, 2nd s. late Col. E Holloway, gs.
Gen. Sir Charles Holloway, m. Caroline, 2nd dau. Edward
Pengelley, Halifax, NS, 13 Oct.1863.   (NS2/15:772)

HOLLOWAY ..., s. C Elphinstone Holloway, b. Halifax, NS,
7 July 1865.   (NS2/19:501)

HOLMES John jr, Belfast, m. Miss Daniell, only dau. Thomas
Daniell, Attorney Gen. Dominica, Snesham, Norfolk, 1 April
1802.   (72:373)

HOLMES John, b.1820, 3rd s. Henry Holmes, solicitor, Romsey,
d. Sandwich, Canada West, 1 Jan.1854.   (NS41:329)

HOLMES Martha, only dau. John Holmes, London, m. Mr Holmes,
merchant, NY, 1797.   (67:710)

HOLMES Richard, St Kitts, d. Jan.1757.   (27:92)

HOLMES Sarah Prescot, dau. Forster Clarke, Barbados, w. J A
Holmes, d. Boulogne-sur-Mer, 30 May 1864.   (NS2/17:122)

HOLMES Thomas, Customs Collector, Grenada, m. Caroline, yngs.
dau. Robert W Benjamin, Demerara, 19 Nov.1841.   (NS17:321)

HOLMES Rev. William, yngs. s. Robert Holmes, Limerick,
St Anne's, Jamaica, d. Jamaica, 1802.   (72:377)

HOLMES Mr, merchant, NY, m. Martha, only dau. John Holmes,
London, 1797.   (67:710)

HOLMESTEAD Margaret Elizabeth, dau. Arthur Holmes, Toronto,
m. Charles Irvine, yngs. s. late Lord William Douglas,
Toronto, 4 March 1862.   (NS2/12:640)

HOLT James, ex Leeward Islands, d.1 June 1748.   (17:284)

HOLWORTHY Rev. Samuel, Croxall, Derby, m. Diana Sarah, dau.
late Nathaniel Bayly, Jamaica, Cheshunt, 6 April 1811.(81:392)

HONEYWOOD Philip, planter, Jamaica, d.2 Aug.1767.   (37:430)

HOOD Dr Alexander, b.1737, Speaker Assembly, d. Montserrat,
7 July 1817.   (87:561)

HOOD William, merchant, Bristol, d. Charleston, SC, 7 July
1837.   (NS8:327)

HOOKE Anna, only dau. Rev. James de la Hooke, Gravenhurst,
Beds., m. Alfred W, 2nd s. late Rev. Dr Otter, Lord Bishop
of Chichester, Goderick, Canada West, 1842.   (NS19:197)

HOOK Sarah, eldest dau. late Richard Hook, Heathfield,
Sussex, m. Alexander James Moore, ex Jamaica, London,
9 Nov.1840.   (NS13:85)

HOOPER Henry Filkes, 76th Reg., yngr. s. late Rev. John
Hooper, Albury, Surrey, m. Anna, dau. late George Coster,
Archdeacon NB, Fredericton, NB, 3 Oct.1860.   (NS2/9:547)

HOPE Brig. Gen., Lt. Gov. Quebec, d. Quebec, 13 April 1789.
                                                     (59:573)

HOPE Rev. H Payne, Christon, Somerset, m. Mary, only dau.
late J Bovell, MD, Barbados, 16 July 1834.   (104:312)

HOPE William, nephew Thomas Lee, London, d. Havanna, 21 June
1846.   (NS26:334)

HOPKINS Anne, b.1821, eldest dau. Cap. Ogden, Sheriff of Three
Rivers, Canada, d. La Chine, Montreal, 24 July 1854.(NS42:408)

HOPKINS Edward M, Hudson Bay Co, m. Ann Ogden, eldest dau.
J Gouvernour Ogden, Sheriff of Three Rivers, ex Cap. 56th
Reg., Three Rivers, Canada East, 31 Aug.1847.   (NS28:630)

HOPKINS Rev. John Henry, b. Dublin, 1792, Bishop of Vermont,
d. Rock Point, Vt., 9 Jan.1868.   (NS3/5:390)

HOPKINS Sally, eldest dau. John Hopkins, Ingastone Hall,
Essex, m. Robert Osborn, Barbados, 18 Sep.1741.   (11:499)

HOPKINS William, 'lately come from Virginia in order to be
called to the bar', d.22 Dec.1734.   (4:703)

HOPKINSON George, b.1830, barrister, d. Charleston, USA,
31 Oct.1854.   (NS43:104)

HOPTON J, 'son of an American loyalist', d. London,
25 Dec.1831.   (101:650)

HORD Mrs John, eldest dau. Alderman Butterworth, Coventry, d.
Boston, America, 1815.   (85:92)

HORE Lt. E G, 2nd s. late Cap. Hore, RN, Pole Hore, Wexford,
m. Maria, 2nd dau. Lt. Col. Reid, Gov. Windwards, Barbados,
17 June 1847.   (NS28:312)

HORLOCK Samuel, b.174C, ex Jamaica, d. London, 1825. (95:187)

HORN Arthur, merchant, Leeward Islands, d.14 Aug.1753(23:372)

HORN Charles Edward, b.1786, London, s. Charles Frederick
Horn, English melodist, d. Boston, NE, 21 Oct.1849. (NS33:99)

HORNE John Gamble m. Ellen, 4th dau. late Maj. Gen. Seymour,
Gov. St Lucia, Kingston, Upper Canada, 15 Nov.1842.(NS19:422)

HORROCKS Rev. James, President College Va., d. Oporto, 1772.
                                                (42:246)

HORSFORD Paul, b.1771, Councillor & Chief Justice, Antigua,
d. Antigua, 16 April 1850.   (NS34:230)

HORSFORD ..., s. Lt. Col. Horsford, Jamaica, d. Spanish Town,
Jamaica, 11 June 1805.   (75:774)

HORSFORD ..., dau. Brig. Gen. Horsford, b. Govt. House,
Bermuda, 15 Jan.1813.   (83:281)

HORSFORD ..., s. Sir R Horsford, Solicitor Gen. Antigua, b.
Antigua, 1843.   (NS20:86)

HORST Elias Vantler, ex US Consul Bristol, d. Clifton,
3 May 1816.   (86:566)

HORT Barbara, w. Maj. Hort, 81st Reg., Lt. Gov. Dominica, d.
Govt. House, Dominica, 16 Aug.1841.   (NS16:558)

HORTON William, barrister, m. Martha, 2nd dau. late Richard
Richardson, Canada, 20 Dec.1842.   (NS19:311)

HORTON Miss, dau. John Horton, merchant, London, m. Angus
Bethune, merchant, ex Charleston, SC, 14 March 1792. (62:278)

HOSKINS Cap. Bradford Smith, late 44th Reg., s. Rev. W E
Hoskins, Chiddingstone, Kent, d. Greenwich, Va., 30 May 1863.
                                                (NS2/15:244)

HOSSACK John, Baff Bay River, Jamaica, d. Dumfries, 20 Sep.
1815.   (85:378)

HOSTE ..., s. Maj. Hoste, RA, b. Hamilton, Canada West,
13 Aug.1862.   (NS2/13:482)

HOUSTON Sir George, d. Ga., 1795.   (65:880)

HOUSTON William, s. Allen Houston, teacher, Glasgow, merchant,
Jamaica, d. Jamaica, 15 Oct.1808.   (79:85)

HOUSTON Dr, botanist, Ga., d. Jamaica, Aug.1733.   (3:662)

HOWARD Henry, British Legation, m. Cecilia, dau. George W
Riggs, Washington, Greenhill, Md., 2 Oct.1867.   (NS3/2:808)

HOWARD Henry George, yngs. s. Earl of Carlisle, m. Mary
Wellesley, dau. John MacTavish, Montreal, London, 29 May 1845.
(NS24:190)

HOWARD Maria, sis. Earl of Effingham, m. Gen. Carlton, Gov.
Quebec, 21 May 1772.   (42:246)

HOWARD Martin, Chief Justice NC, d.24 Nov.1781.   (53:593)

HOWE Elias, b. Mass., 1819, inventor, d. Bridgeport, Conn.,
3 Sep.1867.   (NS3/2:683)

HOWELL Adelaide Anne, 2nd dau. Thomas Howell, Clapham Common,
m. Philip Pritchard, NY, 4th s. Henry Pritchard, Clapham,
19 Sep.1854.   (NS42:619)

HOWTHGATE Miss, dau. Joseph Howthgate, Kingston, Jamaica, m.
Mr Turner, attorney, London, 1791.   (61:582)

HOYLES Harriet Liddell, only dau. Hugh W Hoyles, Attorney Gen.
NFD., m. Lt. Duncan Norton Taylor, RA, eldest s. Cap. Norton
Taylor, London, St Johns, NFD., 19 Oct.1864.   (NS2/17:780)

HOZIER James, b.1793, ex Jamaica, d. London, 22 Nov.1846.
(NS27:102)

HOZIER Jane, wid. James Hozier, Jamaica, m. James O'Loughlin,
MD, London, 11 Sep.1849.   (NS32:530)

HUDSON Miss, London, m. Cap. Falkner, 29th Reg., Sec. NC,
April 1763.   (32:257)

HUGGINS John, Councillor, Nevis, d.21 Nov.1855.   (NS45:99)

HUGGINS Thomas, eldest s. P T Huggins, Nevis, m. Annie, 3rd
dau. David Melville, Nottingham, 17 Nov.1841.   (NS17:92)

HUGHES Cap. William, b.1765, Rose Mount Plant., d. Jamaica,
29 Aug.1836.   (NS6:668)

HUGHES Miss, London, m. James Whitlock, Barbados, 1 July 1773.
(43:359)

HULL P P, ex proprietor 'San Francisco Whig', m. Lola Montes,
Mission Dolores, San Francisco, 2 Aug.1853.   (NS40:404)

HULTON Henry, ex Comm. Customs NA, d. Andover, 12 Feb.1790.
(60:185)

HUMBERT Gen., French Republican Officer, settled US 1812,
'fought with Jackson at New Orleans', d. New Orleans, 1823.
(93:471)

HUMBLEBY John, merchant, Barbados, d.28 Jan.1814.   (84:408)

HUME Benjamin, b.1697, d. Jamaica, 1773.   (43:470)

HUME Robert, yngs. s. late Alexander Hume, Coldingham Law,
d. Bagnals, St Mary's, Jamaica, 12 Jan.1804.   (74:596)

HUMPHREY Catherine, dau. Sir J Humphrey, Boulogne, m.
Jacob Omilius Irving, Jamaica, Paris, 2 Dec.1821.   (91:641)

HUMPHREYS Nathaniel, 2nd s. late William Humphreys, customs
officer, Dominica, gs. late Rev. William Humphreys, Antigua,
d. Dominica, 27 Aug.1845.   (NS24:551)

HUMPHREYS Rev. Philip, Portland, Jamaica, d.16 Jan.1834.
                                                  (104:663)

HUMPHREYS W, Customs officer, yngs. s. late Rev. W Humphreys,
Antigua, d. Dominica, 26 Sep.1835.   (NS4:667)

HUNN Frances Emma, b.1787, dau. Adm. Pickmere, Gov. NFD.,
wid. Cap. Hunn, RN, d. Rolvenden, 8 Jan.1860.   (NS2/8:306)

HUNT D, dau. Robert Hunt, m. Alexander Murray, bro. Earl of
Dunmore, Nassau, Bahamas, 18 May 1811.   (81:184)

HUNT John, Customs Collector, St Kitts, d. Basseterre, St Kitts,
23 Jan.1790.   (60:274)

HUNT Richard, d. Falmouth, Jamaica, 1803.   (73:86)

HUNT William, b.1659, d. Md., 1772.   (42:198)

HUNTER Daniel, s. Robert Hunter, merchant, Bristol, d.
Wilmington, SC, 2 March 1813.   (83:91)

HUNTER D, wid. Dr W Hunter, RI, d. London, 15 Oct.1813.
                                                  (83:506)

HUNTER John, b. America, 1735, d. Leominster, Littlehampton,
7 Nov.1800.   (70:1116)

HUNTER Margery, b.1830, w. Dr Joseph Stewart Hunter, Mayor,
St George's, d. Bermuda, 27 Oct.1853.   (NS41:439)

HUNTER Pauline Rives, eldest dau. William C Hunter, NY, m.
Lt. Augustus W H Atkinson, 99th Reg., Hong Kong, 1 March
1864.   (NS2/17:106)

HUNTER William, d. Savannah, 10 Aug.1802.   (72:1064)

HUNTER Gen., Gov. Jamaica, d.31 March 1734.   (4:330)

HUNTINGFORD ..., dau. Henry Huntingford, b. Huntingford,
Upper Canada, 31 July 1848.   (NS30:420)

HUNTLEY ..., s. Sir R V Huntley, b. Charlottetown, PEI,
5 July 1842.   (NS18:311)

HURD Caroline Wynyard, eldest dau. Thomas Gadwin Hurd, m.
Charles Turville Wilson, Lt. Military Train, s. Maj. Gen.
G J Wilson, Indian Army, Toronto, 7 April 1863. (NS2/14:781)

HUSEY Louisa, only dau. late Henry Husey, Brighton, m. John
Henry, eldest s. late Alexander Murchison, Springfield,
Jamaica, & Elgin, Scotland, London, 5 Aug.1852.   (NS38:411)

HUSKISSON George, b.1789, Customs Collector, St Vincent, bro.
late W Huskisson, d. St Vincent, 7 Feb.1844.   (NS21:558)

HUSTON Thomas, d. Beaufort, SC, 14 March 1808.   (78:367)

HUTCHINGS Hannah, niece Col. Williams, Liverpool, niece Maj.
Skinner, RA, m. Thomas, eldest s. Alderman Bennett,
Shaftesbury, St Johns, NFD., 5 Jan.1828.   (98:175)

HUTCHINS James Henry, s. Rev. James Hutchins, London, d.
Martinique, 13 Aug.1854.   (NS42:638)

HUTCHINSON Anne, wid. William Hutchinson, b.1700, d. East
Windsor, Middlesex Co., America, 1801.   (71:279)

HUTCHINSON Ann F, dau. J Hutchinson, ex Bermuda, m. J P Esten,
barrister, eldest s. J C Esten, Chief Justice Bermuda,
11 Jan.1832.   (102:78)

HUTCHINSON Arthur J, 2nd s. late William Hutchinson,
Cheltenham, m. Maria Marguerite Fernandez, 3rd dau. Louis La
Caze, Castries, St Lucia, 28 Nov.1865.   (NS3/1:267)

HUTCHINSON Catherine, dau. J Hutchinson, m. Cap. F Truscott,
RN, Bermuda, 1815.   (85:274)

HUTCHINSON Foster, b.1761, Mass., Loyalist, Councillor NS,
Judge Supreme Court NS, d. Halifax, 28 Nov.1815.   (86:179)

HUTCHINSON Thomas, Fellow of New College, Oxford, m. Miss
Matson, dau. John Matson, Chief Justice Dominica, 18 July
1799.   (69:1189)

HUTCHINSON Miss m. David Niven, ex Jamaica, Glasgow, 11 Nov.
1800.   (70:1287)

HUTCHISON Frederica Esten, eldest dau. Lt. Col. Hutchison,
97th Reg., m. Erasmus Borrowes, 97th Reg., eldest s. Rev. Sir
G Borrowes, Belleville, Halifax, NS, 14 Aug.1851. (NS36:533)

HUTCHISON Mary, b.1764, wid. Joseph Hutchison, Bermuda, d.
Exeter, 17 March 1838.   (NS9:555)

HUTCHISON Mrs Mary, dau. late M Byam, Antigua, d. Durham,
16 Sep.1826.   (96:379)

HUTCHISON Thomas, ex Gov. Mass., d.3 June 1780.   (50:299)

HUTTON Alexander, Jamaica, m. Miss Coosens, London, 22 Aug.
1775.   (45:406)

HUTTON Charles, Nevis, d. Carlton-on-Trent, 11 Oct.1788.
                                                    (58:938)

HUTTON Cap. Frederick m. Louisa Mary, dau. late Edward Robert
Copeman, New Buckenham, Norfolk, Bermuda, 28 Jan.1858.
                                                    (NS2/4:437)

HYATT Charles, Jamaica, m. Miss Sparks, London, 24 May 1758.
(28:244)

HYDE Edmond, Jamaica, d. 17 Aug.1763.   (33:565)

HYDE George m. Mrs Steele, dau. late Robert Burke, Prospect
Lota, Co. Cork, St Vincent, 7 Oct.1820.   (90:562)

HYDE Dr John, ex Antigua, d. London, 21 Feb.1813.   (83:291)

HYLTON William, b.1749,Co. Durham, settled Jamaica pre 1777,
d. Jamaica, 1837.   (NS8:551)

HYNDMAN Elizabeth Christian, wid. Robert Augustus Hyndman,
Demerara, dau. John Beccles, ex Attorney Gen., Barbados, d.
9 Sep.1834.   (104:554)

HYNDMAN Henry, Sheriff Huron District, yngs. s. late Col. H
Hyndman, HEICS, d. Goderich, Upper Canada, 19 Sep.1844.
(NS22:670)

HYNDMAN Thomas, Antigua, d. Glen Oak, Co. Antrim, 3 Sep.1815.
(85:376)

IBBETSON Denzil John Holt, 3rd s. Denzil Ibbetson, Dep. Comm.
Gen. Malta, m. Clarissa Elizabeth, 3rd dau. Rev. Lansdown
Guilding, St Vincent, Bromley, Kent, 28 May 1846.   (NS26:197)

IFILL William, MD, b.1803, d. Barbados, 9 March 1855.
(NS43:544)

IMAGE ..., dau. Cap. J G Image, Royal North British Fusiliers,
b. Barbados, 2 Dec.1863.   (NS2/16:241)

IMLAH John, poet, d. Jamaica, 1846.   (NS25:670)

INCE John, b.1756, d. Barbados, 28 July 1806.   (76:875)

INGALL ..., dau. Col. Ingall, 62nd Reg., b. Quebec, 17 Sep.
1863.   (NS2/15:632)

INGERSOLL David, American loyalist, d. Hopton, Suffolk,
10 Nov.1796.   (66;971)

INGERSOLL Joseph R, b.1786, s. Jared Ingersoll, Pa., d.
Philadelphia, 20 Feb.1868.   (NS3/5:544)

INGLE Sparkes, 4th s. John Ingle, Ashby-de-la-Zouch, d.
Kingston, Jamaica, 29 Dec.1809.   (80:491)

INGLIS Charles, s. late Rev. John Inglis, Bishop of NS, d.
Aylesford, NS, 24 July 1861.   (NS2/11:335)

INGLES Rev. Charles, b.1780, ex Canada West, d. Bedford,
30 March 1863.   (NS2/14:664)

INGLIS James, ex Kingston, Jamaica, d. Walthamstow, 5 Nov.
1814.   (84:604)

INGLES Col. John, b. Scotland, 1739, d. Raleigh, NC, 10 Oct.
1816.   (86:566)

INGLIS J E W, Lt. Col., 32nd Reg., s. late Bishop of NS, m.
Julia Selina, dau. Sir F Thesiger, London, 17 July 1851.
(NS36:423)

INGLES Thomas, yngs. s. late Charles Ingles, d. Jamaica,
21 Aug.1799.   (69:1193)

INGLIS Katherine, 2nd dau. late Alexander Inglis, SC, m.
Dr James Robertson, physician, Inverness, Edinburgh,
20 Oct.1794.   (64:1148)

INGLES Mrs, Princess Anne Co., m. Dr James Currie, Richmond,
Norfolk, Va., 12 Nov.1789.   (60:178)

INGRAM Herbert, b. Boston, Lincs., 1811, proprietor 'London
Illustrated News', Boston MP, d. Lake Michigan, 8 Sep.1860.
                                                      (NS2/9:555)

INGRAM Miss, only dau. Peter Ingram, ex Provost Marshal
Jamaica, m. Frederick Ravencamp, Moore Park, St George,
Jamaica, Oct.1789.   (60:83)

INMAN Charles, 3rd s. Charles Inman, Liverpool, m. Decima
Isabella Catherina, only dau. late Thomas Davies, MD,
Newbattle, Jamaica, East Barnet, 15 Sep.1853.   (NS40:628)

INNES Alexander, s. Alexander Innes, Bridgend, Glenlivat,
Banffshire, settled America 1840, hotel-keeper, d. Port
Dover, Canada West, 17 April 1860.   (NS2/9:210)

INNES David, Naval Officer, d. Kingston, Jamaica, 20 Aug.1807.
                                                      (77:1075)

INNES George, s. late Col. Innes, d. Grenada, 18 May 1853.
                                                      (NS40:209)

INNES Rev. John, Downe, Hythe, m. Eliza Mary, dau. late John
Laidlaw, Dominica, Hythe, 27 April 1847.   (NS28:80)

INNES Mary, eldest dau. John S Innes, Grafton, Canada West, m.
Charles Spencer, eldest s. late Rev. Arthur Drummond,
Charlton, Kent, Grafton, 28 Oct.1862.   (NS2/13:771)

INNES ..., dau. Cap. W Mitchell Innes, 13th Hussars, b.
Toronto, 15 June 1867.   (NS3/4:234)

IREDELL Rev. Arthur, Trinity College, Cambridge, d. Jamaica,
Nov.1804.   (75:183)

IREDELL Thomas, ex President, Jamaica, d. Jamaica, Sep.1796.
                                                      (66:1057)

IRELAND Charlotte, dau. late Rev. W F Ireland, m. G Allan,
Colonial Bank, Kingston, Jamaica, Cardiff, 15 Nov.1836.
                                                      (NS7:92)

IRONSIDE John Gilbert, s. late Rev. William Ironside, Houghton
le-Spring, Co. Durham, d. Springvale, Pen, Trelawney, Jamaica,
14 Dec.1796.   (66:255)

IRTON Sarah, w. Lt. Col. Irton, Rifle Brigade, dau. late
Joseph Sabine, d. Halifax, NS, 13 Aug.1843.   (NS20:447)

IRVINE Clara Christianna, dau. late Christopher William Irvine,
Bath & Tobago, d. Brompton, 31 Aug.1844.   (NS22:440)

IRVINE Walter, Tobago, m. Catherine, 2nd dau. Alexander
Gordon, Campbelltown, Deebank, 1797.   (67:798)

IRVINE Maj. Gen. William, Revolutionary officer, d.
Philadelphia, 29 July 1804.   (74:882)

IRVING Catherine Diana, dau. late Sir Jere Homfrey, wid.
J A Irving, d. Bonshaw, Canada, 23 Jan.1858.   (NS2/4:449)

IRVING Emma, yngs. dau. Jacob Aemilius Irving of Bonshaw, m.
Rev. Charles Gresford Edmondes, Glamorgan, Newmarket, Upper
Canada, 14 July 1866.   (NS3/2:398)

IRVING Rev. George Clark, b.1828, Bishop's College, Lennoxville, Canada East, d. Riviere du Loup, 11 Aug.1866.
                                                   (NS3/2:551)

IRVING Jacob Omilius, Jamaica, ex 10th Light Dragoons, m.
Catherine, dau. Sir J Humphrey, Boulogne, Paris, 2 Dec.1821.
                                                        (91:641)

IRVING Jacob Aemilius, Jamaica, d. Liverpool, 1816. (86:570)

IRVING Jacob Homilius, b.1791, Ironshore, Jamaica, d.
Niagara, 7 Oct.1856.   (NS2/1:780)

IRVING John Beaufin, Jamaica, only s. late J B Irving, m.
Diana Charlotte, 3rd dau. late Jonathan Williamson, Lakelands,
Co. Dublin, Cheltenham, 6 April 1843.   (NS19:528)

IRVING W, s. James Irving, Rio Bueno, d. Iron Shore Wharf,
Jamaica, 22 June 1798.   (68:811)

IRVING Washington, b. NY, 3 April 1783, author, d. Irvingston,
NY, 28 Nov.1860.   (NS2/8:82)

IRVING William W, PEI, m. Joanna, only ch. late Peter Forrest,
London, Halifax, NA, 17 Nov.1846.   (NS27:195)

IRVING ..., s. Lady Elizabeth Irving, b. Nassau Fort,
Bahamas, 1792.   (62:383)

ISAACS Georgina Ann, only dau. late John C Isaacs, Colonial
Sec. Tortula, m. Charles Osborne Baker, Cap., RM Light Infantry,
Cornwall, 12 Oct.1858.   (NS2/5:629)

ISAACS Rev. Hubert H, m. Augusta, dau. Rev. H S Yates, Henlow,
Beds., Hopeton, Jamaica, 3 Aug.1859.   (NS2/7:414)

ISILL Benjamin, b. Barbados, 1775, d. Barbados, 21 Sep.1835.
                                                     (NS4:667)

IVES Otto, b.1802, s. Edward Otto Ives, Tichfield, Hants., d.
Ancaster, Canada, 2 July 1835.   (NS4:446)

IZARD Miss m. Lord William Campbell, Charleston, SC, 1763.
                                                        (32:313)

JACKMAN Ann Maxwell Hinds, eldest dau. late John Abel Jackman,
niece Samuel Hinds, ex Speaker Barbados Assembly, m. W B
Gibbons, Barbados, 5 April 1845.   (NS23:645)

JACKSON Anna Mary, yngs. dau. late Barnewall Jackson,
St Vincent, niece Sir William Snagg, Chief Justice Antigua,
m. Adam Nicholson, MD, St John, Antigua, 11 June 1863.
(NS2/15:231)

JACKSON Elizabeth, only ch. late William Jackson, Chief Justice
Jamaica, m. Nathaniel Bogle French jr, Dulwich, Surrey,
5 Jan.1811.   (81:85)

JACKSON Elizabeth Gordon, 4th dau. William Walrond Jackson,
Bishop of Antigua, m. Gateward Coleridge Davis, barrister,
eldest s. late Daniel G Davis, Bishop of Antigua, St John,
Antigua, 21 Jan.1864.   (NS2/16:520)

JACKSON Emily, dau. S Jackson, Catherine Hall, Montego Bay, m.
Hugo James, Spanish Town, Jamaica, 1 July 1817.   (87:274)

JACKSON Francis, b.1810, 3rd s. Joseph Jackson, Orpington,
Kent, Provost Marshal Grenada, d.23 Jan.1857.   (NS2/2:371)

JACKSON Frederick George, 21 Royal North British Fusiliers, m.
Alix Marie, 3rd dau. Louis La Caze, Attorney Gen. St Lucia,
Castries, St Lucia, 2 Feb.1864.   (NS2/16:520)

JACKSON Isaac, b.1797, d. Roehampton Est., St James, Jamaica,
3 Aug.1856.   (NS2/1:520)

JACKSON John, Cap., HMS Ariel, d. RI, 1778.   (48:190)

JACKSON Jane Maria, w. W H Jackson, 3rd dau. late Edward
Bullock, Jamaica, d. London, 4 Oct.1852.   (NS38:550)

JACKSON J, wid. J Jackson, Advocate Gen. Jamaica, mo. T Witter,
Attorney Gen. Jamaica, d.4 Sep.1811.   (81:391)

JACKSON Josias, b.1762, ex Councillor, St Vincent, Southampton
MP, d. St Vincent, 30 Aug.1819.   (89:471)

JACKSON J, Special Magistrate, ex Lt., 94th Reg., d. Jamaica,
1835.   (NS5:102)

JACKSON Mary Vardon, eldest dau. Rev. W W Jackson, military
chaplain, m. William Fisher Mends, Dep. Comm. Gen.,
Barbados, 16 Feb.1860.   (NS2/8:506)

JACKSON Rachel, dau. Samuel Jackson, catherine Hall, Jamaica,
m. R Deans, s. Adm. Deans, Spanish Town, Jamaica, 10 April
1820.   (90:562)

JACKSON Robert, Cap., Fort Charlotte, Col. Militia, Supreme
Court Judge, Assemblyman, d. Montego Bay, Jamaica, 26 June
1800.   (70:901)

JACKSON Thomas Jefferson, b. W.Va., Jan.1824, Gen., CS Army,
d. Chancellor's House, Va., 9 May 1863.   (NS2/15:105)

JACKSON William, b.1732, ex Chief Justice Jamaica, d. London,
24 May 1804.   (74:487)

JACKSON Mrs, w. Henry Jackson, sis. late Folliot Magrath,
Dublin, d. Baltimore, America, 12 Aug.1805.   (75:1073)

JACKSON Mr, Attorney Gen. Trinidad, d. Trinidad, 1844.
                                                  (NS23:334)

JACKSON ..., s. John Barclay Jackson, 2nd WI Reg., b.
St Ann's, Jamaica, 24 Dec.1864.   (NS2/18:232)

JACKSON Dr, b.1779, physician, d. NE, 1867.   (NS3/5:124)

JACOB Edwin J, barrister, s. Rev. Dr Jacob, Principal, King's
College, Fredericton, d. Fredericton, NB, 27 May 1859.
                                                  (NS2/9:197)

JACOBS Harriet, wid. William Jacobs, Chale Abbey, Isle-of-
Wight, d. NY, 20 Dec.1848.   (NS31:446)

JACOBS Lionel, 2nd s. J Jacobs, glass manufacturer, Bristol,
d. Spanish Town, Jamaica, 16 Nov.1812.   (83:83)

JACOBSON Joanna Frederica, dau. late Advocate Jacobson,
Altona, step-dau. C D Tolme, Havanna, m. Joseph Tucker
Crawford, HM Consul Gen. Cuba, Havanna, 28 May 1845.(NS24:189)

JACQUET Philip, b.1772, settled Jamaica 1787, d. Jamaica,
26 June 1834.   (104:558)

JAGO Darell Robert, ex Lt., RA, 2nd s. late Darell Jago, Cap.
RA, m. Alice Maude, 2nd dau. William Mills, St John, NB,
St John, 28 March 1865.   (NS2/18:778)

JAMES Catherine Haughton, 2nd dau. J H James, Jamaica, m.
Sir S Haughton Clarke, Jamaica, 9 April 1814.   (84:514)

JAMES Edward, barrister, 2nd s. Edward James, Swedish Vice
Consul Bristol, d. St Kitts, May 1829.   (99:94)

JAMES Edward, barrister, only s. J W James, solicitor,
Devizes, d. St Kitts, May 1829.   (99:190)

JAMES Elizabeth, b.1767, wid. Dr Hugh James, Jamaica, d.
Exeter, 13 Aug.1854.   (NS42:410)

JAMES Elizabeth Haughton, 3rd; dau. late John Haughton James,
Jamaica, d. London, 12 Dec.1850.   (NS35:213)

JAMES Rev. Ewan, London, m. Sarah Anne, dau. late W Paisley,
Jamaica, 15 Oct.1818.   (88:370)

JAMES Henry Eden, ex Bristol, d. Long Island, NY, 6 Sep.
1852.   (NS38:546)

JAMES Hugo, Spanish Town, Jamaica, m. Emily, dau. S Jackson,
Catherine Hall, Montego Bay, 1 July 1817.   (87:274)

JAMES Robert, d. Jamaica, 1790,   (60:1053)

JAMES Mrs, w. William Rhodes James, Spanish Town, Jamaica, d.
on passage to Jamaica, 7 Jan.1815.   (85:373)

JAMESON Peter, Sec. Gov. Jamaica, d.30 April 1773.   (43:203)

JAMESON Robert Sympson, ex Attorney Gen. & Chancellor Canada,
d. Toronto, 1 Aug.1854.   (NS42:409)

JAMIESON Agnes, eldest dau. late Dr Samuel Jamieson, Va., m.
James Neilson, merchant, Glasgow, 19 Oct.1800.   (70:1286)

JAMIESON David, b.1800, London, d. Jamaica, 6 Feb.1843.
                                                    (NS19:556)

JAMIESON John, ex Montreal, d. Edinburgh, 1 Jan.1848.
                                                    (NS29:334)

JAMISON William, ex Jamaica, d. Bath, 1797.   (67:897)

JANSSEN Stephen Theodore m. Miss Soulegre, dau. Col. Soulegre,
Antigua, 13 Dec.1750.   (20:570)

JARDINE Com. William, RN, 2nd s. Sir William Jardine of
Applegirth, m. Louisa Archer, 2nd dau. G Cockburn Harvey,
Halifax, NS, 16 June 1864.   (NS2/17:234)

JARMAIN Edward, b.1817, s. John P Jarmain, Brantham, Chippewa,
Niagara Falls, d. Drummondville, 20 Jan.1853.   (NS39:448)

JARMAN Sarah Maria, b. Essex, 18 Feb.1818, wid. Edward Jarman,
sis. Thomas Allen Blyth, Hamilton, Upper Canada, d. Hamilton,
1866.   (NS3/2:566)

JARRETT Herbert Newton, d. Jamaica, 1790.   (60:1053)

JARRETT Maria, b.1771, wid. Herbert Newton Jarrett, Jamaica,d.
Downton, Wilts., 9 Dec.1831.   (101:573)

JARRETT Mary, dau. John Jarrett, Jamaica, m. John Ashton,
Grange, Cheshire, Liverpool, 1790.   (60:474)

JAQUETTE M Peter, Oneida sachem, d. Philadelphia, 1792,
buried Mulberry St.   (62:674)

JARVIS Bertie Entwistle, Councillor, Antigua, m. Lucy, yngs.
dau. Kilner Brasier, Saffron Hill, Co. Cork, Watergrasshill,
23 Nov.1843.   (NS21:88)

JARVIS B E, Mt. Joshua, Antigua, Councillor, m. Martha Elliot,
3rd dau. late L Oliver, Bristol, Antigua, 6 Dec.1859.
                                                    (NS28:178)

JARVIS Bertie Entwistle, b.1793, Councillor, Antigua, d. at
sea, 15 Oct.1862.   (NS2/13:789)

JARVIS Edward, ex Chief Factor, Albany, Hudson Bay, d. Banbury,
Oxford, 20 July 1798.   (68:812)

JARVIS Sarah Harriet, yngs. dau. W B Jarvis, Sheriff of York,
gdau. W D Powell, Chief Justice Upper Canada, m. Lewis W Ord,
ex Lt., 71st Highlanders, yngs. s. late Maj. R H Ord, RA,
Toronto, 24 June 1854.   (NS42:616)

JARVIS S Peter m. Mary Boyles, dau. D Powell, Chief Justice
Upper Canada, 1818.   (89:80)

JARVIS Thomas, Mt. Joshua, m. Annie, 2nd dau. Stephen J Hill, Gov. Leeward Islands, St Johns, Antigua, 15 Dec.1863.
(NS2/16:244)

JARVIS Mrs, b.1763, w. Thomas Jarvis, eldest dau. late William Whitehead, d. Antigua, 6 Feb.1797.   (67:435)

JARVIS Chief Justice m. Elizabeth, dau. late Robert Gray, ex Judge & Treasurer PEI, Charlottetown, PEI, 12 Dec.1843.
(NS21:309)

JARVIS ..., dau. T Jarvis, b. Antigua, 17 March 1867.
(NS3/3:804)

JAUNCEY James, s. James Jauncey, Assemblyman, NY, m. Miss Elliot, niece Sir Gilbert Elliot, RN Treasurer, 1773. (44:45)

JAY Eliza, dau. Judge William Jay, gdau. late John Jay, Gov. NY, m. Henry Edward, s. Rev. George Pellew, Dean of Norwich, Bedford, Westchester Co., NY, 15 Oct.1858.   (NS2/5:629)

JAY John, b.1745, d. Bedford, Westchester Co., NY, 17 May 1829.
(99:477)

JEFFERIES James, Staunton Dew, Somerset, m. Miss Garth, only dau. Arthur Garth, Jamaica, London, 6 Sep.1796.   (66:789)

JEFFERSON George, ex US Consul Lisbon, partner Gibson & Jefferson, Richmond, Va., d. on passage to USA, 1812.(82:403)

JEFFERSON Sir Robert, judge, Antigua, d. London, 25 June 1807.
(77:686)

JEFFERSON Thomas, b. 2 April 1743, Shadwell, Albemarle Co., Va., ex US President, d.4 July 1826.   (96:271)

JEFFERY John Uniacke, Cap., 81st Reg., eldest s. T N Jeffery, Halifax, NS, d. Tobago, 1841.   (NS16:445)

JEFFREYS George, London mercantile agent, m. Mrs Hayley, wid. George Hayley, sis. John Wilkes MP, America, 1786.   (56:713)

JEKYL John, nephew Sir Joseph Jekyl, Master of the Rolls, Customs Collector, Boston ,NE, d.30 Dec.1732.   (3:102)

JELLICOE Jerimiah, Attorney Gen. Grenada, d. Grenada, 19 Jan. 1817.   (87:374)

JELLY Lt. Frederick, RN, m. Mary Isabella, wid. James Browne, Customs Controller, Savanna-la-Mar, Hatfield Pen, Savanna-la-Mar, Jamaica, 11 Oct.1820.   (91:83)

JEMMETT Barry Lancaster, MD, Grenada, m. Catherine, yngs. dau. late Thomas Kingsley, London, Langley Marsh, Bucks., 10 Dec. 1844.   (NS23:198)

JEMMITT Margaret Ann, dau. Francis Jemmitt, Richmond Est., Grenada, m. Rev. Arthur John Pilgrim Buchanan, Carriacou, s. late Cap. Colin Buchanan, 62nd Reg., St George, Grenada, 4 Feb.1847.   (NS27:542)

JEMMITT Thomas, ex Dominica, d. London, 10 Sep.1815. (85:377)

JENKEN Rosa Henrietta, 2nd dau. late Thomas Jenken, MD,
Zacatecas, Mexico, m. John, s. late John Cross Buchanan,
Auchentoshan, Dunbarton, British Consulate, Mexico,
4 March 1865.   (NS2/18:778)

JENKINS Ann, eldest dau. late Rev. Arnold Jenkins,
Tredlington, Worcs., d. New Orleans, April 1853.   (NS40:97)

JENKINS Rev. C A, m. Lizzie, yngs. dau. H Frith, Stonehaven,
Bermuda, Pembroke, Bermuda, 31 March 1864.   (NS2/16:792)

JENKINS Edward, barrister, eldest s. Rev. John Jenkins,
Montreal, m. Matilda, yngs. dau. P Johnston, Dalriada,
Belfast, Carnmoney, 24 Oct.1867.   (NS3/2:810)

JENKINS Rev. George, Wadhurst, Sussex, military chaplain, d.
Montreal, 26 April 1821.   (91:187)

JENKINS Miss, London, m. Samuel Waterland, Va., 1757.(27:530)

JENNINGS Henrietta Lucy, only dau. late William Robert
Jennings, Bengal Civil Service, m. Albert Parker, Cooksville,
Toronto, yngs. s. late Sir William George Parker, RN,
5 April 1851.   (NS35:658)

JENNINGS Lt., US Army, 'killed in a duel by Cap. Posey at
Vincennes, Indian Territory', 1811.   (81:292)

JENNISON Dr, Mosquito Shore, d.1766.   (36:390)

JERDAN John Stuart, b.1809, eldest s. William Jerdan, Bromton,
Magistrate, Manchioneal, St Thomas-in-the-East, Jamaica, d.
25 Dec.1834.   (105:334)

JERMYN Edmund, Ipswich, m. Millicent Carlton, only ch. Samuel
Abbot, Charleston, SC, 24 May 1818.   (88:464)

JERMYN Edmund, b.1796, yngs. s. late George Jermyn, bookseller,
Ipswich, d. Charleston, SC, 18 Sep.1819.   (89:472)

JERMYN Hugh Turenne, b.1849, 2nd s. Archdeacon Jermyn, d.
Basseterre, St Kitts, 21 May 1855.   (NS54:217)

JERRILL William Downes m. Georgina Bruce, only dau. late Cap.
Colin Buchanan, 62nd Reg., ggdau. James Bruce, Chief Judge
Barbados, Barbados, 26 Nov.1844.   (NS23:420)

JERVIS Martha Mary, b.1835, eldest ch. Cap. Jervis, RN, d.
Boaz Island, Bermuda, 25 Oct.1853.   (NS41:439)

JESSOP Frederick, b.1800, s. late Joseph Shiercliffe Jessop,
Waltham Abbey, Essex, d. St Vincent, 9 June 1820.   (90:186)

JESSOP Henry James, ex Quebec, barrister, m. Anna Maria Bowes
Lyon, sis. Earl of Strathmore, 28 Jan.1788.   (58:177)

JEWELL William, s. John Jewell, Bideford, Devon, d. Montego
Bay, Jamaica, 12 June 1798.   (68:723)

JEWER Thomas, ex Jamaica, late Bath, d.27 April 1798.(68:445)

JOHANNOT Peter, b.1730, Boston, NE, d. London, 8 Aug.1809.
(79:789)

JOHNSON Andrew Cochrane, s. late Earl of Dundonald, s-in-law
Earl of Hopetoun, m. Amelia Constance Gertrude Etienne, only
ch. late Baron de Clugny, Gov. Guadaloupe, wid. M. Raymond
Godet, Martinique, 21 March 1803.   (73:689)

JOHNSON Berkeley, eldest s. Adolphus Pugh Johnson, London, m.
Laura Amanda, only dau. late J H Fleming, Anguilla, London,
17 June 1847.   (NS28:312)

JOHNSON Charles C, Cap., 85th Light Infantry, 3rd s. Sir John
Johnson, Montreal, m. Susan, dau. Rear Adm. Griffith, New
Brook House, Hants., 8 Jan.1818.   (88:81)

JOHNSON Francis, Gray's Inn, m. Miss Hetherington, Durham,
dau. Richard Hetherington, Tortula, 29 Dec.1801.   (71:1210)

JOHNSON Col. Guy, HM Supt. Indian Nations NA, d. London,
5 March 1788.   (58:275)

JOHNSON Jessy, dau. late John Johnson, St Thomas-in-the-East,
Jamaica, m. John Walker, London, 8 Feb.1820.   (90:71)

JOHNSON John, St Vincent, d. on passage from England to
St Vincent on the Oaks, 8 Nov.1820.   (90:570)

JOHNSON Sir John, b.1742, Inspector Gen. Indian Affairs, BNA,
d. St Mary's, Montreal, 4 Jan.1830.   (100:364)

JOHNSON Louisa, 2nd dau. Joshua Johnson, Great Tower Hill, m.
John Quincy Adams, US Ambassador, Court of Berlin, s. John
Adams, US President, 26 July 1797.   (67:709)

JOHNSON Dr Samuel, NE, d.1772.   (42:151)

JOHNSON Samuel, b.1708, ex WI, d. London, 1782.   (52:406)

JOHNSON Stewart Soutar, b.1800, teacher, ex claimant Annandale
peerage, d. Windsor, Sandwich, Canada, 3 Feb.1846. (NS25:559)

JOHNSON Susie, yngs. dau. late Col. Charles C Johnson,
Argenteuil, Canada East, m. Henry Fraser, eldest s. Edward
Stanley Curwen, Workington Hall, Cumberland, London, 30 April
1863.   (NS2/14:784)

JOHNSON Sir William, Johnson Hall, America, d.11 July 1774.
(46:446)

JOHNSON Miss, 2nd dau. Sir John Johnson, m. Col. Bowes, 6th
Reg., Yorks., Montreal, 13 April 1805.   (75:676)

JOHNSON Mrs, b.1754, w. Sir John Johnson, Supt. Gen. Indian
Affairs BNA, d.7 Aug.1815.   (85:376)

JOHNSON Lt. Col. J, ex Bombay Engineers, d. The Retreat, Lake
Erie, Upper Canada, 11 Feb.1846.   (NS25:559)

JOHNSON Lt. Col., Lt. Gov. Quebec, bro. J Johnson, Warrenston, Co. Meath, d. Bath, 23 Dec.1812.   (82:673)

JOHNSON ..., s. Cap. C G Johnson, RA, b. Montreal, 3 April 18 1865.   (NS2/18:634)

JOHNSTON Elizabeth, only dau. late Francis Johnston, London, m. Cap. Blackwell, eldest s. Maj. Gen. Blackwell, Tobago, 26 April 1832.   (102:172)

JOHNSTON George F R, b.1804, yngs. s. Lt. Gen. Gabriel Johnston, HEICS, d. NY, 2 Dec.1854.   (NS43:218) .

JOHNSTON George Milligan, b.1727, Covehead, MD, MAPS Philadel- phia, ex Surgeon Gen. SC & Ga., Loyalist, d.9 March 1799.
                                                       (69:347)

JOHNSTONE Lady Georgina, 2nd dau. Earl of Hopetoun, w. Coch- rane Johnstone, Gov. Dominica, d. Rosseau, Dominica, 17 Sep. 1797.   (67:1069)

JOHNSTONE J C, Theatre Royal, Edinburgh, m. Rebecca, dau. late Alexander Stiven, Tobago, Aberdeen, 1801.   (71:1050)

JOHNSTONE John Edward, MD, m. Amelia, wid. Dr Carter (nephew Sir Isaac Brock), dau. late John Coward, Ordnance storekeeper, Canada, Montreal, 28 Jan.1851.   (NS35:545)

JOHNSTONE Joseph, Bengal, m. Mary Anne Fuller, dau. late John Fuller Brown, Mulberry Garden, Spanish Town, Jamaica, 1797.
                                                       (97:710)

JOHNSTON Matilda, yngs. dau. P Johnston, Dalriada, Belfast, m. Edward, eldest s. Rev. John Jenkins, Montreal, barrister, Carnmony, 24 Oct.1867.   (NS3/2:810)

JOHNSTONE Robert, ex London, Johnstone of Wamphey family, d. Charleston, SC, 1 March 1812.   (82:488)

JOHNSTON Gov., NC, d.30 Sep.1752.   (22:478)

JOHNSTON Mrs, w. Gov. Johnston, d. NC, 2 July 1732.   (2:979)

JOHNSTONE Miss, Liverpool, m. William Smith, Grenada, 5 Nov. 1792.   (62:1054)

JOLLY John, merchant, b.1760, s. T W Jolly, merchant, London, d. St Kitts, 1781.   (52:150)

JONES Agnes, b.1823, dau. Robert Muter, Lt. Col., Royal Canadian Rifles, w. H Stanley Jones, d. Barbados, 22 May 1854.
                                                      (NS42:201)

JONES Andrew Cunningham, b.1850, s. Charles Cunningham Jones, d. Basseterre, St Kitts, 17 Feb.1856.   (NS45:545)

JONES Avonia, b. Richmond, Va., actress, d. NY, 4 Oct.1867.
                                                      (NS3/2:688)

JONES Caroline Martha, yngs. dau. Robert Jones, St Johns, m. Archibald J Arnott, s. George Arnott, Cheltenham, St Johns, Canada East, 19 Nov.1863.   (NS2/16:244)

JONES Charles Cunningham, b.1819, Colonial Bank, d. Basseterre, St Kitts, 11 Feb.1856.   (NS45:434)

JONES Sir Charles Thomas, Cap., HMS Harrier, m. Jane Helen
Melville, only ch. Gilbert Sutton, Customs Collector,
Bermuda, 1817.   (88:272)

JONES Elizabeth, b.1785, wid. Rev. Thomas Arthur Jones, Vere,
Jamaica, d. Bromley, Kent, 6 Feb.1862.   (NS2/12:386)

JONES Emily, dau. Justice Jones, m. Rev. John McCaul, LLD,
ex Dublin, Principal Upper Canada College, Toronto, 1839.
                                                  (NS13:201)

JONES Frances, wid. Rev. William Jones, Nevis, d. Bristol,
12 July 1813.   (83:93)

JONES Gabriel, b.1722, lawyer, d. Rockingham Co., America,
11 Oct.1806.   (76:1169)

JONES H Stanley, Dep. Asst. Comm. Gen., m. Agnes, 2nd dau.
Maj. Muter, Royal Canadian Rifles, Amherstburgh, Canada West,
27 Oct.1846.   (NS27:193)

JONES Rev. James Alfred, d. Falmouth, Jamaica, 8 Feb.1850.
                                                  (NS34:99)

JONES Rev. John, Llangollen, Wales, d. Cincinatti, USA, 1857.
                                                  (NS2/2:368)

JONES John Matthew, barrister, yngs. s. Rear Adm. Sir Charles
T Jones, Fronfraith, Montgomery, m. Mary, yngs. dau. Col. W J
Myers, 71st Highland Light Infantry, Halifax, NS, 23 Oct.1860.
                                                  (NS2/10:200)

JONES Laura, Llanbeblig, Caernarvon, m. Archibald McCorquodale
Kilbride, Argyll, St Johns, NFD., 7 Nov.1813.   (83:20)

JONES Mary Wilhelmina, b.1849, dau. Charles Cunningham Jones,
Colonial Bank, d. Basseterre, St Kitts, 8 Feb.1856.(NS45:434)

JONES Morgan Richard, b.1821, only s. Rev. Morgan Walter Jones,
Ospringe, Kent, drowned Sturgeon Lake, Upper Canada, 16 Dec.
1841.   (NS18:332)

JONES Paul, d. Paris, 1792.   (62:674)

JONES Rev. Peter, Indian missionary & chief, d. Brantford,
Canada West, 29 June 1856.   (NS2/1:254)

JONES Richard Paget Campbell, RA, eldest s. Col. Richard Jones,
RA, m. Eliza Harriet, only dau. Thomas Lane, Colonial Sec.,
Antigua, 23 Nov.1850.   (NS35:196)

JONES Sarah Johnson, yngs. dau. late Maurice Jones, Brompton,
ex Portland, Jamaica, m. Henry William Rolle, London, 5 July
1845.   (NS24:415)

JONES Theophilus, Va., d.2 Aug.1767.   (37:430)

JONES Miss, Mitcham, Surrey, m. Thomas Tichbone, Jamaica, 1758.
                                                  (28:94)

JONES W Edward, barrister, Lincoln's Inn, only s. William
Jones, Springhill, Staffs., m. Ellen, eldest dau. F H Byrne,
PEI, London, 7 Sep.1853.   (NS40:627)

JOPLIN William, Newcastle-on-Tyne, m. Sarah Jameson Harrington,
London, Halifax, NS, 19 Aug.1820.   (90:562)

JOPP Alexander, Kingston, Jamaica, d. Ceres, 26 Jan.1798.
                                                            (68:444)

JORDAN John, ex Cap., 66th Reg., Inspector Niagara District,
d. Niagara, 25 Oct.1840.   (NS13:111)

JORDAN J Kerr, s. late Cap. J Dudley Jordan, gs. Jacob Jordan,
Lower Canada, m. Elizabeth Anne, dau. late Benjamin Lyon,
Jamaica, Clifton, 10 Aug.1845.   (NS24:520)

JORDAN William Leacock, eldest s. William Leacock, m. Mary
Elvira, eldest dau. late Thomas Went, St Lucy's, Barbados,
16 Oct.1860.   (NS2/9:661)

JORDAN Miss, eldest dau. G W Jordan, Colonial Agent Barbados,
m. S P Rigaud, HM Astronomer, Prof. Geometry Oxford, 8 June
1815.   (85:562)

JOYNT John, Cap., RA, bro. Cap. Galbraith James Joynt, RA,
USA, kin Andrew Joynt, surgeon, d. New Orleans, Canada, 1841.
                                                            (NS16:446)

JUDSON Emily C, b.1814, Alderbrook, NY, dau. Mr Chubbock,
authoress, d. America, 1 June 1854.   (NS42:405)

JUGGINS Thomas, ex Jamaica, d. Shootershill, 26 March 1807.
                                                            (77:487)

JULIUS William, d. St Kitts, 19 Feb.1780.   (50:103)

JULYAN Cap. Robert, b.1781, Harbormaster, d. Quebec, 28 Jan.
1856.   (NS45:434)

KADWELL Charles jr., s. Mr Kadwell, Greenwich, m. Caroline,
only dau. James MacDonald, Laprairie, gdau. Maj. William
MacDonald, ex 104th Reg., St Mark's, Laprairie, Canada,
30 July 1850.   (NS34:540)

KALLEY Robert, merchant, Glasgow, m. Mary Boyd, Jamaica,
3 Aug.1795.   (65:702)

KALLIWARNA Erasmus, d. St John's College, NFD., 1856.
                                                            (NS2/1:393)

KEARNEY Cap. Richard, 5th WI Reg., d. on passage from Jamaica
to Honduras, Dec.1803.   (74;374)

KEATE ..., s. Robert William Keate, Gov. Trinidad, b. St Ann's,
Trinidad, 6 March 1862.   (NS2/12:637)

KEEN William, Judge Court Vice Admiralty, St Johns, NFD.,
murdered, 1754.   (24:579)

KEITH Sir Basil, Gov. Jamaica, m. Miss Warren, London,
23 July 1773.   (43:359)

KEITH Sir William, ex Surveyor Gen. Customs America, Gov. Pa.,
d. London, 18 Nov.1749.   (19:524)

KELLERMAN Anne, 3rd dau. Jacob Kellerman, ex Jamaica, m.
Robert Holden, Little Eastcheap, eldest s. R Holden, ex
Jamaica, Watling, Sussex, 17 Jan.1801.   (71:83)

KELLERMAN Mrs E, wid. J Kellerman, Jamaica, m. Joseph Bramly,
Stamford Hill, London, 2 May 1801.   (71:479)

KELLERMAN Miss, dau. Jacob Kellerman, planter, Jamaica, m.
Richard Cooke, Farmhill, Stroud, Glocs., 19 June 1793.(63:575)

KELLY Annie Bruce, yngs. dau. late Robert Kelly, gdau. late
Sir A MacDowall, m. Edmund, yngs. s. late William Deedes,
Sandling Park, Kent, Toronto, 20 Oct.1846.   (NS27:193)

KELLY John, d. Jamaica, 1791.   (61:187)

KELLY John, Tamarind Grove, Househill, d. Jamaica, 28 Oct.
1805.   (75:87)

KELLY John, b.1770, Green Castle, Jamaica, d.4 Nov.1813.
                                                 (83:622)

KELLY William, Cap. Anotto Bay Co., d. St George, Jamaica,
16 Nov.1789.   (60:85)

KELSAL Susan, 2nd dau. Charles Kelsal, Jamaica, m. George
Clarke, Westham, Essex, 12 Feb.1776.   (46:142)

KEMBLE Henry John m. Isabella, yngs. dau. late William James
Stevenson, Receiver Gen. Jamaica, St Andrews, Jamaica,
1 March 1851.   (NS35:545)

KEMBLE John, d. NY, 1798.   (68:1086)

KEMBLE William, b.1780, 3rd s. late Francis Kemble, London,
soldier, editor 'Quebec Mercury', d. Quebec, 5 March 1845.
                                        (NS23:678)(NS24:82)

KEMBLE Miss, Brunswick, m. Col. Gage, NA, 1759. (29:93)

KEMMIS ..., s. William Kemmis, RA, b. St Helen's Island,
Montreal, 3 June 1865.   (NS2/19:229)

KEMP Emma, eldest dau. Maj. Gen. Kemp, East Hothley, Sussex,
m. Alexander Heslop, Inner Temple, only s. W Heslop, Jamaica,
London, 1842.   (NS18:313)

KEMP Dr George, d. Baillou's Plant., Nassau, WI, 24 July 1788,
buried Scotch Cemetery.   (58:752)

KEMPE Rev. Alfred Arrow, Wrexham, Bucks., m. Selina Augusta,
yngs. dau. late James Phipps Woodcock, St Kitts, Tenby,
17 Nov.1846.   (NS27:195)

KENDAL Catherine, 3rd dau. Henry Kendal, m. Rev. Maximilian
Nunez, 2nd s. John Nunez, Jamaica, London, 7 June 1859.
(NS2/9:81)

KENDALL George Wilkins, b.Vermont, 1808, writer & farmer,
d. Boerne, Kendall Co., Texas, 21 Oct.1867.   (NS3/2:827)

KENNEDY Angus, s. Daniel Kennedy, Glasgow, d. St Lucie,
Jamaica, 1803.   (73:86)

KENNEDY Archibald, s. Daniel Kennedy, Glasgow, d. Norfolk,
Va., 1803.   (73:86)

KENNEDY Hugh, s. Daniel Kennedy, Glasgow, d. Philadelphia,
1803.   (73:86)

KENNEDY Jane, dau. late Robert Kennedy, Daljarrock, m.
Robert Thomson, Jamaica, Maybole, 4 Jan.1796.   (66:80)

KENNEDY Jane, b.1777, dau. Alexander Macomb, NY, wid. Robert
Kennedy, d. Leamington, 20 May 1867.   (NS3/4:117)

KENNEDY John, Kirkcudbright, d. on passage from NY, 5 Jan.1797.
(67:165)

KENNEDY Robert, ex Colonial Sec., s. late John Kennedy,
Cultra, Co. Down, d. Bermuda, 17 Oct.1864.   (NS2/17:802)

KENNY Joanna, dau. Edward Kenny, President NS, m. M Bowes, s.
Sir Dominick Daly, Halifax, NS, 4 July 1859.   (NS2/7:302)

KENNEY Mary, b.1817, w. Charles Kenney, ex Cap., 52nd Reg.,
d. Nevis, 16 Dec.1840.   (NS15:558)

KERGINSON Miss, d. NY, 1798.   (68:1086)

KENSINGTON J L, b.1789, judge, d. Tobago, 31 Aug.1837.(NS8:660)

KERR Charles, merchant, d. Antigua, 11 Dec.1796.   (66:168)

KERR Isabella, eldest dau. Rev. Alexander Kerr of Stobo, m.
James Kerr, judge, Quebec, 17 Sep.1818.   (88:370)

KERR James, b.1765, judge, d. Quebec, 5 May 1846. (NS26:222)

KERR John, ex Grenada, d. London, 4 Jan.1816.   (86:183)

KERR Robert Joseph, Grand River, Upper Canada, m. Mary Anne,
gdau. late G Farley, Henwick, Worcs., 7 July 1822.   (92:88)

KERR Robert, Jamaica, d. on passage to WI, 1824.   (94:647)

KERRICH Walter Fitzgerald, Cap., 26th Cameronians, eldest s.
John Kerrich, Geideston Hall, m. Olivia Augusta Gilbert Hanson,
only dau. Jesse Jones, wid. Cap. George Scott Hanson, 56th Reg.
Somerset Isle, Bermuda, 2 July 1857.   (NS2/3:456)

KERRY T N, C-in-C Antigua & Montserrat, d. Antigua, 18 Nov.1819.
(90:186)

KETLAND John, merchant, d. Philadelphia, 29 Aug.1799.(69:993)

KEY John, b.1682, Philadelphia, d.Pa., 5 July 1767. (37:524)

KIDD Adam, b.1802, Co. Londonderry, poet, d. Quebec, 5 July
1831.   (101:477)

KIDD Mrs, b.1755, d.NY, 1858.   (NS2/5:540)

KILMARNOCK Lord, s. Countess of Errol, b. Montreal, 7 Feb.
1852.   (NS37:399)

KINCAID George, ex Charleston, SC, d. Exeter, 5 Jan.1791.
                                                    (61:92)

KINCAID Margaret, dau. late Thomas Kincaid, merchant, Leith,
m. Alexander Rowand, MD, Montreal, Edinburgh, 25 Jan.1844.
                                                    (NS21:309)

KING Christian, dau. Rev. John Campbell, St Andrews, Jamaica,
w. William Brooks King, ex Jamaica, d. Teignmouth, 5 May 1864.
                                                    (NS2/16:812)

KING Francis, d. Jamaica, 1791.   (61:187)

KING George, Southampton, d. Antigua, 1813.   (83:595)

KING George Brodribb, b.1792, eldest s. G King, Bristol,
barrister, d. St Dominica, 16 July 1817.   (87:376)

KING Harriett Nice, wid. Cap. E H King, 59th Reg., m. Thomas
Lett Stahlschmidt, Victoria, Vancouver Island, 26 March 1863.
                                                    (NS2/15:96)

KING Harry, b.1807, barrister, d. Windsor, NS, 24 Oct.1865.
                                                    (NS3/1:143)

KING John Hampden, barrister, Assemblyman, m. Margaret
Hughes, only dau. Adam Cuppage, judge, Barbados, 30 Oct.1850.
                                                    (NS35:195)

KING Joseph, St Kitts, m. Miss Giles, London, Jan.1772.(42:46)

KING Richard, b.1837, 2nd s. Mr King, solicitor, Walsham-le-
Willows, d. Chatham, Canada West, 23 May 1856.   (NS2/1:255)

KING Robert, b.1821, 2nd s. Rev. Robert Francis King, Barbados,
JP & Magistrate St George, d. Barbados, 2 July 1859.(NS2/7:428)

KING Robert Duncan, b.1816, HM Vice Consul Haiti, eldest s.
Cap. J D King, Waterford, d. Port au Prince, Haiti, 8 June
1843.   (NS20:334)

KING William Brooks, b.1824, yngr. s. James Bryan King,
Portland, Jamaica, d. Sydney, NSW, 22 Oct.1849.   (NS33:559)

KING ..., s. Mr King, American minister, b. Jan.1802.(72:180)

KINGDON Roger, MD, s. Rev. Roger King, Holsworthy, Devon, d.
Mariposa, Canada West, 22 April 1854.   (NS42:90)

KINGSLEY Catherine, yngs. dau. late Thomas Kingsley, London,
m. Benjamin Lancaster Jemmett, MD, Grenada, Langley Marsh,
Bucks. 10 Dec.1844.   (NS23:198)

KINNEAR David, b.1807, Edinburgh, proprietor 'Montreal
Herald', d. Montreal, 20 Nov.1862.   (NS2/14:127)

KINNEAR Janet Muir, w. W B Kinnear, Solicitor Gen. NB, d.
Fredericton, NB, 30 Dec.1846.   (NS27:455)

KINNEIR Emily, eldest dau. James Kinneir, MD, NY, m. Rev.
Henry Stuart Fagan, headmaster, Burton-on-Trent Grammar
School, London, 23 July 1851.   (NS36:423)

KIRBY John, Chief Justice Jamaica, d. Spanish Town, Jamaica,
1809.   (79:585)

KIRBY John Malmsbury, b.1826, eldest s. late Rev. J M Kirby,
Stourbridge, d. St Thomas, WI, 29 Sep.1848.   (NS31:222)

KIRKE Elizabeth King, Jamaica, m. Cap. Mayne, 'in the
Jamaica trade', London, 30 Aug.1789.   (59:860)

KIRKE Robert, 'estate owner in WI', m. Miss Bourke, London,
24 Jan.1752.   (22:92)

KIRKHAM Dr, ex Leominster, Hereford, d. Kingston, Jamaica,
20 April 1799.   (69:717)

KIRKPATRICK Robert Faed, 2nd s. William Kirkpatrick, Brighton,
m. Catherine Emma, 3rd dau. William Bradbury, Montreal,
21 May 1852.   (NS38:89)

KIRWAN Patrick, d. Antigua, 1819.   (89:91)

KIRWAN ..., dau. Cap. George Kirwan, b. Montreal, 10 June
1866.   (NS3/2:249)

KITTERMASTER H F J, surgeon, eldest s. Dr Kittermaster,
Meriden, Worcs., d. Warwick, Canada, 10 March 1853.(NS39:672)

KITTOE Mrs, wid. G Kittoe, Antigua, d. Barnstaple, 8 Oct.1811.
                                                  (81:487)

KNIGHT Edward, s. Edward Knight, English comedian, ex London,
settled America 1827, late NY, d. New Orleans, 18 Dec.1833.
                                                  (104:454)

KNIGHT George, Swedish Consul Havanna, d.1843.   (NS20:670)

KNIGHT Lewis, ex Jamaica, d. London, 10 March 1813. (83:389)

KNITT William Henry, eldest s. late Rev. William Smith Knitt,
Bawdrip, Somerset, d. Jamaica, 10 Sep.1851.   (NS36:666)

KNOWLES Sir Charles Henry, b. Jamaica, 24 Aug.1754, only s.
Adm. Sir Charles Knowles, Gov. Jamaica, d.28 Nov.1831.
                                                  (101:564)

KNOX Cap., Royal Emigrants, d. Canada, 1778.   (48:495)

KNOX Gen., d. Warren, America, 25 Oct.1806.   (76:1169)

KNOX Cap. m. Jane Eliza, yngs. dau. G G Gordon, Antigua, niece
late Sir W Ashton, 11 Dec.1817.   (87:628)

KOSSUTH Emilie Zukavaky, b.1817, sis. Louis Kossuth,
settled America 1851, d. Brooklyn, NY, 29 July 1860.
(NS2/9:326)

KUPER Henry George, b.1804, eldest s. Rev. William Kuper,
Royal German chaplain, HM Consul Baltimore, d. Baltimore,
7 Dec.1856.   (NS2/2:249)

KUTIN Rev. Daniel, Christiana Church, Pa., d.9 Oct.1776.
(46:483)

KYAN John Howard, b.1775, inventor, d. NY, 5 Jan.1850.
(NS33:343)

KYTE Mary Loretta, eldest dau. late Charles Kyte, Berbice, m.
Rev. J H Malet, naval chaplain, Bermuda, Fulham, 5 Jan.1842.
(NS17:322)

LABORDE Rev. Horatio William, ex Caius College, Cambridge,
eldest s. William Laborde, m. Georgina Anne, eldest dau.
late Thomas Melville, Kingston, St Vincent, 2 Dec.1845.
(NS25:199)

LA CAZE Alix Marie, 3rd dau. Louis La Caze, Attorney Gen.
St Lucia, m. Frederick George Jackson, 21st Royal North
British Fusiliers, Castries, St Lucia, 2 Feb.1864.(NS2/16:520)

LA CAZE Maria Marguerite Fernande, 3rd dau. Louis La Caze, m.
Arthur J, 2nd s. late William Hutchinson, Cheltenham,
Castries, St Lucia, 28 Nov.1865.   (NS3/1:267)

LA COSTE George, judicial referee, d. Trinidad, 1 Jan.1849.
(NS35:335)

LA FONTAINE Sir Louis Hypolite, b.1862, d. Montreal,
12 May 1867.   (NS3/4:115)

LAIDLAW Eliza Mary, dau. late John Laidlaw, President,
Dominica, m. Rev. John Innes, Downe, Hythe, 27 April 1847.
(NS28:80)

LAIDLAW James, Clerk Council Dominica, d. Dominica, 1 Aug.
1841.   (NS16:668)

LAIDLAW Mary Anne, dau. late John Laidlaw, Dominica, m.
Thomas Denne, Downe, Kent, 19 Oct.1852.   (NS39:86)

LAIDLAW Robert, s. James Laidlaw, Hindleshope, d. Grenada,
1797.   (67:897)

LAING Rev. David, St Peter College Cambridge, s. late David
Laing, Jamaica, m. Mary Elizabeth, dau. John West, Jamaica,
14 April 1824.   (94:368)

LAING John, b.1779, Cap., St George Militia, d. Dominica,
30 Aug.1808.   (78:1126)

LAING Maria, b.1778, wid. John Laing, Dominica & Haddo,
Scotland, d. Jersey, 22 Feb.1853.   (NS39:452)

LAING Mrs, w. James Laing, Jamaica, d. London, 9 Feb.1817.
(87:188)

LAKE Ann, w. J Lake, dau. late Rev. Peregrine Curtois,
Branston, Lincs., d. WI, 8 Jan.1847.   (NS27:455)

LAKE Richard jr., d. Jamaica, 1801.   (71:770)

LAKE W Walton, b.1766, ex NY, late Castle Donington, Leics.,
d. London, 25 Dec.1848.   (NS31:215)

LAMB Alexander, b.1799, d. on passage from WI to GB,
18 Sep.1843.   (NS20:670)

LAMBIE William, Jamaica, m. Elizabeth Dundas, dau. Patrick
Crichton, Jamaica, Edinburgh, 1820.   (90:563)

LA MOTTE Anthony m. Dorcas, only dau. William Randal,
Surveyor Gen. Southern District America, 8 May 1767. (37:279)

LA MOTTE Lewis, barrister, d. Spanish Town, Jamaica,
23 Aug.1814.   (84:498)

LA MOTTE Lewis John, b.1810, eldest s. Lewis La Motte,
Jamaica, d. Bremen, 11 Oct.1848.   (NS30:671)

LAMPKIN Symonds, Jamaica, d. April 1753.   (23:248)

LAND Thomas, solicitor, only s. late Rev. Thomas Land,
Tiverton, d. Spanish Town, Jamaica, Oct.1850.   (NS35:110)

LANE Anne Sarah, 2nd dau. Rev. Ambrose Lane, Pendleton, m.
Ashley Hibberd, ex Lt. Col., Canada Militia, Montreal,
Pendleton, 9 Feb.1864.   (NS2/16:381)

LANE Eliza, yngs. dau. Thomas Lane, London, m. William Dick,
Jamaica, 5 Sep.1811.   (81:284)

LANE Eliza Harriet, only dau. Thomas Lane, Colonial Sec., m.
Richard Paget Campbell, eldest s. Col. Richard Jones, RA,
Antigua, 23 Nov.1850.   (NS35:196)

LANE Maj. Henry Bowyer, RA, m. Jane, dau. Archibald Thomson,
Jamaica, Greenham, Berks., 2 Feb.1825.   (95:177)

LANE Theresa Maria, dau. Cap. Ambrose Lane, PEI, gdau. Charles
Douglas Smith, Lt. Gov. PEI, m. Edward Douglas Harvest, 97th
Reg., s. Maj. Harvest, gs. Charles Douglas Smith, Lt. Gov.
PEI, Charlottetown, PEI, 26 May 1853.   (NS40:304)

LANGDON Eliza, dau. Walter Langdon, gdau. John Jacob Astor,
NY, m. Matthew, s. Rev. Mark Wilks, Paris, gs. late Rev.
Matthew Wilks, London, NY, 3 Oct.1842.   (NS19:197)

LANGDON Micah, only s. Mrs Langdon, Bristol, d. on passage
from Jamaica, 4 July 1806.   (76:874)

LANGHORNE Jeremiah, Chief Justice Pa., d. Philadelphia, 1742.
                                                       (13:51)

LANGLEY Elizabeth, wid.Thomas Langley, MD, ex Jamaica, d.
Henley on Thames, 3 May 1812.   (82:596)

LANGLEY Thomas, MD, d. Jamaica, 1791.   (61:187)

LANGRISHE Esther Isabella, eldest dau. late Lt. Robert
Langrishe, RN, m. William H Mare, NFD., 16 Aug.1821.(NS36:646)

LARDNER Maria, only dau. J Lardner, Barbados, m. Lt. R H
Vetch, RE, Dominica, 29 July 1863.   (NS2/15:498)

LARDY C F, Lt., 4th Reg., m. Mrs Thomasina Pinder, wid.
J Pinder, dau. Gen. Haynes, Barbados, 4 Dec.1823.   (94:456)

LARGE ..., dau. Maj. Large, Rifle Brigade, b. Quebec,
28 Nov.1865.   (NS3/1:114)

LARGE ..., dau. Maj. Large, Rifle Brigade, b. Ottawa,
17 Feb.1868.   (NS3/5:532)

LARKEN William Hare, Lt., 47th Reg., m. Louise, yngs. dau.
Alfred Savage, Montreal, 17 April 1867.   (NS3/3:808)

LARKINS Henry, b.1795, barrister, d. Grenada, 19 Dec.1820.
                                              (91:186)

LASCELLES Miss, niece Adm. Holbourne, m. Godney Clarke jr.,
Barbados, 15 Oct.1762.   (32:503)

LASCO Rev. Francis Joseph, b. Marcianise, Naples, 1819, RC
priest, d. Boston, USA, 3 March 1866.   (NS3/1:754)

LATIMER Richard, ex Kingston, Jamaica, d. Crumlin, Ireland,
30 Oct.1813.   (83:622)

LA TOUCHE Mary, b.1757, wid. John Digges La Touche, Jamaica,
d. Tunbridge Wells, 1842.   (NS19:107)

LA TROBE Frederic Benjamin, b.1804, yngs. s. late Rev. C J
La Trobe, d. Jamaica, 11 Dec.1841.   (NS18:223)

LAURENCE Sophia Anglin, dau. late George Laurence, St James,
Jamaica, m. Rev. John Hambledeon, Holloway, Middlesex,
London, 9 Dec.1834.   (105:204)

LAURENS Henry, b.1723, ex President Continental Congress,
Ambassador to Holland, d. Mepkin, SC, 1792. (62:186)

LAURIE Col. James, b.1720, ex Mosquito Shore, d. Glasgow,
20 Dec.1800.   (70:1298)

LAUZUP Henry William, Ordnance Dept., m. A Tucker, dau.
Henry Tucker, President, Bermuda, 1796.   (66:438)

LAVINGTON Lord, Gov. WI, d. 1 Aug.1807.   (77:889)

LAVINE Isaac, Barbados, d. April 1764.   (34:250)

LAW Elizabeth Lucy, eldest dau. Lt. Col. Law,Royal NFD. Co.,
m. Edmund Heathcote, Lt., HMS Eurydice, 3rd s. Rev. Samuel
Heathcote, New Forest, Hants., St Johns, NFD., 13 July 1844.
                                            (NS22:421)

LAW Joseph, b.1800, only s. Joseph Law, Barbados, d.London,
19 Nov.1816, buried St Michael's, Cornhill. (86:478)

LAW Thomas, b.1756, 8th s. John Law, Bishop of Carlisle, &
Mary Christian, d. Washington, America, 1834. (104:437)

LAWRIE William Kennedy, Redcastle, Galloway, ex Woodhall Est.,
Jamaica, d. Bath, 28 Jan.1811   (81:191)

LAWRENCE Abbott, b. Groton, USA, 16 Dec.1792, late US
Ambassador to GB, d. Boston, USA, 18 Dec.1855.   (NS54:433)

LAWRENCE CHarles, Gov. NS, d. Halifax, NS, 20 Oct.1760.(30:594)

LAWRENCE Elizabeth, b.1829, dau. W H Prescott, historian, w.
James Lawrence, d. Boston, USA, 24 May 1864.   (NS2/17:121)

LAWRENCE Georgina Sarah, w. Cap. Arthur J Lawrence, Rifle
Brigade, eldest dau. G J Pennington, London, d. Halifax, NS,
25 Jan.1846.   (NS25:558)

LAWRENCE James Charles, Hazlenymph & St Ives, d. Hazlenymph,
Jamaica, 1811.   (81:679)

LAWRENCE James, eldest s. Abbott Lawrence, m. Elizabeth, only
dau. W H Prescott, historian, Boston, USA, 16 March 1852.
                                                 (NS37:512)

LAWRENCE Thomas, Kingston, Jamaica, late Cheapside, d. 29 Jan.
1805.   (75:881)

LAWRIE Mrs, sis. late Dr Steele, Jamaica, d. Kentish Town,
7 Aug.1798.   (68:729)

LAWS James, d. Jamaica, 16 April 1732.   (4:330)

LAWS Sir Nicholas, Gov. Jamaica, d. Jamaica, 1731.   (1:355)

LAWSON Sophia Delafosse, b.1836, dau. C Lawson, Archdeacon of
Barbados, d. St James, Barbados, 26 May 1859.   (NS2/9:197)

LAWSON Cap. Thomas Milner, b.1813, ex Whitby, d. Portland,
Maine, 12 Oct.1859.   (NS2/7:654)

LAWTON Charles Henry, 5th s. Rev. J Thomas Lawton, Elmswell,
Suffolk, d. Hampton, Jamaica, 5 March 1846.   (NS25:670)

LAWTON Frederick, s. Rev. J T Lawton, Elmswell, Suffolk, d.
Jamaica, 13 May 1852.   (NS38:211)

LAYBOURNE W, Gov. Grenada, d.1775.   (45:303)

LAYNE Charles, b. Albemarle, Buckingham County, 1700, d.
Campbell Co., Va., 17 May 1821.   (91:91)

LAYTON William Henry, b.1794, magistrate Essex & Suffolk, d.
Zaleski, Vinton Co., Ohio, 29 May 1867.   (NS3/4:120)

LEACH Sarah, yngs. dau. late Hugh Leach, Bristol, m. J A Allen
Colonial Treasurer, Port of Spain, Trinidad, 15 June 1843.
                                                 (NS20:312)

LEACOCK Henrietta Maltby, dau. late Joseph Leacock, Mount
Brevitor, Barbados, d. Lee, Kent, 12 July 1820. (90:93)

LEADER Henry Peregrine, ex 22nd Reg., 2nd s. Henry Leader,
Reaseheath, Cheshire, d. Westwood, Canada West, 20 Feb.1865.
                                                 (NS2/18:660)

LEATHEM.., s. C Leathem, Dominica, b. London, 26 Oct.1858.
                                                 (NS2/5:627)

LEAVER James, ex Halifax, NS, d. London, April 1820. (90:476)

LE BRETON Anne Letitia, eldest dau. Philip Henry Le Breton, Hampstead, m. Frank J Boscoe, Victoria, Vancouver Island, Lyme Regis, 22 Sep.1864.   (NS2/17:648)

LECKIE ..., s. William Leckie, Maj., 39th Reg., b. Bermuda, 30 Nov.1860.   (NS2/10:199)

LECUN Rev. Piancos G, RC Papal Apostolic Prefect WI, d. Kingston, Jamaica, 1808.   (78:170)

LEE George, ex Jamaica, d.4 Oct.1757.   (27:482)

LEE Hannah, dau. Richard Lee, m. Corbal Washington, nephew Gen. Washington, Va., 1787.   (57:933)

LEE Robert, b.1764, Asst. Comm. Gen., d. St George, Bermuda, 22 Feb.1853.   (NS39:560)

LEE William, ex Sheriff of London & Middlesex, d. Green-spring, Va., 27 July 1795.   (65:879)

LEEFE Thomas, b.1803, s. John Leefe, Canal House, Malton, d. New Orleans, 24 Sep.1854.   (NS42:639)

LEES Francis Gerald, ex Lt., 25th Reg., s. George Lees, Werneth, Lancs., m. Sophia Charlotte, only dau. A J Maxham, Quebec, 5 Nov.1867.   (NS3/5:102)

LEES Mary, w. John Campbell Lees, Chief Justice Bahamas, eldest dau. William Vesey Manning, ex Chief Justice Bahamas, d. Nassau, 24 April 1846.   (NS26:222)

LEFFERTS Peter, judge, King's Co., NY, d. Flatbush, Long Island, NY, 1791.   (61:1065)

LEFROY Emily, b.1822, eldest dau. Sir John Beverley Robinson, Chief Justice Upper Canada, w. Col. Lefroy, RA, d. London, 25 Jan.1859.   (NS2/6:330)

LEFROY ..., s. Anthony Lefroy, b. Goderich, Canada West, 30 June 1860.   (NS2/9:312)

LEGARD Richard, yngs. s. late Sir Digby Legard, d. Jamaica, 6 June 1818.   (88:373)

LEGGATT Caroline Mary, eldest dau. late George Leggatt, Guildford, m. Cap. Henry Reynolds Luard, RE, 3rd s. Peter Francis Luard, MD, Warwick, Victoria, Vancouver Island, 8 Oct.1864.   (NS2/16:107)

LEGGE Francis, ex Gov. NS, d. Grove, Pinner, 15 May 1782.
                                                  (53:453)

LE GRAND Sir Samuel, ex Gov. Montserrat, d.1779.   (49:519)

LE GURE Hugh S, US Attorney Gen., d.1843.   (NS20:335)

LEIGH Cap., planter, Jamaica, d.31 Oct.1742.   (12:602)

LEIGH Elizabeth Burke, yngs. dau. Thomas Leigh, d.
Liguena, Jamaica, Nov.1801.   (72:181)

LEIGH Rev. John, b.1790, Ecclesiastical Comm. NFD., d.
St Johns, NFD., 1824.   (94:91)

LEIGH Sir Samuel Egerton, 2nd s. late Sir Egerton Leigh,
Attorney Gen. SC, d. Edinburgh, 11 Jan.1797.   (67:165)

LEITCH Colin, d. Jamaica, 1791.   (61:186)

LEITH Arthur, Cap., 69th Reg., Maj. Brigade Caribees, m.
Charlotte, dau. Gov. Seton, St Vincent, WI, 21 June 1791.
                                                    (61:871)

LEITH Sir James, Gov. Barbados, d. Pilgrim, Barbados,
16 Oct.1816.   (86:566)

LEITH Mrs, wid. Cap. Leith, 69th Reg., only dau. late Gov.
Seton, St Vincent, m. Cap. Henry Evans, 6 Oct.1807. (77:976)

LE MARCHANT ..., dau. Sir John Gasparde Le Marchant, b.
13 June 1848, Govt. House, NFD.,   (NS30:198)

LE MARCHANT ..., s. Sir Gasparde Le Marchant, b. Halifax,
NS, 5 Feb.1854.   (NS41:413)

LENOX George, ex Liverpool, d. Bay of Honduras, 9 June 1817.
                                                    (87:183)

LENTHALL John, b. Chesterfield, Derby, clerk-of-works,
settled USA c1792, d. Washington, NE, 19 Sep.1808. (78:1127)

LEONARD Daniel, b.1740, ex Chief Justice Bermuda, d.27 June
1829.   (99:650)

LEONARD George, Judge Antigua, Councillor Virgin Islands, m.
Miss Martin, dau. Henry Martin, late President, Virgin
Islands, 27 Aug.1791.   (61:872)

LEONARD Mrs Leonara, b.1771, dau. Henry Martin, ex President,
Virgin Islands, w. George Leonard, President, Virgin Islands,
d. 18 Jan.1794.   (64:383)

LEONARD Richard, ex Lt. Col., d. Lundy Lane, Niagara Falls,
Canada, 31 Oct.1833.   (104:556)

LEONI Mr, 'the celebrated singer', d. Jamaica, Oct.1796.
                                                    (67:252)

LESLIE George, b.1780, eldest s. James Leslie, ex Cap., 15th
Reg., d. Spring Gardens, St Thomas-in-the-East, Jamaica,
18 Dec.1800.   (71:185)

LESLY Andrew, President, Antigua, d.26 May 1780.   (50:298)

LE SOUEF Jeremiah, b.1783, US Vice Consul, d. London,
19 Jan.1837.   (NS7:219)

LE SOUEF Laura, eldest dau. late Jeremiah Le Souef, US Consul
London, m. Rev. Abraham Louis Martin, French Weslayan minister,
Calais, Isle of Thanet, 24 July 1841.   (NS16:536)

LE SOUEF Sophia, b.1778, wid. Jeremiah Le Souef jr., US
Vice Consul London, d. Calais, 16 March 1841.   (NS16:110)

LE STRANGE H S, Norfolk, m. Emmeline, dau. late W Austin,
Boston, Mass., Boston, 26 Dec.1866.   (NS3/3:239)

LETHBRIDGE Albert Arthur Erin, ex 13th Light Dragoons, 3rd s.
Sir John Hesketh Lethbridge, m. Jane, only ch. Robert A Hill,
Hamilton, Canada West, 11 Oct.1862.   (NS2/13:770)

LETTSON Pickering, b.1780, yngs. s. Dr Lettson, lawyer, d.
Tortula, 28 Oct.1808.   (78:1127)

LETTSON Mrs, wid. Pickering Lettson, d. Tortula, 24 Jan.1809.
                                                  (79:278)

LEVETT Francis, London, d. Savanna, Ga., Sep.1802. (72:1161)

LEVETT John, b.1785, planter, bro.-in-law Rev. Thomas Bennett,
Lincs., d. Julianstown, SC, 7 Oct.1808.   (78:1189)

LEVI W J, Barbados, m. Rebecca, dau. Levian Hart, London,
2 Feb.1820.   (90:272)

LEVIEN Mary, eldest dau. John Levien, m. John, 3rd s. John
Mewburn, MD, Canada West, Sidmouth, 4 June 1851. (NS36:189)

LEVY Michael, b.1765, ex Kingston, Jamaica, d. London,
12 April 1845.   (NS23:671)

LEVY Thomas, partner Richard Dobson, Liverpool, d. St Pierre,
Martinique, 6 Oct.1794.   (64:1150)

LEVYS Henrietta, b.1772, wid. Philip Levys, Jamaica, d.
Notting Hill, 11 Sep.1852.   (NS38:439)

LEWER Mr, publisher, d. NY, 14 Aug.1838.   (NS10:454)

LEWES James Wrigley, Customs searcher, Bermuda, eldest s.
Lee Lewes, d. St George, Bermuda, 1819.   (89:570)

LEWES Matthew Gregory, d. Gulf of Mexico, on passage from
Jamaica, 16 May 1818.   (88:639)

LEWIS Alexander Calcleugh, 2nd s. Arthur Lewis, Champion Hill,
Surrey, d. Madisonville, NA, 31 May 1845.   (NS24:326)

LEWIS Edwin, d. Jamaica, 1791.   (61:682)

LEWIS George Meade, Madeira, ex NY, m. Eleanor Elizabeth,
eldest dau. Justice McCord, Chancellor Bishop's College,
Lennoxville, Montreal, 24 April 1862.   (NS2/12:775)

LEWIS H L, merchant, d. Kingston, Jamaica, 18 March 1816.
                                                  (86:474)

LEWIS James, b.1778, ex Speaker Jamaica Assembly, Advocate
Gen. Jamaica, d. London, 18 Aug.1847.   (NS28:440)

LEWIS John, printer, d. Jamaica, 1791.   (61:1065)

LEWIS John Bower, barrister, m. Anna, eldest dau. Cap.
Eccles, Dublin & Bath, Niagara, 17 Oct.1840.   (NS15:90)

LEWIS M, Gov. Gen. Upper Canada, d.11 Oct.1809.   (79:1235)

LEWIS Maria Anne, w. Lt. Col. Thomas Lewis, St Pierre,
Monmouth, eldest dau. Thomas Daniel, Bristol, d. on passage
to Barbados, 14 April 1817.   (87:568)

LEWIS Matthew Gregory, b.1773, author, d. on passage from
Jamaica to England, July 1818.   (88:183)

LEWIS Sarah, dau. late William Lewis, Jamaica, m. Robert
Sewell, 1775.   (45:606)

LEWIS William Frederick, b.1814, 2nd s. late James Lewis,
Commissioner Slave Compensation, Supreme Court Judge Jamaica,
d. London, 11 Dec.1856.   (NS2/2:123)

LEWIS William Hoare, b. Gibralter, 1777, 4th s. late Col.
George Lewis, RA, d. Trinidad, 21 Aug.1803.   (74:478)

LEWIS Zachariah, Vice President American Bible Society, d.
Brooklyn, 1840.   (NS15:111)

LEWIS Miss, London, m. Thomas Saunderson, Jamaica, 1757.
                                                    (27:338)

LEWIS Miss, Jamaica, m. Thomas A Woolls, Ostend, 4 May 1789.
                                                    (59:572)

LEWIS ..., dau. Dr W J Lewis, ex RN surgeon, b. Halifax, NS,
3 Feb.1865.   (NS2/18:497)

LEWIS Mrs, w. J Mason Lewis, Naval Comm. Antigua, d. London,
1814.   (84:418)

LEWTHWAITE Rev. Samuel, b.1815, Fellow St Mary Magdalene
College Cambridge, d. Belize, Honduras, 6 Aug.1846. (NS27:99)

LEYBORNE S, s. late Gov. Leyborne, Jamaica, d. Jamaica on
Duke, 1782.   (52:454)

LIGHT Alexander Whalley, ex Col., 25th Reg., d. Woodstock,
Canada West, 17 May 1856.   (NS2/1:255)

LIGHT Jane, b.1787, w. Col. Light, Lytes Carie, Woodstock,
d. Upper Canada, 1 Sep.1853.   (NS40:537)

LIGHT Margaret Lucretia, 4th dau. Col. Light, ex 25th Reg.,
Lytes Carie, Woodstock, Upper Canada, m. Henry, s. Peter
Boyle de Blaquierl, Woodstock, 11 Oct.1848.   (NS31:198)

LIGHTBOURNE Mary, 3rd dau. William Lightbourne, m. Robert
Pennington Sparrow, surgeon, RN, 3rd s. late R G Sparrow, Deal,
Pagets, Bermuda, 22 Dec.1849.   (NS33:430)

LIGHTFOOT Col., SC, d. London, 11 June 1764.   (34:302)

LIGHTFOOT Lt. Col., m. Cornelia, 2nd dau. Cap. Edward Williams
Kingston, Upper Canada, 28 Dec.1819.   (90:272)

LILLICRAP J H A, Cap., Indian Army, 2nd s. late Adm. James
Lillicrap, d. North Douro, Canada, 1 Dec.1861.   (NS2/12:237)

LINCOLN Abraham, b. Hardin Co., Kentucky, 12 Feb.1809, s.
Thomas Lincoln, US President, d. Washington, 15 April 1865.
                                                 (NS2/18:785)

LINDEGREN John, b.1779, HM Consul Porto Rico, d. St Johns,
Porto Rico, 3 Feb.1855.   (NS43:544)

LINDO Esther, dau. Alexander Lindo, m. A M Belisario, Kingston,
Jamaica, 1791.   (61:774)

LINDSAY Charles Philip, b.1820, s. late Philip Yorke Lindsay,
HEICS, d. NY, 8 March 1854.   (NS41:554)

LINDSAY Rev. David, s. late James Lindsay, London, m. Sophia,
dau. Rev. Dr Adamson, Montreal, 30 April 1851.   (NS36:79)

LINDSAY Rev. John, St Catherine, Jamaica, d. Spanish Town,
Jamaica, 3 Nov.1788.   (59:178)

LINDSAY John, emigrated from London on brigantine Gen. Clarke,
d. Nassau, New Providence, 1794.   (64:1155)

LINDSAY William, Gov. Tobago, d.1796.   (66:618)

LINDSAY W, b.1755, ex Antigua, d. Southampton, 19 Feb.1812.
                                                 (82:392)

LINDSAY Miss m. Francis Forbes, Barbuda, 30 April 1764.(34:250)

LINE John m. Miss Shubrick, SC, 22 June 1768.   (38:302)

LINGAN George, b.1742, ex Customs Collector Georgetown, d.
Baltimore, 1812.   (82:404)

LINGING John, b. Kennington, 1788, d. St Anne, Jamaica, 1810.
                                                 (80:192)

LINWOOD S Whalley, 2nd s. Mrs Linwood, Leicester, d. Jamaica,
1801.   (71:770)

LIPSCOMBE Christopher, Bishop of Jamaica, m. Miss Pope, dau.
late E Pope, London, 27 July 1824.   (94:176)

LIPSCOMB Christopher, b.1782, eldest s. Rev. William Lipscomb,
Walbury, Northallerton, Bishop of Jamaica, d. St Thomas,
4 April 1843.   (NS20:201)

LIPSCOMBE E F, b.1805, d. Cades Bay, Antigua, 12 Sep.1853.
                                                 (NS40:649)

LIPSCOMBE Frances Eves, w. Dr Lipscombe, Bishop of Jamaica,
d. Perkins Pen, Jamaica, 27 April 1825.   (95:652)

LISTON Robert, US Plenipotentiary, m. Henrietta, dau. late
Nathaniel Merchant, Antigua, Glasgow, 27 Feb.1796. (66:254)

LITTLE Aaron, d. Jamaica, 1791.   (61:186)

LITTLE James Somerville, surgeon, RA, m. Ellen, dau. Rev. Dr
Porter, Alphington, Exeter, Halifax, NS, 15 Dec.1852.(NS39:196)

LITTLE Michael, b.1739, 40 years NFD., d. Greenwich, 9 Dec.
1819.   (89:571)

LITTLE Philip Francis, NFD. Supreme Court Judge, m. Mary Jane,
dau. Edward Holdright, Monkstown, Kingstown, Dublin, 4 May
1864.   (NS2/16:795)

LITTLE Rev. Robert, ex Gainsboro, Unitarian pastor, Washington,
d. Harrisburg, 1827.   (97:382)

LITTLEWOOD Caroline, w. Rev. William Littlewood, d. Inagua,
Bahamas, 13 July 1856.   (NS2/1:390)

LIVINGSTON Isabella, yngs. dau. Dr Livingston, Aberdeen, m.
Dr Thomas Pym Weeks, physician, Nevis, 21 April 1789.(59:669)

LIVINGSTONE Jasper, Livingstone Manor, NY, m. Matilda, yngs.
dau. Sir John Morris, Shelly Park, Dover, 26 May 1851.
                                                   (NS36:188)

LIVINGSTON Philip, Pa. Congressman, d.1777.   (48:395)

LIVINGSTON Robert, b.1687, Claremont, America, d.27 July 1775.
                                                      (45:407)

LIVINGSTONE William, Gov. Md., d. Elizabethtown, NA,
28 July 1790.   (60:956)

LIVINGSTON Mrs, w. William Livingston, Gov. NJ, d.Elizabeth-
town, America, 1790.   (59:865)

LIVINGSTONE Mr, Congressman NY, fa.-in-law Gen. Montgomery,
d.1776.   (46:142)

LIVIUS Peter, ex Chief Justice Canada, d. Brighton, 23 July
1795.   (65:622)

LIVIUS Miss, Richmond, Surrey, dau. late Peter Livius, Chief
Justice Quebec, m. John Dalby, Derby, 5 Dec.1800.   (70:1288)

LLOYD Rev. F L, Aldworth, Berks., m. Jessy. eldest dau. late
Henry Harding, HM Customs, Nevis, Tamworth, 10 Feb.1859.
                                                   (NS2/6:316)

LLOYD Rev, ex Shrewsbury, d. Chester, America, 25 Feb.1795.
                                                   (65:1054)

LLOYD ..., s. Col. Lloyd, RE, b. St George, Bermuda, 12 June
1862.   (NS2/13:219)

LOCKHART Cap. Allan Elliot, RE, m. Georgina, dau. Maj. Benison,
39th Reg., St George, Bermuda, 4 June 1864.   (NS2/17:234)

LOCKHART Edward, s. late James Potter Lockhart, ex President,
Dominica, m. Louisa, 3rd dau. late Adm. Cumberland, gdau. late
Richard Cumberland, Dominica, 18 May 1843.   (NS20:427)

LOCKHART J P, ex President, Dominica, d. Dominica, 22 Oct.1837.
                                                    (NS9:222)

LOCKHART Mrs, w. James Potter Lockhart, Dominica, d.
Montserrat, 19 June 1807.   (77:888)

LOCKHART ..., dau. James Potter Lockhart, b. Dominica,
15 Oct.1813.   (83:498)

LOCKHART John Dyer, b.1779, Dominica, d. London, 15 Sep.1809.
                                                        (79:894)

LOCKHART Louisa, w. Edward Lockhart, d. Dominica, 5 Aug.1843.
                                                        (NS20:446)

LOCKYER Gerald, s. late Nicholas Lockyer, Plymouth, m.
Charlotte Lucy, eldest dau. late J Spedding, Montreal,
18 Aug.1864.   (NS2/17:512)

LODINGTON Thomas, Court Common Pleas, m. Miss Day, dau. late
John Day, Antigua, 22 Sep.1791.   (61:873)

LOGGIN Marianne Elizabeth, dau. late William Cole Loggin,
Woolfardisworthy, m. Hugh McNeill Dyer, Lt., RN, s. Cap.
Dyer, RN, Bermuda, 15 May 1858.   (NS2/5:185)

LOINSWORTH Auguste Painting, Barbados, eldest s. late A L
Loinsworth, MD, m. Augusta, yngs. dau. Thomas Titt, Brighton,
London, 23 June 1851.   (NS36:315)

LONG Samuel, Assemblyman, Jamaica, d.1757.   (27:189)

LONGDEN ..., dau. Lt. Gov. Longden, b. Dominica, 30 Aug.1866.
                                                        (NS3/2:682)

LONGLANDS Rev. William David m. Judith Campbell, dau. John
Pendville, gdau. W Campbell, New Milns, Jamaica, Walcot,
Bath, 18 Dec.1822.   (92:642)

LONGLEY Maj. John, Lt. Gov. Dominica, d. Dominica, 5 Aug.1838.
                                                        (NS10:566)

LOOSEMORE Rev. Philip Wood, Prince William, m. Elizabeth
Isabella, only dau. John Davidson, Dumfries, NB, 30 Nov.1858.
                                                        (NS2/6:197)

LOPEZ Abraham Rodrigues, Jewish merchant, d. St Jago de la
Vega, Jamaica, 13 March 1788.   (58:933)

LORD Sarah, b.1776, m. Ricard Lord, Nassau, Bahamas, d.
4 Oct.1849.   (NS32:553)

LORENTZ Baron m. Miss Mills, dau. late James Mills, Jamaica,
London, Dec.1825.   (95:560)

LORING Elizabeth, yngs. dau. Lt. Col. Loring, m. John F J
Harris, eldest s. John Harris, RN, Toronto, 9 Nov.1859.
                                                        (NS2/8:176)

LORING George Frederick, b.1829, s. late Lt. Col. Loring,
d. Albany, USA, 24 Jan.1855.   (NS43:438)

LORING Sir John W, b.13 Oct.1775, s. Joshuah Loring, High
Sheriff Mass., Admiral, RN, d. Ryde, Isle of Wight, 29 July
1852   (NS38:312)

LOSACK Adm. George, s. Richard Hawkshaw Losack, St Kitts,
d. Milan, 22 Aug.1829.   (99:465)

LOSACK Richard Hawkshaw, b.1730, St Kitts, Lt. Gov. Leeward
Islands, d.2 Nov.1813.   (83:622)

LOSACK Miss, only dau. Richard Losack, St Kitts, Lt. Gen.
Leeward Islands, m. John White, RN, 22 March 1796.   (66:253)

LOSH Emma Louisa, eldest dau. late W Losh, Trinidad, m.
Com. T Malcolm Sabine Pasley, RN, eldest s. Rear Adm. Sir
Thomas S Pasley, Port of Spain, Trinidad, 13 Feb.1860.
                                                      (NS2/8:506)

LOPEZ Catherine, b.1672, d. Kingston, Jamaica, 28 Aug.1806.
                                                      (76:1075)

LOUGH Charlotte Eleanor Burnaby, dau. Rev. John Lough,
St George, m. William Shedden Barr, St George, Bermuda,
1 Jan.1861.   (NS2/10:454)

LOUGHNAN Andrew, London, m. Mary Ann, dau. late Dr Robert
Hamilton, Grenada, 21 June 1798.   (68:535)

LOUIS Anne Woollcombe, eldest dau. Thomas Louis, Culloden,
Barbados, gdau. Rear Adm. Sir Thomas Bent, Cadwell, m. Sir
Abraham Josias Cloete, CO Windward Islands & Demerara,
Barbados, 8 July 1857.   (NS2/3:328)

LOUIS Thomas, 2nd s. late Admiral Sir Thomas Louis, m.
Elizabeth Grasett, 2nd dau. Foster Clarke, the Garden,
Barbados, 2 Oct.1828.   (98:558)

LOVELL Langford, Antigua, m. Miss Heathcote, eldest dau. Sir
W Heathcote, MP, 28 April 1798.   (68:441)

LOVERING Sarah M, dau. T Lovering, m. George, s. late Cap.
G Truscott, RN, Exeter, Buffalo, NY, 1 Oct.1851.   (NS37:83)

LOW Alexander F, Tizapan, Mexico, m. Mary Ann Julia, yngr. dau.
late James Chabot, Mexico, British Residence, Mexico, 24 July
1852.   (NS38:519)

LOW ..., s. John Low, 15th Reg., b. St Johns, NB, 9 April
1863.   (NS2/14:778)

LOWDEN Frances E, wid. George L Lowden, dau. late James
Stewart, HM Consul, New London, Conn., d. Cheltenham,
22 March 1852.   (NS37:533)

LOWE Alfred, US Consul, Civita Vecchia, Roman States, m. Mary
Ann, eldest dau. Paul Balme, London, Ramsgate, 22 Aug.1851.
                                                      (NS36:647)

LOWE Penelope, Jamaica, m. Roger Tuckfield, Devon, 22 Feb.
1755.   (25:138)

LOWE Mrs, b.1740, wid. Isaac Lowe, ex NY, sis. Sir Cornelius
Cuyler, d. London, Jan.1820.   (90:187)

LOWE ..., s. Maj. R D Lowe, Grenadier Guards, b. Montreal,
3 June 1863.   (NS2/15:95)

LOWER Henry Martyn, Archdeacon NFD., m. Alice Mary Fulford,
only dau. Bishop of Montreal, Hemmingford, Canada East,
12 Aug.1858.   (NS2/5:412)

LOWER ..., s. Archdeacon Lower, b. St Johns, NFD., 22 May 1862.
                                                     (NS2/13:219)

LOWNDES John, b.1755, Surveyor Gen. Dominica, d. Mount
Pleasant, Dominica, 11 Aug.1819.   (89:472)

LOWNDES W, SC Congressman, d. on board Moss on passage from
Philadelphia to England, 27 Oct.1822.   (92:649)

LOWREY Cap. Joseph, ex Jamaica, d. Bristol, 21 Dec.1806.
                                                        (76:185)

LOWTHER John, ex Lancaster, merchant, d. St Thomas, 5 July
1804.   (74:881)

LOWTHER Rev. Ponsonby, eldest s. late George Lowther,
Somerset, d. Montreal, 20 July 1854.   (NS42:407)

LUARD Henry Reynolds, Cap., RE, 3rd s. late Peter Francis
Luard, MD, Warwick, m. Caroline Mary, eldest dau. late George
Leggatt, Guildford, Victoria, Vancouver Island, 8 Oct.1864.
                                                     (NS2/16:107)

LUCAS Charles, ex Antigua, d.5 Aug.1766.   (36:390)

LUCAS John, ex Dominica, d. Cheltenham, 1810.   (80:677)

LUCAS Sampson, ex Kingston, Jamaica, d. London, 14 April 1813.
                                                        (83:492)

LUCE Philip, d. NY, 1798.   (68:1086)

LUDGATER Eliza, yngs. dau. late James Ludgater, Lee, Kent, m.
Rev. Charles Walsh, St Paul's, Harbor Grace, NFD., 29 Nov.1859.
                                                      (NS2/8:177)

LUDWELL Philip, Va., d.25 March 1767.   (37:144)

LUGAR James, Archdeacon Demerara, bro.R & J Lugar, Ardleigh,
Essex, d. Barbados, 26 May 1853.   (NS40:207)

LUNDIE Mary Ann, w. Thomas Lundie, ex Jamaica, d. Liverpool,
16 March 1844.   (NS21:555)

LUNDY F J, Lockington, Yorks., m. Henrietta Eliza, 2nd dau.
J Sewell, Chief Justice Lower Canada, Quebec, 11 May 1837.
                                                        (NS8:192)

LUNDY Henrietta Eliza, w. Rev. Francis James Lundy, dau. late
Jonathan Sewell, Chief Justice Canada East, d. Niagara,
Canada West, 1848.   (NS29:335)

LUNDY Louisa de Quincy, 3rd dau. Rev. F J Lundy, Grimsby,
Upper Canada, gdau. Jonathan Sewell, Chief Justice Lower
Canada, m. Henry, eldest s. Rev. Carre, Raphoe, Ireland,
Stirling, Upper Canada, 9 Aug.1866.   (NS3/2:539)

LUSCOMBE Henry, 3rd s. Dr Samuel Luscombe, Exeter, d.
St Domingo, 1796.   (66:794)

LUSHINGTON G, s. W Lushington, Chislehurst, Kent, d.
Grenada, 1 Feb.1803.   (73:382)

LUSHINGTON Henry, 2nd s. William Lushington, London, d.
Martinique, 17 April 1794.   (64:576)

LUSINIANI Charles, b. Florence, 1719, d. Montreal, 19 May
1825.   (95:94)

LUTENER Dr William R T, b. England, d. Broadway, NY, 1854.
                                                    (NS41:439)

LUTWYCHE Edward Goldston, b. New Bolton, 1737, NB agent, d.
London, 9 Nov.1815.   (85:637)

LUXMOORE ..., s. Rev. Dr Luxmoore, Bishop of Jamaica, b.
Jamaica, 14 May 1836.   (NS6:204)

LYALL Charles, Barbados, yngs. s. John Lyall, Brighton, m.
Charlotte Augusta, dau. late Alexander Bayley, Wood Hall,
Jamaica, Stapleton, Gloucester, 21 Aug.1845.   (NS24:521)

LYDEKKER Rev. Gerhardus, b. America, 1729, ex pastor Dutch
Church NY, American Loyalist, d. London, 1794.   (64:768)

LYLE John, Speaker Barbados Assembly, d. 27 May 1767.(37:382)

LYLES Enoch M, Alexandria, America, d.13 Aug.1805.   (75:971)

LYMAN Daniel, b. Newhaven, Conn., American Loyalist, Maj.,
Royal Invalids, d. London, 3 Nov.1809.   (79:1175)

LYMAN Gen. William, ex US Consul London, d. Cheltenham,
22 Sep.1811.   (81:394)

LYNCH P, d. Jamaica, 30 Sep.1817.   (87:561)

LYNNE Henry, ex Hants. editor, theater manager, d. St Louis,
Mobile, America, 8 Aug.1854.   (NS42:409)

LYNE Sarah Poole, w. Philip Lyne, ex Antigua, d. London,
15 Aug.1825.   (95:188)

LYNEY R T, London, m. Grace, eldest dau. late William
Sutherland, Jamaica, 23 Dec.1819.   (89:635)

LYON Anna Maria Bowes, sis. Earl of Strathmore, m. Henry
James Jessop, ex Quebec, barrister, 28 Jan.1788.   (58:177)

LYON Benjamin, 3rd s. late Benjamin Lyon, Jamaica, d. Spanish
Town, Jamaica, 5 Sep.1800.   (70:1107)

LYON Elizabeth Anne, dau. late Benjamin Lyon, Jamaica, m.
J Kerr, s. late Cap. J Dudley Jordan, gs. Jacob Jordan, Lower
Canada, Clifton, 10 Aug.1845.   (NS24:520)

LYON George, barrister, d. Spanish Town, Jamaica, Jan.1799.
                                                     (69:347)

LYONS Henry, Antigua, d.6 Jan.1747.   (17:47)

LYSAGHT Elizabeth, dau. late Lord Lisle, m. James Hall,
Jamaica, Dawlish, Devon, 1800.   (70:1284)

LYSONS Harriet Sophia, b.1823, w. Col. D Lyssons, d. Montreal,
15 May 1864.   (NS2:17:120)

LYSSONS ..., dau. Col. Lyssons, b. Montreal, 20 Feb.1863.
                                                     (NS2:14:513)

LYSTER Letitia, dau. Col. William Lyster, ex Greenford Manor,
Middlesex, m. John, s. Thomas Higham, Charleston, SC, &
Margate, Kent, Llanlligan, 24 Jan.1844.   (NS21:309)

LYTE Thomas Maximilian, b.1807, 2nd s. late Cap. Thomas Lyte,
Christchurch, Hants., d. Twillingale, NFD., 30 July 1850.
                                                        (S34:566)

LYTTLETON William Henry, Gov. Jamaica, bro. Lord Lyttleton,
m. Miss Macartney, 2 June 1761.   (21:284)

LYTTLETON ..., s. Henry Lyttleton, Gov. Jamaica, b.26 Oct.
1763.   (34:146)

MABANE Isabella, sis. Adam Mabane, judge, Quebec, d. Quebec,
28 Dec.1809.   (80:283)

MABELLE Margaret, dau. F Mabelle, Jamaica, m. W Farquharson,
Lt., RA, Ealing, 22 July 1823.   (93:272)

MACALISTER Katherine Elisabeth, dau. A MacAlister, Torresdale
Castle, Scotland, m. William, eldest s. John Rose, Montreal,
2 Jan.1868.   (NS3/5:385)

MCALISTER Miss m. Walter Colquhoun, Logon, Dominica, 1776.
                                                        (46:435)

MCALPINE Miss, American lady, m. Horatio Robson, paper hanging
manufacturer to Prince of Wales, London, 1790.   (60:178)

MCANDREW Alexander, NY, m. Catherine, 2nd dau. William P
McAndrew, Dulwich, London, 21 Dec.1848.   (NS31:311)

MCANUFF John Clinton, Master of Chancery Jamaica, Supreme Court
Judge Jamaica, d. Hopewell Est., Jamaica, 1819.   (88:655)

MCARTHUR John, Bristol, m. Susan Matilda, 2nd dau. Thomas
Darrell, Barbados, Clifton, 8 Sep.1842.   (NS18:651)

MACARTNEY Miss m. William Henry Lyttleton, Gov. Jamaica, bro.
Lord Lyttleton, 2 June 1761.   (21:284)

MACAULAY D W, b.1815, barrister, d. Canada, 18 Dec.1840.
                                                      (NS16:222)

MACAULAY George Hayter, 2nd s. late Col. J S MacAulay, d.
Toronto, 27 Jan.1859.   (NS2/6:438)

MACAULAY James, ex Honduras, d. Dawlish, Exeter, 1795.(65:174)

MACAULAY Louisa Birchell, yngs. dau. Chief Justice MacAulay,
Toronto, m. Henry Edward, s. Rev. H Bennett, Sparkford,
Somerset, Toronto, 26 Nov.1857.   (NS2/4:207)

MACAULAY ..., three daus. J MacAulay, Inspector Gen.,
Toronto, 1840.   (NS14:310)

MACBEAN Caroline H H, only ch. late Aeneas MacBean, Tomatin,
St Thomas, m. Lt. Col. Robert Ross, 4th Royal Irish Dragoon
Guards, Inverness, 7 April 1819.   (88:368)

MACBEAN John, b.1752, ex Jamaica, d. Brompton, 23 Sep.1834.
                                                   (104:554)

MACBEAN Mary, dau. late William MacBean, Roaring River Est.,
Jamaica, m. Charles Willis jr., Cranbrook, Kent, Oxford,
22 March 1825.   (95:364)

MCCALL John, ex Jamaica, d. Canonbury, Middlesex, 18 May 1808.
                                                   (78:560)

MCCALMAN Duncan, s. Dr McCalman, Islay, Argyll, d. Jamaica,
March 1795.   (65:791)

MCCARTHY Charles, Councillor, d. WI, 1793.   (63:1152)

MCCAUL Rev. John, Principal Upper Canada College, ex Dublin,
m. Emily, dau. Justice Jones, Toronto, 1839.   (NS13:201)

MCCAUSLAND Caroline, 2nd dau. Oliver McCausland, Letterkenny,
d. Union Island, St Vincent, 8 June 1798.   (68:627)

MCCLALAND Sarah, Nottingham, dau. late Joseph McClaland,
Kingston, Jamaica, m. John Mayne, Houndsgate, Nottingham,
Dublin, 16 June 1798.   (68:624)

MCCLELLAN James, surgeon, d. St James, Jamaica, 20 July 1794.
                                                   (64:958)

MCCORD Eleanor Elizabeth, eldest dau. Justice McCord,
Chancellor Bishop's College, Lennoxville, m. George Meade
Lewis, ex NY, Madeira, Montreal, 24 April 1862. (NS2/12:775)

MCCORD John Samuel, b.1801, judge, d. Temple Grove, Montreal,
28 June 1865.   (NS2/19:259)

MCCORD Julia, dau. late David McCord, Columbia, SC, m. Cap.
Henry Wemyss, 2nd s. Sir William H Feilden, Feniscowles,
Lancs., Greenville, SC, 27 Oct.1864.   (NS2/18:234)

MCCORMACK James, b. Co. Cavan, 6 Aug.1751, settled New
Windsor, NY, d. Newburgh, NY, 11 Nov.1865.   (NS3/1:283)

MCCORNOCK Thomas, Custos, St Thomas in the East, Jamaica,
d. Dec.1848.   ⸜NS31:335)

MCCORQUODALE Archibald, Kilbride, Argyll, m. Laura Jones,
Llanbeblig, Caernarvon, St Johns, NFD., 7 Nov.1813. (83:20)

MCCRAE Thomasina, only dau. late Alexander McCrae, Jamaica,
m. T G Maddison, 7th Hussars, 1815.   (85:82)

MCCREADY Andrew, d. NY, 1798.   (68:1086)

MCCULLOCH John, b. Northern Ireland, 1716, settled America,
Provincial officer under Rogers, Comm. Stores Oswego 1756,
d. London, 27 Dec.1793.   (64:89)

MCCULLOCH Thomas, merchant, ex Va., d. Westfield, Bothwell,
4 Nov.1794.   (64:1150)

MCCULLOH Anne, w. Robert McCulloh, dau. George Roupell,
Charleston, SC, d. Charlton, Kent, 1 Nov.1785.   (55:835)

MCCUMMING Price, Grand Valley, ex Cap., 5th WI Reg., d.
Montreal, 13 June 1805.   (75:881)

MACDONALD Allan, ex Cap., 84th Reg., d. Quebec, 13 April 1790.
                                                       (60:668)

MACDONALD Caroline B, only dau. James MacDonald, Laprairie,
gdau. Maj. William MacDonald, ex 104th Reg., m. Charles jr.,
s. Mr Kadwell, Greenwich, Laprairie, Canada, 30 July 1850.
                                                     (NS34:540)

MACDONALD Donald, bro. late Col. Alexander MacDonald of
Kinlochmoidart, d. Banks, St Anne, Jamaica, 19 Aug.1794.
                                                      (64:1054)

MACDONALD Elizabeth R, w. R C MacDonald, Paymaster, 30th Reg.,
Castle Tioram, PEI, d. St John, NB, 22 Jan.1843.   (NS19:557)

MACDONALD J M, Treadie, ex Cap., 84th Reg., d. PEI, 1811.
                                                       (81:679)

MACDONALD Ronald, d. Jamaica, 1790.   (60:1214)

MACDONALD William John m. Catherine Balfour, 2nd dau. Cap.
James Murray Reid, Hudson Bay Co., Fort Victoria, Vancouver
Island, 17 March 1857.   (NS2/3:212)

MACDONALD Maj. m. Miss Graham, only dau. late Charles Graham,
Williamsfield, Jamaica, 27 April 1805.   (75:485)

MCDONALD Mrs, b.1726, wid. Lt. Col. D McDonald, 84th Reg.,
ex America, d. Edinburgh, 1815.   (85:92)

MACDONALD ..., dau. Lt. Col. P J MacDonald, 4th WI Reg., b.
St Eustatia, 17 Oct.1862.   (NS2/14:102)

MACDONALD Miss m. William McGillevray, Montreal, 22 Dec.1800.
                                                      (70:1288)

MCDONELL Rev. Alexander, b.1760, Bishop of Kingston, Upper
Canada, d. Dumfries, 14 Jan.1840.   (NS13:327)

MACDONELL Helen, b.1760, wid. James McKenzie, dau. Allan
MacDonell of Lundie, Mohawk & Glengarry settler, d. Three
Rivers, Canada, 10 Nov.1839.   (NS13:333)

MACDONELL Susan, eldest dau. Charles MacDonell, Upper Canada,
gggdau. late Sir John Johnson, d. London, 21 Feb.1850.
                                                     (NS33:447)

MACDONELL Miss, dau. late Charles MacDonell, Newhall, Co Clare,
m. Charles Hamilton, ex Tobago, 23 Oct.1799.   (69:1192)

MCDONOGH Thomas, HM Consul NE, d. Boston, 24 Oct.1805.(75:282)

MACDOUGALL Celia, w. Rev. Henry MacDougall, military chaplain,
Bahamas, d. Jamaica, 6 Oct.1849.   (NS33:341)

MACDOUGALL Clara Lefanu, b.1846, dau. late Maj. P MacDougall,
d. Montreal, 28 Feb.1864.   (NS2/16:671)

MCDOUGALL Eliza, eldest dau. late Alexander McDougall,
Weston Hall, Grenada, gdau. James MacQueen, London, m.
William Willcocks, eldest s. Robert Baldwin, Canada, London,
29 Aug.1854.   (NS42:617)

MACDOUGALL Rev. Henry, military chaplain, Nassau, Bahamas,
m. Frances Hall, 2nd dau. Maj. Bacon, Seafield, Isle of Man,
26 Aug.1851.   (NS36:647)

MACDOUGALL P, b.1774, ex Maj., 25th Reg., d. Montreal,
26 Oct.1861.   (NS2/11:693)

MACDOWELL Allan, MD, m. Susan Harriet, only dau. Col. Thomas
Browne, St Vincent, 4 July 1818.   (88:273)

MACDOWELL Daniel, b.1748, St Vincent, d.20 May 1829. (99:94)

MCDOWELL Cap. J V V, b.1828, ex 2nd Bengal Cavalry, late
American Federal Army, d.21 Dec.1862.   (NS2/14:257)

MCELHINEY James, b.1766, ex Baltimore, d. Brighton, 2 Jan.1851.
                                                    (NS35:220)

MACEUEN Dr William, d. Jamaica, 1791.   (61:187)

MACFARRAN John, Solicitor Gen. Caribee Islands, d. Grenades,
1 Aug.1770.   (60:393)

MCGAWLEY John, MD, d. Quebec, 1780.   (51:45)

MCGEE Thomas D'Arcy, b.Carlingford, Ireland, 1823, d. Ottawa,
1868.   (NS3/5:690)

MCGHIE Robert, b.1740, ex Jamaica, d. London, 19 June 1806.
                                                    (76:590)

MCGILL Peter, Montreal, Councillor, Lower Canada, m. Eliza,
only dau. John Shuter, Hendon, London, 1832.   (102:267)

MCGILLIVRAY Col. Alexander, b. Inverness, Chief Creeks, d.1792.
                                                    (62:577)

MCGILLIVRAY Mary, sis. William McGillivray, Montreal &
Argyll, d. Elmwood, Montreal, 28 April 1854.   (NS42:90)

MCGILLIVRAY William, Montreal, m. Miss MacDonald, 22 Dec.1800.
                                                    (70:1288)

MCGILLIVRAY William, b.1764, Peine an Ghael, Mull, ex Montreal,
d. London, 16 Oct.1825.   (95:380)

MACGILLIVRAY Mr, Creek Chief,ex Drumnaglass, Inverness-shire,
d. Pensacola, 17 Feb.1793.   (63:767)

MCGOWN Alexander, merchant, s. Baillie Alexander McGown,
Rothesay, d. Kingston, Jamaica, 2 June 1795.   (65:791)

MCGRATH Sara, 2nd dau. George McGrath, Charlemont, Jamaica,
m. Cap. Dawson R Evans, 6th Royal Reg., St Thomas in the Vale,
Jamaica, 4 May 1865.   (NS2/19:106)

MAGRATH Rev. Dr, b. Dublin, ex St Marks, Liverpool, Rector
Trelawney, Jamaica, d.14 June 1852.   (NS38:320)

MCGREGOR Sir E J Murray, Lanric, Perth, b.1785, Gov. & C.in C.
Barbados, St Vincent, Grenada, Tobago, St Lucia & Trinidad,
d. Barbados, 14 June 1841.   (NS16:540)

MACGREGOR ..., dau. Malcolm MacGregor, 2nd WI Reg., b. Up Park
Camp, Jamaica, 16 April 1864.   (NS2/16:789)

MAGRUDER Helen, 2nd dau. Cap. Magruder, m. Lord William
Frederick Abinger, Montreal, 23 Dec.1863.   (NS2/16:245)

MAGRUDER Thomas, b.1747, d. Indianapolis, USA, 1857.(NS2/2:628)

MCGUFFIE James Muir, b.1798, HM Consul Gonaives Haiti, d. NY,
30 Aug.1849.   (NS32:559)

MCGUFFOG Catherine, Jamaica, m. William Duff, London, 1793.
                                                   (63:956)

MCINNES Donald, Hamilton, Upper Canada, m. Mary Amelia, yngs.
dau. late Sir John B Robinson, Toronto, 30 April 1863.
                                                   (NS2/15:97)

MACKAY Sheridan K, barrister, 2nd s. T M Mackay, d. Northfield,
Minnesota, 6 Aug.1867.   (NS3/2:539)

MACKINTOSH Lachlan, b.1738, ex Comm. Gen. St Domingo, d.Bath,
2 Sep.1804.   (74:888)

MACKINTOSH William Lyster Hay, b.1824, 2nd s. J Mackintosh,
Totteridge, Herts., d. Guanasevi, Mexico, 21 May 1856.
                                                   (NS2/1:390)

MCINTOSH Miss, yngs. dau. William McIntosh, Grenada, m.
Chevalier le Sieur de Colleville, French infantry officer, s.
Marchioness de Colleville, Normandy, Ostend, 1791. (61:1061)

MCINTYRE Frances Charlotte, 3rd dau. Rev. John McIntyre,
St James, Jamaica, m. John Salmon Gordon, 96th Reg., London,
22 Feb.1849.   (NS31:535)

MCINTYRE John S, Baldwin Co., Ala., m. Mary Augusta Hardwich,
Baldwin Co., dau. late James Hardwich, Bristol, niece William
Lovell Hardwich, London, Mobile, Ala., 18 Aug.1858.(NS2/5:628)

MACKAY Aeneas, s. James Mackay, Ross-shire, d. Havanna, Cuba,
May 1817.   (87:629)

MACKAY Charles, d. Jamaica, 1791.   (61:186)

MACKAY Daniel, Santa Cruz, m. Mrs John Muir, wid., Demerara,
Edinburgh, 17 Feb.1825.   (95:273)

MACKAY Hector, St Thomas in the Vale, Jamaica, d. London,
21 Dec.1823.   (93:645)

MACKAY James, Paymaster, 1st WI Reg., m. Mrs Catherine Jane
Moore, wid. Dr John Moore, Trinidad, 27 Nov.1823.   (94:176)

MACKAY Robert, Bighouse, Scotland, d. Antigua, 29 Sep.1816.
                                                     (86:566)

MACKAY William, Supt. Indian Affairs Montreal, d. Montreal,
6 Sep.1832.   (103:190)

MACKAY Mrs, ex St Vincent, m. James Seton jr., Bishop
Auckland, 1 Jan.1799.   (69:77)

MCKEAN Thomas, b.1737, Chief Justice Pa., ex Gov. Pa., d.
Philadelphia, 1817.   (87:187)

MACKECHNIE Stuart, eldest s. A MacKechnie, St Austins, Fife,
d. Canada West, 5 May 1853.   (NS40:98)

MACKENZIE Charles Kenneth, b.1788, d. NY, 6 July 1862.
                                                  (NS2/13:504)

MCKENZIE Donald, b. Scotland, 1783, ex Gov. Hudson Bay Co.,
d. Mayville, Chataque Co., 20 Jan.1851.   (NS35:454)

MCKENZIE George, Councillor, Bahamas, d. Long Island, America,
1792.   (62:576)

MACKENZIE George Udny, 2nd s. late Alexander MacKenzie, WS,
d. Clarendon, Jamaica, 6 Aug.1808.   (78:1039)

MACKENZIE Hector, NY State, s. late Kenneth MacKenzie of Redcastle, m. Diana, 2nd dau. Dr Davidson, Leeds, Edinburgh,
29 March 1800.   (70:588)

MACKENZIE John, ex merchant, St Kitts, d. Glasgow, 19 Oct.
1797.   (67:984)

MACKENZIE John Francis, b.1824, yngs. s. late Arthur
MacKenzie, Clarendon, Jamaica, d. Vere, Jamaica, 10 Feb.1856.
                                                   (NS45:545)

MACKENZIE Mrs Margaret, dau. Lord John Oliphant, d. Spanish
Town, Jamaica, 6 April 1800.   (70:797)

MCKENZIE Mary, dau. Earl of Cromarty, wid. Thomas Drayton,
m. John Ainslie, Charleston, SC, 17 June 1762.   (32:390)

MACKENZIE Mary, 2nd dau. G MacKenzie, Clarendon, Jamaica, m.
Arthur Foulks, Brockenhurst House, Downton, Wilts., 20 Oct.
1803.   (73:1252)

MACKENZIE Peter, b.1749, Vere, Jamaica, d. Brighton, 8 Sep.
1807.   (77:894)

MACKENZIE Roderick, s. late Cap. Kenneth MacKenzie of Redcastle, d. Jamaica, 1801.   (71:483)

MACKENZIE R Shelton, ex journalist, Liverpool, d. America,
1856.   (NS45:101)

MACKENZIE Thomas, ex Barbados, d. Dunkirk, 1831.   (101:652)

MACKENZIE William Lyon, b. Dundee, 1794, settled Canada, 1825, political radical, d. Toronto, 28 Aug.1861.   (NS2/11:567)

MACKENZIE Mrs, wid. George MacKenzie, Clarendon, Jamaica, d. Twickenham, 10 Oct.1798.   (68:912)

MCKINSTRY John Henrietta, w. Col. McKinstry, 17th Reg., sis. Charles W O'Hara, Co. Sligo, d. Toronto, 8 Feb.1867.(NS3/3:541)

MACKINTOSH James, inf. s. Robert James Mackintosh, d. Govt. House, St Kitts, 29 Aug.1847.   (NS28:558)

MACKINTOSH John, d. Jamaica, 1791.   (61:682)

MACKINTOSH Marion Susan Anne Reade, only dau. Thomas Mackintosh, Guadaloupe y Calvo, Mexico, m. William Randolph Simpson, RA, Southsea, 13 Aug.1853.   (NS40:522)

MACLACHLAN D. , ex Jamaica, m. Louisa, dau. Duncan Campbell, Ardgair House, 11 May 1794.   (64:480)

MCLACHLAN William, b.1818, 2nd s. late Patrick McLachlan, Stanford Hill, d. NY, 2 June 1852.   (NS38:211)

MACLAE Walter Ewing, s. Walter Ewing MacLae, merchant, Glasgow, d. Charleston, 2 Sep.1797.   (67:1069)

MACLAINE Lady Elizabeth, wid. Gen. Sir Archibald MacLaine, m. Edward Harry, s. late M N Neal, Dover, NH, London, 12 March 1863.   (NS2/14:516)

MCLARTY ..., s. Mr McLarty, Chesterville, Jamaica, b. Greenock, 26 Dec.1801.   (71:1208)

MCLAUCHLAN John, d. Jamaica, 1790.   (60:1148)

MCLEAN John, Councillor, Grenada, d. Limlain Est., Carriacou, 18 Feb.1816.   (86:473)

MCLEAN John, Providence Est., St Thomas in the East, Jamaica, d.1852.   (NS38:322)

MCLEAN Lt. Gen. Lachlan, Lt. Gov. Quebec, d.1829.   (99:477)

MCLEAN Miss, dau. late Maj. McLean, m. C Martyr, R N Hospital Agent, Halifax, NS, Halifax, 3 May 1817.   (87:635)

MCLEOD Janetta Maria, yngs. dau. late Maj. McLeod, Salisbury, NE, m. Charles W Marsh, s. late Rev. M Marsh, Salisbury, New Town, NSW, 16 July 1842.   (NS19:311)

MACLEOD Norman, b. Skye, d. Montreal, 27 Jan.1796.   (66:614)

MCMAHON Mrs Elizabeth Dalrymple, b.1761, ex St Kitts, d. London, 8 Sep.1845.   (NS24:434)

MCMILLEN George Douglas, ex Kingston, Jamaica, d. Barcohennock, 29 Sep.1824.   (94:574)

MCMILLAN William, s. Robert McMillan, Liverpool, d.
Jamaica, 6 Oct.1800.   (71:185)

MCMILLAN Cap., master Europa of Greenock, drowned River
St Lawrence, Oct.1794.   (64:1150)

MCMILLAN Mr, d. on the Jamaica on passage to Jamaica, 10 May
1798.   (68:903)

MCNAB Sir Allan Napier, b. Canada, 19 Feb.1798, s. Lt. Allan
McNab, 3rd Dragoons, ex PM, Upper Canada, d. Toronto,
8 Aug.1862.   (NS2/13:494)

MCNAMARA John, merchant, Jamaica, d. on Snow River on passage
from Jamaica, 2 Aug.1815.   (85:376)

MACNAMARA Miss, eldest dau. John MacNamara, m. Lord Cranstoun,
St Kitts, 25 Aug.1807.   (77:886)

MACNAMARA Mrs, wid. J MacNamara, St Kitts, mo. Lady Cranstoun,
d. 21 June 1818.   (88:643)

MCNEAL Theophilius, ex Barbados, d.18 Sep.1776.   (46:436)

MCNEEL Thomas, Custos, Westmoreland, Jamaica, m. Bathia, 2nd
dau. Charles Barclay, Inchbroom, Moray, Jamaica, 25 Jan.1842.
                                                       (NS17:429)

MCNEEL Miss, dau. Thomas McNeel, Custos, Westmoreland, Jamaica,
m. Henry Turner, Cap. West Indian, Jamaica, 25 Jan.1842.
                                                       (NS17:429)

MACNEIL Hector, ex Kingerloch, d. Pictou, NS, 1810.   (80:395)

MCNEVIN Dr William James, b.1763, 'Irish rebel & companion of
Emmett', d. NY, 1841.   (NS16:447)

MACPHERSON ..., s. Maj. MacPherson, 30th Reg., b. Mt. Carmel,
Quebec, 15 Jan.1868.   (NS3/5:382)

MACQUEEN David, b.1820, s. James MacQueen, London, d. Golden
Lane Est., Tobago, 16 Sep.1848.   (NS30:670)

MACQUEEN John, b.1787, Potosi, Jamaicá, d. Kennington,
Surrey, 27 Feb.1853.   (NS39:453)

MCRAE Alexander, Jamaica, d. Edinburgh, 14 March 1796.(66:352)

MCRAE A, b.1764, Va., d. London, 14 Jan.1841.   (NS15:217)

MCRAE Eliza, dau. late Colin McRae, Jamaica, d. London,
16 May 1853.   (NS40:98)

MACTAGGART John, Civil Engineer, Rideau Canal, Canada, author,
d. Tors, Kirkcudbright, 8 Jan.1830.   (100:285)

MCTAVISH D., b.Stratherick, partner North West Co., Canada,
drowned River Columbia, near Cape Disappointment, 22 May 1815.
                                                       (85:376)

MACTAVISH Emily, yngr. dau. Richard Caton, Md., gdau. Charles
Carroll, d. Baltimore, 2 Feb.1867.   (NS3/3:540)

MACTAVISH Georgina, dau. late J G MacTavish, Montreal, m.
N W Massey, s. George Massey, Pitlochry, 21 Oct.1863.
(NS2/15:773)

MACTAVISH John, b.1787, HM Consul Md., d. Baltimore, 21 June
1852.   (NS38:213)

MCTAVISH Mary, eldest dau. late Simon McTavish, Montreal, m.
Maj. Charles Pasley, HEICS, London, 21 May 1817.   (87:82)

MACTAVISH Mary Wellesley, dau. John MacTavish, Montreal, m.
Henry Howard, yngs. s. Earl of Carlisle, London, 29 May 1845.
(NS24:190)

MACULLUM Rev. John, ex Aberdeen, d. Red River Colony, Hudson
Bay, 3 Oct.1849.   (NS33:546)

MCUWIN Mrs Princess, b.1723, settled Kingston, Jamaica, 1739,
d. Montego Bay, Jamaica, 1840.   (NS15:110)

MCWILLIAMS John, attorney, Grand Bacolet Est., d. Grenada,
1 Aug.1826.   (96:477)

MADDEN Helen Martha, b.1818, eldest dau. Lt. Col. T H Ball,
31st Reg., wid. Charles Madden, Kilkenny, d. London, Canada
West, 28 Nov.1862.   (NS2/14:255)

MADDAN James Strange, b.1813, eldest s. Col. Maddan, d. Jamaica,
13 Dec.1854.   ₍NS41:329)

MADDISON T G, 7th Hussars, m. Thomasina, only dau. late
Alexander McCrae, Jamaica, 1815.   (85:82)

MADDOCK Samuel, d. Nevis, 3 Sep.1755.   (25:428)

MADISON James, b. Va., 1758, ex US President, d. Washington,
30 June 1836.   (NS6:429)

MAGRATH Rev. James, b.1766, Trinity College, Dublin, ex
Shankhill & Castlerea, Rector Toronto, d. Erindale, Upper
Canada, 14 June 1851.   (NS36:327)

MAGUIRE Joseph, printer, ex Baltimore, d. Washington, 1816.
(86:380)

MAHARG J, MD, surgeon, 70th Reg., m. Jane Elizabeth Perkins,
dau. Thomas Trigge, Quebec, wid. J M Perkins, Nicolet, Lower
Canada, 6 Jan.1843.   (NS19:422)

MAHON Bernard, stipendiary justice, St Andrews, Jamaica,
d.1846.   (NS25:335)

MAINE Henry Cracroft, b.1832, eldest s. Rev. J T Maine, Hants.,
d. Montreal, 5 April 1864.   (NS2/16:805)

MAINWAIRING Edward, ex Cap., King's American Rangers, d.
London, 1803.   (73:693)

MAIR Georgina Augusta, yngs. dau. late Rev. W Mair, Fulburn,
m. Charles Hay, Nevis, London, 10 March 1847.   (NS27:648)

MAIR John Hastings, b.12 Oct.1790, Lt. Gov. Grenada, d.
Grenada, 21 March 1836.   (NS6:430)

MAIS Frances Dun, 2nd dau. S W Mais, Custos, Port Royal,
Jamaica, m. Rev. William Edward Pierce, St Davids, Jamaica,
5 July 1864.   (NS2/17:377)

MAIS Henry P, of Messrs John & Henry Mais, Kingston, Jamaica,
d. Jamaica, ᴌ3 Nov.1825.   (96:95)

MAIS John, b.1775, d. Spanish Town, 9 Oct.1853.   (NS41:439)

MAIS Rev. John Leslie, Spanish Town, Jamaica, m. Julia
Caroline, 2nd dau. late Cap. Henry Hill, 57th Reg.,
St Andrews, Jamaica, 29 Jan.1856.   ·   (NS45:512)

MAIS Martha, w. John Mais, Kingston, Jamaica, d. London,
15 April 1841.   (NS15:554)

MAIS Rebekah, 3rd dau. Rev. John Mais, Tintern Parva,
Monmouth, m. Arthur Douglas Capel, Bishop's College, Lennox-
ville, 4th s. Rev. T R Capel, Wareham, Dorset, Lennoxville,
Canada East, 26 Dec.1861.   (NS2/12:220)

MAITLAND Amelia, 3rd dau. William Maitland, ex Exeter, d.
Montreal, 2 April 1832.   (102:479)

MAITLAND James, Jamaica, d.1773.   (43:526)

MAITLAND James William, yngs. s. late Lord Dundrennan, d.
Staten Island, NY, 25 June 1860.   (NS2/9:213)

MAITLAND T, physician, m. Mrs Taynton, wid. Nathaniel Taynton,
Attorney Gen. Grenada, Carricou, 31 July 1813.   (83:620)

MAITLAND William, b.1757, ex Exeter, d. Montreal, 20 Jan.1851.
                                                 (NS35:454)

MALEBONE Godfrey, ex Oxford University, farmer, Pomfret,
Wyndham Co., Conn., d.12 Nov.1785.   (56:266)

MALET Rev. J H, chaplain, HM Dockyard, Bermuda, m. Mary
Loretta, eldest dau. late Charles Kyte, London, 5 Jan.1842.
                                                 (NS17:322)

MALLET Mr, 2nd s. Mr Mallet, Leicester, d. St Pierre,
Martinique, 1794.   (64:768)

MALONE Julia, yngs. dau. E Malone, Plymouth, m. John Bradfoot
Cherriman, Prof. Nat. Phil., Toronto, London, 12 June 1858.
                                                  (NS2/5:84)

MALTBY George, merchant, ex Norwich, d. Baltimore, Sep.1807.
                                                  (77:1075)

MALTBY Richard, merchant, d. Barbados, 12 Sep.1816. (86:465)

MANN Rev. Isaac, Caius College Cambridge 1800, Kingston,
Jamaica, d. Jamaica, 1829.   (99:377)

MANN Mary, wid. Rev. Isaac Mann, Kingston, Jamaica, d. Lee,
30 Aug.1850.   (NS34:452)

MANN Mr, d. Montego Bay, Jamaica, 1800.   (70:905)

MANNERS-SUTTON ..., dau. Lt. Gov. J H T Manners-Sutton, b.
Fredericton, NB, 30 Dec.1857.   (NS2/4:325)

MANNING Rev. James, President, RI College, d. New Providence,
29 July 1791.   (61:969)

MANNING Miss, only dau. late Richard Manning, Antigua, m.
Henry Pearson, merchant, London, Antigua, June 1787. (57:933)

MANNING T J, Barbados, m. Ann Catherine Rose, dau. Frederick
Nassau, St Ostyth Priory, Essex, Kendal, 15 Aug.1825.(95:270)

MANNING Sarah, dau. William Manning, St Mary Axe, m.
Benjamin Vaughan, Jamaica, 30 June 1781.   (51:342)

MANSELL Walter, ex merchant, Charleston, SC, d. Sutton,
Shropshire, 20 Dec.1795.   (65:1113)

MANSEL William Villiers, 2nd s. late Lord Jersey, d.
America, 1814.   (84:299)

MANSFIELD Mr, s. Lord Chief Justice, m. Miss Smith, dau. Gen.
Smith, Baltimore, 1810.   (80:86)

MANSON Daniel, b.1739, shipbuilder, Charleston, SC, Maj. in
Royal Provincial Army during Revolution, d. Berwick, 24 April
1816.   (86:566)

MANTACH Rev. Robert, b.1795, chaplain convict settlement, d.
Boaz Island, Bermuda, 18 Dec.1853.   (NS41:437)

MANWEE Eunice, b. Derby Co., 1757, Princess Pishgachtigok
Indians, dau. Joseph Manwee, gdau. Gideon Manweesemium, d.
Kent Indian Reserve, USA, 11 March 1860.   (NS2/8:526)

MAPLES Thomas, d. Santee, Charleston, USA, 29 July 1805.
                                                       (75:971)

MARBOIS Madame Barbe, dau. T Moore, Gov. Pa., d. Gisors, 1834.
                                                      (104:447)

MARCEY W L, b. Stowbridge, Mass., 1786, Gov. NY, d. Ballston,
Saratoga Co., USA, 4 July 1857.   (NS2/3:221)

MARCH C, d. Jamaica, 1790.   (60:766)

MARCH John, b.1754, ex bookseller & printer, Yarmouth &
Norwich, d. Georgetown, Washington, 21 June 1804.   (74:784)

MARCHANT Henrietta, dau. late Nathaniel Marchant, Antigua, m.
Robert Liston, US Plenipotentiary, Glasgow, 27 Feb.1796.
                                                       (66:254)

MARCHANT Nathaniel, Antigua, d. Sidmouth, Devon, 19 Feb.1804.
                                                       (74:191)

MARCUS Rev. Moses, late Brigstock, Northants, ex NY, d.
London, 25 Nov.1852.   (NS39:215)

MARE William Henry m. Esther Isabella, eldest dau. late Lt.
Robert Langrishe, RN, NFD., 16 Aug.1851.
                                                     (NS36:646)

MARESCAUX Oscar, Inspector Colonial Bank, eldest s. Adolphe
Morescaux, St Omer, France, m. Isabella Anne, 2nd dau.
Hinton East, Councillor, Jamaica, niece Sir Edward Hyde East,
Woodford, Jamaica, 15 March 1864.   (NS2/16:650)

MARIGNY Bernard, b. New Orleans, 1784, d. Washington, 1868.
                                                     (NS3/5:408)

MARKLAND John Edward, b.1792, ex Jamaica, d. Caen, Normandy,
5 July 1863.   (NS2/15:248)

MARLOW John Richard, d. Dunfermline Est., Labay, Grenada,
Nov.1799.   (70:1004)

MARRIOTT Cap. H C m. Rosamond, dau. Rev. Hamilton Carrington,
St Johns, NFD., 18 April 1849.   (NS32:84)

MARRYAT Charlotte, b.1773, 3rd d. Frederick Geyer, merchant,
America, m. Joseph Marryat, Boston, USA, 1788, d. Wimbledon,
Surrey, 13 Dec.1854.   (NS43:219)

MARSH Charles W, s. late Rev. M Marsh, Salisbury, m. Janetta
Maria, yngs. dau. late Maj. McLeod. Salisbury, New England,
New Town, NSW, 16 July 1842.   (NS19:311)

MARSH Emmeline Adriana, b.1792, w. John Milbourne Marsh, Dep.
Postmaster Gen., d. Kingston, Jamaica, 15 Sep.1812. (82:670)

MARSH Frances Lucy, dau. late Milbourne Marsh, Jamaica, niece
late Sir Francis Forbes, Chief Justice, NSW, m. George Foster
Wise, eldest s. Edward Wise, eldest s. Edward Wise, Bembridge,
Isle of Wight, Scone, NSW, 21 June 1842.   (NS19:197)

MARSH John Milbourne Augustus, only s. late J M Marsh, Postmaster Gen., Jamaica, m. Grace Elizabeth, eldest dau. late
Philip Pinnock, Jamaica, London, 26 Jan.1848.   (NS29:422)

MARSH William, b.1791, eldest s. Cornelius Marsh, Yoxford, d.
Kingston, Jamaica, 25 April 1820.   (90:186)

MARSHAL Agnes, dau. Robert Marshal, merchant, Glasgow, m.
Campbell Douglas, Jamaica, Hamilton, 1 July 1793.   (63:670)

MARSHALL Anna, dau. late Rev. Edward Marshall, Jamaica, m.
Lt. J Binney, RN, s. H N Binney, NS, London, 1822.   (92:640)

MARSHALL Edward,(alias Peter Fisher), m. Mary Ann Hamilton,
wid., Edinburgh, St Johns, NFD., 23 Feb.1815.   (85:)

MARSHAL James, Cap., NY Volunteers or Queens Rangers, ex NY,
d. 30 July 1779.   (49:47)

MARSHALL James Ford, eldest s. James Marshall, Bath, d.
Trinidad, 14 Sep.1800.   (70:1107)

MARSHALL Jessy, b.1801, dau. George Marshall, Spanish Town,
Jamaica, d.29 June 1819.   (89:90)

MARSHALL Louisa Philips, 3rd dau. Cap. Sir John Marshall,
Gillingham, m. Cap. George Black, Royal Canadian Rifles,
Gillingham, Kent, 5 Oct.1841.   (NS16:648)

MARSTON Charity Jane, wid. N Marston, Jamaica, d. London,
22 Jan.1832.   (102:185)

MARSTON Nathaniel, ex Jamaica, d. London, 18 Oct.1826.(96:473)

MARTER William, only s. William Marter, Sevenoaks, Kent, d.
Rochester, NA, 20 May 1858.   (NS2/5:91)

MARTIEL Mrs Henrietta, b. Hanover, 1687, resident Hanover,
England, Jamaica, & Virginia, d. Dumfries, Va., 1790.(61:187)

MARTIN Rev. Abraham Louis, French Wesleyan minister, Calais,
m. Laura, eldest dau. late Jeremiah Le Souef, US Consul
London, Isle of Thanet, 24 July 1841.   (NS16:536)

MARTIN Lewis Burwell, b.1737, yngr. bro. Samuel Martin,
Whitehaven, Representative St Elizabeth, judge, Jamaica,
d. Oct.1782.   (53:181)

MARTIN Thomas, bro. Rev. Denny Martin, Fairfax, Leeds Castle,
nephew Lord Thomas Fairfax, Va., d. Va., 1798.   (68:1086)

MARTIN Cap. William, ex Royal NC Highland Reg., d. Edinburgh,
8 March 1791.   (61:285)

MARTIN William Alexander, b.1818, yngs. s. late W A Martin,
WS, Edinburgh, d. Tobago, 24 Jan.1850.   (NS33:558)

MARTIN William Fiennes Wykeham, b.1817, yngs. s. late Fiennes
W Martin, Leeds Castle, Kent, d. on passage from America to
England on SS President, March 1841.   (NS16:334)

MARTIN Miss m. 'TA Esq.', Boston, NE, 1772.   (42:495)

MARTIN Miss, dau. Henry Martin, dec., ex President, Virgin
Islands, m. George Leonard, Vice Adm. Judge Antigua,
Councillor Virgin Islands, 27 Aug.1791.   (61:872)

MARTIN Mrs, w. Samuel Martin, Antigua, ex Egham, d. WI, 1810.
                                                       (80:491)

MARTIN ..., dau. Albin Martin, Silton, Dorset, b. Naples,
Jamaica, 7 Nov.1842.   (NS18:650)

MARTLEY ..., dau. John Martley, Grange, ex Cap., 56th Reg.,
b. Lillooet, BC, 5 Oct.1862.   (NS2/14:102)

MARTYR C, RN Hospital Agent, Halifax, NS, m. Miss McLean, dau.
late Maj. McLean, Halifax, 3 May 1817.   (87:635)

MARTYR John, b.1774, Greenwich, d. Mexico, 11 Aug.1826.
                                                       (96:477)

MARYCHURCH Rev. H W, London, m. Elizabeth, dau. Alexander
Campbell, Jamaica, wid. D Davies, London, 5 Sep.1849.(NS32:529)

MASON Dr David, Councillor, Jamaica, d. Savanna la Mar,
6 April 1862.   (NS2/13:112)

MASON Col. George, b.1725, d. Gunston Hall, Fairfax Co., Va.,
7 Oct.1792.   (63:89)

MASON John, b.1767, d. St Kitts, 23 Sep.1821.   (91:571)

MASON Dr Robert, St Mary, Jamaica, d. Jamaica, Oct.1792.
(62:1220)

MASON Miss, eldest dau. Rev. Edward Mason, Blyth, m. George
Robinson, ex Jamaica, Blyth, Notts., 20 Feb.1793.   (63:280)

MASON ..., s. Cap. Mason, RN, b. St Johns, NFD., 1806.(76:773)

MASSEY Mrs Ingoldsby, Norbiton, Surrey, m. Charles N Palmer,
Jamaica, 2 June 1808.   (78:556)

MASSEY N W, s. George Massey, m. Georgina, dau. late J G
MacTavish, Montreal, Pitlochry, 21 Oct.1863.   (NS2/15:773)

MASSIE Jane, 2nd dau. George Massie, Jamaica, d. Kew, 16 Dec.
1795.   (65:1059)

MASSINGBERD Emily Agnes, dau. Rev. H Massingberd, London, ex
Upton, Lincs., m. John Ronalds, St Catherine, Canada West,
6 April 1859.   (NS2/7:78)

MASTON Richard, Gov. Tobago, d. Martinique, 26 Oct.1801.(71:83)

MATHER Dr, physician, Boston, NE, d. June 1764.   (34:350)

MATHIAS Vincent, Customs Chief Teller, m. Miss Popple, dau.
Alured Popple, Gov. Bermuda, 7 Oct.1752.   (22:478)

MATTHEWS Gov., Antigua, d.30 Sep.1752.   (22:478)

MATKARSIE Herbert Henry, RN, m. Elizabeth Stewart, eldest dau.
Lt. R Cock, RN, Seymour East, Canada West, 7 April 1852.
(NS38:87)

MATSON Judith, b.1779, dau. John Matson, Chief Justice
Dominica, d. Roseau, Dominica, 26 Sep.1794.   (64:1150)

MATSON Miss, dau. John Matson, Chief Justice Dominica, m.
Thomas Hutchinson, Fellow New College, Oxford, 18 July 1799.
(69:1189)

MATSON Mary Roberta, b.1749, wid. John Matson, Chief Justice
Dominica, d. Sandwich, Kent, 7 Oct.1812.   (82:405)

MATHEW Edward F R, b.1833, yngs. s. Rev. E W Mathew,
Pentlowhall, Essex, d. Basseterre, St Kitts, 27 Oct.1858.
(NS2/6:100)

MATTHEWS E K, Cap., 6th WI Reg., eldest s. late Etherington
Thomas Matthews, St Catherine, Jamaica, d. St Lucia, 15 Jan.
1810.   (80:491)

MATHEWS Cap. Frederick, s. late Col. Matthews, Chelsea College,
magistrate, d. Barbados, 15 Sep.1836.   (NS6:668)

MATHEW Greville CB, b.1839, Colonial Sec. British Honduras,
d. Belize, 8 June 1866.   (NS3/2:412)

MATTHEWS Dr James, surgeon, d. Oestrich, Nassau, 9 March 1844.
(NS21:558)

MATTHEWS William, b.1769, eldest s. Mr Matthews, bookseller,
London, barrister, d. Tobago, July 1801.   (71:960)

MATHEWS Rev. William Arnold, Laughton, m. Caroline Sarah
Georgina, dau. William Henry Stuart, Lennoxville, Canada
East, Kirton-in-Lindsay, 11 Aug.1866.   (NS3/2:402)

MATTHISON Gilbert, Judge Grand Court St Jago de la Vega,
Trelawney Assemblyman, Jamaica, d.1774.   (44:390)

MAUDE Cap. Francis, RN, yngs. bro. Vicount Hawarden, m.
Frances, 2nd dau. A H Brooking, Customs Collector, St Johns,
NFD., 4 Sep.1827.   (97:364)

MAULIN Mr, d. Kingston, Jamaica, 1793.   (63:1152)

MAUNDER Henry, b.1822, 4th s. late Frederick Maunder, Exeter
& Port au Prince, d. Port au Prince, 5 Feb.1850.   (NS34:109)

MAUNSELL Lt. Gen. John, b.1724, d. NY, 27 July 1795. (65:879)

MAXHAM Sophia Charlotte, only dau. A J Maxham, m. Francis
Gerald Lees, ex Lt., 25th Reg., s. George Lees, Wernett,
Lancs., Quebec, 5 Nov.1867.   (NS3/5:102)

MAXWELL Cap. Alexander, b.1710, d. Jamaica, 1790.   (60:766)

MAXWELL Ann, 3rd dau. Col. Maxwell, m. Eden Colville, Montreal,
4 Dec.1845.   (NS25:199)

MAXWELL Edward, d. Jamaica, 1790.   (60:476)

MAXWELL John, 2nd s. late William Maxwell of Carriden, d.
Tobago, 22 Oct.1793.   (63:1214)

MAXWELL James, b.1774, Orange Grove, Tobago, d. Cheltenham,
1811.   (81:88)

MAXWELL William, b.1837, 3rd s. J G Maxwell, Oaklands, Devon,
4th Officer, Royal WI Mail Steam Packet Co., d. St Thomas, WI,
20 March 1858.   (NS2/5:89)

MAXWELL Miss, m. Henry Beckels, Barbados, 28 Sep.1762.(32:503)

MAXWELL Miss, dau. Mr Maxwell, Jamaica, m. Thomas Windle,
Symond's Inn, 1 Oct.1788.   (58:932)

MAXWELL Col., Gov. St Kitts & Virgin Islands, m. Miss Douglas,
dau. Col. Douglas of Greencroft, Lockerbie, Dumfries,
5 April 1821.   (91:372)

MAXWELL Mrs, w. Charles William Maxwell, Gov. St Kitts, d.
St Kitts, 9 Jan.1823.   (93:473)

MAXWELL Lt. Col., b.1775, ex 15th Reg., d. St Catherine,
Montreal, 9 May 1857.   (NS2/3:100)

MAY Rev. Charles T, d. Strathnavar, Buff Bay, Jamaica,
29 Sep.1866.   (NS3/2:837)

MAY James Westerman, of Messrs O'Reilly, Hill, May & Co.,
Jamaica, d. London, 8 June 1814.   (84:699)

MAY Louise Polk, b.1826, w. Morgan May, d.New Orleans,
4 Dec.1857.   (NS2/4:225)

MAY Rose Herrins, b.1736, Councillor, Jamaica, d. Spanish
Town, Jamaica, 1791.   (61:971)

MAYERS Benjamin, b.1764, ex Assemblyman, d. Tenby, Barbados,
3 June 1854.   (NS42:201)

MAYHEW Alice Maria Elizabeth, only dau. Rev. William Mayhew,
St Andrews, Jamaica, m. Cap. George Lee Chandler, RA, Halfway
Tree Church, Jamaica, 4 Dec.1862.   (NS2/14:369)

MAYHEW Emily, 2nd dau. Joshua Mayhew, London, m. William
Weyman, NY, London, 3 Aug.1841.   (NS16:424)

MAYNARD Eleanora, w. William Maynard, dau. late Cap. John
Blanshard, d. Woodstock, Upper Canada, 25 April 1855.(NS44:105)

MAYNARD George, Chief Judge Common Plea Court Barbados, d.
Barbados, 30 May 1818.   (88:373)

MAYNE Charles, SC, d.1759.   (29:606)

MAYNE John, Houndsgate, Nottingham, m. Sarah McClaland,
Nottingham, dau. late Joseph McClaland, Kingston, Jamaica,
Dublin, 16 June 1798.   (68:624)

MAYNE Cap., Jamaica trade, m. Elizabeth King Kirke, Jamaica,
London, 30 Aug.1789.   (59:860)

MAZYCK Isaac, Assemblyman, SC, d.1770.   (40:487)

MEACHAM Rev. Thomas, b.1794, ex Shepton Mallet, Somerset,
Episcopal minister, d. Weathersfield Springs, Ontario,
21 Oct.1849.   (NS33:102)

MEAGHER Gen. Thomas Francis, b. Waterford, Ireland, 3 Aug.1823,
Gov. Montana, d. Fort Benton, USA, 1 July 1867.   (NS3/2:397)

MEANY Bryan, Waterford, surgeon, d. Jamaica, 1795. (65:616)

MEDLEY Thomas Sands, Maida Vale & New Orleans, d. NY, 8 Nov.
1855.   (NS45:97)

MEECH William, s. late Mr Meech, surgeon-apothecary,
Sherbourne, Dorset, d. Jamaica, Aug.1800.   (70:1290)

MEFFIAT Simon, merchant, Barbados, m. Deborah Bilenfaite,
1768.   (38:198)

MEIKLEHAM David Scott, MD, b.1805, s. late Prof. Meikleham,
Glasgow, d. NY, 20 Nov.1849.   (NS33:342)

MEIKLEHAM William Stuart, MD, d. Trinidad, 1854.   (NS42:201)

MELHADO Charles, b.1820, Belize, Honduras, d. Margate,
20 Feb.1860.   (NS2/8:524)

MELHADO Judith, b.1788, wid. Daniel Melhado, ex Jamaica, d.
London, 9 Feb.1853.   (NS39:335)

MELLISH William Leigh, Cap., Rifle Brigade, eldest s. late
Edward Mellish, Dean of Hereford, m. Margaret Ann, 2nd dau.
Samuel Cunard, Halifax, NS, 19 Oct.1843.   (NS20:648)

MELMOTH John, yngs. bro. late J P Melmoth, d. Jamaica, 1846.
                                                      (NS25:446)

MELVILLE Gov., the Grenades, d. England, 2 June 1766.(36:294)

MELVILLE Annie, 3rd dau. David Melville, Nottingham, m.
Thomas Huggins, eldest s. P T Huggins, Nevis, Nottingham,
17 Nov.1841.   (NS17:92)

MELVILLE Gansevoort, Sec. US Legation, d. London, 12 May 1846.
                                                      (NS26:104)

MELVILLE Georgina Anne, eldest dau. late Thomas Melville, m.
Rev. Horatio William Laborde, ex Caius College, Cambridge,
eldest s. William Laborde, Kingston, St Vincent, 4 Dec.1845.
                                                      (NS25:199)

MELVILLE Jane, 2nd dau. late Thomas Melville, St Vincent, m.
George Herbert Cox, 53rd Reg., Twickenham, 17 May 1848.
                                                       (NS30:88)

MELVILLE Margaret Elizabeth, eldest dau. Dr Alexander Melville,
MD, St Vincent, m. Joseph Billinghurst, Yapton, Sussex,
St Vincent, 28 March 1827.   (96:557)

MELVILLE ..., dau. Norman Leslie Melville, Cap., Grenadier
Guards, b. Montreal, 10 Jan.1863.   (NS2/14:367)

MENDS William Fisher, Dep. Comm. Gen., m. Mary Vardon, eldest
dau. Rev. W W Jackson, military chaplain, Barbados, 16 Feb.
1860.   (NS2/8:506)

MENTEATH Thomas Loughnan Stuart, Cap., US Army, ex 16th
Lancers, 2nd s. late Sir Charles Granville Stuart Menteath,
d. Canandaqua, Ontario, 22 Feb.1854.   (NS41:554)

MENZIES of CULDAIR Archibald, Customs Com., Scotland, m.
Fanny, only dau. John Rutherford, NC, 17 Oct.1776.   (46:530)

MENZIES Edward, b.1787, ex Kingston, Jamaica, d. New Scone,
Perth, 12 Aug.1852.   (NS38:434)

MERAC John, yngs. s. L Merac, merchant, London, d. St Kitts,
Jan.1803.   (73:283)

MERCER Robert, b.1786, ex Norwood, Surrey, d. Windsor,
Canada West, 29 June 1849.   (NS32:335)

MERCER Col., NA, m. Miss Neville, Lincoln, 15 Aug.1767.
                                                       (37:429)

MERRIFIELD William, d. St Anne, Jamaica, Nov.1801.   (72:181)

MERRITT William John, b.1825, 2nd s. late Rev. Richard
Robinson Merritt, St Michael, Barbados, d.11 June 1842.
                                                      (NS18:335)

MERRY Elizabeth Emily, dau. Walter Merry, Cheltenham, ex
Dep. Sec. War, m. Alexander Haserman, Solicitor Gen. Canada,
London, 15 April 1834.   (104:551)

MERRY Robert, b.1755, s. Robert Merry, Gov. Hudson Bay Co.,
m. Miss Brunton, 1791, d. Baltimore, 24 Dec.1798.   (69:252)

METCALFE Emma Wharton, w. William Hall, Staff Surgeon, d.
Cornwall, Upper Canada, 27 Aug.1840.   (NS14:676)

METZNIER Francis, d. Mass., 1792.   (62:1220)

MEWBURN Henrietta, b.1823, 2nd dau. John Mewburn, surgeon, ex
Whitby, Yorks., d. Stamford, Canada West, 25 Jan.1852.
                                                      (NS37:316)

MEWBURN John, 3rd s. John Mewburn, MD, Canada West, m. Mary,
eldest dau. John Levien, Sidmouth, 4 June 1851.   (NS36:189)

MEYERS Henry, b.1804, 2nd s. T P Meyers, Battle, Sussex, &
Jamaica, d. Kent, 24 Feb.1820.   (90:283)

MEYLER Mrs, w. Jeremiah Meyler, ex Jamaica, d. Bath, 26 Dec.
1788.   (58:1183)

MICHEL Charles Edward, Maj., 66th Reg., m. Emily Spooner,
eldest dau. Sir R B Clarke, Chief Justice Barbados, Barbados,
19 Nov.1850.   (NS35:196)

MICHEL Rachel Mary Lumley Godolphin, eldest dau. Lt. Gen. Sir
John Michel, m. Cap. Raymond Harvey de Montmorency, 32nd
Light Infantry, only s. Viscount Frankfort de Montmorency,
Quebec, 25 April 1866.   (NS3/1:901)

MIDDLETON Emily Wisset, wid. A Middleton, RN marine surveyor,
m. Edward Calvert, headmaster, Trinidad, London, 17 Feb.1859.
                                                      (NS2/6:317)

MIDDLETON Starkey, WI, d.1768.   (38:302)

MIDDLETON Miss, dau. late Arthur Middleton, Congressman, m.
Daniel, s. William Blake, London, SC, 1800.   (70:484)

MIGNOT Elizabeth Croasdaile, eldest dau., David Mignot, MD,
Kingston, Jamaica, m. Henry, yngs. s. William Collick,
Shripney, Sussex, London, 13 Oct.1846.   (NS27:79)

MILES F A, b.1807, Maj., Bengal Artillery, d. Hitchin, NE,
28 Aug.1852.   (NS38:436)

MILLER A, yngs. s. Rev. William Miller, Hasfield, Gloucster,
m. Mrs Sarah Louisa, wid. Judge Ward, Nevis, 31 Jan.1818.
                                                      (88:176)

MILLER David James, shipbuilder, ex Wapping Wall, d.
Toronto, 2 Aug.1854.   (42:409)

MILLER Cap. Dugald Stewart, QM, 67th Reg., eldest s. Dr Miller,
Exeter, m. Elizabeth, 3rd dau. Sir Bowcher Clark, Chief
Justice Barbados, Barbados, 20 May 1858.   (NS2/5:185)

MILLER Eliza, only dau. late Alexander Miller, m. Alexander
Reid Scott, Kingston, Jamaica, Lyston, Essex, 1846.(NS26:420)

MILLER James, ex Stirling, merchant, Charleston, SC, d. on
Rose in Bloom when wrecked Aug.1806.   (76:1168)

MILLER Joseph, b.1797, Carlisle, engineer, d. Charleston,
SC, 23 Feb.1860.   (NS2/8:524)

MILLER S, MD, b.1779, ex physician, Barbados, d. Chelmsford,
15 May 1860.   (NS2/9:106)

MILLER Thomas, b.1728, ex NY, d. North Berwick, 15 July 1814.
                                                  (84:190)

MILLER Thomas, b.1801, 2nd s. late Walter Miller, Highgate,
d. Trinidad, 3 July 1840.   (NS14:446)

MILLER William, ex Jamaica, d. London, 8 March 1837.(NS7:443)

MILLER Miss, niece Judge Winstone, Fredericton, m. W Woodford,
Fredericton, NB, 4 Nov.1812.   (83:179)

MILLER Father, b.1782, d. NY, 20 Dec.1849.   (NS33:342)

MILLETT Elizabeth Mary, 3rd dau. Rev. John Curnow Millett,
Penpoll, m. Frederic Edmonds, MD, Guanaxuato, Mexico,
Phillack, Cornwall, 21 Oct.1846.   (NS27:80)

MILLS Alice Maude, 2nd dau. William Maude, St John, NB, m.
Darrell Robert Jago, ex Lt., RA, 2nd s. late D Jago, Cap., RA,
St John, NB, 28 March 1865.   (NS2/18:778)

MILLS C Hamilton, eldest s. G Galway Mills, m. Frances Jane,
dau. B Brown Davis, St Kitts, St Kitts, 21 July 1820.(90:272)

MILLS George Rice, b.1824, d. Nevis, 9 Dec.1853. (NS41:329)

MILLS Henry James m. Margaret Ann Currie, 2nd dau. Henry M
MacLean, Tortula, wid. Alexander Currie, Port of Spain,
Trinidad, 1 Jan.1863.   (NS2/14:369)

MILLS John Colhoun, ex President, Nevis, d. at sea 15 July 1828.
                                                  (98:286)

MILLS Paixfield, b.1818, Chief Justice Nevis, d. Nevis,
1 Jan.1854.   (NS41:329)

MILLS Rebecca, b.1692, d. St Elizabeth, Jamaica, Dec.1804.
                                                  (75:1171)

MILLS Thomas Richard, ex Lt., 1st Dragoon Guards, eldest s.
William Mills, Saxham Hall, Suffolk, m. Emily, 3rd dau. late
Samuel Hall, Seigneur of Chambly, Chambly, Canada, 31 May 1843.
                                                  (NS20:199)

MILLS Miss, dau. late James Mills, Jamaica, m. Baron Lorentz,
London, Dec.1825.   (95:560)

MILLWARD John Gardner, Lt. Gen. Jamaica Militia, d. Spanish
Town, Jamaica, 24 Dec.1822.   (93:382)

MILNE Alexander David, b.1851, eldest s. Rear Adm. Sir
Alexander Milne, d. Quebec, 7 Sep.1860.   (NS2/9:560)

MILNE Andrew, merchant, ex Thaves Inn, d. on passage to
Jamaica on Augustus Caesar, 6 Jan.1804.   (74:182)

MILNE Sir David, Rear Adm., m. Miss Stephen, dau. late
G Stephen, Grenada, 28 Nov.1819.   (89:563)

MILNE James Alexander, b.1783, only s. Mr Milne, London, d.
Kingston, Jamaica, 13 May 1808.   (78:655)

MILNE Mary Jane, yngs. dau. A G Milne, Eltham, m. Rev. J.
Congdon Shapley, Carricou, Grenada, Eltham, Kent, 13 June 1844.
                                                 (NS22:202)

MILNE Robert, ex merchant, London, d. Cape Henry, Haiti,
19 Sep.1814.   (84:604)

MILNE Mrs Sophia, Pedro River, Jamaica, d. Paris, 17 Sep.1822.
                                                 (92:649)

MILNE Mr, b. Fochabers, Moray, d. Philadelphia, 2 Jan.1845.
                                                 (NS23:223)

MILNER William Shepherd, Cap., 69th Reg., 2nd s. late Cap.
Milner, RN, m. Mary Elizabeth, 4th dau. Lt. Gen. Wood, Comm.
Windward & Leeward Islands, Barbados, 31 July 1855.(NS54:531)

MILROY David, MD, s. Rev. Andrew Milroy, Edinburgh, d.
Bermuda, 3 Sep.1864.   (NS2/17:663)

MILLWARD Thomas Nixon, b.1789, d. Kingston, Jamaica, 1819.
                                                 (89:377)

MILLWARD T, b.1754, ex Jamaica, d. Gosfield Hall, Essex,
12 Oct.1835.   (NS4:556)

MILLWARD Miss, dau. John Gardner Millward, Spanish Town,
Jamaica, m. Francis Rigby Brodbelt, Spanish Town, 25 July 1803.
                                                 (74:277)

MINOS George, Custos, Portland, d. Port Antonio, Jamaica,
6 Jan.1801.   (71:371)

MINSHULL John, b.1745, d. London, 24 April 1822, "many years
a responsible citizen of USA".   (92:476)

MINTO Walter, Prof. Maths., d. Princeton, USA, 21 Oct.1796.
                                                 (67:80)

MINTURN Susan Carter, eldest dau. Robert Bowne Minturn, NY,
m. Thomas Charles Baring, eldest s. Bishop of Gloucester &
Bristol, NY, 15 Nov.1859.   (NS2/8:176)

MITCHELL A P, b.1793, eldest s. Robert Mitchell, Provost-
Marshal Tobago, d. Tobago, Sep.1812.   (82:670)

MITCHELL Alexander, MD, s. John Mitchell, exciseman, Ayr, d.
Bladensburg, America, 29 Sep.1804.   (75:183)

MITCHELL Cary, b.1729, Customs Collector Va. 30 years, d. 26
Dec.1782.   (52:600)

MITCHELL Charles, b.1756, ex Jamaica, d. London, 18 April
1808.   (78:464)

MITCHELL Eliza, eldest dau. Nicolas Mitchell, Plymouth, m.
Christopher Ayre, Marshal Vice Adm. Court NFD, Plymouth,
13 Oct.1847.   (NS29:80)

MITCHELL Hugh, ex surgeon, Jamaica, d. Edinburgh, 22 July 1799.
                                                   (69:718)

MITCHELL James, Receiver Gen. Jamaica, d. Spanish Town,
Jamaica, Aug.1806.   (76:1075)

MITCHELL John, London, d. Jamaica, 20 April 1815. (85:646)

MITCHELL John, b.1812, s. Rowland Smith, London, d. Jamaica,
1 Aug.1840.   (NS14:676)

MITCHELL Samuel, President, Grenada, m. Mary, sis. Thomas
Floud, Mayor of Exeter, 7 Sep.1802.   (72:877)

MITCHELL Samuel, President, Grenada, d. Newport, Exeter,
4 Feb.1805.   (75:189)

MITCHELL William, b. Londonderry, 1 July 1689, Revenue Officer
America, Loyalist, d.1804, buried St Andrew's, Dublin.(74:596)

MITCHELL Mrs, w. Vice Adm. Sir Andrew Mitchell, d. Bermuda,
10 Feb.1803.   (73:382)

MITCHELL Cap., Galway, d. Aux Cayes, St Domingo, 1819.(89:476)

MOE Rev. Samuel Rous, St Johns, Grenada, s. Miles Braithwaite,
Barbados, d. London, 27 May 1842.   (NS18:215)

MOFFAT Thomas, MD, b. Scotland, settled America 1729, ex
Customs Controller New London, Conn., American Loyalist, d.
London, 21 March 1787.   (57:278)

MOLINEAUX Mr, Speaker Assembly Montserrat, d. 2 Oct.1761.
                                                   (21:538)

MOLINEAUX Crisp, Thundersley Hall, Essex, late Sheriff of
Norfolk, d. St Kitts, 4 Dec.1792.   (62:1220)

MOLLE John William, MD, b.1832, Charleston, USA, d. Frankfort
on Main, 18 May 1867.   (NS3/4:116)

MOLSON Mary Anne E, 2nd dau. Thomas Molson, Montreal, m.
W Barrett, surgeon, Montreal, 3 June 1858.   (NS2/5:185)

MONCK ..., dau. R Monck, b. Ottawa, 24 Jan.1868.   (NS3/5:383)

MONK J F, s. Judge Monk, drowned Halifax, NS, 16 July 1813.
                                                   (83:400)

MONKTON W, planter, Va., d.22 Sep.1779.   (49:472)

MONROE James, b. Monroe's Creek, Westmoreland Co., Va., 1758,
ex President USA, d.NY, 4 July 1831.   (101:269)

MONTAGU Lord Charles, bro. Duke of Manchester, d. Halifax,
NS, Jan.1784.   (54:236)

MONTAGUE Charles William, Jamaica, d. England, 1820. (90:379)

MONTAGU Edward, Savannah la Mar, Jamaica, d.1768.   (38:302)

MONTAGUE Ralph, merchant, d. Barbados, 24 Feb.1824. (94:647)

MONTAGUE Jane, w. Edward Montague, d. Blower Hall, St James,
Jamaica, 1820.   (90:97)

MONTAGUE Matthew, b.1768, ex Black River, Jamaica, d.17 March
1816.   (86:375)

MONTEATH Amelia, b.1767, wid. Thomas Monteath, Jamaica, d.
Lympstone, Devon, 20 April 1833.   (103:476)

MONTEATH Andrew, carpenter, d. Falmouth, Jamaica, 11 June 1797.
                                                          (67:800)

MONTES Lola, m. P P Hull, ex proprietor 'San Francisco Whig',
Mission Dolores, San Francisco, 2 Aug.1853.   (NS40:404)

MONTGOMERY Archibald, Kingston, Jamaica, drowned Negril River,
Westmoreland, Jamaica, 1784.   (55:956)

MONTGOMERY Rev. D E, South Gower, Canada West, m. Jane,
eldest dau. Cap. Richard Rennie, Fife Royal Artillery,
Glasgow, on board John Bell, Montreal, 3 Aug.1859.(NS2/7:414)

MONTGOMERY John, Gov. NY, d.1 July 1731.   (1:355)

MONYPENNY Elizabeth Charlotte, yngs. dau. late Robert
Monypenny, Kent, m. Rev. Henry D Sewell, 4th s. late Jonathan
Sewell, Chief Justice Lower Canada, Haddow, Kent, 25 Oct.1843.
                                                         (NS23:90)

MOODIE Benjamin, ex HM Consul SC, d. Charleston, April 1823.
                                                          (93:478)

MOODY Harry m. Florence, yngs. dau. Neville Parker, Fredericton
NB, 28 July 1863.   (NS2/15:498)

MOODY ..., dau. Col. Moody, RE, b. New Westminster, BC,
28 Nov.1861.   (NS2/12:362)

MOODY ..., dau. Col. Moody, RE, b. New Westminster, BC,
20 Jan.1863.   (NS2/14:512)

MOONEY Ida Robe, b.1850, dau. late Harcourt Mooney, d.St John,
NFD., 18 March 1865.   (NS2/18:799)

MOONEY W, d. NY, 1798.   (68:1086)

MOORE Abraham, b. Devon, barrister, ex Shaftesbury MP, d. NY,
1822.   (92:569)

MOORE Alexander James, ex Jamaica, m. Sarah, eldest dau. late
Richard Hook, Sussex, London, 9 Nov.1840.   (NS13:85)

MOORE Mrs Catherine Jane, wid. Dr John Moore, m. James Mackay,
paymaster, 1st WI Reg., Trinidad, 27 Nov.1823.   (94:176)

MOORE Daniel, b.1798, s. Daniel Moore, Jamaica, d.19 Jan.1816.
(86:186)

MOORE Francis Holyoake, Queens College, Cambridge, 3rd s. late
Mr Moore, Warwicks., d. on New Jersey on passage from Savanna,
1839.   (NS13:334)

MOORE Sir Henry, Gov.NY, d.25 Oct.1769.   (39:511)

MOORE James, Montreal, m. Mary, eldest dau. late R Statter,
Knowsley, Huyton, Liverpool, 14 May 1840.   (NS14:89)

MOORE Rev. Richard Channing, Bishop of Va., d. Lynchburg, Va.,
Nov.1841.   (NS17:111)

MOORE Sarah Anne, dau. late William Moore, MD, niece Dr Moore,
ex Bishop of NY, m. Edward Hodges, Doctor of Music, ex Bristol,
NY, 11 April 1844.   (NS21:644)

MORALES Christopher boyd McLarty, b.1842, s. Speaker Jamaica,
d. on passage to England, 17 May 1864.   (NS2/17:120)

MORANT Catherine, yngs. dau. late John Morant, Brockenhurst,
Hants., d. Jamaica, 26 April 1802.   (72:686)

MORETON Anne Louisa, b.1720, wid. late Maj. Charles Moreton,
yngs. s. Matthew, Lord Ducie, maternal gmo. Henry Moreton
Dyer, Vice Adm. Judge Bahamas, d. Nassau, 25 Dec.1811.
(81:395)

MORGAN Anne, b.1762, wid. George Cadogan Morgan, ex Southgate,
Middlesex, d. Hudson, NY, 16 March 1846.   (NS25:670)

MORGAN Emma, yngs. dau. late Peter Morgan, Toronto, m.
Dawson Palgrave Turner, only s. late Gurner Turner, HEICS,
Toronto, 12 March 1867.   (NS3/3:666)

MORGAN Henry R, ex Jamaica, m. Eliza, dau. James Dawson,
London, 10 Dec.1821.   (91:641)

MORGAN Henry Rhodes, Jamaica, d. London, 4 Jan.1836.(NS5:211)

MORGAN James, surgeon, b.1828, eldest s. late Rev. Allen
Morgan, Nant-Y-Derry, Monmouth, d. Barbados, 31 March 1853.
(NS40:97)

MORGAN John, Prof. Physics, Univ. Phila., d. Philadelphia,
Oct.1789.   (61:279)

MORGAN Jonathan, b.1762, ex St Vincent, d. Bath, 24 July 1843.
(NS20:331)

MORGAN Louisa Jane, b.1795, eldest dau. late F Hobson,
Wordsley, Staffs., w. Lt. Morgan, 1st WI Reg., d.8 Feb.1817.
(87:374)

MORGAN R, ex Jamaica, d. London, 30 Jan.1813.   (83:287)

MORICE Rev. Charles m. Augusta Mary Anne, yngs. dau. late
Richard Zouch, Dublin Castle, Quebec, 13 March 1845.(NS24:72)

MORLAND Thomas m. Hannah Eliza, yngs. dau. Maj. Gen.
Servante, Montreal, 13 Aug.1863.   (NS2/15:498)

MORRAH ..., dau. Cap. Morrah, 60th Royal Rifles, b. Montreal,
10 Dec.1863.   (NS2/16:241)

MORRAH ..., dau. Cap. Morrah, 30th Royal Rifles, b.Montreal,
6 Jan.1865.   (NS2/18:362)

MORRIS Fanny, only dau. J Morris, Halifax, m. R G Coles,
Royal Reg., yngs. s. Rev. J Coles, Silchester, Hants.,
Halifax, NS, 22 July 1852.   (NS38:305)

MORRIS Henry Gage, b.1770, s. Lt. Col. Roger Morris,
Councillor, NY, Rear Adm., RN, d. Beverley, 24 Nov.1851.
                                                (NS37:300)

MORRIS John, Customs Controller, Charleston, SC, d.1777.
                                                (48:45)

MORRIS J B, b.1780, Jamaica, d. London, 24 Nov.1846.(NS25:103)

MORRIS Katherine Roberta, b.1825, 2nd dau. Samuel Jackson
Dallas, Jamaica, w. Mowbray Morris, d. London, 3 Nov.1857.
                                                (NS2/3:689)

MORRIS Mary, b.1787, wid. Lt. Col. W Morris, 97th Reg., d.
Lennoxville, Canada East, 27 March 1865.   (NS2/18:664)

MORRIS Matilda, yngs. dau. Sir John Morris, Shelly Park, m.
Jasper Livingstone, NY, Dover, 26 May 1851.   (NS36:188)

MORRIS Robert Hunter, Gov. Pa., d.24 Feb.1764.   (34:146)

MORRIS Gen. S L, Col. 61st Reg., Gov. Quebec, d.1800.(70:699)

MORRIS William, b.1781, ex Lt. Col. 97th Reg., Militia officer
& JP, Lennoxville, Canada, d. Lennoxville, 18 May 1851.
                                                (NS36:218)

MORRISON Alexander, d. Kingston, Jamaica, 1797.   (67:804)

MORRISON Cap. Alexander, b.1717, ex NC Highlanders, d. Greenock
28 Jan.1805.   (75:186)

MORRISON John, planter, Va., d.21 Nov.1777.   (47:556)

MORRISON John, judge, Customs Controller, Bahamas, d. Nassau,
12 Nov.1786.   (41:1093)

MORRISON John jr., Glasgow, m. Mary Beach, 3rd dau. W H Ruan,
MD, St Croix, Southampton, 18 April 1859.   (NS2/6:537)

MORRISON Martin, Greenwich Hospital, m. Miss Beall, Lewisham,
dau. Edward Beall, ex master shipwright, HM Dockyard, Jamaica,
Lewisham, Kent, 16 Feb.1788.   (58:178)

MORSE Edward, ex Chief Judge Senegambia, d. Jamaica, 1794.
                                                (64:768)

MORSE Cap. Ezra, b.1697, d. Dedham. Mass., Dec.1789. (61:279)

MORSE Rev. Jedidiah, Pastor First Church, Charlestown, d.
New Haven, Conn., 9 June 1827.   (97:375)

MORSON Arthur, b.1776, s. William Morson, merchant, ex
Antigua, d. Brompton, 19 May 1793.   (63:485)

MORTIMER Rev. George, Hamilton, Canada, d.1844.   (NS22:437)

MORTON David, MD, b.1731, ex Jamaica, d. London, 18 July 1812.
                                                       (82:93)

MORTON Mrs Mary, b.1742, wid. C Morton, Jamaica, d.
Newington Butts, 11 Oct.1823.   (93:380)

MORTON William J m. Miss Akers, dau. late Aretas Akers,
St Kitts, London, 23 Jan.1799.   (69:78)

MORUGEAN Francois Forgue, b.1709, d. St Rose, Effingham Co.,
America, 1829.   (99:94)

MOSSE James Urquhart, 17th Reg., 3rd s. late Thomas Mosse,
Knockfinne, Queens Co., ex Cap. Royal Scots, gs. late Lt. Gen.
B Forbes Gordon, Balbithan, Aberdeen, m. Catherine Morden,
2nd dau. Col. Edward Kent Strathearn Butler, Hants., Windsor,
NS, 26 Oct.1865.   (NS2/19:1865)

MOSSOP Samuel, b.1794, 3rd s. Rev. John Mossop, Deeping
St James, Lincs., d. St Lucia, Oct.1809.   (79:1235)

MOTTEY Victor, Marchiennes, Officier de la Legion d'Honneur,
m. Georgina, dau. late R P Page, London & New Orleans,
London, 12 Feb.1850.   (NS33:530)

MOUNSHER James Eyles, only s. late James Mounsher, RN, nephew
late Cap. Mounsher, RN, Old Buckenham, Norfolk, d. NY,
20 May 1849.   (NS32:334)

MOUNTAIN Eliza, dau. Bishop of Quebec, m. Cap. Frederick
Arabin, RA, s. H Arabin, Maglove, Co. Meath, Quebec, 31 May
1823.   (93:367)

MOUNTAIN Rev. George Robert, b.1791, 3rd s. Rev. Jacob
Mountain, Bishop of Quebec, bro. Rev. George Jehosephat
Mountain, Bishop of Montreal, Havant, Hants., d. Blackheath,
25 June 1846.   (NS26:216)

MOUNTAIN Rev. Jacob H Brooke, Blunham, eldest s. Bishop of
Quebec, m. Frances Margaretta, wid. Frederic Polhill,
Howbury Hall, Blunham, Beds., 2 April 1850.   (NS33:658)

MOUNTAIN Jacob George, Principal St Johns College, NFD., m.
Sophia, 5th dau. late Robert Bevan, Rougham, 5 Sep.1854.
                                                     (NS42:617)

MOUNTAIN Rev. Jacob George, b.1817, 2nd s. Rev. J H B Mountain
Blunham, Beds., Principal St Johns College, NFD., d. St Johns,
10 Oct.1856.   (NS2/1:775)

MOUNTAIN Rev. J, eldest s. Bishop of Quebec, m. Frances, yngs.
dau. late Rev. William Brooke, Baconthorpe, 12 Oct.1812.
                                                      (82:390)

MOUNTAIN Rev. Jehosaphat, bro. Bishop of Quebec, Bishop's
Officer Lower Canada, d. Montreal, 10 April 1817.   (87:568)

MOUNTAIN Sarah, sis. Bishop Quebec, d. Quebec, 8 May 1808.
                                                    (78:748)

MOWATT James, b.1806, NY, d. London, 15 Feb.1851.   (NS35:447)

MOWATT William, d. Jamaica, 1790.   (60:476)

MOYLAN James, US Agent, d. L'Orient, France, 1784.   (54:475)

MUDIE James, London, m. Jane, dau. late Charles Aitken,
St Croix, North Tarry, Angus, 11 Dec.1798.   (68:1082)

MUHLENBURG Gen. Peter, s. late Henry Muhlenburg, Patriarch
German Lutheran Church Pa., d. Schuylkill, America,
1 Oct.1807.   (77:1172)

MUIRSON Dr James De Lancey, eldest s. George Muirson, ex NY,
d. London, 12 Sep.1791.   (61:877)

MULCASTER Mrs Wilhelmina, w. Frederick George Mulcaster,
Councillor, East Florida, d. St Augustine, 1773.   (43:621)

MUNDAY Marian Catherine, eldest dau. Maj. Robert Miller
Munday, Lt. Gov. Grenada, m. Maj. Charles Knight Pearson,
Somerset, Grenada, 10 April 1866.   (NS3/1:900)

MUNDY Edward Miller, b.1800, s. Edward Miller Mundy, Shipley
Hall, Derby, d. Barbados, 29 Jan.1849.   (NS32:96)

MUNN David, s. late Cap. James Munn, Ulverstone, d.Gibbons
Vere, Clarendon, Jamaica, 1793.   (63:1055)

MUNROE Catherine, b.1784, wid. David Munroe, Quebec, d.
London, 1847.   (NS28:555)

MUNRO David, b.1760, ex Quebec, d. Bath, 3 Sep.1834.(104:445)

MONRO David Arthur, Maj., 12th Lancers, only s. late David
Monro, Quebec, d. Torquay, 7 Sep.1863.   (NS2/15:521)

MUNRO Dorothea, only dau. Hugh Munro, Carriacou, Grenada, m.
John Spain, merchant, Bristol, Clifton, 2 Nov.1796. (66:965)

MUNRO Frances, wid. Alexander Munro, Trinidad, eldest dau.
J Townsend Pasea, m. Lt. Col. Simms, ex 41st Reg., London,
8 July 1847.   (NS28:312)

MUNRO George, Customs officer Jamaica, 2nd s. Sir Harry Munro
of Foulis, d. Kingston, Jamaica, 22 April 1802.   (72:686)

MUNRO Gilbert, b.1778, St Vincent, d. Weymouth, Dorset,
21 June 1843.   (NS20:218)

MUNRO Harry, d. Jamaica, 1791.   (61:186)

MUNRO Hugh, surgeon, St Thomas in the Vale, Jamaica, d.
Spanish Town, Jamaica, 26 Sep.1797.   (67:1136)

MUNRO Cap. Israel, ex shipmaster London-NY trade, d.
Jamaica, 1790.   (60:1214)

MUNRO Rachel Sophia, wid. Gilbert Munro, St Vincent, m. Col.
Sir Richard Doherty, London, 8 July 1845.   (NS24:416)

MUNRO ..., dau. Col. Munro, b. Bermuda, 13 June 1861.
                                                  (NS2/11:194)

MUNRO ..., s. Col. Munro, 39th Reg., b. St George, Bermuda,
27 May 1863.   (NS2/15:228)

MUNT Judith, b.1762, wid. Isaac Munt, Kingston, Jamaica, d.
Cheshunt, Herts., 17 July 1837.   (NS8:325)

MUNT Sarah, dau. Isaac Munt, Jamaica, m. J Early Cook,
Nunnery, Cheshunt, 5 Feb.1820.   (90:272)

MURAT Prince Louis Napoleon Achille, b.1801, s. Joachim Murat,
ex King of Naples, & Caroline Bonaparte, sis. Napoleon,
Florida, 15 April 1847.   (NS28:223)

MURCH Mrs Henry, dau. late William Jackson, St Dorothy's,
Jamaica, d. Naples, 1 March 1847.   (NS27:566)

MURCHISON Dr Alexander, ex Springfield, Jamaica, Custos Vere,
Assemblyman Jamaica, d. Elgin, 10 Oct.1845.   (NS24:663)

MURCHISON John Henry, eldest s. late Alexander Murchison,
Springfield, Jamaica, & Elgin, Scotland, m. Louisa Husey,
only dau. late Henry Husey, Brighton, London, 5 Aug.1852.
                                                  (NS38:411)

MURCOTT Isaac Barnes, b.1812, 2nd s. Mr Murcott, Hinckley,
physician, Jamaica, 1840-1850, d.24 Oct.1850.   (NS35:222)

MURDOCH William, Md., d.1769.   (39:608)

MURE Caroline Louisa, b.1827, dau. Alfred Hennen, w. William
Mure, HM Consul, d. New Orleans, 15 Dec.1851.   (NS37:312)

MURE ..., s. William Mure, HM Consul New Orleans, b. Mudbury,
22 Dec.1857.   (NS2/4:205)

MURRAY Adelaide Coppinger, 2nd dau. Sir John Murray, m. Cap.
G Granville Richardson, s. Thomas Richardson, St Albans, NY,
8 Jan.1863.   (NS2/14:369)

MURRAY Alexander, bro. Earl of Dunmore, m. Miss D Hunt, dau.
Robert Hunt, Nassau, Bahamas, 18 May 1811.   (81:187)

MURRAY Ann, w. Dr Murray, dau. Earl of Cromartie, d.
Charleston, SC, 1768.   (38:142)

MURRAY Catherine, b.1738, wid. George Murray, ex Custos Westmoreland, Assemblyman St Elizabeth, Jamaica, d. London,
14 Aug.1818.   (88:377)

MURRAY Charles Augustus, Consul Gen. Egypt, m. Elizabeth,
only dau. late James Wadsworth, Genesee, NY, Edinburgh,
12 Dec.1850.   (NS35:196)

MURRAY Davidson Munro, s. William Murray, gs. Alexander Bruce,
MD, Edinburgh & Barbados, nephew David Bruce, Kennet, Clackmannan, d. Canada, 1852.   (NS37:530)

MURRAY Edward, 2nd s. Henry Murray, London, gs. late Henry
Murray, Trinidad, m. Grace, only ch. Sir Thomas Elmsley
Croft, g'niece Lord Denman, London, 5 March 1846. (NS25:535)

MURRAY Elizabeth, 2nd dau. William Murray, Barbados, m. Lt.
Col. S H Berkley, 16th Reg., Barbados, 24 Feb.1818. (88:464)

MURRAY Elizabeth Williama, yngs. dau. William Murray,Colonial
Bank, m. John Henry, eldest s. Grant E Thomas, President,
Barbados, Barbados, 4 July 1865.   (NS2/19:373)

MURRAY Dr Hugh, b. Ireland, 1741, d. Bethlem, Conn.,
28 Aug.1815.   (85:634)

MURRAY Cap. James, ex Queen's American Rangers, d. Norfolk,
Va., 29 March 1789.   (59:670)

MURRAY James W McD, Customs officer, Tobago, ex Assemblyman,
proprietor Calder Hall Est., only bro. Mr Murray, Sunderland
Harbour Engineer, d.26 Jan.1841.   (NS15:558)

MURRAY Johanna Maria, Jamaica, m. James Stewart, Judge
Advocate Gen., Bengal, 11 Dec.1777.   (47:611)

MURRAY John J, US Consul, d. Glasgow, 4 April 1805. (75:389)

MURRAY John, b. Jamaica, yngr. s. Walter Murray, Maj. Gen.,
d. Brighton, 21 Feb.1832.   (102:463)

MURRAY Keturah Shephard, b.1769, only ch. Alexander Bruce, MD,
Edinburgh, w. William Murray, d. Barbados, 31 March 1852.
                                                      (NS38:106)

MURRAY Dr Patrick, b.1744, physician, Jamaica, Jamaica Grand
Court Judge, d. Kirkcudbright, 1829.   (99:477)

MURRAY Richard Henry, barrister, eldest s. Thomas Murray, MD,
Trinidad, m. Georgina, yngs. dau. late Robert Woodall, Ardwick,
Lancs., London, 2 Feb.1859.   (NS2/6:315)

MURRAY Robert, merchant, NY, 4th s. late Dr Murray, Norwich,
d. Brickhill, Bucks., 22 Oct.1807.   (77:990)

MURRAY Robert, Knapdale, Jamaica, d. at sea, 21 June 1820.
                                                       (90:639)

MURRAY Walter, b.1772, Dundee, Jamaica, d. Brighton, May 1826.
                                                       (96:573)

MURRAY William, Jamaica, d.1777.   (48:45)

MURRAY William, Edinburgh, ex merchant, Va., d. London,
2 Jan.1791.   (61:91)

MURRAY William, b.1769, St James, Jamaica, d. Southampton,
15 Dec.1846.   (NS25:107)

MURRAY Mrs, b.1784, wid. H Murray. Woodbrook, Trinidad, d.
Port of Spain, Trinidad, 5 Feb.1868.   (NS3/5:684)

MURRAY ..., dau. Alexander Murray, b. Nassau, New Providence, 15 Jan.1812.   (82:288)

MURRAY ..., s. Alexander Murray, b. Nassau, New Providence, 17 Aug.1813.   (83:394)

MURRAY-AYNSLEY ..., s. Cap. Murray-Aynsley, RN, b. Halifax, NS, 27 Oct.1866.   (NS3/3:101)

MURPHY Ellen Sophia, 2nd dau. Francis Murphy, merchant, m. Robert Brown Watson, merchant, Mexico, HM Consulate, Mexico, 19 Dec.1857.   (NS2/4:326)

MUSGRAVE George, ex Customs Controller Carolina & Bahamas, d.10 June 1745.   (15:332)

MUSGRAVE William, eldest s. Anthony Musgrave, MD, Antigua, d. Edinburgh, 26 Nov.1840.   (NS15:221)

MUSSON Alice, dau. late John Musson, Paynter Vale, Bermuda, m. David Turnbull, judge, Jamaica, 1 Aug.1844.   (NS22:538)

MUSSON John T., b.1812, s. G S Musson, Antigua, d. London, 25 April 1847.   (NS27:672)

MUSSON ..., dau. S J Musson, Barbados, b. Upper Norwood, 1 Dec.1867.   (NS3/5:101)

MUTIR Agnes, 2nd dau. Maj. Mutir, Royal Canadian Rifles, m. H Stanley Jones, Dep. Asst. Comm. Gen., Amherstburgh, Canada West, 27 Oct.1846.   (NS27:193)

MYERS Rev. John Morrison, headmaster, d. Linsted, Spanish Town, Jamaica, 2 Feb.1861.   (NS2/10:467)

MYERS Mary, yngs. dau. Col. W J Myers, 71st Highland Light Infantry, m. John Matthew Jones, barrister, yngs. s. Rear Adm. Sir Charles T Jones, Fronfraith, Montgomery, Halifax, NS, 23 Oct.1860.   (NS2/10:200)

MYERS William, ex Col., 71st Reg., d. Halifax, NS, 12 April 1867.   (NS3/3:820)

MYERS William R., m. Helen, 2nd dau. Hinton Spalding, MD, Spanish Town, Jamaica, 29 April 1845.   (NS24:189)

MYERS William Robertson, PC Clerk Jamaica, d. Spanish Town, Jamaica, 9 April 1866.   (NS3/1:915)

MYERS Col., QM Gen. NA, d. Quebec, 3 Nov.1817.   (87:567)

NAILER Charles, Customs Controller, d. Dominica, 25 April 1812.   (82:668)

NAINBY John, Dep. Ordnance Storekeeper, St Johns, NFD., d. 19 March 1834.   (104:671)

NAIRN Francis Thomas, s. Dr Nairn, Dedham, Essex, d. Baltimore, 29 Dec.1851.   (NS37:312)

NAIRNE Lt. Col. John, d. Quebec, 14 July 1802.   (72:974)

NANTON Georgina Rosalie, yngs. dau. late J G Nanton,
St Vincent, m. Fennings Taylor, Councillor, Toronto, 8 Sep.
1858.   (NS2/5:525)

NAPIER Catherine Elizabeth, eldest dau. Lt. Col. Napier, Sec.
Indian Affairs, m. Rev. Frederick Brown, missionary, Montreal,
18 Jan.1842.   (NS17:429)

NAPIER George, d. Whitehall, Clarendon, Jamaica, 25 June
1806.   (76:874)

NAPIER Maria Aletta, dau. Maj. Gen. George Napier, m. John
Frederick Bell, 47th Reg., s. Frederick Brown Bell, Norfolk,
Toronto, 16 Oct.1862.   (NS2/13:770)

NAPLETON George Decimus, b.1814, 5th s. late Rev. T Napleton,
Powderham, Devon, d. Toronto, 27 Nov.1845.   (NS25:558)

NASH Alexander, b.1810, eldest s. late Andrew John Nash,
Edmonton, d. NY, 13 May 1845.   (NS24:103)

NASMYTH Mary Sabina, dau. late Thomas Nash, Jamaica, m.
Count Edward de Melfort, Paris, London, 11 Jan.1826. (96:80)

NASMYTH Robert, b.1798, only s. Mrs Nasmyth, Jamaica, d.
Toulouse, 7 Jan.1817.   (87:91)

NASMYTH Thomas, MD, Rhodeshall, d. Water Valley, Jamaica,
9 June 1806.   (76:874)

NASSAU Ann Catherine Rose, dau. Frederick Nassau, St Osyth
Priory, Essex, m. T J Manning, Barbados, Kendal, 15 Aug.1825.
                                                    (95:270)

NATHAN Eliza, 2nd dau. late J P Nathan, Jamaica, m. Thomas
Maitland Snow, banker, eldest s. Thomas Snow, Franklyn, Little
-ham, 27 Feb.1851.   (NS35:424)

NATHAN Emily, eldest dau. late J P Nathan, Trelawney, Jamaica,
m. Cap. Rocke, 2nd Queen's Royal Reg., Exmouth, 27 June 1850.
                                                    (NS34:320)

NATHAN J P, ex Portsmouth, d. Jamaica, 26 Oct.1831. (102:94)

NEAL Edward Harry, s. late M N Neal, Dover, NH, m. Lady
Elizabeth MacLaine, wid. Gen. Sir Archibald MacLaine,
London, 12 March 1863.   (NS2/14:516)

NEALE Mrs Harriet, yngs. dau. late George Bruere, Gov. Bermuda,
d. Gloucester, 25 May 1801.   (71:482)

NEAME ..., s. Cap. Neame, 16th Reg., b. Halifax, NS, 22 June
1865.   (NS2/19:229)

NEEDHAM Henry, Jamaica, d.1758.   (28:94)

NEIL Andrew, Cap., 99th Reg., m. Louisa, yngs. dau. late Sir
James Patey, Reading, St Vincent, 1813.   (83:87)

NEILD William Camden, b.1777, eldest s. James Neild,
London, Councillor, Antigua, d. Falmouth, 19 Oct.1810.(80:1810)

NEILL Thomas, yngs. s. late T Neill, Turnham Green, Middlesex,
d. Canada West, 6 Feb.1850.   (NS34:109)

NEILL William M., merchant, NY, m. Susan Mary, dau. late John
Abbott, solicitor, London, 22 Nov.1858.   (NS2/6:89)

NEILSON James, merchant, m. Agnes, eldest dau. late Dr
Samuel Jamieson, Va., Glasgow, 19 Oct.1800.   (70:1286)

NELLES Elizabeth, dau. Lt. Col. Nelles, 4th Lincoln Militia,
Upper Canada, m. Rev. B Bridges Stevens, military chaplain,
s. late Rev. Thomas Stevens, Panfield, Essex, d. Grimsby,
Upper Canada, Sep.1820.   (91:180)

NELSON John, d. St Mary's, Jamaica, 1800.   (70:905)

NELSON William, President Council Va., d.1773.   (43:154)

NESBIT Samuel, b.1753, ex Sec. Bahamas, d. Devon, 14 April
1838.   (NS9:555)

NESBIT Lt. Col., d. Quebec, 1776.   (46:578)

NESBIT Dr, ex Nevis, d. Salisbury, 5 Oct.1781.   (51:491)

NETHERSOLE Eliza, eldest dau. John Nethersole, Jamaica, m.
William Cunningham Glen, barrister, London, 15 Dec.1848.
                                                      (NS31:200)

NETTLEFOLD John, planter, d. Martha Brae, Jamaica, 29 June
1798.   (68:811)

NEUFVILLE Jacob, Lymington, Hants., & Jamaica, d. Manchioneal,
Jamaica, 1817.   (87:637)

NEUFVILLE Sibylla Phoebe, wid. Jacob Neufville, Jamaica, d.
Lee, 14 Nov.1831.   (101:475)

NEUMAN Dr, RC Bishop of Philadelphia, b. Bohemia, 1811, d.
Philadelphia, 9 Jan.1860.   (NS2/8:511)

NEVILLE Thomas J., yngs. s. late Brent Neville, Ashbrooke,
Co. Dublin, m. Amelia, eldest dau. Leander Ransom, NY,
Dublin, 16 Dec.1853.   (NS41:309)

NEVILLE Miss, Lincoln, m. Col. Mercer, NA, 15 Aug.1767.(37:429)

NEVILLE ..., dau. Christopher Neville, Lincoln, w. Col. Mercer,
Va., d.6 June 1768.   (38:303)

NEVILLE ..., ex Barbados, d. London, 22 Nov.1777.   (48:551)

NEWALL John, ex Bristol, d. Antigua, Nov.1808.   (79:277)

NEWBERRY William, b.1777, s. late W Newberry, Southwark, d.
Quebec, 31 May 1814.   (84:699)

NEWCOMBE Frederick, s. Dr Newcombe, Dean of Rochester, husband Elizabeth Neate, 3rd dau. Rev. Richard Neate, Whestone, Middlesex, Sec. Grenada, d. Grenada, 25 Nov.1795.
(68:626)

NEWLAND Ann Elizabeth Wood, w. Cap. Newland, RN, d. Boyn Island, Bermuda, 15 March 1861.   (NS2/10:584)

NEWMAN Charles Durnford, s. Rev. Robert Newman, Coryton, Devon, m. Julia Mary, 2nd dau. Robert Carter, RN, Colonial Treasurer, St Johns, NFD., 31 Dec.1850.   (NS35:421)

NEWMAN F., ex North Cadbury, Somerset, d. The Grange, Port Tobacco, Md., 5 March 1818.   (88:468)

NEWMAN Henry, 3rd s. T Harding Newman, Nelmes, Essex, d. Montego Bay, Jamaica, 1846.   (NS25:335)

NEWTON Frances Elizabeth, dau. R Newton, Coldrey, Hants., m. E R Bertrand, Tabery, Dominica, Froyle, Hants., 1 Feb.1823.
(93:272)

NEWTON Gilbert Stuart, b. Halifax, NS, 20 Sep.1794, 12th s. Henry Newton, Customs Collector, NS, d. London, 5 Aug.1835.
(NS4:438)

NEWTON Thomas Henry, b.1823, only s. T G Newton, Hereford, Customs officer & private sec. Lt. Gov. Tobago, d. Tobago, 4 July 1843.   (NS20:446)

NIBBS Jack, ex Antigua, d. Upton House, Hants., 26 Sep.1822.
(92:380)

NIBBS J G, St Anne's, Jamaica, d. London, 1823.   (93:188)

NIBBS Octavius, Councillor, Tobago, d. Tortula, 25 March 1789.
(59:573)

NIBLOCK Dr James, b. Ireland, settled Brunswick Co., Va., 1803, killed 5 July 1810.   (80:491)

NICHOLLS Edward, St Vincent, m. Silias Jane, only ch. late Alexander Wilson, Redhill, Middlesex, Barnwell, 20 May 1847.
(NS28:200)

NICHOLSON Adam, MD, m. Anna Mary, yngs. dau. late Barnewell Jackson, St Vincent, niece Sir William Snagg, Chief Justice Antigua, St Johns, Antigua, 11 June 1863.   (NS2/15:231)

NICHOLSON Samuel, b.1743, Comm. USN, d. Charlestown, Mass., 1812.   (82:499)

NICHOLSON W T, MD, d. Nevis, 2 Sep.1848.   (NS30:558)

NICOLLET Mr, b.1795, surveyor, d. Washington, 11 Sep.1844.
(NS21:670)

NISBET of DEAN Sir Alexander, d. Charleston, SC, Oct.1753.
(24:48)

NIVEN David, writer, Glasgow, d. on passage to WI, 19 Nov.1799.
(70:182)

NIVEN David, ex Jamaica, m. Miss Hutchinson, Greenbank, Glasgow, 11 Nov.1800.   (70:1287)

NIXON John, Supreme Court Judge, Militia Col., Assemblyman,
Jamaica, d.15 April 1774.   (44:287)

NOBLE John, b.Grafton, Yorks., 1764, d. NY, Aug.1853.(NS41:328)

NOCKELLS Charles, Mount Pleasant, Jamaica, d. Edinburgh,
8 Sep.1850.   (NS34:454)

NORMAN Mary Charlotte, only dau. Richard Norman, London, m.
Robert Archibald Young, Quebec, London, 24 Feb.1846.(NS25:535)

NORRIS Edward, b.1664, '20 years a pilot within the Capes' Va.,
d.30 July 1767.   (37:430)

NORRIS Isaac, d. Philadelphia, 1766.   (36:439)

NORRIS J, MD, ex St Croix, d. London, 21 Dec.1815.   (85:643)

NORRIS Rev. T., ex military chaplain, Leeward Islands, d.
London, 6 Oct.1816.   (86:467)

NORTH William, English author, d. NY, 1854.   (NS43:109)

NORTON Rev. Andrew, b.1786, d. Newport, RI, 18 Oct.1853.
                                                     (NS41:215)

NORTON Eardley, b.1817, 2nd s. late Sir John David Norton, ex
15th Hussars, d. Nelson, Canada West, 15 Nov.1852. (NS39:216)

NORTON Thomas, ex Chief Justice NFD., m. Augusta Sophia, wid.
James Hill Albony, London, Paris, 18 Oct.1852.   (NS39:86)

NORTON William, b.1695, ex planter, Dominica, d. Exeter, 1782.
                                                      (52:551)

NOUAILLE Philip, b.1807, yngs. s. late Peter Nouaille,
Sevenoaks, d. Dawn, Upper Canada, 28 Dec.1849.   (NS33:559)

NOWELL Henry Craddock, yngs. s. Vice Adm. Nowell, Iffley,
Oxford, d. Montgomery, Ala., 29 Aug.1836.   (NS6:669)

NOWELL Mrs, wid. J Nowell, Jamaica, d. Southampton, 1814.
                                                       (84:95)

NOWLAN James, bro. Mrs Gilchrist, Stamford, d. St Domingo,
17 Oct.1810.   (80:283)

NUGENT Richard, MD, Dublin, m. Elvira Crichton, eldest dau.
Samuel Sedgwick, MD, Antigua, 29 Feb.1848.   (NS29:538)

NUGENT ..., s. Mr Nugent, Lt. Gov. Jamaica, b. Govt. Pen,
Jamaica, 12 Oct.1802.   (72:1159)

NUGENT ..., dau. Lt. Gov. Nugent, b. Jamaica, 8 Sep.1803.
                                                     (73:1084)

NUNES William George, Comm. Stamps, d. Jamaica, 4 April 1854.
                                                     (NS42:90)

NUNEZ Rev. Maximilian, 2nd s. John Nunez, Jamaica, m.
Catherine, 3rd dau. Henry Kendale, London, 7 June 1859.
                                                    (NS2/9:81)

OATES George Hibbert, eldest s. Mrs Oates, Bath, d. Jamaica,
11 April 1837.   (NS8:326)

OATES Hibbert, b.1796, s. Mr Oates, Sion Hill, Bath, d.
Kingston, Jamaica, 14 Dec.1840.   (NS15:558)

O'BRIEN Mrs, w. Cap. O'Brien, 24th Reg., dau. John Frobisher,
Montreal, d. Exeter, 11 Dec.1800.   (70:1296)

O'BRYAN John, b.1759, ex Barbados, d. Bristol, 20 Sep.1813.
                                                   (83:403)

O'CONNOR James Arthur, MD, b.1796, gnephew Abbe Edgworth, d.
Hamilton, Upper Canada, 1837.   (NS8:660)

O'CONNOR John, Middleton, Co. Cork, d. Honduras, 8 April 1804.
                                                   (74:690)

O'CONNOR Thomas, b. Ireland, exiled 1798, d. NY, 9 Feb.1855.
                                                   (NS43:544)

ODDY Mr, ex merchant, London & St Petersburg, d. Havanna, 1814.
                                                   (84:509)

ODELL Elizabeth Ludlow, w. Dr George M Odell, niece Comm. Gen.
Robinson, d. Fredericton, NB, 19 April 1861.   (NS2/10:705)

O'DONNELL William L., barrister, eldest s. late Nicholas
O'Donnell, Dublin, d. Grenada, 2 Nov.1866.   (NS3/3:115)

O'DONOGHUE Patrick, Irish rebel, d. NY, 1854.   (NS41:445)

O'DRISCOLL Dorinda, eldest dau. John O'Driscoll, Chief
Justice Dominica, m. Edwin Winey, Burton on the Water, Glocs.,
Taunton, 24 Nov.1842.   (NS19:197)

O'DRISCOLL John, Chief Justice Dominica, d. Dominica,
3 June 1828.   (98:94)

OGDEN Anne, eldest dau. J Gouvernour Ogden, Sheriff of Three
Rivers, ex Cap., 56th Reg., m. Edward M Hopkins, Hudson Bay Co.,
Three Rivers, Canada East, 31 Aug.1847.   (NS28:630)

OGDEN Charles Rice, Solicitor Gen. Canada, m. Mary Aston,
yngr. dau. Gen. Coffin, Walmer, Kent, 29 July 1824. (94:176)

OGDEN Isaac, Judge King's BenchLower Canada 29 years, d.
London, 1 Feb.1824.   (94:283)

OGDEN Mary Aston, w. Charles Ogden, Solicitor Gen., yngs. dau.
Gen. J Coffin, d. Montreal, 1827.   (97:478)

OGILBY Rev. John, Prof. Ecclesiastical History, NY, d. Paris,
2 Feb.1851.   (NS35:563)

OGILVY Adam, yngs. s. Sir John Ogilvy, d. Antigua, 29 July
1799.   (69:900)

OGILVY Col. John, HM Comm. under Treaty of Ghent, d. Malden,
America, 28 Sep.1819.   (89:472)

OGILVIE Peter, b.1774, s. Rev. Dr Ogilvie, Midmar, Aberdeen,
asst. surgeon to Dr Henry McLean, St Domingo, d.Sep.1794.
                                                   (64:1150)

OGILVY R., b.1752, ex Assemblyman, Jamaica, d.
London, 31 March 1816.   (86:377)

OGLE Rev. W R, s. late John Ogle, Meeson Hall, Shropshire, m. Julia, eldest dau. late Maj. Tallmadge, NY, Nice, 7 Feb.1850.   (NS33:529)

O'GORMAN Charles T, ex Consul Gen. Mexico, d. London, 29 Sep.1847.   (NS28:552)

O'KEEFE Rev. T, chaplain to Duke of Clarence, only s. Mr O'Keefe, celebrated writer, d. Jamaica, 1805.   (75:677)

OKEY Adeline, only ch. C H Okey, Antigua, m. Sir William Snagg, Chief Justice Antigua & Montserrat, Salisbury, 29 June 1865.   (NS2/19:235)

OLDFIELD Granville Sharp, merchant, ex England, m. Anne, eldest dau. Ralph Higginbotham, Baltimore, 5 Aug.1819.(89:562)

OLDHAM William, merchant, d. Jamaica, 18 June 1800.   (70:798)

OLDMIXON George, Cap., RN, m. Frances Margaret, 2nd dau. John Hodgson, St Johns, NFD., 8 Oct.1854.   (NS43:76)

OLDMIXON Sir John, settled USA 1793, d. USA 1818.   (88:478)

OLDMIXON Lady, 'resident in America over 35 years', d. Philadelphia, 3 Feb.1835.   (105:671)

OLIVER Andrew, b.1706, Lt. Gov. Mass. Bay, d.3 March 1774.
                                                                          (44:239)

OLIVER George, Craigmill, Jamaica, magistrate, d. London, 22 Aug.1818.   (88:378)

OLIVER Harriet, w. Thomas Oliver, ex Gov. Mass., dau. Mr Freeman, Antigua, d. Bristol, 16 July 1808.   (78:662)

OLIVER Martha Elliot, 3rd dau. late L Oliver, Bristol, m. B E Jarvis, Mount Joshua, Antigua, Councillor, Antigua, 6 Dec.1859.   (NS2/8:178)

OLIVER Peter, 3rd s. late P Oliver, Lt. Gov. Mass., surgeon, d. London, 6 April 1795.   (65:358)

OLIVER Richard, ex Alderman of London, d. on Sandwich Packet on passage from Nevis, 16 April 1784.   (54:395)

O'LOUGHLIN James, MD, m. Jane, wid. James Hozier, Jamaica, London, 11 Sep.1849.   (NS32:530)

OLTON J A, d. Barbados, 1 Aug.1810.   (80:387)

OLTON O, eldest dau. late John Allen Olton, Harrowplace, Barbados, m. Cap. William Whitmore, ADC Maj. Gen. Munro, Cabbage Tree Hall, Barbados, 14 April 1811.   (81:589)

ONDERDONK Rev. Benjamin Treadwell, b.1791, Bishop of NY, d. NY, 30 April 1861.   (NS2/11:93)

O'NEAL Mary Ann, 2nd dau. late Thomas Whitfoot O'Neal, Barbados, m. Henry Charles Benyon, only s. late Cap. Robert Cutts Barton, RN, Devon, Cheltenham, 1 July 1845.
                                                                          (NS24:415)

ORD Eliza Dare, w. Col. Ord, RE, d. Montreal, 10 Feb.1858.
(NS2/4:449)

ORD Sir John, ex Gov. Dominica, m. Miss Frere, dau. John
Frere, London, 2 Dec.1793.   (63:1148)

ORD Lewis W, ex Lt., 71st Highlanders, yngs. s. late Maj. Ord,
RA, m. Sarah Harriet, yngs. dau. W B Jarvis, Sheriff of York,
gdau. W D Powell, Chief Justice Upper Canada, Toronto,
24 June 1854.   (NS42:616)

ORDE Thomas, Customs Collector, Militia Col., Receiver Gen.,
St Lucia, d. St Pierre, Martinique, 1799.   (69:819)

ORDERSON Mrs, w. J W Orderson, Barbados, d. on passage to
England, 20 July 1810.   (80:189)

ORGILL Charles Richard, Portland, Jamaica, m. Harriet, dau.
late Rev. John Davies, Pedworth, Berks., Salisbury, 1800.
(70:1284)

O'REILLY Dowell, b.1795, 6th s. Matthew O'Reilly, Knock
Castle, Louth, Attorney Gen. Jamaica, d. St Andrews,
Kingston, Jamaica, 13 Sep.1855.   (NS24:651)

O'REILLY Richard, Judge Jamaica Supreme Court, d. Kingston,
Jamaica, 22 Dec.1860.   (NS2/10:348)

ORIEL H F, b.1798, Asst. Comm. Gen., d. Bermuda, 11 Oct.1853.
(NS41:439)

ORLEBAR John, RN, m. Harriet, yngs. dau. John Hale, Receiver
Gen. Lower Canada, Quebec, 5 Feb.1838.   (NS9:539)

ORMOND Helen, dau. late James Ormond, Leith, d. Florida,
27 Aug.1841.   (NS17:118)

ORMBY Charlotte Anne Seymour, yngs. dau. late Lt. Gen. Ormby,
m. William Carlisle Strather, only s. E Strather, Nevis,
Kotergherry, Neilgherry Hills, 2 May 1837.   (NS8:528)

ORR Charlianna, w. Bryan West Orr, Castle Est., Portland.
Jamaica, London, 26 Sep.1820.   (90:377)

ORR Matthew, d. King's Bay Est., Tobago, 1 Aug.1790. (60:956)

ORR ..., dau. Cap. Orr, RA, b. Montreal, 20 July 1863.
(NS2/15:366)

ORSETT George, Kingston Assemblyman, d. Jamaica, 1845.
(NS24:665)

OSBORN Rev. Daniel, b.1812, St George, Jamaica, d. at sea,
27 Feb.1853.   (NS39:558)

OSBORNE Sir D'Anvers, Gov. NY, d. Dec.1753.   (23:591)

OSBORN Grace Parson, b.1776, eldest dau. Humphrey Osborn,
St Kitts, d. Southampton, 5 Jan.1853.   (NS39:221)

OSBORN John Brownlow, 3rd s. late Sir John Osborn, Chicksands
Priory, d. Toronto, 15 Dec.1853.   (NS41:329)

OSBORNE Robert, Barbados, m. Sally, eldest dau. John Hopkins, Ingastone Hall, Essex, 18 Sep.1741.   (11:499)

OSBORNE Samuel, Barbados, d.2 Aug.1767.   (37:430)

OSGOOD Miss, London, m. James Foxcraft, Dep. Postmaster Gen. NA, 2 Aug.1770.   (40:392)

OTTER Alfred W, 2nd s. late Rev. Dr Otter, Bishop of Chichester, m. Anna, only dau. Rev. James de la Hooke, Gravenhurst, Beds., Goderich, Canada West, 1842.   (NS19:197)

OTTER Alfred W, b.1815, 2nd s. Rev. W Otter, Bishop of Chichester, d. Toronto, 25 Aug.1866.   (NS3/2:556)

OTTLEY Alice, sis. late Dreury Ottley, President, St Vincent, d. Bath, 27 Aug.1843.   (NS20:444)

OTTLEY Dreury, b.1740, St Kitts, d. London, 2 April 1822.   (92:379)

OTTLEY Frederick, 2nd s. Warner Ottley, London & St Vincent, d. St Vincent, 27 Aug.1842.   (NS19:110)

OTTLEY George Wetherill, ex Councillor, Antigua, d. Southampton, 16 July 1856.   (NS2/1:263)

OTTLEY Matilda Elwin, 4th dau. George Weatherill Ottley, Parry's, Antigua, m. George Fenton Fletcher Boughey, Cap., 59th Reg., 3rd s. late Sir J F Boughey, Antigua, 16 Dec.1842.   (NS19:311)

OTTLEY Sarah Elizabeth, wid. Richard Ottley, St Vincent, d. London, 14 March 1825.   (95:379)

OTTLEY W, ex St Kitts, d. Cambridge, 28 Sep.1815.   (85:379)

OTTLEY W, b.1797, s. late Dreury Ottley, President, St Vincent, bro. Sir Richard Ottley, d. St Vincent, 24 April 1820.(90:638)

OTTLEY Warner, b.1775, ex Councillor, St Vincent, d. London, 8 Dec.1846.   (NS27:104)

OVERING Cato, b.1711, d. Newport, RI, 5 Oct.1821.   (91:571)

OVERING John, Attorney Gen. NE, d. Boston, Mass., 1754.(24:435)

OWEN Rev. David, Senior Fellow Trinity College Cambridge, d. NB, 10 Dec.1829.   (100:280)

OWEN James, b.1811, NY, d. St Paul's Hotel, 12 Sep.1858.   (NS2/5:430)

OXNARD Thomas, merchant, grandmaster mason NA, d. Boston, NE, 27 Aug.1754.   (24:388)

PACKWOOD Joseph, b. Bermuda, Post-Cap.RN, d. Naples, 1836.   (NS5:547)

PAGAN William, Dominica, m. Catherine, dau. late Rev. John Hart, Kirkenner, 23 June 1791.   (61:871)

PAGE Adam, b.1745, d. King George Co., Va., 11 March 1867.   (NS3/3:679)

PAGE Charlotte Dorothea, b.1802, yngs. dau. William Page, RN, d. Toronto, 18 Aug.1854.   (NS42:528)

PAGE Georgina, dau. late R P Page, London & New Orleans, m. Victor Mottey, Marchiennes, Officier de la Legion d'Honneur, London, 12 Feb.1850.   (NS33:530)

PAGE Julianna, wid. Dr Page, dau. late Rev. Henry Dawson, Hopton, Suffolk, gdau. late Sir Robert Buxton, Norfolk, d. Racine, Wisc., 12 Sep.1866.   (NS3/2:837)

PAGE John Dupuis, b.1791, s. Mr Page, St Paul's Cathedral, London, d. St Domingo, July 1810.   (80:386)

PAINE Mary Elizabeth, 2nd dau. David Paine, Ingersoll, Canada West, m. Albert Caswell, Troubridge, Wilts., Woodstock, Canada West, 7 Oct.1851.   (NS37:83)

PAINE Thomas, d. NY, 8 June 1809, buried New Rochelle.(79:678)

PAIRMAN James, b.1782, ex Postmaster Gen. Barbados, d. Barbados, 6 Dec.1845.   (NS25:335)

PAISLEY Sarah Anne, dau. late W Paisley, Jamaica, m. Rev. Ewan James, London, 15 Oct.1818.   (88:370)

PAKENHAM T H, Col., 30th Reg., m. Elizabeth Staples, eldest dau. William Clarke, NY, 25 Feb.1862.   (NS2/12:497)

PALACIOS Teresa, 2nd dau. Don Capician Palacios, Castile, m. Lt. Charles Rookes, 2nd WI Reg., Nassau, New Providence, 23 Oct.1846.   (NS25:87)

PALAIRET S H, Cap., 29th Reg., m. Mary Anne, only ch. late Andrew Hamilton, Woodlands, Philadelphia, & Middlesex, Broad Mayne, Dorset, 18 April 1843.   (NS19:643)

PALESKE Charles Godfried, Prussian Consul Gen. USA, m. Hannah Elmslie, Philadelphia, 1792.   (62:574)

PALFORD Mrs, ex WI, d. Richmond, 13 Nov.1784.   (55:878)

PALMER Aphra Maria, dau. John Palmer, Colonial Treasurer, d. Dominica, 17 May 1853.   (NS40:209)

PALMER Charles N, Jamaica, m. Mrs Ingoldsby Massy, Norbiton, Surrey, 2 June 1808.   (78:556)

PALMER Constant Grace, w. Lt. Col. Reynolds Palmer, RA, d. Kingstown, Upper Canada, 16 Oct.1850.   (NS35:111)

PALMER Henry Spencer, Lt., RE, yngs. s. late Col.J F Palmer, Madras Army, Bath, m. Mary Jane Pearson, eldest dau. H P Wrigh Archdeacon of Columbia, New Westminster, BC, 7 Oct.1864.
                                                  (NS2/16:107)

PALMER James, Bristol, Jamaica, d. Hot Wells, 5 July 1806.
                                                     (76:777)

PALMER John, 2nd s. Mr Palmer, St Mary Axe, d. Charleston, SC, 9 Sep.1792.   (62:1054)

PALMER J, b.1742, Jamaica, d.Bath, 1819.   (88:92)

PALMER John, s. John Palmer, Wiltshire Park, Clarendon,
Jamaica, d. Beckington, 18 Feb.1825.   (95:381)

PALMER Mary, b.1787, dau. Mr Gatfield, London, w. H Palmer,
Green Mountains, d. Jamaica, 12 Dec.1810.   (81:293)

PALMER Mary, dau. John Palmer, Colonial Treasurer, d.
Dominica, 17 May 1853.   (NS40:209)

PALMER Mary Anne, sis. John Palmer, Colonial Treasurer, d.
Dominica, 4 May 1853.   (NS40:209)

PALMER Sarah, b.1728, wid. Henry John Palmer, Jamaica, d.
Bath, 2 Aug.1814.   (84:198)

PALMER Thomas, d. Warm Springs, Va., 1797.   (67:805)

PALMER Cap., Guards Reg., s. Sir Charles Palmer, m. Miss
French, dau. Nathaniel French, Antigua, 25 Oct.1752. (22:478)

PALMER Mrs, wid. Herbert Palmer, m. Maj. Cosnan, Quebec, 1762.
                                                         (32:93)

PANTON Annis Rachel, dau. Rev. Dr Panton, Widcombe, niece
Vice Chancellor Jamaica, m. Mayow Short, Chairman Quarter
Sessions, Jamaica, 15 June 1847.   (NS28:311)

PANTON Eliza, Manchioneal, m. J D Andrews, Port Antonio,
Jamaica, 1800.   (70:1283)

PANTON Rev. Richard, Archdeacon of Surrey, Jamaica, d.
30 Aug.1860.   (NS2/9:438)

PAPLEY Miss, Jamaica, m. William Hey, Customs Comm., 5 April
1783.   (53:363)

PAPPS Frances Ann, b.1804, dau. late Alexander Forbes, London,
w. Henry Spencer Papps, d. Hamilton, Canada West, 16 May 1856.
                                                       (NS2/1:123)

PAPPS Henry Spencer, b. Antigua, 1800, eldest s. Henry Papps,
solicitor, Hamilton, Canada West, d. London, 9 March 1867.
                                                       (NS3/3:548)

PARKE Mary, yngs. dau. William Parke, the Thickets, Jamaica,
m. Rev. H Morland Austen, Crayford, Kent, Sturminster,
Dorset, 15 Sep.1853.   (NS40:628)

PARKER Albert, Cooksville, Toronto, yngs. s. late Sir William
George Parker, RN, m. Henrietta Lucy, only dau. late William
Robert Jennings, Bengal Civil Service, 5 April 1851.(NS35:658)

PARKER Florence, yngs. dau. Neville Parker, m. Harry Moody,
Fredericton, NB, 28 July 1863.   (NS2/15:498)

PARKER George, s. John Parker, planter, Jamaica, d. London,
1 Oct.1788.   (58:936)

PARKER Henry, Jamaica, d. London, 9 Nov.1787.   (57:1031)

PARKER Lucy, b.1796, dau. H N Binney, Halifax, NS, wid. Maj.
Edward Parker, 62nd Reg., d. Isleworth, 20 May 1864.(NS2/16:814)

PARKER Robert, b.1796, Chief Justice NB, d. St John, NB,
24 Nov.1865.   (NS3/1:149)

PARKER Susan, dau. Sir William George Parker, ex Plymouth, m.
Sir William Smith, Erdiston House, Worcester, Canada, 1843.
                                                     (NS20:537)

PARKER Thomas, ex naval officer, d. America, 1800.   (70:905)

PARKER Thomas, b.1761, Jamaica, d. London, 3 April 1823.
                                                     (93:382)

PARKER Mrs Isabel, wid. late Henry Parker, Jamaica, m.
James Grierson, London, 1788.   (58:269)

PARKER Mrs, b.1755, wid. John Parker, Lincoln's Inn, sis.
Alexander Croke, Judge High Court Admiralty NS, Studley House,
23 July 1814.   (84:191)

PARKYNS Joseph Wilfred, b. Carlisle, ex Sheriff of London,
d. NY, 12 April 1840.   (NS14:549)

PARKYNS Ann Catherine, niece Vice Adm. Sir John Borlase
Warren, m. William Territt, Judge Bermuda Vice Adm.,
Bermuda, 13 Jan. 1810.   (80:383)

PARNELL T O, b.1801, only s. T O Parnell, Warminster, d.
Jamaica, 19 Sep.1829.   (99:651)

PARR Horton, b.1822, eldest s. John Hamilton Parr, Liverpool,
d. Demerara, 6 Sep.1845.   (NS24:665)

PARR John, b.1725, Gov. NS, d. Halifax, NS, 25 Nov.1791.
                                                     (61:1235)

PARR Thomas, Prof. Languages, SC College, d. Winnsborough,
SC, 16 July 1844.   (NS22:334)

PARRIS James New, b.1767, Councillor, Nevis, Lt. Col. Nevis
Militia, d. Maidstone, 19 Feb.1846.   (NS25:443)

PARRIS Mrs, w. R N Parris, Nevis, ex Cardiff, d. Nevis, 1817.
                                                     (87:646)

PARRY Constance Louisa, 5th dau. Thomas Parry, Bishop of
Barbados, m. John Thomas Dalyell, Maj., 21st Royal North
British Fusiliers, s. Lt. Col. Thomas Dalyell, 42nd Native
Infantry, Barbados, 7 Feb.1861.   (NS2/10:567)

PARRY Henry, Leyden Est., Montego Bay, Jamaica, d. Northrop,
Flint, 18 Jan.1820.   (90:187)

PARSON Rev. James, b.1747, bro. John Parson, Botesdale, d.
St Croix, 10 Aug.1811.   (81:657)

PARTELOW Ada, yngs. dau. John R Partelow, Auditor Gen. NB,
m. Charles Clifton Tabor, 15th Reg., Fredericton, NB,
8 Oct.1862.   (NS2/13:770)

PARTINGTON Charles, ex Charleston, SC, d. 10 Jan.1794.(64:180)

PARYS Michael m. Miss Christie, niece Fairley Christie,
Assemblyman, Kingston, Jamaica, July 1800.   (70:1001)

PASLEY Maj. Charles, HEICS, London, m. Mary, eldest dau. late
Simon McTavish, Montreal, 21 May 1817.   (87:82)

PASLEY Comm. T Malcolm Sabine, RN, eldest s. Rear Adm. Sir
Thomas S Pasley, m. Emma Louisa, eldest dau. late W Losh,
Trinidad, Port of Spain, Trinidad, 13 Feb.1860.   (NS2/8:506)

PATERSON Samuel, NE, m. Miss Wood, dau. late Sir P Wood,
Newington, 23 June 1750.   (20:284)

PATEY Louisa, yngs. dau. Sir James Patey, Reading, m. Cap.
Andrew Neil, 99th Reg., St Vincent, 1813.   (83:87)

PATON ..., s. Maj. Paton, 4th King's Royal Reg., b.
Charlottetown, PEI, 31 Jan.1867.   (NS3/3:663)

PATRICK James Jarman, b.1812, yngs. s. Jarman Patrick, Norwich,
ex Wiggenhall, St Germans, d. Milan, NA, 23 Dec.1843.
                                                     (NS21:334)

PARTRIDGE Mary Julia, b.1807, w. S T Partridge, MD, Barbados,
d. Bath, 1830.   (100:647)

PARTRIDGE Richard, b.1672, Agent of Philadelphia, RI, Conn.,
& East Jersey for 30 years, d.1759.   (29:146)

PARTRIDGE Thomas, estate owner, Jamaica, d.12 May 1759.(29:242)

PARTRIDGE Thomas, London, d. Jamaica, 1820.   (90:379)

PATTEN Ann, b.1838, wid. Joshua Patten, d. Boston, USA,
17 March 1861.   (NS2/10:704)

PATTERSON Maria Jane, dau. late Cap. Theophilius Patterson,
RM, m. James W Sinckler, MD, Barbados, London, 5 Sep.1854.
                                                     (NS42:618)

PATTERSON Marian, eldest dau. late William Patterson, Jamaica,
m. Charles Vardon, Surrey, 15 May 1806.   (76:477)

PATTERSON William, ex Gov. PEI, d. Oxford Market, 6 Sep.1798.
                                                     (68:815)

PATTERSON W D, US Consul Antwerp, d. Antwerp, 4 July 1836.
                                                     (NS6:223)

PATTINSON William, merchant, d. Jamaica, 1791.   (61:1065)

PATTISON Granville Sharp, yngs. s. John Pattison, Kelvingrove,
Prof. Anatomy NY, d. NY, 12 Nov.1851.   (NS37:107)

PATTISON Lt. Col., 2nd WI Reg., d. Nassau, New Providence, 1835.
                                                     (105:446)

PATTON Rev. Henry, Cornwall, Canada West, m. Georgina, dau.
late George Dodson, Lichfield, Staffs., Prescott, Canada West,
3 Dec.1846.   (NS27:303)

PATTON William, Seigneur St Thomas, 2nd s. Late John Patton,
Walthamstow, d. Quebec, 12 Aug.1853.   (NS40:426)

PAUL Anne, eldest dau. Robert Paul, President, St Vincent, m. Maj. Wilby, 90th Reg., St Vincent, 3 Feb.1814.   (84:406)

PAUL Rev. Charles, White Lackington, Somerset, m. Frances Kegan, 3rd dau. John Horne, St Vincent, Bath, 22 May 1827.
(96:557)

PAUL Elizabeth, dau. Gov. St Vincent, m. Cap. Bent, 5th Reg., 1822.   (93:79)

PAXTON Charles, b.1702, ex Comm. Revenue America, d. Norfolk, 1788.   (58:83)

PAYNE Arabella Gertrude, 2nd dau. Lt. Col. Payne, m. Philip Bedingfield, RA, Fredericton, NB, 28 Oct.1851.   (NS37:181)

PAYNE C, 2nd dau. Sir Gillies Payne, m. George Sharpe, St Vincent, Tempsford, Beds., 1788.   (58:1026)

PAYNE Emma, dau. E W Payne, ex NY, m. Robert Zoffanie Beach-croft, London, Mere worth, Kent, 30 Nov.1842.   (NS19:197)

PAYNE George Thomas, bro. Gov., d. Antigua, 1774.   (44:390)

PAYNE Ralph, St Kitts, d.1763.   (32:97)

PAYNE Mrs, wid. John Payne, Dodds, Barbados, d. Odiham, 9 April 1810.   (80:493)

PAYNE Miss, Odiham, dau. late John Payne, Barbados, d.2 March 1814.   (84:812)

PEACAN Matthew, London, merchant, d. Kingston, Jamaica, 1810.
(80:283)

PEACOCK Benjamin, d. Barbados, 1757.   (27:531)

PEARCE John, eldest s. Dr Pearce, surgeon, ex London, d. Kingston, Jamaica, 1783.   (53:451)

PEARCE Robert, estate owner, Antigua & St Kitts, m. Miss Pycraft, 28 Jan.1745.   (15:108)

PEARCE Robert, b.1773, yngs. s. late Cap. Pearce, Woodford, Essex, d. Kingston, Jamaica, 25 Nov.1793.   (64:180)

PEARL Lady Anne, wid. Sir James Pearl, St Johns, NFD., d. 8 Nov.1855.   (NS43:105)

PEARNE Mr, Great Western engineer, d. NY, 1838.   (NS10:111)

PEARSON Maj. Charles Knight, Somerset, m. Marian Catherine, eldest dau. Maj. Robert Miller Munday, Lt. Gov. Grenada, Grenada, 10 April 1866.   (NS3/1:900)

PEARSON Henry, merchant, London, m. Miss Manning, only dau. late Richard Manning, Antigua, June 1787.   (57:933)

PEARSON Sarah, b.1821, dau. Rev. William Henry Rawlins, Fiddington, Somerset, w. George Dance, 71st Reg., d. Chambly, Canada, 27 Aug.1843.   (NS20:670)

PEARSON Thomas, eldest s. Rev. Thomas Pearson, Great Witley,
Worcs., d. Jamaica, 1835.   (105:222)

PEARSON W H, ex clerk Council Jamaica, successor to uncle
T Harrison, d. Kingston, Jamaica, 1813.   (83:183)

PEARSUN Mr, Manchester, d. St Pierre, Martinique, 5 Oct.1794.
                                                      (64:1150)

PEART Frederick, b.1813, 2nd s. John Peart, ex Cheltenham,
d. Newark, Jamaica, 1848.   (NS30:446)

PEAT Frederick m. Ann Margaret Eleanor, elder dau. Joseph
James Swaby, Kilnsey, Yorks., gdau. Joseph James Swaby, ex
Jamaica, Jamaica, 5 March 1842.   (NS17:661)

PEAT Rev. William, Nettleslead, Norfolk, d. Jamaica, 29 Aug.
1815.   (85:634)

PECHELL Edward Rodney Cecil, Royal Canadian Rifle Reg., yngs.
s. late Cap. Samuel George Pechell, RN, m. Alicia Alleyn,
eldest dau. Rev. John Rothwell, Amherst Island, Kingston,
Canada West, 7 Sep.1859.   (NS2/7:638)

PEDDER Eliza, b.1776, ex Isle of Wight, w. James Pedder,
editor 'The Cultivator', d. Boston, USA, 25 July 1854.
                                                      (NS42:316)

PEDLEY Henry, ex Reading, Berks., merchant, d. Kingston,
Jamaica, 17 Dec.1797.   (68:256)

PEDLEY Joseph, b.1817, eldest s. Joseph Pedley, London, d.
Bound Brook, NJ, 2 Feb.1843.   (NS19:557)

PEEL Edmund, only s. late John Peel, the Abbey, Burton on
Trent, d. Philipsburgh, Canada East, 17 Feb.1846. (NS25:559)

PEELE Rembrandt, b.1777, painter, d. Philadelphia, 4 Oct.1860.
                                                      (NS2/9:680)

PEETE William, only s. Richard Peete, Norwich, judge Jamaica,
Assemblyman Kingston, d. Jamaica, 1787.   (57:1194)

PELE Mrs S, eldest dau. late John Heaver, d. Antigua, Nov.1816.
                                                       (86:626)

PELLEW Henry Edward, s. Rev. George Pellew, Dean of Norwich,
m. Eliza, dau. Judge William Jay, gdau. late John Jay, Gov.
NY, Bedford, Westchester Co., NY, 5 Oct.1858.   (NS2/5:629)

PELLY Edward, Hudson Bay Co. Service, m. Anne Rose, 2nd dau.
Edward Clouston, Stromness, Orkney, York Factory, Hudson Bay,
28 Aug.1849.   (NS32:638)

PEMBERTON George Tudor, 2nd s. George Pemberton, Quebec, m.
Sophia Louisa, eldest dau. A C Buchanan, Quebec, 25 Sep.1867.
                                                      (NS3/2:671)

PEMBERTON George, b.1795, Councillor, Quebec, d. Quebec,
21 Feb.1868.   (NS3/5:544)

PEMBERTON Mrs Susannah, b.1754, ex Jamaica, d. Richmond,
7 Nov.1829.   (99:476)

PEMBERTON Thomas, St Kitts, m. Jane, yngs. dau. late John
Blanshard, HEICS, Broadstairs, 12 Aug.1846.   (NS26:420)

PEMBERTON Walter Maynard, b.1789, Spring Hill, Nevis,
Councillor, Nevis, d. wreck Clarendon, off Isle of Wight,
11 Oct.1836.   (NS6:668)

PRENDVILLE Judith Campbell, dau. John Pendville, gdau. W
Campbell, New Milns, Jamaica, m. Rev. William David Longland,
Bath, 18 Dec.1822.   (92:642)

PENGELLEY Caroline, 2nd dau. Edward Pengelley, Halifax, m.
C W Elphinstone Holloway, 2nd s. late Col. E Holloway, gs.
Gen. Sir Charles Holloway, Garrison Chapel, Halifax, NS,
13 Oct.1863.   (NS2/15:772)

PENN Anne, b.1746, wid. John Penn, ex Gov.Pa., d. London,
4 July 1830.   (100:91)

PENN John, s. William Penn, Lord Proprietor Pa., d.28 Oct.
1746.   (16:612)

PENN John, Lt. Gov. Pa., m. Miss Allen, eldest dau. William
Allen, 31 May 1766.   (36:342)

PENN John, ex Gov. Pa., d. Philadelphia, Feb.1795.   (65:347)

PENN John, b.1759, ex Proprietor & Hereditary Gov.Pa., d.
Stoke Park, Bucks., 21 June 1834.   (104:650)

PENN Thomas, Proprietor Pa., m. Lady Juliana Fermor, yngs.
dau. Earl of Pomfret, 22 Aug.1751.   (21:427)

PENN Thomas, s. Thomas Penn, Proprietor Pa., d.1757. (27:436)

PENN William, Proprietor Pa., gs. Sir William Penn, m. Miss
Forbes, dau. Alexander Forbes, merchant, London, 1732.(2:1126)

PENN ..., dau. Lady Juliana Penn, w. Mr Penn, Proprietor Pa.,
b.19 May 1753.   (23:248)

PENN Miss, dau. late Thomas Penn, Proprietor Pa., m. Rev. Dr.
William Stuart, Bishop of St David's, 3 May 1796.   (66:438)

PENN ..., s. Richard Penn, Proprietor Pa., b.5 June 1747.
                                                     (17:296)

PENN ..., s. Thomas & Juliana Penn, Proprietor Pa., b.28 June
1752.   (22:288)

PENN Mrs, wid. Richard Penn, ex Proprietor & Gov. Pa., d.
Latcham, Middlesex, 20 April 1785.   (55:328)

PENNY Rev. John, b.1805, Sandy Point, St Kitts, garrison
chaplain, d. St Kitts, Sep.1840.   (NS14:670)

PENRICE Henry, b.1819, 4th s. George Penrice, MD, Great Yarmouth, d. St Lucia, 21 Sep.1842.   (NS19:556)

PEPLOW Thomas, b.1661, est. owner, St Kitts, d.19 April 1752.
(22:192)

PEPPERELL Lady, wid. Sir William Pepperell, gmo. Sir William
Pepperell, d. Kittery, NE, 25 Nov.1789.   (60:179)

PERCH Sarah Elizabeth, eldest dau. Thomas Perch, Barbados, m.
James Bedford, Loaugharne, South Wales, s. Col. Perch, Bengal
Army, Bath, 3 Feb.1864.   (NS2/16:380)

PERCIVAL James Gates, b. Kensington, Conn., 15 Sep.1795, 2nd
s. Dr James Percival, poet, d. America, 1856.   (NS2/1:121)

PERCIVAL Michael Henry, b.1779, s.-in-law Sir Charles Flower,
Customs Collector Quebec, d. at sea, 12 Oct.1829.   (99:477)

PERCY Marcella, eldest dau. Rev. Gilbert Percy, St Peter's,
Quebec, m. Lt. Edward Ashe, RN, The Observatory, Quebec,
28 May 1851.   (NS36:188)

PERCY Rev. William, b.1744, St Paul's, Charleston, SC, d.1819.
(89:187)

PERINE Bessie, wid. W B Perine, Baltimore, dau. late Z Collin
Lee, Baltimore, m. Comm. Bernard John Cooper, RN, Baltimore,
USA, 15 Aug.1867.   (NS3/2:527)

PERKINS Charlotte, 2nd dau. John Perkins, Blechingly, Surrey,
drowned on passage from Barbados on Atlas, 27 Aug.1809.
(79:1235)

PERKINS Jacob, b.1766, inventor, ex USA, d. London, 30 July
1849.   (NS32:327)

PERKINS Jane Elizabeth, dau. Thomas Trigge, Quebec, wid. J M
Perkins, Nicolet, m. J Maharg, MD, surgeon, 70th Reg.,
Nicolet, Lower Canada, 6 Jan.1843.   (NS19:422)

PERKINS Marianne, 2nd dau. late A T Perkins, London, m. W J
Evans, MD, Barbados, 1 Feb.1838.   (NS9:539)

PERKINS Richard, d. New London, 1798.   (68:1086)

PERKINS Dr, inventor metallic tractor, d. NY, 1799. (69:904)

PERLEY Ada, dau. M H Perley, Comm. NA Fisheries, m. Richard,
2nd s. Charles Simonds, St John, NB, 31 Oct.1860. (NS2/10:95)

PERRIN William, Jamaica, d.1759.   (29:293)

PERROTT Isobel Charlotte, 3rd dau. late Edmund Thomas Perrott,
Worcs., ggs. John, Lord St John, m. Valesius Skipton, eldest
s. Valesius Goldsbury, Longford, Ireland, ggs.IA Goldsbury,
Auchnogare, Barbados, 8 Sep.1867.   (NS2/17:647)

PERROTT A, 2nd s. late G Perrott, Cracombe, Worcs., d. St Kitts
1811.   (81:292)

PERROT James Leigh, North Leigh, Oxford, m. Miss Warkham,
Barbados, 9 Oct.1764.   (34:498)

PERRY Anne, eldest dau. late John Perry, d. Montego Bay,
Jamaica, 29 Dec.1809.   (10:283)

PERRY Elizabeth, 2nd dau. John Perry, ex Bristol, d.
Montego Bay, Jamaica, 5 Jan.1806.   (76:281)

PERRY Elizabeth Charlotte, ex Bristol, w. William Perry, d.
Jamaica, 26 Dec.1814.   (85:179)

PERRY John, Assemblyman, Common Pleas Court Judge Jamaica,
d. Jamaica, 30 April 1809.   (79:984)

PERRY Comm., US Navy, d. Trinidad, 23 Aug.1819.   (89:378)

PESHALL Sir Charles J, ex HM Consul NC, d.24 July 1834.
                                           (104:659)

PETERS Col. John, b. Hebron, Conn., June 1740, ex Queen's
Loyal Rangers, American Loyalist, d. London, 11 Jan.1788,
buried St George, Hanover Square, London. (58:84)

PETERS J, b.1700, d. Adams, Berkshire Co., Mass., 10 Sep.
1807.   (77:1172)

PETER William, b.22 March 1788, s. Henry Peter, Harlyn,
Cornwall, barrister, HM Consul Pa., d. Philadelphia, 6 Feb.
1853.   (NS39:441)

PETION Alexander, President, Haiti, d.28 March 1818. (88:565)

PETIT Rev. John Louis m. Louisa Elizabeth, eldest dau. George
Reid, Jamaica, Wye, Kent, 5 June 1828.   (98:646)

PETRIE Rev. George, Burford & Norwich, Canada West, d.
28 Aug.1847.   (NS28:551)

PETRY Rev. Henry James, Quebec, m. Caroline Josepha, yngs.
dau. late John George Smith, Montreal, 21 Nov.1860.(NS2/10:95)

PETRY Rev. Henry James, Danville cum Tingwick, m. Araminta,
3rd dau. Cap. Hill, 69th Reg., Ottawa, 10 Jan.1867.(NS3/3:377)

PETRY ..., s. Rev. Henry James Petry, b. Quebec, 6 April 1863.
                                           (NS2/14:778)

PEWTNER William, b.1821, yngs. s. J Pewtner, Stockwell & Bank
of England, d. Fergus, Upper Canada, 26 Aug.1843. (NS20:670)

PEWTRESS Sarah Jane, 2nd dau. Ebenezer B Pewtress, Buffalo,
NY, m. Robert Charles Carrington, The Admiralty, Whitehall,
London, 15 June 1861.   (NS2/11:82)

PHELON Patrick, RC Bishop of Toronto, d.6 July 1857.(NS2/3:224)

PHELPS A Peyton m. Rachel Susanna, wid. Alexander Deans, Master
in Chancery, Jamaica, London, 12 May 1835.   (NS4:88)

PHELPS Rev. Joseph Francis, eldest s. Joseph Phelps, Madeira,
m. Fanny Harriot, 4th dau. Justice Robinson, NFD., St Johns,
NFD., 2 Sep.1862.   (NS2/13:627)

PHILLIPS Ann Sisum, dau. late Peter Phillips, Barbados, m.
George Geoffrey, only s. Jeffrey Wyatville, Windsor, London,
17 Jan.1828.   (98:80)

PHILLIPS Anna, wid. Samuel Phillips, Portsmouth, d. Jamaica,
7 Nov.1831.   (102:94)

PHILIPS Rev. Ebenezer, Baptist missionary, d. Jamaica,
12 Oct.1825.   (95:575)

PHILIPS Elizabeth, wid. Rev. E Philips, d. Jamaica,
15 Oct.1825.   (95:575)

PHILIPPS Lt. G G, RN, m. Georgina, dau. late Jonas Wilkinson,
Barbados, London, 3 Aug.1852.   (NS38:411).

PHILIPS Helen, 2nd dau. Rev. Thomas Philips, ex Vice Principal
Upper Canada College, m. Rev. C Dade, Caius College,
Cambridege, Winston, Upper Canada, 14 March 1840. (NS13:645)

PHILIPS Henry, Manchester, m. Sophia, dau. Judge Benjamin
Chew, Philadelphia, 18 Oct.1796.   (66:1054)

PHILIPS James, s. John Philips, Bank, Lancs., d.Philadelphia,
11 July 1808.   (78:852)

PHILLIPS John, Cap., RN, yngs. s. late Frederick Phillips,
Phillipsborough, NY, American Loyalist, d. Bristol, 18 March
1813.   (83:390)

PHILIP John Baptist, MD, d. Trinidad, 16 June 1829. (99:190)

PHILIP Mary, b.1808, w. St Louis Philip, d. Bushy Park,
Nasgarina, Trinidad, 1843.   (NS19:556)

PHILIPS Robert, Jamaica, d.1764.   (34:46)

PHILIPS Sophia Letitia, dau. Hardman Philips, Philipsburg,
Pa., d. Hampton Court, Hereford, 24 April 1837.   (NS8:100)

PHILLIPS Mr, Clifford's Inn, m. Mary, only dau. Rev. Joseph
Stokes, ex Charleston, America, 8 April 1790.   (60:371)

PHILIPS Mrs, b.1732, wid. Frederick Philips, mo. Lady
Strangford, NY, d. Bath, 1817.   (87:184)

PHIPARD William, merchant, d. St Mary's, NFD., 3 July 1830.
                                                     (100:286)

PHIPPS Paul, Assemblyman, Judge, & Militia Col., St Andrew's,
d. Kingston, Jamaica, Oct.1787.   (57:1194)

PHIPPS Paul, Kingston, Jamaica, d. on passage to England on
Grantham Packet, 1788.   (58:1181)

PHIPPS Sarah, wid. Paul Phipps, Kingston, Jamaica, d.9 Feb.
1820.   (90:282)

PICKERING John, ex Lt. Gov. Tortula, Quaker, d.1768. (38:302)

PICKERING John, b. Salem, 17 Feb.1777, s. Col. Pickering,
scholar & jurist, d. Boston, USA, 5 May 1846.   (NS26:321)

PICKWOOD Robert Williams, b.1778, s. Robert Pickwood, Vintry,
d. St Kitts, 8 Feb.1834.   (104:670)

PIDCOCK Harriet Millicent, w. Rev. Richard Pidcock, d.
Texas, 25 June 1851.   (NS36:440)

PIDCOCK Rev. Richard, St John's College Cambridge 1822, ex
Warslow, Staffs., d. Texas, 24 June 1851.   (NS36:440)

PIERCE Earl Horton, b.1826, ex NY, d. Highgate, 5 June 1859.
                                                         (NS2/9:92)

PIERCE Jane M, b.1807, dau. Rev. Dr Appleton, Bowdoin College,
w. ex President Pierce, d. Andover, America, 2 Dec.1863.
                                                       (NS2/16:399)

PIERCE Kate Rebecca, 4th dau. C S Pierce, m. Lt. Edward
Whitacre Davies, Royal Canadian Rifles, only s. Rev. E Acton
Davies, Malvern Link, St Johns, Canada East, 22 Aug.1866.
                                                       (NS3/2:541)

PIERCE Rev. William Edward m. Frances Dun Mais, 2nd dau.
S W Mais, Custos Port Royal Jamaica, St David's, Jamaica,
5 July 1864.   (NS2/17:377)

PIERPONT Rev. John, b. Conn., 1785, poet, d. USA, 1866.
                                                       (NS3/2:708)

PIGEUNIT J G, barrister, m. Mary Anne, eldest dau. George
Tyson, St Kitts, Boxwell, Glocs., Dec.1829.   (99:558)

PIGOT Fanny, only dau. late Cap. George Pigot, RN, m. James
Speyers, NY, Rudstone, Bridlington, 24 June 1841. (NS16:312)

PIGOTT James, Attorney Gen. Tobago, Admiralty Judge Trinidad,
yngs. bro. late Sir A Pigott, Attorney Gen. England, d.
Tobago, 17 Jan.1807.   (77:376)

PILKINGTON John Edward, 2nd s. Maj. Pilkington, d. Jamaica,
24 Feb.1841.   (NS16:111)

PILKINGTON Robert John, Royal military draughtsman, only s.
late Maj. Gen. Pilkington, RE, m. Jane, eldest dau. Andrew
Shaw, Montreal, 8 Jan.1850.   (NS33:528)

PILKINGTON Mary Anne, dau. Edward Pilkington, Urney, King's
Co., m. Richard Potter, Fellow Queen's College, Prof. Maths.,
University of Cambridge, Toronto, London, 11 April 1843.
                                                        (NS20:86)

PINCKNEY Charles, SC, d.1758.   (28:556)

PINCKNEY William, Md. Senator, d. Baltimore, 1822.   (92:478)

PINDER Anne Isabella, b.1818, dau. F F Pinder, Barbados, d.
Bath, 20 Aug.1835.   (NS4:444)

PINDER Elizabeth, b.1779, dau. late W Senhouse, Surveyor Gen.
Customs WI, w. F F Pinder, Barbados, d. Bath, 30 Dec.1836.
                                                        (NS7:221)

PINFOLD Charles, b.1708, ex Gov. Barbados, d. London,
24 Nov.1788.   (58:1127)

PINKNEY Mrs, w. US Ambassador, d.24 Aug.1794.   (64:773)

PINKNEY ..., s. Mr Pinkney, US Minister, b. London, 25 June
1807.   (77:680)

PINCKING Rev. Guy R., b.1811, yngs. s. late Rev. W Pincking,
Carrickmacross, Co. Monaghan, d. Charleston, Miss., 4 Sep.1841.
(NS16:660)

PINDER Mrs Thomasina, wid. J Pinder, dau. Gen. Haynes,
Barbados, m. C F Lardy, Lt., 4th Reg., Barbados, 4 Dec.1823.
(94:456)

PINDER Rev. William Lake, Barbados, m. Harriet, yngs. dau.
late Rev. Dr. Charles Wilson, Prof. Church History, University
of St Andrews, Edinburgh, 8 June 1808.   (78:556)

PINHEY Hamnett K., b.1784, d. Horaceville, Upper Canada,
3 March 1857.   (NS2/2:625)

PINNOCK Grace, only dau. George Pinnock, d. Jamaica, 2 Feb.
1818.   (88:568)

PINNOCK Grace Elizabeth, eldest dau. late Philip Pinnock,
Jamaica, m. John Milbourne Augustus, only s. late J M Marsh,
Postmaster Gen. Jamaica, London, 26 Jan.1848.   (NS29:422)

PINNOCK Philip, Jamaica, d. London, 5 Jan.1817.   (87:91)

PINNOCK Samuel, b.1671, d. Kingston, Jamaica, 1796. (66:615)

PINNOCK Mrs, b.1757, wid. J Pinnock, London & Jamaica, d.
Southampton, 23 Nov.1836.   (NS7:108)

PINTARD John, merchant, NY, d.1752.   -   (22:478)

PITCAIRN Mr, US Minister Hamburg, m. Pamela, wid. Lord Edward
Fitzgerald, Hamburg, 1800,   (70:1283)

PITCHER Miss, dau. Isaac Pitcher, London, m. Nathaniel
Winter, ex Martinique, 1 Nov.1798.   (68:1150)

PITMAN Edward, b.1795, Asst. Comm. Gen., d. Barbados, 18 Sep.
1817.   (87:561)

PITT John, ex Gov. Bermuda, d.23 June 1750.   (20:332)

PLANTER William, d. Jamaica, 1791.   (61:682)

PLAW John, d. PEI, 24 May 1820.   (90:376)

PLAYFORD Arthur, 4th s. late Henry Playford, Northrepps,
Norfolk, d. Jamaica, 30 Oct.1851.   (NS37:208)

PLAYNE ..., dau. Cap. T C Playne, Rifle Brigade, b. Hamilton,
Canada, 14 July 1863.   (NS2/15:366)

PLEASANTS Edward, b.1671, 'who had married 7 Indian wives',
d. Va., 1767.   (37:524)

PLEYDELL John, merchant, s. late Samuel Pleydell, MD, Jamaica,
d. Edinburgh, 23 March 1807.   (77:385)

PLUM Thomas, b. America, 1724, American Loyalist, army surgeon,
d. London, 25 Aug.1832.   (102:282)

PLUMMER William jr., b.1772, d. St James, Jamaica, 10 Jan.
1801.   (71:372)

POLDEN Rev. Thomas Bolch, b.1819, ex missionary & teacher NFD,
d. Tewkesbury, 11 May 1847.   (NS28:328)

POLHILL Frances Margaretta, wid. Frederic Polhill, Howbury
Hall, m. Rev. Jacob H Brooke Mountain, Blunham, eldest s.
Bishop of Quebec, Blunham, Beds., 2 April 1850.   (NS33:658)

POLK James Knox, b. Mecklenburg, NC, 2 Nov.1795, ex US
President, d. Nashville, Tenn., 16 June 1849.   (NS32:207)

POLK Leonidas, Bishop of Louisiana, d. Ga., 14 June 1864.
                                                  (NS2/17:256)

POLLARD Rev. H S, 2nd s. R B Pollard, Brompton, m. Anne
Isabella, dau. late W Snagg, St Vincent, London, 15 May 1838.
                                                     (NS10:92)

POLLARD Mrs M, b.1664, d. Barbados, 1779.   (49:566)

POLLARD Mrs, wid. Dr Pollard, Barbados, d. London, 11 Nov.1808.
                                                     (78:1128)

POLSON David, Sec. Gov. Dominica, d.1777.   (48:607)

PONSFORD ..., s. Rev. W Ponsford, military chaplain, b.
Airey Cottage, Barbados, 6 April 1865.   (NS2/18:775)

POORE Archdeacon, b.1816, d. St Kitts, 28 Aug.1861.(NS2/11:570)

POORE ..., s. Sir Edward Poore, b. Coburg, Canada West,
7 July 1853.   (NS40:304)

POMPEY ..., b.1684, d. Dover, USA, 28 Aug.1804.   (74:979)

POOLE Rev. Thomas, Clarendon, d. Jamaica, 1791.   (61:682)

POOLE Miss, dau. James Poole, Gov. St Kitts, m. John Prowse,
Norton Fitzwarren, Somerset, 14 Aug.1777.   (48:439)

POPE Charlotte Frances, dau. late Edward Pope, Archdeacon of
Jamaica, m. Cap. George Frederick Campbell Bray, 96th Reg.,
2nd s. Col. Bray, 39th Reg., Guildford, 27 April 1859.
                                                   (NS2/6:638)

POPE Rev. John, ex St John's College Oxford, Barriefield,
Kingston, Upper Canada, d.22 April 1846.   (NS26:101)

POPE Miss, dau. late E Pope, m. Rev. Christopher Lipscombe,
Bishop of Jamaica, London, 27 July 1824.   (94:176)

POPHAM Honora Alica Lambart, b.1803, 2nd dau. Lt. Col. S T
Popham, d. Collymore House, Barbados, 3 Dec.1820.   (91:185)

POPHAM Miss, dau. Sir Home Popham, d. Jamaica, March 1820.
                                                     (90:568)

POPKIN William Bassett, b.1788, s. John Popkin, Talygreen,
Glamorgan, settled Jamaica 1822, d. Montego Bay, Jamaica,
1845.   (NS23:679)

POPPLE Sophia, London, sis. late Alured Popple, Gov. Bermuda,
d. 2 Sep.1778.   (48:439)

POPPLE William, Gov. Bermuda, d.8 Feb.1764.   (34:97)

POPPLE Miss, dau. Alured Popple, Gov. Bermuda, m. Vincent
Mathias, Customs Receiver Chief Teller, 7 Oct.1752. (22:478)

PORTER Charles Collier, b.1828, 2nd s. David Charles Porter,
d. Panama, 17 July 1852.   (NS42:200)

PORTER Charles Rain, Antigua, m. Miss Rowland, Parham Hill,
11 Feb.1762.   (32:93)

PORTER Elizabeth, London, m. Robert Swete Tompion, Jamaica,
April 1752.   (22:240)

PORTER Ellen, dau. Rev. Dr Porter, Alphington, Exeter, m.
James Somerville Little, surgeon, RA, Halifax, NS, 15 Dec.1852.
                                                     (NS39:196)

PORTER James, 'the first planter who cultivated indigo in NC',
d.1767.   (37:478)

PORTER Mary Maud, 2nd dau. Rev. Dr Porter, Alphington, Exeter,
ex President, NS, m. John B Bland, Halifax, NS, 30 May 1848.
                                                     (NS30:198)

PORTER Robert, d. Adelphi Est., St Vincent, 14 Jan.1820.
                                                     (90:281)

PORTER Miss, Cheshunt, m. Thomas Baynton, Jamaica, 4 Nov.1758.
                                                     (28:556)

PORTER Comm., US Minister Plenipotentiary, d. Constantinople,
3 March 1843.   (NS19:558)

PORTEOUS James, b.1809, ex Councillor, Jamaica, & Custos of
St Andrews, Jamaica, d. London, 5 Oct.1861.   (NS2/11:692)

PORTMAN Edward Napier Berkeley, b.1836, eldest s. Maj. Portman,
Dorset, d. Victoria, BC, 3 Feb.1861.   (NS2/10:584)

PORTMAN Mrs Maurice, d. London, Canada West, 30 March 1860.
                                                  (NS2/8:638)

PORTMAN ..., s. Maurice Portman, b. London, Canada West, 10
Oct.1858.   (NS2/5:627)

POSSON Anthony Cole, ex Liverpool, d. Kingston, Jamaica, 1793.
                                                     (63:1152)

POTHLER Anne, w. T Pothler, dau. late Col. Bruyeres, RE, d.
Montreal, 1840.   (NS13:669)

POTTER Richard, Fellow Queen's College, Prof. Maths.,Cambridge,
Toronto, m. Mary Anne, dau. Edward Pilkington, Utney, King's
Co., London, 11 April 1843.   (NS20:86)

POTTS Ralph H, Lt., 1st WI Reg., yngs. s. late Radford Potts,
Beverley, m. Frances Sarah, yngs. dau. late James W Farrington,
Nassau, 20 Dec.1864.   (NS2/18:364)

POTTS Thomas, b.1739, settled Honduras 1762, Senior Magistrate,
d, Honduras, 8 Nov.1806.   (77:179)

POULDEN Richard M, ex Maj., RA, s. late Rear Adm. Poulden,
m. Elizabeth, yngs. dau. Sir Brenton Haliburton, late Chief
Justice, Halifax, NS, 5 June 1861.   (NS2/11:196)

POWELL Anne, b.1755, sis. late Charles Murray, Petworth, wid.
William Dummer Powell, Chief Justice Upper Canada, d. Toronto,
7 March 1849.   (NS31:558)

POWELL Henry Cottrell, eldest s. Henry Folliott Powell,
Brandlesholme Hall, Lancs., d. Fort Union, New Mexico,
1 March 1858.   (NS2/6:546)

POWELL Mary Boyles, dau. D Powell, Chief Justice Upper
Canada, m. S Peter Jarvis, Upper Canada, 1818.   (89:80)

POWELL T, b.1791, Asst. Comm. Gen., d. Grenada, 17 Sep.1817.
                                                     (87:561)

POWELL Miss, dau. Col. Powell, m. Charles Augustus Stewart,
Charleston, SC, 29 July 1769.   (39:414)

POWELL Mr, b.1755, actor, d. Upper Canada, May 1836.(NS6:223)

POWELL Mrs, wid. Thomas Powell, ex Henley Grove, Westbury, d.
Ballynure, Jamaica, Nov.1843.   (NS21:334)

POWER Helen Elizabeth, yngs. dau. Robert Power, Tasmania, m.
Charles A Henderson, HM Consul Panama, Surbiton, 14 Nov.1860.
                                                     (NS2/9:664)

POWER Rev. Michael, RC Bishop of Toronto, d. Toronto, 1 Nov.
1847.   (NS28:671)

POWNALL Sir George, b.1755, Provost Marshal Gen. Leeward
Islands, d. Brighton, 17 Oct.1834.   (104:556)

POWNALL James Corne, d. Kingston, Jamaica, 4 Sep.1825.(95:478)

POWNALL Mrs Mary Anne, late Mrs Wrighton, b.1756, d. Charleston,
SC, 11 Aug.1796.   (66:880)

POWYS ..., s. Cap. W C Powys, 22nd Reg., b. Fredericton, NB,
28 Aug.1867.   (NS3/2:525)

POYER Maria Jane, wid. John P Poyer, Barbados, m. Rev. Thomas
Griffith Connell, Barbados, Windsor, 1 Sep.1853.   (NS40:626)

POYNTELL William, b.1756, Chipping Norton, Oxford, merchant,
Councillor, Pa., d. Philadelphia, 10 Sep.1811.   (82:294)

POYNTELL Miss, eldest dau. William Poyntell, m. Samuel Relf,
Philadelphia, 9 Oct.1800.   (70:1286)

PRANT Dominic James, b.1775, d. Montserrat, 10 Dec.1803.
                                                     (74:182)

PRARL Miss, 5th dau. P Prarl, Hampton Court, Conn., m. G P
Holbrook, Surveyor Gen. NFD, St Johns, NFD.,4 June 1817.
                                                     (87:274)

PRATER Elizabeth MacLean, b.1804, w. Henry Prater, eldest dau.
Charles Kyd Bishop, Barbados, d. London, 31 Aug.1846.
(NS26:441)

PRATT Benjamin, Chief Justice NY, d.1763.   (32:145)

PRATT Frederick, merchant, Baltimore, eldest s. late Josiah
Pratt, Birmingham, d. Va., 13 Oct.1800.   (70:1214)

PRATT Orson, Mormon leader, d. Van Buren, Arkansas, 1857.
(NS2/3:226)

PRATT Thomas, d. Jamaica, 1791.   (61:1065)

PRESCOTT Mrs Catherine Creighton, 2nd dau. Sir Thomas Mills,
Gov. Quebec, d. Paris, 6 April 1832.   (102:574)

PRESCOTT Elizabeth, only dau. W H Prescott, historian, m.
James, eldest s. Abbot Lawrence, Boston, USA, 16 March 1852.
(NS37:512)

PRESCOTT William Hickling, b. Salem, Mass., 4 May 1796,
historian, d. Boston, Mass., 28 Jan.1859.   (NS2/6:324)

PRESCOTT ..., s. Albert Knight Prescott, b. Montreal,
17 Aug.1863.   (NS2/15:496)

PRESCOTT Miss, dau. Gov.BA, m. Cap. Baldwin, King's Own (4th)
Reg., Quebec Chateau, Aug.1797.   (67:979)

PRESTON Plunkett Standish Lyne, merchant, Bridgetown, m.
Rachael Susan, only dau. late John Grayfoot, Bridgetown,
Barbados, 3 Jan.1846.   (NS25:421)

PRETTEJOHN John, Barbados, m. Augusta Buckley, 23 Nov.1801.
(71:1209)

PRETTEJOHN John, b.1730, d. Barbados, 29 June 1803. (73:882)

PRETTEJOHN John, Barbados & Harehatch, Berks., m. Laura, yngs.
dau. Charles Cole, Paston Hall, Northants., 8 April 1840.
(NS13:536)

PRETTEJOHN Miss, dau. John Prettejohn jr., Barbados, b. Bath,
19 Aug.1802.   (72:778)

PRETTEJOHN ..., dau. John Prettejohn, Barbados, b. Bath, 29
July 1803.   (73:787)

PREVOTT Miss, b. Govt. House, Dominica, 27 April 1803.(73:594)

PRICE Anna, b.1818, w. Thomas Price, s. Sir R Price, Cornwall,
d. Tortula, 13 July 1857.   (NS2/3:347)

PRICE Sir Charles, d. Jamaica, 1772.   (42:542)

PRICE Sir Charles, Maj. Gen. Militia, Assemblyman St Thomas in
the Vale, St Catherine Magistrate, d. Spanish Town, Jamaica,
18 Oct.1788.   (59:178)

PRICE Emily Valentina, dau. Edward, Lord Dunsany, w. George
Price, d. Ellerslie, Jamaica, 30 Sep.1864.   (NS2/17:798)

PRICE George, b.1803, ex Bennett's Bridge, Co. Kilkenny,
d, Tulloch Est., Jamaica, 15 April 1848.   (NS30:110)

PRICE Gilbert, Tobago, d. Bath, 3 March 1807.   (77:381)

PRICE Jane, b.1793, w. John Banner Price, Asst. Comm. Gen.,
d. Montreal, 4 June 1832.   (102:94)

PRICE Stafford B, eldest s. S Price, Hendon, Middlesex, d.
Canada, 7 April 1835.   (NS4:223)

PRICE Thomas MacNamara Rose, b.1847, eldest s. Lt. Gov. Price,
gs. late Sir Rose Price, d. Dominica, 16 April 1864.
                                                  (NS2/16:807)

PRIESTLEY Fanny, Northumberland, USA, ggdau. late Rev. Dr
Priestley, m. Maj. Harry Toulmin, Mobile, Ala., gs. late Rev.
Dr Toulmin, Taunton, Northumberland, USA, 13 Sep.1859.
                                                  (NS2/7:638)

PRIESTLEY Joseph, b. Leeds, 1718, settled USA 1794, d.
Nothumberland, Susquehannah River, Pa., 6 Feb.1804. (74:374)

PRIESTLY Thomas, Jamaica, m. Henrietta Carteret, Gloucester,
18 Oct.1767.   (37:523)

PRIESTMAN Charles, b.1783, yngs. s. William Priestman, d.
Philadelphia, 21 Aug.1811.   (81:657)

PRIMROSE Francis Neil, b.1832, eldest s. Francis Ward Primrose,
d. Quebec, 24 Nov.1864.   (NS2/18:119)

PRIMROSE Francis W, bro. Earl of Roseberry, d. Quebec,
26 May 1860.   (NS2/9:211)

PRINCE Rev., Boston, NE, d.1759.   (29:94)

PRINCE Mrs M, w. Thomas Prince jr., Jamaica, gdau. late Sir
Christopher Hales, d. Portland, Jamaica, 1 Nov.1807. (78:86)

PRINCE Mary Anne, b.1803, eldest dau. late T Prince, Jamaica
& Bath, d. Jamaica, 3 July 1826.   (96:191)

PRINCE Thomas jr., Jamaica, m. Marianne Sanderson, niece late
Sir John Hales, Blashford, Hants., London, 31 Oct.1803.
                                                  (73:1254)

PRINGLE John Alexander Gordon, 3rd WI Reg., b.1833, eldest s.
Mark Pringle, Oakenden, Sussex, d. Jamaica, 31 July 1853.
                                                  (NS40:426)

PRINGLE Margaret, wid. Thomas Pringle, d. Coburg, Canada West,
15 Nov.1852.   (NS39:216)

PRINN John, RE Clerk of Works, d. Dominica, 4 Aug.1853.
                                                  (NS40:426)

PRIOLEAU Philip, b.1715, settled Jamaica pre-1742, d. Jamaica,
1790.   (60:1148)

PRIOR Cap. Elisha, b.1746, d. Sag's Head Harbor, NA, 6 Dec.
1818.   (88:87)

PRITCHARD Henry, London, m. Sybil, dau. late John Robley,
Tobago, Clifton, 7 April 1859.   (NS2/6:536)

PRITCHARD Philip, NY, 4th s. Henry Pritchard, Clapham, m.
Adelaide Anne, 2nd dau. Thomas Howell, Clapham, 19 Sep.1854.
                                                   (NS42:619)

PROBY Miss, dau. Dean of Lichfield, d. on Atlas on passage to
Bristol from Barbados, 6 Aug.1804.   (74:790)

PROBYN Jane, b. Abergavenny, 1775, w. Edward Probyn, merchant,
Bristol & Merthyr Tydvil, d. NY, 14 July 1832.   (102:191)

PROBYN Thomas, Gov. St Kitts, d. 10 Jan.1819.   (88:182)

PROCTOR Toney, b.1743, d. Tallahasee, Fla., June 1855.
                                                   (NS54:552)

PROCTOR Rev., Amelia Co., Va., d.1762.   (32:145)

PROTHEROE James, Bristol, m. Caroline, eldest dau. James
Choppin, St Vincent, Bath, 27 Aug.1806.   (76:873)

PROTHEROE Mary Matilda, 3rd dau. Thomas S Protheroe, Clifton,
m. John S Gaskin, Bushy Park, Barbados, Jersey, 4 June 1844.
                                                   (NS23:311)

PROTHEROE Sophia, b.1815, dau. Philip Protheroe, d. on passage
to WI, 9 May 1833.   (103:190)

PROTHEROE William Evan Garrick, eldest s. late Cap. Protheroe,
Carmarthan, d. Brighton, Canada West, 2 Jan.1866. (NS3/1:595)

PROUDFOOT Edmund, Grenada, d. Martinique, 8 May 1794.(64:671)

PROVOST Rev. Samuel, b.1744, Bishop of NY, d. NY, 1816.
                                                    (86:638)

PROWSE John, Norton Fitzwarren, Somerset, m. Miss Poole, dau.
James Poole, Gov. St Kitts, 14 Aug.1777.   (48:439)

PRYCE Francis Horatio, 4th s. Cap. Henry Pryce, RN, m. Lucy
Jane, 3rd dau. late Charles Favey, merchant, Antigua, 13 Jan.
1848.   (NS29:421)

PRYCE Marianne Emilia Frances, eldest dau. Cap. Henry Pryce,
RN, m. Melcher Gamer Todd, St Lucia, Clifton, 7 Oct.1845.
                                                   (NS24:650)

PULLEN Louise Frances, only dau. Cap. W J S Pullen, RN, d.
Bermuda, 30 Sep.1864.   (NS2/17:798)

PULTENEY Daniel, b.1751, ex Bramber MP, Customs Collector
Dominica, Senior Fellow King's College, Cambridge, d.1811.
                                                    (81:194)

PURCELL Elizabeth, yngs. dau. Rev. Dr Purcell, Charleston, d.
Charleston, SC, 1792.   (62:577)

PURCELL Rev. Dr Henry, 26 years Rector St Michael's, Charleston
d. Charleston, SC, March 1802.   (72:584)

PURCELL Mrs, w. Rev. Dr Henry Purcell, St Michael's, Charleston, d. Charleston, SC, 24 July 1792.   (62:1054)

PURDIGO Francis, b. Greece, 1632, d. Jamaica, 1742. (13:443)

PURKIS Rev. Isaac, b.1786, Southampton, Presbyterian minister,
Osnabruck, Canada, d.16 Oct.1852.   (NS39:216)

PURVES John Home, b.1785, eldest s. Sir Alexander Purves,
Purves Hall, Berwickshire, HM Consul Pensacola, d. Pensacola,
30 Sep.1827.   (97:573)

PUTNAM Ellinor, wid. Charles S Putnam, Fredericton, NB,
Councillor, d. London, 3 June 1843.   (NS20:104)

PUTNAM Frances Anna, yngs. dau. late Charles S Putnam,
barrister, m. Rev. W H Shore, s. late George Shore, Councillor,
NB, London, 29 April 1852.   (NS38:87)

PUTNAM Israel, b.1717, Maj. Gen., Continental Army, d.
Brooklyn, America, 29 May 1790.   (60:669)

PUTNAM Gen. Rufus, Revolutionary Army Officer, d. Marietta,
Ohio, 1 May 1823.   (94:574)

PYCRAFT Miss m. Robert Pearce, estate owner, Antigua & St
St Kitts, 28 Jan.1745.   (15:108)

PYKE Caroline, dau. late Rev. G Pyke, Essex, m. Sir R Chapman,
Gov. Bermuda, Boyton, Wilts., 9 Nov.1835.   (NS4:646)

PYM J E, s. J Pym, London, Provost Marshal Grenada, d.
Grenada, 17 Oct.1802.   (72:1161)

PYTON Miss, b.1773, ex America, gdau. Mr Roberts, 'late city
garbler', d. Enfield Highway, 13 Aug.1783.   (53:717)

QUELCH Cap. James Spencer, b.1779, d. Basseterre, St Kitts,
28 July 1856.   (NS2/1:520)

QUENEBOROUGH Samuel, ex Assemblyman St Johns, Jamaica, d.
Dunstable, 13 Oct.1815.   (85:382)

QUINCY John, ex Speaker NE Assembly, d.1767.   (37:478)

QUINCEY Joshua jr., Boston, d.1775.   (45:303)

QUINCEY Samuel, barrister, d. on passage from Tortula to
England on the Sally, 9 Aug.1789.   (59:861)

QUINCY Miss, Boston, m. John Hancock, President Continental
Congress America, 1775.   (45:502)

RABO Father, Jesuit explorer, d. Canada, 1767.   (37:524)

RACEY John, b.1783, ex Quebec, d. Bath, 19 May 1856.(NS2/1:123)

RADDOCK Samuel, apothecary, d. Annapolis Royal, 1769.(39:318)

RAIKES Thomas jr., London, m. Sophia Maria, dau. late N Bayly,
Bayly's Vale, Jamaica, 24 May 1802.   (72:469)

RAINALS Cap. Henry, US Army, yngs. s. late John Rainals,
Brentwood, Essex, d. Washington, 14 Feb.1867.   (NS3/3:564)

RAINALS Mark Oswald, b.1812, ex Columbo, Ceylon, s. late
John Rainals, US Consul Gen. Copenhagen, d. London, 12 Oct.
1844.   (NS22:553)

RALEY W, b.1740, emigrated from Hull to America on the Venus,
June 1819, d. Philadelphia, 30 Aug.1819.   (89:568)

RALSTON Gerard, Philadelphia, m. Isabel, 2nd dau. William
Crawshay, Cyfartha Castle, Pendeylan, Glamorgan, 18 Sep.1838.
                                                   (NS10:656)

RAM Joseph, b.1669, d. Jamaica, Dec.1809.   (79:277)

RAMSEY Ann, 2nd dau. late Nathaniel Thomas Ramsey, Barbados,
m. Robert, 5th s. late Joseph Henry, Dublin, London, 10 Nov.
1853.   (NS41:185)

RAMSAY Col. Nathaniel, Baltimore, bro. late Dr David Ramsay,
d. SC, 24 Oct.1818.   (88:87)

RAMSAY Sir Thomas, Balmain, m. Miss Steele, dau. late Rev.
Dr Steele, Jamaica, 29 June 1809.   (79:676)

RAMSAY ..., dau. William Ramsay, Jamaica, b. Hanwell,
Middlesex, 10 Oct.1806.   (76:977)

RAMSAY Miss, b.1791, only dau. Gen. Ramsay, Leeward & Windward
Islands, d. Port Royal, Martinique, 5 May 1809.   (79:678)

RAMSAY Dr, author, killed Charleston, SC, 1815.   (85:284)

RAMSON Sophie, b.1830, yngs. dau. late William Torrance,
Quebec, w. F W Wallace Ramson, d. Toronto, 5 Dec.1855.
                                                   (NS45:208)

RANDAL Dorcas, only dau. William Randal, Surveyor Gen.
Southern District America, m. Anthony la Motte, 8 May 1767.
                                                    (37:279)

RANDALL J Colvin, Philadelphia, m. Fanny E, yngs. dau. late
Alfred Harrold, Birmingham, Edgbaston, 7 Nov.1860.(NS2/9:663)

RANDOLPH John, American orator & statesman, d. Philadelphia,
24 May 1833.   (103:190)

RANDOLPH Peter, Surveyor Gen. Middle District America, d.1767.
                                                    (37:478)

RANDOLPH Peyton, President Continental Congress Va., d.
22 Dec.1775.   (45:607)

RANKIN Ann, eldest dau. Robert Rankin, NY, d. Royston,
16 Feb.1851.   (NS35:450)

RANKINS Mrs Catherine, b. Va., 1724, American Loyalist, d.Va.,
27 Oct.1833.   (103:556)

RANKIN George, d. Jamaica, 1791.   (61:1065)

RANKIN William, s. James Rankin, Hendon, Middlesex, d.
Grenada, 27 Dec.1820.   (91:378)

RANNEY W P, b.1794, d. St John, NB, 26 Oct.1843.   (NS20:671)

RANSFORD Thomas, b.1765, ex Cheltenham, d. SC, 17 Dec.1837.
(NS9:559)

RANSOM Amelia, eldest dau. Leander Ransom, NY, m. Thomas J,
yngs. s. late Brent Neville, Ashbrooke, Co. Dublin, Dublin,
16 Dec.1853.   (NS41:309)

RANSOM Edward, NY, 4th s. late William Ransom, Stowmarket,
m. Elizabeth, 4th dau. James Roberts, West Bromwich, Staffs.,
25 June 1853.   (NS40:305)

RAPALJE John, b.1728, ex Long Island, NY, d.London, 19 Jan.
1802.   (72:182)

RAPER ..., dau. A H Raper, 39th Reg., b. St George, Bermuda,
12 April 1860.   (NS2/8:619)

RAREY J S, b. Franklin Co., Ohio, 1828, horse-tamer, d.
Cleveland, USA, 4 Oct.1866.   (NS3/2:703)

RATCLIFFE Thomas Wilkinson, b.1791, Castle Coakley, St Croix,
d. London, 21 Dec.1854.   (NS43:221)

RATTRAY David, ex Helensburgh, d. Hamilton, Canada West,
5 Sep.1859.   (NS2/7:541)

RATTRAY John, Judge Court Vice Admiralty Charleston, d.
30 Sep.1761.   (21:603)

RAVENCAMP Frederick m. Miss Ingram, only dau. Peter Ingram,
ex Provost Marshal Jamaica, Moore Park, St George, Jamaica,
Oct.1789.   (60:83)

RAWLINGS Miss, dau. Stidman Rawlings, m. Cap. Anthony Young,
St Kitts, 21 June 1787.   (57:738)

RAWLINS Ann Taylor, dau. late Stedman Rawlins, St Kitts, m.
Cap. Rawlins, 30th Reg., Eltham, Kent, 22 Aug.1803. (73:788)

RAWLINS Francis Ironside, 15th Reg., m. Eliza Mary, eldest
dau. Col. Butler, Hants, NS, Windsor, NS, 16 Nov.1865.
(NS3/1:117)

RAWLINS Stephen, b.1778, s. John Rawlins, Yeovil, Somerset,
d. Barbados, 18 Aug.1803.   (73:987)

RAWLINS William Wharton, d. St Kitts, 9 Dec.1840. (NS15:558)

RAWLINS Cap., 30th Reg., m. Ann Taylor, dau. late Stedman
Rawlins, St Kitts, Eltham, Kent, 22 Aug.1803.   (73:788)

RAWSON Evelyn, 2nd dau. Christopher Rawson, Lennoxville, m.
Cap. De Winton, RA, Lennoxville, Canada East, 9 June 1864.
(NS2/17:234)

RAWSON Frances Emily, eldest dau. Christopher Rawson, Helmwood,
Lennoxville, m. Dudley Raikes de Chair, s. Rev. Frederick de
Chair, East Langdon, Kent, Lennoxville, Canada East, 10 Dec.
1863.   (NS2/16:244)

RAYMOND Cap., 21st Light Dragoons, m. Miss Broadbett, Jamaica,
Chudleigh, Devon, 25 April 1798.   (68:441)

RAYNELL Sir Richard Lyttleton, s. Thomas L. Raynell, d.
Baltimore, 4 Sep.1830.   (100:381)

REA Dr George, surgeon, d. La Guayra, WI, 31 Dec.1852.
                                                         (NS39:329)

READE Alfred, 3rd s. late Frederick Reade, London, m. Frances
Elizabeth, eldest dau. Sir William MacBean George Colebrooke,
NB, 8 Oct.1844.   (NS23:311)

READE Polly, NY, m. Francis Stephens, 1768.   (38:302)

READMAN John, Boston, NE, d.14 May 1775.   (45:450)

READY Mrs, w. Lt. Col. Ready, Gov. PEI, d. Brighton, April
1825.   (95:651)

REDHEAD Ellen, dau. late George Redhead, Antigua, ex Cap.,
3rd Guards Reg., m. James Athill, Lt., RN, London, 13 March
1850.   (NS33:657)

REDHEAD George, b.1737, Antigua, d. London, 5 Dec.1801.
                                                         (71:1155)

REDKNAP Emily, w. Henry S Redknap, ex Tobago, d. Twickenham,
8 March 1857.   (NS2/2:501)

REDMAN Patty, London, m. Laurence Crawford, Jamaica, May 1750.
                                                         (20:284)

REDWOOD J L, b.1766, ex St Vincent, d.28 June 1807.   (77:593)

REDWOOD Ledeatt, eldest s. George Washington Ledeatt,
Antigua, m. Elizabeth Jane, eldest dau. Miles Brathwaite,
Barbados, London, 13 Jan.1846.   (NS25:308)

REDWOOD Philip, b.1750, ex Chief Justice Jamaica, Speaker
Assembly Jamaica, d. London, 1810.   (80:287)

REECE Sarah Isabella, dau. R Reece, Barbados, w. Rev. J C
Corlette, d. Illawarra, NSW, 28 Oct.1863.   (NS2/16:262)

REED Cadington Baynes, b.1841, 4th s. Dr Baynes Reed, Exeter,
d. Toronto, 1 March 1862.   (NS2/12:652)

REED Catherine, dau. late James Reed, Partridge Island, m.
Cobourg Corrington, Customs officer, St Johns, yngs. s. Cap.
William Henry Corrington, barrackmaster, Dorchester, England,
St Johns, NB, 23 Dec.1843.   (NS21:309)

REED Leonora Matilda, only dau. late W Reed, St Vincent, m.
W Talbot Agar, only s. late W Agar, QC, Lymington, 29 July
1843.   (NS20:428)

REED Rev., b. Scotland, d. Erie Co., Pa., 1858.   (NS2/4:684)

REEKIE Isabella, dau. Rev. David Ross, Burntisland, w. J R
Reekie, Quebec, d. Burntisland, 3 July 1859.   (NS2/9:199)

REES Evan, b.1774, ex St Vincent, d. Llanidloes, 19 Aug.1855.
(NS54:443)

REID Caroline, only dau. late E James Reid, Saltpool, Spanish
Town, Jamaica, m. Joseph Dods, Stanford, Hornsey, 31 May 1860.
(NS2/9:86)

REID Catherine Balfour, 2nd dau. Cap. James Murray Reid,
Hudson Bay Co., m. William John MacDonald, Fort Victoria,
Vancouver Island, 17 March 1857.   (NS2/3:212)

REID Dr David Boswell, b.Edinburgh, gs. Hugh Arnot, d.
Washington, DC, 5 April 1863.   (NS2/14:803)

REID Edward Mathew, 2nd s. late E J Reid, Jamaica, m. Sarah
Fenwick, only ch. W S Bowen, Naseby Woolley, Northants, gdau.
late Thomas Fenwick, Barrow Hall, Lancs., Naseby, 6 Oct.1841.
(NS16:648)

REID Elizabeth m. Alexander Roberts, Kingston, Jamaica, 1800.
(70:483)

REID Henry Solomans, b.1793, ex Cap. Bengal Establishment, d.
Darlington, Canada West, 28 Nov.1852.   (NS39:217)

REID James, b.1769, ex Chief Justice, d. Montreal, 19 Jan.
1848.   (NS29:566)

REID James, Lennoxville, Canada East, m. Mary Jane, only ch.
late Maj. Thomas Reid, 33rd Reg., Edinburgh, 19 April 1865.
(NS2/18:779)

REID John Lynch, Queen's College, Cambridge, & John's Hall,
Brown Town, Jamaica, m. Christiana, 4th dau. J W Robey,
Kentish Town, London, 15 July 1848.   (NS30:316)

REID Louisa Elizabeth, eldest dau. George Reid, Jamaica, m.
Rev. John Louis Petit, Wye, Kent, 5 June 1828.   (98:646)

REID Maria, 2nd dau. Lt. Col. Reid, Gov. Windward Islands, m.
Lt. E G Hore, 2nd s. late Cap. Hore, RN, Pole Hore, Wexford,
Barbados, 17 June 1847.   (NS28:312)

REID Mary Jane, only ch. late Maj. Thomas Reid, 33rd Reg., m.
James Reid, Lennoxville, Canada East, Edinburgh, 19 April 1865.
(NS2/18:779)

REID Robert, b.1740, ex High Sheriff of Northumberland, d.
Chatham, NA, 15 April 1828.   (98:477)

REID Sophia Lonsdale, 3rd dau. Lt. Col. Reid, Gov. Bermuda, m.
Edmond G Hallewell, Lt., 20th Reg., Bermuda, 11 May 1843.
(NS20:87)

REID Cap. Washington, USSVixen, d. Jamaica, March 1813.
(83:660)

REILLY Barnaby, Jamaica, d. Westminster, 13 Aug.1790.(60:769)

RELF Samuel, Philadelphia, m. Miss Poyntell, eldest dau.
William Poyntell, 9 Oct.1800.   (70:1286)

RENAGLE Alexander, b.1749, manager Philadelphia & Baltimore
theaters, d. America, Nov.1809.   (80:283)

RENNALLS Dr J P, ex Spanish Town, Jamaica, d. Clapton,
12 Sep.1813.   (83:402)

RENNELL William, inf. s. Bishop of Barbados, gs. Dean of
Winchester, d. Barbados, 1827.   (97:285)

RENNIE Jane, eldest dau. Cap. Richard Rennie, Fife Royal
Artillery, Glasgow, m. Rev. D E Montgomerie, South Grove,
Canada West, Montreal, on board John Bell, 3 Aug.1859.
                                                    (NS2/7:414)

RETALLACK ..., dau. Cap. Retallack, 63rd Reg., b. Quebec,
26 Aug.1862.   (NS2/13:482)

REYNOLDS Ebenezer, b.1778, d. Amhertsburg, Upper Canada,
11 Feb.1854.   (NS41:554)

REYNOLDS Elizabeth Harnett, 2nd dau. Thomas Reynolds, Montreal, ex Snaresbrook, Essex, m. William George Swinhoe,
Rifle Brigade, s. Gen. Swinhoe, Bengal Army, Montreal,
17 March 1864.   (NS2/16:651)

REYNOLDS Margaret, b.1765, eldest dau. late Thomas Reynolds,
Comm. Dept., d. Amherstburg, Upper Canada, 5 May 1855.
                                                    (NS54:329)

REYNOLDS Thomas, 3rd s. late William Reynolds, Catherine Mount
Est., d. Jamaica, 1 March 1850.   (NS33:558)

RHODES Mr, Barbados, d. Bath, Oct.1761.   (21:538)

RIALL Maj. Gen., Gov. Grenada, m. Miss Scarlett, eldest dau.
late James Scarlett, Jamaica, Dec.1819.   (89:635)

RICE J R, actor, d. NY, 19 Sep.1860.   (NS2/9:562)

RICE Cap. S, only s. late J Rice, Shoreham, Sussex, d.
Charlottetown, PEI, 2 May 1857.   (NS2/3:100)

RICHARDS Cap. Joseph, Hudson Bay Co. ship Sea Horse, d.
19 June 1782.   (52:358)

RICHARDS Robert, Carrickmacross, d. Kingston, Jamaica, 1790.
                                                        (60:373)

RICHARDSON Bowes, ex Darlington, Co. Durham, d. Bethel,
Philadelphia, 4 Sep.1798.   (68:1083)

RICHARDSON Euretta, dau. late James Richardson, Belle River,
Montreal, m. Col. William Denny, 71st Highland Light Infantry,
gnephew late Sir Barry Denny, Montreal, 15 Dec.1846.(27:418)

RICHARDSON Cap. G Granville, s. Thomas Richardson, St Albans,
m. Adelaide Coppinger , 2nd dau. Sir John Murray, NY, 8 Jan.
1863.   (NS2/14:369)

RICHARDSON Hannah, wid. Anthony Richardson, ex Grenada, d.
Welshpool, 3 Feb.1798.   (68:175)

RICHARDSON James, Jamaica, d.1758.   (28:94)

RICHARDSON Sir James, d. Paradise, Savanna-la-Mar, Jamaica,
24 Nov.1788.   (59:178)

RICHARDSON Maria Caroline, w. Maj. Richardson, Police Superintendent, Welland Canal, 2nd dau. William Drayson, Brompton,
Kent, d. St Catherine's, Canada, 16 Aug.1845.   (NS24:665)

RICHARDSON Martha, 2nd dau. late Richard Richardson, m.
William Horton, barrister, Canada, 20 Dec.1842.   (NS19:311)

RICHARDSON William, ex St Vincent, m. Elizabeth, dau. David
Gardiner of Kirktonhill, Kirktonhill, 7 Oct.1789.   (59:954)

RICHARDSON Maj. Gen. m. Mrs Scott, wid. David Scott, Antigua,
Bath, 9 Nov.1808.   (78:1039)

RICHIE Rev. David, b. Perth, Roseau, Dominica, d.22 Sep.1801.
                                                    (72:181)

RICHMOND Dean, b.1803, d. NY, 27 Aug.1866.   (NS3/2:558)

RICHMOND Rev. J P, s. late Rev. C G Richmond, Sixhills, Lincs.,
m. Mary, 3rd dau. John Ross, Leeds, Megantic Co., Quebec,
Inverness, 7 Oct.1867.   (NS3/2:808)

RICKELL Charles William, b.1810, yngs. s. late Joseph Rickell,
Oundle, d. Falmouth, Jamaica, 2 Feb.1853.   (NS39:560)

RICKETTS John Crawford, b.1705, coachman G C Ricketts,
Attorney Gen. Jamaica, d. Spanish Town, Jamaica, 1847.
                                                    (NS27:334)

RICKETTS Mrs Mary, b.1738, wid. William Henry Ricketts,
Canaan, Jamaica, mo. Viscount St Vincent, d.Bath, 12 March
1828.   (98:570)

RICKETTS William Henry, d. Jamaica, 30 June 1790.   (60:669)

RICKETTS William Henry, Councillor, Canaan, Westmoreland,
Jamaica, ex Longwood, Hants., d. Jamaica, 5 Oct.1798. (69:78)

RICKETTS Miss, only dau. Gov. Ricketts, Barbados, m.
Stanlake Batson, Winfield, Berks., 14 Sep.1818.   (88:274)

RIDDOCH James, Montego Bay, d. Jamaica, 10 Sep.1796. (67:164)

RIDOUT Horace, 3rd s. Thomas Ridout, York, Upper Canada, d.
London, March 1826.   (96:283)

RIGAUD Rev. S Jordan, Bishop of Antigua, s. late Stephen
Peter Rigaud, d. Antigua, 16 May 1859.   (NS2/9:84)

RIGAUD S P, HM Astronomer Richmond, Prof. Geometry Oxford, m.
Miss Jordan, eldest dau. G W Jordan, Barbados, 8 June 1815.
                                                    (85:562)

RIGGS Cecilia, dau. George W Riggs, Washington, m. Henry
Howard, British Legation, Greenhill, Md., 2 Oct.1867.
                                                    (NS3/2:808)

RILEY Thomas, ex St Anne, Jamaica, d. Liverpool, 23 Jan.1801.
                                                    (71:186)

RIPLEY Rev. William Honywood, b.1816, eldest s. Rev. Thomas
Hyde Ripley, Wootten Basset, Wilts., Toronto, master Canada
College, d.22 Oct.1849.   (NS33:102)

RITCHIE Alexander, attorney, d. Kingston, Jamaica, April 1807.
                                                      (77:682)

RITCHIE Cornelia, wid. Col. Ritchie, USA, dau. Gen. Wadsworth,
Geneseo, USA, m. John George Adair, Queens Co., Paris,
30 May 1867.   (NS3/4:102)

RITTENHOUSE David, b. Pa., 1732, philosopher, d. 10 July 1796.
                                                      (66:791)

RIVINGTON James sr, Senior Liveryman Stationers Company,
London, bro. late John Rivington, d. NY, 1803.   (73:87)

ROB Mary Pattison, 3rd dau. Dr Rob, Water Valley, Jamaica, m.
Rev. Thomas Barry Cahusae, Jamaica, 1 May 1845.   (NS24:189)

ROBBINS Thomas, b. Tewkesbury, St Mary's, Jamaica, d. Jamaica,
29 Dec.1802.   (73:381)

ROBE John, Bristol, d. St Vincent, 16 Nov.1806.   (77:376)

ROBERTS Alexander m. Elizabeth Reid, Kingston, Jamaica, 1800.
                                                      (70:483)

ROBERTS Charles, b. Oxfordshire, 1680, settled America 1716,
d. Berkeley Co., Va., 17 Feb.1796.   (66:789)

ROBERTS Elizabeth, 4th dau. James Roberts, West Bromwich, m.
Edward Ransom, NY, 4th s. late William Ransom, Stowmarket,
West Bromwich, 25 June 1853.   (NS40:305)

ROBERTS Fanny Kemp, yngs. dau. J Roberts, Customs Surveyor,
Bristol, m. Alexander B Cleland, MD, Royal Canadian Rifle Reg.,
NY, 3 June 1845.   (NS24:190)

ROBERTS Louisa Margaret, w. Rev. Frederick Roberts, 4th dau.
late Rev. Francis Baker, Wylye, Wilts., Charlottetown, PEI,
4 April 1842.   (NS18:333)

ROBERTS Walter, eldest s. late Samuel Roberts, Great Borzell,
Sussex, d. Kingston, Jamaica, 18 Feb.1813.   (83:660)

ROBERTS Walter, Lt., 3rd WI Reg., m. Julia Mary, only dau.
P Herbert Delamere, Cap., 3rd WI Reg., Kingston, Jamaica,
6 July 1867.   (NS3/2:383)

ROBERTSON Alexander, Naval Officer Jamaica, d. Jamaica, 1791.
                                                      (61:1235)

ROBERTSON Alexander, surgeon, late Jamaica, m. Lilias, dau.
Alexander Wilson, merchant, Inverness, 25 Oct.1802. (72:1224)

ROBERTSON Andrew, ex merchant, Charleston, SC, d. Streatham,
18 Jan.1791.   (61:190)

ROBERTSON Duncan, Councillor, d. Gilnock Hall, Jamaica,
9 May 1850.   (NS34:230)

ROBERTSON Francis, b.Aberdeenshire, 1747, lawyer, settled SC
pre 1789, d. Charleston, SC, Oct.1819.   (90:281)

ROBERTSON George, the Guina Bank, nephew late James Robertson
Chief Judge Virgin Islands, d. St Thomas, on passage to
England, 26 Feb.1843.   (NS19:558)

ROBERTSON Dr James, physician, Inverness, m. Katherine, 2nd
dau. late Alexander Inglis, SC, Edinburgh, 20 Oct.1794.
                                                         (64:1148)

ROBERTSON James, Clerk Signet, d. Kingston, Jamaica, 1794.
                                                          (64:768)

ROBERTSON James, b.1750, Chief Justice Virgin Islands, d.
Tortula, 23 Nov.1818.   (88:87)

ROBERTSON John, d. Jamaica, 1791.   (61:971)

ROBERTSON John, Judge Adm. Court Martinique, d. St Vincent,
1794.   (64:865)

ROBERTSON Dr John, d. Antigua, 1797.   (67:804)

ROBERTSON Mary Margaret Adam, dau. late John Robertson,
Belmont, Jamaica, m. Chevalier Thomas Francis Sargent,
Chamberlain to Duke of Lucca, Paris, 29 May 1841.   (NS16:199)

ROBERTSON Robert Henry, 2nd s. Duncan Robertson, St Elizabeth,
Jamaica, m. Elizabeth Frances, only dau. late Matthew
Farquharson, St Elizabeth, London, 19 March 1864.(NS2/16:521)

ROBERTSON William, d. Windy Hill, Tortula, 26 Jan.1807.
                                                          (77:376)

ROBERTSON William, b.1737, ex St Ann, Jamaica, d. Brighton,
14 Sep.1825.   (95:286)

ROBERTSON Miss, dau. Gen. Robertson, Gov.NY, m. John, s. Sir
Robert Henderson, 1781.   (51:242)

ROBERTSON Mrs, w. G Robertson, HM Consul, d. Philadelphia,
29 Aug.1834.   (104:659)

ROBERTSON-ROSS ..., s. Lt.Col.Robertson-Ross of Glenmoidart,
25th Reg., b. Quebec, 17 March 1865.   (NS2/18:632)

ROBEY Christiana, 4th dau. J W Robey, Kentish Town, m. John
Lynch Reid, Queens College, Cambridge, John's Hall, Brown's
Town, Jamaica, London, 15 July 1848.   (NS30:316)

ROBBILLIARD Cap., RN, m. Martha, dau. Thomas Clarke,
Antigua, 12 July 1820.   (90:84)

ROBINSON Alexander, Naval Officer Kingston, 3rd s. James
Robinson, Bishopmill, Moray, d. Port Royal, Jamaica,
19 Sep.1791.   (61:1062)

ROBINSON Arthur Lambert, b.1815, yngs. s. S S Robinson, Surrey,
d. Three Rivers, Lower Canada, 18 Jan.1842.   (NS18:332)

ROBINSON Col. Beverley, b.Va., 1722, American Loyalist, nephew
John Robinson, Bishop of Bristol, d. Bath, 9 April 1792.
                                                          (62:479)

ROBINSON ..., s. Bryan Robinson, QC, St Johns, NFD., b.
Clifton, 6 April 1848.   (NS29:538)

ROBINSON Caroline, dau. George Christopher, Chiswick, Middlesex, w. Nelson George Robinson, ex Hendon Lodge, Sunderland,
d. Britannia, Bytown, Lower Canada, 20 Oct.1848.   (NS31:223)

ROBINSON Charles, 3rd s. late George Robinson, London, d.
Copse Est., Montego Bay, Jamaica, 14 Sep.1853.   (NS40:649)

ROBINSON D, ex England, d. Jamaica, 1791.   (61:187)

ROBINSON Emma, wid. Sir John Beverley Robinson, ex Chief
Justice Upper Canada, d. Beverley House, Toronto, 29 May
1865.   (NS2/19:123)

ROBINSON Fanny Harriot, 4th dau. Justice Robinson, NFD, m.
Rev. Joseph Francis Philps, eldest s. Joseph Philps, Madeira,
St Johns, NFD., 2 Sep.1862.   (NS2/13:627)

ROBINSON Gen. Sir F P, b. Highlands, NY, Sep.1763, 4th s.
Col. Beverley Robinson, Va., Col. 39th Reg., d. Brighton,
1 Jan.1852.   (NS37:188)

ROBINSON George, ex Jamaica, m. Miss Mason, eldest dau. Rev.
Edward Mason, Blyth, Notts., 20 Feb.1793.   (63:280)

ROBINSON Jeremiah, barrister & recorder, d. Appleby,
Westmoreland, Jamaica, 21 Jan.1792.   (63:94)

ROBINSON John, Dep. Gov. Va., d.3 Oct.1749.   (19:476)

ROBINSON John, d. Williamsburg, Va., 14 May 1766.   (36:342)

ROBINSON John, ex Dominica, d. Epsom, Surrey, 6 July 1809.
                                                     (79:685)

ROBINSON John Beverley, Solicitor Gen. Upper Canada, m. Emma,
only dau. Charles Walker, niece Dep. Sec. War, 5 June 1817.
                                                     (87:635)

ROBINSON Laura, wid. Thomas Pickering Robinson, Darlington,
m. J M Trew, Archdeacon of Bahamas, Cheltenham, 17 Aug.1843.
                                                   (NS20:430)

ROBINSON Mary Amelia, yngs. dau. late Sir John B Robinson, m.
Donald McInnes, Hamilton, Upper Canada, Toronto, 30 April
1863.   (NS2/15:97)

ROBINSON Miss, dau. Comm. Gen. Robinson, m. Lt. Col. Smelt, 1
103rd Reg., Quebec, 26 Dec.1814.   (85:370)

ROBINSON Lt. Col., Councillor, d. Prince of Wales Island, Gulf
of St Lawrence, Sep.1807.   (77:1075)

ROBINSON ..., s. William Robinson, President, Montserrat, b.
Govt. House, Montserrat, 12 Aug.1864.   (NS2/17:643)

ROBLEY John, President, Tobago, d. Golden Grove, Tobago,
3 Nov.1821.   (92:91)

ROBLEY Sybil, dau. late John Robley, Tobago, m. Henry
Pritchard, London, Clifton, 7 April 1859.   (NS2/6:536)

ROBSON Horatio, 'paper-hanging manufacturer to Prince of
Wales', London, m. Miss McAlpine, an American lady, 1790.
                                                   (60:178)

ROBSON Mary, dau. late William Wealands Robson, Bishopwearmouth,m. Robert Thornton, staff surgeon, Kingston, Jamaica,
24 March 1860.   (NS2/8:507)

ROBSON Mr, Speaker Assembly Va., d.1766.   (36:342)

ROCHE Patrick, estate owner, Montserrat, d.1763.   (33:518)

ROCHEFORD Robert, d. Montego Bay, Jamaica, 31 Oct.1801.(72:181)

ROCHESTER Anne, b.1698, d. Tophill, Jamaica, 24 Dec.1822.
                                                   (92:574)

ROCKE Cap., 2nd Queen's Royal Reg., m. Emily, eldest dau. late
J P Nathan, Trelawney, Jamaica, Exmouth, 27 June 1850.
                                                   (NS34:320)

ROEBUCK Charles Augustus, b.1845, s. late Jarvis Roebuck,
St Croix, d. London, 9 Sep.1859.   (NS2/7:434)

ROEBUCK ..., s. Cap. F A Disney Roebuck, 23rd Royal Welsh
Fusiliers, b. Trinidad, 7 Oct.1846.   (NS25:86)

ROESWYSS Elizabeth, b.1718, wid. Nicholas Roeswyss, d. The
Alps, Trelawney, Jamaica, 1824.   (94:190)

ROGERS Rev. Edward Jordan, Nassau, New Providence, m. Fanny,
yngs. dau. Thomas Fitzgerald, Greenbank, Falmouth, 3 Aug.1843.
                                                   (NS20:428)

ROGERS Helen, yngs. dau. late John Rogers, m. R Beckles, 3rd
WI Reg., only s. Robert Beckles, Barbados, gs. late John
Alleyne Beckles, Barbados, Westbury on Trym, 20 Jan.1852.
                                                   (NS37:401)

ROGERS Rev. H, ex Bumpstead Hellion, Essex, missionary, d.
Layton, St Vincent, 1812.   (82:603)

ROGERS Woods, Gov. Barbados, d.16 July 1732.   (2:979)

ROGERS Miss, London, m. C B Wyatt, Surveyor Gen. Upper Canada,
29 March 1805.   (75:383)

ROLLE Henry William, Stockwell, m. Sarah Johnson, yngs. dau.
late Maurice Jones, Brompton, ex Portland, Jamaica, London,
5 July 1845.   (NS24:415)

ROLLESTON George Alexander, b.1777, s. Samuel Rolleston,
Whippington, d. on _Jamaica_, on passage to Jamaica, 10 May
1798.   (68:903)

RONALDS Hugh, ex Hammersmith, m. Mary Catherine, dau. Richard
Flower, ex Marden, Herts., Albion, Illinois, 29 March 1820.
                                                   (90:562)

RONALDS John m. Emily Agnes, dau. Rev. H Massingberd, Upton,
Lincs.,St Catherine , Canada West, 6 April 1859.   (NS2/7:78)

ROOKES Lt. Charles, 2nd WI Reg., m. Teresa, 2nd dau. Don
Capician Palacios, Castile, Spain, Nassau, New Providence,
23 Oct.1846.   (NS25:87)

ROOKS Samuel Nicholas, HM Solicitor Gen. Tobago, d. on passage
to WI, 14 Oct.1849.   (NS32:671)

ROOME Sarah Frances, b.1782, dau. late David Shakespear,
Jamaica, wid. Maj. Gen. William Roome, Bombay Army, d.
London, 2 Jan.1858.   (NS2/4:228)

ROPER Sarah, yngs. dau. T Roper, West Cowes, m. Joseph
Rodney Croskey, US Consul Cowes, Northwood, 25 Sep.1843.
                                                        (NS20:539)

ROSCOE Frank J, Victoria, Vancouver Island, m. Anne Letitia,
eldest dau. Philip Henry Le Breton, London, Lyme Regis,
22 Sep.1864.   (NS2/17:648)

ROSE Mrs Anne Bromley, 3rd dau. late Thomas Rose, Vineyard,
Jamaica, d. London, 13 Dec.1841.   (NS17:222)

ROSE Lt. Charles, and wife, drowned wreck Annie Jane an
emigrant ship on route to Canada, 1853.   (NS40:654)

ROSE Charlotte Amy, yngs. dau. John Rose, Montreal, m.
Frances Sloane Stanley, Hants., Montreal, 15 Aug.1866.
                                                        (NS3/2:539)

ROSE John, b.1722, emigrated SC, American Loyalist, settled
Jamaica, d. London, 16 June 1805.   (75:590)

ROSE Roderick, Grenada, d. Norfolk, Va., 13 Oct.1799.(69:1087)

ROSE William, eldest s. John Rose, Montreal, m. Katherine
Elisabeth MacAlister, dau. A MacAlister, Torresdale Castle,
Scotland, Montreal, 2 Jan.1868.   (NS3/5:385)

ROSE William Baillie m. Miss Cockburn, eldest dau. Dr Alex.
Cockburn, Grenada, Edinburgh, 23 April 1798.   (68:441)

ROSS David R, b.22 March 1797, Rosstrevor, Co. Down, Lt. Gov.
Tobago, d. Tobago, 27 July 1851.   (NS36:542)

ROSS Elizabeth Ann, b.1767, wid. John Ross, ex Jamaica, d.
London, 18 May 1843.   (NS20:103)

ROSS Elizabeth Garrett, only ch. John Crosbie, Antigua, w.
Rev. James Way, Adwell, Oxford, d.16 May 1810.   (80:594)

ROSS John Dawes, b.1769, eldest s. late Rev. J D Ross, Syston,
Leics., d. Pa., May 1841.   (NS16:335)

ROSS Mary, 3rd dau. John Ross, Leeds, Megantic Co., Quebec, m.
Rev. J P Richmond, s. late Rev. C G Richmond, Sixhills, Lincs.,
Inverness, 7 Oct.1867.   (NS3/2:808)

ROSS Lt. Col. Robert, 4th Royal Irish Dragoon Guards, m.
Caroline, only ch. late Aeneas MacBean, Tomatin, St Thomas,
Inverness, 7 April 1819.   (88:368)

ROSS William, b.1771, ex Attorney Gen. Jamaica, d. Bath, 16 Sep.1845.   (NS24:548)

ROSS Miss, London, dau. late Peter Ross, Dominica, m.Mr Adams, Newington, Surrey, 18 July 1799.   (69:1189)

ROSSITER Rev. Rodney, b.1786, d. Monroe, Canada, 25 Dec.1846.
                                                           (NS27:444)

ROTHWELL Alicia Alleyn, eldest dau. Rev. John Rothwell, Amherst Island, m. Edward Rodney Cecil Pechell, Royal Canadian Rifle Reg., yngs. s. late Cap. Samuel George Pechell, RN, Amherst Island, Kingston, Canada West, 7 Sep. 1859.   (NS2/7:638)

ROULSTONE Lavinia, b.1791, d. Morristown, America, 1811.
                                                              (81:658)

ROUPELL George, b.1756, Postmaster Gen. southern NA, Customs searcher Charleston, SC, d. SC, Oct.1794.   (64:1150)

ROUSE Joshua, b.1765, ex Jamaica, d. Southampton, 18 April 1842.   (NS17:674)

ROUTH Miss, b.1773, dau. late Richard Routh, Chief Justice NFD., d. Camberwell, Surrey, 1809.   (79:183)

ROW Benjamin, MD, b.1720, d. Kensington, NH, April 1790.
                                                              (61:279)

ROWAN John J, eldest s. Rev. R W Rowan, Ahogill, Co. Antrim, m. Mary, eldest dau. George Wright, Colonial Treasurer PEI, Charlottetown, PEI, 5 Nov.1866.   (NS3/3:104)

ROWAND Alexander, MD, Montreal, m. Margaret, dau. late Thomas Kincaid, merchant, Leith, Edinburgh, 25 Jan.1844. (NS21:309)

ROWBOTHAM Charles, s. late Mr Rowbotham, Bristol Theater, d. Antigua, 17 Oct.1810.   (80:659)

ROWBOTHAM John, s. late Mr Rowbotham, Bristol Theater, d. Antigua, 10 Nov.1810.   (80:659)

ROWCROFT Julia Clara, yngs. dau. late Charles Rowcroft, HM Consul Cincinatti, m. Maj. Charles Warley, SC, London, 11 Nov., 1858.   (NS2/5:632)

ROWE Rev. George Wilkinson, St Dorothy, Jamaica, b.1808, s. Joshua Rowe, Devonport, d. Bideford, Devon, 1 Jan.1867.
                                                           (NS3/3:261)

ROWE ..., b.1788, s. John Rowe, d. Sunderland, Mass., 19 July 1807.   (77:977)

ROWE Cap., RN, Barbados, d. Bath, 1819.   (88:92)

ROWLAND Miss, Jamaica, m. Maj. Fraser, ADC Lt Gen. Nugent, Liverpool, 13 April 1807.   (77:375)

ROWLANDS Mrs Esther, w. Dr Rowlands, surgeon, d. Halifax, NS, 28 Feb.1817.   (87:473)

ROWLAND Richard, planter, St Kitts, d.27 June 1761. (21:334)

ROWLAND Miss, Parham Hill, m. Charles Ram Porter, Antigua,
11 Feb.1762.   (32:93)

ROWLEY George, 23rd Royal Welsh Fusiliers, m. Alicia, dau.
late Cap. Hollis, King's Gragoon Guards, Montreal, 27 Sep.
1867.   (NS3/2:808)

ROWORTH ..., s. C E W Roworth, 6th Reg., b. Newcastle,
Jamaica, 9 Aug.1865.   (NS2/19:635)

ROY George, b. Banff, 1751, early settler Halifax, NA, d.
Merigomish, Halifax, 1831.   (101:477)

RUAN Frances, yngs. dau. late William Ruan, MD, St Croix, m.
James Caw jr., St Thomas, St Croix, 14 Sep.1859. (NS2/7:529)

RUAN Mary Beech, 3rd dau. W H Ruan, MD, St Croix, m. John
Morrison jr., Glasgow, Southampton, 18 April 1859.(NS2/6:537)

RUDD John, b.1765, Cap. American ship <u>Richmond</u>, d. Hull, June
1803.   (73:693)

RUDDACH Charles, ex Tobago, d. Totteridge, Herts., 6 July
1811.   (81:91)

RUDDACH Elizabeth Cecilia, only dau. late Alexander Ruddach,
Tobago, m. William Fitch Arnold, 19 May 1819.   (88:480)

RUDVERD Charlotte, dau. Henry Rudverd, Colne House, m. Henry
John Boulton, s. Henry J Boulton, Toronto, late Chief Justice
NFD., Iver, Bucks., 23 Sep.1852.   (NS38:631)

RUE C W, MD, Hudson Bay Co., m. Catherine Jane Alicia, 3rd
dau. Maj. G A Thompson, 85th King's Light Infantry, Toronto,
25 Feb.1860.   (NS2/8:402)

RULE James, Craggy Mount, St Thomas in the Vale, Jamaica, d.
1797.   (67:986)

RUMBOLD Horace, Sec. British Legation, m. Caroline Barney,
dau. George Harrington, US Minister Switzerland, Berne,
15 July 1867.   (NS3/2:383)

RUMSEY James Crook, b.1809, eldest s. Nathaniel Rumsey, MD,
Henley on Thames, d. Clifden, Lobo, Upper Canada, 19 Oct.1841.
                                                      (NS17:229)

RUMSEY Robert Murray, Colonial Sec., m. Louisa Frances, 3rd
dau. late William Wharton, Councillor, St Kitts, St Kitts,
12 Dec.1844.   (NS23:311)

RUSH Dr Benjamin, American physician, d.26 April 1813.(83:194)

RUSSELL Daphne, b.1694, d. Spanish Town, Jamaica, 1801.(71:376)

RUSSELL H, Caenwood Est., St George, Jamaica, d. on passage
from Bristol to Jamaica, 1813.   (83:670)

RUSSELL Henry Chambers, Adm. Court Judge NE, d.22 Nov.1766.
(36:599)

RUSSELL Lucy, b.1788, sis. late William Ellery Channing, wid.
William W Russell, d. New Windsor, NY, 26 Nov.1863.(NS2/16:399)

RUSSELL Thomas, d. Boston, NE, April 1796.   (66:524)

RUSSELL W C. b.1793, ex Lt., 6th Reg., d. Quebec, 8 Sep.1832.
(103:190)

RUSSELL Col., ex Gov. Bermuda, d.1 Oct.1740.   (10:525)

RUTHERFORD Fanny, only dau. John Rutherford, NC, m.Archibald
Menzies of Culdair, Customs Comm. Scotland, 17 Oct.1776.
(46:530)

RUTHERFORD James, d. Jamaica, 1791.   (61:682)

RUTHERFORD William, planter, Jamaica, d.1754.   (24:579)

RYDER Isabella Maxwell, wid. Thomas Ryder, dau. Thomas
Nasmyth, MD, Jamaica, d. Hale End, 3 Aug.1832.   (102:188)

RYLAND Herman Witsius, Sec. Lord Dorchester, m. Miss Warwick,
niece Alderman Robinson, Stamford, Montreal, 15 Dec.1794.
(65:437)

RYLAND H W, b.1761, s. late Rev. John Ryland, Northampton,
bro. late Rev. Dr Ryland, Bristol, d. Beauport, Quebec,
21 July 1838.   (NS10:454)

RYND ..., s. Maj. McKay Rynd, b. Fredericton, NB, 24 Sep.1861.
(NS2/11:555)

RYND ..., dau. Maj. McKay Rynd, 62nd Reg., b. Quebec, 19 May
1863.   (NS2/15:94)

SABAZAN Joseph, b.1781, d. Black Bay Est., Grenada, 28 Nov.
1820.   (91:185)

SADLER James, b.1772, London, ex Weyhill Plant., Jamaica, d.
Jamaica, 26 Aug.1838.   (NS10:671)

SADLER John, b.1800, ex Oajaca, Mexico, d. Torquay, 22 March
1854.   (NS41:556)

SADLER Lucy, b.1791, wid. James Sadler, Jamaica, d. Highgate,
8 Oct.1850.   (NS34:559)

ST CLAIR Charles James Chisholm, b.1844, 2nd s. Cap. St Clair,
RN, d. Nassau, New Providence, 4 Aug.1861.   (NS2/11:453)

ST CLAIR Col. Sir John, Elizabethtown, NY, d.1768.   (38:47)

ST CLAIR William, Barbados, d.6 June 1757.   (27:290)

ST GEORGE Julia Anne Caroline, eldest dau. James D N St George,
m. Lt. John L Utterton, 47th Reg., eldest s. Archdeacon Utterton, Farnham, Halifax, NS, 2 April 1867.   (NS3/3:808)

ST QUINTIN Francis John, ex Brevet Maj., 85th Light Infantry,
yngs. s. late William Thomas St Quintin, Yorks., d. Rice Lake,
Coburg, Canada, 7 Feb.1857.   (NS2/2:624)

SALMON Maria Mulgrave, yngs. dau. John Salmon, President,
Jamaica, m. George Wilson, Royal Monmouth Light Infantry,
Elgin, 22 Dec.1859.   (NS2/8:179)

SALMON Thomas Stokes, d. Archibald Pen, St Elizabeth, Jamaica,
1793.   (63:1152)

SALMONSON Frederick, d. NY, 17 Oct.1849.   (NS33:342)

SALTER Dinah Adams, wid. Rev. John Salter, Stratton, Wilts.,
d. Maxwell, Upper Canada, 25 Jan.1843.   (NS19:557)

SALTER William, b.1796, ex Exeter, Customs Landing Surveyor,
d. St Lucia, 30 Sep.1739.   (NS13:333)

SALTONHILL Richard, d. Philadelphia, 1798.   (68:1086)

SALVADOR Joseph, Elder Portuguese Jews London, d. NC, 1786.
                                                    (57:89)

SAMBOURNE Thomas, ex attorney, Sheffield, d. Raleigh, NC, 1808.
                                                    (78:170)

SAMPSON John, 2nd s. late Rev. George Sampson, Leven, Yorks.,
d. Cal., 22 Sep.1850.   (NS35:223)

SAMPSON Rev. William, b.1790, eldest s. Rev. Dr Sampson,
Petersham, Surrey, d. Grimsby, Upper Canada, 1822. (92:644)

SAMPSON Mrs, w. James Sampson, NFD. Fencibles, 3rd dau. Rev.
Charles Edward Stewart, ex Metford, Suffolk, d. Kingston,
Upper Canada, 30 Aug.1813.   (83:621)

SAMUDA Alice, dau. Benjamin Samuda, ex Jamaica, m. Lyndon
Howard Evelyn, Customs Collector Savanna la Mar, Lund,
Westmoreland, Jamaica, 3 March 1821.   (91:467)

SANDERSON Edward Dyer, b.1810, Chief Justice Tobago, d.
Tobago, 20 April 1861.   (NS2/10:705)

SANDERSON Marianne, niece late Sir John Hale, Blashford, Hants,
m. Thomas Prince jr., Jamaica, London, 31 Oct.1803. (73:1254)

SANDERSON Prof., d. Philadelphia, 5 May 1844.   (NS22:446)

SANDIFORD Rowland, b.1755, yngr. bro. Archdeacon Sandiford, &
Dr Sandiford, Fulmodestone, d. Philadelphia, 16 Sep.1827.
                                                    (97:477)
SANDILANDS John, East Barnet, d. Jamaica, April 1806.(76:583)

SARGENT Chevalier Thomas Francis, Chamberlain to Duke of Lucca,
m. Mary Margaret Adam, dau. late John Robertson, Belmont,
Jamaica, Paris, 29 May 1841.   (NS16:199)

SARTI Signor, b. Florence, Italy, anatomical modeller, d.
America, 1850.   (NS34:566)

SAXBY George, b.1714, Receiver Gen. Quit Rents SC, d. 26 Oct.1786.   (56:1000)

SAUNDERS George Nicholson, Bengal Army, s. late Robert John Saunders, Eltham, m. Rachel, elder dau. R D Cullen, Philadelphia, Brighton, 7 Aug.1862.   (NS2/13:358)

SAUNDERS Henry Chalmers, b.1835, yngs. s. John S Saunders, d. Fredericton, NB, 11 July 1856.   (NS2/1:656)

SAUNDERS Rev. James, Week St Mary, Cornwall, m. Mary, yngr. dau. W B Seaman, Vere, Jamaica, East Teignmouth, 29 June 1853.   (NS40:305)

SAUNDERS Sophia Storie, dau. John Simcoe Saunders, m. G Montgomery Campbell, Fredericton, NB, 9 June 1858.(NS2/5:185)

SAUNDERS Thomas J C, b.1826, d. Saratoga Springs, USA, 3 July 1856.   (NS2/1:260)

SAUNDERSON Thomas, Jamaica, m. Miss Lewis, London, 1757.
                                                          (27:338)

SAVAGE Arthure, b.1731, ex Boston, NE, d.21 March 1801.
                                                          (71:373)

SAVAGE Arthur, b.1767, d. Strawberryhill Plant., Port Royal, Jamaica, 24 Dec.1814.   (85:278)

SAVAGE Louise, yngs. dau. Alfred Savage, Montreal, m. Lt. William Hare Larken, 47th Reg., Montreal, 17 April 1867.
                                                          (NS3/3:808)

SAVAGE John, b. Bermuda, 1715, merchant, Charleston, SC, American Loyalist, settled England, d. London, 13 May 1804.
                                                          (74:486)

SAVAGE Mrs, wid. George Savage, d. Antigua, 1 May 1806.
                                                          (76:583)

SAVARY W Tawzia, yngs. s. late Col. W J T Savary, m. Frances Eliza, only dau. late William Hall Durham, barrister, St Vincent, London, 1828.   (98:267)

SAVARY W T, Maj. Bengal Service, m. Mary Elizabeth, dau. late Allan Dalzell, Barbados, Leckhampton, Glocs., 4 April 1850.
                                                          (NS33:658)

SAWBRIDGE James, 3rd s. S E Sawbridge, Olanteigh, Kent, d. Chippawa, Upper Canada, 5 Sep.1841.   (NS17:119)

SAWYER Miss, dau. Adm. Sawyer, d.Halifax, NS, 1788. (58:562)

SAYER Edward Kyrwood, d. Jamaica, 24 March 1814.   (84:697)

SAYRE Stephen, b. Long Island, 1734, banker & merchant, private sec. Benjamin Franklin, d. Va., 7 Sep.1818. (88:89)

SCADDING Harriet Eugenia, b.1823, w. Rev. Henry Scadding, chaplain Bishop of Toronto, d. Toronto, 26 Sep.1843.(NS20:670)

SCANDELLA J B, MD, b. Venice, 1771, d.NY, 16 Sep.1798.(69:252)

SCARLETT Elizabeth, dau. late Philip Anglin Scarlett, Jamaica,
d. Bristol, 14 Nov.1831.   (101:571)

SCARLETT James m. Miss Gallimore, dau. Jarvis Gallimore,
Jamaica, 28 July 1791.   (61:774)

SCARLETT Miss, eldest dau. late James Scarlett, Jamaica, m.
Maj. Gen. Riall, Gov. Grenada, Dec.1819.   (89:635)

SCHAW Mrs, wid. Charles Schaw, Schawfield, Jamaica, m. William,
Cruchley, London, 19 Oct.1795.   (65:878)

SCHENLEY Jane Maria, b.1814, dau. Sir W T Pole, Shute House,
Devon, w. Edward Wyndham Harrington Schenley, HM Commissioner
of Arbitration Cuba, d. Havanna, 23 April 1837.   (NS8:103)

SCHLATTER Fanny, dau. Col. C L Schlatter, m. Eardley Graham
Westmoreland, HM Vice Consul, Brunswick, Ga., 5 July 1867.
                                                         (NS3/2:383)

SCHNELL Francis MacDonald, ex Kew Green, only s. late Cap.
Charles Vaughn, HEICS, d. Cincinatti, Ohio, 14 Feb.1852.
                                                          (NS37:529)

SCHREIBER Lemuel, b.1831, 3rd s. Rev. T Schreiber, Stokes Hall,
Essex, d. Cincinatti, NA, 28 June 1850.   (NS34:565)

SCHREIBER Sarah, b.1805, 3rd dau. late Adm. Bingham,
Lymington, d. Toronto, 15 March 1856.   (NS45:546)

SCHRIMSHAW Mr, ex WI, d.18 Nov.1785.   (55:921)

SCHUYLER Col. Peter, NJ, d.24 Jan.1762.   (32:194)

SCHUYLER Peter, Senator Western NY, d. Montgomery Co., NA,
4 Jan.1792.   (62:182)

SCHWEIGHAUSER Nicholas, merchant, NY, d. Elizabeth, 1799.
                                                        (69:903)

SCHYLER Brant, Mayor of NY, d.1752.   (22:478)

SCLATER William Salisbury, b.1800, ex Barbados, d.Greenwich,
12 Jan.1842.   (NS17:336)

SCOTLAND Rev. John, St John's College, Oxford, 2nd s. John
Scotland, Chief Judge Trinidad, m. Elizabeth Snow, 2nd dau.
Thomas Heath, Putney, 10 Jan.1849.   (NS31:312)

SCOTLAND Lt. Thomas C, RN, s. Thomas Scotland, Antigua, d.
Antigua, Dec.1812.   (83:284)

SCOTLAND Mrs, w. Thomas Scotland, Antigua, d. Hextable House,
Kent, 23 Aug.1815.   (85:281)

SCOTT Alexander, Councillor, d. Grenada, 1 June 1806.(76:978)

SCOTT Alexander Reid, Kingston, Jamaica, m. Eliza, only dau.
late Alexander Miller, Lyston, essex, 1846.   (NS26:420)

SCOTT Mrs, wid. David Scott, Antigua, m. Maj. Gen. Richardson,
Bath, 9 Nov.1808.   (78:1039)

SCOTT Frances, dau. late Rev. Scott, Port Royal, Jamaica, m.
Lt. Alexander Bocher, HMS Prosperine, Port Royal, 1793.(63:860)

SCOTT Francis Carteret, Customs Collector, Montego Bay,
Jamaica, m. Charlotte Elizabeth, eldest dau. Col. Cunningham,
the Scots Brigade, 1801.   (71:1051)

SCOTT G H C, London, m. Mary Favell, 2nd dau. late George
Dehany, Jamaica, London, 27 Nov.1833.   (104:102)

SCOTT George, Gov. Dominica, d.1768.   (38:47)

SCOTT James, Kingston, Jamaica, d.1759.   (29:146)

SCOTT James, Comiestoun, d. Jamaica, 14 Oct.1801.   (72:83)

SCOTT John Gregory, b.1801, d. on board Henry Wellesley
during passage from Jamaica, 1820.   (90:571)

SCOTT Maria Litchfield, b. NA, m. Peter Pedersen, Danish
Charge d'Affairs, d. 7 Nov.1814.   (85:88)

SCOTT Matthew Henry, b. Jamaica, 1767, Vive Adm., d. Southampton, 31 Oct.1836.   (NS7:321)

SCOTT Mrs, wid. Michael Scott, Grenada, m. Count de la
Basecque, Artois, France, Nov.1792.   (84:697)

SCOTT Richard, planter, Va., d.1766.   (36:439)

SCOTT Mrs, wid. Robert Scott, Nassau, New Providence, m.
Robert William, MD, London, 1800.   (70:1003)

SCOTT Thomas, Paymaster, 70th Reg., bro. Sir Walter Scott, d.
Quebec, 14 Feb.1823.   (93:478)

SCOTT Cap. T, RM, m. Elizabeth, dau. late S Francis,
Newington Est., Jamaica, London, 26 Oct.1837.   (NS8:648)

SCOTT William, b.1759, ex North Devon Bank, Barnstaple, d.
NB, 1832.   (102:649)

SCOTT Winfield, b. Petersburg, Va., 13 June 1786, ex C in C
US Army, d. West Point, 29 May 1866.   (NS3/2:118)

SCOTT Rev. Dr, Bishop of Oregon, d.1867.   (NS3/2:833)

SCRIPPS William, b.1750, London, d. Cape Girardou, Missouri,
8 Nov.1824.   (94:574)

SCRIVEN Thomas, ex Henbury, Bristol, d. Buff Bay, Jamaica,
29 Aug.1810.   (80:492)

SEABROOK Thomas, only bro. John Seabrook, St Paul's Churchyard,
d. Bermuda, 1819.   (89:570)

SEABURY Rev. Samuel, Bishop of Protestant Episcopal Church
USA, d. Norwich, Conn., 1797.   (67:442)

SEAGER Mrs Edward, ex Longfleet, dau. Robert Pack, merchant,
Carboner, NFD., d.Constantinople, 7 Aug.1848.   (NS30:447)

SEALE Lt. F S, RA, yngs. s. late Sir J H Seale, m. Harriett,
2nd dau. J A Harvey, Ordnance storekeeper, Kingston, Canada,
24 April 1851.   (NS36:78)

SEALY George Augustus, 2nd s. John Sealy, Attorney Gen.
Barbados, m. Agnes Senhouse, 2nd dau. James Walker, Barbados,
15 Nov.1866.   (NS3/3:238)

SEALEY Richard, b. London, 1805, paper-maker, d. Cockeyville,
Md., 13 Oct.1852.   (NS38:657)

SEAMAN Catherine, eldest dau. late Rev. John Campbell,
St Andrews, Jamaica, wid. Dr W B Seaman, Vere, Jamaica, d.
Teignmouth, 30 April 1864.   (NS2/16:810)

SEAMAN Mary, yngr. dau. W B Seaman, Vere, Jamaica, m. Rev.
James Saunders, Week St Mary, Cornwall, East Teignmouth,
29 June 1853.   (NS40:305)

SEAMAN W G, b.1784, eldest s. W Seaman, Great Yarmouth,
surgeon, Vere, Jamaica, d. Spanish Town, Jamaica, 15 Jan.1819.
                                                      (88:279)

SEARS Mrs, w. Maj. Sears, HEICS, d. Md., 1787.   (57:934)

SEDGWICK Catherine Maria, b.1789, writer, d. Roxbury, Mass.,
31 July 1867.   (NS3/2:403)

SEDGWICK Elvira Crichton, eldest dau. Samuel Sedgwick, MD, m.
Richard Nugent, MD, Dublin, Antigua, 29 Feb.1848. (NS29:538)

SEGUIN Edward, opera singer, d. NY, 1853.   (NS39:556)

SELBY James Hall, 5th s. Prideaux Selby, Maidenhead, d.
Quebec, 24 May 1847.   (NS28:558)

SELBY Samuel, b.1729, d. Goshenhill, Union, SC, 6 July 1830.
                                                     (100:286)

SELDEN Josephine, yngr. dau. late Lt. Col. Selden, US Army,
Va., m. Graham Willmore, barrister, Middle Temple, London,
14 Aug.1845.   (NS24:521)

SELF Fanny, yngs. dau. late Samuel Self, m. Frederic Singleton
Kingston, Jamaica, London, 11 Aug.1853.   (NS40:521)

SELFE James, Trowbridge, Wilts., m. Grace Camilla, dau. late
Thomas Cottle, Nevis, Camberwell, Surrey, 14 Nov.1797.(67:1126)

SELLON Rev. John, s. Serjeant Sellon, d. Albany, NY, 2 March
1830.   (100:571)

SELWYN Henry Charles, Lt. Gov. Montserrat, d. Gloucester, 1807.
                                                      (77:684)

SENILH Joseph, French Protestant, merchant, Quebec, d.
12 Aug.1764.   (34:545)

SENIOR James Christopher, b.1827, eldest s. James Gale Senior,
Richmond, Surrey, d. Black River, Jamaica, 12 Oct.1860.
                                                    (NS2/9:681)

SERVANTE Hannah Eliza, yngs. dau. Maj. Gen. Servante, m.
Thomas Morland, Montreal, 13 Aug.1863.   (NS2/15:498)

SETON Charlotte, dau. Gov. Seton, St Vincent, m. Arthur Leith,
Cap., 69th Reg., Maj. Brigade in Caribees, 21 June 1791.
                                              (61:871)

SETON G, 2nd s. Gov. Seton, d. St Vincent, 21 Aug.1795.
                                              (65:968)

SETON James jr., m. Mrs Mackay, ex St Vincent, Bishop
Auckland, 1 Jan.1799.   (69:77)

SEWELL Constantia Caroline, 2nd dau. late Robert Shore Milnes
Sewell, Quebec, gdau. Jonathan Sewell, Chief Justice Quebec,
m. Dr Francis, s. Edward Bowen, Chief Justice Quebec,
Chilvers Cotton Vicarage, 8 Jan.1861.   (NS2/10:201)

SEWELL Rev. Edmond Willoughby, 2nd s. Chief Justice Sewell, m.
Susan, 2nd dau. Montgomerie Stewart, niece Earl of Galloway,
niece Bishop of Quebec, Quebec, 12 Nov.1828. (99:80)

SEWELL Henrietta Eliza, 2nd dau. J Sewell, Chief Justice
Lower Canada, m. F J Lundy, Lockington, Yorks., Quebec,
11 May 1837.   (NS8:192)

SEWELL Rev. Henry D, 4th s. late Jonathan Sewell, Chief
Justice Lower Canada, m. Elizabeth Charlotte, yngs. dau. late
Robert Moneypenny, Kent, Haddow, Kent, 25 Oct.1843. (NS23:90)

SEWELL Jonathan, b.1766, ex Chief Justice Quebec, d. Quebec,
12 Nov.1839.   (NS13:334)

SEWELL Martin, d. Jamaica, 1791.   (61:186)

SEWELL Maud Lavinia, dau. late W S Sewell, Sheriff of Quebec,
gdau. Chief Justice Sewell, m. Lt. Henry Burton Winter, 7th
Royal Fusiliers, Quebec, 11 July 1867.   (NS3/2:383)

SEWELL Mrs M J, w. William J Sewell, Sheriff of Canada, d.
Quebec, 1842.   (NS18:332)

SEWELL Stephen, ex Hancock Prof. Hebrew, d.Cambridge, USA,
23 July 1804.   (74:881)

SEWELL Robert m. Sarah, dau. late William Lewis, Jamaica,
1775.   (45:606)

SEWELL Rev. Willoughby, 2nd s. late Chief Justice Sewell, m.
Elizabeth, 3rd dau. Maj. Gen. Dunford, RE, Montreal, 24 July
1843.   (NS19:85)

SEYMOUR Ellen, 4th dau. late Maj. Gen. Seymour, Gov.St Lucia,
m. John Gamble Horne, Kingston, Upper Canada, 15 Nov.1842.
                                              (NS19:422)

SEYMOUR John William m. Ellen Tobin, yngs. dau. Michael Tobin,
Halifax, NS, Jersey, 1 May 1849.   (NS31:646)

SHACKELFORD Henry, b.1733, ex Jamaica, d. Peterfield, Hants.
6 Nov.1821.   (91:478)

SHAND John, Cap., 51st Reg. Madras Native Inf., m. Eliza
Jane, yngs. dau. late Hinton Spalding, MD, Kingston, Jamaica,
Munich, 23 Feb.1859.   (NS2/6:422)

SHANLY Ellen, only ch. late James Shanly, Thondale, Middlesex
Co., Canada West, ex Normangrove, Co. Meath, m. Maj. Charles
Courtenay Villiers, 47th Reg., Montreal, 5 Feb.1863.
                                                (NS2/14:515)

SHANNON Maria Jane, dau. late W C Shannon, Co. Clare, m.
George W Garden, Jamaica, London, 28 Oct.1846.   (NS27:193)

SHANNON Mr, b.1786, merchant, Kingston, Jamaica, d. on the
Pelican when attacked by the privateer Marengo, 1811.(81:658)

SHAPLEY Rev. J Congdon, Carricou, Grenada, m. Mary Jane, yngs.
dau. A G Milne, Eltham, Kent, 13 June 1844.   (NS22:202)

SHAPLEY Rev. J C, ex Carricou, d. Tenby, 13 June 1862.
                                                 (NS2/13:112)

SHARPE Frances, b.1760, wid. John MacArtha Sharpe, Solicitor
Gen. Grenada, sis. late Sir Peter Payne, d. Bedford, 9 Feb.
1844.   (NS21:444)

SHARPE George, St Vincent, m. C Payne, 2nd dau. Sir Gillies
Payne, Tempsford, Beds., 1788.   (58:1026)

SHARPE George Henry, b.1804, St Vincent, d. Bedford, 25 Oct.
1853.   (NS40:652)

SHARPE Laura, yngs. dau. Henry Edward Sharpe, Chief Justice
St Vincent, m. Charles Lionell John Fitzgerald, Lt., 1st WI
Reg., eldest s. Lt. Col. Fitzgerald, RA, St George, St Vincent,
12 March 1863.   (NS2/14:781)

SHARPE Maria, eldest dau. John Sharpe, ex Attorney Gen. Grenada,
m. Rev. L Calder, Tempsford, Beds., 1812.   (82:288)

SHARP Rebecca, dau. Richard Sharp, Maidstone, Kent, m. Rev.
Charles Campe, Port of Spain, Trinidad, only s. late Charles
Campe, Esses, Trinidad, 15 April 1847.   (NS28:198)

SHAW Alexander, s. late Rev. John Shaw, Greenock, d. Jamaica,
10 Aug.1804.   (74:1071)

SHAW Henry Thomas, b.1823, 4th s. Lee Shaw, nephew Sir Robert
Shaw, Bushy Park, Dublin, Kingston, Jamaica, June 1844.
                                                  (NS22:446)

SHAW Jane, eldest dau. Andrew Shaw, m. Robert John Pilkington,
Royal Military draughtsman, only s. late Maj. Gen. Pilkington,
RE, Montreal, 8 Jan.1850.   (NS33:528)

SHAW John Hercy, eldest s. John Shaw, Jersey, d. Jamaica,
16 Feb.1843.   (NS20:110)

SHAW Mrs, w. Dr James Shaw, d. Kingston, Jamaica, 22 Feb.1797.
                                                  (67:435)

SHEA John Augustus, b. Cork, 1800, poet, settled America 1830,
d. NY, 16 Aug.1845.   (NS24:429)

SHEA Matthew, d. Kingston, Jamaica, 6 July 1803.   (73:882)

SHEA Mrs, actress, gdau. Stephen Kemble, gniece Mrs Siddons,
d. St Louis Theater, America, 6 July 1851.   (NS36:329)

SHEARMAN Mrs Caroline, w. Henry Shearman, 3rd dau. James Bate,
Exeter, d. PEI, 12 July 1838.   (NS10:454)

SHEDDEN T, ex Cap., 91st Reg., d. Toronto, 1837.   (NS7:558)

SHEEPSHANKS Mr, ex merchant, Leeds, d. America, 1798.(68:172)

SHEIL Edward, ex merchant, Belize, bro. Richard Lalor Sheil,
MP, d. on passage to Honduras, 7 May 1843.   (NS20:222)

SHEKELL J H, b.1822, eldest s. T Shekell, Pebworth, Glocs.,
d. Havanna, Sep.1846.   (NS26:670)

SHELLY Miss, b.1796, dau. Seba Shelly, St Anne, Jamaica, niece
Mr Tippetts, surgeon, London, d.1817.   (87:184)

SHERGOLD William Whitmore, d. St Vincent, 21 Aug.1804.
     (74:1168)

SHELTON Frederick Richard, eldest s. Robert Shelton,
Kennington, d. Serge Island Est., Jamaica, 3 Nov.1817.(87:629)

SHENANDON, b.1706, Chief Oneida, d. Oneida, 11 March 1816.
     (86:473)

SHEPHERD John, b.1728, d. Akron, Ohio, 3 March 1847.(NS27:567)

SHEPHERD Mrs J, Barbados, d.1768.   (38:143)

SHEPPARD Grace, w. George Sheppard, ex editor 'Eastern
Counties Herald' & 'Newcastle Courier', d. Hamilton, Canada
West, 13 June 1854.   (NS42:202)

SHEPPARD Harriot Frances Josephine, yngs. dau. late William
Sheppard, Clifton, Bristol, m. Lt. R W Brettingham, St Johns,
NFD., 22 June 1846.   (NS26:314)

SHEPPARD ..., dau. Cap. T W Sheppard, 25th Reg., b. Quebec,
28 Nov.1864.   (NS2/18:93)

SHERIFF James Watson, b. Antigua, President Nevis, d. Nevis,
9 March 1866.   (NS3/1:754)

SHERIFF Joyce Clandia, only dau. James Watson Sheriff,
Attorney Gen. Antigua, d. London, 24 Aug.1853.   (NS40:428)

SHERLEY Judith, dau. Gov.NE, d.27 Nov.1754.   (24:530)

SHERMAN Mrs Elizabeth, b.1774, wid. Roger Minott Sherman,
Judge Supreme Court, sis. James Gould, Judge Supreme Court,
sis. Maj. Samuel Gould, d. Fairfield, Conn., 1848. (NS30:671)

SHERRARD Noble jr., Bristol, d. Jamaica, 1818.   (88:90)

SHERWEN Mrs Douglas, w. John Sherwen, MD, Enfield, Middlesex,
dau. Dugald Campbell, Saltspring, Jamaica, d.Bath, 16 June 1804.
     (74:601)

SHERWOOD Mary Helen, 2nd dau. H Sherwood, Attorney Gen.
Upper Canada, m. Lawrence William, eldest s. Rev. W Herchmond,
Kingston, Canada, 8 Nov.1866.   (NS3/3:238)

SHERWOOD ..., s. Lt. T H Sherwood, 21st Fusiliers, b.
Barbados, 28 Feb.1861.   (NS2/10:565)

SHICKLE Ann, wid. John Hayle Shickle, ex Jamaica, d.Laugharne,
Carmarthen, 27 Oct.1840.   (NS14:675)

SHIFFNER Mr, merchant, Jamaica, d.30 June 1762.   (32:448)

SHILLITO Benjamin, b.1789, ex RM Artillery, settled NS 1829,
d. Windsor, NS, 23 Sep.1834.   (104:654)

SHILLETO W, b.1784, Jamaica, d.London, 11 June 1838.(NS10:224)

SHIPLEY Sir Charles, b.1757, Gov. Grenada, d. Grenada,
30 Nov.1815.   (86:276)

SHIPLEY Mordaunt James, b.1781, 2nd s. Dean of St Asaph, d.
Russell's Rest, Nevis, 27 Nov.1806.   (77:179)

SHIPPEN Edward, b.1728, ex Chief Justice Supreme Court Pa.,
d.15 April 1806.   (76:583)

SHIRLEY Henry, Craycombe House, Worcs., d. Hyde Hall, Jamaica,
1848.   (NS30:558)

SHIRLEY Sir Thomas, Oathall, Sussex, ex Gov. Antigua & St Kitts,
d. Bath, 21 Feb.1800.   (70:286)

SHIRLEY Mrs, b.1759, wid. Edward Shirley, Petersfield,
Jamaica, d. Clifton, 15 March 1808.   (78:367)

SHIRLING George, d. Jamaica, 1790.   (60:1053)

SHIRREFFS David, Assemblyman Jamaica, 2nd s. Convenor
Shirreffs, Aberdeen, d. Kingston, Jamaica, 4 Sep.1805.
                                                   (75:1171)

SHOOLBRED Elizabeth, wid. David Shoolbred, Quebec, d.
London, 8 June 1811.   (81:680)

SHOOLBRED Henry, bro. Mr Shoolbred, London, d. Nassan, NE,
1790.   (60:373)

SHOOLBRED Sybelea, w. J N Shoolbred, Chief Comm. United
Mexican Mining Co., d. Guanaxuato, Mexico, 2 Sep.1850.
                                                   (NS35:110)

SHORDICHE John Cleveland, 2nd s. Paul Rycaut Shordiche,
nephew Lt. Gen. Cleveland, Madras, & late Col. Baird, 66th
Reg., d. Antigua, 6 Nov.1864.   (NS2/18:116)

SHORDICHE Paul Rycaut, s. late Paul Rycaut Shordiche, gs. late
Michael Shordiche, Middlesex, nephew Lt. Gen. John W Cleveland,
Madras Army, & Lt. Col. Baird, 66th Reg., d. Antigua, 13 July
1865.   (NS2/19:392)

SHORE Eliza Saunders, dau. George Shore, Fredericton, m. W L
Stewart, Cap., Royal Reg., s. Lt. Col. Stewart, HEICS,
Fredericton, NB, 10 April 1849.   (NS32:84)

SHORE Rev. W H, s. late George Shore, Councillor, NB, m. Frances Anna, yngs. dau. late Charles S Putnam, barrister, London, 29 April 1852.   (NS38:87)

SHORT Christina, b. NA, 1745, American Loyalist, settled England, w. Rev. Dr Short, d. Bath, 22 Nov.1819.   (88:89)

SHORT Mayow, Quarter Sessions Chairman, m. Annis Rachel, dau. Rev. Dr Panton, Widcombe, niece Vice Chancellor Jamaica, Jamaica, 15 June 1847.   (NS28:311)

SHUBRICK Miss, SC, m. John Line, 22 June 1768.   (38:302)

SHULTZ M, NY, m. Anne, wid. Sir H R Bishop, London, 20 Dec. 1859.   (NS2/6:91)

SHUTER Eliza, only dau. John Shuter, Hendon, m. Peter McGill, Montreal, Councillor, Lower Canada, London, 1832.   (102:267)

SIBBALD A, b.1763, ex Barbados, d. London, 10 Jan.1820.(90:93)

SIBREE Robert, MD, b.1803, bro. Rev. James Sibree, Hull, d. NY, 30 Nov.1847.   (NS29:334)

SIGOURNEY Mrs Lydia Huntley, b.1 Sep.1791, authoress, d. Hartford, Conn., 10 June 1865.   (NS2/19:255)

SILL John, planter, Jamaica, d. Dent, Yorks., 29 March 1803.   (73:386)

SILLIMAN Prof. Benjamin, s. Gen. Gold Sellack Silliman, d. Newhaven, USA, 24 Nov.1864.   (NS2/18:118)

SILVESTER Robert, ex Chard, Somerset, d. Jamaica, 19 April 1841.   (NS16:222)

SIM John, MD, London, m. Ann Eliza, eldest dau. James Clark, MD, Dominica, 9 Oct.1817.   (87:466)

SIMBLET James, Jamaica, d. Bath, 22 July 1757.   (27:386)

SIMMONS John Alleyne, Vaucluse, Barbados, m. Caroline, 2nd dau. Robert Gresham, Beds., Campton, Beds., 8 Feb.1855.
                                                      (NS43:410)

SIMMONS Thomas W, b.1810, Chief Clerk of Works, RE, d. Nassau, New Providence, 30 Oct.1846.   (NS25:110)

SIMMONS Lt. Col., ex 41st Reg., m. Frances, wid. Alexander Munro, Trinidad, eldest dau. J Townshend Pasea, London, 8 July 1847.   (NS28:312)

SIMONDS Helen, only dau. Charles Simonds, m. Thomas Howard Fletcher, 15th Reg., St John, NB, 27 April 1867. (NS3/2:383)

SIMONDS Henry George, eldest s. Charles Simonds, St John, NB, m. Gertrude Anne, yngs. dau. Rev. Randall Ward, Coltishall, Norfolk, Moulton, Northants., 3 May 1849(NS32:86)

SIMONDS Henry George, b.1828, eldest s. late Charles Simonds, St John, NB, d. River Kennebecasis, 8 Nov.1860. (NS2/10:111)

SIMONDS Richard, 2nd s. Charles Simonds, m. Ada, dau. M H
Perley, Comm. NA Fisheries, St John, NB, 31 Oct.1860.
(NS2/10:95)

SIMONDSON Mary, b.1727, d. Shippensburg, Pa., 1853.(NS40:541)

SIMPSON Eleanor Lawrence, eldest dau. John Simpson, Tilston,
Jamaica, m. William Henry Bradley, Bombay Medical Staff,
Bycullah, 16 Nov.1840.   (NS15:311)

SIMPSON Cap. George, b.1801, yngs. s. Henry Simpson, Whitby,
Yorks., master Palaniban of London, d. St Elizabeth, Jamaica,
10 June 1824.   (94:478)

SIMPSON Sir George, b.1792, Gov. Hudson Bay Co., d. Lachine,
Montreal, 7 Sep.1860.   (NS2/9:445)

SIMPSON ..., s. Sir G Simpson, Lachine, Quebec, b. Montreal,
14 June 1850.   (NS34:318)

SIMPSON Cap. Houstoun, master Cumberland of Leith, ship-
wrecked on passage from Jamaica, 22 Aug.1806, d.Baltimore,
24 Sep.1806.   (76:1168)

SIMPSON Thomas, b.Dingwall, 1808, educated Aberdeen University,
settled Hudson Bay, 1829, d. Turtle River, Canada, 28 June
1840.   (NS14:548)

SIMPSON William H Randolph, RA, m. Marion Susan Annie Peade,
only dau. Thomas Mackintosh, Guadaloupe-y-Calvo, Mexico,
Southsea, 13 Aug.1853.   (NS40:522)

SIMS Rev. C A J, ex schoolmaster, Monkton, Farley, Wilts., d.
St Lucia, 1842.   (NS18:669)

SIMS C J, only s. J Sims, Walthamstow, Essex, Assemblyman,
d. Kingston, Jamaica, 1813.   (83:595)

SIMS Frances, wid. C J Sims, Jamaica, d.Walthamstow, 5 July
1816.   (86:93)

SIMS Frances Cockburn, only dau. C J Sims, Jamaica, m.
Viscount Valentia, only s. Earl of Mountnorris, Brighton,
21 Oct.1837.   (NS8:648)

SINCKLER James W, MD, Barbados, m. Maria Jane, dau. late Cap.
Theophilius Patterson, RM, London, 5 Sep.1854.   (NS42:618)

SINCKLER Maria Jane, w. J W Sinckler, MD, dau. late Cap.
Patterson, RM, Dublin, d. Barbados, 25 Oct.1855.   (NS45:96)

SINCLAIR William, MD, Hospital Purveyor, d. Port au Prince,
17 June 1795.   (66:255)

SINCLAIR ..., dau. Lt. Col. R Bligh Sinclair, b. Dartmouth,
NS, 6 March 1862.   (NS2/12:637)

SINGER Mrs M K, wid. George Singer, Jamaica, d. London, July
1809.   (79:785)

SINGLETON Frederic jr., Kingston, Jamaica, m. Fanny, yngs.
dau. Samuel Self, London, 11 Aug.1853.   (NS40:521)

SINNOTT Pierce, ex Lt. Gov. Niagara, d.London, 30 May 1794.
(64:482)

SISSON Mary, w. A Sisson, 3rd dau. T Neale, Reigate, Surrey,
d. Rosseau, Dominica, 24 Aug.1841.   (NS16:558)

SKAIFE Joseph, b.1799, yngs. s. late Thomas Skaife, Little-
thorp, Yorks., d. NY, 1841.   (NS16:446)

SKEETE Agnes, niece William Bishop, Gov. Barbados, m. Lt.Col.
Bonham, 69th Reg., Bridgetown, Barbados, 26 Feb.1800(70:588)

SKEETE Agnes Bonham, 3rd dau. late E Skeete, Barbados, m.
S L Gower, Little Hempston, Devon, Wells, 1 Sep.1840.
(NS14:424)

SKEETE Margaret, dau. late J B Skeete, President, Barbados,
m. John C Russell, Warminster, Wilts., Brighton, 15 Dec.1864.
(NS2/18:98)

SKEETE Thomas, MD, b. Barbados, 1757, d. London, 1789.(59:575)

SKEETE Mrs, wid., John Braithwaite Skeete, Barbados, d.
Mangrove Est., Barbados, 26.Sep.1816.   (86:566)

SKENE Andrew Philip, Halyards, Fife, & Kilmacoo, Wicklow, b.
1753, only s. Gov. Skene, Skenesboro, NA, & Northants., d.
Durham, 18 Jan.1826.   (96:572)

SKENE Col. Philip, ex Skenesboro, Lt. Gov. Crown Point &
Ticonderoga, NY, British Army officer 1739-1782, d. Stoke
Goldingham, Bucks., 9 July 1810.   (80:672)

SKETCHLEY James, ex Birmingham, d. Pekipsy, NY, 1801.(71:1153)

SKIDDY William, NY, m. Mary Anne, only ch. James Anderson,
London, Isleworth, 26 Nov.1841.   (NS17:205)

SKINNER Charles, Chief Justice SC, d.1768.   (38:199)

SKINNER Dorothy Griffith, b.28 Feb.1765, dau. William Rollock,
w. Isaac Skinner, Barbados, d. Barbados, 16 July 1852.
(NS38:655)

SKINNER Mrs Elizabeth, b.1773, wid. J D Skinner, ex Jamaica,
d. Little Ealing, Middlesex, 28 Dec.1823.   (94:188)

SKIPWITH Sir Peyton, d. Presswould, Va., 9 Oct.1805.(75:1238)

SKIPWITH Sir William, Prestwood, Va., d.26 Feb.1764. (34:450)

SKURRAY Charles Thomas, b.1777, St George, Jamaica, d. 1 Oct.
1814.   (84:604)

SLANEY Moreton Aglionby, ex Shifnal, Shropshire, d. Charlottetown, PEI, 1 March 1817.   (87:568)

SLADE James, b.1802, partner David & James Slade, merchants,
NFD., d. Poole, 22 Sep.1847.   (NS28:554)

SLATER Charlotte, dau. late William Slater, Nassau, New
Providence, d.Westrop House, Wilts., 9 Aug.1844. (NS22:222)

SLATER Isabella, b.1793, dau. Charles MacAlester, Philadelphia,
ex Campbelltown, Argyll, w. Anthony Slater, Chesterfield,
Derby, d. Philadelphia, 4 Jan.1851.   (NS36:216)

SLATER John, d. Kingston, Jamaica, 1789.   (59:1209)

SLATER Mrs, Richmond, m. Duncan Fraser, Jamaica, 1 Aug.1794.
                                                        (64:764)
SLEATER Thomas, d. Jamaica, 1790.   (60:766)

SMEAR Miss, eldest dau. Rev. Christopher Smear, Frostenden, m.
John Berry, NY, Frostenden, Suffolk, 24 Oct.1795.   (65:878)

SLOCOMBE Jemima, yngs. dau. Mr Slocombe, HM Customs, Jamaica,
d. St Anne, Jamaica, 8 Oct.1810.   (81:85)

SLOCOMBE Rupert, 4th s. late Joseph Slocombe, Stockwell, d.
Barbados, 30 June 1852.   (NS38:433)

SMALL Charles Coxwell, b.1802, Clerk of Court, d. Toronto,
17 March 1864.   (NS2/16:671)

SMART Henry Dalton, Maj., 76th Reg., m. Louisa, dau. John
Wallace, Halifax, NS, 28 June 1854.   (NS42:385)

SMART Robert, d. Kingston, Jamaica, 5 June 1817.   (87:183)

SMART Mrs, wid. R Smart, Jamaica, eldest dau. John Willis,
London, m. James Cunningham, Jamaica, 17 Nov.1818.   (89:80)

SMEATHMAN Rev. Charles, ex Melbourne, Australia, eldest s.
late Maj. Smeathman, d. St Kitts, 17 June 1855.   (NS54:439)

SMEDLEY Joseph Valentine, s. late Thomas J Smedley, gs.
Valentine Smedley, m. Alice A, eldest dau. late Thomas Clarke,
Norfolk, Va., Hawesville, Kentucky, 8 June 1854.   (NS42:294)

SMELT Lt. Col., 103rd Reg., m. Miss Robinson, dau. Comm. Gen.
Robinson, Quebec, 26 Dec.1814.   (85:370)

SMITH Alicia, Barbados, m. Thomas Tindall, Bristol, Aug.1756.
                                                        (26:450)
SMITH Anne, b.1812, w. I Delap Wilson, niece Robert Claxton,
St Kitts, d. Milford, 20 Jan.1836.   (NS5:214)

SMITH Arthur, d. Beaufort, SC, 14 March 1808.   (78:367)

SMITH Rev. Augustus Francis, eldest s. Rev. Rowland Smith,
Ilston, Glamorgan, m. Elizabeth, yngst. dau. late Thomas
James, Enfield, Jamaica, Littlebourne, 13 May 1863.(NS2/14:785)

SMITH Caroline Josepha, yngs. dau. late John George Smith, m.
Rev. Henry James Petry, Quebec, Montreal, 21 Nov.1860.
                                                    (NS2/10:95)
SMITH Charles, bro. Mr Smith, apothecary, Bath, d. Tobago,
1801.   (71:1149)

SMITH Charles, merchant, Curacao, d. Portsmouth, 16 Sep.1809.
                                                        (79:894)

SMITH Charles William, b.1828, 3rd s. Rev. Jeremiah Smith,
Long Buckley, Lichfield, d. New London, Canada, 18 Sep.1849.
                                                    (NS33:341)

SMITH Charlotte, dau. Robert Smith, MD, Speaker Tobago Assembly,
m. Charles Simpson Hanson, Constanipol, Woodford, Essex, Sep.
1829.   (99:270)

SMITH David, New Providence, m. Miss Tucker, eldest dau.
Jeremiah Tucker, London, 20 Nov.1802.   (72:1160)

SMITH Dr E H, physician, d. NY, 1798.   (68:1086)

SMITH Dr Eli, American missionary, d. Beirut, 12 Jan.1857.
                                                   (NS2/2:367)

SMITH Elishu Hubbard, b. Lichfield, Conn., educated Newhaven
College, NY, physician, d. NY, 19 Sep.1798.   (69:252)

SMITH E, ex Eastley, Kent, Kingston, Jamaica, drowned off
America, Oct.1834.   (105:222)

SMITH George, dockyard clerk, Port Royal, Jamaica, d.
20 Oct.1814.   (84:604)

SMITH Maj. Gen. G S, Lt. Gov. NB, d. Fredericton, NB,
27 March 1823.   (93:382)

SMITH Mrs, w. Maj. Gen. G S Smith, Lt. Gov. NB, d. Halifax,
1817.   (87:637)

SMITH Henry, b.1830, s. Robert Smith, Acaster Malbis, York,
d. Hong Town, Cal., 6 Feb.1852.   (NS37:529)

SMITH Henry Bowyer, ex Customs Collector St Johns, b.1801,
4th s. late C D Smith, nephew late Adm. Sir W S Smith, d.
St Johns, NFD., 3 Jan.1868.   (NS3/5:396)

SMITH Isabella, w. Col. Smith, RA, d. Port Royal, Jamaica,
1815.   (85:379)

SMITH James, b.1742, d. Springhill Est., Jamaica, 24 Feb.1813.
                                                    (83:490)

SMITH Rev. J, Christ Curch, Oxford, House of Commons chaplain,
m. Miss Barnett, yngs. dau. W Barnett, Jamaica, 9 Aug.1803.
                                                    (73:788)

SMITH James Lamond, Glen Millan, Aberdeen, m. Isabella, 3rd
dau. late George Barker, Leamington Prior, Warwick, Guelph,
22 Oct.1844.   (NS23:196)

SMITH John, ex Hanover, Jamaica, m. Jeannie, dau. late William
Brown, glover, Glasgow, 1792.   (62:181)

SMITH J F, WS, Edinburgh, m. Caroline, 3rd dau. D S Turner,
Clarendon, Jamaica, London, 12 June 1830.   (100:554)

SMITH John Lucie, b.1795, Demerara, d. Barbados, 10 April 1844.
                                                    (NS22:110)

SMITH Martin, b.1784, only s. Cap. M Smith, London, d. on
passage from NC, 1 Aug.1826.   (96:477)

SMITH Mary Anne, yngs. dau. James Smith, gdau. Alexander
Aikman, m. Henry Forbes jr, Kingston, Jamaica, 2 Nov.1831.
(101:644)

SMITH Mary Shaftesbury, w. Rev. C J Smith, ex Archdeacon of
Jamaica, Erith, Kent, dau. Rev. Aubrey George Spencer,
Bishop of Jamaica, d. Hastings, 20 May 1854.   (NS42:91)

SMITH Miles, b.1756, ex Sunderlandwick, Driffield, Yorks.,
d. Ross Hall, Jersey, America, 7 June 1838.   (NS10:566)

SMITH Nicholas, d. Kingston, Jamaica, 1799.   (69:719)

SMITH Peter, b.1751, Ayrshire, d. Jamaica, 1831.   (101:477)

SMITH Robert, ex Speaker Tobago Assembly, d.1814.   (84:525)

SMITH Richard, Md., d.29 April 1759.   (29:194)

SMITH Susanna Elizabeth, dau. Lt. Gov. Smith, m. Hector
Harvest, Shepperton, PEI, 18 Nov.1819.   (90:368)

SMITH Thomas Waterford, s. late Mr Smith, chemist, Salisbury,
d. on passage from St Vincent to England, 1795.   (65:971)

SMITH William, Grenada, m. Miss Johnstone, Liverpool, 5 Nov.
1792.   (62:1054)

SMITH William, Chief Justice Lower Canada, d. Quebec, Dec.
1793.   (64:180)

SMITH William, d. Philadelphia, 1798.   (68:1086)

SMITH Sir William, Erdiston House, Worcester, m. Susan, dau.
Sir William George Parker, ex Plymouth, Canada, 1843.
(NS20:537)

SMITH William, s. James Smith, Bishopmill, Scotland, Whitehall,
St Thomas in the East, Jamaica, d. Jamaica, 17 Oct.1865.
(NS3/1:143)

SMITH William Castle, MD, Bideford, m. Sophia Caroline, 3rd
dau. William Jekyll Anstey, ex PMG, Jamaica, London, 19 Nov.
1846.   (NS27:195)

SMITH William Sidney, ex Havanna, HM Consul Trinidad de Cuba,
d. Trinidad de Cuba, 8 Jan.1865.   (NS2/18:388)

SMITH William Tabois m. Eliza Gay, eldest dau. Stephen
Hannaford, Jamaica, 7 April 1846.   (NS26:528)

SMITH Dr, 50 years resident, d. Jamaica, 31 July 1764.(33:415)

SMITH Mrs, w. Miles Smith, Sunderlandwick, Yorks., eldest dau.,
late Sir Digby Legard, Ganton, d. Blackhall, NJ, 11 Sep.1795.
(65:968)

SMITH Lt., 57th Reg., m. Miss Burrow, only dau. late James
Burrow, Councillor, NS, Halifax, NS, 27 Oct.1791.   (61:1157)

SMITH Rev. Prof., Queen's College, Canada, d. Garelochhead,
8 Aug.1856.   (NS2/1:390)

SMITH Maj., Prince Edward Co., Va., m. Charlotte B Brodie,
ex Preceptress Raleigh Academy, Williamsburgh, Granville
Co., America, 1812.   (81:188)

SMITH Miss, dau. Gen. Smith, m. Mr Mansfield, s. Lord Chief
Justice, Baltimore, 1810.   (80:86)

SMITH ..., dau. Maj. Astley Smith, 25th Reg., b. Montreal,
17 Sep.1865.   (NS2/19:635)

SMITHERS Deborah, w. Alfred Smithers, d. St John, NB, 11 June,
1845.   (NS24:214)

SMYTH Benjamin, b.1789, ex Colonial Sec. Cape Breton, & Naval
Officer Gen. Antigua & Bermuda, d. Westbury, Bucks., 27 Dec,
1840.   (NS15:330)

SMYTH E St George, Cap., 30th Reg., m. Marie Victoria
Harline de Sinier, only dau. Olivier Perrault de Sinier,
Montreal, 9 July 1867.   (NS3/2:383)

SMYTH Harriet, b.1838, 2nd dau. Thomas Sheppard Smyth,
Niagara Falls, gdau. late Lt. Col. Delatre, d. Fulham,
11 July 1859.   (NS2/9:201)

SMYTHE Cap., RE, d. Pa., 5 Jan.1842.   (NS18:332)

SMYTHSON James, ex NY, d.15 Aug.1775.

SNAGG Ann, w. Sir William Snagg, Chief Justice, d. Antigua,
16 Feb.1861.   (NS2/10:470)

SNAGG Anne Isabella, dau. late W Snagg, St Vincent, m. Rev.
H S Pollard, 2nd s. R B Pollard, Brompton, London, 15 May 1838.
                                                   (NS10:92)

SNAGG Sir William, Chief Justice Antigua & Montserrat, m.
Adeline, only ch. C H Okey, Antigua, Salisbury, 29 June 1865.
                                                 (NS2/19:235)

SNELL James, b.1795, surgeon, d. Kingston, St Vincent,
6 July 1850.   (NS34:331)

SNODGRASS ..., s. Lt. Col. J J Snodgrass, b. Govt. House,
Frederickton, NB, 1832.   (102:266)

SNOW Thomas Maitland, banker, eldest s. Thomas Snow, Franklyn,
m. Eliza, 2nd dau. late J P Nathan, Jamaica, Littleham,
27 Feb.1851.   (NS35:424)

SOBER John, Barbados, m. Penelope Blake, Sevenoaks, Kent,
6 Nov.1760.   (30:542)

SOCKETT George, s. late Rev. T Sockett, Petworth, Sussex, d.
Eramosa, Guelph, Canad, 6 Nov.1860.   (NS2/10:111)

SOMERFIELD Charles, Barbados, d.10 May 1758.   (28:244)

SOMERVILLE Rev. James, ex Prof. Theology, King's College,
Fredericton, NB, d. Brechin, 10 Sep.1852.   (NS38:545)

SOMERVILLE Mrs, w. Alexander Somerville, emigrated Liverpool
to Canad, July 1858, d. Quebec, 29 May 1859.   (NS2/9:197)

SONTAG Henrietta, b. Coblentz, 13 May 1805, vocalist &
musician, d. Mexico, 17 June 1854.   (NS42:197)

SOULBY Alfred, b.1814, 4th s. late Anthony Soulby, Crouchend,
Middlesex, d. San Francisco, 20 Sep.1850.   (NS35:110)

SOULEGRE ..., dau. Col. Soulegre, Antigua, m. Stephen
Theodore Janssen, 13 Dec.1750.   (20:570)

SOUTHERLAND Christiana, b.1800, dau. late Rev. James Coffin,
Linkinhorn, Cornwall, w. Edward Southerland, Fort Major, d.
Sydney, Cape Breton, 4 June 1852.   (NS38:211)

SOUTHWELL Rev. Henry George, ex Trinity College, Dublin, d.
Barbados, 25 Feb.1854.   (NS41:552)

SOUTHWELL Marcus Richmond, b.1828, s. Rev. M R Southwell,
St Albans, d. Montreal, 2 May 1860.   (NS2/8:643)

SPALDING Eliza Jane, yngs. dau. late Hinton Spalding, MD,
Kingston, Jamaica, m. John Shavel, Cap., 51st Reg. Madras
Native Inf., Munich, 23 Feb.1859.   (NS2/6:422)

SPALDING Helen, 2nd dau. Hinton Spalding, MD, m. William
R Myers, Spanish Town, Jamaica, 29 April 1845.   (NS24:189)

SPALDING Jane Rankin, b.1791, w. Hinton Spalding, St Andrews,
Jamaica, d. Elie, Fife, 19 May 1861.   (NS2/11:94)

SPALDING Robert, surgeon gen., Surry Co. Militia, d. Liguanea,
Jamaica, 17 June 1792.   (62:766)

SPALDING Stewart, Jamaica, m. Anne, dau. Charles Spalding,
merchant, Edinburgh, 29 July 1796.   (66:701)

SPAN Harriet, w. Samuel Span, Bristol, d. Trinidad, 3 Nov.
1809.   (79:1236)

SPAN John, merchant, Bristol, m. Dorothea, dau. Hugh Munro,
Carricou, Grenada, 2 Nov.1796.   (66:965)

SPARKE William, Islington, m. Agnes Prowse, dau. Ewen Stabb,
St Johns, NFD., St Ives, Cornwall, 6 July 1854.   (NS42:385)

SPARKS Jared, b. Wilmington, Conn., 10 May 1789, author &
historian, d.15 March 1866.   (NS3/1:755)

SPARKS Miss, London, m. Charles Hyatt, Jamaica, 24 May 1758.
(28:244)

SPARROW Robert Pennington, asst. surgeon, RN, 3rd s. late
R G Sparrow, Deal, m. Mary, 3rd dau. William Lightbourne,
Pagets, Bermuda, 22 Dec.1849.   (NS33:430)

SPEARE R, b.1782, Sec. Rear Adm. J E Douglas, d. Jamaica,
14 Nov.1815.   (86:181)

SPEARS William, d. St Lucia, 2 May 1794.   (64:767)

SPEDDING Charlotte Lucy, eldest dau. late J Spedding, m.
Gerald, s. late Nicholas Lockyer, Plymouth, Montreal,
18 Aug.1864.   (NS2/17:512)

SPEER Wilfred Dakin, Cap., 3rd Surrey Militia, d. Quebec, 1867.
                                                      (NS3/2:408)

SPENCE George, Chief Judge Hanover parish, d. Lucea, Hanover,
Jamaica, 30 Sep.1790.   (60:1213)

SPENCER Augustus Almeric, Cap., 43rd Light Inf., 3rd s. Lord
Churchill, m. Helen, 2nd dau. Maj. Gen. Sir Archibald
Campbell, Lt. Gov. NB, Government House, Fredericton, NB,
6 Feb.1836.   (NS5:544)

SPEYERS James, NY, m. Fanny, only dau. late Cap. George
Pigot, RN, Rudstone, Bridlington, 24 June 1841.   (NS16:312)

SPIER Thomas Thorneville, d. St Vincent, 7 Nov.1806. (77:277)

SPOONER John jr., ex Barbados, d. London, 6 April 1819.
                                                      (88:381)

SPOTSWOOD Col., Va., d.7 June 1740.   (10:413)

SPOTTISWOODE Thomson, Tobago, d. Falmouth, 24 Oct.1796.
                                                      (66:1059)

SPRAGGE Harriet Eliza, eldest dau. Vice Chancellor John
Godfrey Spragge, Toronto, m. Lt. Henry Fyers Turner, RE,
Toronto, 7 Sep.1864.   (NS2/17:647)

SPRAT Mrs, w. Mr Sprat, merchant, NFD, 2nd dau. Rev. Howell,
Yeovil, d. NFD., 1787.   (57:547)

SPROULL Andrew, merchant, Kingston, Jamaica, d. on passage
to Jamaica, 1802.   (72:785)

SPRING Thomas, farmer & nurseryman, Sheffield, d. Washington,
Pa., 1 Aug.1820.   (90:376)

SPRY William, Gov. Barbados, d.1772.   (42:495)

SPURING Richard sr., b.1767, d. Antigua, June 1804.   (74:784)

SQUIRE S J, ex attorney, Plymouth, d. Tortula, 9 Jan.1804.
                                                      (74:374)

SQUIRE Rev. W, Superintendent Weslayan Missions Eastern
Canada, d. Montreal, 17 Oct.1852.   (NS38:658)

STABB Agnes Prowse, dau. Ewen Stabb, St Johns, NFD., m.
William Sparke, Islington, St Ives, Cornwall, 6 July 1854.
                                                      (NS42:385)

STAFFORD Frederick, b.1822, 7th s. late Brabazon Stafford,
Dublin, d. Port of Spain, Trinidad, 5 Nov.1857.   (NS2/4:112)

STAHLSCHMIDT Thomas Lett, Victoria, Vancouver Island, m.
Harriett Nice, wid. Cap. E H King, 59th Reg., Victoria,
26 March 1863.   (NS2/15:96)

STANDBRIDGE Fanny, w. Mr Standbridge, 5th dau. late Rev.
George Lillington, Warwick, d. Philadelphia, May 1846.
(NS26:447)

STANDIFORD Mrs, w. English Standiford, d. Port Royal,
Martinique, 18 Oct.1800.   (71:275)

STANLEY Francis Sloane, Hants., m. Charlotte Amy, yngs. dau.
John Rose, Montreal, 15 Aug.1866.   (NS3/2:539)

STANLEY Lt Gen. Thomas, bro. Earl of Derby, d. Jamaica, 1779.
(50:50)

STANTON Dr James, d. Jamaica, 1790.   (60:1053)

STATTER Mary, eldest dau. late R Statter, Knowsley, m. James
Moore, Montreal, Huyton, Liverpool, 14 May 1840.   (NS14:89)

STAYNER Charles, Gov. Churchill Factory, Hudson Bay, m.
Sarah Elizabeth Bayliss, London, 5 Jan.1798.   (68:83)

STEBBINS Caroline, yngs. dau. late John Stebbins, NY, m.
John R Tilten, Rome, London, 27 May 1858.   (NS2/5:82)

STEDMAN Elizabeth, w. William Stedman, MD, d. St Croix,
20 Sep.1843.   (NS20:670)

STEDMAN Lucretia Gordon, eldest dau. William Stedman, MD,
St Croix, d. Portobello, Edinburgh, 1 March 1841.   (NS15:669)

STEDMAN William, MD, b.1764, Knight of Dannebrog, d. St Croix,
7 April 1844.   (NS21:670)

STEELE Charles James, b.1827, 2nd s. James Steele, London,
d. Ironshore Est., Jamaica, 7 Aug.1845.   (NS24:551)

STEELE Joshua, Councillor, Barbados, d. Barbados, Oct.1796.
(67:80)

STEEL William, Councillor, NS, d.1754.   (24:579)

STEELE Miss, yngr. dau. late Rev. Dr Steele, Jamaica, m.
Sir Thomas Ramsay of Balmain, 29 June 1809.   (79:676)

STEELE Mrs, dau. late Robert Burke, Prospect Lota, Co. Cork,
m. George Hyde, St Vincent, 7 Oct.1820.   (90;562)

STEENBERGEN Miss, ex St Kitts, m. Sir Thomas Durrant,
Scottow, Norfolk, 5 Oct.1799.   (69:900)

STEERS G H, shipbuilder, d. Brooklyn, USA, 25 Aug.1856.
(NS2/1:656)

STEHELIN Cap., RA, m. Miss French, Spanish Town, Jamaica,
Nov.1790.   (60:1213)

STEPHEN Miss, dau. late G Stephen, Grenada, m. Rear Adm. Sir
David Milne, 28 Nov.1819.   (89:563)

STEPHENS Catherine, w. Laurence Reade Stephens, d. Jamaica,
28 July 1818.   (88:469)

STEPHENS Catherine, yngs. dau. late Col. Stephens, St Lucia,
m. Rev. W J Heale, Berrow, Worcs., 28 Nov.1837.   (NS9:88)

STEPHENS Francis m. Polly Reade, NY, 1768.   (38:302)

STEPHENS Frances Young, eldest dau. William Stephens, St Kitts,
m. Robert Claxton, barrister, St Kitts, 26 Oct.1816. (86:622)

STEPHENS Thomas William, b.1754, clerk, d. St Jago de la Vega,
6 Sep.1800.   (70:1107)

STEPHEN William, b. Aberdeen, 1772, d. on passage from
Jamaica on board Orpheus, 7 July 1808.   (78:1039)

STEPHENS William C, Sec. Great Western Railway of Canada, 2nd
s. late Cap. Edward L Stephens, RN, m. Jessie Isabella, 4th
dau. late Edward Durham, Cape of Good Hope, Hamilton, Canada
West, 15 June 1858.   (NS2/5:304)

STEPHENS Zachariah, b.1718, Customs Controller Bridgetown
Barbados, d. Barbados, 16 June 1793.   (63:768)

STEPHENSON Daniel, b.1734, ex Bladensburg, America, merchant,
London, d.10 May 1818.   (88:572)

STEVENS George, b.1834, s. Mrs Stevens, Hoxton, merchant, d.
Castries, St Lucia, 18 Sep.1852.   (NS38:656)

STEVENS Henry, b.1833, s. Mrs Stevens, Hoxton, merchant, d.
Castries, St Lucia, 18 Sep.1852.   (NS38:656)

STEVENS Susan Gertrude, w. T Woodhouse Stevens, Philadelphia,
d. Tows, 30 Aug.1853.   (NS40:429)

STEVENSON Elizabeth, eldest dau. William Stevenson, Quebec,
m. Salway Browne, ex Cap., 68th Reg., s. late William Browne,
Herts., Quebec, 11 May 1848.   (NS30:314)

STEVENSON Rev. Henry James, b.1820, d. St Thomas in the Vale,
Jamaica, 10 Jan.1854.   (NS41:437)

STEVENSON Isabella, yngs. dau. late William James Stevenson,
Receiver Gen. Jamaica, m. Henry John Kemble, St Andrews,
Jamaica, 1 March 1851.   (NS35:545)

STEVENSON Justice, Judge Jamaica Supreme Court, m. Caroline
Octavia, yngs. dau. late Joseph Seymour Biscoe, Pendhill,
Surrey, Barnwood, 9 June 1852.   (NS38:195)

STEVENSON Mary Charlotte, b.1813, w. Justice Stevenson, d.
Spanish Town, Jamaica, 16 Dec.1850.   (NS35:334)

STEVENSON Mary Laurence, wid. William James Stevenson, Receiver
Gen. Jamaica, d. Clifton, 27 Feb.1850.   (NS33:450)

STEWART Alexander, Customs Collector Barbados, d. on passage
to Barbados, 27 Sep.1848.   (NS30:670)

STEWART Alexander, b.1793, Admiralty Court Judge NS, d.Halifax,
NS, 1 Jan.1865.   (NS2/18:258)

STEVENS Rev. B Bridges, military chaplain, s. late Rev.
Thomas Stevens, Panfield, Essex, m. Elizabeth, dau. Lt.Col.
Nelles, 4th Lincoln Militia, Upper Canada, Grimsby, Upper
Canada, Sep.1820.   (91:180)

STEVENS Isaac, merchant, d. Jamaica, 1791.   (61:1065)

STEVENS John, merchant, ex London, late New Providence,
Bahamas, d. Ga., 29 Aug.1820.   (91:91)

STEVENS Josiah, WI, m. Jane Maria Holdford, London, 13 March
1752.   (22:191)

STEVENSON James, d. Grenada, 24 June 1795.   (65:879)

STEWART Lt. Col. Allan, ex NC Highlanders, d.Invernahyce,
2 April 1793.   (63:378)

STEWART Charles, b.1725, ex Receiver Gen. Customs America,
d. Edinburgh, 27 Nov.1797.   (68:443)

STEWART Charles Augustus, Charleston, SC, m. Miss Powell,
dau. Col. Powell, 29 July 1769.   (39:414)

STEWART Charles, Llandovery, Custos St Anne Jamaica, d.
30 June 1854.   (NS42:314)

STEWART Charles E, 5th s. T A Stewart, Douro, Canada West, m.
Charlotte Mary Jane, 2nd dau. late Cap. F W Ellis, RN,
Southwold, Suffolk, 9 Aug.1860.   (NS2/9:318)

STEWART Charles, bro. Mr Stewart, London, d. Queen Anne Co.,
Md., 1803.   (73:1254)

STEWART C, b.1760, Attorney Gen. PEI, d. Charlottetown, PEI,
6 Jan.1813.   (83:490)

STEWART Duncan, b.1796, Attorney Gen. Bermuda, d. Bermuda,
9 Feb.1861.   (NS2/10:469)

STEWART James, Judge Advocate Gen. Bengal, m. Johanna Maria
Murray, Jamaica, 11 Dec.1777.   (47:611)

STEWART James Affleck, b.1840, yngr. s. Henry Stewart, St Fort,
Fife, d. Brantford, Canada West, 15 May 1867.   (NS3/4:115)

STEWART John, b.1769, ex President, Bermuda, Customs Collector
Bermuda, d. London, 3 Feb.1832.   (102:185)

STEWART John, Speaker NFD Assembly, NFD Vice Armiralty Court
Marshal, d. PEI, 22 June 1834.   (104:558)

STEWART Cap. Kenneth, ex NC Highland Reg., d. Edinburgh, 1814.
                                                     (84:609)

STEWART K, Comm. HMS Ringdove, bro. Earl of Galloway, m. Mary
Caroline, only dau. Sir Charles Fitzroy, niece Duke of Richmond, PEI, 9 July 1841.   (NS16:422)

STEWART Maria Augusta Catherine Campbell, dau. Alexander
Stewart, MD, Inspector Gen. Army Hospitals, m. Rowland
Webster, Paymaster, 72nd Highlanders, Barbados, 24 April
1851.   (NS36:78)

STEWART Mary, eldest dau. Walter George Stewart, Island Sec.,
m. Cap. Barker, RA, ADC Gov., Spanish Town, Jamaica,
16 March 1852.   (NS37:612)

STEWART Mary Elizabeth, dau. Rev. Thomas Stewart, Kingston,
m. Henry Westmoreland, Kingston, Jamaica, 30 April 1859.
                                                        (NS2/7:79)

STEWART Peter, b.1724, Chief Justice PEI, d. PEI, 10 Nov.1805.
                                                        (76:182)

STEWART Peter D, ex Lt. Col., RA, s. Charles Stewart, ex
Attorney Gen. PEI, d. Springbank, PEI, 1 Nov.1867.(NS3/2:830)

STEWART Robert Farquhar Shaw, s. late Sir Michael Shaw
Stewart, Ardgowan, Renfrew, m. Isabella Jane, eldest dau.
Charles W Warner, Attorney Gen. Trinidad, Port of Spain,
Trinidad, 10 Feb.1859.   (NS2/6:534)

STEWART Sarah, 4th dau. late Rev. S H Stewart, Trelawney,
m. Rev. T Garrett, Vere, Spanish Town, Jamaica, 8 July 1854.
                                                        (NS42:385)

STEWART Susan, 2nd dau. Montgomerie Stewart, niece Earl of
Galloway, niece Bishop of Quebec, m. Rev. Edmund Willoughby S
Sewell, 2nd s. Chief Justice Sewell, Quebec, 12 Nov.1828.
                                                        (99.80)

STEWART Susan, w. W G Stewart, Island Sec., d. Spanish Town,
Jamaica, 25 Jan.1856.   (NS45:434)

STEWART W, d. New London, 1798.   (68:1086)

STEWART William, 3rd s. William Stewart, Shambelly, d.Jamaica,
20 June 1799.   (69:812)

STEWART William, b.1768, ex Inverkeithing & Hammersmith, d.
Stamford, Upper Canada, 3 July 1838.   (NS10:343)

STEWART William, PEI, m. Annie Eliza, dau. late Henry Green,
Titley, Herts., Pavenham, 4 May 1844.   (NS21:646)

STEWART Cap. W L, Royal Reg., s. late Lt. Col. Stewart, HEICS,
m. Eliza Saunders, dau. George Shore, Rosehall, Fredericton,
NB, 19 April 1849.   (NS32:84)

STEWART Col., 1st WI Reg., d. Barbados, 21 Oct.1799. (70:283)

STEWART Mrs, ex St Vincent, d. London, 23 Aug.1820. (90:283)

STEWART Mrs, w. Dr Alexander Stewart, d. Dominica, 11 May 1844.
                                                        (NS22:110)

STILES Olive Ann, wid. Cap. J W Stiles, Bengal Army, d.
Jamaica, 21 July 1840.   (NS14:676)

STIRLING Rev. John Mayne, eldest s. William Stirling,
Harbor Grace, NFD., d. Maugerville, Fredericton, NB,
1 July 1850.   (NS34:446)

STIRLING Thomas Cochrane, b.1807, s. late Rev. Alexander
Stirling, Tillicoutry, Clackmannan, d. Mexico, Sep.1833.
                                                    (104:343)
STIRLING William, d. Jamaica, 1791.   (61:186)

STIVEN Rebecca, dau. late Alexander Stiven, Tobago, m. J C
Johnstone, Theater Royal, Edinburgh, Aberdeen, 1801.(71:1050)

STODDART George Alexander, St Kitts, d. NY, 31 Aug.1796.
                                                    (67:252)

STOGDON John, d. Martha Brae, Jamaica, 19 Oct.1792. (62:1220)

STOKES Mrs Elizabeth, b.1733, wid. Anthony Stokes, ex Chief
Justice Ga., d. London, 18 July 1818.   (88:187)

STOKES Cap. James, d. Jamaica, 1791.   (61:1065)

STOKES Mary, only dau. Rev. Joseph Stokes, Charlestown,
America, m. Mr Philips, London, 8 April 1790.   (60:371)

STOKES Mary, London, yngs. dau. late Anthony Stokes, ex Chief
Justice Ga., m. Robert Butler, 13 Oct.1800.   (70:1003)

STONE Ebenezer, b.1682, d. Newton, NE, 1754.   (24:579)

STONE Gen. John Hoskins, ex Gov.Md., d. Annapolis, 1804.
                                                    (74:1174)

STONE Mrs Margaret, b.1757, d. Harrisburg, Pa., 3 Nov.1867.
                                                  (NS3/2:830)

STONE Rev. William Murray, Bishop of Md., d. Salisbury,
Somerset Co., USA, 25 Feb.1838.   (NS9:664)

STONE ..., dau. William A Stone, b. Ireland Island, Bermuda,
18 May 1864.   (NS2/17:104)

STONEY Rev. Joseph, Trelawney, Jamaica, d. July 1789.(59:955)

STORER Anthony Gilbert, Purley Park, Berks., & Westmoreland,
Jamaica, d. Nassau, New Providence, 13 June 1818.   (88:373)

STORER Charlotte, 3rd dau. late Anthony Gilbert Storer,
Berks., d. Jamaica, 7 July 1831.   (101:286)

STORER Thomas, d. Golden Square, Westmoreland, Jamaica,
11 July 1793.   (63:1149)

STORER Miss, dau. Thomas Storer, Golden Square, m. John
Campbell, Jamaica, 10 March 1774.   (44:141)

STOREY Margaret Gillies, dau. Robert Gillies, Arcot,
Northumberland, m. S Barrett, Jamaica, 7 March 1812. (82:288)

STORMONTH James, surgeon, d. St Mary, Jamaica, 1 Oct.1801.
                                                  (71:1211)

STORY Joseph, b.1779, US Supreme Court Judge, d. Boston, USA, 10 Sep.1845.   (NS24:536)

STOTHARD Cap. Matthew, b.1779, d. St Croix, 28 May 1817.
(87:183)

STOTHERD ..., s. Cap. Stotherd, RE, b. Montreal, 26 March 1864.   (NS2/16:648)

STOTT William sr., merchant planter, ex Kingston & Port Royal, Jamaica, d.1 Nov.1809.   (79:1175)

STOTT Mrs, wid., d. Jamaica, Jan.1784.   (54:395)

STOUT H E, b.1778, s. Mr Stout, Lynn, surgeon, d. WI, 26 Feb.1799.   (69:716)

STRACHAN Archibald, b.1782, d. Manchioneal, Jamaica, 13 Nov. 1828.   (99:190)

STRACHAN Charlotte Mary Elizabeth Brace, only dau. Rev. William Strachan, Christ Church, Nassau, m. Lt. Edward Hinton East, RA, Nassau, New Providence, 5 Nov.1850.(NS35:195)

STRACHAN Rev. John, b. Aberdeen, 12 April 1778, Bishop of Toronto, d. Toronto, 1 Nov.1867.   (NS3/5:105)

STRACHAN Simpson, d. Mortendue, Grenada, 20 Oct.1801. (71:83)

STRAKER Thomas James, b. Barbados, 1782, Customs Controller Barbados & St Lucia, d. on passage to Lisbon on Duke of Kent, 6 March 1814.   (84:412)

STRANGWAYS ..., dau. Cap. Fox Strangways, b. St John, NB, 20 May 1867.   (NS3/4:98)

STRATHER William Carlisle, only s. E Strather, Nevis, Lt. Paymaster & Interpreter, 1st Grenadier Reg., Bombay, m. Charlotte Anne Seymour, yngs. dau. late Lt. Gen. Ormsby, Kotergherry, Neilgherry Hills, 2 May 1837.   (NS8:528)

STRATTON D, b.1782, s. J Stratton, d. Bennington, Vermont, 17 Nov.1802.   (72:1225)

STRATTON Thomas, MD, surgeon, RN, m. Elizabeth Mary, eldest dau. William Winder, MD, Montreal, 29 Dec.1847.   (NS29:421)

STRATTON ..., dau. Dr Stratton, RN, b. Montreal, 8 Feb.1849.
(NS31:418)

STREET Charles, ex Bath, d. on passage from WI, Oct.1799.
(70:82)

STREET Jeremy, ex Jamaica, d. London, 21 Sep.1781.   (51:443)

STREET John Ambrose, ex Attorney Gen. NB, Fredericton, NB, d. St John, NB, 3 May 1865.   (NS2/19:119)

STREET Thomas George, b.1824, King's College, Fredericton, NB, eldest s. J A Street, Fredericton, d. London, 29 Dec.1846.
(NS25:216)

STRETTON Henry, b.1808, 2nd s. William T Stretton, London,
Ramsgate, d. New Orleans, 1 Sep.1852.   (NS38:661)

STRICKLAND Frederick, b.1820, s. Sir George Strickland, d.
White Mountains, NH, 31 Oct.1849.   (NS33:342)

STRICKLAND Robert Alexander, Duoro, Canada West, eldest s.
Maj. Strickland, m. Caroline Charlotte, eldest dau. Cap. F W
Ellis, RN, Southwold, Suffolk, 25 March 1856.   (NS45:514)

STRODE Miss, dau. Nathaniel Strode, St Croix, d. Bristol,
25 Dec.1813.   (84:96)

STRUTH Charles, s. Sir W Struth, St Vincent, d. NY, 1834.
                                                    (104:671)

STUART Alexander, MD, b.1735, d. Grenada, Aug.1797. (67:1069)

STUART Mrs Anne, b. America, w. Rev. James Stuart, ex Georgetown, SC, d. Lyme Regis, Dorset, 12 July 1805.   (75:775)

STUART Caroline E, dau. John Stuart, Windsor, Canada West, m.
Alfred, 2nd s. A W Wyndham, Blandford, Dorset, Toronto,
1 June 1859.   (NS2/9:182)

STUART Caroline Sarah Georgina, dau. William Henry Stuart,
Lennoxville, Canada East, m. Rev. William Arnold Matthews,
Laughton, Kirkton in Lindsay, 11 Aug.1866.   (NS3/2:402)

STUART Henry, bro. Col. Stuart, Superintent Indian Affairs,
ex America, d. London, 21 May 1783.   (53:454)

STUART James, b. Charleston, SC, 25 Dec.1728, d. Berwick on
Tweed, 11 April 1844.   (NS22:101)

STUART Sir James, b.1780, 3rd s. Rev. John Stuart, Kingston,
Quebec, Chief Justice Lower Canada, d. Quebec, 16 July 1853.
                                                    (NS40:531)

STUART Julia Maria, yngr. dau. James Cuthbert, Seignior,
Berthier, Canada East, w. Simeon Henry Stuart, Royal Canadian
Rifles, eldest s. Sir Simeon Stuart, d. Brockville, Canada
West, 10 Jan.1848.   (NS29:566)

STUART Moses, b.1781, Prof. Theology, d. Andover, Mass.,1852.
                                                    (NS37:429)

STUART Robert, b.1770, 2nd s. John Stuart, Birkenburn, Banff,
ex Port Morant, Jamaica, d. Hazely Heath, Hants., 29 June 1813.
                                                     (83:666)

STUART Rev. Dr William, Bishop of St David's, m. Miss Penn,
dau. late Thomas Penn, Proprietor Pa., 3 May 1796.   (66:438)

STUART ..., s. Col. J Ramsay Stuart, 21st Fusiliers, b. Bush
Hall, Barbados, 10 June 1864.   (NS2/17:231)

STUBBS Robert Baynes, 2nd s. late Richmond Robert Stubbs,
surgeon, Bengal, d. Welford, NA, 10 March 1852.   (NS37:632)

STURGESS Charles William, HMS Cornwallis, m. Emma Louisa,
eldest dau. Martin J Wilkins, Solicitor Gen. NS, Banff,
28 Feb.1861.   (NS2/10:455)

SUCH Georgina, w. James Such, ex London, d. NY, 5 Aug.1854.
(NS42:528)

SUCKLING George, Attorney Gen. Quebec, d.1769.   (39:270)

SUTHERLAND Robert, St Vincent, d. Hastings, 1828.   (98:476)

SUTTON George, America, d. Montpellier, France, 1788.(58:751)

SUTTON Jane Helen Melville, only ch. Gilbert Sutton, Customs
Collector Bermuda, m. Sir Charles Thomas Jones, HMS Harrier,
Bermuda, 1817.   (88:272)

SUTTON Margaret Frederica Georgina, dau. J H T Manners Sutton,
Lt. Gov. NB, d. Govt. House, Fredericton, 5 April 1858.
(NS2/4:682)

SUTTON Lt., 86th Reg., s. Lord George Sutton, d. Tobago,1781.
(51:442)

SWABY Ann Margaret Eleanor, elder dau. Joseph James Swaby,
Kilnsey, Yorks., gdau. Joseph James Swaby, ex Jamaica, m.
Frederick Peat, Jamaica, 5 March 1842.   (NS17:661)

SWABEY Caroline, 2nd dau. William Swabey, PEI, ex Royal Horse
Artillery, m. Henry Beaumont Cattley, Doctors Commons,
London, 12 June 1854.   (NS42:294)

SWAIN Catherina, b.1788, w. William Swain, mo. P W Swain,
Devonport, d. Auburn, NY, 13 Jan.1853.   (NS39:330)

SWAINE Harry, b.1818, yngs. s. T Swaine, MD, Rochford, Essex,
d. Jamaica, 1840.   (NS13:559)

SWANADITHIT, b.1800, last of the Boethicks, d. St John, NB,
6 June 1829.   (99:477)

SWANN Marianne Hamilton, b.1827, dau. John M Trew, Archdeacon
of the Bahamas, w. Rev. Robert Swann, Christchurch, d. Nassau,
New Providence, 12 May 1856.   (NS2/1:255)

SWARTON William, Jamaica, d.30 June 1762.   (32:448)

SWINBURNE Henry, yngs. s. late Sir John Swinburne, Capheaton,
Northumberland, d. Trinidad, April 1803.   (73:479)

SWINEY Matthew, Customs Collector, d. Savanna la Mar,
24 Dec.1792.   (62:279)

SWINHOE William George, Rifle Brigade, s. Gen. Swinhoe, Bengal
Army, m. Elizabeth Harnett Reynolds, 2nd dau. Thomas Reynolds,
Montreal, ex Snaresbrook, Essex, Montreal, 17 March 1864.
(NS2/16:651)

SWINHOE ..., dau. W G Swinhoe, Rifle Brigade, b. Montreal,
14 May 1865.   (NS2/19:103)

SWYMMER Anthony Langley, d. Jamaica, 1760.   (30:154)

SYDSERF Walter, Antigua, d.13 March 1760.   (30:154)

SYLVESTER James, Jamaica, d. Oct.1757.   (27:577)

SYM Dr Robert, d. Montreal, 3 Sep.1807.   (77:1075)

SYMES William Leigh, Offord Hall, Northants., d. Oxford Est.,
St Mary, Jamaica, 20 Dec.1796.   (67:350)

SYMPSON Dr Archibald, Assemblyman, d. Jamaica, 1791.(61:1065)

SYMPSON Edward, b.1812, ex RN, d. Monymusk, Jamaica, 1846.
                                                 (NS25:670)

SYNGE William Webb Follett, British Attache, m. Henrietta
Mary, yngs. dau. Col. Wainwright, USMC, British Legation,
Washington, 27 Jan.1853.   (NS39:426)

TAAFFE Dr, d. Jamaica, 1791.   (61:971)

TABOR Charles Clifton, 15th Reg., m. Ada, yngs. dau. John R
Partelow, Auditor Gen. NB, Fredericton, NB, 8 Oct.1862.
                                                 (NS2/13:770)

TACHE Sir Etienne Pascal, Prime Minister Canada, d. St Thomas,
Quebec, 30 July 1865.   (NS2/19:396)

TADDY Charles, 2nd s. Rev. John Taddy, Northill, Beds., m.
Margaret, 2nd dau. late George Barclay, Barbados, Clifton,
8 May 1843.   (NS20:87)

TAGGART Robert, d. Philadelphia, 1798.   (68:1086)

TAILER William, Lt. Gov. NE, d. Dorchester, NE, 1 March 1732.
                                                 (2:724)

TAIT George, s. James Tait, exciseman, Glasgow, d. Sullivan's
Island, Charleston, SC, 30 Aug.1801.   (71:1053)

TALBOT Henry, Barbados, m. Miss Craddock, Bridgenorth,
3 Dec.1758.   (28:611)

TALFOURD Froome, bro. late Judge Talfourd, Superintendent
Indian Affairs, m. Jane, 2nd dau. Allan Thornton, Whitby,
Sarnia, Canada West, 17 Sep.1857.   (NS2/3:556)

TALLMADGE Julia, eldest dau. late Maj. Tallmadge, NY, m.
Rev. W R Ogle, s. late John Ogle, Meeson Hall, Shropshire,
Nice, 7 Feb.1850.   (NS33:529)

TANEY Roger B, b.1768, Chief Justice US, d. Washington,
12 Oct.1864.   (NS2/17:801)

TAPPAN Susan, sis. Col. Aspinwall, US Consul London, w. Lewis
Tappan, d. Brooklyn, NY, 24 March 1853.   (NS39:563)

TASKER Benjamin, President, Va., d.Annapolis, Md.,1768.
                                                 (38:446)

TATE Rev. Matthew, b.1749, d. Beaufort, SC, 6 Oct.1795.
                                                 (66:524)

TATHAM William, s. late John Tatham, London, d. Kingston,
Jamaica, 18 Feb.1794.   (64:384)

TATHAM Col. W, d. Richmond, Va., 22 Feb.1819.   (88:376)

TATTNALL Josiah, ex Councillor, Bahamas, d.27 May 1813.(83:592)

TATTNALL Maria Frances, wid. John Mulrynet, ex Bonadventure,
Ga., d. Jersey, 13 Oct.1842.   (NS19:109)

TATTNALL, w. Josiah Tattnall, Bahamas, d. London, 12 March
1794.   (64:285)

TAWS John, planter, d. Lady Mayo's Est., St John, Jamaica,
1800.   (70:905)

TAYLOR Alexander, Assemblyman, Nassau, New Providence, d.
Edinburgh, 1801.   (71:576)

TAYLOR Charles, barrister, Grenada, d.1774.   (45:46)

TAYLOR Duncan Norton, Lt., RA, eldest s. Cap. Norton Taylor,
RN, London, m. Harriet Liddell, only dau. Hugh W Hoyles,
Attorney Gen. NFD., St Johns, NFD., 19 Oct.1864. (NS2/17:780)

TAYLOR Eliza, 2nd dau. John Taylor, Good Hope, Jamaica, m.
Cap. William Grove Annesley, 6th Reg., 4th s. late Gen. A G
Annesley, Co. Cork, St Michael, Port Royal Mountains,
Jamaica, 8 March 1866.   (NS3/1:737)

TAYLOR Fennings, Councillor, m. Georgina Rosalie, yngs. dau.
late J G Nanton, St Vincent, Toronto, 8 Sep.1858. (NS2/5:525)

TAYLOR G L, m. Sybilla, dau. late Jacob Neufville, Jamaica,
8 June 1820.   (90:635)

TAYLOR George, b.1812, nephew Arthur Foulks, Jamaica, d.
Jamaica, 25 Oct.1833.   (104:118)

TAYLOR George Cavendish, ex 95th Reg., m. Louisa, 2nd dau.
Col. Charles Carroll, Md., gggdau. Charles Carroll of
Carrollton, Baltimore, Md., 28 Dec.1858.   (NS2/6:313)

TAYLOR Harriett Elizabeth, eldest dau. late George Taylor,
London, m. Rev. J Ellegood, St Ann, Montreal, 3rd s. late
Jacob Ellegood, Dumfries, Fredericton, NB, 10 Sep.1849.
                                                    (NS32:638)

TAYLOR Henry, ex Chibburn, Northumberland, d. Savannah,
America, 19 Jan.1841.   (NS15:670)

TAYLOR Sir John, d. Kingston, Jamaica, 6 May 1786.   (56:619)

TAYLOR Cap. John Duncombe, 46th Reg., m. Miss Van Der Horst,
2nd dau. Elias Van Der Horst, US Consul, 5 May 1798. (68:533)

TAYLOR John Duncombe, b. Antigua, ex Clifton, Glocs., d. Sion
Hill, Antigua, 28 Feb.1835.   (105:558)

TAYLOR Margaret, dau. late N Taylor, Antigua, m. Rev. John
Halton, Chester, 1822.   (92:88)

TAYLOR Mary, 3rd dau. George N Taylor, Barbados, m. James R
Holligan, barrister, West Teignmouth, 3 Dec.1853. (NS41:308)

TAYLOR Richard Cowling, b. Hinton, Suffolk, 18 Jan.1789,
geologist, d. Philadelphia, 26 Oct.1851.   (NS37:201)

TAYLOR Simon, b.1740, Assemblyman, d. Port Royal, Jamaica,
14 April 1813.   (83:660)

TAYLOR William, London, m. Miss Van Cortlandt, dau. Maj.
Van Cortlandt, Halifax, NS, Cowley, 6 May 1791.   (61:488)

TAYLOR Zachary , b. Orange Co., Va., 24 Nov.1786, President
USA, d. Washington, 9 July 1850.   (NS34:321)

TAYLOR Mr, s. Mr Taylor, merchant, NY, s. in law Gov. Clinton,
d. Falmouth, England, 1791.   (61:1162)

TAYLOR Mrs, w. John Taylor, Jamaica, d. London, 1803. (73:89)

TAYNTON Nathaniel, Attorney Gen. Grenada, d. Grenada, Nov.
1810.   (81:187)

TAYNTON Mrs, wid. Nathaniel Taynton, Attorney Gen. Grenada, m.
T Maitland, physician, Carricou, 31 July 1813.   (83:620)

TAZEWELL Littlejohn Waller, b. Williamsburg, Va., 1775, ex
Gov. Va., d. Norfolk, Va., 6 May 1860.   (NS2/10:336)

TELFER Mr, ex Trelawney, Jamaica, d. London, 30 Oct.1812.
                                                  (82:498)

TEMPLE Sir John, HM Consul, d. NY, Nov.1798.   (68:1152)

TEMPLE Miss, dau. John Temple, HM Consul, NY, m. Lindal
Winthrop, Boston, NE, 1786.   (56:906)

TEMPLE Matilda Margaret, b. Paris, 4 Jan.1824, yngs. dau. Sir
Grenville Temple & his first wife Elizabeth, dau. George
Watson, Mass.   (94:382)

TERRITT Sarah, b.1757, w. Dr Territt, sis. Crawford Ricketts,
Kingston, Jamaica, d.21 Sep.1802.   (72:886)

TERRITT William, Vice Admiralty Court Judge Bermuda, m. Ann
Catherine Parkyns, niece Vice Admiral Sir John Borlase
Warren, Bermuda, 13 Jan.1810.   (80:383)

TESSIER Peter German m. Jane Caroline, 3rd dau. Robert Carter,
RN, Assemblyman, St Johns, NFD., 4 Feb.1849.   (NS31:534)

THACKER Mrs Ann, w. William Thacker, Penn, Staffs., only dau.
Col. William Henry Mills, Peedee, SC, d.21 Dec.1806. (77:89)

THADY Miss, sis. Col. Thady, m. Cap. Byrne, NY, 1763.(33:313)

THARP Benjamin H, Hampton, Jamaica, d.24 July 1851.(NS36:442)

THARP Thomas Reid, only ch. late Benjamin H Tharp, d. Jamaica,
3 Sep.1851.   (NS36:553)

THARP William, Lt. Col. St James Militia Reg., d. Windsor
Castle Est., Montego Bay, Jamaica, 2 March 1809.   (79:677)

THESIGER Julia Selina, dau. Sir F Thesiger, m. Lt. Col. J E
W Inglis, 32nd Reg., s. late Bishop of NS, London, 17 July 1851.
                                                  (NS36:423)

THESIGER Maj. Gen., d. Quebec, Aug.1812.   (82:400)

THIBOU Esther, Antigua, m. George Blount, London, 2 Jan.1753.
                                                  (23:51)

THOM James, b. Ayrshire, 1799, sculptor, d. NY, 17 April 1850.
                                                  (NS34:98)

THOM John, land surveyor, bro. late Robert Thom, HM Counsul
Ningpo, d. Clarendon, Jamaica, 15 May 1851.   (NS36:100)

THOMAS Abigail Jane, wid. William Carter Thomas, Barbados,
d. Clifton, 7 July 1846.   (NS26:331)

THOMAS Frances Brooking, only dau. Henry P Thomas, merchant,
m. R J Dacres, Cap., RA, s. late Vice Adm. Sir R Dacres,
St Johns, NFD., 3 Nov.1840.   (NS15:90)

THOMAS James, b.1675, d. America, April 1804.   (75:281)

THOMAS John Henry, eldest s. Grant E Thomas, President,
Barbados, m. Elizabeth Williama, yngs. dau. William Murray,
Colonial Bank, Barbados, 4 July 1865.   (NS2/19:373)

THOMAS Richard Morris, ex President, Virgin Islands, d.
Heddington, 10 Sep.1843.   (NS20:444)

THOMAS Robert, ex merchant, Grenada, d. Liverpool, 1801.
                                                  (71:89)

THOMAS S jr., ex Ordnance storekeeper, Bytown, Canada West,
d.30 Dec.1850.   (NS35:215)

THOMAS William Lloyd, b.1837, only s. John Thomas, Clydach
Iron Works, Brecon, d. Barbados, 27 Nov.1858.   (NS2/6:216)

THOMASON James B, s. Thomas Thomason, HM Consul, Tortula, m.
Maria Bourke, St Croix, 15 Oct.1791.   (61:1157)

THOMPSON Alexander, NY, d.1770.   (40:591)

THOMSON Alexander Dingwall, Cap., 16th Reg., s. Lt. Col.
Thomson, m. Mary Ann, dau. John Duffus, Halifax, NS, 17 Aug.
1864.   (NS2/17:512)

THOMSON Cap. Andrew, 2nd WI Reg., only s. James Thomson,
baker, Edinburgh, d. Trinidad, 15 Dec.1800.   (71:275)

THOMPSON Archibald, merchant, d. Liguenea, Jamaica, 11 Nov.
1792.   (62:1220)

THOMSON C, Attorney Gen. St Kitts, eldest s. late C Thomson,
m. Maria, only dau. N Byrne, London, 10 Jan.1832. (102:78)

THOMPSON Catherine Alicia, 3rd dau. Maj. G A Thompson, 85th
King's Light Inf., m. C W Rue, MD, Hudson Bay Co., Toronto,
25 Feb.1860.   (NS2/8:402)

THOMSON Charles, b.1793, ex Attorney Gen. Leeward Islands,
d. Liverpool, 19 March 1848.   (NS29:562)

THOMPSON James, ex planter, Barbados, m. L Watson, London,
13 Nov.1781.   (53:541)

THOMPSON James, Halifax, NS, m. Margaret Maria, dau. late
George Thomas Baxter, step dau. James Anderton, London,
14 May 1850.   (NS34:200)

THOMSON Jane, dau. Archibald Thomson, Jamaica, m. Maj. Henry
Bowyer Lane, RA, Greenham, Berks., 2 Feb.1825.   (95:94)

THOMPSON Rev. J H, Prof. Theology, Bishop's College, m. Mary
Lavinia, yngs. dau. James Waldron, Wivelscombe, Somerset,
Lennoxville, Canada, 14 July 1859.   (NS2/7:302)

THOMPSON Margaret, dau. John Thompson, Spring Garden, m.
James Bruce, Lt. Gov. Jamaica, Edinburgh, 1798.   (68:1147)

THOMSON Peter, eldest s. Baillie John Thomson, Burntisland,
d. Kingston, Jamaica, 11 Feb.1803.   (72:374)

THOMSON Robert, Jamaica, m. Jane, dau. late Robert Kennedy,
Daljarrock, Maybole, 4 Jan.1796.   (66:80)

THOMSON Robert, b.1738, ex Gov. Leeward Islands, President,
St Kitts, d. London, 2 March 1816.   (86:372)

THOMSON Robert Craig, d. Manchester, Jamaica, 9 Feb.1854.
                                                     (NS41:554)

THOMPSON Tannatt Houstoun, Dep. Comm. Gen., d. Toronto,
3 Feb.1851.   (NS35:455)

THOMPSON William, Jamaica, d.4 Nov.1767.   (37:563)

THOMPSON Rev. William, 3rd s. Ebenezer Thompson, Norwood,
Surrey, d. Christieville, Upper Canada, 15 June 1848.
                                                     (NS30:325)

THOMPSON Miss, Tooting, Surrey, m. Archibald Gloster, Attorney
Gen. Trinidad, 22 Oct.1806.   (76:978)

THOMPSON ..., dau. Cap. Thompson, RA, b. Montreal, 4 June
1865.   (NS2/19:105)

THOMKINS Harriet, b.1813, 2nd dau. Rev. F Woodcock, Moreton,
Hereford, d. NFD., 30 Nov.1833.   (104:343)

THORBURN Helen, eldest dau. Alexander Thorburn, ex Alexandria,
Egypt, m. John Higgenson, Douro, Canada West, 5 Dec.1861.
                                                    (NS2/12:220)

THORN Louisa, dau. late William Thorn, Turnham Green, m.
Abel, yngs. s. George Easton, Strathfieldsaye, Hants.,
Broadway, NY, 5 July 1860.   (NS2/9:314)

THORN Nathaniel, s. Rev. T Thorn, Gloucester, d. St Lucia,
Jamaica, 1814.   (84:197)

THORNBURY C, b.1787, s. Rev. N Thornbury, Avening, Glocs.,
d. Port Royal, Jamaica, 1813.   (83:595)

THORNHILL John, mechanic, d. Philadelphia, 1783.   (53:181)

THORNHILL Tim, d. Barbados, 21 April 1813.   (83:660)

THORNLEY Montague, Lt. Col. Royal WI Rangers, d.St Lucia, April 1807.   (77:682)

THORNTON Abraham, settled America 1818, d.1820.   (90:475)

THORNTON Daniel, ex St Kitts, d.21 July 1777.   (48:335)

THORNTON Jane, 2nd dau. Allan Thornton, Whitby, m. Froome Talfourd, bro. late Judge Talfourd, Superintendent Indian Affairs, d.Sarnie, Canada West, 17 Sep.1857.   (NS2/3:556)

THORNTON John Paul, Colonial Sec., 3rd s. late Thomas Thornton, Constantinople, nephew Sir Edward Thornton, m. Frances Sarah, eldest dau. Maj. Lawrence Graeme, Lt. Gov. Tobago, Tobago, 25 May 1846.   (NS26:196)

THORNTON Robert, staff surgeon, m. Mary, dau. late William Wealands Robson, Bishopwearmouth, Kingston, Jamaica, 24 March 1860.   (NS2/8:507)

THORNTON ..., dau. Robert Thornton, staff surgeon, b. Corosal, British Honduras, 8 Dec.1860.   (NS2/10:329)

THORPE John, Chippenham Hall, Cambridge, merchant, d. Jamaica, 1804.   (74:1175)

THOYER Arodi, b.1773, d. Boston, NE, 1789.   (59:955)

TIBBETS Cap., master brigantine Nancie of Tobago, d. Portsmouth, America, Dec.1798.   (69:165)

TICHBONE Thomas, Jamaica, m. Miss Jones, Mitcham, Surrey, 1758.
                                                           (28:94)

TICKELL Richard, eldest s. late R Tickell, d. Upper Canada, 16 Nov.1795.   (65:1112)

TIDY Mrs, dau. late Chief Justice Pinder, Barbados, wid. Col. Francis Skelly Tidy, 24th Reg., d. Portsmouth, Hants., 12 March 1849.   (NS31:666)

TIDYMAN Dr Philip, b.1778, Charleston, SC, d. Aberdeen, 11 May 1850.   (NS34:229)

TIERNEY James, d. Kingston, Jamaica, 18 July 1784.   (53:797)

TILLETT Marianne Ellen, 2nd dau. John Edward Tillett, ex Liverpool, m. Henry Curle, Barbados, London, 23 Dec.1848.
                                                         (NS31:311)

TILTEN John R, Rome, m. Caroline, yngs. dau. late John Stebbins, NY, London, 27 May 1858.   (NS2/5:82)

TINCHBURNE Thomas, ex planter, WI, d. London, 23 Dec.1785.
                                                         (55:1008)

TINDALL Thomas, Bristol, m. Alicia Smith, Barbados, Aug.1756.
                                                          (26:450)

TINLEY Dr, President, NJ College, d. Philadelphia, 1766. (36:439)

TITT Augusta, yngs. dau. late Thomas Titt, Brighton, m.
Augustus Panting Loinsworth, Barbados, eldest s. late A L
Loinsworth, MD, London, 23 June 1851.   (NS36:315)

TOBIN Ellen, yngs. dau. Michael Tobin, Halifax, NS, m. John
William Seymour, Jersey, 1 May 1849.   (NS31:646)

TOBIN James Webb, s. James Tobin, Bristol, d. Nevis,
30 Oct.1814.   (84:675)

TOBIN James Webb, d. Nevis, 30 Oct.1814.   (85:178)

TODD Eliza, eldest dau. Utten J Todd, The Ridge, Jamaica, &
Upper Halliford, Middlesex, m. Henry John Blagrove, s. late
F R Coore, London, Jamaica, 25 July 1850.   (NS34:540)

TODD Isaac, b.1742, ex Montreal, d. Bath, 22 April 1819.
                                                      (88:488)

TODD Melchior Garner, St Lucia, m. Marianne Emilia Frances,
eldest dau. Cap. Henry Pryce, RN, Clifton, 7 Oct.1845.
                                                     (NS24:650)

TODD Melchior Garner, ex Councillor, d. Castries, St Lucia,
20 Sep.1866.   (NS3/2:698)

TODD ..., s. Melchior Garner Todd, b. Union Est., St Lucia,
18 May 1847.   (NS28:198)

TOKER Claude Buck, s. Edward Toker, The Oaks, Faversham, Kent,
d. Newcastle, Upper Canda, 22 Oct.1841.   (NS17:229)

TOKER George John, b.1817, yngs. s. Edward Toker, The Oaks,
Ospringe, Kent, d. Upper Canada, 18 Sep.1842.   (NS19:110)

TOLME C H, b.1831, s. C D Tolme, London, d. Havanna, 3 Dec.
1858.   (NS2/6:216)

TOLMIE Joanna, 2nd dau. late James Tolmie, Campbelltown,
Argyll, m. Montague William, 2nd s. late Rev. George Tyrwhitt
Drake, Malpas, Cheshire, Victoria, Vancouver Island, 12 March
1862.   (NS2/13:222)

TOMKIN Alfred Boyce, s. T Tomkin, MD, Witham, Essex, m. Martha
Frances, only dau. J A Forbes, Santa Clara, Cal., Santa Clara,
24 Aug.1859.   (NS2/8:176)

TOMKIN Georgina Maria, w. John Royce Tomkin, barrister, dau.
late John McDonald, Grenada, d. Boulogne, 29 April 1857.
                                                    (NS2/2:740)

TOMKINS Philip, Jamaica, d.1753.   (23:591)

TOMKINS Lt. Col., Gov. New Providence, d. Nassau, Aug.1820.
                                                      (91:91)

TOMLINSON John, Dep. Gov. Antigua, d.20 Sep.1753.   (23:445)

TOMMAS N B, ex Bristol, d. Perth, Upper Canada, 14 Oct.1823.
                                                      (93:382)

TOMPION Robert Swete, Jamaica, m. Elizabeth Porter, London,
April 1752.   (22:240)

TOMPSON George, b.1755, Militia Maj., Dep. Judge Advocate, d. Honduras, 19 April 1807.   (77:780)

TONYN Col., Gov. West Florida, d.1774.   (44:598)

TOOLEY Miss, ex London, d. Barbados, 23 May 1799.   (69:621)

TOPPIN George Pilgrim m. Mary Blanche, yngr. dau. Rev. F R Brathwaite, St George, Basseterre, St Kitts, London, 23 July 1863.   (NS2/15:369)

TORRANCE William C, b.1822, eldest s. Mr Torrance, Excise Collector, Greenock, surgeon, Port Royal, Jamaica, d.24 Oct. 1848.   (NS31:222)

TORRES ..., b.1687, a Jewess, d. Spanish Town, Jamaica, 1799.   (69:624)

TORRES Manuel, Columbian envoy, d. Philadelphia, 1822.(92:382)

TORY Netlam, b.1783, ex Jamaica, d. Everton, 16 Feb.1855.   (NS43:444)

TOULMIN Maj. Harry, Mobile, Ala., gs. late Rev. Dr Toulmin, Taunton, m. Fanny Priestly, Northumberland, USA, ggdau. late Rev. Dr Priestly, Northumberland, USA, 13 Sep.1859.(NS2/7:638)

TOULMIN Joshua, 2nd s. Judge Toulmin, gs. Rev. Dr Toulmin, d. Milledgeville, NA, 1818.   (88:478)

TOVEY Alexander, Lt., RE, s. Alexander Tovey, 24th Reg., m. Maria Elizabeth, dau. E J Goodhue, London, Canada West, London, Canada West, 14 April 1864.   (NS2/16:792)

TOVEY E, Somerset, m. Mrs Duncan, wid. John Duncan, Jamaica, 4 Jan.1817.   (87:32)

TOVEY ..., dau. Lt. Hamilton Tovey, RE, b. Halifax, NS, 11 April 1865.   (NS2/18:775)

TOWLE William Henry, b.1835, surgeon, Nuneaton, d. St Thomas, WI, 28 June 1860.   (NS2/9:323)

TOWN Anne, dau. late George Town, Aberdeen, d. St Croix, 8 Jan.1843.   (NS19:556)

TOWNSHEND Flora, wid. William Townshend, PEI, d. Amherst, NS, 1 Nov.1843.   (NS21:110)

TOWNSEND James, US Congressman, d. Jericho, Long Island, May 1790.   (60:668)

TOWNSHEND Lord James, yngs. s. Marquis of Townshend, Cap. HMS Eulus, m. Elizabeth, dau. P Wallis, Halifax, NS, 8 May 1813.   (83:586)

TOWSON Nathan Paymaster Gen, US Army, d. Washington, 20 July 1854.   (NS42:408)

TRACEY Uriah, b.1753, Senator Conn., d. NY, 19 July 1807.   (77:889)

TRACEY Miss m. Dr DJH Dickson, naval physician, Leeward Islands, 1812.   (82:188)

TRAIL Dr David, d. Jamaica, 1791.   (61:187)

TRANT James, Montserrat, m. Miss Barrett, only dau. late
Wisdom Barrett, Jamaica, London, 1798.   (68:1147)

TRAVERS Horace, Asst. Comm. Gen., d. Jamaica, 25 June 1867.
                                                    (NS3/2:397)

TRAVERS John Taylor, eldest s. Joseph Travers, d. Jamaica,
23 July 1845.   (NS24:438)

TRELAWNEY Edward, Gov. Jamaica, m. Miss Crawford, niece
Countess of Dartmouth, 8 Nov.1737.   (7:701)

TRELAWNEY Edward, Gov. Jamaica, s. Sir John Trelawney,
Winchester, d.16 Jan.1754.   (24:47)

TRELAWNEY Mrs, w. Gov. Edward Trelawney, Jamaica, d.Jan.1742.
                                                    (12:107)

TRELAWNEY Sir William, Gov. Jamaica, d.1773.   (43:103)

TRELAWNEY Mrs, wid. late Col. Trelawney, Gov.Jamaica, d.
13 May 1782.   (52:263)

TREMAYNE John, MD, ex Helston, Cornwall, d. New Lancaster, Pa.,
31 May 1844.   (NS22:223)

TREW Ann, w. Rev. JM Trew, ex St Thomas in the East, Jamaica,
d. Grenada, 29 March 1842.   (NS18:223)

TREW Fanny, b.1823, eldest dau. Rev. JM Trew, St Thomas in the
East, Jamaica, d. Grenada, 24 March 1842.   (NS18:223)

TREW JM, Archdeacon of Bahamas, m. Laura, wid. Thomas Pickering
Robinson, Darlington, Cheltenham, 17 Aug.1843.   (NS20:430)

TREW Sophia, dau. Rev. JM Trew, ex St Thomas in the East,
Jamaica, d. Grenada, 24 Feb.1842.   (NS18:223)

TREZEVANT Peter, b.1768, ex Charleston, SC, d. Brighton,
20 June 1854.   (NS42:203)

TRICKETT Matthew, and w. Mary, Isle of Wight, d. Kingston,
Jamaica, Aug.1853.   (NS40:429)

TRIGGE ..., dau. Cap. Trigge, 100th Reg., b. Montreal,
23 May 1867.   (NS3/4:98)

TRIPE Algernon S, b.1820, 5th s. C Tripe, Devonport, Clerk,
Ordnance Dept., Jamaica, d. Ordnance Island, WI, 8 June 1850.
                                                    (NS34:230)

TROTMAN Mrs, w. Thomas Trotman, ex Barbados, d. London, 1793.
                                                    (63:867)

TROUP Miss, Jamaica, m. Henry Darlot, Foreign Post Office,
6 March 1800.   (70:282)

TROUTBECK Sarah, b.1760, eldest dau. late Rev. John Troutbeck,
Blencoe, ex King's Chaplain, Boston, Mass., d. Exeter, 1 July
1846.   (NS26:218)

TRUMBALL Jonathan, Gov. Conn., d. America, 1783.   (53:978)

TRUMBALL Gov., b.1741, Gov. Conn., d. Conn., 2 Aug.1809.
(79:886)

TRUSCOTT Eliza, b.1835, yngs. dau. late Cap. George Truscott,
RN, d. Buffalo, NY, 9 Oct.1853.   (NS40:650)

TRUSCOTT F, Cap., RN, m. Catherine, dau. J Hutchison,
Bermuda, 1815.   (85:274)

TRUSCOTT George, s. late Cap. George Truscott, RN, Exeter, m.
Sarah, dau. T Lovering, Buffalo, NY, 1 Oct.1851.   (NS37:83)

TRUSCOTT Dr, b.1780, 3rd s. late Adm. Truscott, Exeter, d.
Jamaica, 1813.   (83:183)

TRYON Cap., 43rd Light Infantry, Northants., m. Elizabeth,
only dau. Sir John Harvey, Lt. Gov. NB, niece Gen. Lord Lake,
NB, 25 Nov.1837.   (NS9:205)

TUCKER A, dau. Henry Tucker, President, Bermuda, m. Henry
William Lauzup, Ordnance Dept., 1796.   (66:438)

TUCKER Henry St George, b. Bermuda, Feb.1771, Director, HEICS,
d. London, 14 June 1851.   (NS36:204)

TUCKER John Harvey, eldest s. James Tucker, Bermuda, m. Mary,
yngs. dau. late William Brown, ex Gov. Bermuda, 1 Aug.1803.
(73:788)

TUCKER John Scott, 3rd s. late Joseph Tucker, naval surveyor,
m. Unity Isabella, 2nd dau. Lt. Henry Hire, RN, Bermuda,
6 March 1845.   (NS23:538)

TUCKER M, eldest dau. J Tucker, Speaker Bermuda Assembly, m.
John Noble Harvey, Bermuda, 1800.   (70:484)

TUCKER Nathaniel, b. Bermuda, 1750, graduated Leyden 1776, MD,
d. Hull, 1807.   (77:1174)

TUCKER Richard Alexander, Dep. Paymaster Gen. NS, m. Mary,
eldest dau. J Bruere, London, 10 March 1808.   (78:270)

TUCKER St George, d. Norfolk, Va., March 1828.   (98:471)

TUCKER Col., merchant, Va., d.1767.   (37:478)

TUCKER Miss, eldest dau. Jeremiah Tucker, London, m. David
Smith, New Providence, 20 Nov.1802.   (72:1160)

TUCKETT JW, St Vincent, m. Miss Twigg, London, 15 Aug.1803.
(73:985)

TUCKFIELD Roger, Devon, m. Penelope Lowe, Jamaica, 22 Feb.
1755.   (25:138)

TUDOR Frederick, b.1784, merchant, d. Boston, USA, 1864.
(NS2/16:671)

TUELS ..., (twins), b.1796, ch. Enoch Tuels, Middletown, USA,
(66:787)

TULLOCH Alexander Francis Tannachie, s. Francis Tulloch, ex
Maj., Inverness Militia, d. Jamaica, 23 March 1835. (NS4:102)

TULLOH Henry Bowyer, Col. Sec. Dominica, 2nd s. Lt. Col. Tulloh,
RA, d. Dominica, 12 July 1823.   (93:647)

TULLOH Margaret Isabella, b.1804, w. Lt. Alexander Tulloh, RA,
dau. William Bremner, President, Dominica, d. Dominica,
11 Sep.1826.   (96:574)

TULLOH Mary, dau. Cap. Tulloh, RN, m. Henry King Dickenson,
St Johns, NFD., Waterford, 16 July 1851.   (NS36:316)

TULLY Adelaide Elizabeth, yngs. dau. late James Dillon Tully,
MD, Inspector Gen. Hospitals Jamaica, m. Edward, 2nd s. Sir
Robert Graham, Esk, Cumberland, London, 3 Aug.1844.(NS22:422)

TULLY Dr, Hospital Inspector, d. Jamaica, 3 Sep.1827.(97:477)

TURING of FOVERAN Rev Sir Inglis, St Thomas in the Vale,
Jamaica, d. Jamaica, Nov.1791.   (61:1235)

TURNBULL Dr Andrew, b. Annan, 1719, physician, d. Charleston,
SC, 16 March 1792.   (62:673)

TURNBULL David, Judge, m. Alice, dau. late John Marshall,
Paynter Vale, Bermuda, Jamaica, 1 Aug.1844.   (NS22:538)

TURNER Caroline, 3rd dau. DS Turner, Clarendon, Jamaica, m.
JF Smith, WS, Edinburgh, London, 12 June 1830.   (100:554)

TURNER Charles, London, m. Miss Athill, dau. Samuel Athill,
Antigua, London, 13 Jan.1804.   (74:86)

TURNER Col. Charles Barker, settled Canada 1845, d. Toronto,
1853.   (NS40:97)

TURNER Dawson Palgrave, only s. late Gurner Turner, HEICS, m.
Emma, yngs. dau. late Peter Morgan, Toronto, 12 March 1867.
                                                     (NS3/3:666)

TURNER EP Bingham, Cap., RA, yngs. s. late Lt. Gen. Turner,
19th Reg., m. Helen, eldest dau. CS Gzowski, Toronto,
20 Aug.1863.   (NS2/15:499)

TURNER Cap. Henry, master West India, m. Miss McNeal, dau.
Thomas McNeal, Custos, Westmoreland, Jamaica, 25 Jan.1842.
                                                     (NS17:429)

TURNER Henry Fyers, Lt., RE, s. Col. Henry A Turner, RA, m.
Harriet Eliza, eldest dau. Vice Chancellor John Godfrey Spragge,
Toronto, 7 Sep.1864.   (NS2/17:647)

TURNER Sarah, w. Rev. Thomas Bryett Turner, Port Royal, d.
Kingston, Jamaica, 20 July 1856.   (NS2/1:519)

TURNER William, b.1745, Boston, NE, d. London, 1792. (62:90)

TURNER Mr, attorney, London, m. Miss Howthgate, dau. Joseph
Howthgate, Jamaica, 1791.   (61:582)

TURNER ..., dau. Cap. Turner, 39th Reg., b. Hamilton, Bermuda,
31 March 1863.   (NS2/14:778)

TURNER ..., dau. Cap. Bingham Turner, RA, b. Toronto, 30 June 1864.   (NS2/17:232)

TURNER ..., dau. Cap. Bingham Turner, b. Montreal, 27 Sep. 1865.   (NS2/19:636)

TURNER ..., dau. Lt. Henry F Turner, RE, b. Toronto, 15 Dec. 1865.   (NS3/1:264)

TURQUAND Bernard, b.1791, Dep. Receiver Gen. Canada, d. Montreal, 8 Dec.1848.   (NS31:223)

TUSON George Haviland, eldest s. Rev. GB Tuson, Huish, Langport, Somerset, d. on passage to Upper Canada, May 1833.
                                                                (103:190)

TWIGG Miss, London, m. JW Tuckett, St Vincent, 15 Aug.1803.
                                                                 (73:985)

TWINING Rev. JT, military chaplain, Halifax, NS, d. 8 Nov. 1860.   (NS2/10:110)

TWISS Adelaide Louisa, b.1830, w. Lt. Twiss, RA, d. Bermuda, 26 June 1852.   (NS38:322)

TWISS AW, Lt., RA, m. Ann Eliza, eldest dau. Rev. TD Winslow, Warwickshire, St George, Bermuda, 11 Sep.1853.   (NS40:628)

TWISLETON Mrs, d. Burlington on route to Canada, 1816.(86:380)

TYDDESLEY Thomas, b.1776, Friery, Isle of Man, d. on passage from St Vincent on board Elizabeth, 1798.   (68:814)

TYE Lucy, 3rd dau. Daniel Tye, Wilmot, m. William Dyne Harrison, Stratford, s. Rev. W M Harrison, Clayhanger, Devon, Galt, Upper Canada, 10 May 1851.   (NS36:29)

TYNDALL Dr, ex Plymouth, d. St Thomas, WI, 24 Jan.1851.
                                                                (NS35:574)

TYRRELL James, Portland, Jamaica, m. Anne, only dau. John Codrington, Machioneal, 23 June 1792.   (62:1151)

TYSON Mary Anne, eldest dau. George Tyson, St Kitts, m. JG Pigeunit, barrister, Boxwell, Glocs., Dec.1829. (99:558)

TYSON Peter Thomas, Speaker St Kitts Assembly, d.25 March 1767.
                                                                 (37:192)

TYSSEN Caroline, 3rd dau. late William George Daniel Tyssen, Foley House, Kent, m. CA Hagerman, judge, Canada, London, 12 Aug.1846.   (NS26:420)

UNDERHILL James, Boston, d.1775.   (45:607)

UNIACKE Crofton, b.1784, 2nd s. late Richard John Uniacke, d. Mount Uniacke, Halifax, NS, 26 Oct.1852.   (NS39:104)

UNIACKE Crofton James, yngs. s. Andrew Mitchell Uniacke, Halifax, NS, m. Frances Elizabeth, dau. Maj. J Campbell, 60th Rifles, London, 16 Nov.1865.   (NS3/1:117)

UNIACKE Helen Maria, eldest dau. late Richard Uniacke, judge, NS, d. London, 21 Dec.1845.   (NS25:217)

UNIACKE Mary Mitchell, dau. late RJ Uniacke, judge, NS, m.
Charles William Watkins, Badby House, Northants., ex 38th
Reg., London, 6 Nov.1851.   (NS37:182)

UNIACKE Norman Fitzgerald, b.1777, eldest s. late Richard
John Uniacke, Attorney Gen. NS, Attorney Gen. Lower Canada,
d. Halifax, NS, 11 Dec.1846.   (NS27:223)

UNIACKE Rev. Richard John, St Alban's Hall, Oxford, m. Ann
Jane, yngs. dau. Robert Willis, Archdeacon of NS, London,
1 June 1847.   (NS28:310)

URQUHART James, Cap., 14th Reg., m. Miss Flucker, dau.
Thomas Flucker, Sec. Mass. Bay, 1774.   (45:46)

URQUHART Robert, b. Cadboll, Ross, d. Charleston, SC,
11 Aug.1800.   (70:1107)

USBORNE Mary, 2nd dau. George Usborne, Portage-du-fort,
Quebec, m. Henry John Fourdrinnier, Montreal, Portage-du-
fort, 9 May 1860.   (NS2/9:84)

USSHER Herbert Taylor, s. Thomas Neville Ussher, Consul Gen.
Haiti, m. Julia Sarah Hicks, dau. Cap. A Bond, wid. Cap. GWS
Hicks, Tunbridge Wells, 17 Oct.1854.   (NS43:76)

USHER Townsend, ex Bristol, d. Kingston, Jamaica, Nov.1810.
                                                         (81:34)

USSHER Lady, w. Cap. Sir Thomas Ussher, RN, d. Halifax, NS,
11 Jan.1835.   (105:446)

UTTEN Harriot, wid. James P Utten, dau. late Duncan Campbell,
Jamaica, d. Brompton, 11 Nov.1845.   (NS24:658)

UTTEN JP, d. Jamaica, 15 Nov.1841.   (NS17:231)

UTTERTON John L, Lt., 47th Reg., eldest s. Archdeacon
Utterton, m. Julia Anne Caroline, eldest dau. James DN St George,
Halifax, NS, 2 April 1867.   (NS3/3:808)

VAIL Emilie Laurencie, b.1818, w. Aaron Vail, ex US Charge
d'Affaires London, d. Geneva, 17 Nov.1860.   (NS2/10:111)

VALENTIA Viscount, only s. Earl of Mountnorris, m. Frances
Cockburn, only dau. late CJ Sims, Jamaica, Brighton, 21 Oct.
1837.   (NS8:648)

VALLETTE Peter, Jamaica, d.1762.   (32:45)

VAN ALLEN Mr, Pittsburgh, d.1803.   (73:87)

VAN BEELEN John, d. St Elizabeth, Jamaica, 15 Aug.1793.
                                                       (63:1051)

VAN BUREN Martin, b. Kinderhook, Columbia Co., NY, 5 Dec.1782,
ex President USA, d.24 July 1862.   (NS2/13:370)

VAN CORTLANDT Gertrude m. Cap. Edward Buller, RN, Halifax, NS,
15 March 1789.   (59:371)

VAN CORTLANDT Miss, dau. Maj. Van Cortlandt, Halifax, NS, m.
William Taylor, London, Cowley, 6 May 1791.   (61:488)

VAN COSTLAND Catherine, dau. Maj. Philip Van Costland, NY, m.
Dr William Gourlay, physician, Madeira, Madeira, 25 April
1787.   (57:637)

VAN DER HORST Miss, 2nd dau. Elias Van Der Horst, US Consul,
m. John Duncombe Taylor, Antigua, Cap., 46th Reg., 5 May 1798.
                                                       (68:533)

VAN DER LINDE John, merchant, d. Curacao, 4 Jan.1816.(86:473)

VAN DER LYN John, b. Kingston on Hudson, NY, 1776, painter,
d. Kingston on Hudson, NY, 23 Sep.1852.   (NS39:103)

VAN KOUGHNET Philipinna, eldest dau. Col. Philip Van Koughnet,
m. Philip, 2nd s. Francis Coleman Harris, Cornwall, Canada,
12 Oct.1845.   (NS24:650)

VAN SITTART C Augustus, Lt., RN, 2nd s. late Rev. William Van
Sittart, Shottesbrooke, Carlisle, d. NY, 14 Aug.1849.
                                                      (NS33:341)

VAN SITTART Mary, w. Adm. Van Sittart, Bisham Abbey, Berks.,
d. Saratoga Springs, 1 July 1834.   (104:559)

VAN SITTART Rear Adm., b.1779, d. Eastwood, Woodstock, Canada,
21 March 1843.   (NS20:110)

VAN ZANDT James, s. late Jacobus Van Zandt, NY, d. Taunton,
26 Oct.1823.   (93:574)

VARDON Charles, Battersearise, Surrey, m. Marian, eldest dau.
late William Patterson, Jamaica, 15 May 1806.   (76:477)

VASS Catherine Leonard Margaret, 2nd dau. late Alexander Home
Vass, m. Cap. RJW Birch, 30th Reg., 2nd s. GW Birch, Wretham.
Norfolk, Montreal, 31 Oct.1867.   (NS3/5:102)

VASSALL John m. E Athill, yngs. dau. late James Athill,
Antigua, 13 May 1799.   (69:526)

VASSALL Richard, b.1732, Jamaica, d. London, 28 Feb.1795.
                                                      (65:349)

VAUGHAN Benjamin, Jamaica, m. Sarah, dau. William Manning,
St Mary Axe, 30 June 1781.   (51:342)

VAUGHAN Benjamin, b.1750, ex London, d. Hallowell, Maine,
8 Dec.1835.   (NS5:445)

VAUGHAN John, b. London, 1756, settled Philadelphia 1782,
Treasurer American Philosophical Society, d. Philadelphia,
30 Dec.1841.   (NS18:332)

VAUGHAN Samuel, 58 years in Jamaica, St James Assemblyman,
Cornwall Co. judge, d. Ridgeland Est., Jamaica, 9 Feb.1827.
                                                      (96:478)

VAUGHAN W Welby, 5th s. Dr Vaughan, Leicester, d. Spanish
Town, Jamaica, 1803.   (73:1254)

VAUGHAN William, NE, 'besieger of Cape Breton', d.Bagshot,
11 Dec.1746.   (16:668)

VAUGHTON John, estate owner, Barbados, d.8 Nov.1754. (24:530)

VEITCH Henry, Madeira, m. Margaret Antoinetta, dau. late
Thomas Harrison, Attorney Gen., Jamaica, 1808.   (78:1187)

VERMONT Thomas Robert, b.1802, ex Hayes, Middlesex, magistrate,
Trelawney, Jamaica, d. Falmouth, Jamaica, 6 Sep.1864.
                                                (NS2:18:114)

VETCH RH, Lt., RE, m. Marian, only dau. J Lardner, Barbados,
Dominica, 29 July 1863.   (NS2:15:498)

VIALL Nathaniel, merchant, NE, d. Dec.1753.   (23:591)

VIDAL Eliza, w. Dr William Henry Vidal, niece Jesse Foot,
Ilfracombe, Devon, d. St Mary, Jamaica, 21 Nov.1825. (96:94)

VIDAL John James, ex Assemblyman St Thomas in the Vale,
Jamaica, judge Jamaica, d. Clifton, 22 Oct.1823.   (93:572)

VILLETTES Gen. William A, lt. Gov. Jamaica, d. Port Antonio,
Jamaica, 3 July 1808.   (78:852)

VILLIERS Charles Courtenay, Maj., 47th Reg., m. Ellen, only
dau. late James Shanly, Thorndale, Middlesex, Canada West,
ex Normansgrove, Co. Meath, Montreal, 5 Feb.1863.(NS2:14:515)

VILLIERS ..., dau. Maj. CC Villiers, 47th Reg., b. Kingston,
Canada West, 7 April 1864.   (NS2:16:789)

VIRGIN Samuel, b.1737, ex Jamaica, d. London, 22 Feb.1815.
                                                    (85:280)

VIRGO James, d. Jamaica, 1791.   (61:186)

VISGER Harman, b.1767, US Consul Bristol, d. Ilfracombe,
4 June 1833.   (103:572)

VYSE William, b.1810, s. Thomas Vyse, Hernehill Abbey, Surrey,
d. NY, 29 Dec.1843.   (NS21:223)

WADE Andrew, Barbados, d. Demerara, 4 June 1798.   (68:811)

WADE Isaac, b.1762, d. Springfield, NJ, 19 Sep.1809.(79:1174)

WADMAN Miss m. Laurence Grenholme, 60th Reg., Bridgetown, WI,
May 1790.   (60:667)

WADSWORTH Elizabeth, only dau. late James Wadsworth, Genesee,
NY, m. Charles Augustus Murray, Consul Gen. Egypt, Edinburgh,
12 Dec.1850.   (NS35:196)

WAGNER John Mitchel, ex Bristol, d. Three Rivers, Quebec,
31 July 1811.   (81:195)

WAHAB Thomas, MD, b.1780, surgeon, 37th Reg., d. Halifax, NS,
1840.   (NS13:335)

WAINWRIGHT Arnold Francis, only s. Arnold Wainwright,
Grafton Manor, Oxford, d. NY, 9 Dec.1847.   (NS29:334)

WAINWRIGHT Henrietta Mary, yngs. dau. Col. Wainwright, USMC,
m. William Webb Follett Synge, British Attache, British
Legation, Washington, 27 Jan.1853.   (NS39:426)

WAINWRIGHT Rev. JM, b. Liverpool, Asst. Bishop of NY, d.
21 Sep.1854.   (NS4/3:104)

WAIT Samuel, 2nd s. Samuel Wait, Sanford, Somerset, d.
Montgomery, NY, 30 July 1847.   (NS28:446)

WAKEFIELD G, b.1780, eldest s. late Rev. G Wakefield,
ordnance storekeeper, Kingston, Upper Canada, d. Barnstaple,
Devon, 16 Sep.1837.   (NS8:435)

WALCOT John Richard, Black Bay Est., m. Aline, yngs. dau.
Thomas Bell, President, Dominica, ex Stockton on Tees,
Grenada, 15 Dec.1859.   (NS2/8:289)

WALDEGROVE Augustus, b.1802, yngs. s. late Adm. Lord Radstock,
d. Mexico, Nov.1825.   (96:95)

WALDO Francis, ex Customs Collector, Falmouth, Casco Bay, NA,
Assemblyman Mass., d.9 June 1784.   (54:477)

WALFORD Emma Louisa, dau. JT Walford, ex 64th Reg., m.
Charles Binney, RE, Halifax, NS, 27 Nov.1845.   (NS25:199)

WALKER Agnes Senhouse, 2nd dau. James Walker, m. George
Augustus, 2nd s. John Sealy, Attorney Gen. Barbados,
Barbados, 15 Nov.1866.   (NS3/3:238)

WALKER Benjamin, St Thomas, Canada West, m. Caroline, 2nd dau.
late Edward Howard Gibbons, Arundel, Sussex, London, Canada
West, 6 Nov.1858.   (NS2/6:88)

WALKER Emma, only dau. Charles Walker, niece Dep. Sec. War, m.
John Beverley Robinson, Solicitor Gen. Upper Canada, 5 June
1817.   (87:635)

WALKER Henry, b.1805, Jamaica, d. Northumberland, 1827.
                                                  (97:188)

WALKER John, b.1729, 35 years in Jamaica, proprietor
'Jamaica Gazette', d. Kingston, Jamaica, 20 June 1786.(56:810)

WALKER John, London, m. Jessy, dau. late John Johnson,
St Thomas in the east, Jamaica, 8 Feb.1820.   (90:71)

WALKER William, Lt., RA, b.1829, s. Andrew Walker, Ceylon
Civil Service, d. Kingston, Upper Canada, 24 March 1852.
                                                  (NS37:632)

WALKINSHAW Francisca Gamez, wid. Robert Walkinshaw, New
Almaden, Cal., d. Liverpool, 20 Oct.1859.   (NS2/7:547)

WALL John, 45th Reg., m. Miss Winslow, Boston, NY, 4 Dec.1777.
                                                  (48:93)

WALLACE Hugh, ex merchant, NY, Councillor NY, d. Waterford,
1788.   (58:178)

WALLACE John, HM Consul Ga., d. Savannah, 1804.   (74:1174)

WALLACE Louisa, dau. John Wallace, m. Henry Dalton Smart,
Maj., 76th Reg., Halifax, NS, 28 June 1854.   (NS42:385)

WALLACE Robert John, b.1834, s. Col. Robert T Wallace, Madras
Army, ex 26th Reg., d. Panama, 21 Feb.1860.   (NS2/8:524)

WALLACK James William, b. London, 1794, s. William Wallack &
Elizabeth Field, actor, d. NY, 25 Dec.1865.   (NS2/18:387)

WALLER Margaret, w. Rev. Edmund Waller, dau. late Rev. John
Findlater, St Vincent, d. Brookheath, Hants., 4 May 1848.
                                                 (NS29:675)

WALLIN James, s. late Joseph Wallin, Leicester, d. Tobago,
1811.   (81:679)

WALLIS Elizabeth, dau. P Wallis, m. Lord James Townsend, yngs.
s. Marquis of Townsend, Cap. HMS Eolus, Halifax, NS, 8 May 1813.
                                                 (83:586)

WALLIS ..., s. Allan Wallis, HM Consul, b, San Jose, Costa
Rica, 13 June 1863.   (NS2/15:228)

WALLIS ..., s. William Beale Wallis, surgeon, b. Kingston,
Jamaica, 7 June 1864.   (NS2/17:231)

WALLOP Newton Ward, b.1810, 2nd s. late Maj. Barton Powlett
Wallop, cousin Earl of Portsmouth, husband Elizabeth
Gilliard, 2nd dau. Dr McBride, SC, d. Savanna, 10 April 1850.
                                                 (NS34:110)

WALROND Amabel, dau. late Nathaniel Walrond, w. Barwick Bruce,
d. Hartford, Conn., 29 July 1841.   (NS18:331)

WALROND Benjamin, b.1787, Provost Marshal Barbados, d.
Barbados, 16 July 1844.   (NS22:334)

WALROND Benjamin, s. late George Walrond, d. Barbados, 28 Sep.
1851.   (NS37:105)

WALDRON Mary Lavinia, yngs. dau. James Waldron, Wivelscombe,
Somerset, m. Rev. JH Thompson, Professor Theology, Bishop's
College, Lennoxville, Canada, 14 July 1859.   (NS2/7:302)

WALROND Nicholas Humphrey, Barbados, d. London, 27 Oct.1846.
                                                 (NS26:664)

WALSH Rev. Charles m. Eliza, yngs. dau. late James Ludgater,
Lee, Kent, St Paul's, Harbor Grace, NFD., 29 Nov.1859.
                                                 (NS2/8:177)

WALSH John Adams, eldest s. late Jonathan W Walsh, Walsh Park,
Tipperary, m. Ada Campbell, yngs. dau. James Hackett,
Lennoxville, Canada East, 2 Sep.1861.   (NS2/11:557)

WALTER Eleanor Elizabeth, w. James Walter, ex Liverpool, d.
Jersey, USA, 31 Jan.1851.   (NS35:454)

WALTER John Jacob, Antigua, d. London, 21 Dec.1828. (98:649)

WALTON Jacob, b.1821, s. Rear Adm. Walton, RN, d. NY,
13 Feb.1843.   (NS19:558)

WALTON Jacob, b.1767, Rear Adm., RN, d. NY, 11 April 1844.
                                                   (NS22:110)

WALTON William, NY, d.1768.   (38:446)

WALTON Miss, Barbados, d. London, 18 Aug.1814.   (84:294)

WALWYN Anne, wid. Rev. John Hutchinson Walwyn, St Kitts, 2nd
dau. late Rev. Henry Hunter, Norfolk, d. Mount Pleasant,
St Kitts, 27 Oct.1854.   (NS43:105)

WALWYN Anne Frances, b.1763, 3rd dau. late William Walwyn,
St Kitts, d. London, 17 Oct.1841.   (NS16:661)

WALWYN John Hunter, eldest s. late Rev. JHWalwyn, St Kitts,
d. Mount Pleasant, St Kitts, 19 April 1849.   (NS32:110)

WANHILL Thomas, Cap. ship Garland, Poole, Dorset, d. Baltimore,
1819.   (89:476)

WANTON William, Gov. RI, d. July 1737.   (7:514)

WARCUP Isabella, b.1768, wid. William Warcup, surgeon, St
Vincent, d. East Dereham, 22 Feb.1853.   (NS39:452)

WARD Caroline, w. Henry V Ward, late Frederick Hath & Co.,
Valparaiso, Chile, d. Boston, USA, 13 Feb.1857.   (NS2/2:624)

WARD Gertrude Anne, yngst. dau. Rev. Randall Ward, Coltishall,
Norfolk, m. Henry George, eldest s. Charles Simonds, St John,
NB, Moulton, Northants., 3 May 1849.   (NS32:86)

WARD Mrs Sarah Louisa, wid. Judge Ward, Nevis, m. A Miller,
yngst. s. Rev. W Miller, Hasfield, Gloucester, 31 Jan.1818.
                                                   (88:176)

WARD Rev. Valentine, Gen. Superintendant Weslayan Mission
WI, Jamaica, d.26 March 1835.   (NS4:102)

WARD Dr W, ex physician Bristol, d. Kingston, Jamaica, 1811.
                                                   (81:656)

WARDEN Susannah, b.March 1701, Pennsburg Manor, Pa., wid.
Virgil Warden, house servant William Penn, d. Philadelphia,
30 June 1809.   (79:885)

WARING Elijah, b.1826, Philadelphia, nephew late Edward
Waring, Bristol, d. Abingdon, Pa., 31 May 1850.   (NS34:230)

WARKHAM Miss, Barbados, m. James Leigh Perrot, North Leigh,
Oxford, 9 Oct.1764.   (34:498)

WARLEY Maj. Charles, SC, m. Julia Clara, yngs. dau. late
Charles Rowcroft, HM Consul Cincinatti, London, 11 Nov.1858.
                                                   (NS2/5:632)

WARNEFORD Catherine, 3rd dau. Rev. John Warneford, Caldicott
Hill, Herts., m. Rev. S Oliver Crosby, St Philips, Barbados,
Barbados, 30 May 1848.   (NS30:314)

WARNER Ashton, b.1780, Chief Justice Trinidad, d.Trinidad,
4 Sep.1830.   (100:645)

WARNER Eliza Jane, 2nd dau. late Henry Warner, barrister,
Trinidad, m. Maj. William Hanbury Hawley, 14th Reg., Port of
Spain, Trinidad, 10 March 1864.   (NS2/16:680)

WARNER Frederick, 3rd s. late Ashton Warner, Chief Justice
Trinidad, m. Jeanetta Maria, 3rd dau. late Rev. William
Gunthorpe, Antigua, London, 20 June 1843.   (NS20:200)

WARNER George Godwin, yngs. s. late Joseph Warner, Chudleigh,
d. Goderich, Canada West, 20 Aug.1851.   (NS36:665)

WARNER Georgina, dau. Ashton Warner, late Chief Justice
Trinidad, m. Anthony Clogstoun, Marshal of Trinidad,
Trinidad, 1840.   (NS14:650)

WARNER Henry, barrister, 2nd s. late Ashton Warner, Chief
Justice Trinidad, d. Jamaica, 25 July 1843.   (NS20:446)

WARNER Isabella Jane, eldest dau. Charles W Warner, Attorney
Gen. Trinidad, m. Robert Farquhar Shaw, s. late Sir Michael
S Stewart, Ardgowan, Renfrew, Port of Spain, Trinidad,
10 Feb.1859.   (NS2/6:534)

WARNER Mildred, b.1751, wid. William Warner, Dominica, d.
Eltham, 1 Nov.1833.   (103:476)

WARNER Rev. Richard Albert, b.1817, Tobago, yngs. s. Ashton
Warner, Chief Justice Trinidad, d. Plymouth, Tobago, Dec.
1845.   (NS25:326)

WARREN Dawson Stockley, Cap., 14th Reg., m. Barbara Mary,
yngs. dau. G Colquhoun Grant, Treasurer St Vincent, Morne
Fortune, St Lucia, 24 Feb.1863.   (NS2/14:515)

WARREN Edward B, b.1781, magistrate, Port Royal, Jamaica,
only bro. Thomas Warren, wholesale druggist Bristol, d.
Jamaica, 27 June 1836.   (NS6:668)

WARREN Peregrine, b.1807, ex Cap., 60th Reg., ex Militia Maj.,
Niagara Frontier, d.25 June 1840.   (NS14:446)

WARREN Thomas, b.1716, Attorney Gen. Leeward Islands, d.
Antigua, 2 June 1779.   (49:423)

WARREN Thomas Fullerton, b.1780, ex Jamaica, d. Brompton,
Middlesex, 30 Dec.1813.   (84:97)

WARREN Miss, Wotton, Berks., m. William Collier, Barbados,
18 Sep.1760.   (30:490)

WARREN Miss, London, m. Sir Basil Keith, Gov.Jamaica, 23 July
1773.   (43:359)

WARREN Mrs, late Miss Brunton, eldest sis. Countess of Craven,
w. Mr Warren, manager Baltimore & Philadelphia theaters, d.
Alexandria, America, 28 May 1808.   (78:749)

WARWICK Miss, niece Alderman Robinson, Stamford, m. Herman
Witsius Ryland, Sec. Lord Dorchester, Montreal, 15 Dec.1794.
(65:437)

WASHINGTON Corbal, nephew Gen. Washington, m. Hannah, dau.
Richard Lee, Va., 1787.   (57:933)

WASHINGTON George, d. Mount Vernon, 14 Dec.1799.   (70:84)

WASHINGTON Col. George C, b.1799, Rockville, Md., d.
Washington, 18 July 1854.   (NS42:408)

WASHINGTON J Marshall, Bermuda MP, m. Frances, only dau. late
Rev. William Wilson, Greenbank, Partick, Glasgow, 8 July 1845.
(NS24:416)

WASHINGTON Martha, wid. late President Washington, d. Mount
Vernon, 23 May 1802.   (72:686)

WASHINGTON Mrs, b.1707, mo. George Washington, d.Fredericksburg,
NA, 25 Aug.1789.   (59:1052)

WATERHOUSE John, b.1789, s. late Benjamin Waterhouse, Jamaica,
d.27 March 1854.   (NS41:557)

WATERHOUSE Julia Alice Wraxall, 2nd dau. late John Waterhouse,
Kingston, Jamaica, m. Thomas Benyon, Thorp Arch, Yorks.,
Brenchley, Kent, 9 July 1862.   (NS2/13:225)

WATERHOUSE Susannah, wid. Benjamin Waterhouse, Jamaica, d.
London, 20 March 1809.   (79:386)

WATERHOUSE Susan, dau. late Benjamin Waterhouse, Kingston,
Jamaica, m. RW Carpenter, Bath, 3 April 1846.   (NS25:639)

WATERLAND If., Jamaica, d.7 Dec.1757.   (27:577)

WATERLAND Samuel, Virginia, m. Miss Jenkins, London, 1757.
(27:530)

WATERS William O, Comm. Dept. Barbados, d. Barbados, 15 Oct.
1805.   (75:1171)

WATKINS Charles William, Badby House, Northants, ex 38th Reg.,
m. Mary Mitchell, dau. late RJ Uniacke, judge, NS, London,
6 Nov.1851.   (NS37:182)

WATKINS Price, b.1802, barrister, ex Greenwich Park, Jamaica,
d. Shrewsbury, March 1836.   (NS5:675)

WATKINS Sophia Louisa Henrietta, b.1803, 2nd dau. Edward Long,
Jamaica, w. Col. Lloyd Watkins, Pennoyre, d. Bath, 27 May 1851.
(NS36:102)

WATKINS Rev. William, Antigua, d.1776.   (47:47)

WATLEY Caroline, w. Joseph Watley, Solicitor Gen. Tobago, d.
Pepper Hill, Tobago, 24 Sep.1844.   (NS23:222)

WATSON Adele, wid. NJ Watson, Burnopfield, d. Barbados,
22 April 1854.   (NS42:200)

WATSON Mrs Dorothea, d. Dominica, 16 Nov.1827.   (98:94)

WATSON Elizabeth, b.1758, only dau. John Watson,
St Elizabeth, Jamaica, d. London, 10 April 1800.   (70:390)

WATSON James, Jamaica, d.1763.   (33:518)

WATSON Dr James, b.1766, conspirator - tried for High
Treason in England, 1817, d. NY, 12 Feb.1838.   (NS10:219)

WATSON James, eldest s. late James Watson, WS, Edinburgh,
d. Toronto, 9 April 1845.   (NS24:103)

WATSON John, b.1769, ex Trelawney, Jamaica, d. Fortrose,
5 Dec.1810.   (81:492)

WATSON Miss L, London, m. James Thompson, ex planter,
Barbados, 13 Nov.1781.   (53:541)

WATSON Robert Brown, merchant, Mexico, m. Ellen Sophia, 2nd
dau. Francis Murphy, merchant, HM Consulate, Mexico,
19 Dec.1857.   (NS2/4:326)

WATSON William, 2nd s. David Watson, Stamford, Lincs., d.
WI, 1794.   (64:675)

WATT Ann, yngs. dau. Robert Watt, Jamaica, m. James Anderson,
Edinburgh, Stratford Bow, 30 Dec.1840.   (NS15:199)

WATTS Catherine, wid. Thomas Watts, HEICS, m. Henry R Cassin,
MD, Antigua, 30 May 1819.   (89:271)

WATTS John, ex Councillor NY, d.15 Aug.1789.   (59:769)

WATTS John Turner, b.1767, ex London Stock Exchange, d.
Boston, Mass., 16 March 1853.   (NS39:562)

WAY Edward, Montreal, m. Sarah Garway, yngs. dau. late Lt.
William Fynmore, Southampton, 22 April 1851.   (NS35:659)

WAYNE Gen., US Army, d. Presque Isle, 15 Dec.1796. (67:252)

WEBB Amelia, b.1825, w. George Webb, ex Lt., 21st Royal Scots
Fusiliers, d. Brooklyn, NY, 31 March 1853.   (NS39:673)

WEBB George, merchant, Nevis, d. Cambridgeshire, 22 June 1804.
                                                    (74:694)
WEBB John, ex Jamaica, d. London, 1779.   (49:48)

WEBB Nathaniel, Customs Collector Montserrat, d. Somerset,
29 Jan.1741.   (11:108)

WEBB Thomas, b.1798, d. Jamaica, 30 July 1845.   (NS24:438)

WEBBER Matthew, b.1805, bro. John Webber, Manningtree, Essex,
ex treasurer Washington Co., d. Potosi, Missouri, 12 Jan.1853.
                                                  (NS39:448)
WEBLEY Edward, Chief Justice Jamaica, Assemblyman, d.1777.
                                                    (47:555)
WEBSTER Andrew, b.1778, d. Grenada, 1822.   (92:478)

WEBSTER AF, b. Grenada, 1781, d. Grenada, 1823.   (93:287)

WEBSTER Prof. John White, b.1793, s. Dr Redford Webster, Boston, Prof. Chemistry & Mineralogy Harvard, d. Boston, USA, 30 Aug.1850.   (NS34:567)

WEBSTER Noah, b. West Hartford, Conn., 16 Oct.1758, dictionary author, d. New Haven, USA, 27 May 1843.   (NS20:208)

WEBSTER Rowland, paymaster, 72nd Highlanders, m. Maria Augusta Catherine Campbell, dau. Alexander Stewart, MD, Army Hospital Inspector, Barbados, 24 April 1851. (NS36:78)

WEBSTER William, b. Scotland, 1826, Crown Agent, Assembly Speaker, d. Honolulu, Sandwich Islands, 23 March 1864.
                                                       (NS2/17:119)

WEBSTER Mrs, wid. Prof. Webster, d. NY, 10 Oct.1853.(NS40:650)

WEDDERBURN James, attorney & proprietor, d. Jamaica, July 1797.
                                                           (67:889)

WEEDEN Thomas Saxby, b.1823, eldest s. Thomas Weeden, Ripe, Sussex, d. Warwick, Canada West, 5 Dec.1857.   (NS2/4:225)

WEEKS James jr., Bristol, m. Miss Chambers, eldest dau. late Edward Chambers, Bachelorshall, Jamaica, 4 July 1792.(62:672)

WEGG Edmund Rush, Attorney Gen. Bahamas, d, Nassau, New Providence, 23 Sep.1789.   (59:1147)

WEEKS Dr Thomas Pym, physician, Nevis, m. Isabella, yngs. dau. Dr Livingston, Aberdeen,21 April 1789.   (59:669)

WEIR Daniel, Comm. Gen., d. NY, 1781.   (51:593)

WEIR John, Comm. Gen. Dominica, m. Elizabeth, dau. Elizabeth Grove, Ashgrove, 1776.   (46:578)

WELCH George AW, Comm., RN, eldest s. George Asser White Welch, Cheltenham, m. Mary Catherine, yngs. dau. late Maj. England, 75th Reg., niece Gen. Sir Richard England, Montreal, 1 June 1864.   (NS2/17:108)

WELCH Richard, planter, WI, d. Bath, 14 Oct.1782.   (52:504)

WELCH Susanna, 2nd dau. late William ·Welch, Stoke Newington, m. William Jay Bolton, Caius College, Cambridge, 2nd s. Rev. R Bolton, NY, Lynn, 26 Sep.1849.   (NS32:639)

WELLARD Col., Councillor, d. Boston, NE, 11 Feb.1753.(23:100)

WELLESLEY Marianne, dau. Richard Caton, Md., wid. Robert Paterson, merchant, NY, w. Richard Marquess Wellesley, Hampton Court, 17 Dec.1853.   (NS41:188)

WELLS Grissy, b. Charleston, SC, 1754, dau. Robert Wells, merchant, sis. late William Wells, MD, aunt Rev. R Wells Whitford, HEICS chaplain Madras, d.19 April 1843. (NS19:665)

WELSH Mary, w. John Welsh jr., Philadelphia, d. London, 9 Oct.1852.   (NS38:551)

WELSH Piers, Lt., 29th Reg., d. Montreal, 14 Oct.1785.(55:76)

WELSH William James, b.1813, only s. Maj. Gen. Welsh, Madras, d. St Louis, Missouri, 12 Sep.1846.   (NS27:110)

WEMYSS Alexander, d. Jamaica, 1791.   (61:1065)

WENT Mary Elvira, eldest dau. late Thomas Went, m. William Leacock, eldest s. William Jordan, St Lucy's, Barbados, 16 Oct.1860.   (NS2/9:661)

WENTWORTH William Fitzwilliam, yngs. s. Lt. Wentworth, RN, Deptford, d. Port au Prince, Haiti, 28 May 1853.   (NS40:209)

WENTWORTH Mr, Gov.NH, m. Miss Hilton, 15 March 1760. (30:297)

WENTWORTH Lady, w. Sir John Wentworth, Surveyor Gen. HM Woods BNA, ex Gov. NS, d. Sunninghill, 13 April 1813.   (83:290)

WERSFOLDF, ex Montserrat, d. Winchcomb, Glocs., 20 Aug.1811.
                                                   (81:287)

WERGE Frances Henrietta, b.1836, eldest dau. John Unett, Edgebaston, w. Maj. Werge, 2nd Reg., d. Bermuda, 7 Sep.1864.
                                                  (NS2/17:663)

WEST Charles Augustus, b.1754, surgeon, Tortula, d. Tortula, Jan.1793.   (63:767)

WEST James, ex Theater Royal, Bath, m. Mrs Bignall, joint proprietor theaters Charleston, Norfolk & Richmond, Norfolk, SC, 22 May 1795.   (65:701)

WEST Joseph, b.1728, Quaker, d. Wilmington, Del., 7 May 1790.
                                                   (60:669)

WEST Mary Ann, wid. Dr West, Antigua, d. Montserrat, July 1852.   (NS39:104)

WEST Mary Elizabeth, dau. John West, Jamaica, m. Rev. David Laing, St Peter's College Cambridge, s. late David Laing, Jamaica, 14 April 1824.   (94:368)

WEST Robert, b.1690, Long Crandon, Bucks., Quaker, settled Pa., 1715, returned to England, 1764, d.1776.   (46:483)

WEST Rosina, 4th dau. late Dr West, Antigua, m. Francis West, Montserrat, 22 Oct.1844.   (NS23:196)

WEST Sarah, only dau. late William Henry West, Jamaica, m. John Campbell, Colesburg, Cape of Good Hope, London, 1 Nov.1842.
                                                  (NS19:86)

WEST Thomas, WI, d. Bath, 1780.   (50:394)

WEST William, b.1798, 2nd s. John West, Jamaica & Surrey, d. Portland, Jamaica, 27 Nov.1833.   (104:343)

WEST William, MD, d. Antigua, 23 July 1835.   (NS4:446)

WEST Mrs jr., 'the Melpomene of the Va. co. of comedians' d. Richmond, America, 15 Jan.1805.   (75:282)

WESTCOTE Thomas Pottenger, barrister, ex Attorney Gen.NFD.,
d. Bristol, 30 March 1835.   (105:556)

WESTERN Cap., RN, m. Miss Burch, dau. late Mr Burch, Bermuda,
Bermuda, 4 Oct.1794.   (64:1148)

WESTMACOTT Richard m. Miss D Wilkinson, Jamaica, 20 Feb.1798.
                                                    (68:255)

WESTMORELAND Eardley Graham, HM Vice Consul, m. Fanny, dau.
Col. Schlatter, Brunswick, Ga., 5 July 1867.   (NS3/2:383)

WESTMORELAND Henry m. Mary Elizabeth, dau. Rev. Thomas
Stewart, Kingston, Jamaica, 30 April 1859.   (NS2/7:79)

WESTMORLAND Herbert, b.1827, 5th s. Isaac Westmorland,
Camberwell Green, d. Ettingen Est., Trelawney, Jamaica,
16 April 1846.   (NS25:670)

WETHERELL Robert Alexander, b.1820, 5th s. Rev. Richard
Wetherell, Hawkhurst, Kent, d. Woodstock, Canada West,
27 Feb.1856.   (NS45:660)

WEYMAN William, NY, m. Emily, 2nd dau. Joshua Mayhew, London,
3 Aug.1841.   (NS16:424)

WEYONOMON Mahomet, Sachem of Moheagons, Conn., ggs. Sachem
Onkass, d. Aldermanbury, 8 Aug.1736.   (6:487)

WHARTON Louisa Frances, 3rd dau. late William Wharton,
Councillor St Kitts, m. Robert Murray Rumsey, Colonial Sec.,
St Kitts, 12 Dec.1844.   (NS23:311)

WHARTON Thomas, President, Pa., d.1777.   (48:395)

WHEATE Lady, wid. Sir John Wheate, m. Alexander Cochrane, bro.
Earl of Dundonald, NY, April 1788.   (58:561)

WHEATLY Nathaniel, Boston, NE, m. Miss Enderby, London,
10 Nov.1773.   (43:581)

WHITALL Benjamin, s. Job Whitall, d. Philadelphia, 1 Oct.1797.
                                                    (67:1069)

WHITALL Rebecca, wid. James Whitall, d. Redbank, Philadelphia,
1 Oct.1797.   (67:1069)

WHITALL Sarah, gdau. Job Whitall, d. Redbank, Philadelphia,
1 Oct.1797.   (67:1069)

WHITCHURCH William, b.1659, d. Va., 1766.   (36:405)

WHITCOMB Samuel, Lillington, Dorset, m. Miss Allin, dau.
Jacob Allin, Jamaica, 27 May 1749.   (19:236)

WHITE Arthur, ex Colonial Sec. Trinidad, d. Paris, 24 March
1856.   (NS45:548)

WHITE Charlotte, wid. D White, Madras Civil Service, eldest
dau. S Nicholls, Tiverton, m. Rev. William Duckett, St Agnes,
Nassau, Forest of Dean, 8 Jan.1855.   (NS43:302)

WHITE Daniel, b.1789, ex Lt., 60th Reg., d. Montreal,
11 Sep.1832.   (103:190)

WHITE Elizabeth Gould, dau. late David White, Jamaica, d.
Brighton, 23 Aug.1808.   (78:855)

WHITE George Rusby, b.1779, ex solicitor & town-clerk,
Cambridge, d. Ribley, USA, 18 Nov.1851.   (NS37:208)

WHITE Harriet, yngs. dau. Rev. FH White, m. Rev. William
Grey, chaplain Bishop NFD., Hants., 25 June 1849. (NS32:313)

WHITE Henry, ex Councillor, NY, d. London, 23 Nov.1786.
                                                         (56:1095)

WHITE James Clayton, Custos Portland, Militia Maj. Gen., d.
Jamaica, 13 July 1834.   (104:558)

WHITE John William, ex clerk, Boston, Lincs., d.WI, 1794.
                                                          (64:386)

WHITE John, RN, m. Miss Losack, only dau. Richard Losack,
St Kitts, Lt. Gen. Leeward Islands, 22 March 1796. (66:253)

WHITE Mrs Mary, d. Kingston, Jamaica, 1793.   (63:1152)

WHITE Mary, b.1727, wid. Michael White, Gov. Montserrat, d.
London, Aug.1832.   (102:187)

WHITE Mrs, w. Michael White, St Vincent, d. Brighton,
26 Jan.1802.   (72:185)

WHITE Samuel, Councillor, NE, d.1769.   (39:270)

WHITE Stephenson, ex Belfast, d. Baltimore, USA, Feb.1826.
                                                          (96:287)

WHITE T, eldest s. Mrs White, Grantham, Lincs., d. Spanish
Town, Jamaica, 24 May 1794.   (64:671)

WHITE Rev. William, b.1748, Bishop of Pa., d. Philadelphia,
17 July 1836.   (NS6:429)

WHITE Lt. Col., 80th Reg., m. Miss Greig, only dau. late
W Greig, St Vincent, 1810.   (80:383)

WHITEFOORD Rev. Caleb, b.1842, s. Rev. C Whitefoord, Whitton,
Shropshire, d. Fullerswood, Jamaica, 5 Aug.1866. (NS3/2:551)

WHITEMAN Andrew, b.1760, London, ex Grenada, d.1813. (83:85)

WHITEMAN Eliza, dau. late Andrew Whiteman, Grenada, m. Richard
Fall, 17 June 1820.   (90:636)

WHITFIELD Rev., Methodist preacher, d. Ga., April 1748.
                                                          (18:236)

WHITFIELD Rev. George, d. Newburyport, NE, 1 Oct.1770.(40:542)

WHITFIELD George, b.1776, barrister, d. St Vincent, 23 Aug.
1819.   (89:472)

WHITFORD Mrs Helena, w. Edward Whitford, dau. Robert & Mary
Wells, Scots who settled Carolina 1753, sis. Dr William
Charles Wells, d. London, 6 July 1824.   (94:569)

WHITEHEAD William, d. Antigua, 1791.   (61:1235)

WHITEHEAD Mrs, wid. William Whitehead, Antigua, d.Winchester,
1 Sep.1800.   (70:908)

WHITEHORNE James Risby, judge, d. St Anne, Jamaica, 1789.
                                                (59:573)

WHITEHORNE Samuel, judge, St Catherine Representative,
barrister, d. Carravina, Jamaica, Dec.1796.   (67:350)

WHITEHOUSE Fanny, yngs. dau. Edward Whitehouse, Walsworth,
Surrey, m. Charles Ashwell, Grenada, 18 Aug.1792. (62:766)

WHITEHOUSE William Frederick, d. Chiswick, St Thomas in the
East, Jamaica, 8 Sep.1846.   (NS26:559)

WHITELEY Frederick, surgeon, 3rd s. late Rev. Joseph Whiteley,
Leeds, d. Jamaica, 16 Oct.1832.   (102:382)

WHITLOCK Charles, ex comedian company manager, England,
husband E Kemble, sis. Mrs Siddons, d. America, 1799.(69:440)

WHITLOCK James, Barbados, m. Miss Hughes, London, 1 July 1773.
                                                (43:359)

WHITMORE Georgina Maria Louisa Philis, b.1830, w. Lt.
Montagu Whitmore, RE, d. St George, Bermuda, 22 Sep.1853.
                                                (NS40:649)

WHITMORE Cap. William, ADC Gen. Munro, m. Miss Olton, eldest
dau. late John Allen Olton, Harrow Place, Barbados, Cabbage
Tree Hall, Barbados, 14 April 1811.   (81:589)

WHITNEY Stephen, b.1775, merchant, d. NY, 23 Feb.1860.
                                                (NS2/8:418)

WHITTALL Ann, 3rd dau. late Thomas Whittall, Bailey Irvon,
Radnor, m. John Whittall, St Vincent, Builth, Brecon,
15 Sep.1842.   (NS18:535)

WHITTALL John, St Vincent, m. Ann, 3rd dau. late Thomas
Whittall, Bailey Irvon, Radnor, Builth, Brecon, 15 Sep.1842.
                                                (NS18:535)

WHYTE Margaret, yngs. dau. Robert Whyte, ex Philadelphia,
d. London, 3 Sep.1795.   (65:795)

WHYTE Lt. Col., 7th Hussars, m. Mary Ann Jessy, 3rd dau. late
M. de Montenach, Patrician of Fribourg, & of Mary Elizabeth,
gdau. late Baroness de Longeuil, Montreal, 9 Sep.1842.
                                                (NS18:651)

WICKHAM Samuel, Chief Justice & Admiralty Court Judge, NY,
d. April 1753.   (23:248)

WICKLOW Philip, Barbados, d. London, 8 Jan.1783.   (53:94)

WIDDER Blanche Anne, yngs. dau. Frederick Widder, Chief Comm.
Canada Land Co., m. Cap. Henry L Balfour, Toronto, 12 May 1863.
                                                (NS2/15:97)

WIDMER Christopher, MD, d. Toronto, 3 May 1858.   (NS2/5:90)

WIGGLESWORTH Mr, ex Comm. Gen. St Domingo, d.Jamaica,
21 March 1800.   (70:486)

WIGNELL Mr, manager Philadelphia Theater, d.23 Feb.1803.
                                                      (73:382)

WILBRAHAM Corbin, Antigua, d.11 Nov.1757.   (27:531)

WILBY Maj., 90th Reg., m. Anne, eldest dau. Robert Paul,
President, St Vincent, St Vincent, 3 Feb.1814.   (84:406)

WILCKENS Jacob Frederick, b.1757, d. Kingston, Jamaica,
12 June 1826.   (96:574)

WILKES Israel, bro. late John Wilkes, Chamberlain of London,
d. NY, 25 Nov.1805.   (75:1238)

WILKIE Robert Ball, b.1817, 2nd s. Maj. Wilkie, Horfield,
Bristol, d. Hanover, Jamaica, 13 Jan.1850.   (NS33:343)

WILKINS Emma Louisa, eldest dau. Martin J Wilkins, Solicitor
Gen. NS, m. Charles William Sturgess, HMS Cornwallis, Banff,
28 Feb.1861.   (NS2/10:455)

WILKINS Sarah, b.1771, wid. Judge Wilkins, NS, d. Windsor,
NS, 3 Nov.1859.   (NS2/8:190)

WILKINSON Charles, eldest s. Edward Wilkinson, London, d.
St Lawrence River, Canada, 23 Sep.1844.   (NS22:670)

WILKINSON Miss D, Jamaica, m. Richard Westmacott, 20 Feb.
1798.   (68:255)

WILKINSON Daniel Weir, 2nd s. late Jacob Wilkinson, d.
Tobago, 5 July 1800.   (70:902)

WILKINSON George Browne, s. late G Browne, London, d.
Trinidad, 17 Dec.1841.   (NS18:223)

WILKINSON Georgina, dau. late Jonas Wilkinson, Barbados, m.
Lt. G G Philipps, RN, London, 3 Aug.1852.   (NS38:411)

WILKINSON James, Jamaica, d.2 June 1779.   (49:327)

WILKINSON Rev. J B, St Paul's, Antigua, d.1851.   (NS35:325)

WILKINSON Jemima, b.1753, d.Pennyann, NY, 1 July 1819.(89:185)

WILKINSON William, Antigua, d.King's Bench Prison, 24 Aug.1798.
                                                      (68:730)

WILKINSON Rev., ex Savoy, d. on passage to America, 1757.
                                                      (27:482)

WILKS Francis, merchant, Mass. Bay agent, m. Miss Jeffereys,
London, 8 April 1731.   (1:177)

WILKS Mrs, w. Francis Wilks, NE agent, d. child-bed,10 Feb.1732.
                                                       (2:631)

WILKS Matthew, s. Rev. Mark Wilks, Paris, gs. late Rev.
Matthew Wilks, London, m. Eliza, dau. Walter Langdon,
gdau. John Jacob Astor, NY, NY, 3 Oct.1842.   (NS19:197)

WILLAN Robert, MD, London, m. Mrs Scott, wid. Robert Scott,
ex Nassau, New Providence, 1800.   (70:1003)

WILLARD Annie, yngs. dau. late Charles Willard, Kingston,
Canada West, m. Thomas M Bruce-Gardyne, Middleton, Angus,
ex Lt., 40th Reg., Kingston, 6 April 1858.   (NS2/4:185)

WILLARD Mrs Martha, b.1694, wid. Maj. Joseph Willard, d.
Grafton, Mass., 25 July 1794.   (64:767)

WILLIAMS Abigail, wid. John Williams, ex St Johns, NFD., d.
London, 22 Feb.1843.   (NS19:442)

WILLIAMS Amelia Caroline, eldest dau. Lt. Col. Montgomery
Williams, RE, Bermuda, m. Lt. Frederick Hall, RA, s. Lt. Col.
Hall, RE, St George, Bermuda, 15 Feb.1855.   (NS43:519)

WILLIAMS Caroline, w. Thomas Robinson Williams, RI, d.
London, 2 March 1830.   (100:282)

WILLIAMS Charles, Lt., 24th Reg., prisoner, d. Va., 1780.
                                                 (50:589)

WILLIAMS Cornelia, 2nd dau. Cap. Edward Williams, m. Lt. Col.
Lightfoot, Kingston, Upper Canada, 28 Dec.1819. (90:272)

WILLIAMS Elizabeth, w. Charles Williams, Asst. Comm. Gen.,
d. St Lucia, 1 Feb.1846.   (NS25:446)

WILLIAMS George Parker, b.1783, s. late Robert Williams, SC,
d. London, 14 Nov.1846.   (NS27:102)

WILLIAMS Henry, estate owner, Jamaica, m. Miss Knight, dau.
James Knight, Stoke Newington, 6 Dec.1739.   (9:666)

WILLIAMS James, b. WI 1803.   (73:1254)

WILLIAMS Jenkins, Councillor, Judge King's Bench Quebec, d.
Quebec, 30 Oct.1819.   (89:638)

WILLIAMS John, estate owner, Jamaica, d. London, 5 Dec.1744.
                                                 (14:676)

WILLIAMS Rev. John Robert, eldest s. Rev. Henry Williams,
Llanedi, Carmarthen, d. NY, 23 March 1854.   (NS41:552)

WILLIAMS Mrs Mary, b.1738, w. William Williams, Pensacola,
d.14 Jan.1791.   (61:189)

WILLIAMS Mrs Mary, b.1795, eldest dau. Sir Stephen Shairp, w.
Cap. John Thomas Williams, 2nd Reg., d. Grenada, 14 March 1819.
                                                 (88:585)

WILLIAMS Michael, Nevis, d. Bath, 6 Feb.1758.   (28:94)

WILLIAMS Pinckney, w. Cap. WG Williams, US Army Engineers,
dau. late Thomas Peter, ggdau. Gen. Curtis & Mrs Washington,
d. Buffalo, USA, 1842.   (NS18:333)

WILLIAMS Robert, b.1732, ex SC, d.1808.   (78:370)

WILLIAMS RE, Weston Green & Antigua, d. Surrey, 28 Nov.1826.
                                                 (96:573)

WILLIAMS Cap. Rowland Edward, b.1784, ex Thames Ditton, Surrey,
d. Antigua, 30 May 1852.   (NS38:321)

WILLIAMS Samuel, Sec. Jamaica, d. May 1751.   (21:284)

WILLIAMS Samuel, Tortula, d.14 Dec.1757.   (27:577)

WILLIAMS Samuel, b.1760, ex London, d. Boston, USA, 16 Feb.
1841.   (NS15:670)

WILLIAMS Sarah, b.1721, wid. Samuel Williams, Grenada, d.
Dundee, 14 Sep.1809.   (79:984)

WILLIAMS Susan Mary, dau. late Benjamin Williams, m. Jerome
Napoleon Buonaparte, Baltimore, 2 Nov.1829.   (99:558)

WILLIAMS Thomas Bull, b.1788, ex London, d. Orange Grove,
Jamaica, 25 Nov.1840.   (NS15:558)

WILLIAMS Mrs Phillipa, ex Barbados, d. Kingsdown, Somerset,
1813.   (83:668)

WILLIAMS Thomas, Jamaica, d.17 Jan.1762.   (32:145)

WILLIAMS Thomas, Barbados, d. Bristol, 13 Nov.1773. (43:582)

WILLIAMS Thomas B, Jamaica, m. Mary Sophia, dau. late John
Forbes, New Providence, 24 June 1820.   (90:636)

WILLIAMS William, merchant, ex Halifax, NS, d. Liverpool,
7 Sep.1802.   (72:885)

WILLIAMS William, d. Jamaica, 27 Jan.1749.   (19:92)

WILLIAMSON Diana Charlotte, 3rd dau. late Jonathan Williamson,
Lakelands, Co. Dublin, m. John Beaufin Irving, Jamaica, only
s. late JB Irving, Cheltenham, 6 April 1843.   (NS19:528)

WILLIAMSON Jonathan, planter, Va., d.10 June 1770. (40:279)

WILLIAMSON Joseph, planter, Barbados, d.13 Dec.1770. (40:591)

WILLIAMSON Peter, b. Aberdeen, kidnapped & taken to America,
lived amongst the Cherokees, d. Edinburgh, 19 Jan.1799.
                                                 (69:167)

WILLIAMSON Mrs, w. Maj. Gen. Williamson, Lt. Gov. Jamaica, d.
King's House, Spanish Town, Jamaica, 19 Sep.1794. (64:1150)

WILLIS Dr Adam, d. Good Hope, Trelawney, Jamaica, 15 Oct.1801.
                                                 (71:1211)

WILLIS Ann Jane, yngs. dau. Robert Willis, Archdeacon NS, m.
Rev. Richard John Uniacke, St Alban's Hall, Oxford, London,
1 June 1847.   (NS28:310)

WILLIS Charles jr., Cranbrook, Kent, m. Mary, dau. late
William McBean, Roaring River Est., Jamaica, Oxford,
22 March 1825.   (95:364)

WILLIS James, London, d. Jamaica, Dec.1793.   (64:180)

WILLIS Nathaniel Parker, b. Portland, USA, author, d. NY,
1867.   (NS3/3:390)

WILLIS Robert, Archdeacon NS, d. 21 April 1865.   (NS2/19:117)

WILLIS Samuel, SC Assemblyman, d.30 May 1755.   (25:333)

WILLISTON Eliza Jane, eldest dau. John Williston, m. James
Charles Edward, only s. late John Edward Carmichael, gs.
Charles Douglas Smith, ex Lt. Gov. PEI, Miramachi, NB,
19 May 1853.   (NS40:304)

WILLOCK Mr, merchant, Antigua, m. Fanny Atkinson, Lancaster,
16 March 1777.   (47:147)

WILLMORE Graham, barrister, Middle Temple, m. Josephine, yngr.
dau. late Lt. Col. Selden, US Army, Va., Highgate, 14 Aug.1845.
                                                    (NS24:521)

WILLOUGHBY Rev. Mark, b.1797, s. William Hall Willoughby, Chew
Magna, Somerset, minister, Trinity Church, Montreal, Church of
England school superintendent NFD., d. Montreal, 1847.
                                                    (NS28:549)

WILMOT Montagu, Gov. NS, d.23 May 1766.   (36:342)

WILMOT Thomas, yngs. s. T Wilmot, builder, Bristol, d.
Dominica, 1 Nov.1807.   (78:86)

WILMSHURST Laura Borthwick, 3rd dau. Thomas Wilmshurst,
Walton on Naze, Essex, d. Albany, USA, 1 Sep.1852. (NS38:546)

WILSON Andrew, b. Edinburgh, 1806, s. Andrew Wilson, d.
Toronto, 18 Oct.1864.   (NS3/1:141)

WILSON Anne, yngs. dau. late R Wilson, St Kitts, m. John
Baillie, Sherwood Park, Southampton, 16 July 1806.   (76:774)

WILSON Charles, d. Boston, NE, Aug.1754.   (24:435)

WILSON Charles Turville, Lt., Military Train, s. Maj. Gen.
GJ Wilson, Indian Army, m. Caroline Wynyard, eldest dau.
Thomas Gadwin Hurd, Toronto, 7 April 1863.   (NS2/14:781)

WILSON David, b.1749, d. Madison, Indiana, 1856.   (NS2/1:260)

WILSON Fleetwood, b.1817, ex Cap., 8th Hussars, Auditor Gen.
Barbados, d. Barbados, 13 Sep.1862.   (NS2/13:788)

WILSON Frances W, only dau. late Rev. William Wilson, m.
J Marshall Washington, Bermuda MP, Greenbank, Partick,
8 July 1845.   (NS24:416)

WILSON Dr George, Stoteneleugh, ex Edinburgh, m. Marianne,
dau. John Bannister, ex Congressman, niece Theodore Bane, Va,
Congressman, 19 March 1789.   (59:761)

WILSON George, Royal Monmouth Light Inf., m. Maria Mulgrave,
yngs. dau. John Salmon, President, Jamaica, Elgin, 22 Dec.
1859.   (NS2/8:179)

WILSON Harriet, yngs. dau. late Rev. Dr. Charles Wilson,
Prof. Church History, Univ. St Andrews, m. Rev. William Lake
Pinder, Barbados, Edinburgh, 8 June 1808.   (78:556)

WILSON Harry, ex Lloyds Coffee House, many years Jamaica, d.
Spanish Town, Jamaica, 20 March 1821.   (91:475)

WILSON John, b. Edinburgh, 1800, vocalist, d. Quebec,
8 July 1849.   (NS32:547)

WILSON John, Deputy Postmaster Gen. Jamaica, d. Kingston,
2 July 1850.   (NS34:454)

WILSON John Manyon, Lt., 3rd WI Reg., eldest s. JM Wilson,
Fitzjohns, Essex, d. Jamaica, 13 Aug.1853.   (NS40:426)

WILSON Lilias, dau. Alexander Wilson, merchant, Inverness, m.
Alexander Robertson, surgeon, ex Jamaica, 25 Oct.1802.
                                                   (72:1224)

WILSON Richard, judge, Antigua, d.1759.   (29:497)

WILSON Robert, Liverpool, d. Charleston, NA, 1822. (92:478)

WILSON Selina Irwin, 3rd dau. late JWD Wilson, President,
St Kitts, niece Dr Davis, Bath, d. Lymington, 3 Sep.1833.
                                                  (103:284)

WILSON Silias Jane, only ch. late Alexander Wilson, Redhill,
Middlesex, m. Edward Nicholls, St Vincent, Barnwell, 20 May
1847.   (NS28:200)

WILSON Mrs, w. John Wilson, b. SC, Loyalist, d. London, 1814.
                                                   (84:98)

WILSON Mrs, w. J Wilson, Proprietor European Museum, niece
late Gen. Gadsden, cousin William Hazell Gibbs, Col.
Charleston Artillery, Chancellor SC, d.7 Jan.1814. (84:200)

WINDE Scudamore, judge, Assemblyman, Jamaica, d.14 Oct.1775.
                                                   (45:607)

WINDER Elizabeth Mary, eldest dau. William Winder, MD, m.
Thomas Stratton, MD, surgeon, RN, Montreal, 29 Dec.1847.
                                                  (NS29:421)

WINDER Thomas, b.1757, St Anne, Jamaica, d. London, 6 Jan.1816.
                                                   (86:184)

WINDLE Thomas, Symond's Inn, m. Miss Maxwell, dau. Mr Maxwell,
Jamaica, 1 Oct.1788.   (58:932)

WING Edwin, Bourton on the Water, Glocs., m. Dorinda, eldest
dau. John O'Driscol, Chief Justice Dominica, Taunton,
24 Nov.1842.   (NS19:197)

WINGATE Rev. John, St George, Grenada, d. Grenada, 1789.
                                                   (59:955)

WINPENNY RC, surgeon, 2nd s. Rev. Richard Cooke Winpenny, Market Weighton, Yorks., d. Carriacou, 3 Jan.1851. (NS35:334)

WINKWORTH William Samuel, surgeon, eldest s. late Rev. William Winkworth, Southwark, d. Trinidad, 4 Sep.1817.(87:629)

WINSLOE Richard William Charles, Cap., 21st Royal North British Fusiliers, m. Constance Edwards, 2nd dau. FM Cromartie, Dep. Superintendent Military Stores, Barbados, 12 Sep.1861.   (NS2/11:557)

WINSLOW Ann Eliza, eldest dau. Rev. TD Winslow, Napton on Hill, Warwick, m. Lt. W Twiss, RA, St George, Bermuda, 11 Sep.1853.
(NS40:628)

WINSLOW Thomas, Lt., 47th Reg., m. Mary Forbes, Bermuda, 6 Sep.1794.   (64:1052)

WINSLOW Cap. T, NY, Loyalist, d. London, 18 Nov.1815.(85:639)

WINSLOW Miss, Boston, m. John Wall, 45th Reg., NY, 4 Dec.1777.
(48:93)

WINDSOR Leonora, eldest dau. SB Windsor, Solicitor Gen. St Vincent, m. Archibald Bannatyne, St Vincent, 1814.(84:674)

WINSTANLEY Rev. Charles, b.1778, ex St Edmund Hall, Oxford, d. Scarborough, Toronto, 19 Aug.1847.   (NS28:550)

WINSTANLEY Ozias Stanley, b.1822, 2nd s. Rev. C Winstanley, Toronto, 2nd master HMS Avon, d. River Ramosa, Africa, 2 April 1846.   (NS26:334)

WINTER George, d. Jamaica, 29 July 1800.   (70:1004)

WINTER Henry Burton, Lt., 7th Royal Fusiliers, m. Maud Lavinia, dau. late WS Sewell, Sheriff of Quebec, gdau. Chief Justice Sewell, Quebec, 11 July 1867.   (NS3/2:383)

WINTER Nathaniel, ex Martinique, m. Miss Pitcher, eldest dau. Isaac Pitcher, London, 1 Nov.1798.   (68:1150)

WINTHROP Lindal Thomas m. Miss Temple, dau. John Temple, HM Consul, NY, Boston, NE, 1786.   (56:906)

WISE Emma Jane, yngs. dau. Lt. John Wise, RN, Chatham, m. Horatio Nelson Dickson, Halifax, NS, Chatham, 8 Feb.1853.
(NS39:427)

WISE George Foster, eldest s. Edward Wise, Bembridge, Isle of Wight, m. Frances Lucy, dau. late Milbourne Marsh, Jamaica, niece late Sir Francis Forbes, Chief Justice NSW, Scone, New South Wales, 21 June 1842.   (NS19:197)

WISE James, b.1784, eldest s. JB Wise, Maidenhead, Thicket, St Croix, d. on passage from St Bartholemew's to Grenada, 16 Sep.1816.   (87:183)

WISE T, ex Claremont, Jamaica, d. Hillbank, Dundee, 25 Jan. 1819.   (88:185)

WITHERSPOON Rev. Dr, President NJ College, m. Mrs Anne Dill,
wid. Dr Dill, York Co., NY, Philadelphia, 1791.   (61:774)

WITHERSPOON Dr John, b.1722, President NJ College, d. Princeton,
15 Nov.1794.   (64:1150)

WITHY Rev. H m. Christian Dottin, 4th dau. late John Gay
Alleyne, Barbados, Cheltenham, 26 April 1829.   (99:366)

WOOLFF Maximilian, Manchester, Jamaica, m. Maria, dau.
Hyman Cohen, London, 19 Sep.1821.   (91:372)

WOLHAUPTER Caroline Jane, only dau. late Benjamin Wolhaupter,
Sheriff of York, m. Rev. TE Dowling, Douglas, NB, 2nd s.late
Rev. JG Dowling, Gloucester, Frederickton, 4 April 1864.
                                                  (NS2/16:792)

WOLLASTON Frederick Hyde, 4th s. Rev. Francis Wollaston,
Chislehurst, Kent, d. St Kitts, 1810.   (80:501)

WOOD Charles Henry, b.1801, s. Rev. H Wood, Grenton, Somerset,
d. Longville, Jamaica, 1820.   •   (90:476)

WOOD Rev. Edward Dix, b.1825, 2nd s. Lt. Gen. Wood, C in C,
Windward & Leeward Islands, ex Burton, Dorset, d. Queen's
House, Barbados, 31 Oct.1852.   (NS39:214)

WOOD Emily Frances, 3rd dau. Lt. Gen. Wood, C in C, Windward
& Leeward Islands, m. Alfred Bury, 69th Reg., 3rd s. Earl of
Charleville, Barbados, 20 June 1854.   (NS42:384)

WOOD Frederick James, b.1819, s. late Richard Wood, London,
d. Tobago, 9 Feb.1851.   (NS35:334)

WOOD George, eldest s. Lord Wood, Edinburgh, m. Emma, eldest
dau. Barnard Henry, Philadelphia, 17 April 1845.   (NS24:72)

WOOD John, eldest s. late Rev. Alexander Wood, Rosemarkie,
Ross, d. Trelawney, Jamaica, 3 May 1811.   (81:88)

WOOD Joseph, bro. late Rev. Alexander Wood, Rosemarkie, d.
Jamaica, March 1819.   (89:472)

WOOD Mary Elizabeth, 4th dau. Lt. Gen. Wood, C in C, Windward
& Leeward Islands, m. William Shepherd Milner, Cap., 69th Reg.,
2nd s. late Cap. Milner, RN, Barbados, 31 July 1855.(NS54:531)

WOOD Dr Robert, surgeon, Port Royal, Jamaica, d.24 Feb.1795.
                                                   (65:439)

WOOD Thomas, b.1784, s. William Wood, Tetbury, Glocs., d.
Curacao, 13 Oct.1811.   (81:657)

WOOD Thomas, ex Col. SC Rangers, Superintendent Indian Affairs,
d. St Vincent, 3 Aug.1825.   (95:382)

WOOD Thomas Charles, yngs. s. Archdeacon of Chester, d. Nevis,
4 Nov.1864.   (NS2/18:115)

WOOD William, HM Consul Baltimore, d.15 Oct.1812. (83:83)

WOOD Miss, dau. late Sir P Wood, Newington, m. Samuel
Patterson, NE, 23 June 1750.   (20:284)

WOOD Miss, London, m. Gregory Grant, Quebec, 1777.   (48:606)

WOOD Mrs, wid. J Wood, m. Cap. Sir William Barnaby, RN,
Bermuda, 2 May 1816.   (86:632)

WOODALL Georgina, yngs. dau. late Robert Woodall, Ardwick,
Lancs., m. Richard Henry Murray, barrister, eldest s. Thomas
Murray, Trinidad, London, 2 Feb.1859.   (NS2/6:315)

WOODBRIDGE Edward Herbert, eldest s. Edward Collins Woodbridge,
d. Dominica, 2 Feb.1850.   (NS33:558)

WOODCOCK James, Jamaica, m. Miss Croft, eldest dau. Sir
Arthur Croft, Berks., 1777.   (48:237)

WOODCOCK Selina Augusta, yngs. dau. late James Phipps Woodcock, St Kitts, m. Rev. Alfred Arrow Kempe, Woxham, Bucks.,
Tenby, 17 Nov.1846.   (NS27:195)

WOODELY J, ex Carolina, d. 6 Nov.1764.   (34:546)

WOODFALL W, Chief Justice Cape Breton, s. W Woodfall, printer,
d. Cape Breton, 1806.   (76:483)

WOODFORDE W, m. Miss Millar, niece Judge Winstone, Fredericton,
NB, 4 Nov.1812.   (83:179)

WOODLEY Catherine, b.1780, w. John Woodley, Councillor,
St Kitts, dau. Rev. Dr Horne, Chiswick, d. St Kitts, 15 July
1818.   (83:374)

WOODLEY Charles, b.1776, yngs. s. late William Woodley, Gov.
Leeward Islands, d. Plymouth, 22 Feb.1859.   (NS2/6:439)

WOODLEY Gen., Gov. Leeward Islands, d. St Kitts, June 1793.
                                                    (63:768)

WOODLEY Mrs, wid. late William Woodley, Gov. Leeward Islands,
d. Bloxworth, Dorset, 29 March 1813.   (83:393)

WOODRUFF Elias A, 2nd s. G Woodruff, Oakland, Trenton, NJ,
d. Liverpool, 8 Aug.1819.   (89:281)

WOODRUFFE Samuel, America, d.1768.   (38:494)

WOODS Rev. James, b.1831, ex Halifax, NS, Paget & Warwick,
Bermuda, d. Bermuda, 11 Sep.1864.   (NS2/17:661)

WOODS Thomas, d. Charlottetown, PEI, 28 June 1809. (79:885)

WOODYEAR Mary, w. William Woodyear, Customs Controller Fort
Royal, d. Martinique, 13 Dec.1801.   (72:182)

WOODYER Thomas, St Kitts, m. Miss Boyfield, 1785. (55:1005)

WOOFFENDALE Mrs, w. Robert Wooffendale, dentist, ex London, d.
NY, 1809.   (79:389)

WOOLING Miss, Jamaica, m. William Barnet, Jamaica, 11 Sep.
1764.   (34:497)

WOOLERY Edward, Isleworth, m. Frances Barnett, Jamaica, 18 Sep.
1760.   (30:490)

WOOLLERY John, d. Jamaica, 1757.   (27:189)

WOOLLERY William, planter, WI, d. Bristol, 1 April 1789.
                                                     (59:374)

WOOLLERY William Stone, Midgham, Long Pond Est., Westmoreland,
Jamaica, d. on passage from Jamaica on Augustus Caesar,
9 June 1805.   (75:881)

WOOLLEY Edward ,MD, b.1817, 6th s. George Woolley, London,
d. Wrights Corner, Indiana, 31 July 1857.   (NS2/3:467)

WOOLLS Thomas A m. Miss Lewis, Jamaica, Ostend, 4 May 1789.
                                                     (59:572)

WOOLRICH EP, Quebec, m. Harriett, wid. Lt. Col. Leslie Walker,
London, 10 Feb.1840.   (NS13:314)

WOOLRIDGE Rev. John, London Missionary Society, ex Bristol, d.
Manchester, Jamaica, 1841.   (NS15:324)

WOOTTEN William, b.1662, old soldier, d. Va., 1773. (43:203)

WOOTTON William, Customs Inspector NA, d.25 June 1781.(51:343)

WORKMAN Thomas, Barbados, m. Mrs Cholmley, wid. Robert
Cholmley, Barbados, 1757.   (27:530)

WORMELY Ariana Randolph, yngs. dau. late Rear Adm. RR Wormely,
RN, m. Daniel Sargent Curtis, Boston, USA, Newport, RI,
3 Nov.1853.   (NS41:185)

WORMELEY James Preble, b.1825, only s. Rear Adm. Ralph
Randolph Wormeley, d. NY en route to Cuba, 10 Jan.1851.
                                                    (NS35:454)

WORMELEY Ralph Richard, b.Va., 1786, Rear Adm., RN, d. Utica,
NY, 26 June 1852.   (NS38:530)

WORRELL Rebecca, b.1776, wid. Jonathan Worrell, ex Barbados,
d. East Grinstead, 23 April 1851.   (NS35:685)

WORSAM Richard, Councillor Barbados, d. Philadelphia,
10 May 1766.   (36:342)

WORSLEY Henry, ex Envoy to Portugal, Gov. Barbados, d.
15 March 1740.   (9:148)

WOTTON George, d. Jamaica, 1790.   (60:1053)

WRAGG Priscilla, b.1678, d. St Jago de la Vega, 1799.(69:257)

WRANGHAM Cap., master Gipsy of Hull, d. NY, 10 Aug.1803.
                                                     (73:1086)

WRIGHT George, b.1788, Assemblyman, St David, Jamaica,
Greenwall Est., Jamaica, 4 Oct.1846.   (NS26:670)

WRIGHT Helen Frances, only ch. late W Burt Wright, Jamaica,
m. Rev. George Hill Clifton, Ripple, Worcs., London, 16 Aug.
1842.   (NS18:421)

WRIGHT Isabella, only dau. William Wright, Advocate Gen.NB,
m. BE Allhusen, 15th Reg., 2nd s. Christian Allhusen,
Newcatle on Tyne, Fredericton, NB, 18 Oct.1864. (NS2/17:780)

WRIGHT JC, b.1768, Wilmington, NC, judge, d. Charleston,
10 July 1811.   (81:192)

WRIGHT J, ex Cambridge, d. Montreal, 1813.   (83:183)

WRIGHT John, MD, Inspector Hospitals Canada, d. on passage to
NY, 1827.   (97:647)

WRIGHT Mary, b.1793, dau. Rev. George Wright, Halifax, NS,
d. Lisbon, 13 Dec.1811.   (81:659)

WRIGHT Mary, w. Lt. Col. Wright, RE, d. Barbados, 6 Nov.1852.
                                                (NS39:216)

WRIGHT Mary A, eldest dau. George Wright, Colonial Treasurer
PEI, m. John J Rowan, eldest s. Rev. RW Rowan, Ahogill,
Co Antrim, Charlottetown, PEI, 5 Nov.1866.   (NS3/3:104)

WRIGHT Mary Jane Pearson, eldest dau. HP Wright, Archdeacon of
Columbia, m. Lt. Henry Spencer Palmer, RE, yngs. s. late Col.
JF Palmer, Madras Army, Bath, New Westminster, BC, 7 Oct.1864.
                                                (NS2/16:107)

WRIGHT P, Customs Collector, d. Windsor, Canada, 19 Feb.1841.
                                                (NS16:222)

WRIGHT ..., s. Archdeacon Wright, b. Victoria, Vancouver Island,
16 May 1862.   (NS2/13:351)

WYATT CB, Surveyor Gen. Upper Canada, m. Miss Rogers, London,
29 March 1805.   (75:383)

WYATT Emma, eldest dau. Henry Wyatt, ex Long Ditton, Surrey,
m. Hugh Cossart Baker, Canada, 15 Nov.1845.   (NS25:199)

WYATT George, London, m. Miss Bainbridge, only dau. late
Thomas Bainbridge, Jamaica, 25 July 1796.   (66:614)

WYATVILLE George Geoffrey, only s. Jeffrey Wyatville, Windsor,
m. Ann Sisum, dau. late Peter Phillips, Barbados, London,
17 Jan.1828.   (98:80)

WYBAULT SR, london, m. Frances Maria, 2nd dau. John Rycroft
Best, Barbados, Charlton Kings, 2 June 1846.   (NS26:197)

WYKE Anthony, Lt. Col. Caribinies, judge, d. Montserrat, 1777.
                                                (48:141)

WYLLIE Robert Crichton, b. Dunlop, 13 Oct.1798, 2nd s.
Alexander Wyllie of Hazelbank, Minister Foreign Affairs, Hawaii,
d. Honolulu, 24 Nov.1865.   (NS3/1:284)

WYLIE William, Cambridge graduate, d. Quebec, 7 Aug.1853.
                                                (NS40:426)

WYLLY Susan Matilda, eldest dau. William Wylly, Attorney
Gen. Bahamas, m. Cap. Samuel Chambers, RN, Nassau, New
Providence, 10 March 1807.   (77:585)

WYNDHAM Alfred, 2nd s. AW Wyndham, Blandford, Dorset, m.
Caroline E, dau. John Stuart, Windsor, Canada West,
Toronto, 1 June 1859.   (NS2/9:182)

WYNDHAM Rev. John, Sutton Mandeville, m. Caroline Delia, only
dau. Edward Kielley, St Johns, NFD., Orcheston St Marys,
Wilts., 31 May 1853.   (NS40:86)

WYNDHAM ..., s. Alfred Wyndham, b. Toronto, 27 July 1860.
                                                      (NS2/9:312)

WYNN Isaac Lascelles, b.1735, Quaker, d. Montego Bay,
Jamaica, 4 April 1808.   (78:557)

WYNNE Robert, St Vincent, d. Little Ealing, Middlesex,
20 Feb.1795.   (65:348)

WYNNE Thomas, Councillor, Tobago, d. St Vincent, 11 Sep.1842.
                                                       (NS19:110)

WYNTER William, Councillor, Jamaica, d.1772.   (42:342)

YARWOOD Stephen, purser RN, emigration agent at Montreal,
d. Montreal, 29 June 1847.   (NS28:335)

YATES Thomas, d. Jamaica, 1735.   (NS5:335)

YATES Dr William, b. England, 1767, d. Morris, Otsego Co.,
NY, 7 March 1857.   (NS2/2:737)

YEATS Grant David, b. Fla., 1773, s. Dr David Yeats, d.
Tonbridge Wells, Kent, 14 Nov.1836.   (NS6:666)

YORKE Cap. Frederick Augustus, d. Trinidad, 26 April 1817.
                                                        (87:568)

YORKE Philip, Chief Clerk, Jamaica Supreme Court, d.8 Jan.1741.
                                                        (11:50)

YOUNG Andrew Houston, Quebec, m. Janet, 2nd dau. Thomas
Greenshields, Kilmarnock, 12 Jan.1841.   (NS15:200)

YOUNG Cap. Anthony m. Miss Rawlings, dau. Stidman Rawlings,
St Kitts, 21 June 1787.   (57:738)

YOUNG Sir Aretas William, b.1777, Gov. PEI, d. Government
House, PEI, 1 Dec.1835.   (NS5:661)

YOUNG Dr George, b.1727, physician, WI, d. London, 11 March
1803.   (73:292)

YOUNG George, London, d. NY, 24 June 1819.   (89:185)

YOUNG Georgina, 2nd dau. late Rev. George Young, Spanish Town,
Jamaica, d. London, 29 May 1865.   (NS2/19:123)

YOUNG Jane Frances, b.1816, eldest dau. TH Brooking, London,
w. George Rennie Young, d. Halifax, NS, 28 Dec.1841.(NS18:332)

YOUNG Robert Archibald, Quebec, m. Mary Charlotte, only dau.
Richard Norman, London, 24 Feb.1846.   (NS25:535)

YOUNG Sir William, b.1726, d. St Vincent, 8 April 1788.
                                                  (58:562)

YOUNG Sir William, b.1749, Gov. Tobago, d. Government House,
Tobago, 10 Jan.1815.   (85:373)

YOUNG Willington Lemprieve, b.1841, eldest s. William Young,
NY, gs. late Vice Adm. Young, d. Brighton, 22 Feb.1854.
                                                  (NS41:443)

YOUNG Cap., b. America, d. London, 13 July 1812. (82:92)

YOUNGER Thomas, ex Glasgow, Wilmington, NC, d. Lucie,
Jamaica, 1795.   (65:794)

ZACARA Mrs Martha, b.1685, Mohegan agent, Conn., d. Mohegan,
America, 1805.   (75:877)

ZANDER Rev. Christian, d. Jamaica, 1790.   (60:1148)

ZIMMER John D, b.1811, HM Consul Aux Cayes, d. Aux Cayes,
Haiti, 5 Feb.1840.   (NS13:668)

ZOUCH Augusta Mary Anne, yngs. dau. late Richard Zouch,
Dublin Castle, m. Rev. Charles Morice, Quebec, 13 March 1845.
                                                  (NS24:72)